TRAVELS WITH TOCQUEVILLE BEYOND AMERICA

Travels *with* Tocqueville Beyond America

JEREMY JENNINGS

Harvard University Press

CAMBRIDGE, MASSACHUSETTS | LONDON, ENGLAND 2023

Printed in the United States of America

First printing

Library of Congress Cataloging-in-Publication Data

Names: Jennings, Jeremy, 1952– author.
Title: Travels with Tocqueville Beyond America / Jeremy Jennings.
Description: Cambridge, Massachusetts : Harvard University Press, 2023. |
Includes bibliographical references and index.
Identifiers: LCCN 2022028396 | ISBN 9780674275607 (cloth)
Subjects: LCSH: Tocqueville, Alexis de, 1805–1859—Travel. |
Travel writers—History—19th century.
Classification: LCC DC36.98.T63 J46 2023 | DDC 944.007202—dc23 / eng / 20220707
LC record available at https://lccn.loc.gov/2022028396

For my dear friend Aurelian Craiutu,
Without whom this book would not have been written,
And there would have been much less fun.

Contents

TRAVELS WITH TOCQUEVILLE
BEYOND AMERICA

CHAPTER ONE

Embarking

In a recent work entitled *O My America!* the British travel writer Sara Wheeler refers to Alexis de Tocqueville as the "high priest of European tourists." For Tocqueville specialists, let alone a broader readership, this would probably not be the first description of him that comes to mind. Yet, Wheeler tells us, when she was writing her book about British women who fled to the United States in the nineteenth century, she "could scarcely get through a day without crossing paths" with the Frenchman.[1]

There are many Tocquevilles available to us. The most obvious of these is the nineteenth-century liberal political theorist who has been much admired as a forerunner of later critics of modern totalitarianism.[2] There is, in the words of Robert Putnam, Tocqueville the "patron saint of American communitarians," the advocate of the merits of a vibrant "civil society."[3] So, too, there is Tocqueville the sociologist and social scientist, the first analyst of democracy as a social state characterised by an equality of conditions.[4] To this can be added Tocqueville the historian and Tocqueville the politician and statesman. Less evidently, there is Tocqueville the member of a distinguished aristocratic family (with which he was frequently in disagreement) and Tocqueville the faithful and devoted friend. It was to these friends, as well as to an astonishingly wide range of correspondents, that Tocqueville sent innumerable letters brimming with reflections about politics, philosophy, religion, contemporary affairs, and much else.

However, in line with Sara Wheeler's remark, this book intends to take Tocqueville seriously as a traveller. It does so for a variety of reasons and with a range of different intentions. As a starting point, it is interested in the question of why people travel and how people travel, recognising that the latter changed very significantly over the course of Tocqueville's lifetime. In so doing, it sets itself against the contemporary zeitgeist that mistakenly believes that simply to travel is to learn something. Rather, it assumes that, to be a voyage of discovery, travel amounts less to visiting new places than in seeing those places with new eyes. It also recognises that this is not a gift lightly given or possessed by all but that it was a gift granted to Tocqueville.

Nonetheless, this book is not intended merely to be an account of the travels of someone not known previously to have been an assiduous and tireless nineteenth-century traveller. Tocqueville himself wrote as his intended first line to his most famous text, *De la démocratie en Amérique,* that it was not to be read as a travelogue.[5] Rather, in exploring why, where, and how Tocqueville travelled, this volume seeks to show that travel played an integral role in framing and informing his intellectual enquiries. Here, there is an element of scholarly controversy. Critics have argued that Tocqueville frequently did not see beyond what his first impressions were and that these were often based upon scant empirical evidence. All too often, it has been argued, Tocqueville learned nothing from his travels and was more interested in mixing with the social elites of the country he was visiting than in learning about it to any significant degree. More damaging still is the charge that Tocqueville's writings, like the travel genre in general, are infused with the spirit and gaze of European colonialism. There can be no doubt that Tocqueville was not without his imperfections as a traveller, and to these arguments we will return, but here it is sufficient to assert that the places Tocqueville visited, the people he met, and the detailed observations he arrived at on his journeys were not matters of idle curiosity but the source of new perspectives and new avenues of thought that informed the conclusions he reached about the world he inhabited. Examples abound of how seriously Tocqueville took the activity of travel. Journeys were meticulously prepared and researched. Where possible, the language of the country was learned. Friends were interrogated when they returned from a foreign trip. What was seen and heard on a journey was reflected upon and distilled afterwards at length. Importantly, Tocqueville never shied away from eyewitness, first person testimony in his analysis of the countries he was writing about.

More than this, this book hopes to provide a new perspective on both the man and his work. To that extent, it does not limit itself to recounting Tocqueville's actual travels (as extensive and as varied as these were). Rather, it seeks to explore the development of Tocqueville's ideas through the prism of travel. If, for example, he did not return to America after his only trip there in the early 1830s, he continued to think about the country for the rest of his life. The subject of this book is nothing less than the journey of Tocqueville's mind.

Here we should pause to introduce the central character of our story.[6] Alexis de Tocqueville was born on 29 April 1805 into an aristocratic family from the Cotentin Peninsula in Normandy where Alexis was subsequently to inherit his father's château, a property he was later to describe to his English friend Lord Hatherton as "a small French manor house."[7] Tocqueville's father, Hervé de Tocqueville, had narrowly escaped being guillotined in the French Revolution of 1789. Other members of his family perished in the Jacobin-inspired Terror of 1793–1794. Like many a young man of his privileged social background, Tocqueville was educated privately by a Catholic priest, the pious and devoted Abbé Lesueur. Nonetheless, Tocqueville lost his religious faith in his youth, producing, as he was later to tell his confidante Madame de Swetchine, a "fund of melancholy and discontent" and a "universal doubt" that was never to leave him. "I was seized," he wrote, "with the blackest depression."[8] It also seems possible that Tocqueville fathered a child by one of the maidservants at the Préfecture in Metz where his father was posted as a government official. After some hesitation Tocqueville trained for the law and in 1827 was appointed an unpaid *juge-auditeur* at the law courts of Versailles, just outside Paris.

The July Revolution of 1830—when, in the space of "three glorious days," the Bourbon monarch Charles X was replaced by the Orleanist Louis-Philippe as king and a new constitutional monarchy came into existence—put Tocqueville in a difficult situation. What was a man of such impeccable legitimist credentials and loyalty to the Bourbon royal family to do? How could he serve under the new regime? Tocqueville's solution to this dilemma, as improbable as it might seem, was to study the penitentiary system of the United States. Accordingly, Tocqueville, with his close friend Gustave de Beaumont, set out for America in May 1831, returning the following February.

It was this journey that provided the prelude to Tocqueville's famous account of the principles and practices of American democracy, published in two volumes in 1835 and 1840, the first appearing when Tocqueville was still only twenty-nine years old. To *De la démocratie en Amérique* we will return; at this point it is enough to cite the opinion of one of Tocqueville's biographers, Hugh Brogan. *De la démocratie en Amérique,* he writes, "is the greatest book ever written on the United States."[9] Moreover, from the evidence Tocqueville saw before him in America, he became convinced that democracy, with its potential ills, would triumph not just in the United States but beyond. As he wrote to one of his English correspondents, Mrs. Sarah Austin, in November 1835, "I am an adherent of democracy without being blind to its defects and its dangers. . . . I am intimately convinced that nothing will prevent its ultimate triumph, and that it is only by going with the current, and trying to direct it as far as possible towards progress, that the evils may be diminished and the possible good developed."[10] This was a view from which Tocqueville did not waver for the remainder of his life.

With the first part of *De la démocratie en Amérique* acclaimed a triumph and membership of the illustrious Académie française a distinct possibility, Tocqueville resumed his travels—visiting England and Ireland in the summer of 1835—and soon began what turned out to be the arduous writing of the second volume. When this eventually appeared in print in 1840, by Tocqueville's own admission it was far from enjoying the popular success of the first volume. Less directly focused on the depiction of democratic institutions in the United States, he had tried, Tocqueville told the British philosopher John Stuart Mill, "to describe the general traits of democratic societies of which no complete model yet exists," and it was here, he conceded, that he had lost "the ordinary reader."[11] Posterity has confirmed this judgement.

By the time that the second volume of *De la démocratie en Amérique* appeared in 1840, Tocqueville had not only married his Protestant-born English wife Mary Mottley (much to his family's disapproval),[12] but he had begun a political career, serving as a parliamentary deputy in what amounted to his family constituency in Normandy. He also came to play a prominent role in local politics. In pursuing this course, it is hard not to see a waste of Tocqueville's considerable talents. Throughout the 1840s he struggled, largely unsuccessfully, to define a coherent political position, rarely impressing due to his poor oratorical skills.[13] His efforts as a journalist (in 1844 Tocqueville briefly became part owner of a newspaper named *Le commerce*) were also something of a failure. It was in these years that Tocqueville developed a strong interest in France's attempted colonisation of Algeria, a country he visited twice in the 1840s.

The Revolution of 1848 saw Tocqueville thrust into the constitutional debates surrounding the birth of the new Second Republic. For the most part Tocqueville failed to win the argument. Furthermore, in the heated polemics of the day he showed little or no sympathy for the demands of the workers to the right to work and even less for the principles of socialism. In 1849 he served as minister of foreign affairs, during which time there was a marked deterioration of diplomatic relations with the United States. The irony was not lost on Tocqueville.

The Second Republic came to an end with the coup d'état masterminded by the future Napoleon III on 2 December 1851 and the subsequent creation of the Second Empire in the following year. Tocqueville (along with Gustave de Beaumont and many other members of the French Parliament, as well as government ministers and generals) was briefly imprisoned. Having foreseen this political outcome, and in despair at the indignity that had befallen France and its people, Tocqueville retired from political life. "I feel," he told his brother Édouard, "like a foreigner in my own country."[14] Prior to this, and in his "solitude," Tocqueville had set about the writing of a volume of memoirs, focusing upon the period that had led up to these traumatic events. The government of France, he recognised, had become little more than a joint stock company of a small bourgeois oligarchy. Never quite finished, and written not for "public viewing" but as a form of "mental relaxation," a first (imperfect) edition of his *Souvenirs* was not published until 1893.[15]

Tocqueville's second great text—*L'ancien régime et la révolution*—was published in 1856. It was an instant best seller, with separate English and American editions appearing in the year of its publication and a German edition published in 1857. Part historical scholarship and part political tract, its central thesis was that the governmental centralisation that famously characterised French society was not a product of the French Revolution or of the rule of Napoleon Bonaparte (as had been widely believed) but of the absolutism of the French monarchy in the period prior to 1789. Slow in gestation, this argument never succeeded in convincing everyone, then as now.[16] Nor, it has been said, was it as original as Tocqueville himself believed it to be.[17] Nonetheless, it did provide an important explanation as to why repeated attempts to establish liberty in France had ended in bitter failure and despotism. "We have limited ourselves," he wrote, "to placing liberty's head on a servile body."[18] The planned second volume of *L'ancien régime et la révolution* was unfinished at the time of Tocqueville's death.

Reflecting on the sorry outcome of his political career, Tocqueville was led to conclude that "my true value lies above all in works of the mind . . . more in my thoughts than in my deeds."[19] In this he was surely correct, and what today secures his reputation are his books and his ideas. Tocqueville was only one of many Frenchmen to write about America in the nineteenth century, but his is by far the best and the most read account. Tocqueville did not get everything right, and there was much that he simply turned a blind eye to; but he saw, more clearly than anyone else, that "we are travelling towards unlimited democracy" and that America offered the key to that future. And it is this that takes us to the heart of the significance of Alexis de Tocqueville as both a man and a writer. Through his many fruitless projects and arduous journeys shine the core principles that guided him during his entire life. "Liberty," he wrote, "is the first of my passions" and so much so that he was inclined to worship it.[20] Moreover, he told his readers, "whoever seeks for anything from freedom but itself is made for slavery." Those who understood this knew that liberty was "a good so precious and so necessary" that nothing could console them for its loss.[21]

Tocqueville died after a long illness, in Cannes on the French Riviera, on 16 April 1859.

Travelling and writing about travel are not unproblematic activities.[22] Almost from the very beginning of Western civilisation, doubts about the virtues and benefits of travel have been expressed. The Stoic philosopher Seneca could not have been more forthright in its condemnation. "What good," he wrote, "has travel ever been able to do anyone? . . . It has not granted us the gift of judgement; it has not put an end to mistaken attitudes." Indeed, all travel had ever done, in Seneca's opinion, was "distract us for a little while . . . like children fascinated by something they haven't come across before." All this hurrying from place to place, he concluded, had certainly not made us better or saner human beings. "Take my word for it," Seneca wrote, "the trip doesn't exist that can set you beyond the reach of cravings, fits of temper, or fears."[23]

These grave misgivings have persisted. "I have been reading books of travels all my life," Jean-Jacques Rousseau wrote, "but I have never found two that gave me the same idea of the same nation." Those who "travel best," he added, "travel least," and, in Rousseau's opinion, they travelled not by coach but on foot.[24] Others have agreed. Writing at the end of the eighteenth century, Xavier de Maistre (brother to the more famous Joseph) resolved only to journey for forty-two days around his own room, "safe from the restless jealousy of men." "We will travel slowly," he wrote, "laughing as we go at those travellers who have visited Rome and Paris." Heading north, Maistre discovered his bed.[25] On this view, one travelled best by moving hardly at all. In the nineteenth century, John Stuart Mill displayed a similarly dismissive attitude. "In travelling," he wrote, "men usually see only what they already had in their own minds."[26]

Yet, from the Renaissance onwards, travel became an ever more popular activity. At the outset, it served largely utilitarian purposes. Scientists travelled to collect data on fauna and flora, philosophers to observe people and their customs. Young, usually aristocratic men (much like Tocqueville) were sent abroad by their families or by their governments with the express purpose of studying the political institutions and military capacities of their neighbours and rivals. Only later did travel feature as an integral and indispensable part of the cultural and aesthetic education of the European elite, reaching its apogee in the seventeenth and eighteenth centuries with the so-called Grand Tour. Although the itinerary varied over the time, the focus throughout remained firmly on Italy, with the intention of introducing young men of wealth to the artistic glories of classical antiquity and the Renaissance. Many a young traveller also took the opportunity of being abroad to indulge in gambling, drinking, and sex of various exotic kinds. The continental wars that followed the French Revolution and the rise to power of Napoleon Bonaparte effectively put an end to travel to mainland Europe (encouraging the more adventurous to visit the eastern Mediterranean) but, with the return to peace in 1815, something akin to the Grand Tour reappeared and, despite the advent of mass travel, continued to exist in a much truncated form into the twentieth century. Here travel featured as a rite of passage. Without the knowledge and connoisseurship provided by the Grand Tour, an aspiring gentleman felt a sense of cultural inferiority. The young Alexis de Tocqueville was to make this journey when he visited Italy in 1826.

Yet the Grand Tour was not without its rivals. Not everyone embraced the ideals of "noble simplicity and calm grandeur" espoused by Johann Winkelmann in his *Reflections on the Imitation of Greek Art* of 1755.[27] Indeed, that same decade Edmund Burke set out the principles of an entirely different aesthetic in his *Philosophical Enquiry into the Origins of the Sublime and Beautiful.* This newly emerging Romantic sensibility took several forms. One was an attraction to things dark and terrifying, to the unconscious and supernatural that came to be associated with Gothic literature and art more generally. Ruins featured prominently, as did storms and tempests.[28] Another was an interest in what became known as the *pittoresque,* or picturesque. This, too, took a variety of guises—in art, literature, music, architecture, gardens, and the like—but the central idea was to draw inspiration not from high art but from nature. This in turn gave rise to the phenomenon of *pittoresque* travel. Here, instead of heading towards Italy and the warm south, the traveller was much more likely to head north to the English Lake District or the Scottish Highlands in search of wild, natural beauty, all preferably enhanced by a reading of the medieval romances of Walter Scott and a dose of melancholia at the passing of time.[29] One such traveller was Tocqueville's elder brother, Édouard. Armed with the obligatory sketchbook, he set off for England, Scotland, and Ireland in 1824.[30] A decade later, Alexis was to follow in his footsteps.

Over time, travel became not only more accessible but also less costly and less hazardous (especially with the introduction of rail travel from the 1840s onwards). The first of the famous Baedeker guides was published in 1835 (star ratings for sights and accommodation were introduced in 1846) whilst the first Murray guide, *A Handbook for Travellers on the Continent,* appeared in 1836.

The French equivalent, the *Guides jaunes* (later better known as the *Guides bleus*) began publication in 1841. All were essential reading for a new travelling public eager to know, as Murray put it, what "ought to be seen."

The words *tourist* and *tourism* had entered our vocabulary by the early nineteenth century, with the novelist Stendhal publishing his two-volume *Mémoires d'un touriste* in 1838. To that extent, there is little new about today's guidebooks, with their tips on hotels and practical hints on how to get there and what to eat, except perhaps that they are now more numerous and less well informed than Stendhal's descriptions of the wonders of Florence and southern France. Even by this early date, there was awareness that the new tourism would destroy the beauty—and, no less importantly, the social exclusiveness—of the places and locations being visited.[31] The German poet and literary critic Heinrich Heine was not alone in voicing the complaint that one could not visit Italy without seeing English tourists "swarming everywhere."[32] Tocqueville noted something similar when, writing to his close friend Francisque de Corcelle from Germany in 1854, he remarked, "Where can one not meet the English?"[33] It goes without saying that, despite some notable exceptions, travel remained an activity largely denied to women, especially if they travelled alone.[34]

But what is it that impels people to travel? Why, as Bruce Chatwin muses, do people wander rather than stand still?[35] In the nineteenth century, as remains the case today, the motives were often prosaic in the extreme: the delights of a warmer climate, living cheaply, escaping disastrous marriages or sexual scandal, or simply having nothing much else better to do. Similarly, then as now, travel sometimes took the form of an attempted step back into a simpler and seemingly more authentic past, a journey infused with the sentiment of melancholic belatedness and nostalgia for what the world was once like. Wandering into the primeval forests of North America was a case in point. More seriously, travel has been and continues to be enforced as a fleeing into exile or a means of escaping persecution.[36] In other cases, the traveller engages in the hazardous (and often fruitless) activity of self-discovery, an attempt to reveal the secrets of a soul that is often not there.[37] In its less spiritual form, the traveller looks for something missing, for the unfamiliar, for distance and distraction from the monotonies or relentless challenges of everyday life. The poet Charles Baudelaire, following Blaise

Pascal, spoke of the restlessness associated with "the horror of home." Tocqueville's contemporary, the writer Gustave Flaubert, was a case in point. He left France for the Orient largely out of boredom and contempt for the grey provincial surroundings in Rouen, the place of his birth in northern France. The chaos and colour (not to mention the brothels and other erotic entertainments) of Cairo were more to his sensualist tastes.[38] Here travel served as the pursuit of happiness and as an expression, however misguided, of freedom.

For others, travel has taken the form of political pilgrimage and an opportunity to embrace a foreign cause.[39] Often driven by a heady mixture of self-hatred and ideological fanaticism, the spirit of radiant optimism and naive faith (not to mention personal suffering) with which these resolute voyagers make their pilgrim's progress towards a promised land is not easily extinguished.[40] What they see and describe is often a utopia of their own imaginings.

Such naive and dangerous idealism flourished in the nineteenth century. Socialists such as Charles Fourier and Étienne Cabet, doubting the possibility of radical reform at home, were only too eager to send their followers to the unpopulated and virgin territories of the American West in the hope of establishing model communities based on their principles. In America, Cabet wrote, "there would be the most beautiful roads, the most perfect towns and villages, the most magnificent workshops, perfection in housing, furniture, clothing, food, hygiene, and education, in a word, in everything!"[41] The reality of disease and internal dissent—as well as the authoritarian tendencies of their leaders—ensured that hardly any of these communities lasted more than a few years.[42] The contradiction between real life and idealism has continued to be a feature of such communities to this day, the traveller's pursuit of brotherly and sisterly love frequently descending into violence, persecution, and schism.[43]

Conversely, as Joseph Conrad's famous novella *Heart of Darkness* recounts, travel can be a journey into such darkness, to a place of fear and profound disquiet. To quote Baudelaire again, he spoke of a "taste for the abyss." For Conrad, writing "at the sea-reach of the Thames," the location of this unsettling vision was a journey up the Congo River in search of Mr. Kurtz, but in the nineteenth century it was often Russia that attracted adventurers and outcasts, those drawn to its vast emptiness and thrilled by the idea of living on and beyond the edge of civilisation. To travel there was to move from the known world to its borders, to leave Europe behind for a vast and mysterious continent where nature and brutality held sway. The Spain of the so-called black legend attracted similar negative stereotypical descriptions. "Artists wishing to portray violent passions," Paul Preston has written recently, "drew upon a view of Spain, its history and its people as the embodiment of fanaticism, cruelty and uncontrolled passion." The imagined savagery of both its landscape and inhabitants proved an irresistible attraction to French and British travellers alike.[44]

America has for long been the subject of such dystopian forms of travel. This is how Frances Trollope described her first sighting of the United States in 1827: "I never beheld a scene so utterly desolate as [the] entrance to the Mississippi. Had Dante seen it, he might have drawn images of another Bolgia from its horrors." For the unfortunate Mrs. Trollope things scarcely got better during the remainder of her stay.[45] All too often, descriptions of America were reduced to a catalogue of bestial eating habits and boorish behaviour. Writing in the early 1840s, the English novelist Charles Dickens described the nation's capital as "the headquarters of tobacco-tinctured saliva." As for the "political machinery" he saw in Washington, DC, these, he assured his English readers, were "the worst tools ever wrought: despicable trickery at elections; under-handed tampering with public officers, cowardly attacks upon opponents, with scurrilous newspapers for shields, and hired pens for daggers."[46]

A similarly critical appraisal of America can be found in the writings of Tocqueville's near contemporary, Victor Jacquemont.[47] Having returned to France disillusioned after his visit to America in 1826–1827, Jacquemont gave clear expression to these pessimistic sentiments. In America, he wrote, it was impossible for any political leader to rise above the level of the masses. No country was so lacking in originality and no population less colourful. Everyone came from the same mould, in much the same way as "houses are all built exactly to the same plan." Americans, Jacquemont continued, were humourless. Relations between the sexes were characterised by "coldness" and a lack of intimacy. Parents treated their children without tenderness and manners were "stiff, flat and vulgar." In addition, Americans had no taste for art or poetry, and no appreciation of what was beautiful—only a sense of material pleasures and the pursuit of wealth. They might buy copies of the works of Lord Byron and Walter Scott, Jacquemont wrote, but they never read them. As for New York, from a literary and scientific point of view, it was more "wretched" than the small French provincial towns of Pointoise or Melun.

The horrors of America have been a staple of French and British literature ever since. So, if Tocqueville was one of the first to observe the tendency towards conformism in American society, it has been a commonplace to compare a superior French civilisation to the wasteland of American mass culture and consumerism. "In the United States," Georges Duhamel was later to write, "what strikes the European traveller is the progressive approximation of human life to what we know of the way of life of insects—the same effacement of the individual, the same progressive reduction and unification of social types, the same organization of the group into special castes."[48] Disliking a place that one has had the misfortune to visit is therefore nothing new.

Moreover, travel is all too frequently not a cause of discovery and excitement, let alone of astonished arrival, but a source of suffering and tedium. We know that behind the smiling faces captured on today's holiday photos and selfies lie cancelled flights, dodgy hotel plumbing, predatory locals, indescribable food, and diseases one previously did not know existed. Replace the reference to airports and flights with stagecoaches and paddle boats, and one has a pretty accurate picture of the hardships and inconveniences experienced by travellers during their time in America in the early years of the new republic, and indeed of travel most everywhere at the time. Of her experience aboard a steamboat, the indomitable Mrs. Trollope wrote, "I would infinitely prefer sharing the apartment of a party of well-conditioned pigs to being confined to its cabin."[49] In Tocqueville's case, the steamboat he and Beaumont were travelling on down the Ohio River hit a reef in the middle of the night and sank.

But all travellers, be they explorers or simple visitors, face the problems of trying to understand a culture and a country that is not their own and, in whatever accounts that may follow, of representing other people.[50] Some fail miserably; others succeed brilliantly. Those that succeed usually possess a generosity of spirit and a degree of empathy for what they see before them.

They see more than what is outside the window and do so through something akin to a transparent lens. For such travellers, travel shows us otherness and expands our knowledge of the variety and diversity of the world.[51] By contrast, those that fail often do so because they judge a place by its dissimilarities with their own country and by its failure to meet their own standards. Writing after his return from America in 1793, Jacques-Pierre Brissot de Warville commented that "the greater part of Frenchmen who travel and emigrate have little information and are not prepared in the art of observation. Presumptuous to a fault, and admirers of their own customs and manners, they ridicule those of other nations."[52] Many nineteenth-century European visitors to America could not see beyond the dreadful food, grimy hotels, and uncouth manners. The spittoon figured prominently in their accounts.

In a similar vein, many of those who have either chosen or been paid to recount their travels have had no intention of producing anything more than a list of interesting locations to visit, no matter how little or long they stayed in a place. Some writers, out of laziness or fear, or a mixture of both, simply describe places they have never visited or cared to visit, secure in the knowledge that their inattentive readers will never catch them out. Here travel writing, far from being a work of nonfiction, becomes entangled with fabrication and invention.

This was as true in the nineteenth century as it is in our own age of the fake travel blog and the faux spontaneity of Instagram. Lady Emmeline Stuart-Wortley spoke rather disarmingly of her account of her visit to America as an instance of "the gossip of travel," of appeal only to those for whom "gossip is welcome."[53] The American critic John Graham Brooks, writing in 1908, remarked that he could think of at least twenty books by French visitors to America from which "one could remove the various and picturesque titles, replacing them by 'A Whole Afternoon in the United States.'" Too many of these writers, he continued, "begin to write on the steamer coming out; take their first impressions as a finality, giving them literary form so rapidly that the book is on the Boulevards soon after their return."[54] Both the novelist Stendhal and the jurist Édouard Laboulaye wrote with great authority and insight about America without ever going there.[55]

Others of a loftier disposition have turned their journeys into art. Mixing fact with fiction, literature with autobiography, such writers fashion largely imaginary journeys which, for all their factual inaccuracies, are on occasion hugely influential. One notorious case of the latter is the work of Tocqueville's cousin, Francois-René de Chateaubriand. For almost a century, doubt has been cast upon the account presented by Chateaubriand in his *Voyage en Amérique,* but in his day, his largely invented descriptions of an American wilderness "as old as the world" and of the native peoples who inhabited it were largely accepted as being true.[56] Tocqueville arrived in America with Chateaubriand's account of America at the forefront of his mind. Nonetheless, such infelicities help us to understand why the celebrated anthropologist Claude Lévi-Strauss could begin his account of his time in Brazil, *Tristes tropiques,* with the memorable phrase, "I hate travelling and explorers."[57] The suspicion that writing about one's travels has been the work of self-indulgent fantasists has not been easy to dispel.

Another all-too-frequent characteristic of the travel genre has been and remains reliant upon a set of concepts and categories that are taken to be self-evident and self-explanatory. Beginning in the eighteenth century, it was widely assumed that nations possessed a national genius or character. References abound to Mediterranean joyousness, Latin clarity, German spirituality, and English pragmatism. If one understood the national character, one understood the country and its people. Such forms of argument are easily found in the writings of both the Baron de Montesquieu and Rousseau, but a work such as Astolphe de Custine's *La Russie en 1839* provided a portrayal of the gloomy and violent Russian character that was as influential and enduring among Europeans as were the stereotypical images of the amorous and morally dubious Italian. Madame de Stäel did much the same with her widely read *De l'Allemagne,* first published in 1813. Not until the Franco-Prussian War of 1870–1871 brought home the truth of German militarism could any educated French man or woman conceive of Germany and its people as anything other than a temple to literature and philosophy.

In the case of the American nation, and despite considerable ignorance of American realities, among French observers its character was quickly established and was taken to include patriotism, optimism, energy, versatility, excessive hospitality, and, of course, a love of hard work and making money. As

Achille Murat observed in his *Esquisse morale et politique des États-Unis de l'Amérique du Nord,* first published in 1832, most travellers to America returned to Europe convinced that Americans were "very polite and very adroit and that the government continues to exist because everyone, being busy with their own affairs, leaves it alone."[58] Tocqueville was to be one of these travellers.

In contrast to the British, who tended to see Americans as unsophisticated Englishmen living abroad, the French were always immediately struck by the stark differences between the French and American national characters. There seemed to be little in common between the sophisticated and elegant habitué of the Parisian salon and the brash self-made millionaire from Pittsburgh. French sociability and American coarseness seemed the marks of opposing civilisations. This explains why many French writers identified so readily with the culture of a leisured aristocracy then existing in the southern states. The fear of an Americanisation of French society set in early—certainly by the 1850s—but this did not stop the French, like their British counterparts, taking American money when it was offered.

All of this begged the question of which part or segment of a society provided the most authentic insight into a nation's identity: was it the rich, the poor, the city dweller, the peasant? One recurring theme in the debate about national character was that it was often most clearly disclosed through the behaviour and place of women in society. If, as was largely agreed, the essential clue to a nation's character lay in its *moeurs,* or mores, then women were deemed to be one of the principal instruments through which these were forged. How women played out their social and familial roles and how, in particular, they educated the young was a measure of how good a nation's character was and how that nation's future might be shaped. Again, Montesquieu and Rousseau figured prominently in these discussions—especially with regard to what they saw as the propensity of women to enjoy and value luxury—but later French visitors to America were quick to perceive the very distinctive qualities and special role of women in American society. Once more, Tocqueville (as well as his travelling companion, Beaumont) was among the many French travellers who saw that there was something very distinctive about the family structure in America and the place occupied by women within it. They also saw that relations between the sexes were of a decidedly different and less amorous nature than those they had observed at home.[59]

In addition to references to a—often partly hidden—national character or genius, it was also believed that a country could be understood by reference to its physical shape and its climate. The title alone of the comte de Volney's *Tableau du climat et du sol des États-Unis,* first published in 1803, is enough to illustrate the point. As Volney explained, his "method" told him that one began with geography and climate before moving on, in order, to size and distribution of population, varieties of work and occupation, the mores "resulting from these occupations," and finally the combination of these practices with the ideas and preconceptions derived from a society's origins.[60] It was in no way unusual, therefore, for Tocqueville to begin the first volume of *De la démocratie en Amérique* with a chapter looking at America's "exterior configuration." America's vast continent, it was widely agreed, was an expression of its destiny.

The same applied to climate. Temperature and humidity were thought to shape character from one climate to another. Captain Marryat, in his *Diary of America,* wrote that "the excitement so general throughout the Union and forming so remarkable a feature of the American character, is occasioned much more by climate than by any other cause." Climate explained the difference between the "hot-blooded Southerner" and the "cold-calculating Yankee," and why the farmer from the Eastern Seaboard became "indolent, reckless and often intemperate" when he moved to the warmer temperatures of the South and West. It also explained why Americans were so prone to "the use of tobacco and of spirituous liquors." "Their climate," Marryat concluded, "I unhesitatingly pronounce to be bad, being injurious to them in two important points, of healthy vigour in the body, and healthy action of the mind; enervating the one and tending to demoralize the other."[61] Again, Tocqueville was not immune from this tendency. Having seen firsthand both the "calm, moral, pious" French of Canada and the "restless, dissolute, lax" French of Louisiana, Tocqueville informed Ernest de Chabrol that "should you encounter anyone alleging that climate has no effect on the constitution of a people, assure them they are wrong."[62]

But few imagined that climate was all-determining. "Many things govern men," Montesquieu wrote in *The Spirit of the Laws,* "climate, religion, laws, the maxims of government, examples of past things, mores, and manners."[63] And what the dominant factor was would change over time and from place to place. Of note here was that, from the eighteenth century onwards, French authors increasingly came to emphasise that it was political institutions that played a decisive role in shaping a people. "No people," Rousseau wrote in his *Confessions,* "would ever be anything other than what its Government made of it."[64] If Tocqueville did not entirely agree, when he looked at America he certainly saw that the nature of the country's political institutions played an important part in shaping the lives of its people.

Yet foreign countries and places exist as ideas and symbols. If the unfortunate Ottoman Empire figured in the European imagination for centuries as a land of despotism and misery, China could not escape its portrayal as a backward, stagnant nation. In the case of America, it came to symbolise many things and arguably has done so since the time of the discovery of the Americas by Christopher Columbus.[65] For Europeans, America has often existed as a kind of dream, as a tabula rasa, a providential promised land, a primitive and pre-lapsarian garden of Eden, where a new chapter of our history could be acted out and written.[66] For many, America could not exist simply as America. It was taken as a given—and not only by Americans imbued with a spirit of manifest destiny—that the future course of American civilisation would have a bearing upon the rest of the world. America was the authentic form of modernity. That it is now argued by some that America would have been better had Columbus never set sail across the Atlantic Ocean and that what marks America as exceptional is not the nature of its democracy but the institution of slavery does not diminish what was the historic power of these ideas.

Tocqueville was only one among many who shared these preconceptions. Concluding his very first chapter of *De la démocratie en Amérique,* he wrote that America "is where civilized men had to try to build society on new foundations. Applying, for the first time, theories until then unknown or considered inapplicable, civilized men were going to present a spectacle for which past history had not prepared the world."[67] In a very real sense, America was as much invented as it was discovered.

Where does Alexis de Tocqueville fit into this picture of travel?[68] Was he just another young aristocrat journeying overseas with nothing much better to do? Or was he, like many a traveller both before and since, someone who felt the pressing need to be elsewhere? Did he see travel to exotic locations as an opportunity for personal reinvention? Was he in search of an idealised vision of the future?

The first thing to point out is that Tocqueville spent a considerable amount of his time travelling within the borders of France. This was due largely, but not exclusively, to the fact that his family home was situated at the northern extremity of the Cotentin Peninsula in Normandy. Getting to Paris from there was no easy matter, and for the greater part of his life this was a journey undertaken largely by stagecoach, an experience that was never anything less than uncomfortable and exhausting. In July 1841 Tocqueville wrote to his father in a mood of considerable triumph to report that he had completed the journey in only twenty-four hours.[69] All too often these journeys were dogged by logistical difficulties involving extensive delays. Another route was to travel from the nearby port of Cherbourg by ship to Le Havre and then boat down the River Seine to Paris. This might explain why one of Tocqueville's later obsessions was his campaign to secure the completion of the Paris-to-Cherbourg railway.[70] A journey to Marseilles—made by Tocqueville on several occasions—would commence with a carriage or *diligence* from Paris and conclude with a boat journey down the River Rhône by boat, all subject to possible delay due to bad weather or a flooding river.[71] Even travelling around Tocqueville's parliamentary constituency, usually done on horseback, was fraught with difficulties—especially in the winter, when what passed for roads were swamped by mud and rain.

Moreover, as numerous nineteenth-century testimonies recounted, for many inhabitants of Paris to travel beyond the Île-de-France often felt like visiting an unknown and unhospitable foreign country. This can be illustrated by citing the opening sentence of Eugen Weber's classic text *Peasants into Frenchmen.* It is a quotation from Honoré de Balzac's novel, *Les paysans,* written in 1844: "You don't need to go to America to see savages. . . . Here are the Redskins of Fenimore Cooper."[72] No doubt Balzac's tale of brutal, thieving, and vindictive peasants in Burgundy contained an element of literary exaggeration—his friend, the novelist George Sand, certainly thought so—but it captured something of the view that large sections of France's vast rural population were relatively untouched by the values of modern civilisation, living an unchanging and isolated life dominated by poverty and superstition. Until well into the nineteenth century, the majority of France's inhabitants did not actually speak French.

Did Tocqueville share this Parisian horror of rural life? He certainly found the long journeys to his family home to be something of a trial, especially as his health deteriorated in the 1850s. He was also aware that the view from Paris and the view from *la France profonde* were often very different, especially when it came to politics. Having returned to Tocqueville from Paris in the spring of 1848, he informed his wife that "I cannot tell you what a singular impression seeing the countryside and even the towns made upon me. You would have thought yourself in another country than the France of Paris. People going about their affairs, artisans, labourers, all peaceably; the tranquillity of the open country, the carefree countenance of the peasants, all this presented such a massive contrast with what I had left behind me that I asked myself whether it was me who was seeing things incorrectly or the remarkably peaceful people I was meeting."[73]

But it is beyond doubt that Tocqueville's fondness for life at his family home in Normandy and for the surrounding countryside was always strong. "The more I travel around this world," Tocqueville wrote from Philadelphia in 1831, "the more I am inclined to think that it is only domestic happiness that counts."[74] Writing to his wife in 1837, he commented that "dear Tocqueville" had always figured in his imagination as "a haven of peace and happiness, a port providing shelter amidst the storms."[75] Two decades later this sentiment was undiminished. It was at Tocqueville, he told his wife, that "I have spent the happiest days of my life."[76]

Tocqueville undoubtedly enjoyed aspects of country life, especially as he got older.[77] Writing from Tocqueville in the summer of 1850, he told Jean-Jacques Ampère, "I greatly enjoy the place where I live, as old and as ugly as it might be. I definitely have a weakness for these meadows, for these hedges, for this wet and green labyrinth which surrounds me: I feel calm and relaxed here."[78] To his friend Madame de Circourt he wrote in 1857 that "my day is divided into two parts: up to lunchtime I am a scribbler who is fairly discontented with himself; from lunchtime until the evening I become a peasant; I am outside in all weathers and always find that time is too short; when evening comes I return home as tired as the labourer who has finished his day's work."[79]

And there can be no doubt that Tocqueville threw himself at times into the life and activities of his estate. Returning to Tocqueville after an extended absence and finding it, as he told Beaumont, returned to a "Wilderness," he eagerly set to on the work required to get things back in order. Five weeks later he told Beaumont that he had been right to suggest that the thousand little tasks of a property owner would keep him busy and away from his writing. What with "obligatory visits to make, workers to watch over, orders to give, and a house to put back into shape" there was time for little else.[80] Three months later Tocqueville reported that, despite the expense and the time involved, he was pleased with what had been achieved.

Correspondence with Tocqueville's English friends also shows how seriously he took the practical matters of agricultural life. There is, for example, a marvellous exchange of letters between Tocqueville and the distinguished English writer Harriet Grote that largely concerns iron fences and hurdles and which includes Tocqueville's request to be sent the manufacturer's specimen catalogue, with illustrated patterns. "I cannot prevent myself from laughing," Tocqueville wrote, "in thinking about the subject of this correspondence: a member of the Académie française, writing to one of the most brilliant women in England, and talking about horses, cows and sheep." For the moment, at least, Tocqueville told Mrs. Grote, he had completely given up the trade of author and had become "a man of the fields."[81] A year later he told Nassau Senior that he was living the life of a "*gentleman farmer*" and enjoying it more by the day.[82] Following Tocqueville's visit to England in 1857 there was also a correspondence with Lord Radnor about the acquisition of two of the latter's finest pigs, the magnificent beasts duly arriving in August 1857. "I was expecting to see two small animals in a basket," he told Radnor, "instead of which I saw coming out of two large lattice-work boxes two very lucky animals that immediately attracted the admiration of all our neighbours." None of the inhabitants of the village, it seems, had ever seen such fine porcine specimens.[83] Writing to Louis de Loménie at the end of the year, Tocqueville reported that, while he was working seriously on his next book, he was also building a stable for these pigs. Which of the two, he mused, would survive the longest, his book or his pigsty with its strong walls?[84] A visit to Lord Hatherton's model farm at Teddesley in Staffordshire engendered not only wild enthusiasm on Tocqueville's part—he was especially impressed by the living quarters of both "*messieurs les cochons*" and the farm labourers—but also a later correspondence about how to produce the best "*farmyard manure*" and the working of Hatherton's new agricultural steam engine.[85]

Nor is there any shortage of evidence to show that Tocqueville took his duties as a landowner very seriously, not least with regard to the welfare of the local population. A letter written to Tocqueville's father as the winter approached in 1855 informed him that "we are employing a certain number of men whose age is such that they cannot secure gainful work anywhere else but with us." The same letter expressed Tocqueville's annoyance that he had been unable to get the local priest and mayor to cooperate over the provision of regular charitable support to the local population. Tocqueville's solution was to suggest that they should increase the amount of bread they distributed for free every fortnight.[86]

Yet for all the affection that Tocqueville felt towards his family home in Normandy, as well as the people and landscape that surrounded it, there is no doubt that this, and this alone, would not have satisfied him. Many of Tocqueville's early letters from Normandy contain accounts of his election campaigns, arduous activities that included not only too many copious meals for his taste (and fragile stomach) but also mixing with his constituents. If Tocqueville undoubtedly admired their good sense and capacity for hard work, he was only too pleased to get back to his château at the end of the day. He also was fully aware of the limitations of their vision of the world. Writing to Francisque de Corcelle at the time of the Crimean War, he reported that if, since their arrival at Tocqueville, he and his wife had been living a solitary existence, he felt that he had acquired a fairly accurate picture of how people saw things. "The war," he wrote, "is something of a worry; above all people fear a rise in the cost of living; when they have the time, they moan about the loss of children who have joined the army; but at bottom they are so delighted to sell their livestock and their wheat at a good price that all the rest gets drowned out by a general joy." He now understood, he explained, how people who spent their entire lives in this "heavy and debilitating atmosphere" came little by little to feel "enervated" and "weighed down." Although, he wrote, "I *rub along* happily enough in this land of cattle and cattle dealers. . . . I hope nevertheless that I can resist this contagion and continue to find the happiness with which these people are so contented to be unsatisfactory."[87]

The truth of the matter was that Tocqueville felt torn between the two worlds he inhabited. A letter written to Camille d'Orglandes in 1835 revealed that he could only conceive of two types of life: that of "distant travel or the fireside."[88] This was a feeling that was never to leave him. "I need to return to Paris," he told his cousin Eugénie de Grancey in February 1858, "but it will pain me to leave my fields, the trees I plant, the meadows I have improved, and above all my dear wild countryside to which I become more attached by the day. So, I want to leave and I want to stay. This is the history of my life, but who is the man who has not wanted at least two things at the same time?"[89]

Tocqueville certainly missed the intellectual stimulation that came from the company and conversation of his many friends. Letter after letter sent by him from his home included an invitation to stay in Normandy, and many recorded his disappointment when this did not come to pass. Indeed, like many a person both then and since, Tocqueville's ideal appears to have been the halfway house of life in the country but proximity to the metropolis. "In many respects," he told Adolphe de Circourt, "I confess that I much prefer to live a hundred leagues from Paris than at its gates. . . . I have almost no desire to live in the capital (as they say in the provinces) but to live an hour's journey away would be very useful for me at the moment: close enough to be able to find the old papers, books and people I need; far enough away to gather one's thoughts in country life, taking from Paris what it can give of use without being subjected to what it produces that is empty and boring." Unfortunately, Tocqueville added, fate had arranged things differently.[90]

Nevertheless, there can be no doubt that throughout his life Tocqueville longed to travel. A letter written in 1834 to his then wife-to-be, Mary Mottley, gave a clear sense of the restlessness that drove Tocqueville to travel. Written from the country home of the Beaumont family, and delighted by the warm reception he had received, he was struck by the care and attention his hosts devoted to their trees and the growing of their crops. They wished for nothing more, Tocqueville commented, and lived life with a "tranquil heart." This, he added, was something he could understand: "I love to look at fields; at the sight of a beautiful summer evening in a remote and peaceful countryside, listening to the different sounds which are heard at long intervals and the silence which follows them." But, he went on, the thought of resigning himself to a life of such sweet and monotonous pleasures had no appeal. Displaying to the full the enthusiasm of the Romantics for travel, Tocqueville concluded, "I would prefer life's roughest storms to such peacefulness. . . . With limited abilities I yet feel vast desires; with delicate health, an inexpressible desire for action and emotion."[91]

This was to be a frequent theme in his letters. Writing from Tocqueville over twenty years later, he wrote to Francisque de Corcelle, "Here I am in the place that I love the most, surrounded by the objects that are to me the most agreeable of the physical things that one might find on this earth, amongst people that I like to meet, in a community that suits me best; nevertheless, for all the sweetness of this life, I feel myself gripped by this vague agitation of the spirit from which I have suffered so much in the past."[92]

Time and time again in his letters to Gustave de Beaumont and to others, Tocqueville expressed how strongly he wanted to travel and how much he envied their opportunity to do so. Travel was certainly more appealing, he told Beaumont in 1845, than the life of "sterile agitation" he was living as a member of parliament in France.[93] This desire to travel did not diminish with either age or illness. "I am beginning," he wrote to Lord Hatherton in March 1858, "no longer willingly to undertake long journeys or long absences; nevertheless, both my curiosity and temperament often push me to want to cross the English Channel."[94] But, for Tocqueville, there was more to travel than mere curiosity; it was written into the human condition. "I liken man in this world," he wrote to his friend Louis de Kergorlay, "to a traveller who is walking constantly toward an increasingly cold region and who is forced to move more as he advances."[95]

Yet the tensions between the pull of the domestic hearth and the lure of distant places were never far from the surface. In his earliest travel notes, Tocqueville spoke rather self-pityingly—he was temporarily marooned on a small island in the Mediterranean—of "the horror of exile," of the demoralisation arising from a sense of "abandonment and isolation," and of how being in a foreign country inspired a powerful sense of the beauty and charms of one's homeland.[96] Newly arrived in New York, he told his mother of the "most agonizing worries" arising from the "almost two months and fifteen hundred leagues of sea" that separated them from each other.[97] Later he told his father that "absence has begun to weigh heavily upon me." Never, he continued, had his heart been as heavy as on the day of his departure from France.[98]

Did Tocqueville revel in the sensation of being an anonymous stranger and in the loneliness and solitude that can make travel an intense and rewarding experience? Again, this seems doubtful. In a letter of 1856 to Madame Swetchine, Tocqueville commented "Isolation has always frightened me." It was to him, he added, that could be applied the words (taken from the second chapter of the book of Genesis) that 'It is not good for the man to be alone.'"[99] Writing to his friend Madame de Circourt in 1853, he commented, "when travelling have you not felt on the morning of your arrival in a foreign town where everything—the people, the language, the mores—is new and unknown to you that, although you are surrounded by crowds, you are more overwhelmed by the sentiment of loneliness than if you were lost in a wood"?[100] Likewise, upon arriving in London in 1857 and finding himself temporarily unable to find a hotel room, he wrote to his wife, "I have still to see anyone. At this moment in time I am therefore lost in this vast city, more overwhelmed by the sense of isolation than I ever was in my youth in the midst of the forests of the New World. I hope this feeling passes soon, as it is very painful."[101]

To compensate for this sense of isolation, wherever he went Tocqueville wrote voluminous letters to his family and friends in France and longed, in return, to receive news from them. Hearing nothing, if only for two weeks, he told his mother from Switzerland, "destroys the joy of travel."[102] Yet, for all of that, Tocqueville could see the other side of the coin. To Charles Stoffels (who had just returned from travelling alone in Germany and who had clearly not enjoyed the experience), Tocqueville remarked that "a travelling companion is a useful thing to have and often necessary in a foreign country, particularly in a country where you have no knowledge of the language"; but except in such a case, he continued, they could often spoil the journey. "In travelling alone," he wrote, "I have sometimes felt a sudden and inexpressible sense of unease and a truly awful sense of isolation, but these feelings were fleeting. For the remainder of the time, I have felt a sense of liberty and independence, a liveliness and sharpness of sensation that I would not have experienced in the company of another." "I would not want to spend my entire life in this way," he concluded, "but to break, if only for a moment, all the links that attach one to society: to think, to will, to act according to one's own impulses, this, in truth, is a great pleasure."[103]

Yet Tocqueville did not seem to take much delight in being an unknown outsider. Upon his arrival in New York, he clearly enjoyed the celebrity status with which he and Beaumont were received into polite society. The same applied to his visits to London in 1833 and 1835, when Tocqueville was wined and dined by the cream of England's Whig aristocracy and much impressed by the splendour of the Athenaeum on London's Pall Mall.[104] Rarely did he arrive anywhere without a letter of introduction in his pocket. It is interesting to note that Tocqueville never returned to America, despite frequent invitations from his friends to do so. He seemed happy to leave it to others to verify or contradict his conclusions and predictions.

Tocqueville also frequently broke one of the golden rules of those for whom travel is a form of escape and flight: he rarely travelled alone. To his father he confided that he thought the best way to travel was with one's servant, as the "sense of isolation and abandonment" associated with falling ill while travelling was "awful." Unfortunately, he added, he was not wealthy enough to afford such arrangements.[105] Therefore, Tocqueville usually had to rely on one of his many friends or, upon occasion, his wife.

Nor is it hard to conclude that for Tocqueville travel was at times something of a physical ordeal, and one frequently accompanied by exhaustion and illness—and, sometimes, depression.[106] We catch the earliest glimpse of this at the end of his first visit to Switzerland. In a long letter to Gustave de Beaumont, dated 25 October 1829, Tocqueville reported that, although now partially recovered, he had been ill for four days with stomach pains and a fever. "My health," he told Beaumont, "seems far from improving with the years, and physical exertion seems to take more out of me than in the past." "I am frightened of being frightened," he added.[107]

These concerns were to prove more serious than even Tocqueville might have feared. Most dangerously of all, he fell ill in America. Travelling in the bitter cold between Nashville and Memphis, he came down with what reads like a life-threatening fever. It was the devoted Beaumont who cared for him, building an enormous fire in their log cabin, piling Tocqueville's bed with all the covers he could find and feeding him with rabbit stew.[108] Of that challenging journey across the American continent in winter, from Chesapeake Bay Tocqueville told Ernest de Chabrol that it had routinely been characterised by "broken and overturned carriages, washed away bridges, flooded rivers, and nowhere to stay."[109] He again fell seriously ill in May 1835 when staying in England and was obliged to spend two weeks "in almost complete isolation," convalescing at the home of his future translator Henry Reeve in Hampstead.[110] When on his return journey to France he landed on the island of Guernsey, he was so ill and weak from the voyage that he had to take immediately to his bed.[111] Tocqueville's trip to Algeria with Beaumont and Hippolyte de Tocqueville in the spring of 1841 had to be cut short as, after a series of debilitating illnesses, he came down with dysentery. "My body," he told his wife Mary when he safely returned to the port of Toulon, on France's Mediterranean coast, "is quite definitely an old piece of rubbish for which nothing can be done." It was, he continued, "a machine that needs rest" and was fit for neither physical effort nor emotional excitement.[112]

Later, and especially after Tocqueville displayed the first overt symptoms of tuberculosis, travel abroad was sometimes undertaken to provide rest and to improve his health. If wintering in Sorrento with his wife and friends proved a delight—their house, he told his brother Édouard, was surrounded by "a veritable forest of orange and lemon trees"[113]—a visit to Bonn and to a dreary spa in the Black Forest, where he and his wife knew no one, proved much less so. Tocqueville also fell ill when he visited London in the summer of 1857, an illness upon this occasion that he attributed to the "irregular life" he had been living.[114] More often than not when they travelled together, Madame de Tocqueville was ill and confined to her bed.[115] Writing to Jean-Jacques Ampère in July 1855 to confirm that he and his wife had safely returned home to Normandy, Tocqueville commented that they had arrived "slowly but surely," adding "you know that these two adverbs characterise our manner of travelling."[116] It is hard not to conclude that, for Tocqueville, travel and illness all too frequently went hand in hand.[117]

One thing we know for sure is that Tocqueville and his wife enjoyed nothing more than spending their evenings reading travel books together.[118] Another is that travelling by boat was the form of travel that he most disliked.[119] Still another is that Tocqueville, in the words of his friend, Henry Reeve, was "a great walker."[120]

Gustave de Beaumont not only travelled to America with Tocqueville but accompanied him on trips to England and Ireland and to Algeria. No one was better able to assess how Tocqueville travelled. Tocqueville's way of travelling, Beaumont wrote, was "peculiar." Everything was "a matter for observation." Each day Tocqueville framed in his head the questions he wanted to ask and resolve. Every idea that came into his mind was noted down, without delay, and regardless of where he was. For Tocqueville, Beaumont continued, travelling was never just a form of bodily exercise or simply an agreeable way to pass the time. "Rest," Beaumont wrote, "was foreign to his nature." Whether or not his body was actively employed, Tocqueville's mind was always working. Never could he undertake a walk as a simple distraction or engage in conversation as a form of relaxation. The "most agreeable" discussion was the "most useful" discussion. The worst day was "the day lost or ill-spent." Any loss of time was an inconvenience. Consequently, Tocqueville travelled in a "constant state of tension," never arriving in a place without knowing that he would be able to leave it.[121]

A relatively unimportant episode nicely illustrates Tocqueville's desire to make the most of whatever journey he undertook. In 1852 he made what was then the still arduous and long trip from Gustave de Beaumont's home in the west of France to the château de Tocqueville in Normandy. On the day of his departure, he subsequently told Beaumont, he arrived in Beaufossé (the home of his friend Francisque de Corcelle) at eleven o'clock at night, having had a four-hour stopover in Le Mans. There, he reported, he had visited all the "nooks and crannies" and, most importantly, the town's Gothic cathedral. "You see," Tocqueville told Beaumont, "I fulfilled my profession of traveller dutifully." The next day Tocqueville had set off for another overnight stop in Caen and then on to his home on the Cotentin Peninsula.[122]

This relentless activity, Beaumont wrote, was all the more remarkable when one considered Tocqueville's "frail and delicate" health.[123] Tocqueville, he continued, always wanted to submit himself "to the severest, and even to the most perilous of trials." It was this that led Tocqueville, despite advice to the contrary, to decide to go out into the American wilderness, "to pass whole days without rest, and nights without sleep or even shelter."[124]

Nor was it true that Tocqueville only travelled in search of ideas, that he "remained insensible and cold before the sublime scenes of nature." No one, Beaumont argued, felt more strongly the attractions of nature than Tocqueville, and nowhere had this been more so than before "the irresistible spell of the immense wilderness of America, where everything comes together to intoxicate the senses and benumb the intellect."[125] But so, too, is it evident in the account of an ascent up the Mer de Glace on the northern slopes of Mont Blanc, a place, the young Tocqueville wrote, "so different from the habitable world that one felt oneself at the very edge of creation."[126]

According to Beaumont, this spirit of inquiry and exploration was present in Tocqueville from the time of his visit to Italy and Sicily. The same spirit, he added, was evident in his trips to England, Ireland, Germany and Algeria. So was the interminable taking of notes and recording of conversations. Tocqueville continued the practice in England in 1833, in England and Ireland in 1835, in Algeria in 1841, and again in 1846. He even did so in Switzerland in 1836 when he and his new wife went on a belated honeymoon. Some way or another Tocqueville managed to find time to study the Swiss political system. And, of course, Tocqueville took very extensive notes in America. It was in these notes, according to Beaumont, that were to be found, "in embryo," all the "leading ideas" of *De la démocratie en Amérique*.[127]

As these notes and his letters reveal, Tocqueville was always concerned to get below the surface of what he saw and to find the general principles operating within the society he was observing. Peering through the London fog, he told his father that his ambition was to understand "the vast chaos" constituted by British society, a chaos made all the more impenetrable by the fact that there was not one principle from which the consequences inescapably followed.[128] On that same visit he told his sister-in-law Alexandrine that he had not come to England "to dream, but to think and to see."[129] As for

Ireland and its "five centuries of oppression," Tocqueville spoke of it from Dublin as "a frightful labyrinth" through which he was finding his way only with difficulty.[130] Algiers, he told his wife two days after arriving there, was a place "so different from anything I have seen . . . that my mind remains completely confused and I do not know what to think and say."[131] His trip to Algeria in 1846, he informed Beaumont, was in no way intended to be *pittoresque* but a serious endeavour to understand what was going on there.[132] Delayed in the French port of Toulon for ten days, Tocqueville immediately set to work, reading a stack of documents on colonisation designed to make his trip all the more productive.[133] Even towards the end of his life this same spirit endured. Writing from Portsmouth, England, in July 1857 as he was about to return to France, he told his friend Lord Radnor, "I am an inquiring traveller, and among the things which excite my curiosity the most there is nothing which interests me more than the condition of men and the class relations between them."[134]

Much of this spirit of inquiry was nicely summarised in a letter Tocqueville wrote to one of his closest friends, Louis de Kergorlay, in the autumn of 1836. After much hesitation and soul-searching—he was concerned about whether he should marry or not—Kergorlay had set out on an extended trip to Germany. Not only did Tocqueville exhort his friend to find out as much as he could about the Prussian system of administration (vital, he believed, in helping France escape from "the antiliberal swamp"), but he also provided a set of guidelines on how Kergorlay should travel. The first of these was that Kergorlay should meet as many people as possible and that he should get them to speak as much as he could about the things they knew best. Next, as Kergorlay's name and letters of recommendation would gain him easy access to the aristocracy, he should make every effort to mix with the "middle and literary classes." Moreover, he should keep his opinions to himself—as a foreigner, Tocqueville wrote, Kergorlay was not obliged to have an opinion about what was happening in Prussia—and only say what would best encourage his interlocutors to develop their ideas. He should not, Tocqueville continued, only frequent people he found pleasing, and he should "write a lot," as it was only through writing that he would best understand his own ideas and those of others and get to the heart of things. Above all, Tocqueville advised, Kergorlay should do everything he could to avoid a display of "the nonchalance typical of almost all travellers" and to which he was particularly prone.[135] Charles Stoffels received a letter giving similar advice that same year before he set out for Rome, only this time Tocqueville added that Stoffels should do everything he could to avoid the English and the French. If Stoffels wanted to understand "the real Italy," he should mix as much as possible with the people, and to do that he must learn the language.[136]

Tocqueville returned to this theme the following year in another letter to Kergorlay. What defined someone as a traveller, Tocqueville wrote, were the questions he asked. "When people see that you seek to cast an inquisitive eye not over the surface but over the heart of a society," he continued, "they will not take you for a *flâneur*."[137] Here it is interesting to note that Tocqueville later paid a compliment to his good friend Jean-Jacques Ampère by telling him that he was not "a flâneur" who had no need to account for his days but someone engaged in serious work.[138]

In sum, Tocqueville was always seeking to look beyond the external appearance of a place or country he was travelling through and, in so doing, to understand the changing and unfolding world he saw before him. In studying and critically appraising other societies he came better to know his own country and came better to comprehend the challenges and dilemmas it would face. So, too, it might be suggested, it helped Tocqueville find a place for himself within that changing world. None of this was undertaken in a tone of condescension but in a spirit of intellectual generosity and imaginative sympathy. At all times he approached his subject matter with a broad philosophical and creative sweep, and never just as a scientific investigator. Imagination played as important a part as observation. Moreover, Tocqueville's inquiries were driven by a passionate commitment to liberty and an equally passionate desire to understand how it could be preserved and flourish in the democratic society of equals he saw emerging all around him.

This is not to suggest that Tocqueville was not without his weaknesses and failings as both an observer and a commentator. That would be far from the truth. But it does help to explain why *De la démocratie en Amérique* was immediately seen as capturing something profound in the American spirit and why, despite myths to the contrary, it has since remained a continuous presence in American intellectual life.[139] Few would dispute

Tocqueville's seminal role in fashioning what has been an enduring and distinctive portrayal of America.

Having initially considered a trip to England—abandoned due to a lack of both money and parental approval—Tocqueville's first journey outside France (made when he was only twenty-one years old) was to Italy and (unusually for his day) Sicily between December 1826 and the late spring of the following year.[140] On this occasion his elder brother Édouard was his companion. We know relatively little of Tocqueville's stay on the Italian Peninsula, as the travel diary recording his journey has since been lost. However, Gustave de Beaumont did see and read these notes when he was assembling the first edition of Tocqueville's complete works after Tocqueville's death in 1859. His brief remarks indicate that much of Tocqueville's time, like that of many a first visitor to Italy, was spent sightseeing.[141] True to the traditions of the Grand Tour, all the principal cities were visited. The contents of museums were observed "meticulously." Paintings, medals, and great works of art were admired. Tocqueville even began an in-depth study of the principles of classical architecture in order to help him better make sense of what he saw. A letter dated 15 March 1830 and written to Édouard and Alexandrine de Tocqueville on their honeymoon in Italy recalled how much Alexis had enjoyed his visit to Naples. Nothing had ever given him such "sweet and agreeable sensations" as its sky and shoreline.[142] Yet Holy Week in Rome, Tocqueville advised, was best seen from a distance.

Happily, an edited fragment (roughly twenty pages in total) of what was originally a 350-page manuscript devoted to the trip to Sicily has survived. The real drama (and Gothic quality) in Tocqueville's Sicilian narrative appears in the vivid description of the violent storm encountered on board ship from Naples to Palermo. Amidst a raging nighttime sea and in torrential rain, passengers, crew, and a solitary howling dog feared shipwreck and the loss of their lives. Such was the ferocity of the storm that Tocqueville was reduced to crawling along the deck to avoid being washed overboard by the towering waves. Adding to the discomfort was an old sailor's remark that their travails were Tocqueville's fault because he had insisted that they set sail despite the weather.

When everyone was eventually allowed to disembark—in Sicily, Tocqueville remarked, police measures against travellers were increased in proportion as they were reduced against thieves—it was only to discover that their ship had been blown off course to the east and had landed in the small port of Oliveri. For the weary travellers, Tocqueville continued, no sight could have been more "delicious" than that of the fig trees, olive groves, and bushes with their colourful and perfumed flowers. All the colours and fragrances of spring were spread before them. The next day, they and their mule train set off towards the island's capital, accompanied by an armed military escort ("gun in hand, dagger in his belt") and three barefoot young peasant boys. Remarkably, the contract Tocqueville signed with his guide, Guiseppe Campo, has survived, and from this we know that Tocqueville, having made his way to Palermo, travelled on to Segesta (where, in amazement, he stood before its famous Doric temple), Selinunte, and Syracuse and then to Catania on the east coast.[143]

From these remaining notes we learn not only that Tocqueville climbed Mount Vesuvius but also that, in the manner of the Romantic traveller seeking an experience of fear and terror, he and his brother made a night-time ascent of Mount Etna.[144] As Tocqueville recorded, despite the sulphurous fumes, the high altitude, and a pathway deep in volcanic ash, they made it to the summit in time to see the sunrise. "It was," Tocqueville wrote in his diary, "a sight the like of which one sees only once in a lifetime, one of those severe and terrible beauties of nature that drive you in upon yourself and that crush you with a sense of your own smallness." This, he imagined, "is how we will rise on the last day of the world." The two brothers then stared down into the depths of the smoke-filled crater with "a kind of dread." Here is a perfect example of what Edmund Burke meant by the sublime.

Tocqueville ended his account of the ascent of Etna with a veritable rhetorical display worthy of any young man intent on impressing himself with his own erudition and emotional profundity. He had felt himself in the presence of "the first ages of the world, those ages of simplicity and of innocence where men were not saddened by the memory of the past or frightened by the uncertainty of the future" but "were content with present happiness." Here, he continued, was "the birthplace of the deities of Greek mythology," where Prosperina had been abducted by Pluto, king of the

Mount Etna, Sicily, c. 1833, artist unknown
(Heritage Image Partnership Ltd / Alamy Stock Photo)

underworld, where Ceres sought in vain for her daughter, and where Apollo had guarded his sheep. "These groves," Tocqueville wrote, "had resounded to the sound of Pan's flute; nymphs had wandered in their shadow and had breathed in their perfume." In the distance, he concluded, could be seen the lake of Hercules and the rocks of the Cyclops. Sicily was indeed "the land of the Gods and of heroes." A few days later, having completed their expedition across the island and visited many of the famous historical sites, Tocqueville and his brother set sail for the island of Stromboli in the Tyrrhenian Sea north of Sicily and the ascent of a third active volcano.

According to Beaumont, Tocqueville wrote "very mediocre" on the cover of the manuscript of his *Voyage en Sicile.* We do not know when he did this, but one can imagine that, as a mature man, he might well have looked critically at these early literary efforts.[145] Like many a young writer, Tocqueville was seeking to find his own voice, only to find himself imitating the literary conventions of his day. Yet, even in this piece of juvenilia, what was to become Tocqueville's authentic voice—that of the perceptive observer and commentator—was already visible.

Although hard to believe, Tocqueville wrote shortly after leaving Selinunte, "there are no villages in Sicily, only towns, and not many of these. After having crossed an almost completely empty space for eight or ten leagues one is surprised suddenly to find oneself enter a town of 20,000 people, which no highway or outdoor noise had announced from a distance. It is to here that what little industry or well-being has retreated, much as the warmth in a paralytic body retreats little by little to the heart." The cause of this was all too easy to discern: "The only great landowners in Sicily," Tocqueville explained, "are nobles and, above all, monasteries." Both showed no interest in the improvement of their properties. The nobles dissipated their wealth in Palermo and Naples, and it was said of many, Tocqueville reported, that they had never visited their estates. As for the monks, they were content to live off whatever income they had without thought of increasing it. Worse still, the people—having little or no interest in the land and being unable to find a market for their crops—were, little by little, abandoning their fields. "Someone who saw the coast of Sicily from the sea," Tocqueville concluded, "could easily believe that it was rich and flourishing, but there is no more miserable country in the world; they would think it densely populated, but the countryside is deserted and will remain so until the division of land and the flow of produce gives the people sufficient interest to return."[146]

Perhaps surprisingly, in subsequent years Tocqueville displayed very little interest in political developments in Italy. As French foreign minister in 1849, he sought largely to limit France's military intervention in the affairs of the newly created Roman Republic, seeking above all to avoid outright war with Austria and to save France from the justified contempt of the Roman populace.[147] "The holy cause of liberty," Tocqueville told one Italian correspondent, had been betrayed by the absence in Italy of "a liberal and moderate party wise enough to want only what was possible and strong enough to contain this movement within its proper limits."[148] In the following decade, the rise of Italian nationalism went without commentary. By then Tocqueville was preoccupied with issues closer to home. What seems to have endured is what often remains for the visitor to Italy, then as now: a sense of the unique charm and beauty of the country. Writing to Auguste de la Rive in the spring of 1857, Tocqueville remarked, "Of all the countries of the world, Italy is the one where one best encounters sights agreeable to the eyes and those which speak to the spirit."[149]

Tocqueville's next foreign adventure was a more modest walking holiday in the manner of the *pittoresque* with Louis de Kergorlay in the mountains of Switzerland in the late autumn of 1829. Despite the fact that they had to abandon their intention to climb up to the high valleys because there was too much snow, the itinerary outlined by Tocqueville to his mother still involved a journey across the Grison Alps to Lake Como in Italy and then back to Geneva by the Simplon Pass (an altitude of nearly seven thousand feet). This, he told her as they were about to set out,[150] looked reasonable enough as a plan and hopefully would dissuade family and friends from making the usual accusation that he and Kergorlay were both "harebrained" individuals. From what we know, their walking tour passed off without serious incident, although Tocqueville became ill through overexertion.[151] This rugged physical determination and obvious fascination with distant places—not to mention a keen eye for natural landscapes—were equally, if not more, visible during Tocqueville's trip to America.

CHAPTER TWO

An American Journey

What can we make of Alexis de Tocqueville's voyage to America, and how did he come to understand his journey?[1] First, we must acknowledge that when and why Tocqueville decided to undertake this hazardous enterprise is difficult to gauge. What we do know is that, after the July Revolution of 1830 and the inauguration of the Orleanist regime of King Louis-Philippe, the young Tocqueville found himself in a politically and personally difficult position, as well as the subject of criticism from friends and family.[2] In a letter dated 17 August 1830 to his future wife, Mary Mottley, Tocqueville gave clear expression to his anguish. Having, as required, signed the oath of allegiance to the new regime, Tocqueville explained that he felt "at war" with himself and that he had let down those of his family who had supported and died for the legitimist cause of the Bourbon monarchy.[3] A day later, and in a similarly distressed frame of mind, he told his brother Hippolyte that after such a "disagreeable moment," and with his "pride hurt," he would consider taking up another career if one became available.[4] In a letter to Charles Stoffels, Tocqueville suggested that he might join the army.[5]

Tocqueville's solution to his problems was to suggest to his employers, the French government, that he might be allowed to make a study of the American penitentiary system, and it was with this project in mind that the young magistrate and his friend Gustave de Beaumont were initially granted eighteen months' leave of absence from their legal duties in France. As Tocqueville explained to Stoffels, he had neither wife nor children to keep him in France, and he had therefore decided "to flee the idleness of private life and to take up again the restless existence of the traveller for a few years." In his memoir dedicated to Tocqueville's life, Beaumont made a similar point, suggesting that there were no strong ties to keep Tocqueville in France and that "an irresistible curiosity of spirit pushed him towards America."[6] Nonetheless, a letter to Stoffels written later in the year clearly indicated that Tocqueville thought a period of absence might be a smart career move. His present prospects, Tocqueville conceded, looked bad from whatever angle they were viewed, but a successful trip to America might lift him above the crowd and "some publication or other" might help make his reputation. To that extent, he acknowledged, examining the penitentiary system was a "pretext," but it was a "very honourable" one, and one that might incline whatever government was in power to look favourably upon him when he returned. Moreover, as he and Beaumont would be crossing the United States in the name of France, they would have "an incontestable advantage over all other travellers."[7] Even so, doubts remained until they departed about whether the two young friends would make their journey.[8]

When the idea of writing a book about American democracy first came to Tocqueville is likewise unclear. Beaumont was to suggest that "the study of the institutions and mores of American society" was "the real and premeditated object" of the voyage.[9] This was seemingly confirmed in a letter written by Tocqueville to another of his childhood friends immediately prior to his departure. "For us," he told Eugène Stoffels in February 1831, "it will not be a matter of seeing great cities and beautiful rivers. We are leaving with the intention of examining in detail and as scientifically as possible all the mainsprings of that vast American society which everyone talks about and no one knows. And if events leave us the time, we are counting on bringing back the elements of a fine work, or, at the very least, a new work."[10] However, this does not accord with views later expressed by Tocqueville himself. Whilst he again accepted that the study of the penitentiary system was only ever a "pretext" and one he had used as a "passport" that allowed him to travel across America, he nevertheless told his cousin Camille d'Orglandes after his return that "I did not go there with the idea of writing a book; the idea of the book came to me there."[11]

We should remember that Tocqueville was only one of many Frenchmen (and, less frequently, Frenchwomen) who, throughout the nineteenth century, crossed the Atlantic to witness the New World firsthand. We should then note that Tocqueville's journey was in many ways not dissimilar to that of substantial numbers of his compatriots. By the 1820s the Hudson River valley had already become a major tourist attraction, complete with fine hotels and travel infrastructure. In 1822 Gideon Minor Davison published the first tourist guidebook in America, entitled *The Fashionable Tour, or a Trip to the Springs, Niagara, Quebeck, and Boston.* Cheaply produced, Gideon's guide was not only regularly reprinted with updated information but would also appear in French translation in 1829.[12] Soon after its initial publication, Davison's book faced competition from the rival guidebooks of Theodore Dwight and Henry Gilpin, both published in 1825. Although we cannot be sure, it is possible that Tocqueville was familiar with Davison's guidebook. Writing to his childhood tutor, the Abbé Lesueur, and as he and Beaumont contemplated their departure from New York City for Albany, he announced that they were about to embark upon "what is known here as the *fashionable tour.*" During the summer, he continued, "lots of people do it."[13]

Most European visitors—and, here again, Tocqueville was no exception—arrived by way of New York and were immediately overwhelmed by its sense of feverish and perpetual activity. Educated visitors tended to make their way to Boston and Philadelphia (the latter always being the favourite American city for the French). Substantial numbers duly set off up the Hudson valley tourist trail, visited their French-speaking compatriots in Lower Canada and, like Tocqueville, wondered at the startling beauty of Niagara Falls. Few ventured to the South, preferring rather to satisfy their curiosity on the Eastern Seaboard, and even fewer had any significant contact or exchanges with the Black population. Typically, people came for an extended stay, but it was unusual for it to last longer than three to six months. Rarely did the French come alone—characteristically, they came with a friend or member of the family—and even more rarely did they decide not to return home. With only few exceptions, French visitors to America were, like Tocqueville, financially well off, or at least their families were.

For all of them, having said their sad farewells to family and friends, America began the moment they boarded ship and set sail, most often (as in Tocqueville's case) from Le Havre. With the advent of the steamship the travel time was reduced to between one and two weeks and could be undertaken in relative comfort. In Tocqueville's day a journey of between six and seven weeks was quite normal, and it was not without hazard or hardship.[14] As Jacques Portes recounts, travellers used their enforced leisure to read books about the United States, to meet Americans, and to improve their often very poor English.[15]

A long letter to Tocqueville's mother, written on board ship and begun on 26 April 1831, and another, written in New York to Eugène Stoffels, vividly portray what reads as an almost existential experience as Tocqueville and Beaumont sailed across what then was perceived as an unknowable void, a place of profound mystery and inhospitable to human life.[16] Armed with copies of Basil Hall's *Travels in North America* and the comte de Volney's *Tableau du climat et du sol des États-Unis d'Amérique,* Tocqueville and Beaumont boarded the ship at Le Havre on 2 April 1831, setting sail to their evident surprise and delight shortly after midnight. No sooner was Tocqueville out of sight of the French coast than he, along with most of the other 181 passengers and crew, was laid low by seasickness. When, on the sixth day, everyone finally came on deck, he told his mother, they "made a fine collection of pale, yellow and green faces." As a group, the animals of Noah's ark did not contain a more diverse collection. Quickly Tocqueville began to doubt that he would see dry land again. "I hope that it exists somewhere," he wrote.

After only a few days, birds, fish and other boats vanished. The ocean took on a gloomy aspect, its monotony impressing by its vastness. Above and below there was only "a complete silence." Day after day, the experience was "oppressive" and "heavy on the soul." No longer, Tocqueville reported, did he scan the horizon in anticipation of seeing something, as he now had become used to seeing nothing. The vessel came to take on the form of a separate universe, with its own rituals and codes of behaviour. Although tightly confined, people acted as if they were completely alone, displaying an informality and freedom unknown on dry land. "Everyone," he wrote, "drinks, laughs, eats or cries as the fancy takes them." The drawback was that it was a freedom that could be enjoyed only within the narrow and closed circle of the ship. Thus, most of his fellow travellers had a miserable time, "distilling their boredom drop by drop," watching a passing cloud or a change in the ship's direction with intense interest. Privacy was almost nonexistent, and one washed and dressed for all to see. The experience, Tocqueville suggested, was akin to living on the public square like the ancients.

Upon occasion, however, those on board witnessed what Tocqueville described to both his mother and to Eugène Stoffels as sights worthy of a painter, sights so "sublime" that he could not do justice to them. One stormy and dark night, as the ship's bow threw up foam to a height of twenty feet, the sea began "to sparkle" as if it was on fire, producing an effect of "indescribable beauty." "The solitude of the middle of the ocean," Tocqueville commented, "is a very remarkable thing to experience." Gales, one lasting thirty-six hours, reminded him of the wild night he had endured when sailing to Sicily four years earlier. This time, though, the only danger was that a servant would spill sauce down his shirt. Weather permitting, he and Beaumont tried to work as usual. After dinner they spoke English to "all those prepared to listen."

Their first sense of coming within reach of America came when an injured, sky-blue bird became trapped in the ship's rigging. You could not imagine, he told his mother, the joy caused by such a small animal, which "seemed to have been sent with the express intent of announcing the approach of land." Later came more birds and fish and, finally, marine vegetation. And then came the first sighting of land and the "delicious spectacle" of grass and trees. Soon afterwards, with their fresh provisions almost exhausted and several passengers unwell, the ship dropped anchor not at New York, as anticipated, but at Newport, Rhode Island, and the passengers went ashore. Never, Tocqueville wrote, had people been so happy; "we leapt onto land and each of us took a dozen unsteady steps before coming to stand solidly on our feet."[17] Swiftly they made their way to a local inn, the captain treating everyone to dinner. For Tocqueville the greatest pleasure came from drinking fresh water. That evening, in a spirit of "French gallantry," they returned to the ship around midnight with supplies for those who had stayed on board. No one, Tocqueville reported to his mother, had gone to bed and so, "in triumph," they went down to the "ladies' saloon" and recommenced their celebrations.

The next day they returned to the town. At first glance, it seemed quite pretty and, for someone from France, unimaginably clean. More striking still, in exterior appearance the inhabitants were not noticeably different from the French. They dressed the same way, but their features were so varied it would be difficult to know from what people they came. "I believe," Tocqueville ventured, "that this must be the case throughout the United States." It was 10 May, and Tocqueville had arrived. His journey into America had begun.

It is from this point that Tocqueville's journey can be read in part as a travelogue, his letters bristling with detail, his mood never less than one of fascination and enthusiasm. A new world passed before him, he told one of his sisters-in-law, as if it were seen through a magic lantern.[18] "Never," he wrote to his cousin Louis de Kergorlay, "has a people found itself in such happy and advantageous conditions of existence."[19] The houses along the coast, Tocqueville reported, were small and clean, like "chicken coops." The coastline was low and lacking in beauty—so much so that it was hard to believe that it had attracted the first visitors from Europe three hundred years earlier. No description was adequate to portray the interior of the "immense" steamship that conveyed Tocqueville and Beaumont over sixty leagues in only eighteen hours, "despite a heavy sea and head winds," from Newport to New York City. Up to eight hundred people, he informed his mother, could "eat and sleep comfortably" aboard.

Arriving at sunrise on 11 May 1831, and after thirty-five days at sea, the passengers greeted New York with "cries of admiration." Tocqueville told his mother to picture "a pleasantly jagged shoreline, grassy slopes and flowering trees running down to the sea, and, more than this, an unimaginable multitude of candy-box country cottages, all neat and proper; then, if you can, add a sea dotted with sails and you have the entrance to New York by way of the [Long Island] Sound."[20] Tocqueville's description to Eugène Stoffels was more matter-of-fact. New York, he wrote, "is located in the most admirable location I could think of, at the mouth of a river that warships could sail up to a distance of thirty leagues. It is the key to northern America." Through it, Tocqueville understood immediately, would pass the thousands of foreigners who would people the wildernesses of the West.[21] Nevertheless, he informed his mother, "for a Frenchman" the external aspect of New York was "bizarre and not very agreeable": "one sees not a dome, a steeple, or a large building, such that one would think one was in a suburb." Houses were built monotonously of brick, and none had cornices, balustrades, or carriage gateways. Pedestrians did however, have pavements to walk on.

As was often to prove to be the case on Tocqueville's travels, he initially had great difficulty finding somewhere to stay. This was eventually resolved when he and Beaumont found lodgings in a boarding house on Broadway, "the most fashionable street" in town (as he reassured his mother). Fortunately, Tocqueville discovered, people liked the French, and he was immediately struck by the hospitality of the average American. Everyone they met seemed to be competing to help them. All doors were open and all public documents they wanted to see were placed at their disposal. "I," Tocqueville told his mother, "find these new conditions very agreeable." A day later, and having attended High Mass at what he observed to be one of the many Catholic churches in the city, he added that he was "enjoying the most wonderful journey that one could imagine."[22]

Nor was Tocqueville slow in starting to draw conclusions from what he observed around him. "You will understand", he wrote to Eugène Stoffels on 28 July 1831, "that I have yet to arrive at a fixed opinion about these people." What he saw at first glance was that, in their mixture of virtues and vices, Americans were as difficult to classify as those people of any other nation. On the plus side, morals were very pure; the marriage bond was more sacred than anywhere else on earth; respect for religion was scrupulously observed. On the minus side was "an immoderate longing to make money and to do so quickly, a permanent instability in desires, a continual need for change, a complete absence of old traditions and old mores, and a commercial and mercantile spirit applied to everything." Such, he concluded, are "the external features of New York."[23] Tocqueville also saw, not unimportantly, that the Catholic Church was well established in New York and that, by all accounts, its numbers were increasing across the nation. "I would not be surprised," he wrote, "if a religion so assailed in Europe did not make great steps forward in this country."[24]

It was also from New York at the end of July 1831 that Tocqueville sketched out to Eugène Stoffels the journey that he and Beaumont now proposed to make. After much discussion and advice, they had resolved not to go directly to Boston but instead to travel up the North River and Hudson Valley as far as Albany, head west to see Niagara Falls, and then travel across Lake Erie in search of "Indian tribes." They would then return via Canada to Boston and New York, from whence they would "leave again for a new trip."[25] This turned out not exactly to be the case; having reached Buffalo, New York, they immediately crossed Lake Erie and then Lake Michigan; and visited Niagara Falls on their return. They then sailed down the Saint Lawrence River and, upon their return, set out on another trip. This and more was all meticulously recorded in letters home, in notebooks, and, upon occasion, in Beaumont's beautiful sketches and illustrations.

The speed at which journeys were completed never ceased to astound Tocqueville, especially when his steamship unexpectedly raced past West Point on its way up the Hudson. The navigation of rivers and canals, he wrote, meant that distance was regarded with "unbelievable contempt." Americans would undertake a journey from Pittsburgh to New Orleans with less hesitation than a Frenchman would undertake a trip from Paris to Dijon or Lyons. Tocqueville was less impressed by travel via stagecoach. "One feels exhausted after a few miles," he told his mother.[26]

The "art of cookery," Tocqueville reported to the Abbé Lesueur, was in its infancy. No wine was drunk at meals, and eating habits left much to be desired, with Americans consuming "vegetables and fish before meat, and oysters for dessert—as much to say, complete barbarism." The quality of the "dreadful music" Tocqueville and Beaumont heard was not much better. Laughter was rare and came only in the form of "the world's most ponderous merriment."[27] Like many a visitor, Tocqueville observed disapprovingly that Americans smoked, chewed tobacco, and spat in public. Generally, they lacked grace, refinement and elegance; but this, in Tocqueville's opinion, did not mean that they were not a "quite remarkable race of men."[28] For all of that, this was "a republican land," and Americans were unduly impressed by all the titles and "baubles" of European nobility.

Tocqueville saw immediately that marriage in America was a serious business. "When a woman marries," he informed one of his sisters-in-law, "it is as if she were entering a convent, except that it is not frowned upon that she should have children, and even many children." However, to Tocqueville's great delight, it was possible to call on a lady at nine o'clock in the morning without impropriety. "Picture," he wrote, "the daughters of leading families, dressed in their finest before one in the afternoon, scampering about through all the streets of New York from shop to shop or out riding without father or mother, uncle or aunt, or even a servant."[29] Nonetheless, as Tocqueville quickly realised to his evident dissatisfaction, this was no place for amorous flirtation. In these matters, straightforwardness was the rule. Young Americans, he observed, enjoyed the most proper of courtships.

The cost of living was lower than in Paris, although the price of manufactured goods (Tocqueville was especially exercised about the price of much-needed yellow kid gloves and silk stockings for evening wear) was exorbitant. Nothing was more beautiful than the sight offered by the Hudson River, disappearing as it did in the high, blue mountains to the north—"we envy the first Europeans," Tocqueville wrote, "who discovered the mouth of the Hudson two hundred years ago and sailed upriver when both banks were covered with immense forests"[30]—nor anything as sublime as the "perfect calm" and "complete tranquillity" of the wilderness around Lake Oneida. Autumn, with its great variety of colours and its "pure and sparkling sky," was "the moment when America appeared in all her glory."[31] Even the flies that lit up the nighttime sky were a source of fascination.

Nothing had quite prepared Tocqueville for the extraordinary Shaker ceremony he witnessed in the woods not far from Albany, with men and women dancing and singing wildly for over two hours. "Just imagine," he wrote to his mother, "what aberrations the human mind can fall into when left to its own devices."[32] Or for the Fourth of July celebrations a day later, all carried out in "perfect order" and where vulgarity was mixed "with a loftiness of purpose that spoke to the heart." In recalling a people to the moment of its birth, Tocqueville wrote, "there was something deeply felt and truly great."[33] Nor could he but be moved by the lamentable and mournful sight he witnessed, as he travelled down the Mississippi River, of the Choctaw Indians being transported from their homeland to probable "ruin and destruction," the men with nothing but their weapons, the women with their children on their backs. Among the old folk, he recounted, was a woman over one hundred years old, "naked except for a blanket which in places revealed the most emaciated body one could imagine." The "whole spectacle," he told his mother, was not something one could watch "without a heavy heart."[34]

It is easy to forget just how far Tocqueville and Beaumont travelled during their nine-month stay in North America. On the Great Lakes the two men journeyed as far west as Green Bay. They crossed the border into Lower Canada and travelled down the Saint Lawrence River to the city of Quebec.

They made the obligatory excursion to see Niagara Falls, and they were duly impressed. They went swimming in the Hudson River near Sing Sing. In blizzard conditions they traversed the Alleghenies, passed through Pittsburgh, and next sailed the Ohio River to Cincinnati, Ohio. From Memphis, Tennessee, they went downriver on the Mississippi to New Orleans. From there they crossed the South, through Alabama, Georgia, and the Carolinas, before reaching Norfolk, Virginia: a journey of a thousand miles in twelve days. In addition to New York City, they spent time in Boston, Philadelphia, Baltimore, and Washington DC (where they attended meetings of the US Congress and met President Andrew Jackson at the White House).

As Leo Damrosch has pointed out, Tocqueville and Beaumont visited seventeen of the then twenty-four states, plus those that would later become the states of Wisconsin, Michigan, and West Virginia.[35] If much of this traveling was done on steamboats—one of which struck a rock and sank in the icy Ohio[36]—the rest was undertaken either on horseback through uncharted forests or (to quote Tocqueville) over "abominable" roads and in uncomfortable stagecoaches that constantly broke down. Along the way, Tocqueville and Beaumont somehow found plenty of time to indulge their passion for hunting, the colourful and unsuspecting birds of America paying a heavy price as a result. These extensive travels were all the more impressive as they were frequently undertaken in appalling weather. From Louisville, Kentucky, Tocqueville wrote to Ernest de Chabrol that it was so cold that your ears froze if you did so much as to stick your head outdoors. Although they were on the latitude of Palermo and it was only early December, it was as cold as Russia.[37] Trapped by ice on the Mississippi, Tocqueville reported later that month that he and Beaumont had been forced to spend "a week without newspapers, without news, in total isolation from the rest of humanity [and] in a miserable state."[38] Having almost reached the end of what he described as "a strange and very tiring journey" across the South from New Orleans, Tocqueville told Chabrol that he and Beaumont had endured "a thousand vexations." These included "broken and overturned wagons, washed-away bridges, flooded rivers, and unavailability of accommodation." Such, Tocqueville wrote, had been their "everyday experiences."[39] Moreover, Tocqueville and Beaumont were in the United States to write a report on the penitentiary system and therefore were obliged to spend considerable amounts of their time inspecting prisons.

Above all, it was the sheer newness and novelty of America that came increasingly to press itself upon Tocqueville. Writing to his sister-in-law Émilie, a month to the day after his arrival, he informed her that he was visiting "the most singular country in the world."[40] To his cousin, comtesse Eugénie de Grancey, he wrote that "in the United States, there are no wars, no plagues, no literature, no eloquence, no revolutions, no fine arts, and few serious crimes, none of the things that attracted attention in Europe." People enjoyed "the most insipid happiness" one could imagine.[41] To his brother Édouard he reported that he was now living in "another world," where political passions were superficial and where "the only passion that deeply move[s] the human heart is the acquisition of wealth." There were a thousand ways of doing this without troubling the state.[42]

A letter written to Ernest de Chabrol encapsulated Tocqueville's feelings wonderfully: "I am quite simply dazed by all I see and hear." He asked Chabrol to imagine "a society formed of all the nations of the world . . . : in a word, a society lacking roots, memories, prejudices, habits, common ideas, a national character." Without a common language, beliefs, and opinions, it was a society held together only by individual self-interest and by the fact that its physical situation was so fortunate that private interest never acted contrary to general interest. There was no public power and, given what Tocqueville took to be the absence of enemies, no need of one. Consequently, there was no army, no taxation, and no central government. Executive authority was "only the transient executor of the will of elected bodies," possessing neither money nor influence.[43]

Moreover, America was a land where "the restlessness of the human spirit" did not mobilise political passions and where change seemed "man's natural state." "Here," Tocqueville wrote, "the earth itself wears a new face every day." Amidst such "universal commotion," the American could not stand still. "Nothing," he wrote, "is easier than enriching oneself in America." The Americans as a people "put one in mind of merchants who have convened as a nation just to do business."[44]

The Americans were not, therefore, "a virtuous nation in the strict sense of the word." The ancient European traditions of family pride, honour, and virtue did not exist. But Americans were disciplined, and their morals were pure. They had none of the vices arising from idle wealth, and women were "valued only as mothers and household managers."[45]

These first impressions were supplemented by further insights contained in an early letter to his close friend and cousin, Louis de Kergorlay. Having then travelled only as far as Yonkers, twenty miles from New York, Tocqueville announced that he was struck by "the broad communality of certain opinions" existing in American society. "I have yet to hear anyone," he wrote, "whatever their social rank, publicly express misgivings about the republic being the best of all possible governments or challenge the proposition that a nation has the right to live under a government of its own choosing." The vast majority in America, Tocqueville observed, understood republicanism "in the most democratic sense." All Americans shared a faith in man's good sense and wisdom and embraced the doctrine of human perfectibility. "While everyone acknowledges," Tocqueville wrote, "that the majority may err on rare occasions, no one questions the necessary rightness of its decisions in the long run, or disputes the fact that it is not only the sole legal judge of its interests but also the surest and most infallible." By way of summary, Tocqueville remarked that Americans "sincerely believe in the excellence of their government; they believe in the wisdom of the masses, assuming the latter are well informed; and appear to be unclouded by suspicions that the populace may never share in a special kind of knowledge indispensable for governing a state."[46]

The same letter—now being written from Colwells, twenty-five miles further from New York City—highlighted what, at first glance, Tocqueville took to be two other aspects of American society. One was the special place occupied by religion. "I was struck upon arriving here," Tocqueville told Kergorlay, "by the precise practical measures associated with religious worship." The Sabbath was strictly observed and public opinion, as much as the law, obliged people to abstain from all forms of entertainment.[47] These external forms, in Tocqueville's opinion, concealed "a reservoir of doubt and indifference." Faith was "inert," and religion failed to "move people to the depths of their soul." Enter any Protestant church, "and you will hear sermons about morals, but not a word about dogma." Unitarianism—which Tocqueville regarded as pure deism and "Christian in name only"—was daily making ground, especially among the upper classes. For all of that, Tocqueville also saw that the "Christian religion has stronger underpinnings here than in any other country." "I am sure," he continued, "that it influences every political administration." As a result, the spirit of innovation was held in check and recklessness was discouraged. Rare was the disposition, so common in France, to achieve one's goals by "fair means or foul."[48]

The second aspect highlighted by Tocqueville derived from the laws determining inheritance. The abolition of primogeniture, he believed, had produced "almost magical results." The aristocratic bias of the early American republic had been "replaced by a democratic thrust of irresistible force." Consequently, democracy "informs mores, laws, [and] the opinion of the majority." The effects were visible everywhere: "a perpetual instability in men and laws, an external equality pushed to the limit, a uniform way of behaving and of conceiving ideas." Nor was this a process that could be arrested or reversed. Tocqueville wrote that, henceforth, democracy "will be a fact that a government may pretend to regulate but not to halt." To this he added that "what I see in this country tells me that, even in the most favourable of circumstances, and they exist here, the government of the multitude is not a good thing." In general, he wrote, the people favoured "those who flatter its passions and descend to its level." All in all, Tocqueville told Kergorlay, "this country presents an admirable spectacle" and it "gripped the imagination."[49]

A similar set of conclusions was listed in a note entitled "First Impressions," dated 15 May 1831. The Americans, Tocqueville recorded, "carried national pride to quite excessive lengths" and, on the whole, exhibited a "small-town" outlook. They seemed "a religious people," but how far religion governed their conduct and whether the diversity of religious sects led to indifference was unclear to him. The whole of society seemed to be composed of one enormous middle class. The elegant manners and polite refinement of the European upper classes were lacking, but no one was "downright ill-mannered." All Americans, "right down to the simplest shop assistant," seemed to have been brought up well and to be "serious, poised and reserved." Betraying what was to be one of his abiding preoccupations, Tocqueville again commented upon the way women dressed and the causes of chaste morals.[50]

This sense of the newness of what he was seeing remained with Tocqueville throughout his journey. Writing to his mother from Louisville in December later that year, Tocqueville recorded his impressions of the society he was seeing emerge in the new cities of the Midwest. The Europeans who had first arrived in America had built a society that was analogous to that of Europe but which "at bottom" was "radically different" from it. They had left behind "the traditions of the past, the institutions and the mores of their homeland" and were now "connected to Europe only by language." Everything in America, Tocqueville wrote, was "abrupt, exaggerated, nothing has yet to find its final place; society grows faster than man." Everywhere there was a sense of "the bustle of life, of a feverishly active population." It was here, too, that people were carving out institutions, as they were roads in the forests, sure in the knowledge that they faced neither obstacles nor limits. It was a society that as yet lacked any bonds, where "each individual is as it pleases him to be, regardless of his neighbour." With time, their job done, this "race of men known as *pioneers*" would uproot themselves again, heading ever westward beyond the Mississippi, "pushing back the Indian, destroying big game, probing the forests, finally opening the road to the civilisation that will follow." It was in these western states that "democracy displays all its distinctive attributes, its fickleness, its violent passions, its instability and its restless character." "Everything that is good and bad in American society," Tocqueville told his mother, "is here found in bold relief."[51]

How these various ideas emerged is captured vividly in Tocqueville's letters. To his father he explained that, despite his mental confusion, two ideas had already come to him. The first was that the American people were the happiest in the world. The second was that America owed its prosperity less to its own virtues and even less to a form of government that was superior to all others but rather to the particular circumstances in which it found itself. This in turn told Tocqueville that political institutions were neither good nor bad in themselves and that everything depended upon the physical conditions and social state of the people where they applied. What might work in America might not work in France, and vice versa.[52]

To Louis de Kergorlay he explained that there were two things about America he had come to admire especially. The first was an extreme respect for the law. "Without display and the police," he wrote, "it exercises an irresistible command." The second was the ease with which Americans dispensed with government.[53] America, Tocqueville told Kergorlay, was a society that "walks on its own" and where "the art of government" was in its infancy.[54] The same language was used later in 1831 in another letter to Ernest de Chabrol. "What strikes the traveller most in this country," Tocqueville wrote, "is the spectacle of a society that walks on its own, without benefit of a guide or a crutch." Trying to locate government made no sense as, "in a manner of speaking," it did not exist.[55]

The mistake is to believe (primarily on the basis of the letters written to Chabrol and Kergorlay in June 1831) that Tocqueville quickly settled his mind on what he had seen of American society.[56] Although both letters undoubtedly contained strong intimations of what would in due course form the content of *De la démocratie en Amérique,* it is clear that Tocqueville's journey across the continent forced him to rethink his impressions and conclusions on an almost daily basis. To his father in early June 1831 Tocqueville wrote that he could not tell him what most struck him about America; "a whole volume would be necessary to tell you; and, in any case, I would perhaps not think the same tomorrow."[57] In September, writing from Boston, he told his mother, "Everything I see, everything that I hear, everything that I see from a distance, forms a confused mass in my brain which I will perhaps never have the time nor the strength to unravel. It would be an immense undertaking to present a picture of a society that is as large and as lacking in homogeneity as this one."[58] A month later, this time writing from Hartford, Connecticut, he reaffirmed the observation earlier passed on to his father. "I will know what I think of America only when I am no longer here," he wrote. "One has to give up any idea of studying things deeply when one sees so many things, when one impression drives out the one that preceded it; at best there remain a few general ideas, a few general conclusions, which much later can enable you to understand details when one has the time to study them."[59] From Philadelphia in late October he told his mother that the clearest outcome of his trip would be that, upon leaving America, he would be equipped to understand the documents that he had collected but not yet studied. "For the rest," he continued, "on this country I have only disordered and disconnected notes, disjointed ideas to which only I hold the key, isolated facts which recall a mass of others." The few general ideas he had expressed on America, he admitted, were to be found in his correspondence to family and friends in France; but even these had been written in haste, on a steamboat or in a corner, with his knees serving as a desk. Would he ever write a book on this country? "The truth is," Tocqueville concluded, "I do not know. It seems to me that I have good ideas: but I'm not yet sure how to arrange them and airing them in public frightens me."[60]

James Schleifer, in particular, has drawn our attention to the language used by Tocqueville to indicate moments of surprise in his account. Schleifer specifically refers us to the numerous occasions in *De la démocratie en Amérique* when Tocqueville admits that he found something to be "striking." The best example of this occurs in the very first sentence of the published text, where Tocqueville states, "Among the new objects that attracted my attention during my stay in the United States, none struck me more vividly than the equality of conditions."[61] By extending this analysis of the actual words used by Tocqueville in his account we gain a further insight into the importance of his journey and the manner in which it shaped the content of his argument about America.

If we limit ourselves only to the later chapters of the first volume of *De la démocratie en Amérique,* published in 1835, it is noticeable how many times Tocqueville wrote in the first person. We read such phrases as "I sometimes met in the United States," "I met rich inhabitants of New England who," "As I prolonged my journey, I noticed the great political consequences that flowed from these new facts"; "I saw with my own eyes"; "I remember that"; "I realised with surprise that"; "I discovered that"; "I asked myself how it could happen that"; "What I saw among the Anglo-Americans leads me to believe that," and so on. In essence, what Tocqueville is saying, time and time again, is, "This is what I found."

Many more similar phrases and expressions can be found that testify to the impact upon Tocqueville of his voyage, but to confirm the point we might care to consider the following short paragraph: "Thus *I found* in the United States the restlessness of heart that is natural to man when, all conditions being more or less equal, each one sees the same chances to rise. There *I encountered* the democratic sentiment of envy expressed in a thousand different ways. *I observed* that the people often showed, in the conduct of affairs, a great blend of presumption and ignorance, and *I concluded* that in

America, as among us, men were subject to the same imperfections and exposed to the same miseries."[62] We see clearly how Tocqueville combined a series of observations and reflections drawn directly from what he had seen as he travelled across the United States in order to reach a substantive conclusion.

By dint of considerable effort and imaginative intuition, therefore, Tocqueville came, in fits and starts, to make sense of these confusing and diverse impressions. Yet, as George Wilson Pierson observed many years ago, the very tone of Tocqueville's letters and notes "prophesized the book that one day would result." Tocqueville showed himself not to be interested greatly in individuals, and least of all in their physical appearance. There were no descriptions of domestic interiors. Nor were his observations those of a sightseeing tourist. His subject from the beginning was "the real character of the American people," and with that came necessarily a fascination with the patterns of behaviour and institutions of a democratic society.[63]

What, then, did Tocqueville come to learn from his journey through America? Here we can build upon a summary provided by Schleifer.[64] Tocqueville learned first of the equality of conditions in all its assorted forms and of the importance of laws of inheritance in fostering such equality. This was an equality that extended beyond political mores and laws to all aspects of civil society. It made relations between individuals simpler and easier; it diminished paternal authority within the family and increased the independence of young girls—"I was often surprised and almost frightened," Tocqueville wrote, "by seeing the singular dexterity and happy boldness with which the American young girls knew how to direct their thoughts and their words amid the pitfalls of a lively conversation"[65]—and turned the relationship between master and servant into a purely contractual relationship. Less obviously, the equality of conditions modified the use of the English language, made writers and orators more bombastic, and made all honest professions honourable. From this he concluded that it seemed "beyond doubt that sooner or later we will arrive, like the Americans, at a nearly complete equality of conditions."[66]

Tocqueville also grasped something of the uniqueness of motion and mobility in American life. He observed,

> A man, in the United States, carefully builds a house in which to spend his old age, and he sells it while the ridgepole is being set; he plants a garden and he rents it as he is about to taste its fruits. . . . He settles in a place that he soon leaves in order to carry his changing desires elsewhere. . . . And when, near the end of a year filled with work, he still has a little leisure, he takes his restless curiosity here and there across the vast limits of the United States. He will do as much as five hundred leagues in a few days in order to distract himself better from his happiness."[67]

Phrased in the terminology of Tocqueville's published text, this sense of constant movement appeared in his conclusion that "there is something precipitous, one could almost say revolutionary, in the progress that society makes in America."[68]

Tocqueville discovered some of the key institutional and constitutional mechanisms for moderating democracy—most notably, the federal system and an independent judiciary. He noticed and noted the importance of administrative decentralization and the vigour of local government, observing, "Administrative power in the United States presents nothing either centralized or hierarchical in its constitution; that is why you do not see it." He understood the significance of the habit of association: "Americans of all ages, of all conditions, of all minds, constantly unite." He also saw that, in democratic societies, "the science of association" was "the mother science." Just as importantly, Tocqueville saw the centrality to American life of the fact that Americans "almost always knew how to combine their own well-being with that of their fellow citizens." This was, he theorised, the doctrine of "self-interest well understood." Such behaviour, he noted, did not make "a man virtuous, but it forms a multitude of steady, temperate, moderate, far-sighted citizens who have self-control."[69]

Another key discovery, and one that must have come as a great surprise to a Frenchman, was that religion acted as a guarantor of liberty and democracy: "At the same time that the law allows Americans to do everything, religion prevents them from conceiving of everything and forbids them to dare everything."[70] Tocqueville also came to the conclusion that "in no country in the civilized world is there less interest in philosophy than in the United States."[71] Americans were interested in the practical application of ideas rather than in abstract truths. They had as yet not produced a literature of their own.

Above all, Tocqueville came to appreciate that America was distinguished from all other nations by the fact that there "the principle of the sovereignty of the people is not hidden or sterile." "The people," he wrote, "rule the American political world as God rules the universe. They are the cause and end of all things."[72] Of course, Tocqueville saw the disadvantages and the flaws in such a system: "You must go to America to understand the power material well-being exercises over political actions."[73] Most well known is the fact that Tocqueville saw the potential for a "tyranny of the majority." "In the United States," he wrote, "the majority takes charge of providing individuals with a host of ready-made opinions, and thus relieves them of the obligation to form for themselves opinions that are their own."[74] "I know of no other country," Tocqueville continued, "where, in general, there reigns less independence of mind and true freedom of discussion than in America."[75] Nevertheless, as Schleifer concludes correctly, for Tocqueville the United States could be seen as "a model of a well-regulated democratic republic."[76]

Crucially, Tocqueville brought these things home with him to France. Many examples could be cited, but here it is perhaps enough to refer to just one instance: the electoral address prepared by Tocqueville for the electors of the Valognes constituency in 1837. "I am," he wrote, "a friend of liberty both by taste and by reason. I believe that it is in the interest of the entire world to see it extended, guaranteed and progressive. I love it so profoundly and so sincerely that I would not like to live in a country where it did not exist. I held this view before I went to America, but it was strengthened there. The study of the United States showed me that republican institutions do not suit us but, despite that, it made me see all that free institutions could give a people by way of power, wealth and glory."[77]

Yet Tocqueville also went to America to see the wilderness. And he did so with a set of preconceived notions of what he imagined this primitive and largely uninhabited space would look like, most of which were drawn from the writings of his distant cousin, François René de Chateaubriand.[78] A forerunner of Romanticism, Chateaubriand's writings had an enormous influence upon Tocqueville's generation. If this was true of *Le génie du Christianisme,* a work which inspired a widespread revival of Catholic faith in postrevolutionary France, so too was it the case with the descriptions of America provided in Chateaubriand's novellas *Atala* and *René* and his later *Voyage en Amérique,* published some thirty-five years after his visit to the country in 1791. For all that these descriptions were largely fictitious and a product of his fertile imagination—it is extremely doubtful that Chateaubriand visited many of the American locations he wrote about—Chateaubriand's America was, for many, the true America, and it remained so despite his own admission that the virgin landscape and civilisation of the Native Americans he had encountered had already begun to disappear. As Chateaubriand wrote, "the liberty of the United States" was replacing "the liberty of the Indian."[79]

Nonetheless, Chateaubriand left his many readers with a deep sense of the splendour of "eternal" forests as "old as the world" and "as if left in the hands of God."[80] He also provided a vivid picture of the way in which the soul was replenished by the silence and solitude that accompanied an encounter with a "sublime nature." "Run and shut yourself up in your cities, go and subject yourselves to your petty laws," he wrote; "here I am as the Almighty created me, the sovereign of nature, borne triumphantly by the waters, while the inhabitants of the waters accompany my course."[81] And of all the descriptions provided by Chateaubriand, the most lyrical and unquestionably the most remembered was that of Niagara Falls. First deployed in Chateaubriand's *Essai sur les révolutions* of 1797 and in the epilogue of *Atala,* it resurfaced in his *Voyage en Amérique* and then again in *Mémoires d'outre-tombe.* His heart, Chateaubriand wrote, beat with a mixture of joy and terror as he approached "one of the most-awe inspiring sights that Nature has offered to mankind." In its "sublime disorder" Niagara eclipsed everything.[82]

Chateaubriand also provided an account of the character of Native Americans and their civilisation that left an indelible mark upon his contemporaries. The mistake, he suggested, had been to confuse a state of nature with a primitive state, and thus to imagine that the "savages" found in North America had no religion, no government to speak of, no sophisticated languages or ideas, and knew not how to cultivate their land. For all that the people he described were cruel, naturally indolent and warlike, the customs and practices of the Native American tribes Chateaubriand claimed to have observed were of considerable sophistication. The tragedy of the two young Indian lovers portrayed in *Atala* suggested a capacity for purity and nobility of sentiment.

Little of this civilisation and dignity remained by the time Tocqueville and Beaumont set forth in search of what in French he described as "*le désert*." Tocqueville's "alphabetic notebooks" record that their first sighting of "Indians" took place on 20 July 1831 as they approached Buffalo, northwest of New York City. "I do not think," he wrote, "that I have ever been as disappointed as I was at the sight of these Indians. My mind was full of memories of M. de Ch[ateaubriand] and of [James Fenimore] Cooper, and I was expecting to see savages in the natives of America but savages on whom nature had left traces of some of the lofty virtues to which the spirit of liberty gives birth." He had anticipated seeing "a race of men," Tocqueville continued, not greatly different from Europeans, with bodies made strong by hunting and war and who "would not suffer from being seen in the nude." Nothing could have been further from the truth. "The Indians I saw," Tocqueville explained, "were small in stature; their limbs . . . were thin and weak; their skin, rather than being red as is commonly believed, was dark bronze. . . . Their black hair hung stiffly about their necks and sometimes down to their shoulders. Mostly their mouths were inordinately large and their faces looked ignoble and malicious." If there was a resemblance to Europeans, it was only to "the lowest dregs of our large European cities." Worse still, to the vices they had acquired from European civilisation, the Native Americans had added "something barbarous and uncivilised," making them "one hundred times more repulsive." "At first sight," Tocqueville concluded, "it would have been tempting to see in each of them a beast from the forest that had been brought up to have something of the appearance of a human being but which nevertheless remained an animal." Moving beyond the town, Tocqueville recorded, he and Beaumont met a large group of Indians. Most were drunk. An Indian woman rolled in the dirt. A young man lay motionless by the side of the road, as if dead, occasionally groaning. Those who passed by left him there. "For the rest of my life," Tocqueville wrote, "I will always remember a young Indian woman, who at first seemed to show some interest in him." When she could not rouse the young man, he recalled, she set about him in a rage, banging his head against the ground and kicking him, all the time uttering savage and wild cries. After she moved off, she broke out into "barbarous laughter."[83]

The same sense of shock and profound disappointment was evident in a letter sent by Tocqueville to his sister-in-law, Émilie, on 7 September 1831. Again, the point of reference was to Chateaubriand and the picture he had provided of the beautiful and graceful Atala. Returned from the journey that had taken Tocqueville and Beaumont over many days as far as Green Bay on Lake Michigan, where they had seen "millions of acres of woods to which no one has ever taken an axe and a great number of Indian tribes," he asked if his sister-in-law knew anything of "Atala and her kind." "I will have to give a description of her to you," he continued, "so that you can judge her resemblance to that provided by M. de Ch[ateaubriand]." In brief, there was scarcely any resemblance at all. Atala was "an Indian woman the colour of dark milk coffee . . . usually with a big fat hooked nose . . . a large tin ring in her nostrils . . . and pigeon toed." "All that I know," Tocqueville wrote, "is that I would not want to play the role of Chactas with one of these women for all the gold in the world."[84]

Tocqueville was quickly to concede that it had been a mistake to judge the "Indian race" based on his first encounter. Subsequently, as Tocqueville and Beaumont set out to reach what they believed would be "the limits of civilisation," they met many more Indians. Some of them followed the two men with great agility through the forests; others acted as their guides "like wildcats," negotiating every obstacle in their path, their heads held high. The Native American, Tocqueville observed, looked with contempt at the desire of Europeans for comfort and useless riches. "What we call industry," he wrote, "he calls shameful subjection," the conveniences of life being for him no more than "children's toys and women's fineries." The only things of ours he envied were "our weapons."[85]

Yet Tocqueville also saw that the Indian races were "vanishing in the presence of European civilisation as snow vanishes in the rays of the sun."[86] And this was so, as he heard said on the evening of his first encounter, because Americans, for all the Bible told them that all men were brothers, believed that the continent belonged to them and therefore the Indians must die.[87] As Tocqueville related to his mother, "reason indicates that wherever civilised men are able to establish themselves, the savages must give up their territory."[88] "Every ten years or so," he noted in Utica, New York, on 6 July 1831, "the Indian tribes that have been driven into the wilderness of the West realise that retreat has gained them nothing, and that the white race still advances more rapidly than they retreat." Vexed by their own impotence or the latest insult, they rebel, whereupon "civilisation" temporarily recedes, only for an army to march out to meet them and for the Indians to "resume their westward journey, pausing only when they reach a new wilderness, where soon the white man's axe will be heard anew." "One might say," Tocqueville wrote, "that the European is to the other human races what man is in general to all animate nature. When he cannot bend others to his purposes or make them contribute indirectly to his well-being, he destroys them and little by little makes them disappear before him."[89]

Thus, as Tocqueville reported to Eugénie de Grancey after he had returned to New York City, getting to see the wilderness and Indians in America was more difficult than he and Beaumont had imagined; and what self-respecting Frenchman, he added, would wish to return to France without an image "in his head of a savage and a virgin forest?"[90] Here chance played a part. No sooner had Tocqueville and Beaumont arrived in Buffalo than they discovered that a steamboat, the *Ohio,* was about to leave for Detroit (then, in Tocqueville's words, "a small town of some two to three thousand souls"), where they arrived some four days later (Tocqueville having, as usual, suffered from seasickness). The following day, having hired two horses and with rifles slung over their shoulders, Tocqueville and Beaumont set out into the impenetrable forest "as carefree and lighthearted as a couple of schoolboys setting out from school for a holiday at home." What awaited them were mosquitoes aplenty and the log cabins of the pioneer. Of that "anonymous individual," Tocqueville wrote, he was the representative of "a nation of conquerors that is willing to subject itself to life in the wild without ever being seduced by its appeal; that loves only those aspects of civilisation and enlightenment that are useful to well-being; and that plunges into America's wilderness with an axe and newspapers." His wife and children were "his companion in misery and danger": his home was "the ark of a lost civilisation in an ocean of foliage." Only a hundred paces away lay the shadows of the "eternal forest" and "solitude." As for the mosquitoes, they reduced life in the wilderness to an unbearable torture. "Any part of the body left uncovered," Tocqueville wrote, "immediately became their gathering place."[91]

Yet, as Tocqueville and Beaumont ventured forth towards Saginaw (described to them by an innkeeper in Pontiac as "the last inhabited place between here and the Pacific Ocean") it was not to be long before they "beheld what [they] had been looking for: virgin forest."[92] For Tocqueville it was an overwhelming experience. "Nature's repose is no less impressive in the emptiness of the New World," he wrote, "than on the immensity of the sea." He continued,

> In the middle of the day, one can frequently hear what sounds like a long sigh in the depths of the woods, a plaintive cry echoing in the distance. This is the last gasp of the dying wind. All around the forest then subsides into a silence so deep, a stillness so complete, that a kind of religious terror grips the soul. The traveller stops, he looks: pressed one against the other, their branches intertwined, the trees of the forest seem to form but a single whole, an immense and indestructible edifice, beneath whose vaults reigns an eternal darkness. . . . He listens. Trembling, he holds his breath, the better to hear the least sound of life, but not a whisper, not a murmur can be detected. . . . Thus, in the woods, everything is still, everything silent beneath its foliage. It is as if the Creator has for a moment turned his face away and as if the forces of nature are paralysed."

This, Tocqueville concluded, "was not the only time that we remarked on the striking similarity that exists between the ocean and the wild forest. With the sight of both an idea of immensity takes hold of you. The repetition of the same scenes and their monotony astonishes and overwhelms the imagination. We felt an even stronger and perhaps even more poignant sense of isolation and abandonment in the wilderness of the New World than had weighed upon us in the middle of the Atlantic."[93]

Once reached, Saginaw also gave cause for much reflection on Tocqueville's part. Situated on the Michigan Peninsula, it could be seen, he wrote, "as an outpost, a sort of sentry post that the whites have stationed amidst the Indian nations." Perched between "a beautiful, tranquil river" and the forest, the nascent town had "as yet nothing to awaken an idea of either the past or the future," its population amounting to no more than thirty people, each drawn to this tiny embryonic society by "chance, self-interest and passion" and obliged to live on whatever the wilderness might provide. However, what struck Tocqueville above all about these thirty people—"men, women, the elderly and children. . . . Canadians, Americans, Indians and half-castes"—was that there existed no common bond between them and they differed profoundly from one another. "A few exiled members of the great human family," he wrote, "have come together in the vastness of the forests. Their needs are common. Together they must struggle against the animals of the woods, against hunger and the inclemency of the seasons. . . . Yet they regard each other only with hatred and suspicion. The colour of their skin, their poverty or their wealth, their ignorance or their enlightenment, have already established indestructible classifications among them; national prejudices, the prejudices of education and of birth, divide and isolate them." "Where else," he observed, "can one find in such a confined setting a fuller portrait of the wretchedness of human nature?"[94]

But Tocqueville was also powerfully aware of the momentary and transient character of what he saw in and around Saginaw. Returning to their canoe after a trip upriver to shoot wildfowl, Tocqueville and Beaumont were struck by the fact that the wilderness before them was much as it would have appeared six thousand years earlier. They both fell, Tocqueville recalled, "into a quiet reverie, contemplating the ineffable charm" of their surroundings. Yet Tocqueville knew that soon the impenetrable forests would be felled and the sound of industry would disturb the silence of Saginaw. Quays would line the riverbanks, and the previously undisturbed waters would be pushed back by the bows of ships. "We are," he reflected, "possibly the last travellers who will have been given the chance to contemplate this solitude in all its primitive splendour." "It is," Tocqueville wrote, "this idea of destruction, this sense of imminent and inevitable change, that gives to the American wilderness its unique character and its so very touching beauty; one must lose no time in admiring it."[95]

Back in Detroit, their journey took another unexpected turn. This time they learned that a steamboat, the *Superior,* was about to set sail for an excursion across Lake Huron and Lake Michigan. Again, Tocqueville could not resist temptation, but this time the decision was to prove something of a disappointment. "We set out at six in the morning," his travel note for 4 August recorded. "An absolutely insignificant day. Towards evening we lose all sight of land." The entry for 11 August was hardly more encouraging: "A monotonous day on the lake." Having reached Green Bay, neither Tocqueville nor Beaumont knew what to do. So Tocqueville went hunting alone and for a swim. Two days later he did at least meet a "civilised savage" dressed like a French peasant from whom he learnt much about the religion of the Indians ("God; immortality of the soul. An Indian paradise. Obey the commandments").[96] As Tocqueville told Eugénie de Grancey, the trip did at least give him and Beaumont the satisfaction of travelling past "vast stretches of shoreline where no white man has as yet felled a single tree."[97]

But there remained Niagara Falls to see. Tocqueville and Beaumont stayed for only one hour in Buffalo before they set out for the falls. From a distance, Tocqueville told his mother, the noise was as loud as a storm. The next morning, they arrived in perfect weather. "I would inevitably indulge in pathos," he wrote, "if I were to attempt to describe the spectacle that lay before us. Niagara Falls surpasses all that had been said and written about it in Europe, as well as any idea that the imagination can conceive in advance.... The sublimity of the view ... is without equal, especially at night (as we discovered), when you can no longer see the bottom of the abyss and the moon creates a rainbow above the cloud." Looking out from under the sheet of water, the darkness was deep and terrifying, the occasional fleeting light making possible a view of the entire river as it passed over the spectator's head. "It is hard," Tocqueville's account concluded, "to describe the impression produced by this ray of light when, after it has allowed you a momentary glimpse of the vast chaos that surrounds you, it once again abandons you to darkness and the roar of the cataract."[98]

As Tocqueville commented to another of his French friends a week or so later, "I give the Americans ten years before they build a sawmill or a flour mill at the base of the cataract."[99] Still, for all that the wilderness and its original inhabitants were already disappearing, Tocqueville had, if only briefly, witnessed America in its undefiled and sublime natural form, experiencing for himself the solitude that many Europeans imagined to be an archetypical, and regenerative, form of life in the New World. He had undoubtedly felt what Ralph Waldo Emerson, only five years later in his essay "Nature," was to describe as "the wild delight" that runs through a person "in the presence of nature," even if he understood that Americans saw in nature only something they could use to enhance their material prosperity and that, without any regret or anguish, they were intent on destroying an indigenous population which had occupied the vast solitudes of the New World for millennia. It was four months later that Tocqueville came wholly to see the full horror of the fate that the philanthropic, humane, and moderate Americans intended to visit upon those they were happy to condemn to exile and oblivion. "There can be no doubt," he wrote to his mother on Christmas Day 1831, "that within a hundred years there will not remain in North America either a single tribe or even a single man belonging to the most remarkable of Indian races."[100]

For now, Tocqueville and Beaumont travelled down the Saint Lawrence River into Lower Canada and then back over land to Boston. After stopping again in New York City, they then went on to Philadelphia, with more prisons to visit.

To bring this part of our account to a close I wish to suggest that it is in the final two chapters of the first volume of *De la démocratie en Amérique,* devoted to the "Principal Causes Tending to Maintain a Democratic Republic in the United States" and the "Present and Probable Future of the Three Races," that the impact of Tocqueville's journey appears in its most unmediated published form. This is true of the latter chapter in particular. As Eduardo Nolla has informed us, this part of the book was written as late as the spring or summer of 1834, and (unusually) was not the subject of commentary from either Tocqueville's friends or family. There were few drafts, and there are no great differences between the manuscript and the published version, attesting, in Nolla's opinion, to "a rapid composition."[101] Tocqueville himself also recognised the distinctiveness of this concluding section within the book as a whole, explaining, "You encounter in America something more than an immense and complete democracy: the peoples who inhabit the New World can be seen from more than one point of view." Issues relating to the future of the Americans as a trading people and the dangers threatening the permanence of republican institutions, he noted, "touch on my subject, but do not enter into it . . . and above all I wanted to portray democracy. So I had to put them aside at first; but I must return to them as I finish."[102] In other words, these were specifically American issues and had to be addressed as such.

In what was originally intended to be the last chapter of his first volume, Tocqueville highlighted three causal factors which, in his opinion, explained the survival of a democratic republic in the United States. These were laws, habits and mores, and "the particular and accidental situation in which Providence placed the Americans." After much hesitation and uncertainty, Tocqueville concluded that laws and mores were more important than circumstances and it was to these, rather than to physical causes beyond human influence, that the "Anglo-Americans" owed their "grandeur."[103]

Tocqueville's comments on the influence of the laws at this point in his text were brief, but they built upon conclusions reached after lengthy examination in the main body of the book. Three institutions, he argued, contributed more than all the others to maintain democracy in America. The first was the "federal form," which "allows the Union to enjoy the power of a large republic and the security of a small one." The second were township institutions, witnessed firsthand by Tocqueville in New England. These gave the people "the taste for liberty" and taught them "the art of being free." The third (unknown in Tocqueville's France) was an independent judiciary capable of correcting "the errors of democracy" and of "slowing and directing" the movements of the democratic majority. "The power granted to the American courts to rule on the unconstitutionality of laws," Tocqueville wrote, "forms one of the most powerful barriers that has ever been raised against the tyranny of political assemblies."[104]

In each case these were subjects that had received extensive discussion with those that Tocqueville had met in America. Joel Poinsett told Tocqueville that "I, for one, do not believe that any large republic that is not a federation can survive."[105] For his part, Jared Sparks provided Tocqueville and Beaumont with answers to a long list of questions about the town governments of Massachusetts, as well as informing Tocqueville that in America "our ancestors founded *towns before there was a state.*"[106] As for the notion that an independent judiciary could act as a counterweight to the sovereignty of the people, this was a theme to which Tocqueville repeatedly returned in his conversations and readings whilst in America. To the

Massachusetts senator, Francis Calley Gray, Tocqueville posed the question, "Do judges have much political power?" Gray's affirmation of the special and important role played by the American judiciary could not have been any clearer. "Our courts," he replied, "are the leading power in the state. Everyone concedes that they can refuse to enforce laws they deem unconstitutional, and in fact they do refuse such laws daily. I regard the grant of such powers to judges as one of the greatest guarantees of liberty that a people can have."[107]

When Tocqueville spoke of mores, what he had in mind was "the whole moral and intellectual state of a people."[108] Here, while Tocqueville admitted to an admiration of the "experience" and "good sense" of Americans, he paid particular attention to the influence of religious beliefs upon the maintenance of democracy, arguing specifically that, among Americans, religion "must be considered as the first of their political institutions." If, Tocqueville insisted, religion did not give them "a taste for liberty," it certainly "facilitate[d] their use of it." Again, this was a sentiment awakened vividly by his stay in America: "When I arrived in the United States, it was the religious aspect of the country that first struck my eyes." And the more he looked, the more he perceived that, whilst each of the "innumerable multitude of sects" differed in their form of worship, none showed themselves hostile to democratic and republican institutions.[109]

In order to understand this, Tocqueville explained, he questioned "the faithful of all communions," seeking out the "company of priests," only to discover that, in America, the spirit of religion and the spirit of liberty were "intimately joined the one to the other." Not a single person he had met, laymen or clergy, he reported, dissented from this view. For Tocqueville much followed from this, not least the conclusion that it was by distancing itself from government that religion preserved its power over men's souls. The respect accorded to the marriage bond in American society, Tocqueville believed, was one case in point. These "new facts" also told Tocqueville that the philosophers of the eighteenth century had been wrong to imagine that religious belief would decline with the advance of enlightenment and freedom, as it was in America that "you see one of the most free and enlightened peoples in the world fulfill with ardor all the external duties of religion."[110]

Tocqueville's discussion of "the particular and accidental situation in which Providence placed Americans" was intriguing.[111] Notably missing was any reference to climate. This is surprising not only because one of the early themes in French accounts of America had been that of the damaging effects of the American climate upon humans and beasts alike but also because, in private correspondence, Tocqueville had acknowledged its importance in shaping the character of the calm Quebecois and the restless Louisianan. In addition, Tocqueville and Beaumont had suffered greatly at the hands of the extreme summer heat and biting winter cold during their stay.

Rather, Tocqueville focused upon the geographical isolation and size of America and upon what he had learnt from his conversations with his American acquaintances to regard as America's "point of departure." The great benefit deriving from isolation was that America had no powerful neighbours and thus had no wars, no financial crises and no fear of conquest. America, therefore, needed "neither heavy taxes nor a numerous army, nor great generals" and so could vote for a soldier of such "middling capacity" as Andrew Jackson without fear that the scourge of military glory would undermine its republican institutions.[112] It likewise meant that America had no large capital capable of exerting either its direct or indirect influence over the whole extent of its territory. Consequently, it was able to preserve the "representative system" and, most importantly, to avoid the principal "defect of the republics of antiquity" (none of which, according to Tocqueville, had known such a system).[113]

To these "fortunate circumstances," Tocqueville then added "the good fortunes of birth."[114] "I seem to see," he wrote, "the whole destiny of America contained in the first Puritan who landed on its shores." This was so, he explained, because their fathers had taught the Americans both a love of equality and a love of freedom. They thereby created not only "a republican social state" but also gave to their descendants a set of "habits, ideas and mores" most appropriate for the flourishing of a republic.[115] It was, however, "God himself" who had held "the boundless continent" of America in reserve and who thus had provided the Americans with "the means to remain free and equal for a long time." Tocqueville's point here was that, in America, nature itself worked for the people, that there was an empty continent, "a wilderness land," into which America's inhabitants could pour in pursuit of material well-being. "It would be difficult," Tocqueville wrote, "to depict the avidity with which the American throws himself on the immense prey that fortune offers him." He remarked, "one must go to America" properly to understand why and how this was so.[116]

It was to the question of race that Tocqueville finally turned before finishing the first volume of *De la démocratie en Amérique.* And no question seemed more important in determining the future of the United States. From the first, Tocqueville observed, one saw that people who lived on the American continent made up three "naturally distinct" and "enemy races." Gathered upon the same soil, each pursued its destiny separately. "The first who attracts attention," Tocqueville continued, was "the white man, the European, man *par excellence.*" Below him came "the Negro and the Indian." Both occupied an equally inferior position, and both suffered the effects of tyranny. "If their miseries are different," Tocqueville wrote, "they can blame the same authors for them."[117]

There can be no doubt that Tocqueville, like so many of his compatriots, was deeply moved by the plight of Native Americans. Referring back to the incident of the forced removal of the Choctaw so vividly described in a letter to his mother, he denied that the picture he had drawn was exaggerated, adding that "I have gazed upon evils that would be impossible for me to recount." But these evils, he believed, were irredeemable, and it seemed inevitable that the "Indian race of North America is condemned to perish." Whether they continued to wander through the wilderness or decided to settle made no difference to their prospects, as the relentless and prodigious advance of the European settler population condemned them to destruction and extinction. If the individual states sought their complete expulsion, the Union, exuding the spirit of philanthropy and respect for the law, made this possible by promising them a refuge in the West. "The Spanish, with the help of monstrous crimes without precedents," Tocqueville wrote, echoing what he had written to his mother, "were not able to succeed in exterminating the Indian race, nor even in preventing it from sharing their rights; the Americans of the United States have achieved this double result with a marvelous ease, without violating a single one of the great principles of morality in the eyes of the world."[118]

If then the Native American was fated to live on only in our memories, the same could not be said of the slave population of the South. Here was "the most formidable of all the evils that threaten the future of the United States."[119] Nor should we be in any doubt as to Tocqueville's sense of the awfulness of the oppression visited upon the black population. In an instant, he wrote, they were deprived of "nearly all the privileges of humanity." The "Negro of the United States," he continued, had lost both the memory of his country and his religion and no longer understood the language of his fathers. He had no family and could see in women nothing other than "the temporary companion of his pleasures." Worse still, "plunged into this abyss of evils . . . the practice of servitude has given him the thoughts and ambition of a slave."[120]

Tocqueville's description of the situation of black people and his deep sense of foreboding about the future were structured around his own experience of travelling from the Ohio River down to the mouth of the Mississippi. Such a "traveller," Tocqueville wrote "navigates, so to speak, between liberty and servitude; and he has only to glance around him to judge in an instant which one is most favorable to humanity."[121] He also drew upon the numerous conversations he had had on the subject while in America, conversations that convinced Tocqueville that many people, including "some of the most enlightened," believed that "Negroes belong to an inferior species." An entry in one of his notebooks read simply, "In Philadelphia, blacks are not buried in the same cemeteries as whites."[122] The same entry recorded that, in prisons, black people were kept separate from white people, "even during evening meals." Another recorded that in Massachusetts, where slavery did not exist, a marriage between a white person and a person of colour was legally invalid. In the same state, he learned, prejudice against black people was so strong that their children were not admitted to schools. From this he could see how slavery penetrated the souls of the masters. Among southerners, Tocqueville recorded in his notebooks, slavery made work "dishonourable" and had turned "the entire white race into a leisure class."[123] What he described in *De la démocratie en Amérique* was a reality where even the free slave enjoyed no political rights, had no recourse to the law for protection, and—whether it be at the theatre, church, or school—lived segregated from the white person. If the practices associated with slavery were receding, Tocqueville observed, the prejudices to which it had given birth were unmoving.[124]

The acute dilemmas and difficulties of this situation did not escape Tocqueville. Slavery neither could nor should endure, he argued. It defied economic reason. It amounted to a reversal of the order of nature. Viewed from a Christian perspective, it was unjust. But, as a deleted passage from the original manuscript of *De la démocratie en Amérique* reveals, it also told us something profound about American society: "The Americans are, of all modern peoples, those who have pushed equality and inequality furthest among men. They have combined universal suffrage and servitude. They seem to have wanted to prove . . . the advantages of equality by opposite arguments. It is claimed that the Americans, by establishing universal suffrage and the dogma of sovereignty . . . , have made clear to the world the advantages of equality. As for me, I think that they have above all proved this by establishing servitude, and I find that they establish the advantages of equality much less by democracy than by slavery."[125]

The prospects of a resolution to this terrible question were, in Tocqueville's view, slim indeed. Slavery was integral to the cotton and tobacco growing economy of the South. In line with what he had been told on a regular basis and had seen for himself, he saw no possibility that the white and black races would merge. Nor did he believe that a return to Africa was either a serious or viable option. Either the slave population in the South would seize their own freedom (by violent means, if necessary) or, if freedom were granted to them, they would undoubtedly abuse it. "I summon up all of my hatred," Tocqueville wrote, "against those who after more than a thousand years of equality introduced servitude again into the world."[126]

This, in turn, raised the question of the future viability of the United States itself. In his lengthy meditation on this subject, we see the extent to which during his nine-month stay Tocqueville had taken note of the key political questions agitating America at the time. He commented, at some considerable length, not only upon the character of President Andrew Jackson—referred to in Tocqueville's travel notebooks as "a mediocre individual"—but also upon the intense debates over the renewal of the charter of the Second Bank of the United States, tariff reform, and the nullification crisis engineered by James Calhoun and his supporters in South Carolina. Jackson was "a slave of the majority; he follows it in its will, in its desires, in its half-discovered instincts, or rather he divines it and runs to put himself at its head." In so doing, Tocqueville wrote, "he belittles himself, he hides, he stands aside" but, at the same time, he "tramples underfoot his personal enemies . . . with an ease no President has found."[127] The present union, Tocqueville observed, will last for only as long as its constituent states wish it to.

Yet, as ever, Tocqueville's preoccupation was not with the fleeting questions of the day but with the long-term future. His focus remained on the enduring trends which would decide and determine the course of American history. If he saw the threats to the Union that came from the different temperaments of the southerner and the northerner—the one spontaneous and aristocratic, the other active and middle class—he believed (incorrectly, as it turned out) that all Americans recognised the commercial and political incentives to remain united. Within the Union, Tocqueville argued, Americans had "no invasion to fear, no army to maintain, no taxes to levy." No material advantages would be derived from splitting off from the rest. Americans, "from Maine to Florida, from the Missouri to the Atlantic Ocean," agreed about the general principles which should govern society and about the sources of moral authority. They had the same ideas about liberty and equality. They believed that self-interest well understood was sufficient to guide their fellow citizens. Everyone shared a faith in human perfectibility. All, Tocqueville wrote, "admit that what seems good to them today can be replaced tomorrow by something better that is still hidden." Not only this, but Americans possessed an immense pride in their nation and were "not far from believing that they form a species apart in the human race."[128]

The greatest threats to the United States, therefore, came from its extension beyond the original thirteen states—as the number of states increased one saw "the chance to gather the assent of all to the same laws diminish"—and what Tocqueville termed "the continual displacement of forces that takes place within it." "This gradual and continuous march of the European race towards the Rocky Mountains," he wrote, "is like a flood of men that rises unceasingly and that swells each day by the hand of God." The rapidity and extent of this internal movement, driven forward by the search for material prosperity, only accentuated the danger. Within a hundred years, Tocqueville predicted, the United States would have a population of more than one hundred million and would be divided into forty states.[129]

Countering these tendencies towards dissolution were the forces of greater economic integration—the civilisation of the North, Tocqueville contended, would become the norm—and the Constitution itself. Around the latter, Tocqueville wrote, there existed a "*consensus universalis.*" What was meant by the republic in the United States was "the slow and tranquil action of society upon itself," and these principles had deep roots in American society. Tocqueville believed, therefore, that it could only be with extreme difficulty that the practices of monarchy and aristocracy could be received into American customs. Nothing indicated that America would take this path. Indeed, Tocqueville believed that federal power was weakening rather than strengthening and thus that talk of presidential despotism was unfounded. The fears of Americans on this subject, he wrote, were "entirely imaginary."[130]

It was at the very end of these reflections that Tocqueville provided a glimpse of what he clearly perceived to be the forces likely to transform America in the decades to come. He first turned his attention to the causes of America's commercial greatness, and here he captured something of the all-conquering spirit of American capitalism: "I cannot express my thoughts better than by saying that Americans put a kind of heroism in their way of doing commerce." They constantly adapted their labours to satisfy their needs and were never hampered by old methods and old attitudes. Nowhere did they see limits to the actions of humankind. They lived in "a land of wonders" where everything was in motion and where change was a step forward. Newness was associated with improvement. Americans lived in a state of "feverish agitation," keeping them above "the common level of humanity." For an American, Tocqueville wrote, "all of life happens like a game of chance, a time of revolution, a day of battle." Choose any American at random and you would find someone of ardent desires, of initiative, of enterprise, and, above all, "an innovator." In consequence, America was destined to become a major maritime and naval power. As a matter of course, it would gain dominance over South America. Commercial greatness would soon generate military power.[131]

It was then with the gaze of someone he described as "a traveller who, while coming outside the walls of a vast city, climbs up an adjacent hill" that

Tocqueville concluded the first volume of *De la démocratie en Amérique* by providing "a clear idea of the whole." America, he thought, would drag the whole North American continent into its orbit. He saw that the United States would soon break its treaty obligations with Mexico. Its people would make their way into these solitary lands, intent on snatching ownership from their rightful owners. Texas, although still under Mexican rule, was day by day being infiltrated by Americans, imposing their language and way of life. Soon no Mexicans would be found there. The same was happening wherever the "Anglo-Americans" came into contact with other peoples. "It must not be believed," Tocqueville wrote, "that it is possible to stop the expansion of the English race of the New World," for such was its inevitable destiny. Neither bad laws, nor revolutions, nor anarchy could prevent its spread from "the strands of the Atlantic Ocean to the shores of the Pacific"; and soon the entire continent would belong to a people sharing "the same point of departure, the same civilisation, the same language, the same religion, the same habits, the same mores." This much was certain, Tocqueville believed, and it was something entirely novel in the world.[132]

It was for this reason that Tocqueville ended the first volume of *De la démocratie en Amérique* with what has since become his famous comparison between America and Russia. Here, he suggested, were two great peoples who, from different starting points, shared the same destination. All other peoples appeared to have reached the outer limits of their natural development, but the Americans and the Russians—the first with the farmer's plough, the second with the soldier's sword—seemed called by "a secret design of Providence" one day to determine "the destinies of half the world."[133]

When the first volume of *De la démocratie en Amérique* was published in France in late January 1835 it was an immediate success and turned Tocqueville into a celebrity. Writing in *Le courrier français,* the well-known journalist Léon Faucher commented that it "will strike its readers as a revelation."[134] For *Le journal des débats* it was an "unrivalled book" that honoured not only its author but the country and the age in which it was written.[135] Another review described it as "one of the most remarkable books to have appeared in our time." The same review also developed a theme that was to be frequently repeated elsewhere. The author of *De la démocratie en Amérique* combined "the imagination of a young man with the patient observation of maturity." [136] The Protestant *Le semeur* was of a similar opinion. Few books, it commented, revealed "such a serious-minded search for the truth."[137] Tocqueville, it was widely agreed, had described what he had seen in America and had done so with honesty, impartiality, and, according to *Le courrier français,* "a rare wisdom." In the eyes of the prorepublican *Le bon sens,* Tocqueville's book could "properly be considered a historical document worthy of belief; it is neither an apology nor a satire."[138] *Le semeur* developed the same argument. Tocqueville, its reviewer wrote, had not written a "panegyric" in praise of democracy but had been sensitive "to its faults and its beauties, its vices as well as its virtues."[139]

In brief, by his compatriots Tocqueville was taken to have provided an accurate picture of America and to have done so with great lucidity and honesty. Here, *L'écho français* commented, "is a conscientious book that reveals to us a society so different in real life from the pictures of our imagination."[140] *Le national* made the same point at greater length. "Books about the mores of North Americans and the accounts of travellers, some excessive in their praise, some inspired by the opposite sentiment," it announced, "are not lacking: but what did not exist . . . was a work explaining the life of democracy in America in detail, which reveals the mainsprings of society in the United States." Monsieur Alexis de Tocqueville, the review concluded, had filled that lacuna.[141] By common consent, Tocqueville was the Blackstone of America.[142] Favourable comparisons with Montesquieu, author of *The Spirit of the Laws,* were not in short supply.

Moreover, the most attentive reviewers were fully aware of the significance of Tocqueville's achievement. From the eighteenth century onwards, the French had been told to turn their gaze in admiration towards England. Tocqueville told them to look elsewhere, to a new civilisation and a new people, to a country where the obstacles of the past were being overcome and where an unparalleled form of government was taking shape. Not everyone liked what was described to them. *Le moniteur du commerce* was only too ready to dismiss democracy as the "sovereignty of number" and therefore of ignorance and mediocrity.[143] Not for the first or last time, America was derided as a country of materialistic individualism with no concern for moral and intellectual well-being. Others were convinced that American institutions could not be adapted to French circumstances, that only a fundamental transformation of the French people could make it safe to embrace the institutions of republican democracy. Nonetheless, Tocqueville's compatriots agreed that, for those who cared to reflect, *De la démocratie en Amérique* was clearly written with lessons in mind for Europe.[144]

Almost immediately Tocqueville turned his thoughts to securing the publication of the first volume of the book in English translation. In London this was quickly secured through the efforts of a young Englishman named Henry Reeve.[145] In America there was no such immediate success. Several of Tocqueville's American friends tried to find a publisher in the United States, but to no avail. As Olivier Zunz has explained, political squabbles between France and the United States at the time meant that American opinion was particularly hostile to all things French and the American press had picked up what were seen as Tocqueville's negative comments on aspects of American democracy from the reviews that had appeared in Britain.[146] So it was not until 1838 that an American edition saw the light of day. And when it did, the company of Scatcherd and Adams in New York simply ignored international copyright and reprinted the Reeve translation without permission. One consequence was that Tocqueville earned no money from the American edition of his book.

Upon its publication there was one article on *De la démocratie en Amérique* that particularly pleased Tocqueville: that written by eminent Harvard University professor Edward Everett for the *North American Review.*[147] To his translator Henry Reeve, Tocqueville wrote that "I have been extremely happy for the past two days because of an article I have read in the July issue of the *North American Review.* My book is reviewed in the most flattering of terms. The author . . . says several times that I am the first European to have grasped the spirit of American institutions and offered an accurate description of them. I read this with genuine pleasure."[148] A letter written the next day to Gustave de Beaumont expressed similar sentiments. "What particularly impressed me," Tocqueville wrote, "was the praise for my impartiality and above all for the great *truthfulness* of my portraits. . . . I was afraid that I might at times be making monumental errors, principally in the eyes of the people of the country."[149]

He was right to be happy. While pointing out that Tocqueville was sometimes "led away by the desire to generalize,"[150] and that the book contained factual errors ("some of considerable importance"), Everett did indeed affirm that Tocqueville's work was "by far the most philosophical, ingenious and instructive, which has been produced in Europe on the subject of America." Tocqueville "came to this country," he continued, "to study with impartiality its institutions, to ascertain its condition, and to trace the existing phenomena to their principles." He was correct to place the equality of conditions as "the parent principle of our institutions" and to have diagnosed the sovereignty of the people as "the master-principle of our politics." He had penetrated, "with great accuracy, the municipal system of New England." Just as importantly, in Everett's view, Tocqueville had dispelled the "European prejudice" that religion "can have no substantial foothold" in America and that "the people of the United States are an irreligious people."[151]

Everett could not help but compare what he described as Tocqueville's "manly love of truth" with "the vulgar error of foreigners" whose many works on America had of late caused "much mischief." At issue was what Everett described as "the scandal and gossip of the travellers in our own country." "How gentlemen and ladies," he wrote, "can find in the mere fact, that they are foreign tourists . . . a reason for liberating themselves from those restraints of good breeding, which would operate on a person travelling from city to city in his own country, we have never been able to conceive." There was "a sin of a deeper dye," Everett wrote, by which "we mean that of undertaking the voyage expressly and for the avowed purpose of political effect at home, and consequently to find and . . . to make the materials for vilifying this country." If Tocqueville had "no partiality for the experiment" of American democracy, "he has at least no prejudice against it." There was neither "eulogy" nor "detraction." To that extent, Everett concluded, "M. de Tocqueville's work exhibits more insight into our system than any European publication we have seen."[152]

There was, though, one specific part of *De la démocratie en Amérique* that Everett felt deserved praise: Tocqueville's introduction, where, in Everett's words, Tocqueville "traced the growth of the democratic principle" and glanced at "our future fortunes." It was with this in mind that Everett showed himself to be among the first truly to understand the greatness of the book. "It would be underrating the importance of Tocqueville's work," he wrote, "to regard it merely as a book on America. It is a work of deep significance and startling import for Europe and for the modern civilized world."[153]

Yet the praise heaped upon *De la démocratie en Amérique* by American readers often came with significant reservations. For example, the American edition came complete with a preface and notes written by one of the people Tocqueville had met while in America, the prominent lawyer and politician John Canfield Spencer.[154] Whilst full of praise, Spencer did not disguise the purpose of his additions. "The work of M. de Tocqueville," he began, "is universally regarded as a sound, philosophical, impartial, and remarkably clear and distinct view of our political institutions, and of our manners, opinions and habits, as influencing or influenced by those institutions." "His views of our political institutions," Spencer went on, "are more general, comprehensive, and philosophic, than have been presented by any writer, domestic or foreign. He has traced them from their source, democracy—the power of the people—and has steadily pursued this foundation-principle in all its forms and modifications: in the frame of our governments, in their administration by different executives, in our legislation, in the arrangements of our judiciary, in our manners, in religion, in the freedom and licentiousness of the press, in the influence of public opinion, and in various subtle recesses, where its existence was scarcely suspected." "The intelligent American reader," Spencer therefore concluded, "will find no better guide than M. de Tocqueville."[155]

Nevertheless, Spencer added, among the "distinguished men" eager to see a copy of *De la démocratie en Amérique* before an American public, "it seemed . . . that a reprint in America of the views of an author so well entitled to regard and confidence, without any correction of the few errors or mistakes that might be found, would be in effect to give authenticity to the whole work, and that foreign readers especially, would consider silence under such circumstances as strong evidence of the accuracy of its statements." Spencer self-declared task, in other words, was "to correct any erroneous impressions." "With very few exceptions," Spencer explained, his corrections were limited to "what appeared to be misapprehensions of the author in regard to some matters of fact or some principles of law" and excluded "comments on the theoretical views of our author." As Spencer's notes confirm, this was largely true. Where this was not true was with regard to "the very sore subject" of "the tyranny of public opinion."[156]

To this sore subject we will return, as it was to be one of the topics frequently raised by Tocqueville's critics. Here it is sufficient to say that in Spencer's additional notes to the text his view was that Tocqueville's "fundamental error" arose largely from the unusual political circumstances of Andrew Jackson's Presidency. "In reference to this particular subject," Spencer explained, Tocqueville "visited the United States at a particular time, when a successful political chieftain had succeeded in establishing his party in power, as it seemed firmly and permanently, when the preponderance of that party was immense, and when there seemed little prospect of any change." Consequently, Tocqueville "mistook a temporary state of affairs for a permanent and ordinary result" and, in doing so, used "a style of exaggeration . . . so different from the well-considered and nicely-adjusted language employed by him on all other occasions."[157] "At all events," Spencer concluded in his Preface, "it is to be hoped that the citizens of the United States will patiently read and candidly consider the views of this accomplished foreigner, however hostile they may be to their own pre-conceived opinions or prejudices."[158]

With typical courtesy, Tocqueville made a point of thanking Spencer for his remarks. "I have always set the greatest value on the judgement of enlightened Americans," he wrote from the château de Tocqueville in September 1838, adding that "a great number of your critiques appear to me to be just and I propose taking advantage of them in the seventh edition of my work."[159] Nonetheless, the critical comments did not cease. Indeed, they have continued to this day.[160]

All Tocqueville scholars are familiar with Garry Wills's charge that Tocqueville did not "get" America. "A fact usually omitted in discussions of Tocqueville," Wills writes, "is the shallow empirical basis of his study." "It is," he continues, "as if [Tocqueville] ghosted his way directly into the American spirit, bypassing the body of the nation." In Tocqueville's *De la démocratie en Amérique,* Wills points out, there is virtually nothing about American capitalism, manufacturing, banking, or technology. Moreover, during their nine months in America, Tocqueville and Beaumont spent around two months "narrowly focused on prison life" and, in addition, devoted time to trips "only remotely connected, or not connected at all, with what went into *Democracy.*" These included a trip to what we now know as French-speaking Quebec and two weeks in the forests of the West. Most of the remaining seven months, Wills tells us, were spent in the North, where "almost all of *Democracy*'s conclusions" were "formed while Tocqueville was fresh in the country and seemed particularly impressionable." Wills further contends that Tocqueville was extremely selective—not to say, snobbish—about those with whom he chose to converse, showing little interest in "ordinary people."[161] Wills is likewise less than charitable in his assessment of the impact of these meetings with the superior minds of the East Coast. "Tocqueville," he writes, "took many of his views from the last remnants of the Federalists, who supplied him with what he thought necessary to democracy, a moderating counter to extreme egalitarianism." Accordingly, Wills affirms, Tocqueville "parroted" the views of the Federalists in his "scathing" comments on Andrew Jackson and upon populist leaders such as Sam Houston and Davy Crockett.[162] The implication of Wills's comments is that not only were these views of dubious worth—damned, as they were, by their lofty social origin—but that Tocqueville would have discovered an altogether different America had he chosen occasionally to mix with his social inferiors.

The criticism does not cease there. "In his erratic traversing of the country," Wills writes, "what Tocqueville did not see is often more interesting than what he did."[163] Tocqueville never visited a New England town meeting. He never saw an American university. He made no efforts to become familiar with American intellectual life. The only state capital he visited was Albany, New York.[164] His journey through the South to New Orleans was hasty in the extreme and diminished as a source of potential information by Tocqueville's debilitating illness.

Wills's conclusion is clear. Tocqueville "would probably not have benefited by a longer stay in America." His ideas were formed upon the basis of first encounters and rarely changed afterwards. He had a propensity to form "instant judgments." He "concluded things about America because of the prejudices he brought with him from France." He was not seeking to write "an objective account of what he saw in America." His pronouncements were made "*de haut en bas.*" The whole book, like Tocqueville's work in general, was characterised by "the taste for grand simplification."[165]

The surprise is that these conclusions find an echo in what would normally be regarded among Tocqueville scholars as a friendly source—namely, George Wilson Pierson's magisterial reconstruction *Tocqueville and Beaumont in America.* Published first in 1938, Pierson devoted a set of four chapters to a consideration of the overall character of Tocqueville's achievement. Let it first be clear that Pierson believed that Tocqueville drew "some useful conclusions" from his American experiences. Indeed, Pierson goes so far as to say that "one may without exaggeration insist that there is not a single chapter in the first two volumes of his commentary that did not draw most of its basic ideas and many illustrative details directly from the study that he and Beaumont had made, personally, in the United States, on the spot." In particular, Pierson wrote, Tocqueville saw that "there seemed to exist in the United States certain habits, certain institutional practices, which increased the good effects obtainable from self-government at the same time that they mitigated or even altogether eliminated the dangers inherent in mass control." Second, if Pierson acknowledged that Tocqueville "had carried some prejudices to America," he countered this by asserting that "the Americans themselves had again and again supplied the corroborating information."[166]

Yet Pierson did not seek to disguise or hide the "defects" to be found in *De la démocratie en Amérique.* Of these, Pierson suggested, the principal deficiency was to be found in Tocqueville's philosophical method. Tocqueville was "neither a historian nor a scientist but a philosopher, and a philosopher whose concepts and whose habits were not well calculated, if he wanted, rigorously, to find the truth." It was this, Pierson concluded, that "injected into his classic the strong dose of mortality that it undoubtedly contains." Pierson was also of the view that Tocqueville was "unscientific in his use, or rather in his failure to use, contemporary literature" and that he was "not sufficiently inquisitive."[167]

So too, Tocqueville was guilty of "errors of observation." What follows is a pared-down version of the lengthy list highlighted by Pierson: Tocqueville misread the American inheritance laws. He neglected American material development, in the process ignoring "the one great factor that was going to transform his chosen civilization almost overnight." He failed properly to acknowledge the nationalizing influence of American commerce and underestimated the centralizing tendency in American politics. He did not foresee the rise of American cities and therefore did not appreciate the strain that would be placed upon institutions of local self-government. In his appraisal of American institutions, he failed to obtain "sufficient knowledge of their historical background," and so was unable correctly to discuss the dispute over slavery and the bitterness between the North and South. In the field of politics he made "two considerable errors of omission": he failed to notice the growth of a two-party system (the wealthy New Yorker, Peter Schermerhorn, had convinced Tocqueville aboard ship that there were no parties in America), and he neglected the intermediate unit of American politics, the state, thus closing his eyes to "its significant possibilities as a balancing force and experimental laboratory." "Both of these mistakes," Pierson concluded, "can be traced to his visit to Albany and his failures of observation there." More than this, because of his experience with President Andrew Jackson—a man that both Tocqueville and Beaumont found to be far from impressive—Tocqueville "underestimated the power of the executive branch in American government." Most alarming of all, Tocqueville failed "to give adequate credit to American enthusiasm for liberty" and, worse still, he "perhaps overestimated the tendency of democracy, at least as practised in the United States, to degenerate into tyranny by the majority."[168]

Here we might pause to consider the justice and substance of some of these critical remarks. There is no shortage of evidence to support the view that Tocqueville quickly made up his mind about what he saw in America. Letters to two of his closest friends, Ernest de Chabrol and Louis de Kergorlay, written shortly after his arrival in the United States, gave a strong indication of what would become many of the themes of his famous book. Likewise, Tocqueville's pattern of mixing in the best social circles was also quickly evident, even if he was of the opinion that he and Beaumont mixed with people of all classes. During their voyage from Le Havre, most attention was lavished upon Peter Schermerhorn, a distinguished shipping merchant and banker from New York, and his family. Once on dry land Schermerhorn lost no time in introducing the two visitors to his wealthy friends and relatives. Tocqueville and Beaumont were clearly delighted by the way they were received, and soon found themselves the toast of New York society, their hosts seemingly "competing" as to who might be the most friendly and useful.[169] After an initially chilly welcome and a difficult first few days, the doors of the Bostonian elite were similarly opened to them, with Tocqueville making the acquaintance of, among others, Josiah Quincy, the president of Harvard University; the "distinguished Boston literary man" Jared Sparks; the eminent Everett brothers, Alexander the diplomat and Edward the future governor of Massachusetts and US senator, the much-travelled and cultivated George Ticknor; and, last but not least, former president John Quincy Adams.

A reading of Tocqueville's notebooks reveals just how much he learned from his conversations with those he told his mother were "the most distinguished men of this country." From one Joseph Coolidge he learnt of the democratic nature of Catholicism in America. From John Quincy Adams he heard that religion was "one of the most important safeguards of American society." Adams also told Tocqueville something of "the spirit of the Americans of the South"—"Every white man in the South," he told Tocqueville, "is equally privileged, in that he has the right to put Negroes to work while doing none himself"—and of the significance of the movement of the population towards the West. Most importantly, it was Jared Sparks who explained to Tocqueville that the "political dogma" of America was "that the majority is always right," and it was Alexander Everett who informed Tocqueville one evening that "a people's point of departure is a matter of immense importance." In the course of his stay in Boston Tocqueville recorded a similar remark from Jared Sparks to the effect that "I believe that our government and mores are best explained by our origins."[170] It was this idea, as Tocqueville was later to inform readers of *De la démocratie en Amérique,* which provided "the key to nearly the whole book."[171]

What of the potentially more serious, and often repeated, charge that Tocqueville showed no interest in and failed to perceive the growing industrialisation of the American economy? This assertion can often figure as part of a broader argument alleging that Tocqueville knew nothing of economics and displayed a near total indifference to the social issues and problems of his day. That this general contention is largely false has been amply shown by the work of Michael Drolet and Richard Swedberg,[172] but does it hold true for the specifics of Tocqueville's examination of America?

This is the way the evidence has been presented by Seymour Drescher, one of the most perceptive of commentators upon Tocqueville's work. Tocqueville and Beaumont, he writes, "visited prisons until they felt themselves imprisoned by their own mission. They sacrificed comfort, and almost their lives, to view the American West firsthand. But though they knew of the world-famous industrial experiment at Lowell, Massachusetts, they simply passed it by. Their one hour in Pittsburgh . . . was spent catching up on correspondence. They were deeply impressed by Cincinnati's throbbing industry but spent their extremely rationed time there with its lawyers rather than its industrial classes."[173]

How, on Tocqueville's behalf, might we respond? The failure to visit Lowell was undoubtedly a notable omission. Despite its recent creation in the early 1820s it had already achieved notoriety as a purpose-built mill town and regularly received foreign visitors, including some from France. Among these was Michel Chevalier, author of *Lettres sur l'Amérique du Nord,* first published in 1836.[174] Regarding Tocqueville's visit to Pittsburgh, Tocqueville arrived there only after an arduous journey fraught with considerable difficulty in blizzard conditions. Moreover, following a request from the French Ministry of Justice, he and Beaumont had now been obliged to cut short their visit to America and were hurrying in order to return to France within a year.[175]

A similar observation might be made about their four-day stay in Cincinnati. While it is undeniably true that Tocqueville used his letters of recommendation in order to secure interviews with lawyers—and also Supreme Court Justice John McLean—these conversations were wide-ranging and led Tocqueville to reflect extensively upon the character of the rapidly expanding American West. "More than any of the other parts of the union," he confided in his notebook, "Ohio strikes me as a society totally occupied with its own affairs and, through work, with rapid growth."[176] The whole of society, he observed, was an industry and everyone had come there to make money. Of Cincinnati, in particular, Tocqueville remarked,

> It is always difficult to know exactly why cities develop and grow. Chance always plays a part. Cincinnati is situated in one of the most fertile plains of the New World, and because of this advantage it began to attract settlers. Factories were built to supply the needs of these settlers and before

View of Cincinnati from the Ohio River (The Protected Art Archive / Alamy Stock Photo)

> long of a whole region of the West, and the success of these industries attracted new industries and more settlers than ever. Cincinnati was, and I believe still is, a transit point for many shipments to and from the Mississippi and the Missouri valleys to Europe and for trade between New York and the northern states and Louisiana."[177]

From this and other observations in his notebooks, it would be difficult to conclude that Tocqueville neither observed nor appreciated the importance of the rapid industrial and commercial progress that was transforming America and pushing its population ever westward.

Nevertheless, this material does not on the whole appear in *De la démocratie en Amérique.* Indeed, in his printed text, this part of Tocqueville's journey into America figured largely as the occasion for him to reflect upon how, when travelling down the Ohio River, the "traveller . . . navigates, so to speak, between liberty and servitude." The white man of the right bank of the Ohio River, "obliged to live by his own efforts, made material well-being the principal goal of his existence. . . . The American of the left bank scorns not only work, but all the enterprises that work brings to success, . . . So slavery not only prevents whites from making a fortune, it turns them away from wanting to do so."[178] These remarks were anticipated in his notebooks and in a letter written from Memphis to his father, dated 20 December 1831.[179]

Yet, if one looks a little closer at this section of the text of *De la démocratie en Amérique,* one also sees a note where Tocqueville makes reference to the efforts of the state of Ohio to ensure the building of a canal between Lake Erie and the Ohio River, thanks to which "the merchandise of Europe that arrives in New York can descend by water as far as New Orleans across more than five hundred leagues of the continent."[180] This observation is also prefigured in his travel notes.

The fact of the matter is that Tocqueville was not unfamiliar with these aspects of the American economic infrastructure. In his Notebook E, the section recording his impressions of Cincinnati and Ohio is followed almost immediately by a section entitled "Means of Increasing Public Prosperity," in which he wrote, "The roads, the canals and the post play a prodigious part in the prosperity of the union." America not only enjoyed a greater sum of prosperity than any other country but had also "made the greatest effort to supply itself with . . . free communications." One of the first things done in a new state was to create a postal service such that "there is no cabin so isolated, no valley so wild, that letters and newspapers don't arrive at least once a week." Main roads were built "in the middle of a wilderness" and almost always before the arrival of those whom they were meant to serve. America, Tocqueville further observed, "has undertaken and finished the construction of some immense canals. It already has more railways than France; no one fails to see that the discovery of steam has incredibly increased the power and prosperity of the union; and that is because it facilitates speedy communications between different parts of that immense land." As Americans were not a sedentary people, they felt the need for means of communication with a liveliness and zeal unknown in France. As to the means employed to open up communications in America, Tocqueville saw that, whilst "the American government does not interfere in everything," when it came to "great works of public utility" they were seldom left to the "care of private persons." Individual states led the way, the canal linking Lake Erie to the Mississippi being funded by the state of New York, and so on.[181]

Why did Tocqueville not include these observations in *De la démocratie en Amérique*? The fact is that, despite assertions to the contrary, in part he did.

The 1840 volume of the book contains a chapter entitled "What Makes Nearly All Americans Tend toward Industrial Professions." The primary theme is that the equality of conditions associated with democratic society inclined people away from agriculture and towards industry and commerce. The result, Tocqueville noted, was that "there is no people on earth which has made as rapid progress as the Americans in commerce and industry. They form today the second maritime nation of the world; and, although their manufacturing has to struggle against almost insurmountable natural obstacles, it does not fail to make new gains every day." To this Tocqueville then added that, although they had only recently arrived on the North American continent, the Americans had "already overturned the whole natural order to their profit. They have united the Hudson with the Mississippi and connected the Atlantic Ocean with the Gulf of Mexico, across more than five hundred leagues of the continent that separates these two seas. The longest railroads that have been constructed until now are in America." The key to this astonishing achievement, according to Tocqueville, lay in "the innumerable multitude of small enterprises" that characterised the American economy. "The Americans," he wrote, "make immense progress in industry, because they are all involved in industry at the same time."[182]

But let us put these comments aside and return to the question of why Tocqueville might have ignored these important developments in his published account. Garry Wills has a simple answer. "Tocqueville," he tells us, "took some notes on these matters, but did not consider them important enough to reflect on in *Democracy.*" There might be another explanation. In his notebooks Tocqueville himself made the following remark: "To return to roads and all the other means of bringing the achievements of industry or of thought quickly from one place to another, I make no claim to have discovered that they contribute to the prosperity of a people; it is a truth universally felt and recognised."[183] In other words, as far as Tocqueville was concerned, these facts were so well known that they did not require additional comment or inclusion in his own text.

There is a further, and equally compelling, reason why Tocqueville chose to exclude these issues from his account. In a first version of the drafts of *De la démocratie en Amérique,* Tocqueville wrote in the margin, "I have not said everything that I saw, but I have said everything that I believed at the same time true and useful [v: profitable] to make known, and without wanting to write a treatise on America, I thought only to help my fellow citizens resolve a question that must interest us deeply." He went on to add, "I see around me facts without number, but I notice one of them that dominates all the others: it is old; it is stronger than laws, more powerful than men; it seems to be a direct product of the divine will; it is the gradual development of democracy in the Christian world." He further clarified, "When I say 'democracy' here I do not mean to speak only about a political form of government, but of a social state."[184] This, and not railways and canals, was the subject of Tocqueville's book.

The process by which this subject came progressively to displace all other considerations in Tocqueville's mind can be seen by consulting the Tocqueville material held at Yale University's Beinecke Rare Book and Manuscript Library and assembled by Eduardo Nolla. In his introduction to his bilingual edition of *De la démocratie en Amérique,* Nolla includes Tocqueville's first plan for the contents of his book.[185] The list of subjects to be considered was truly daunting, falling into three broad categories: political society, civil society, and religious society. In the political society section were clearly listed such topics as canals, roads, banks, and other related material such as maritime commerce and free trade. The section detailing the elements of civil society included not only civil and criminal law but also commercial law. As Nolla observes, some of the topics on this long list—most notably, canals and roads—were subsequently excluded from consideration, whilst others not on the list—for example, the army and Catholicism—were included for discussion in the second volume.

In brief, if on Tocqueville's part there was recognition that "no nation on earth has made such swift progress in trade and industry as the Americans," he came to see that these matters were not integral to the argument that he wished to develop. As Tocqueville made plain in a letter to Gustave de Beaumont, in which he asked his friend specifically for commentary on Michel Chevalier's rival text on America, his own study was intended to be an "*ouvrage philosophique-politique.*"[186] It is therefore no surprise that, if Chevalier's account opened with a delightfully instructive map of America's railroads and canals, the first editions of *De la démocratie en Amérique* provided a map on which could be identified the location of slave and nonslave states.

The second substantive criticism—and one with which we are already familiar—is that Tocqueville overestimated the potential of American democracy to degenerate into the tyranny or despotism of the majority. On this issue, Pierson wrote, Tocqueville's American readers were of one opinion: "The conscientious Frenchman was entirely wrong."[187] Such was the view of Tocqueville's American friend, Jared Sparks. In August 1833 Sparks told Tocqueville that in Tocqueville's forthcoming book he anticipated "a more accurate and judicious account of the United States than has yet appeared from the pen of any European traveller."[188] After its publication in France, and in the face of irritation in America about the way the English press had drawn attention to Tocqueville's remarks on "the defects of Democratic institutions," Sparks similarly assured his French colleague that "all the intelligent persons among us who have read your treatise have applauded its ability and candor."[189] Nevertheless, in a letter to William Smyth, a professor at Cambridge University, dated 13 October 1841, Sparks wrote that, on the subject of the tyranny of the majority, Tocqueville's imagination

> leads him far astray. In practice we perceive no such consequences as he supposes. If the majority were large and always consisted of the same individuals, such a thing might be possible; but with us, as in all free governments, parties are nearly equal, and the elections are so frequent that a man who is in the majority at one time is likely to find himself in the minority a few months afterwards. What inducement has a majority thus constituted to be oppressive? Moreover, M. de Tocqueville often confounds the majority with public opinion, which has the same tendency, or nearly so, in all civilized countries, whatever may be the form of government.[190]

The strange thing here is that it was Sparks who first introduced Tocqueville to the idea of the tyranny of the majority when they met in September 1831. "In this country," Tocqueville recorded Sparks as saying, "the political dogma is that the majority is always right. All things considered, we were correct to adopt this principle but there is no denying that experience has shown it to be wrong. (He cited examples.) Sometimes the majority has sought to oppress the minority."[191] Subsequent conversations with others that Tocqueville met in America seemed to confirm that there was some substance to this claim. The distinguished Baltimore physician, Richard Spring Stewart, told Tocqueville in November of that year that "public opinion here accomplishes what the Inquisition was never able to do."[192] In a footnote to the text Tocqueville cited two examples of the abuses associated with majority tyranny. The first concerned the use of mob violence during the War of 1812 to ransack the offices of a Baltimore newspaper which had opposed the war. The second related to the fact that emancipated black people in Pennsylvania failed to exercise their right to vote, as the law was nothing if it did not have the support of public opinion.[193] In both instances the examples were provided for Tocqueville by Americans he met in late 1831: a journalist by the name of Peter Hoffman Cruse and a Quaker from Philadelphia by the name of Smith.[194]

Yet it is easy to see how Tocqueville's use of language might have offended the sensibilities of his American readers. "What I most criticise about democratic government as it has been organised in the United States," he wrote, "is not its weaknesses, as many people in Europe claim, but, on the contrary, its irresistible strength. And what repels me the most in America is not the extreme liberty that reigns there; it is the slight guarantee against tyranny that is found." Where, he asked, could someone turn who suffered an injustice? To public opinion? To the legislative body? To the executive power? To the police? To the law? All, in one way or another, were subject to the power and authority of the majority. There was therefore no alternative for the individual but to submit.[195] Worst of all was the tyranny exercised by the majority over thought: "As long as the majority is uncertain, people speak; but as soon as the majority has irrevocably decided, everyone is silent." The majority, in short, lived in what Tocqueville described as a state of "perpetual self-adoration," drawing "a formidable circle around thought."[196] To this Tocqueville then added a comment that could easily have been read as a gratuitous insult: "If America has not yet had any great writers, we do not have to look elsewhere for the reasons: literary genius does not exist without freedom of the mind, and there is no freedom of the mind in America."[197] He also remarked that the effect of the tyranny of the majority on the national character of the Americans was to produce "a general debasing of souls" and what he described as the development of a "courtier spirit" unknown among the distinguished American figures of the past.[198]

Tocqueville was under no illusion about how these critical remarks would be received: "If these lines ever reach America, I am sure of two things: first, that readers will raise all their voices to condemn me; second, that many among them will absolve me deep down in their conscience." He was certainly right about the first point. Was he right about the second? It is obviously difficult to judge. Here we might cite one of the foremost contemporary commentators on Tocqueville's *De la démocratie en Amérique,* James Schleifer. Schleifer's argument is that Tocqueville's idea of the tyranny of the majority is not persuasive if the focus falls on shifting political majorities. However, if the focus is upon unchanging or slowly changing "majority opinions, ideas, prejudices, especially when the majority is more or less exempt from how the minority is treated, the case is much stronger." The whole matter of race would be a case in point. "Considered from this perspective," Schleifer argues, "Tocqueville's concept of the despotism of the majority becomes a key to understanding much of the long history of racial and ethnic injustice in America."[199]

The fact remains that it is not easy to dislodge the criticism that errors in central aspects of Tocqueville's analysis arose due to both the brevity of his stay in America and to the fact that he could not escape his own inherited prejudices. And here let us remember that he was an outsider in America not only because he was French and an aristocrat but also because he was a Catholic. On this view, the odds were well and truly stacked against Tocqueville ever producing an account of America that rose above shallow empiricism and vague theoretical generalization. Thus forewarned, it might be argued, we are better placed to make sense of Tocqueville's well-known remark that "in America I saw more than America."[200] Had he not been only interested in France all along?

It is not simple to unravel the complex relationship between Tocqueville's impressions of America and his thoughts on the future of European civilisation. Even its earliest reviewers—for example, Edward Everett—realised that *De la démocratie en Amérique* was not *merely* a book about America. The fact that it is not so explains why we continue to read it for instruction and enlightenment (unlike the vast majority of nineteenth-century accounts of America that, if read at all, are done so for entertainment and amusement alone). A letter to Louis de Kergorlay helps us to understand Tocqueville's intentions: "Although I rarely spoke of France in that book, I did not write a page without thinking of her and without always having her, as it were, before my eyes. And above all, what I tried to highlight in the United States and to explain was less a complete picture of that foreign society than the contrasts and resemblances with our own. It was always, either through opposition or analogy with the one, that I endeavoured to present a fair and, above all, interesting image of the other. . . . In my opinion, the return that I constantly made, without making it known, to France was one of the main causes of the success of the book."[201]

Few would disagree with the assessment presented here of the place occupied by France within Tocqueville's study, but two important points need to be made. First, he was very aware of the limits regarding what nations could learn from one another. Less than a month into his stay in America, Tocqueville wrote to his father, "The more I see of this country, the more I am persuaded by this truth: there are virtually no political institutions that are radically good or bad in themselves and that everything depends upon the physical conditions and social state of the people to which they are applied. I see institutions work here that would inevitably cause chaos in France; others that suit us would be certainly harmful in America." This was not, he added, because people were better or worse on either side of the Atlantic. Rather, they were just differently placed.[202] He likewise told his brother Édouard, "In my opinion, one must be truly blind to want to compare this country to Europe and to impose on one what works in the other. I believed this before I left France; I believe it more and more in examining the country in the midst of which I now live."[203] Second, that Tocqueville had France in mind when he wrote *De la démocratie en Amérique* does not and did not reduce the journey to America to either insignificance or irrelevance. To his father he reported that since their arrival, he and Beaumont had had "in truth, only one idea. . . . This idea is to understand the country through which we are travelling."[204]

Next, Tocqueville was only too aware of his own prejudices and of the difficulties involved in freeing himself from them. In his essay *A Fortnight in the Wilderness,* written as Tocqueville traversed the Great Lakes by steamboat, we find the following remark: "As for me, in my traveler's illusions—and what class of man does not have them—I imagined something entirely different." America, he had believed, would "present all the conditions of existence and offer the image of a society across all the ages." Nothing of this picture, he now realised, had any truth. Indeed, America was "the least appropriate for providing the spectacle that I was coming to find there."[205]

Tocqueville was in turn utterly damning in his attitude towards those of his French compatriots who had not bothered themselves with doing anything other than observing America from a lofty and disdainful distance. In a letter to his beloved former tutor, the Abbé Lesueur, he warned that his compatriot, a man called Édouard Schérer, "will paint you an unfavourable picture of America: the fact is that he has made the most stupid journey in the world. He came here without any other end than to stroll about, knowing nothing about either the language or the customs of the country."[206] He later repeated the advice to his mother, condemning a person (possibly the same man) for deriving all he knew of the country from a "particular class of Frenchmen whom he saw exclusively and who, in America as elsewhere, seem to represent all the defects that can be found in the French mind."[207] For his own part, Tocqueville was rather proud of the fact that, from the moment he and Beaumont had boarded ship, they had only mixed with Americans. "We have already shed most of our national prejudices about this nation," he told Ernest de Chabrol on 18 May 1831.[208]

Nor were Tocqueville and Beaumont lacking in inquisitiveness. Since their arrival, Tocqueville told his cousin Félix Le Peletier d'Aunay that he and Beaumont had become "the world's most merciless questioners."[209] To his brother Édouard he remarked that "our minds are constantly striving for the acquisition of useful knowledge."[210] From Sing Sing he told his father only a few days later that they were "now *examining machines.*"[211] As a letter to Ernest de Chabrol illustrates, they also worked hard at their task, rising at five o'clock in the morning and often working into the evening.[212] A reading of Tocqueville's notebooks and letters, therefore, reveals a mind not closed to new experiences, but someone overwhelmed by the novelty and importance of what he was seeing and eager to learn as much as he could.

Nor was Tocqueville under any illusions as to the limits of his knowledge and acquaintance with the United States. Writing from Washington, DC, as his time in America reached its end, he confided in separate letters to both his father and his brother Édouard that he had only a "superficial" knowledge of the South and that a minimum stay of two years was required to prepare a "complete and accurate picture" of the whole country. To attempt to take in the whole, he continued, would be madness, as he had simply not seen enough. In any case, such a work would be as "boring as it was instructive."[213] The same point was made to an unidentified correspondent in November 1831. Providing a "general portrait" of a country that remained to that day as unknown as Japan, he wrote, would be a massive undertaking and one completely beyond his capacities. "I believe," he continued, that it would be "impossible to provide a full account of the impression produced upon the foreigner by their first sight of American society."[214] Similarly, Tocqueville was acutely aware that, given the differences that existed among the then twenty-four states, he could speak only with anything resembling authority about those he had actually seen with his own eyes.[215] Tocqueville also conceded that the decision of the French government to recall Beaumont and himself had deprived them of "an essential part of their journey"—namely, the opportunity to study Louisiana in detail.[216]

For all of that, Tocqueville felt that his time in America had been spent usefully. He had collected numerous documents, spoken with many people, and thought much about what he had seen. Furthermore, he had come to believe that he knew more about America than was generally known in France, and some of what he knew might not only be of great but also current interest. "I believe," he wrote modestly, "that if, upon my return I have the leisure, I might write something passable on the United States."[217] Less than four years later the first volume of the French edition of *De la démocratie en Amérique* was published to instant acclaim.

Furthermore, the meticulously researched edition of *De la démocratie en Amérique* established by Eduardo Nolla provides an invaluable insight into how Tocqueville's text was written and how, as its content evolved over time, the experience of what had been seen and heard in America was distilled into its final written form. Tocqueville began with the notebooks and letters he had written while in America, and worked his way through the extensive collection of printed material he had accumulated. He continued to communicate and interrogate his American acquaintances by mail. To help him complete his research he employed two young Americans, Francis Lippitt and Theodore Sedgwick, as his assistants. The manuscript was passed on to his family, to Gustave de Beaumont and to Louis de Kergorlay, and in turn received extensive, expert comment.[218] Certain sections were read out loud to close friends. Tocqueville's letters to Beaumont make clear what a painstaking and painful process this was. At one point in 1839, and as he neared the completion of the second volume, Tocqueville commented that it was "a fight to the death: either I will kill it or it will kill me."[219]

Given this thoroughness, it is difficult to know what to make of the charge that Tocqueville was unscientific in his use of contemporary sources. Specifically, we know that his long reflection upon his investigation of America convinced Tocqueville that "a new political science is needed for a world entirely new."[220] Why was a new science of politics required? For the simple reason, as Tocqueville pointed out in his introduction to *De la démocratie en Amérique,* that "a great democratic revolution is taking place" and this was a revolution where "the generating fact from which each particular fact seemed to derive" was revealed in American society.[221] The corollary to this, as Schleifer has observed, is that Tocqueville discounted "the traditional inclination to draw lessons about democracy from ancient and Renaissance texts."[222]

There is much that might be said and asked about the merits and character of this avowedly new political science.[223] To what extent was it genuinely novel and innovative? Was it to be value free? Did it possess predictive power? To what extent was it philosophically and empirically flawed? Whatever the answer to these questions, there can be no doubt that Tocqueville did not imagine that his new political science amounted (as Sheldon Wolin has suggested) to a form of political impressionism.[224] The guiding assumption was that, sooner or later, Europe would also arrive at something near to the equality of conditions. This did not mean, Tocqueville argued, that Europe would be obliged to draw the same political conclusions from this social state as had been done in America, or that democracy would produce only one form of government. It had therefore been no part of his purpose to write a panegyric on America. Rather, Tocqueville's hypothesis was that, beyond a legitimate curiosity, one could "find lessons there from which we would be able to profit."[225]

This was achieved with a level of methodological self-awareness and sophistication that was unusual for the age and certainly unusual for the subject matter. In the printed text of *De la démocratie en Amérique,* as well as in his notes and his letters, Tocqueville acknowledged that both he and his book could, and would, be criticised. To his friend Francisque de Corcelle he wrote, "I know that those who will want to attack me will not fail to direct two criticisms at me. . . . First, they will say that I have only general ideas that are not supported by all the details and, second, they will claim that I draw so heavily upon the details of American government that I want to see everything from this perspective." "You can be sure," he then added, "that I will do my best to defend myself and to prove that the criticisms directed at me on these two points are without foundation."[226]

In *De la démocratie en Amérique* itself, Tocqueville wrote that "despite my care, nothing will be easier than to criticize this book, if anyone ever thinks to examine it critically." Someone determined "to contrast an isolated fact to the whole of the facts I cite, a detached idea to the whole of the ideas" could do so with "without difficulty." To this he responded with a clear explanation of his methodology: "When a point could be established with the help of written documents, I have taken care to turn to original texts and to the most authentic and respected works. I have indicated my sources in notes, and everyone will be able to verify them. When it was a matter of opinions, of political customs, of observations of mores, I sought to consult the most enlightened men. If something happened to be important or doubtful, I was not content with one witness, but decided only on the basis of the body of testimonies." Tocqueville remained adamant that he had "never yielded, except unknowingly, to the need to adapt facts to ideas, instead of subjecting ideas to facts." To an extent, Tocqueville willingly conceded, this had to be taken on trust, as it needed also not to be forgotten that "the author who wants to make himself understood is obliged to push each of his ideas to all of their theoretical consequences, and often to the limits of what is false and impractical." Not without some justification, therefore, Tocqueville made a plea for generosity on the part of the reader: "I would like you to grant me the favor of reading me with the same spirit that presided over my work, and would like you to judge this book by the general impression that it leaves, as I myself came to a decision, not due to a particular reason but due to a mass of reasons."[227]

In his unpublished notes, Tocqueville added, "To whoever will do that and then does not agree with me, I am ready to submit. For if I am sure of having sincerely sought the truth, I am far from considering myself as certain to have found it."[228] Tocqueville's modesty in this and with regard to other elements of his inquiry on America seems frequently to have been overlooked by his critics.[229] The surprise is that it should have been suggested that he saw nothing in America and that he might just as well have stayed at home.

A similar mistake has been to imagine that Tocqueville, having published the second volume of *De la démocratie en Amérique* in 1840, turned his back for good upon the country that had so contributed to his fame and renown. This fits in well with the opinion that derides the value and significance of his journey to America. Nothing could be further from the truth. Not only did Tocqueville keep in touch with many of those he had met on his travels across the North American continent, but his interest in America was fuelled by the visits to America of those he knew. Time upon time, he referred to America in his published writings and parliamentary speeches, always reminding his readers and listeners of what there was to learn from the American experience. More intriguing still, as time passed, Tocqueville focused his attention ever more upon the issues he had raised in the final chapters of the 1835 edition of *De la démocratie en Amérique.* His journey through America continued, even if not in person.

What is more, the memories of Tocqueville's visit to America never lost their power to move him. Writing to Beaumont from Compiègne, north of Paris, during the harsh winter of 1855, he reminisced,

> For the last week I have not stopped from going, once a day, for a walk of an hour or more in the forest. These enormous trees, seen through the snow, remind me of the woods of Tennessee that we travelled through, almost 25 years ago, in weather still more severe.[230] What was most different in the picture was myself. . . . This little retrospective review put

me back in good humour and, to finish the job of cheering me up again, I thought how I had kept to this day the same friend with whom I had hunted the parrots of Memphis and that the passing of time had only strengthened the ties of trust and of friendship which then existed between us. This thought seemed to me more heartening to reflect upon than all the others.[231]

CHAPTER THREE

Prisons, Slavery, and a Trip to Canada

Born in 1802, Gustave de Beaumont was three years older than Alexis de Tocqueville. Like Tocqueville, he came from a distinguished aristocratic family from the west of France and, moreover, one that remained loyal to the Bourbon monarchy and proud of its legitimist credentials. He, too, chose to enter the legal profession.

When Tocqueville and Beaumont first met is not exactly clear. A letter written to Louis de Kergorlay, dated 23 July 1827, indicates that in his new role as *juge auditeur* in Versailles, Tocqueville had found "one or two young men" worthy of respect, but we cannot be certain that one of these was Beaumont. Nevertheless, sometime during the first months of January 1828 Tocqueville took up lodgings with Beaumont in the Rue d'Anjou and this remained the case until Beaumont secured a new appointment in Paris in September 1829.

The two men quickly became firm friends and, despite the occasional later political disagreement, remained so for the rest of their lives. Their friendship, Tocqueville told Beaumont, was "born already old."[1] Nor would it be long before Tocqueville was referring to Beaumont as his "dear future collaborator."[2] They read together (the first letter we have from Tocqueville to Beaumont consists of a very long commentary on John Lingard's *A History of England from the First Invasion of the Romans to the Commencement of the Reign of William III*), attended the celebrated lectures of François Guizot on the history of France at the Sorbonne, went for long walks and, like many young men of their age, gossiped about the women they were courting.

Beaumont, Tocqueville told him, was the only person in whose judgement he had complete confidence and the only one on whom he could count always to tell him the truth. Both quickly concluded that their individual destinies were conjoined. "The same studies, the same plans, the same places unite us," Tocqueville told Beaumont in May 1830.[3] Tocqueville was plainly very upset when Beaumont moved out to new accommodation in the French capital. Nothing, he moaned, would ever be the same again.[4]

Gustave de Beaumont has lived in Tocqueville's shadow ever since. The widespread assumption, both then and more recently, has been that, whatever Beaumont said, Tocqueville said it much better.[5] This, in truth, seems at times also to have been Beaumont's view. Indeed, his admiration for Tocqueville appears to have been almost boundless. Tocqueville, he told his father whilst sailing to the United States, "is a truly distinguished man. There is a great loftiness in his ideas and great nobility in his soul."[6] Much later, in 1848, Beaumont told Tocqueville that he was "the only politician in whose judgement and honesty he had complete faith."[7] Likewise, he held Tocqueville in the deepest affection. On the banks of the Hudson River, Beaumont presented Tocqueville with an intentionally amusing character sketch, congratulating his friend on the affability and graciousness with which he had responded to what had been a dreadful and lengthy musical interlude presented by a lady far from young in years. It ended, "I attest that the said Alexis is the best friend one could find on this earth."[8] In 1850, as Tocqueville began to show signs of the illness that would eventually kill him, Beaumont wrote that theirs was "the only perfect friendship" of his life.[9] Four years later he reflected that their early work together had been the best part of his life.[10] The future Lord Houghton, Richard Monckton Milnes, was to record that "Tocqueville and Beaumont are so united that they are called Messrs Tocquemont and Beauville."[11] Above all, as Tocqueville wrote to his father in 1835, Beaumont was his "excellent travelling companion."[12]

It would be wrong to assume, as Seymour Drescher correctly pointed out some fifty years ago, that Beaumont's work is no more than "merely a mechanism for the clarification of Tocqueville's ideas."[13] If Beaumont travelled with Tocqueville, then so, too, Tocqueville travelled with Beaumont, and they did so in continuous dialogue—such that it is never easy to discern from whom an idea originated. Nevertheless, as inseparable as they undoubtedly were, each had his own tastes and each his own distinctive character and passions. Meeting both men for the first time in 1835, Nassau Senior's daughter Minnie later recalled that "even then I was more amused with [Beaumont], who had all the fire and gesticulation of the Southerner, while Tocqueville's manner had all the sobriety usually characteristic of an Englishman."[14]

These differences in personality and taste become immediately apparent upon reading Beaumont's own account of his travels to America. Like Tocqueville, Beaumont wrote many letters to family and friends, some of considerable length. Both men frequently wrote about the same subject matter—the Fourth of July celebrations they witnessed in Albany, New York, for example—but the tone and content of Beaumont's letters are subtly different from those of Tocqueville with which we are already familiar. Where Tocqueville is frequently serious, Beaumont is often lighthearted. Where Tocqueville habitually focuses on beliefs and values, Beaumont more readily discusses people, social events, and locations.

One example suffices to illustrate this. Upon their arrival in the United States, both Tocqueville and Beaumont were forcefully struck by the novel position held by women in American society. Both wrote about this in their letters and, in Tocqueville's case, it figured prominently in the second volume of *De la démocratie en Amérique.* "If the young girl is less restrained [in the United States] than anywhere else," he wrote, "the wife submits to the strictest obligations." If, he added, "society is more tranquil and better ordered because of it, private life has fewer charms." Here were clues to the character of what Tocqueville termed "the democratic family."[15]

Beaumont was of a similar mind. Everyone agreed, he observed, that among Americans morals were "chaste" and few were the women in America whose conduct was not "beyond reproach." If young women enjoyed "an extreme liberty"—they spent their time "strolling, reading, making music" and frequently went out alone and unchaperoned, engaging in conversation with the men they met in the street—[16]once married they devoted themselves entirely to their husbands. Domestic contentment, Beaumont commented, appeared to be the norm. No doubt somewhat surprised, he discovered that unmarried men only directed their attentions to single women.[17]

For all that Beaumont concluded that the upbringing of American women made for happy families, if rather dull wives, he could not help but let his head be turned by the pretty women he met, be it the beautiful Miss Fulton in New York, the charming daughters of John Canfield Spencer—"I have not seen such beautiful eyes as theirs in the United States," he told his mother[18]—or the attractive niece of the extremely wealthy David Sears of Boston. The whiteness of their complexion—so unlike anything he saw in France—Beaumont deemed especially attractive. Philadelphia, he later reported, was full of fine-looking women. They dressed like their French counterparts and were covered in jewels, even if, he added less gallantly, their taste was not on a par with that of the "*princesses des boulevards*" he had seen many times in Paris.[19] Similar praise was lavished on the "agreeable" and "excessively coquettish" girls of Baltimore. The "mischievous" and "scatter-brained" Miss Mary Randolph seems particularly to have caught Beaumont's eye.[20] However, as troubled and as "inflamed" as he might have been, the young Beaumont soberly concluded that all these distractions were a "mere bagatelle" and that he would "much prefer to be hanged than to get married in a foreign country."[21] On these pressing matters Tocqueville maintained a studied silence.

Thus, from Beaumont we learn that, on their voyage out, not only did he and Tocqueville prepare themselves for their arrival by studying the history of America and by speaking English whenever they could, but that they drank fine wines from Bordeaux and Madeira, not to mention the occasional glass of champagne. Among their "fellow passengers," he reported, were a cow, sheep, and donkey, all of which at some point found their way onto their table. So too did duck, chicken, turkey, and fresh bread, all ruined by their dreadful cook.

In Beaumont's case, this was the first time he had travelled outside France and he, like Tocqueville, was homesick. The only thing that consoled him on his long voyage, he lamented mid-Atlantic, was that he was not forgotten by those he loved. In fleeing to a foreign country, he told his father, he feared that he was in pursuit of a chimera. Yet Beaumont seemed to adapt well (probably better than Tocqueville) to his new environment: rising at five o'clock in the morning, breakfasting at nine, lunching at three, walking on board deck (weather permitting) in the afternoon, and conversing with the other passengers (some of whom, he noted, not without a hint of snobbery, were "truly distinguished"). On occasion, and to the delight of his companions (who merrily danced the quadrille), he played his flute. And there was always "the beautiful spectacle" of the sea to stir his imagination. Sometimes he and Tocqueville managed to sleep; at others they were so thrown about by the waves that it was impossible to close their eyes. But sleep gave them the opportunity to dream. "We have great projects in mind," he told his father from the mid-Atlantic.[22]

Like Tocqueville, Beaumont was overjoyed when he first caught sight of land and was thrilled with excitement (and a slight tinge of fear) as they travelled at great speed on an immense steamboat from Newport, Rhode Island, to New York City. The first difference between France and America noted by Beaumont was that their trunks were subject to the most rudimentary search by American customs officers. His first disappointment was that the women of Newport were not as "famously beautiful" as promised.

Their arrival in New York, Beaumont told his mother, caused a sensation. It was covered in all the American newspapers. The two men were showered with kindness and attention from all they met, receiving so many invitations that they had no time to catch their breath. Their hosts, he reported, ranged from the baron de Saint-André (the French consul) and Enos T. Throop (the governor of the state of New York) to various aldermen and magistrates, as well as some of the richest and most influential families of the city. He told his brother Jules that if he could see the "grand role" that Beaumont and Tocqueville played, Jules's "fraternal pride" would be "agreeably flattered."[23]

None of this was without the occasional mishap. His and Tocqueville's command of English was so poor, Beaumont reported, that it was not uncommon for them to mistake the day or time of their invitation, arriving for tea when a copious lunch had been prepared or simply not turning up at all. The family of Edward Livingston seems to have been a regular victim of these social faux pas. A similar mishap meant that Tocqueville and Beaumont failed to meet the famous American novelist Catherine Sedgwick.

As Beaumont readily admitted, this relentless socialising about town kept him and Tocqueville away from the all-important business of work. Nevertheless, an unabashed Beaumont easily convinced himself that being seen at the best houses in New York complemented rather than hindered their "public mission." If nothing else, it improved their English. Only by mixing with people would they come to understand the manners, habits, and character of the nation. Crucially, the most enlightened minds were to be found in the best society. To his father, Beaumont was even more to the point: meeting "the richest and most influential" people provided "useful contacts."[24]

From Beaumont, therefore, we learn that Americans had the misfortune to love music but to be poor musicians. Nor did they possess a talent for painting. Cultural life in general was in its infancy. Going to the theatre was not the thing to do, and in any case the quality of the acting was dreadful. If there were libraries, they had neither books nor readers. What passed for museums contained nothing more than magic lantern shows and stuffed birds. There was no interest in literature. Indeed, from what Beaumont could see, the only thing read by all Americans were newspapers, and these were mostly full of advertisements.

None of this Beaumont later discovered was the case in Boston and Philadelphia. In Boston he saw for the first time houses built with "taste and elegance." Here was a place where one could "live with all the amenities provided by an advanced civilization." Above all, he told his mother, there existed "a superior class possessing the tone and manners to be found in European societies," men who did not need to engage in commerce and industry to earn their living. Admittedly this class was small and, within the egalitarian culture of the United States, it felt like a "strange anomaly," but in Boston there was a vibrant intellectual life with a genuine interest in the fine arts. It was there, Beaumont told one of his brothers, that he and Tocqueville met Francis Lieber, the German-born editor of the *Encyclopaedia americana,* and the historian Jared Sparks.[25]

If Beaumont had a complaint, it was that for all that one ate extremely well in Boston, people drank too much. Like the English, Bostonians remained at the table to drink and converse. However, from Beaumont there were no complaints about the numerous "*soirées dansantes*" he and Tocqueville attended.[26]

Beaumont was similarly impressed by the charm and cleanliness of Philadelphia, even if the "geometrical precision" of its streets produced a "monotonous beauty." But it was here that he saw not only the many German immigrants, with their distinctive and separate ways of life, but also "people of colour": men and women who enjoyed equal rights with white people but who nonetheless continued to be treated like slaves.[27]

As for the week he and Tocqueville spent in Baltimore, it reads as one big party. If they were not at the horse races—here, too, Beaumont clearly had a good eye—they were going from banquet to banquet. Not once, he boasted to his brother Achille, did they dine at their guest house, and at each festivity they were received with "incredible luxury." By the end of their stay the American enthusiasm for drinking toasts had rather gotten the better of them.[28]

Not every aspect of this social calendar was as appealing as dancing the night away. In addition to the awkwardness engendered by repeated toasts to the American republic, Beaumont quickly tired—as did many a traveller to the United States—of the seemingly insatiable desire of Americans for praise and their unbounded sense of national pride. The latter, he believed, derived from the eulogies heaped upon their institutions of government by Europeans. Seeing the truth behind this boastfulness, Beaumont observed, was not always easy. He was also taken aback that such ardent "champions of equality" should so readily seek the distinctions of social superiority, boasting of their ancient lineage, and sporting coats of arms on their carriages and seals.[29]

Beaumont did, however, quickly adopt the American habit of drinking tea—wine was so expensive—and he was especially pleased to learn that Americans did not have the high opinion of France imagined by "our revolutionaries." He took particular delight in hearing that, for all of the praise heaped upon him, most Americans regarded the Marquis de La Fayette—the so-called Hero of the Two Worlds—as being misguided and lacking in political judgement, if not actually dangerous.[30] That even the "smallest village" in Michigan followed Paris fashions he found astonishing. Not finding a comfortable bed in America, he reported to one of his brothers, did not prevent him from sleeping the sleep of the blessed.[31]

Yet for all of Beaumont's jollity, he was no less a shrewd and conscientious observer of American society than Tocqueville. To his sister Eugénie he explained that if he wrote to her about "a dinner, a ball or a concert," it was because these were things that could be described in a couple of words. Were he to portray to her the things that were really interesting, on the other hand, he would not be able to stop. "I am reduced to providing you," he explained, "with a description . . . of the four walls of a building without saying anything about the arrangement of the furniture and the ornaments." Like Tocqueville, he was indefatigable in taking notes and filled his diary with observations about everything he saw.[32]

Nor did Beaumont have any doubts about the seriousness of the work that he and Tocqueville were undertaking. Perhaps, he wrote in late May 1831, "this journey will be useful to me: it will, I think, extend my knowledge, improve my judgement, and possibly put me in a position to be useful to my country." To his father he explained that "in studying the penitentiary system we will see America; in examining its prisons we will examine its inhabitants, its towns, its institutions, and its mores; we will understand the machinery of its republican government." "Would it not be a good book," he added, "that gave an accurate idea of the American people, sketched out its history, painted the main features of its character, analysed its social state, and corrected any number of erroneous opinions on this matter?"[33]

Like Tocqueville, Beaumont enthusiastically recorded his first impressions. There was nothing picturesque about the coastline he and Tocqueville saw. It was flat and monotonous. But immediately upon landing he observed that American society was like nothing to be found in Europe. Its people were neither English, nor French, nor German, but "a mixture of nations." He also concluded that it was a people preoccupied by commerce. "In the small town of Newport," he wrote, "there are four or five banks." This, he asserted confidently (and presumably without a shred of evidence), was true of all the towns in the country. By the time Beaumont reached New York City two days later, the feverish animation he had seen in Long Island Sound had convinced him that Americans were a "merchant people . . . devoured by an appetite for riches." This, he wrote, brought with it "many less than honourable passions, such as greed, fraud, and dishonesty."[34]

This substantially remained Beaumont's view throughout his stay. "Money," he wrote to his brother Jules, "is the divinity everyone burns incense to, and it is so easy in this country to make a fortune that, in truth, one can forgive the Americans for having such a great thirst for wealth." To his and Tocqueville's friend, Ernest de Chabrol, he commented from Lake Huron that

America was "a uniform society, with neither head nor tail, neither low nor high; it has nothing wretched about it but nor does it have anything distinguished." It was, he believed, "the happiest of societies . . . but not the most agreeable."[35]

Like Tocqueville, Beaumont saw that America was a deeply moral society. And he was intrigued to know why. His first answer built upon the observation that in America there was no "idle class." In contrast to France, he reported to his father, "there exists no body of men who, if there were not kept busy by seducing women, would have nothing to do." In short, commerce and industry absorbed every moment. There simply was not time to behave badly. Moreover, Americans had a colder temperament than the French.[36]

Beaumont's second suggestion had more substance. Religion, he saw immediately, had a special place in American society, and it was one quite unlike anything to be found in France. Nothing in America, Beaumont observed, was "done without the assistance of religion." Moreover, all religions were tolerated and honoured. How a "lively and sincere faith" could coexist with an "equal respect" for religions with such differing beliefs was not something Beaumont claimed to understand, nor was he sure how deep an impact on individual behaviour—beyond a strict observance of the Sabbath—it truly had, but there could be no doubting that religious sentiment flourished.[37] A man with no religion was regarded as a beast.

Later, as the two men travelled westward, Beaumont came to see that religious toleration had its limits—a Catholic priest described Presbyterians to him as being as "nasty as vipers"—but, like Tocqueville, he saw that Catholicism prospered in an environment where it was freed from control by the state. So, too, as he learned from his visit to Boston, did Unitarianism. Although it was not as "mad and absurd" as the Shaker ceremony he and Tocqueville witnessed, Beaumont was clearly unimpressed by what he described as a "sect of philosophers" which, "under the cloak of religion, attacked all doctrines." "The truth is," he concluded ruefully, "that I have never felt so attached to my own religion since I have seen the aberrations of other forms of worship."[38]

Surprisingly, Beaumont's letters to his family and friends in France made little reference to either politics or political institutions. Like Tocqueville, he observed that political parties scarcely existed and that American citizens were generally disinterested in seeking public office. He noted that America had no need of an army and that the actions of government were scarcely felt. He also found himself strangely moved by the (often comic) Fourth of July ceremony he and Tocqueville witnessed in Albany, with its ragbag of an orchestra and procession of ordinary town- and tradespeople. There was, he told his sister Eugénie, "something of grandeur in its simplicity." What was certain, Beaumont added, was that the system of government established in the United States was favourable to both the prosperity of the country and the well-being of its inhabitants.[39]

This endorsement came with significant qualification. This might not remain the case, Beaumont suggested, when the population had reached forty million, when the natural resources that produced such wealth had diminished, or when the activity presently devoted to commerce and industry was directed to intellectual labour and political interests. Then, he wrote, "I ask myself if we will not see the beginning of political quarrels, parties with their divisions, etc, and I do not know what will become of a central power that has no strength."[40] It would, Beaumont concluded, be both impossible and dangerous for France to imitate America's political institutions.

Indeed, Beaumont's doubts only seem to have increased as he and Tocqueville made their way down the Ohio River. Like his friend, Beaumont was struck by the sheer novelty of Cincinnati. It was, he told his brother Jules, "the most curious town" he had ever seen. No other place in the world, he ventured, had experienced such prodigious growth. "The character of this society," he wrote, "is not to have a character." It was here that democracy was pushed to its most "rigorous conclusions." An equality of political rights existed, and no one was denied the right to vote. This, he observed, might be ideal if "the people were never wrong," but their judgement was less strong than their passions and they frequently gave themselves up to whoever flattered them most. So, everyone elected to public office by the people of Ohio was "more or less mediocre."[41]

But there was arguably a much deeper cause for concern. In such a "society of the moment," where "memories have no hold over a people," no one knew each other and no one was subject to the influence of "age-old mores" or "domestic virtues." "Each person," Beaumont concluded, "proceeds and moves forwards in complete liberty, with nothing to restrain his interests and his passions." As a matter of fact, he acknowledged, Ohio was prosperous and thriving but this, he argued, was due to "material causes" and the prohibition of slavery and not, as "European demagogues" maintained, its "extreme democracy." At bottom, Beaumont's worry was that it was difficult to identify or portray "the moral being" of such a society.[42]

Whether on Beaumont's part this was a case of misplaced nostalgia for an imaginary earlier age is difficult to say, but he was undoubtedly using what he took to be the values of an aristocratic past to criticise a democratic present. As critics have often remarked, this was something Tocqueville did throughout *De la démocratie en Amérique.* However, neither man was sufficiently naive as to believe that such a past could be resurrected—the tide of democratic equality could not be turned back—but what is evident is that, as they travelled together across the United States, both came to the conclusion that they had found something resembling such a past in North America—in French-speaking Quebec.

A visit to what was then known as Lower Canada had not been part of Tocqueville's and Beaumont's original itinerary, but both men ultimately found a visit to the land of their abandoned countrymen to be irresistible. Writing to his mother on 19 June 1831 from New York, Tocqueville told her, "Quebec piques our curiosity greatly." There, he had heard, "the French nation has been preserved intact: the people have the mores and speak the language of the century of Louis XIV." A clergyman by the name of Power, he added, had told him "some very interesting things about the progress of Catholicism in this part of the world."[43] Tocqueville and Beaumont were not to be disappointed. As always, they set off with letters of introduction and were, as Beaumont wrote, received with "open arms" by "the most distinguished men of the country."[44] Arriving in Montreal on or about 23 August 1831, they then spent five days in the city of Quebec before returning to Montreal on board the steamer *Richelieu* and leaving Canada on 2 September.

"Of all the parts of America we have visited so far," Tocqueville wrote as he and Beaumont travelled down the Saint Lawrence River, "Canada is without doubt the most comparable to Europe, and especially to France." The banks of the river were "thoroughly cultivated and covered with houses

Quebec City, Old Town (Old Images / Alamy Stock Photo)

and villages in every way similar to our own." All vestiges of the "wilderness" had disappeared, to be replaced by "tended fields, steeples, and a population as numerous as that found in our provinces." Montreal bore a "striking resemblance" to a French provincial city. As for the city of Quebec, although ugly (so they deemed), it had nothing in common with American cities and was positioned "in a very picturesque location, surrounded by rich, fertile country." "I have never seen in Europe," Tocqueville observed, "a place more animated than the area around Quebec."[45] The Saint Lawrence River, Tocqueville told the Abbé Lesueur with a sense of amazement, was the widest river existing in the world. It was as if the English Channel had been moved inland. Six months previously, Tocqueville confessed, he had believed like everyone else that Canada was "completely English."[46]

There—to their evident delight, and as John Power had promised—Tocqueville and Beaumont encountered, in Beaumont's words, a people who had "preserved their language, their mores and their nationality."[47] French Canadians, Beaumont continued, had none of the "glacial coolness" he associated with Americans and they were more "gay" than the French had now become. The reason for the latter was not difficult to comprehend: unlike the French, the Quebecois had not passed through the French Revolution of 1789 and had not had to endure the changes to society it had brought about. In brief, in terms of their character, they were now more French than the French.[48]

In his letters and notebooks, Tocqueville took up the same refrain. To the Abbé Lesueur, he wrote that the Quebecois resembled the French more than Americans resembled the English. It was in Lower Canada that "the old France" existed. There, far from the towns, were to be found "the old customs and old French mores." The villages—with "a church topped by a cock and a cross with the fleur-de-lis"—resembled the handsome villages of provincial France. "Four times a day," he continued, "the family, consisting of vigorous parents and plump, joyful, children, gathers about a round table. After supper they sing old French songs. . . . On Sundays they play and sing after services. The priest himself shares in the communal gaiety."[49] Touring the countryside on horseback, Tocqueville saw well-built houses that, with their excellent beds, clean furniture and white walls, "breathed comfort." "A small mirror and a crucifix or a few engravings from Holy Scripture," he noted, "complete the picture." Churches were richly decorated but in "very good taste."[50] The population paid not a penny of taxes.

What else did Tocqueville and Beaumont describe as part of this seemingly idyllic society? According to Tocqueville, the French Canadians were not touched by the mercantile spirit of their neighbours. Doing little to cultivate their minds, Tocqueville wrote, "they make fine warriors and are fonder of noise than of money." In his notebooks, he confided that the population was "markedly more handsome" than that of the United States, being strong and solidly built, adding for good measure that "the women lack the delicate, sickly appearance of most American women." French Canadians were polite without being servile and possessed something "distinguished" in their manners. In contrast to their neighbours, they were "cheerful, lively, bantering, fond of glory and noise, intelligent and eminently sociable." It was only in Canada, Tocqueville concluded, that one could find people who in France would be described as "*bon enfant*," or good-natured. The Quebecois were governed by their hearts, the Americans by their heads.[51]

For his part, Beaumont noted the remnants of feudalism, with land divided into *seigneuries,* the *seigneur* having his own pew in church, and the priest taking a tithe on the harvest. "This state of affairs," Beaumont concluded, "served the interests of the inhabitants," their homes displaying "an air of comfort and well-being that indicates a thoroughly happy condition." This was not all that attracted Beaumont and Tocqueville to the French-speaking population of Lower Canada. Beaumont did not mince his words: "There is a uniformity of religion: everyone is Catholic." Not only were the Catholic clergy "universally respected," but there was "not one philosopher" who was not "also a religious man or at any rate who dares to appear otherwise."[52]

Tocqueville was of a similar mind. The Catholic priest, he observed, was "the oracle, the friend and the advisor of the population."[53] The people saw in him their most constant source of support, the first to oppose their oppression. Tocqueville also noted that here the Catholic religion had none of the "bizarre and ridiculous" accessories associated with southern Europe. There were no monasteries and no shrines to the Madonna at the side of the road. Rather, it was an "enlightened" religion and one he found more satisfying than the Protestantism he had recently encountered in the United States. "The priest," he wrote, "is truly pastor of his flock and not an entrepreneur in the religious industry like most American ministers."[54]

This, both men agreed, was not without significant consequences. "The purity of morals that prevails in all the villages," Beaumont wrote, "would be hard to believe if one were talking of our European cities," adding that "crime and public indecency" were unknown.[55] Tocqueville voiced an almost identical opinion. "Along with religious ideas," he wrote, "mores have been preserved."[56] There could be no doubting, he commented in his notebooks, that "the people in general are more moral, more hospitable, and more religious than in France."[57] To the Abbé Lesueur, Tocqueville noted, "Public opinion has incredible power in these villages. The people would never turn a thief over to the authorities, but the minute suspicions are raised against a man, he is forced to leave town. Nothing is rarer than a girl who has been seduced."[58] In French-speaking Canada, in other words, the ancien régime seemed alive and well. That it came with its own version of the tyranny of the majority seems to have troubled neither Tocqueville nor Beaumont.

Nonetheless, Tocqueville saw that, for all that French speakers formed most of the population, they were a "vanquished people." Although, he observed, "French is almost universally spoken, most newspapers, street posters, and even shop signs of French merchants are in English." More troubling was the fact that the people themselves were only dimly aware of their status as a "defeated nation." For the time being, at least, Tocqueville believed that the distinctiveness of this society was preserved through what he saw as the strict separation of the French and English populations. "Fortunately," he observed, religion stood as "an obstacle" to intermarriage and created an educated clergy "with an interest in speaking French and absorbing French literature and ideas."[59]

However, there already existed a class of men who bridged the gap between the French and the English. If, Tocqueville argued, these people abandoned the French Canadians and allowed themselves to be drawn into the orbit of the English, "the French race is lost in America." Nor was the Canadian peasant immune from the "spirit of equality and democracy." There, Tocqueville noted, was "the breach through which the enemy will enter." And this could "only be to the detriment of the French, their language and their customs."[60]

For his part, Beaumont emphasised the stark economic realities of the situation. The English controlled trade and industry and populated the cities of Montreal and Quebec. The wealthy of Lower Canada were entirely English. Each year there arrived a throng of "adventurers" from England, Scotland, and Ireland in search of cheap land, increasing the likelihood that the French would be overwhelmed by a "foreign majority." The English, he concluded, were doing everything they could to crush a population whose "poverty they scorned and whose happiness they could not understand."[61]

Despite this, both Beaumont and Tocqueville believed that if the Quebecois could overcome their apathy, the French-speaking population would probably survive, and that Lower Canada would ultimately become "an entirely French nation." "I still hope," Tocqueville wrote in his notebooks, "that the French, despite the conquest, will one day create a beautiful empire of their own in the New World, more enlightened perhaps and more moral and happier than that of their ancestors."[62] If so, it would never be a populous nation and it would most likely be nothing more than a "drop" in an

Anglophone "ocean." "I am sorely afraid," Tocqueville concluded, "that fortune has indeed decided that North America will be English."[63]

Yet Beaumont and Tocqueville had travelled to the United States to do work, and not just to enjoy the warm welcome from their compatriots in Canada and the feeling of being at home. Already by the end of May 1831 they had visited a house of refuge for juvenile offenders, an asylum for the insane, a poorhouse, and the newly built prison on Blackwell's Island in New York City's East River. They then set off up the Hudson River valley to spend ten days visiting the celebrated penitentiary at Sing Sing.

The two men were at once both impressed and disturbed by what they first saw of the prison system in America. They were not convinced that such a system—resting as it did on the principles of absolute silence among inmates and frequent resort to corporal punishment—could be transposed successfully to France. They did, however, throw themselves into their enquiries and continued to do so as they crisscrossed the country, visiting the Auburn Penitentiary in upstate New York; the Massachusetts State Penitentiary in Charlestown, near Boston; and the Eastern State Penitentiary outside Philadelphia. At the latter Tocqueville and Beaumont carried out a series of detailed and, for the time, innovative interviews with prison inmates.[64] And as government employees they had to write periodic reports on their progress to their masters back in Paris.[65] To his brother Jules, Beaumont commented that they would be "incontestably the world's leading *pénitentiers* [penitentiary experts]."[66]

Tocqueville subsequently remarked that the inquiry into prisons was only a pretext for visiting America. The letter by Beaumont to his father, written from the mid-Atlantic on 25 April 1831, similarly suggested that studying the penitentiary system would provide the two men with the opportunity to "see America," adding that he and Tocqueville might perhaps write a book about the American people. Beaumont made a further reference to the possibility of a jointly authored book on American government in another letter to his father dated 16 May 1831. To his sister Eugénie two months later he referred to "our great book" on political institutions which she would one day read.[67]

At some imprecise point a division of labour came into existence. By the end of October 1831 Beaumont was speaking of publishing "my work" and a week or so later (having visited Baltimore and witnessed slavery firsthand) he alluded to "the work that will immortalise me."[68] In his letters to friends and family Tocqueville increasingly spoke in the first person about the book he might write on the subject of the United States, even if its character and content remained decidedly vague. Certainly by the time Beaumont and Tocqueville returned to France in the spring of 1832 the idea of two books—what would become Tocqueville's *De la démocratie en Amérique* and Beaumont's novel about slavery, *Marie*—had taken shape. Nevertheless, as late as February 1833 Tocqueville informed one of his American correspondents, Edward Everett, that he and Beaumont were "composing a more general work on America."[69]

For all of that, Beaumont and Tocqueville's first task upon returning home was to write their report on the American penitentiary system. If Beaumont set to work, Tocqueville was struck down with a dose of what he referred to as "imbecility" and what we might be inclined to attribute to nervous exhaustion. Every day, he told Beaumont, "the ailment takes on more and more the character of a chronic illness." He sat down in the large armchair given him by his father, with paper in hand and a pile of books at his side, but everything came to his mind "except prisons."[70]

An outbreak of cholera in Paris did little to improve Tocqueville's spirits; his cousin, the Marquis de Chauvelin, he told Beaumont, had been carried away by the disease and five people had died at the corner of the (rather posh) street where he lived.[71] Whether Beaumont's exhortation that Tocqueville needed to free himself from his state of "moral torpor" had any effect is hard to judge,[72] but in mid-May 1832 Tocqueville inspected one of the notorious prison ships at Toulon and, in the following month, he visited prisons in Geneva and Lausanne.[73] During the summer Tocqueville and Beaumont made further visits to several penal institutions in France, and they finally submitted their report in October of that year.

Within three months it had been published, and to considerable critical acclaim if not commercial success.[74] Not long afterwards it appeared in English translation in the United States, although Tocqueville, for one, was far from happy with the work of their translator, the German-born Francis

Lieber. Not for the last time, Lieber seemed intent on proving that he knew more about the subject of America than the book's authors and in defending America from the least criticism. Here, Tocqueville told Beaumont, was another case of the "incorrigible pride" of the Americans.[75] Tocqueville and Beaumont's text was also immediately translated into German, enjoying a similar critical success. It likewise received much by way of favourable commentary in Italy.

Beaumont clearly undertook the lion's share of the writing of what became the *Système pénitentiarei aux États-Unis et son application en France,* and subsequently Tocqueville was to downplay his own contribution, suggesting as late as 1841 (when Beaumont's candidacy for the prestigious Académie des sciences morales et politiques was under consideration) that Beaumont was its sole author. This is palpably untrue: at least a third of the text was directly written by Tocqueville. Moreover, as James Schleifer has written, "Tocqueville's official mission cannot be divorced from his larger American experience."[76] Nor, indeed, can it be divorced from his broader concerns about the future of French society.

This is immediately apparent from the very first sentence of the *mémoire* written by Tocqueville and Beaumont to justify their projected journey to America. "Like all societies that have arrived at a high degree of civilization," it reads, "society in France is tormented by an inner illness that attacks the very principle of its existence."[77] And that illness was "the progressive increase in crimes and misdemeanours." As the population grew, Tocqueville and Beaumont contended, so too did crime. Unemployment and the ignorance of the "poor classes" only added to the gravity and scale of the problem. An equally significant contributing factor were the failings of France's prison system. In no country, they argued, were criminals as quick to reoffend as they were in France. In short, a good prison system was one that punished and reformed the criminal. It also had to be good value for money.

Where, Tocqueville and Beaumont asked, could France look for guidance? Not to England, and not to the Netherlands nor to Switzerland, where, for all its undoubted success in securing the moral reform of the prisoner, prisons were both expensive to run and small in scale. The only country was America. There, for twenty years, principles of prison reform had been put in practice. States, with limited financial means, had succeeded in building vast penitentiaries. Reoffending rates were low. Moreover, for the eager investigator, America presented not one prison system but several, and their results and practices could be compared. But reading about these prisons in books and reports was not enough. They had to be seen and visited. Here was Tocqueville and Beaumont's justification to their superiors of their momentous trip to the United States.

The research for their report was undertaken with typical thoroughness. "Hardly had we arrived at Sing Sing," Beaumont told his mother, "than people appeared offering us every conceivable service: the prison warden, the guards, all of the employees, catered for all our needs. All records were delivered to us and all doors opened. We were installed in a room intended for overseers and made ourselves at home, working every day. We observed a lot and did some important research."[78] Tocqueville made the same point to his cousin, Félix Le Peletier d'Aunay, but in slightly more graphic prose: "Apart from sleeping in the cells and being whipped by rope," Tocqueville wrote, "we are leading almost the same life as the inmates. That's what I call throwing oneself wholeheartedly into the penitentiary system."[79]

The same theme surfaced in a letter written two weeks later by Tocqueville to Ernest de Chabrol: "The life we lead here suits us very well, except for the penitentiary system about which we are beginning to feel weary. We are carrying out an enormous amount of work on prisons."[80] Yet, for all of their efforts, both men recognised that too often they were working in "near complete darkness." Everything in America was so different from France and what was better or worse was almost impossible to decide.[81]

The letters and reports sent back to France by Tocqueville and Beaumont also enable us to appreciate the seriousness both men attached to the issues raised by their enquiries. To Le Peletier d'Aunay, Tocqueville noted that he and Beaumont had already reached some firm convictions. First, the prisons they had visited so far "cost the State nothing and often make a profit." In Sing Sing, over nine hundred prisoners were supervised by only twenty-two guards. Second, mortality rates among prisoners were lower than among the general population. Third, "discipline is extremely strict and is designed to isolate the prisoner from his fellows." This was achieved through the imposition of silence and constant work, the latter absorbing all the physical and moral efforts of the inmate. Tocqueville also saw that this system ultimately rested on "the unlimited arbitrary power to inflict corporal punishment."[82]

Moreover, Tocqueville and Beaumont were reasonably confident that the American system decreased the numbers of reoffenders. "It seems to be proven," they told the French minister of the interior, "that those who enter into it never become worse as a consequence." Nonetheless, Tocqueville and Beaumont also expressed doubts about what they saw. Enormous power, they noticed, was being handed over to a small group of prison administrators. It seemed unlikely that this level of strict discipline among the inmates could be maintained. Nor, even if the French were prepared to meet the initial costs of implementing such a system, could it be assumed that French mores and public opinion would accept the widespread use of corporal punishment.

Tocqueville and Beaumont did, however, reach one very controversial conclusion. At Sing Sing they saw a prison based upon a principle of partial solitary confinement, with inmates working together during the day. In Philadelphia they observed a different system and one, in their words, where the "guiding principle" was "solitary confinement day and night and the complete isolation of the criminal." Corporal punishment was never used, but "the prisoner is cut off from the entire world," his time divided between the reading of religious tracts and work. Four times a day a guard brought the prisoner what he required, and on Sunday he received a visit from a minister to bring consolation.[83]

Tocqueville and Beaumont were fully aware of the disapproval directed against such a harsh regime. For its critics, they acknowledged, "a man reduced to such a wretched state must soon lose either his reason or his life." Tocqueville and Beaumont would have nothing of this. Nearly all the prisoners they spoke to, they reported in November 1831, were "in the best of health" and "nothing in their conversation gave any sign of mental derangement." With the passing of time, they insisted, the solitude became easier to bear and after a year the prisoner was "perfectly calm." Moreover, the range of work that could be performed in solitude, if not profitable, was enough to keep an inmate busy. There was reason to believe, Tocqueville and Beaumont concluded, that the Philadelphia penitentiary offered "the most powerful and most complete scheme for the reform of the convict ever created." For good measure, in no other prison was it easier to maintain discipline and no special skills and effort were required of the guards.[84]

It was this system that Tocqueville and Beaumont broadly commended to their employers and to their readers, and they did so, as Tocqueville told one of his political allies in Normandy, based on having seen the two rival systems in operation. Prior to his visit to America, he confirmed, he had been of the contrary opinion.[85] Moreover, Tocqueville and Beaumont did so while acknowledging that it "offered the spectacle of the most complete despotism."[86] Separated from the moral contagion of his fellows, reduced to silence and compelled to work, the inmate was justifiably deprived of his liberty and left alone with only his conscience to reflect upon his past crimes and transgressions.[87] Tocqueville and Beaumont wrote that they were "not animated by that misguided philanthropy which, if it is to be believed, would make of prison an agreeable stay."[88]

Tocqueville and Beaumont's published text was scarcely the most thrilling read. It was, however, testimony to the willingness of both men to immerse themselves as far as possible in the daily realities of American life. Their notes of their meetings with prisoners in the Philadelphia penitentiary were particularly revealing. Moreover, they showed again an acute awareness of the difficulties involved not only in the comparative analysis of both countries but also of transferring institutions from one country to another. Many actions treated as crimes in America—incest, fornication, drunkenness, and so on—went unpunished in France, and vice versa. The same crime was treated with different levels of severity. It was virtually impossible to compare statistics on reoffenders. Indeed, given the movement of population in America these figures were largely unknown. Women made up a far smaller proportion of the prison population in America than they did in France. This Tocqueville and Beaumont attributed to "the extraordinary morality of the women who belonged to the white race."[89] At best, they avowed, the success or otherwise of one American prison could only be compared to another American prison. They also made it clear that it had never been part of their intention to study those prisons—the vast majority—untouched by penal reform or those of the American South. What mattered was to study institutions that might serve as a model for France.

The challenges facing those wishing to learn from the American experience were likewise not to be underestimated. Two stood out. First, much of the impetus behind the drive to secure the moral improvement of the prisoner, Tocqueville and Beaumont recognised, was religious in inspiration and it was to this, they believed, that American prisons owed much of their success. In France, by contrast, such was the pervasive antipathy towards religion that it was doubtful that this invaluable resource could be called upon. Moreover, the general influence of religion in French society was much less than it was in America. Once released, the prisoner would easily escape religion's sway. Second, prison reforms in the United States were invariably the result of local initiatives. The whole community was involved, and success inspired emulation. Any attempt to introduce reforms in France would come up against the dead hand of administrative centralisation. Here were important themes that would resurface in *De la démocratie en Amérique.* For good measure, Tocqueville and Beaumont added that, while Americans—even those in prison—displayed an attitude of "obedience to the law," the French had "a penchant for insubordination."[90]

Tocqueville and Beaumont's recommendations were therefore modest ones. "It has never been our belief," they concluded, "that France should abruptly attempt a wholesale revolution in its prison system, raze old institutions to the ground, suddenly build new ones, and devote enormous sums to this single objective." Nonetheless, to both men it did seem that "without adopting the American prison system in its entirety" there were principles that could be borrowed and ideas from which one could learn. "Do we not see," they wrote, "prisons which successfully reform the wicked in a country where, fifteen years ago, the prisons were worse than our own."[91]

Prisons and their reform made only one brief appearance in *De la démocratie en Amérique,* and this was in the context of Tocqueville's thoughts on the legislative and administrative instability resulting from the political omnipotence of the majority. "Several years ago," Tocqueville wrote, "some religious men undertook to improve the condition of prisons." The public, he continued, "was roused by their voice, and the regeneration of criminals became a popular undertaking" but the majority, preoccupied by the idea of building new institutions, forgot about the old ones that already existed. And so, Tocqueville concluded, alongside monuments to "the mildness and enlightenment of our time" was found "a dungeon that recalled the barbarism of the Middle Ages."[92]

This passing comment should not be taken to mean that prison reform was only a matter of fleeting interest for either Tocqueville or Beaumont.[93] Here, too, we can see the long-term impact of travelling across America and of learning from what was seen and investigated there with such thoroughness.

In 1837 both men ran unsuccessfully for the French Chamber of Deputies, but two years later they were successful in their candidacies. Neither, it should be said, had a particularly glorious parliamentary career, and both ended badly when Tocqueville and Beaumont were briefly imprisoned after the future Napoleon III's coup d'état in 1851. However, in 1840 they were asked to sit on a commission composed of parliamentarians and outside experts to investigate the problem of prison reform. Another commission was established three years later, with Tocqueville appointed as rapporteur. Accordingly, in July of that year he presented a long and meticulous report before his parliamentary colleagues.[94] Beaumont provided moral support with four anonymous articles in *Le siècle* supporting his friend's proposals.[95]

There is no need here to dwell in detail on the content of these texts. It is enough to note that Tocqueville drew heavily upon his and Beaumont's earlier investigations in America and that he argued for the adoption of what amounted to a modified and improved version of the Philadelphia system. The emphasis was to fall not upon the complete isolation of the prisoner but upon his separation from his fellow criminals. Again, there was an awareness of the difficulties of implementing reform and of the dangers of seeking to transplant institutions wholesale from one country to another. But Tocqueville insisted that there were things to learn and to borrow from America.

This was most evident in the frank exchange of views that occurred at a meeting of the Académie des sciences morales et politiques in March of the following year where Tocqueville found himself in discussion with an old rival, Charles Lucas. In 1830 Lucas had been appointed inspector of prisons in France, and prior to the departure of Tocqueville and Beaumont for America he had counselled them not to exaggerate what might be learnt from the American experience.[96] Now, as one of the acknowledged authorities in the field, he sought to demolish the entire basis upon which Tocqueville and Beaumont had built their argument.

Tocqueville was unrepentant. His and Beaumont's aim in writing their book, he responded, had been only to examine the different systems that existed in America and nothing more. It was not true that, through lack of knowledge of his own country's penal system, he had recommended a "servile imitation" of what was done elsewhere. His ambitions were not the same as those of Pennsylvanian Quakers who had sought to condemn the prisoner to a "monastic discipline." More interesting still, Tocqueville accepted that, when it came to political constitutions, transposing institutions from one nation to another was not without its dangers. But what, he asked, was at issue here? It was, he responded, "a matter of the physical constitution of a man and of his health." Was the European transported to the New World a different man from someone who remained on our continent? Could a source of health for one person be a cause of sickness and death for another? When it came to prisons, therefore, it was perfectly legitimate to make comparisons between America and France.[97]

Beaumont's published work on America was not limited to his joint writings with Tocqueville on prisons and prison reform. There remains his famous novel *Marie,* first published to great critical acclaim in 1835. Its subtitle, not insignificantly, is *L'esclavage aux États-Unis: Tableau des mœurs américaines.* As Christine Dunn Henderson has observed, "That Beaumont would ultimately concentrate on America's racial situation is not surprising, for the plight of freed blacks and of Indians seems to have captured his attention quite early during his voyage to America." As she further observes, Beaumont's concern with the fate of the downtrodden was to remain throughout his public life, most notably in the book he was later to publish on Ireland.[98]

Beaumont's text was the product of the curious division of labour that emerged as he and Tocqueville travelled across America. Tocqueville's two references to Beaumont's text in *De la démocratie en Amérique* were brief and consigned to footnotes, but they left no doubt as to the importance he attached to this work. "The principal goal of M. de Beaumont's text," he wrote, "was to bring out and make known the situation of Negroes within Anglo-American society. His work will throw a bright and new light on the question of slavery, a vital question for the united republics." At the beginning of his own discussion on the probable future of the Black race in America, he added that his "travelling companion . . . M. de Beaumont has thoroughly treated a question that my subject has only allowed me to touch upon. . . . [It] should be read by those who want to understand to what excesses of tyranny men are pushed little by little once they have begun to go beyond nature and humanity."[99]

Nevertheless, history has been rather harsh on Beaumont's literary endeavours. After initial success and prize-winning public acclaim, *Marie* quickly sank without a trace. It took over one hundred years for it to be translated into English.[100] It is not hard to see why. In his own introduction, Beaumont explained that it had not been his intention to write a novel. He did not, he willingly admitted, have the skill of a "fiction writer." The reader, he continued, must not expect anything that might "excite, sustain or suspend his interest." By offering truth in the form of fiction, he accepted that he ran the risk of "pleasing no one." He was proved to be largely right.[101]

The story Beaumont tells of the love of a young Frenchman, Ludovic, for a beautiful American woman, Marie, of mixed-race ancestry is sentimentally formulaic, to say the least, and scarcely a page turner. After much by way of trial and tribulation, the couple try to marry; they are thwarted by race riots in New York; fatigued, she dies of a broken heart; her brother is killed in a rebellion by Black slaves and Native Americans in the South; and Ludovic, grieving and distraught, leaves for the wilderness and the open prairies, embracing a life of solitude beyond "civilised" America. "The greatest of all my errors," the forlorn lover remarks, "was to believe that man is greater than he is."[102]

For all of his lack of literary talent, Beaumont's courage lay in choosing the love of a white man for a woman of colour as his controversial subject. There have been few more powerful themes in American history. So it is easy to see why an American audience, eager to celebrate what they saw as the praise of the United States in *De la démocratie en Amérique,* would have felt distinctly uneasy with the deeply troubling vision of American society provided by Beaumont.

"During my stay in the United States," Beaumont began, "I saw a society which, like our own, displayed both harmonies and contrasts" and, he continued, "it seemed to me that if I could succeed in doing justice to the impressions I had of America my account would not be entirely without purpose."[103] At bottom, he insisted, what he described, even though it was in fictional form, was true to life. By way of clarification, Beaumont then added that there were principally two things that needed to be observed in a foreign people: their institutions and their mores. His friend Tocqueville, he acknowledged, had brilliantly analysed the "democratic institutions" of the United States; Beaumont, therefore, would focus on mores alone.

The first time he entered a theatre in America, Beaumont recalled in the novel's preface, he was surprised to see how the white members of the audience were separated from the Black members. In the dress circle were the white people; in the upper circle were the mulattos; and in the gallery were the Black people. As Tocqueville's own notebooks make clear, this occurred on New Year's Day 1832 in New Orleans. Both men, according to Tocqueville, went dancing afterwards where, it seems, they were struck by the lax morals and ease of familiarity exhibited between the white men present and the Black women of all ages: mothers, young girls, and children.[104]

Beaumont took the story in another direction. An American sitting next to him, he remembered, insisted that the dignity of the white race required such physical separation. Always one to spot a pretty girl, Beaumont then noticed a young woman of "astonishing beauty" and pure white skin sitting in the upper circle among the audience of mixed-race people. Why, he asked, was this woman of obvious English extraction sitting among Africans? Because she was coloured, came the answer, and she was deemed to be coloured because, as everyone knew, she counted a person of mixed race among her ancestors. Undaunted, Beaumont pressed on, next asking why a woman whose appearance was nonwhite was sitting among the white people in the dress circle. Again, there was no hesitation in the answer. The lady who now attracts your attention, he was told, is white and she is white because "the blood that flows through her veins is Spanish." The evident absurdity of these answers clearly escaped Beaumont's fellow theatregoer.

Yet, as Beaumont next made clear, these were not "frivolous distinctions" but slurs rooted in deep and enduring racial prejudice towards the Black population of the United States. Each day, Beaumont wrote, this prejudice "deepens the abyss which separates the two races and pursues them in every part of social and political life; it determines the mutual relations of white people and people of colour; corrupting the habits of the first whom it accustoms to domination and tyranny, ruling the fate of the Negroes, whom it condemns to the persecution of the white people; and it gives rise between them to hatreds so violent, resentments so lasting, clashes so dangerous, that one may rightly say that its influence will stretch across the entire future of American society."[105]

What follows is a curious text, part novel, part documentary, and one full of detail drawn from Beaumont's and Tocqueville's travels across America. Here we read again that Americans have an insatiable desire for flattery and that they are poor musicians. A visit to the theatre, made by Tocqueville and Beaumont in Philadelphia in October 1831 to see a play entitled *Napoléon ou Schoenbrunn et Sainte-Hélène,* appears in the novel as a visit made in New York.[106] In Beaumont's letters the episode figures as no more than an opportunity to comment on the poor acting and awful auditorium, whilst in *Marie* it provides the background to an expression of violent racial prejudice directed against Marie's brother, Georges. An overlong, chapter-length monologue by Ludovic details why Americans have no taste for the arts and literature. The first preoccupation of all Americans, we are reminded, is to make money. With Marie, Ludovic undertakes the same journey up the Hudson Valley and then to Saginaw through the forests and by boat that Beaumont and Tocqueville had made together. Above all, the novel draws upon what Beaumont and Tocqueville had seen of the treatment of Black people in Baltimore and Philadelphia. It was here that Beaumont came to understand that even a freed Black person was still treated as a slave. Being white was a form of nobility, even in a society supposedly committed to the principle of "absolute equality."

Most obviously, the novel's hero, Ludovic, is a mirror image of Beaumont himself. At age twenty-five (Beaumont was twenty-nine) Ludovic leaves from Le Havre for New York, without a career and bored by what he found in Europe. He did so, like Beaumont, to see a country where, each day, he heard people "praise the wisdom of its institutions, its love of liberty, the wonders of its industry, the greatness of its future."[107] The big difference was that the fictional Ludovic, unlike the real-life Beaumont, there found the woman of his dreams.

Beaumont's tale, then, is of an idealistic young Frenchman who comes to America in search of a radiant future. And this is what he thinks he has found until the moment he is told that the woman he loves is a woman of colour and therefore that there could be no possibility of them becoming man and wife. It is only then, as Marie's father explains their tainted family history, that he begins to understand the full extent of racial prejudice in the United States. In one dramatic revelation, the reader, like Ludovic, is confronted by the horror of a society where many of its members are seen as being less than human.

After the close of the novel, Beaumont added several detailed appendices, the first of which was devoted to an examination entitled "Social and Political Condition of Negro Slaves and Freed People of Colour." It began by explaining that, in the United States, there existed two million people denied all political, civil and natural rights. Excluded from political life, deprived of even the right to marry and to care for his children, the slave was reduced to a "material object" and a form of "moveable property." If a slave killed his master, he would be sentenced to death. A master who killed his slave would pay nothing more than a small fine. As Beaumont saw, the very question of how a slave might be punished was itself revealing of the slave's situation and of the society in which he lived. A slave could not be fined for a misdemeanour, as he owned no property. To imprison him was to deprive his owner of his labour. So only the alternative of corporal punishment remained. Whipping punished the slave without harming the interests of the master.[108]

Yet Beaumont understood that beyond the question of slavery lay the "more serious" question of race. In vain was the Black man set free for, in the eyes of the white population, he retained all the characteristics of a slave. Even in those states where slavery had long been abolished, white and Black people lived distinctly separate existences. They had their own schools, their own churches, and, as Tocqueville had similarly observed, their own cemeteries. Even in prisons they were kept apart. Nor would the white prostitute accept the embraces of a Black man. An "unbreakable barrier" existed between the white and Black populations.[109]

It was this enduring separation, rather than the existence of slavery itself, that lay at the heart of Beaumont's novel. An uncomprehending Ludovic listens in near disbelief as Marie's father—himself a man who believes that Black people are intellectually inferior to white people—tells him that "the Black race is despised in America because it is a race of slaves: it is hated because it aspires to liberty." To this he then adds that "no people is more devoted to the principle of equality than we are, but we cannot accept that a race inferior to ours can share in our rights."[110] The ending of slavery, therefore, would at best be a poisoned chalice. Left to their own devices, the Black population would not know how to survive. Thus, even the emancipated Black had no place in society. He was shunned, humiliated, and treated with public contempt. Being a person of colour was the only crime that an individual could not expunge.

It is at this point that the reader sees with greatest clarity the fruits of Beaumont and Tocqueville's common journey across the United States. What sustained racial prejudice, Beaumont realised, was not the law but public opinion and mores. And in America, as Tocqueville had appreciated, the power of majority opinion knew no bounds. Changing the legal status of the Black population would therefore have little effect, for the simple reason, Beaumont believed, that an "all-powerful" public opinion wanted "the oppression of a hated race and nothing would impede it." "The people who hated the Negroes," he continued, is "the one who makes the laws." The power of popular sovereignty was irresistible. Its least desires were turned into commands. There was no moderating influence, no countervailing force, to hold back the impulses of popular sentiment. It was truly the people, with its passions, who governed, and consequently "the Black race" suffered from "the sovereignty of hate and scorn." Everywhere, Beaumont has Ludovic announce, "I found again and again the tyrannies of the popular will."[111]

When *De la démocratie en Amérique* was first published, there were many among Tocqueville's American friends and admirers who felt that he had exaggerated the power of the majority. Majorities, they argued, came and went, and to talk of a tyranny of the majority was misplaced. But here, as Beaumont saw, was an unchanging majority opinion and one that showed little aversion to condemning a minority to permanent silence and oppression. When it came to understanding America's long history of racial injustice, Tocqueville looks to have had a point, and sadly a not unimportant one.

This, Beaumont understood, was deeply disquieting. In the countries of the East, he wrote—clearly echoing the arguments advanced by Montesquieu in *The Spirit of the Laws*—one was not surprised to find lands where the arbitrary power of a tyrant held sway over the lives of his people and where caprice, force, and universal misery were the order of the day. In such countries the existence of millions of slaves was only to be expected. But one expected something different among a free people and in a civilised and religious society. There people understood what slavery was because they lived a life of liberty. Surely they would detest injustice and persecution because they enjoyed the benefits of fairness and tolerance. Thus, the shock of seeing slavery in the United States was all the greater and the more unfathomable. "In a land of equality," Beaumont wrote, "all citizens are responsible for social injustices; each is a party to them. Not a white man exists in America who is not a barbarous, iniquitous persecutor of the Black race. In Turkey . . . there is but one tyrant; in the United States, for each act of tyranny, there are ten million tyrants."[112] In short, the iniquitous treatment of the Black population was the great contradiction of American democracy.

With Beaumont's tragic tale at an end, he then asked the fundamental question: Could slavery be abolished in the United States? He saw two reasons why it should be. The morals of a Christian society condemned slavery, and slavery was economically inefficient. But could it be abolished? Many contended—incorrectly, in Beaumont's view—that the African race was intellectually inferior to the European race. Others believed that the work carried out by Black people in the heat of the South was not possible for white people. In purely financial terms, there was the question of potentially massive compensation for the slave owners. Another concern related to the future of the Black population once emancipation had been achieved. How could they live among those who had formerly enslaved them? Could they be transported back to Africa, or might a portion of American territory be assigned to them? Most grave of all was the question of whether the slave states of the South would agree to the abolition of slavery, for, as Beaumont correctly observed, this could only be achieved with the sovereign consent of those individual states. Given that the entire wealth of the South depended upon slave labour, this seemed extremely unlikely.

So for all that Beaumont believed it was "impossible" that slavery would not sooner or later completely disappear from North America, this did not stop him from wondering whether the future would bring "a crisis of extermination." White people in the South, he concluded, had the "habit of power" and they were certain of finding support in the North. Was the Black population then destined to lose the fight if it came to war? No one, Beaumont replied, could answer this question. What was certain was that the storm was gathering and that it could be heard in the distance. No one, he concluded, "could say where the lightning would strike."[113]

The first volume of *De la démocratie en Amérique* was published in 1835. Beaumont's *Marie* was published the same year. By the time that the second volume of *De la démocratie en Amérique* was published, both Tocqueville and Beaumont had been elected to the French Chamber of Deputies in 1839. In July of that same year, a matter of weeks after his election, Tocqueville presented a report to the French Parliament on the abolition of slavery in the colonies.[114] True to their usual practice of a division of labour, Beaumont presented the report to the chamber on behalf of the Société française pour l'abolition de l'esclavage.

That Tocqueville's report was largely ignored by his fellow legislators does not diminish its importance for the insights it provides as to how both Tocqueville and Beaumont applied the lessons they had learned in America to the situation faced by France.[115] Without any equivocation, Tocqueville called not for the gradual but the immediate abolition of slavery. "It is not," the report announced, "a question of whether slavery is an evil and whether it should end but when and how it can best be brought to an end." Specifically, Tocqueville denied that the slave could only be set free once he had been educated to be free. "It seems scarcely reasonable to believe," the report stated, "that the vices naturally and necessarily produced by servitude can be destroyed in a condition of servitude." In brief, it was "only the experience of liberty" that could give a person "the opinions, the virtues and the habits appropriate to a citizen in a free country." No theme was dearer to Tocqueville's heart. For good measure, the report added that the abolition of slavery was also in the interests of the French colonies.[116]

What followed was a careful consideration of the practical measures required to end French colonial slavery, and one that openly drew upon the experiences of those "who have travelled through those lands where slavery exists." Recognising that "a man has never had the right of possessing another man," the report nonetheless "unanimously" recommended that it would be neither "humane, equitable nor wise" for the French state not to compensate the slave owners for their inevitable financial losses. The ambition was to create former colonies that were "civilised, industrious and peaceable" and this could only be done if the colonial settler was kept on board. Above all else, interracial violence had to be avoided. The biggest challenge would be to encourage the former slaves to adopt diligent habits.[117]

Four years later, Tocqueville again went on the attack, this time in a series of articles published in *Le siècle*.[118] In the intervening years, another report had been prepared—this time chaired by the duc de Broglie and described by Tocqueville in a letter to Beaumont as "a masterpiece"[119]—but the opposition to the abolition of slavery in the French colonies remained unshaken. "The colonists," Tocqueville wrote, "constitute one of the most exclusive aristocracies that has ever existed in the world," and no aristocracy had ever given up its privileges willingly.[120] Now Tocqueville sought to influence not his parliamentary colleagues but public opinion. And he did so, first, by reassuring his fellow citizens that the experience of emancipation in the British colonies had largely been successful—there had been no accompanying civil disorder or economic collapse—and, second, by appealing to French national pride and honour. Only if slavery was abolished, Tocqueville argued, could the French Empire be preserved and defended from external attack. It was the French in 1789 who had turned the Christian idea that all people were born equal into a political programme. But Tocqueville also argued for a set of transitional arrangements designed to facilitate a smooth route towards emancipation. These included preventing former slaves from leaving the colony where they resided and from owning property. This, he asserted, was in no way a form of tyranny, and "the man on whom only this constraint was imposed upon leaving slavery would seem to have little right to complain."[121]

This dubious proposition did not figure in the speech made to the Chamber of Deputies almost two years later when Tocqueville again argued that the abolition of slavery in the French colonies served France's political and moral interests.[122] In a fit of rhetorical excess, he assured his enthusiastic audience that it was the French, and not the English, who were "the true authors of the abolition of slavery" and the French who had shown that "slavery was not only contrary to the laws of God [but] should disappear from the laws of men."[123]

What is most of interest is that Tocqueville explicitly framed his argument in terms of what he and Beaumont had seen in the United States. First, when challenged by one of his fellow deputies, he explicitly endorsed views he had expressed in *De la démocratie en Amérique.* For as long as the "two races" lived separated from each other and did not form "one and the same people," he responded, the only alternatives were "subjection and death." Next, he denied that the attitudes of French slave owners merited particular reproach, adding "I have seen similar opinions and like prejudices—prejudices even more extraordinary—prevail in a country I have been able to visit and see firsthand: the United States of America." This in turn allowed him to expand upon one of his and Beaumont's oft-repeated themes: the glaring and fateful contradiction that lay at the heart of American democracy. "I have seen," Tocqueville proclaimed, "these two singular extremes; I have seen men who loved equality with such passion that they do not want even to allow the appearance of those inequalities and natural differences that arise from fortunes, education, taste and mores; and these same men find it perfectly natural to own and place under their feet millions of their fellow creatures in an eternal and irredeemable servitude." It was these identical people who were covering the United States with public schools where their own children could be educated and who, at the same time, believed that teaching a Black person to read and write should properly be a crime punishable by death. "I have seen them," he continued, "wish to raise all men of their colour to the level of European society" whilst making "a common effort, an energetic effort, to push down almost to the condition of beasts the entire mass of their slaves." Were these people to be detested, to be insulted? No, Tocqueville replied, they were to be pitied, for they were only obeying "a universal law of human nature" and following an example that was many centuries old.[124]

For all of Tocqueville's and Beaumont's efforts, it took the French Revolution of 1848 and the establishment of the Second Republic for slavery finally to be abolished in the French colonies. Once more, however, the importance of Tocqueville's travels in the framing of ideas that remained with him throughout his life cannot be denied.

CHAPTER FOUR

England, Ireland, and Switzerland

After their return from America in March 1832, neither Alexis de Tocqueville nor Gustave de Beaumont were particularly overjoyed to be back in France. A cholera epidemic ravaged the country, and, in Tocqueville's view, France seemed enveloped by political apathy and indifference. Worse still, a month after his return Beaumont was dismissed by the government from his post in Paris. Out of personal loyalty, Tocqueville tendered his resignation. Yet, although now without gainful employment, they continued to travel, either singly or together, and as they did so America was never to be far from their thoughts. Hence, in the summer of 1833 Tocqueville was to make a five-week visit to England,[1] while Beaumont took a long vacation in Spain. With typical self-mockery, Beaumont commented that, while Tocqueville had witnessed the great orators of the English Parliament—in fact, Tocqueville observed little more than the boring oratory of the aged Duke of Wellington—he himself had only seen bullfights. Beaumont did, however, admit that one benefit of his visit to a country where one did little more than cross one's arms and sit in the sun was that he now swam less badly than he had done in the Hudson River. As for Tocqueville, he told one of his many cousins, Laurette de Pisieux, that he was travelling to England in order to flee the "insipid spectacle" presented by his homeland and "to relieve his boredom." He also told her that, with the threat of revolution in the air, he was hastening to England like someone rushing to see "the last performance of a well-produced play."[2] Once more, Tocqueville's travels were to shape his ideas on what the future held.

Setting out for England in early August 1833, Tocqueville wrote immediately to his mother providing details of his journey. Having spent three days in nearby Cherbourg waiting for a boat to take him across the English Channel, he was fortunate enough to meet an English colonel who kindly offered to transport him on his yacht to the British island of Guernsey off the coast of Normandy. Not only this, but the colonel generously offered his accommodation to Tocqueville (accommodation akin, he confided to his mother, to "the boudoir of a fine lady"). For once in Tocqueville's life he travelled on a calm sea, and six hours later he was in the harbour of Saint Peter Port. The following morning a steamship left for Weymouth on the English coast where he arrived without mishap after a journey of some ten and a half hours.

As had been the case when he first arrived in America, Tocqueville was overwhelmed and dazed by the huge variety of things he saw in England and by the vastness of London in particular. He stayed in the "small but fairly pretty town" of Weymouth for only one night, the following day setting off for Southampton in a "superb carriage . . . drawn by four magnificent horses, each very brightly harnessed." The countryside he crossed, Tocqueville reported to his mother, had "nothing of the picturesque," but, he continued, "you find me still stunned by the excessive wealth that one notices . . . a universal luxury which, people say, often hides poverty but which at least hides it wonderfully well from the eyes of the foreigner." To his surprise, the port of Southampton had shops as beautiful as those in Paris.[3]

On 8 August Tocqueville set off for London by way of Portsmouth (where, presumably in connection with the impending admission of his future wife, Mary Mottley, to the Catholic Church, he recorded a conversation with a Catholic priest). London, he told Mary, was always engulfed in smoke (although, happily, for once it was not raining). Never had he visited somewhere as expensive. If the English could tax the air one breathed, he commented, they would. Nevertheless, it was "a magnificent city" and, even if the new districts were "a little monotonous" in appearance, one sensed an "air of universal wealth." In Paris there were beautiful things of all kinds, but in London there was simply more of them.[4] Above all, it was the immensity of London that Tocqueville found difficult to grasp. It gave him, he told Gustave de Beaumont, "a profound sense of being a nobody." He felt like "a gnat on a haystack."[5]

Nonetheless, and as he always did, Tocqueville set himself immediately to work, with the intention, he told his father, "of returning with more accurate ideas about England than I had upon my departure from France."[6]

This, he indicated to Beaumont, he had done with courage, but it was not easy, as the distances to be covered travelling across London were "prodigious."[7] His letters of introduction, for the most part (and by his own admission) to members of the upper aristocracy, proved to be of little use, as people had either left London for the summer or were about to do so; but among the few who remained, he reported, he had been politely received. What had undoubtedly helped to secure him entry into this world, he informed his father, was his and Beaumont's book on prisons, which, to Tocqueville's delight, was both well known and frequently cited. Indeed, such was its notoriety that he was invited to a "*dîner pénitentiare*" attended by no less a figure than the Anglican Archbishop of Dublin (accompanied, Tocqueville observed, by his wife and several very pretty daughters, all of which, he confessed, he found difficult to reconcile with any idea he had of the episcopate).[8] One project, abandoned due to lack of time, was a visit to Liverpool to see the newly opened railway.

Once out of London and having made the sixty-mile journey on top of a (very uncomfortable) public stagecoach, Tocqueville was spellbound by the medieval charms of Oxford. Turn off Oxford's High Street, he told Mary Mottley, and one was immediately transported back into the fourteenth century. He was shocked at how well and how copiously the Fellows of Oxford's Colleges ate and drank. Fortunately, Tocqueville's own fragile stomach withstood the test.[9]

A day or so later he fell into lyrical raptures at the sight of Warwick and Kenilworth castles. Of Warwick, he wrote that there was nothing in France that so "recalled feudal times, those centuries of liberty and oppression, of great crimes and sublime virtues, of enthusiasm and energy which will live on in the imagination of men for as long as there remains a little poetry here on earth." What a "magnificent idea" it gave of the "savage grandeur" of those days. Leaving the castle, and in a state of "intellectual excitement," Tocqueville then hired a horse and rode the six or seven miles to Kenilworth. "Imagine," he wrote to Mary, "a light breeze, a cloudless sky, a full moon; add to this a fiery and agile horse between my thighs, centuries of chivalry in my head, and some of the fire of youth in my veins; and you will know that I didn't touch the ground." Eventually, and after disturbing the inhabitants of the sleeping village, Tocqueville found his way into the ruins of the castle. It was, he wrote, "a great and solemn spectacle" where there reigned "a silence and inexpressible air of desolation." He felt he was in "the domain of Death." "I sat upon a stone," he wrote, "and fell into a kind of somnambulism, during which it seemed that my soul was carried towards the past with an overwhelming force." Moreover, the ruins of Kenilworth, seen in the dead of night, led him to recall the famous novel of Walter Scott and the fate of its tragic heroine, Amy Robsart, murdered by her husband, the Earl of Dudley. Interestingly, when Tocqueville's elder brother, Édouard, had visited the ruins of Kenilworth Castle on 16 June 1824 he, too, had recalled Scott's novel and the sad fate of sweet Amy Robsart.[10] The spirit of *pittoresque* travel had clearly been passed on from brother to brother.

If the visit to Warwick and Kenilworth castles was one of the most memorable evenings of Alexis de Tocqueville's life, the impression did not last. The next day he woke to coal fumes and rain. "Once again," he told his wife-to-be, "I saw that in this life poetry was only met by chance and that the core of our existence is only base prose." Tocqueville was quickly returned, as he saw it, to the real world.[11]

Then, like many both before and since, Tocqueville was seduced by the charms and attractions of the English aristocracy (in this case, the hospitality of Lord Radnor on his country estate near Salisbury, in Wiltshire). As Tocqueville told his father, he was pleased to meet Radnor, as he had the rare quality of being both a member of the top echelon of the aristocracy and a radical. These things, he commented, might seem mutually exclusive but upon occasion they were reconciled in England.[12] Of equal attraction, as Tocqueville informed both his father and his future wife, was that he would be arriving at Longford Castle for the start of the shooting season. His journey to England would therefore "end precisely as [he] would have hoped, by seeing a great English lord on his land."

Tocqueville was also impressed by the magnificence of Radnor's house. "I have seen and stayed in several of the most beautiful châteaux in France," he told Mary Motley, "but this clearly surpasses them in the art of bringing together all the agreeable little things in life."[13] "Concentrate your attention on roads, canals and railways [and] what role government has played in [their] construction," the ever-practical Beaumont advised Tocqueville by way of reply when asked for guidance on how he should fill his time.[14]

Of course, this journey to England took place while Tocqueville and Beaumont were still immersed in their reflections on what they had seen in the United States. It is therefore no surprise to discover that, with his habitual thoroughness, Tocqueville continued to inquire about topics such as inheritance laws, the place of religion in English society, and the workings of local government and administration. He also witnessed the rowdy scenes that accompanied a parliamentary election in the City of London's Guildhall. The impression made upon him by this "saturnalia of English liberty," he noted, was one of "distaste rather than fear."[15] As he had been in America, he was rather proud of the fact that he met and spoke with people of all classes. However, as Tocqueville confided to Beaumont, when he looked at England, "nowhere do I recognise our America." This was so precisely because, in contrast to the United States, where mores were democratic, in England they remained resolutely aristocratic.[16] Yet, as Beaumont responded, Tocqueville had been right to visit England. It was not only the country that interested them most after the United States but it was, above all, "the father of the Americans."[17]

And it was as the father of the Americans that England was to figure in the opening chapters of *De la démocratie en Amérique.* The English experience, Tocqueville affirmed, was America's point of departure. The first emigrants to America not only spoke the same language but "they were all children of the same people." All were born in a country troubled by political and religious strife and where, consequently, people had been obliged "to place themselves under the protection of the laws." They brought with them, therefore, "the fertile seed of free institutions" and what Tocqueville did not hesitate to describe as the "germ of a complete democracy." None of these emigrants, Tocqueville contended, departed from their mother country with a sense of their own superiority over others, and it was for this reason that, when attempts were made to establish a hierarchy of ranks on American soil, all claims to territorial aristocracy were rejected. So, Tocqueville concluded, all the "English colonies" shared "a great family resemblance. All, from their beginning, seemed destined to present the development of liberty, not the aristocratic liberty of their mother country, but the bourgeois and democratic liberty of which the history of the world did not yet offer a complete model."[18] It was not by accident that he spoke repeatedly of the Anglo-Americans or of an "Anglo-American civilisation" whose genius had been to combine the spirit of religion and the spirit of liberty.

Tocqueville published relatively little on England, but his initial impressions on visiting it were disclosed in one of his more untypical, and arguably least successful, texts, "Mémoire sur le paupérisme," first delivered as a public lecture in Cherbourg in the spring of 1835.[19] Travel across the English countryside, he told his Norman audience, and one would think oneself "transported into the Eden of modern civilisation." Everywhere one saw well-maintained roads, bright new houses, animals grazing in rich meadows, and a wealth more dazzling than anywhere else in the world. There was a feeling of universal prosperity that made one's heart give a start with every step. But look more closely, he continued, and "with unutterable astonishment you will discover that one-sixth of the inhabitants of this flourishing kingdom live at the expense of public charity."[20]

In part Tocqueville found an answer to this paradox in an account of the general development of civilisation. Over time, our needs multiplied and diversified infinitely, and our sense of insecurity grew. The richer a nation was, in other words, the more people felt the lack of what they did not possess and the more they would call upon the support of their fellows to satisfy the needs they had created for themselves. As England enjoyed the highest standard of living in the world, it followed that those expectations would there be the greatest and that more and more people would consider that they lived in poverty.

However, in Tocqueville's opinion, there were causes of pauperism specific to England alone. The first derived from the fact that no other country in Europe had done more to institutionalise public charity. As Tocqueville recognised, this was a consequence of the near-complete closure of all charitable institutions in the wake of Henry VIII's break with the Catholic Church. The second cause arose from industrialisation and the parallel development of large-scale agriculture. As Tocqueville explained, "The English industrial class provides for not only the necessities and pleasures of the English people but for a large part of humanity." So its prosperity depended not just upon what happened in Great Britain but upon almost every event in the world. "When an inhabitant of the Indies reduces his expenditure or cuts back his consumption," he told his audience, "it is an

English manufacturer who suffers." The English labourer, in short, was the "most exposed to the vicissitudes of fortune."[21]

But the broad thrust of Tocqueville's presentation in Cherbourg was to warn his audience of the dangers of establishing public or legal charity on a permanent basis. The result, he argued, would be to create "an idle and lazy class, living at the expense of the industrial and working class." Nowhere, he believed, was this more in evidence than in Great Britain, where "the number of illegitimate children and criminals grows continuously and rapidly; the indigent population expands beyond measure; the spirit of foresight and of saving becomes more and more alien to the poor." The lower classes, Tocqueville concluded bleakly, remained motionless, reverting to barbarism, emulating the ideas and inclinations of the savage. Yet all of this was occurring in a country where among the rest of the nation morals improved, tastes became more refined, and manners were ever more polished.[22]

Tocqueville was obviously troubled and perplexed by what he saw in England. As his travel notes reveal, there was something about the inner dynamic of English society that eluded him. Upon arrival in England, Tocqueville wrote, the first thing that struck a Frenchman was the "sense of ease" he saw all around him. The "immense riches" of the colleges Tocqueville visited in Oxford was a case in point. So, too, was Lord Radnor's magnificent Elizabethan Longford Castle on the banks of the River Avon in Wiltshire. As he also confided to his notebooks, he had arrived expecting to see a country on the brink of violent revolution, but this proved not to be the case.[23]

The immediate political context was the popular agitation surrounding demands for the reform of the British Parliament and the extension of the franchise associated with the Great Reform Act of 1832. But Tocqueville also brought with him a perspective drawn directly from his journey through America and which he was grappling to understand as he set about the writing of the first volume of *De la démocratie en Amérique*. It is a perspective with which we are familiar, but this is how it was expressed in a long note composed as Tocqueville was about to leave England for France in September 1833. Our century, the note read, is "eminently democratic." "Democracy," it continued, "resembles a rising sea; it withdraws only to come back with greater force on its path; and, after a certain amount of time, one sees that, for all its ebb and flow, it has not ceased to gain ground." In short, the gradual development of the democratic principle was irresistible, and each day brought with it a new attack upon the privileges of aristocracy.[24]

Yet, in stark contrast to what Tocqueville had seen in America, in England the aristocracy remained the dominant class (not least in politics), and aristocratic values informed the prevailing morals and manners of the country. Surely, he thought, this could not endure. Was it not evident that the aristocratic principle was losing its strength each day? In Tocqueville's view, the people of England were beginning to understand that they could involve themselves in matters of government. There was also "a spirit of innovation" present in English society, driven on by "dissatisfaction with the present and a hatred of the past."[25] But, although shaken and undoubtedly declining, the power of the English aristocracy endured. Why?

Tocqueville had several answers. First, unlike the prerevolutionary French aristocracy, the English aristocracy continued to perform a useful function, and it was therefore spared the "violent hatreds" that had been directed at its French counterpart. Second, it was an open aristocracy rather than an exclusive caste. Here Tocqueville made much of the distinction between the respective understandings of the words *gentleman* and *gentilhomme*. If the latter was defined by birth, the former denoted someone of good manners and education. Next, if the English were prone to criticising this or that member of the aristocracy or a particular position taken by the House of Lords, they did not criticise the aristocracy in general nor the principle of a hereditary chamber. Indeed, if anything, the English middle classes reserved their contempt for the people. If one thing had powerfully struck him during his stay, Tocqueville wrote, it was that the "aristocratic principle" was deeply embedded in English mores.[26]

So, if the situation of the English aristocracy was not without its dangers, there was every reason to believe that, if things followed their "natural course," a violent revolution or civil war of the kind that had engulfed the French aristocracy could be avoided. In a very real sense, Tocqueville concluded, the fate of the English aristocracy was largely in its own hands.

Tocqueville left England in early September 1833 having had what he described to his future wife's aunt as an "exceedingly pleasant" stay. As he wrote in his best English, "The country is generally very pretty, and the inhabitants receive the foreigners with the greatest ease and attention."[27] It is clear nonetheless that at least one unfavourable impression of England stayed with him. Writing to a German correspondent, Léon von Thun-Hohenstein, in the spring of 1835 Tocqueville remarked, "Perhaps like me you will finish by concluding that England should not be judged by its appearance and that much squalor and poverty lies hidden beneath a brilliant exterior."[28]

Only a few months after writing this letter, Tocqueville was back again in England, and this time he returned with his loyal companion Gustave de Beaumont. Once again, the journey they had both made to America was never far from their thoughts.

As was often the case, Tocqueville's journey was not without its mishaps or disappointments. Upon arrival in London in May 1835, it was only after considerable effort and at great expense that he and Beaumont were able to find what Tocqueville described as a "shabby" apartment at 101 Regent Street. He did nonetheless have the good grace to admit to his father that this was the part of London where "fashionable" society lived (adding, one would hope with a sense of self-irony, that he and Beaumont were "extremely fashionable"). The weather was dreadful. When the sun shone through the fog, Tocqueville commented, it was akin to a lamp that cast light into a mine shaft.[29] Despite the warm reception they received (Tocqueville had to break off writing one letter to his father due to an unscheduled appearance of the Marquess of Lansdowne at his door) there were aspects of English life and manners not always to his liking. He mixed with all classes, he told Virginie Ancelot, but not one pleased him without reservation. If he was attracted by the lofty sentiments and manners of the upper classes, he was bored and repulsed by the luxury and pomp in which they lived. He admired the simplicity of the middle classes but found their vulgarity unbearable. As for servants, they treated him with undisguised insolence upon his arrival and "prodigious servility" after he had been greeted by their master.[30] The respect that the English showed towards wealth, he told his English fiancée, was "a heartbreaking thing to see."[31]

Tocqueville was also put out by the fact that, as before, most of the people he hoped to see had departed for the country during the parliamentary recess. So there were no balls or society gatherings, just lots of "semiofficial" dinners that would have been of interest were it not for the fact that they started so late and went on for so long with innumerable speeches.[32] On one occasion, and not without fascination, he found himself sitting next to a twenty-year-old Lady Ada Byron, daughter of the infamous poet and future distinguished mathematician. It was not without some wry amusement that Tocqueville noted that, for all of their resemblance to Americans, his English hosts ceaselessly mocked the bad manners of Americans. Three weeks into his stay, Tocqueville felt sufficiently confident in his judgement to tell both his father and Virginie Ancelot that England was without doubt "the true home of spleen," adding that there was nothing like the fog to turn one's mind to philosophising.[33] His journey from London to the Midlands town of Coventry, he reported to John Stuart Mill, was about as awful as one could imagine: ten hours on top of a stagecoach in a howling gale and pouring rain. In the middle of the most civilised country on earth, he added, it was enough to make one miss the "Wilderness of America."[34]

Not for the first or last time, Tocqueville fell ill with stomach problems, and on this occasion he spent two weeks recuperating at the home of his future translator, Henry Reeve, in "the charming village" of Hampstead, then just north of the capital. The ever-loyal Beaumont stayed in town, beavering away on their inquiries, dining with Tocqueville every other day. Writing to his sister-in-law, Alexandrine, Tocqueville explained that, although forbidden to walk, he was allowed to take the air. "My little house," Tocqueville continued, "is surrounded by bushes in flower; on the horizon can be seen London and its smoke; the whole area in between consists of delightful countryside that spring has covered with all its pretty colours." He wrote; he read; but, above all, he dreamed "in a kind of semisleep of the body and soul." He would, he confided to Alexandrine, leave Hampstead and the Reeve family with much regret, were it not for the fact that he had come to England "to think and to see." It was by far "the most agreeable time" he had spent in England.[35]

Tocqueville was also immensely impressed by what he saw on his visit to one of London's grandest of gentlemen's clubs, the Athenaeum on Pall Mall, telling his father about its beautiful drawing rooms, excellent library and fine restaurant.[36]

In other respects, this visit was not dissimilar to that which the two men had made to America. First, Tocqueville took extensive notes that contain frequent comparisons between France and England. Tocqueville and Beaumont kept themselves constantly busy, ploughing through as many documents as they could, attending events, making visits, rising early and finishing late.[37] Even when sick, Tocqueville cross-examined the unfortunate Henry Reeve on the careers open to the aristocracy, the tendency in England towards centralisation, whether people were paid for the performance of administrative functions (largely they were not), and the nature of religious dissent. From the latter discussion Tocqueville concluded that England possessed "not only an aristocratic and a democratic politics but an aristocratic and a democratic religion." This, he recorded, was "a fatal sign for the future."[38] He also learned from Reeve that the British Empire in India was a source of great wealth for the scions of the English aristocracy.

And, of course, Tocqueville conversed with as many people as possible, all the while taking notes and recording his comments. We know that he not only exchanged views with a distinguished cross-section of the English Whig aristocracy—Lords Holland, Minto, and Radnor, the Marquess of Lansdowne, and Lady Charlemont—but also with John Stuart Mill, the historian Henry Hallam, and the radical member of parliament John Roebuck. It was to Mill that Tocqueville observed that there existed a fundamental difference between French and English democrats. Whereas the latter wished not to put the exclusive control of society in the hands of the people but in the hands of a select group, the latter, Tocqueville contended, wished "to put the majority of the people in a position to govern and to make them capable of governing."[39] We also know that Tocqueville renewed his acquaintance with someone whom he had first met in London in 1833 and who was later to become a close personal and family friend, the political economist Nassau Senior.[40] Nor had Tocqueville lost his eye for observing the occasional bizarre incident. Just before dinner with Lord Radnor and his family at their London residence, Tocqueville recorded, all the domestic staff of the household (governess, housekeeper, maids, head butler, grooms, and so on) filed into the room, knelt on their knees, and turned their faces to the wall, whereupon Lord Radnor, also kneeling, read out a prayer to the accompanying responses of his servants. This brief interlude over, the domestic staff filed out of the room in the same order they had arrived and went back to work. Tocqueville listed this cameo under the category of "religious habits."[41] Tocqueville also presented evidence (in French) to a parliamentary committee investigating the issue of electoral corruption.[42]

Yet for all of his and Beaumont's efforts, Tocqueville had to confess to his father that England still appeared to him as a "vast chaos." In contrast to America, he wrote, "there is not a single principle which follows easily from its results; they are like lines which cross each other in all directions, a labyrinth in which we are completely lost."[43] He so wanted God to shout out "Fiat lux!" One "anomaly" Tocqueville rightly observed, was between "the spirit of association" and the "spirit of exclusion" that ran through English society. He could not understand, he recorded in his notebooks, how both "could exist in such a developed way in the same people, and how they are often combined so closely." To illustrate this, Tocqueville chose membership of the gentleman's club. "What better example of association," he wrote, "than the union of individuals who form a club? What is more exclusionary than the individual represented by the club?" The same clash was visible in almost all civil and political associations in England. "Look at families," he continued, "and how they break up as soon as the birds are ready to leave the nest." The more he thought about it, Tocqueville reflected, the more he was inclined to believe that "the spirit of individuality is the foundation stone of the English character."[44]

Yet, time and time again, Tocqueville kept returning to the enormous privileges that attended the possession of wealth in English society. If he could see that the Reform Bill of 1832, with its modest extension of the suffrage, had shifted political power away from the House of Lords to the House of Commons, he saw no parallel movement outside the British Parliament. "The whole of English society," he wrote in his notebook, "is built upon the privilege of money." Money was the outward sign not only of wealth but of power, esteem, and glory. Someone had to be rich to become a member of parliament, because the cost of an election was considerable; to be a justice of the peace or a lord lieutenant, because no salary was received; to be a judge, because the cost of the education required was so expensive; and, to crown it all, the rich had easier access to capital and to positions that enabled them to be rich. If anything, English mores went more in this direction than laws.

Virtue counted for little without money. Tocqueville also saw how the poor were effectively excluded from owning landed property. As he told the comte de Molé, only people already rich acquired land because its ownership had become nothing more than a sign of wealth and status. In contrast to France, any English "peasant" with a modicum of education and capital went into trade.[45] Tocqueville summarised the situation as follows: "Apparent equality; real privileges of wealth; perhaps greater than any other country in the world."[46] To this, five weeks later, he added, "When I weigh up the level of greatness arrived at by the English people, I see among the causes of this greatness many virtues, but I wonder if it should not be attributed still more to vices."[47]

In one respect Tocqueville and Beaumont's trip to England differed significantly from their earlier voyage to America. It will be recalled that one of the criticisms levelled at Tocqueville by later critics has been that he failed to visit the Massachusetts mill town of Lowell. This has been taken to denote a lack of interest in the process of industrialisation. Tocqueville's first trip to England conformed to this pattern when, apart from London, he took in only the historic country towns of Oxford, Warwick, and Salisbury, all blessed with beautiful medieval architecture. His second visit broke this pattern. This time he made his way to the great manufacturing cities of Birmingham and Manchester, as well as the port of Liverpool, then one of the largest and most modern in the world.

For many foreign visitors to Britain's new and growing industrial cities the arrival of the machine age and the factory amounted to the birth of a new kind of civilisation. All too often, and especially for French visitors who readily accepted the popular portrayal of England as the country of inequality, it was taken to be synonymous with poverty, disease, poor housing, and prostitution. Yet even the French could at times see that enormous wealth was being created in what the English themselves, in William Blake's words, came to see later with nostalgia and affection as "the dark, Satanic mills." Tocqueville was similarly taken aback by what he discovered.

Arriving in Birmingham at the end of June 1835, he saw immediately that it bore no resemblance to what he had seen in London. Here, he observed, the people had not a moment to themselves. They worked as if they would become rich today and die tomorrow. When Tocqueville asked whether there

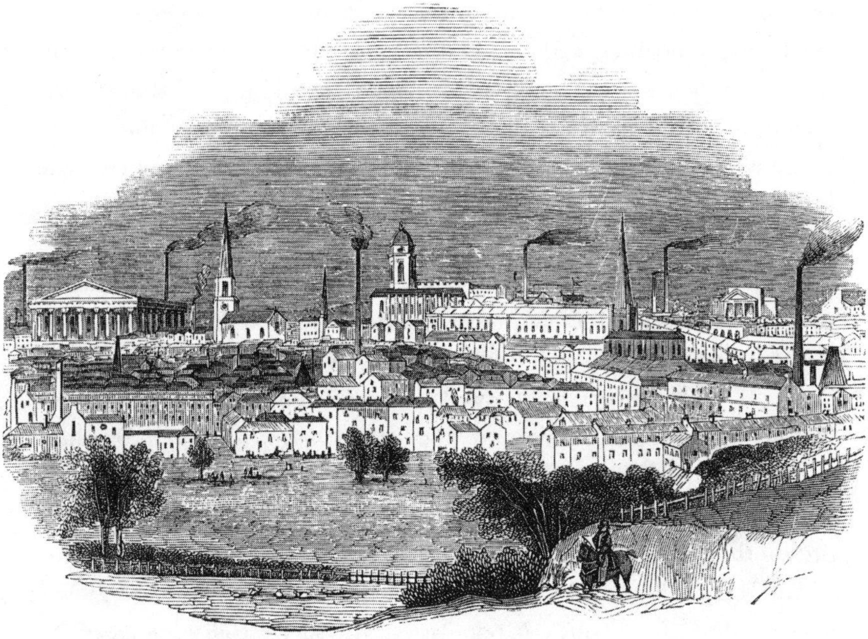

Birmingham, West Midlands, 1844 (The Print Collector / Alamy Stock Photo)

was a class of people in Birmingham without an occupation, his respondent, a Mr. Carter, replied, "No, everyone works to get rich. Their fortune made, they go elsewhere to spend it." In general, Tocqueville wrote, "they are intelligent people, but in the manner of Americans." As for the city itself, it was one immense workshop and foundry. In the streets were only people going about their business, their faces blackened by the smoke. One heard only the sound of hammers and the hissing of steam. Here, he noted, "everything is black, dirty and dark."[48]

Tocqueville saw at once (and correctly) that Manchester was a very different city from Birmingham. In Birmingham the population produced iron and steel and worked in small workshops or at home; in Manchester, they made textiles and cotton goods in factories housing thousands of people. Significantly, if in Birmingham the workforce was mostly male, in Manchester it was largely composed of women and children. The immigrant Irish population of Manchester was much greater than that of Birmingham. Tocqueville also noted that Manchester—in contrast to Birmingham, where small manufacturing companies predominated—had no middle class, only grand capitalists and thousands of poor workers, and that people tended to live thirteen or fourteen to a room, whereas in Birmingham houses tended to be occupied by single families. Everything in Manchester had the air of being incomplete and hastily built; everywhere there were piles of rubbish and pools of stagnant water. Roads were either not paved or badly paved. How, Tocqueville asked, could the "receptacles of vice and misery" inhabited by the poor be described? Down narrow, tortuous lanes were to be found badly built houses standing like the last refuge of someone between destitution and death. Beneath these miserable dwellings were damp and hideous basements, in each of which a dozen or more human beings were crowded together.[49] Nearby a river slowly carried away the putrid and polluted water turned into myriad colours by the surrounding factories. "It is," Tocqueville wrote, "the Styx of the new Hell."[50]

But Tocqueville could also see why a city like Manchester was growing and would continue to grow in population with such astonishing speed. Not only was it located close to the largest port in England, but from here it could import cotton from America. Nearby were mines producing cheap coal to drive machines, as were also the best manufacturers of machines in the world. Three canals and a railway ensured that Manchester's products could be quickly transported across England and to all points of the globe. Furthermore, there was a plentiful supply of cheap labour. Those who arrived for work from the countryside did so "with needs . . . reduced almost to those of a savage." Thus, Tocqueville commented, in Manchester one saw "a bringing together of a poor people and a rich people, an enlightened people and an ignorant people, of civilisation and barbarism."[51]

Nonetheless, with typical perspicacity, Tocqueville saw something of greater significance in the filthy hovels and the poverty of the city's inhabitants. "Look up," he wrote in a note dated 2 July 1835, "and all around this place you will see huge palaces of industry," six storey factories that prevented light and air getting through to the surrounding human habitations, from each of which could be heard the sound of furnaces and the whistle of steam. Here, "among the passing activities of a population eager for gain," was to be found the slave and the master, the wealth of some and the poverty of the many, the organised efforts of thousands to the profit of one man. Here too an individual appeared even weaker and alone than in the middle of a wilderness. Yet this "exterior appearance" attested to what Tocqueville described as "the individual powers of man." At every turn, he wrote, "human liberty shows its capricious creative force." Nowhere was there evident "the directing power of society" or "the slow continuous action of government." From "this foul sewer," Tocqueville concluded, "flowed pure gold," the human spirit was both perfected and brutalised, and civilised man returned "almost to a savage state."[52]

Newly arrived in Dublin, Tocqueville had the opportunity to reflect upon what he had seen of the new civilisation emerging in the industrial heartlands of England. In England, he concluded, money was the real power in the land and, with that, a new "aristocracy of money" had not been slow to emerge. Nothing like this had been seen anywhere else in the world or in any previous century. In other countries, one sought wealth to enjoy life. In England people sought wealth simply to live, as an end in itself. "Imagine," Tocqueville wrote, a similar attitude "operating with growing strength for centuries upon millions of people, and without difficulty you will understand how these people should have become the most fearless seafarers and the most capable industrialists on earth," for it was industry and commerce that provided the quickest and surest means to become rich. If one wanted to know, he wrote in his notebook on 7 July, if a people are commercially and industrially minded, one should not look at its ports, its forests, and the produce of its land (all very French perspectives at the time), but instead ask "whether the laws of this people give people the courage to seek prosperity, the liberty to pursue it, the knowledge and habits to find it, and the confidence that they will enjoy it after having found it." This is what Tocqueville saw in England and this—not its ports, its coal, or its iron—was the cause of its commercial prosperity. To this he added, "In truth, liberty is a *saintly* thing. There is only one other thing that better merits this name: and this is virtue. But what is virtue if not the *free* choice of what is good."[53]

As Seymour Drescher remarked quite a few years ago, it is doubtful that Tocqueville's visit to the industrial Midlands and north of the country seriously affected his general impression of England.[54] Writing to Lord Lansdowne from the elegant seaside town of Cowes on the Isle of Wight as he made his way back to France at the end of August, his admiration of England seemed undiminished. "If," Tocqueville wrote, not without a hint of flattery, "the statesmen of other countries could learn from you the difficult art of making power and wealth accessible and the secret of enhancing real merit through simplicity and the graciousness of manners, this alone would make it worth coming to England."[55] But what Tocqueville also saw was a mutual incomprehension that marked relations between England and France. During the twenty years of "profound peace" that had existed between Great Britain and France, he wrote in the *London and Westminster Review* the following year, both countries had "derived many things from each other." "From the laws of England," he argued, "the French have drawn the principles of constitutional liberty and the idea, previously unknown to them, of a government of law as distinguished from one of arbitrary will; whilst certain of the democratic tastes which are to be met with in England, and of the principles of political and social equality which are there promulgated, seem to be of French origin." Nevertheless, Tocqueville concluded, "such marked differences exist between the natural genius of the two nations, that in ceasing to be enemies they have yet to learn to know each other: they have imitated without understanding one another."[56]

Yet what Tocqueville saw in Manchester in particular and in England more generally of an "aristocracy of money" arguably found its way into the second volume of *De la démocratie en Amérique.* At the end of the second part of that volume there appears an intriguing chapter entitled "How Aristocracy Could Emerge from Industry." We know from Tocqueville's notes that he struggled to decide where best to place these pages. Most obviously, the chapter's theme posed a problem because it ran the risk of contradicting his central thesis about the equality of conditions in a democratic society.

Tocqueville's initial insight came directly from Adam Smith and his famous case of the pin factory in the opening chapter of *The Wealth of Nations:* the progress of the division of labour in modern industry was such as to diminish the intellectual powers of the artisan. The worker, Tocqueville wrote, had become "weaker, more limited, and more dependent." Yet, he observed, at the same time a new breed of educated men, eager to deploy science and their genius to make their fortunes, were exploiting the newfound power of industrial production. In such a situation, he continued, "the master and the worker are not in any way similar," and those differences would only grow by the day. "The one," he wrote, "is in continual, narrow and necessary dependence on the other, and seems born to obey, as the latter to command." While the vast mass of the people showed themselves to be more and more alike, among a small section of society differences and inequality grew. What, he asked, was this if not aristocracy?[57]

It was Tocqueville's firm opinion that this aristocracy did not resemble any that had preceded it. Moreover, viewed from the perspective of the democratic social state, it was "an exception, a monstrosity." First, unlike their aristocratic predecessors, the class of the rich could not be said properly to exist, as its members possessed neither common spirit nor common traditions. Next, the relationship between master and worker was a purely financial and temporary one. Neither was bound to the other by a permanent bond of habit or duty. Nor did this aristocracy of trade and commerce live amidst the industrial population. "Its goal," Tocqueville wrote, "is not to govern the latter, but to make use of it." Finally, the manufacturing aristocracy, in contrast to the landed aristocracy of the past, felt under no moral obligation to relieve the misery of their latter-day servants. "After impoverishing and brutalizing the men it uses," he observed, it "delivers them in times of crisis to public charity to be fed." In summary, this new aristocracy was "one of the harshest that has appeared on the earth."[58]

This was to be a theme to which Tocqueville would return in his final reflections on America during the 1850s. In the writing of *De la démocratie en Amérique,* however, these observations were deployed to develop a powerful warning against the possible rise of a new form of despotism, a despotism that was milder than those that had preceded it but which, for all of that, remained despotism. "The thing is new," Tocqueville wrote, "so I must try to define it, since I cannot name it."[59]

Again, the experience of visiting England provided crucial evidence in support of the argument Tocqueville was to advance. When Tocqueville and Beaumont arrived in England, the most important issue of the day was reform of the Poor Law. The Poor Law Amendment Act of 1834 had not only sought to relieve local rate (or tax) payers of the financial burden of caring for the poor and destitute but did so via a significant increase in administrative centralisation on the part of the state. This was an issue that Tocqueville discussed with both the economist Nassau Senior and with John Stuart Mill, and it figures prominently in the notes he kept during his visit. After a conversation with Henry Reeve on 11 May 1835, he wrote "Centralisation, a democratic instinct; instinct of a society that has succeeded in escaping from the individualistic system of the Middle Ages." To this he added the comment, "A preparation for despotism."[60]

Reworking these thoughts into the final part of *De la démocratie en Amérique,* Tocqueville argued that the charitable establishments of "old Europe" had almost everywhere fallen into decay. In consequence, "it is the State that has undertaken almost alone to give bread to those who are hungry, relief and a refuge to the sick, work to those without it." It had become "the almost unique repairer of all miseries." In parallel to this, Tocqueville noted, individuals more and more called the state "to their aid in all their needs," at every moment "setting their sight on it as on a tutor or on a guide." Much of this development could be accounted for by advances in public administration, which right across Europe had become more efficient, intrusive and detailed—"everywhere," Tocqueville wrote, "it penetrates more than formerly into private affairs"—but its principal driver, he now argued, was the development of industry.[61]

As he had seen in Birmingham and Manchester, industry not only brought a multitude of people together in one place but exposed them to great and sudden increases of misery and poverty. It also endangered their health. Furthermore, as industry continued to develop, this new "industrial class" would become more, not less, dependent upon the aid of others. It would need, in Tocqueville's words, to be more "regulated, supervised, and restrained than all the other classes" and with this it was only natural that the attributions of government would grow. In brief, the industrial class carried "despotism within it."[62]

Ahead of us, therefore, Tocqueville saw a world peopled by "an innumerable crowd of similar and equal men who spin around endlessly." Withdrawn and apart, they existed only for themselves, living among their fellows but not seeing them, focused only on satisfying their "small and vulgar pleasures." Above them would be "an immense and tutelary power," farseeing and mild, working for their happiness and security, providing for their needs, but fixing them "irrevocably in childhood." Such a power would not tyrannise but hinder and control and, in so doing, would reduce "each nation to being nothing more than a flock of timid and industrious animals, of which government is the shepherd."[63]

These remarks feature only a matter of a few pages before the very end of the second, and final, volume of *De la démocratie en Amérique*. The world he had sought to describe, Tocqueville wrote by way of conclusion, lay "still half caught in the ruins of the world that is falling." No one could safely predict what the outcome would be, what would survive of the past and what would be destroyed, but, Tocqueville confessed, when he surveyed "the innumerable crowd composed of similar beings," that "the spectacle of this universal uniformity saddens and chills me." As he understood only too well, there could be no possibility of reconstructing the aristocratic society of the past. Our task was to make freedom issue from the bosom of the democratic society in which God had placed us to live. Nevertheless, Tocqueville wrote, "I do not trust . . . the spirit of liberty which seems to animate my contemporaries; I see well that the nations of today are turbulent; but I do not find that they are liberal, and I am afraid that at the end of these agitations, which make all thrones totter, sovereigns will find themselves stronger than they were."[64]

After Manchester, Tocqueville's next stop was the port of Liverpool, some thirty miles or so to the west. He and Beaumont stayed here for no more than a day or two. It was, Tocqueville wrote in his notebook, a beautiful city, destined to become the centre of English commerce, and one that hid its poverty and poor much better than Manchester. It was also, he remarked correctly, a city that owed much of its original wealth to the transportation of slaves. The establishment of America, the development of manufacturing in Birmingham and Manchester, and the extension of English trade throughout the world had done the rest.

Next came a short trip by boat across the Irish Sea and a visit to Ireland (since 1801 an integral part of Great Britain), with the two Frenchmen arriving in Dublin.[65] Why Tocqueville and Beaumont chose to visit Ireland is not immediately apparent, but Tocqueville's notebooks include an account of a conversation between Nassau Senior and John Revans, secretary to the Irish Poor Law Commission, which took place in London a month before their arrival.[66] Revans's description of a country mired in poverty and hunger, prone to lawlessness, and driven by a fierce hatred of the English might have been enough to whet their appetites for a journey across the Irish Sea.[67] Evidence also suggests that Tocqueville had spoken with John Stuart Mill about Ireland. Whatever the explanation, the visit was to have a lasting impact upon both men.

Tocqueville and Beaumont stayed in Ireland for six weeks, travelling through the southeast and south of the country to Cork, on the way stopping off in Carlow, Waterford, and Kilkenny, then up through County Clare and Galway, getting as far north as Castlebar in County Mayo before returning to Dublin and departure for England on 15 August 1835. Thus, with the exception of Donegal in the far northwest and the largely Protestant province of Ulster, Tocqueville and Beaumont saw most of the country in a relatively short period of time As was their habit, they went about their travels armed with numerous letters of introduction (mostly, it turned out, to Catholic and Protestant priests), travelling with no fixed plan or itinerary, taking the opportunity both to speak with any number of people and to visit a variety of institutions. These included schools, court sessions, churches, a refuge for beggars, and Trinity College Dublin. One memorable dinner in Carlow was as guests of a Catholic archbishop, four bishops, and assorted clergy. Tocqueville and Beaumont even managed to attend a meeting of the British Association for the Advancement of Science. As he had done in America, Tocqueville quickly concluded that to understand the country he would need to stay far longer than he had planned or allowed.

When he arrived in Dublin on 7 July, Tocqueville was clearly still reflecting on what he had seen in England. His first notes consist largely of a commentary on the connection between liberty and commerce, suggesting, contra Montesquieu, that it is the first which precedes the second and citing the English case to prove his point. Two days later his intellectual preoccupations had shifted dramatically. On 9 July, he saw firsthand the hideous condition and misery of the Dublin poor when he and Beaumont visited a workhouse. One struggled, Tocqueville wrote, not to step on a half-naked person. The poor were laid out on the floor like pigs in the mud of their pigsty. Nearby were the old and infirm who neither spoke nor moved, awaiting only their dinner and death. Further off were those fit enough to work. They sat on the earth and, with a small hammer, broke stones. For this, Tocqueville recorded, they received a penny a day.

Upon leaving the workhouse Tocqueville and Beaumont met two poor chaps with a wheelbarrow and learned that their job was to collect waste food from the doors of the rich houses of Dublin and bring it back to the workhouse. Then Tocqueville and Beaumont were led to the precincts of Trinity College and what awaited them was "an immense and magnificent garden maintained like that of a great landowner. A stone palace; a superb church; a splendid library; footmen in livery . . . immense wealth." The contrast could not have been more startling and shocking. "This university," Tocqueville wrote, "was founded by [Queen] Elizabeth on the proceeds from land seized from Catholics, the fathers of those we had just seen wallowing in their dirt at the poor house." At the end of his notes for that day is to be found the following statement: "If you want to know what can be produced by the spirit

Homes of Ireland's nineteenth-century rural poor (De Luan / Alamy Stock Photo)

of conquest and religious hatred combined with the abuses of aristocracy, without any of its advantages, come to Ireland."[68]

This set the tone for what was to follow. Rarely commenting on the beautiful landscape he and Beaumont passed through, Tocqueville saw only an impoverished people, without work, reduced to near starvation, and living in mud hovels without windows or a chimney or any human comforts, protected from the elements only by a poorly constructed thatched roof. Men, women, and children went about their lives for the most part barefoot and in rags. Derelict houses were everywhere to be seen. Time and time again across Ireland, Tocqueville observed the same thing. Inside these miserable houses were only bare walls, a wooden stool, a peat fire burning slowly and obscurely, and, to Tocqueville's initial dismay, the family pig (usually surrounded by playing children). Seeing this, he told his cousin Eugénie de Grancey, reminded him of the longhouses of "his friends, the Iroquois." If anything, he wrote, it was the Iroquois who were the better housed.[69]

Separated from them was a Protestant landowning aristocracy, living off the rents from their huge estates, largely absent, and openly contemptuous of their Catholic compatriots. "To hear them speak," Tocqueville wrote, one would think that the Catholic population were no more than "savages incapable of understanding what was good for them, fanatics led on to all manner of disorder by their priests."[70] Here, in short, was a country ruined by the tyranny of the English government, the demands of its largely absent English aristocracy, and the greed of a Protestant clergy who, in contrast to their Catholic counterparts, lived a life of idle luxury.

And so it was that on one late July evening in Kilkenny, Tocqueville and Beaumont sat down to compare and contrast the English and Irish aristocracies. In Tocqueville's case, this produced an extended parable entitled "Comment l'aristocratie peut former un des meilleurs et un des plus mauvais gouvernements qui soient au monde."[71] Imagine, Tocqueville began, an aristocracy which had been born on the soil it dominated and whose origin was lost in the distant past. Give to this aristocracy an interest in uniting with the people to resist a power that could oppress them if they stood alone, such that the richer and more enlightened the people were, the more assured was the existence of the aristocracy, the more the rights of the aristocracy were respected, the more also were the rights of the people. Imagine also, he continued, that this aristocracy shared the same language, the same mores and the same religion as the people. Add to this a rising middle class that by degrees comes to share and enjoy the power and privileges of that ancient aristocracy, thereby encouraging the belief that inequality favours the wealth of all. Finally, make this country the centre of commerce, thus allowing everyone to hope that through their hard work they might share in its wealth. If, Tocqueville concluded, you could imagine these things, you would see a people where the upper classes were more brilliant and enlightened, the middle classes richer, and the poor more comfortably off than elsewhere; where the state rested upon the free will of all its citizens; where the people willingly submitted themselves to the law; and where order reigned.

By contrast, Tocqueville continued, imagine a country where the aristocracy was established as conquerors only recently and where the memories of that conquest lived on. Give to this aristocracy a different religion to the conquered and no reason to unite with them but cause to oppress them. Ensure furthermore that this aristocracy has the exclusive power to govern and to enrich itself and prevent the people from having any hopes of improving their condition such that the best they can hope for is not to die. In such a dreadful society, Tocqueville wrote, the aristocracy would have all the faults of oppressors and the people have all the vices of slaves, the law would serve to destroy what it should protect, violence would serve to protect what it should destroy, and religion draw strength from passions it should combat.

These two societies, Tocqueville concluded, both rested upon the principle of aristocracy. The paradox was that, if the two aristocracies had the same origins and the same mores, "the one has for centuries given the English one of the best governments in the world whilst the other has given the Irish one of the most detestable that could ever be imagined." The truth, Tocqueville wrote, was that the character and outcomes of aristocracy were conditioned by circumstances. In England these had been particularly happy ones, in Ireland especially bad ones.[72] Of course, the truth was that the two aristocracies of which Tocqueville spoke were one and the same.

Tocqueville and Beaumont left Ireland on 13 August 1835. Beaumont (for reasons unknown) made his way to Scotland, whilst Tocqueville travelled across Wales from the port of Holyhead and down through central England to Southampton to take the boat to the island of Guernsey and then on to Cherbourg and home. If Tocqueville found himself in awe at the sight of Thomas Telford's massive Menai Suspension Bridge and the nearby Pontcysylite canal aqueduct (both masterpieces of early nineteenth-century engineering) he was less impressed by the English border town of Shrewsbury. Not only, he told his father, was the latter impossible to pronounce (which is true), but it was also "an ugly little town" (which is unfair). Tocqueville's ill humour can partly be accounted for by the fact that he had again fallen ill. As he remarked to Beaumont, the remedy of having to rest up was almost as annoying as the illness itself.[73] Tocqueville had also run out of money.[74]

Worse was to follow when he crossed the English Channel to the island of Guernsey. It was, he recounted, one of the worst nights he could ever remember. Never had he been so sick. A letter to Eugénie de Grancey provides further details of this unpleasant experience. His fellow travellers stank, Tocqueville told her, and so much so that he envied the pigs of Ireland.[75] Fortunately a French cutter took him back to Cherbourg the following day, whereupon Tocqueville took to his bed for two days.[76] His private correspondence gives reason to think that he had more serious matters of concern: all was far from well between his wife-to-be and his family (who remained opposed to his plans to marry). Clearly anxious, a rather desperate note from Tocqueville to Mary Mottley assured her that they were "bound together *for life, until death.*"[77]

Tocqueville was never to work up his notes on Ireland for publication. As he made clear in a letter to Mathieu Molé after his return, this had never been his intention. He had travelled to England, he explained, with one goal in mind: to restore himself to full health and to have the pleasure of observing "a great people" living through "a great Revolution," and this was what he had stuck to. Moreover, he wrote, one would need to be blessed with "an enormous philosophical conceit" to imagine that one could "pass sentence on England in six months."[78] Back in France, Tocqueville therefore quickly threw himself into the writing of volume 2 of *De la démocratie en Amérique* and, as he explained to John Stuart Mill, he had little time for anything but this "*très grand travail.*"[79] Nonetheless, when he arrived in Paris at the end of August he took the time to summarise what he had seen and the conclusions he had drawn. He did this in a long letter to his friend Lord Radnor.

In Ireland, Tocqueville told Radnor, "I saw scenes of misery the memory of which I shall never forget, misery that I have only witnessed among the savage and half-destroyed tribes of the New World." As he had travelled up the Atlantic coast, he had found whole populations reduced to near starvation, entire families sleeping half naked upon the bare earth. Nor did Tocqueville believe that this misery would diminish. Its principal cause, he told Radnor, was the extraordinary separation that existed between the aristocracy and the people, a division that left them at best indifferent to each other, if not enemies. Never, he believed, had the hatred between these classes been as strong as it now was. Landowners, be they Catholic or Protestant, displayed an inhuman insensitivity and visceral loathing of the people. For overtly political reasons the great landowners were chasing their tenant farmers from their land. The population was increasing but manufacturing industry was almost wiped out.[80]

In the remainder of the letter Tocqueville chose to focus on Ireland's Catholic population, drawing heavily upon the conversations he had had with Catholic clergy. Also evident was Tocqueville's sense of self-identification with the oppressed plight of his fellow Catholics. The Catholics of Ireland, Tocqueville began, had many of the seeds of a great nation. But, he continued, they had many of the vices of the oppressed. They feared the law and had a complete contempt for the truth. They displayed servility before those in power but had an exaggerated sense of their own strength, leading them frequently to be arrogant and to commit many mistakes. Good fortune was something new and previously unknown to them and therefore something they yet did not know how to make good use of.[81]

Above all—and here there were clear echoes of the conclusions he had reached in America—Tocqueville saw "an intimate union" between Catholicism and democracy. The "Catholic party," he wrote, was perhaps even more "a democratic party" than it was "a religious faction," and this, he believed, was largely down to the influence of the clergy. "Of all the things I have seen in Ireland," he told Radnor, "the thing it appears to me that most merits the attention of the English government is the Catholic clergy." If, Tocqueville added, it was the aristocracy who possessed the land, it was the clergy who possessed the hearts and the minds of the people. It was they who educated the people and who, "with heart and soul," cared for them and who spoke to them of their liberty and their political rights. And they too who, in their ambition, fostered a hatred against the landowners and the English. Never had he seen a country where religious hatred and political passions combined so dangerously. Poverty, ignorance, fanaticism, memories of persecution, fear and oppression: all these and more convinced him that Ireland was ripe for civil war. Did England, Tocqueville asked, have remedies for these ills? This, he told Radnor, was a question to which he had neither a clear answer nor the pretension to offer a reply.[82]

Tocqueville was not to visit Ireland again. Indeed, he was to make little use of his observations and reflections on Ireland in his future writings and political interventions. It seems likely that he published two unsigned articles on Ireland in October 1844 issues of the journal he owned, *Le commerce*. Both amounted to a damning critique of the power and privileges (and the vices) of the English aristocracy and a Protestant monopoly of power.[83] Again he observed that the people of Ireland were being sacrificed without pity at the altar of the "implacable egoism" of a foreign aristocracy. It can also be argued that what Tocqueville had seen of a closed and parasitic aristocracy in Ireland helped him to conceptualise the character of the aristocracy in prerevolutionary France, thus informing one of the central arguments of his second masterpiece, *L'ancien régime et la révolution*.[84] Beyond this there is little trace.

This was not to be so with Beaumont. As is often the case with the Tocqueville and Beaumont relationship, it is not clear when or how it was decided that it would be Beaumont who would explore Irish issues in greater detail. A letter from Tocqueville to his father, dated 7 May 1835 and written from London, speaks of a mutually advantageous arrangement through which, if they both so chose, Tocqueville would write about America and Beaumont would write about England. Obviously neither had at this point set foot in Ireland but, given that Tocqueville generally referred to the British Isles as England, it is conceivable that Ireland was included in this arrangement. Whatever the case, it was Beaumont who returned (this time with his new wife, Clémentine, and his brother-in-law, Edmond de Lafayette) to England and Ireland during the summer of 1837 and Beaumont who in 1839 was to publish what he himself regarded (with justification) as his best book, *L'Irlande, sociale, politique et religieuse.*[85]

Although strictly speaking this book and Beaumont's accompanying journey fall outside our compass, they merit brief attention if only because both were informed by Tocquevillian perspectives and the experiences of Tocqueville and Beaumont's travels together. Here we can see how Tocqueville might have written a book about Ireland had he chosen to do so or if, as he had done successfully before, he had chosen to collaborate with Beaumont in the writing of such a book.

As he always did, Beaumont kept Tocqueville fully informed of his journey's progress. If there was one thing he could not get accustomed to in Ireland, Beaumont told Tocqueville from Dublin, it was the squalor. Everywhere there were rats, mice, and filthy servants.[86] He also told Tocqueville that, for all of the inconveniences he faced, the trip was extremely productive—more productive, he told Tocqueville, than the trip they had made together in 1835. By his own account, he met all the most eminent people in Dublin. He also went to Ulster, in the north of the country, to witness the Orange Order celebrations of Protestant victory at the Battle of the Boyne. Cries of "No Popery" were hurled at his face and, along with the pope, he was sent to hell. From a French perspective, he told Tocqueville, it was hard to conceive of such an explosion of religious fervour.[87] Later he was to tell Tocqueville that, for all its merits, his book on Ireland did not bear comparison with *De la démocratie en Amérique.*[88] Nonetheless, it was most certainly a book that owed much to Tocqueville and Beaumont's travels together.

If, then, in true Tocquevillian vein, Beaumont believed that there was no alternative but to travel to the country oneself and to try to see it and judge it through one's own eyes and to always seek the truth, to examine the evidence as fairly and as objectively as possible, his overarching explanatory framework for an understanding of the Irish situation was precisely the one that he and Tocqueville had come to identify when they were in America—namely, the providential fact of the advent and development of democracy.

"In our times," Beaumont wrote in his preface, "there exists no phenomenon more significant or worthier of attention than the advance of the democratic principle in all modern societies." In every country it carried forth the "dogma of civil and political equality." It touched everyone, whatever their condition. It penetrated all classes and ranks. It had established itself in mores and, through mores, it had passed into law. It was changing the face of the world, Beaumont wrote. But, if the manner of its working was "constant and universal, it was not everywhere the same."[89]

Here again the impact of Beaumont and Tocqueville's travels together was immediately visible. As a consequence of this democratic principle, Beaumont continued, "most European aristocracies are declining" but "there exists one country, England, where the aristocracy is still full of life, where civil and political inequality, embodied in the law, is preserved in its entirety in mores; where old feudal privilege finds itself so particularly intermingled with the youngest and boldest of liberties; such that, on seeing the absolute authority exercised in this country by birth and wealth, one would think it behind all other nations, whilst solely on the basis of the well-being and liberty of the people, one would think it in advance of all others." The English aristocracy, Beaumont continued, was "the only noble and worthy adversary of modern democracy." It fought valiantly to defend its rights and, by its energy and skill, showed that it would defend its privileges until its last breath. No aristocracy was more popular, nor more criticised, because none was more popular or capable of provoking more hostility. Whereas other aristocracies vegetated or expired in the shadows, the English aristocracy lived and fought in broad daylight. It stood alone against "all the forces of modern equality." England, then, had a great role to play in the battle that was taking place between two fundamentally opposed principles of social organisation.[90]

It was precisely at this point that Ireland entered the story. In Beaumont's opinion, Ireland would be "the principal theatre" in which this drama would unfold. It was, he wrote, "from Ireland that democracy blows its most ardent passions upon England, from Ireland that come the blows most capable of shaking the old edifice of the British constitution to its foundations." Ireland, he continued, had suffered seven centuries of oppression under the "English yoke." It had been invaded, seen its religion prescribed, and been deprived of its existence as a nation. Its people had suffered violence, persecution, suffering, and poverty. But this people "had finally escaped from its servitude" and now demanded recompense from the country that had been the source of all its woes. It was this people who "worked to destroy the institutions that England wants to preserve." There was, Beaumont wrote, not one of the sufferings of Ireland that did not "serve to embarrass the English aristocracy."[91]

The task that Beaumont set himself, therefore, was to understand what he described as "this extraordinary situation" and to do so in all its various dimensions. The first of those dimensions was that of politics. "If," he wrote, "it is important to understand how democracies come into existence, it is not without value to know how aristocracies decline or sustain themselves." Nothing more merited our attention than seeing how the government of a people that played such a determining role in the destiny of the world would respond in this struggle. Nor was it without interest to observe how religion aided the cause of liberty. We were, Beaumont argued, witnesses to a process that had begun fifty years earlier and that would continue for at least another half century.[92]

The book itself began with a long historical introduction, framing what, in the terminology of Tocqueville's *De la démocratie en Amérique,* amounted to a sketch of Ireland's "point of departure." And that point of departure was bleak indeed. Here is the very first sentence of Beaumont's account: "The dominion of the English in Ireland, from their invasion of the country in 1169, to the close of the last century, has been nothing but a tyranny."[93] The aim over the centuries had been the complete conquest of the country. The ambition had been to convert Ireland to Protestantism. To that end, the Catholic population was driven from the soil and expelled from the cities. The Irish, Beaumont wrote, "were struck with death or isolation."[94]

Immediately Beaumont observed an important difference between the American and Irish experience of colonisation. In contrast to the United States, where success had depended upon distance from the native soil, in Ireland the English emigrant did not see a permanent home. "To the Norman lord," he commented, "Ireland was a farm; to the British merchant, merely an office." All bore the same dislike of the country in which they temporarily found themselves.[95]

If such was the origin of English power over Ireland, what followed was legal persecution and what Beaumont described, in a phrase redolent of the argument of Tocqueville's *De la démocratie en Amérique,* as "legislative despotism."[96] Violent persecution ceased, to be replaced by a semblance of regularity, but it was, in Beaumont's opinion, no less odious: it killed silently and in cold blood, striking "most deeply into the soul." The people of Ireland were held in a position of debasement and misery. Moreover, and in another argument with clear echoes of what had been learned in America, Beaumont was adamant that legal persecution was not restrained by the limits of the law. "Where tyrannical laws failed," he wrote, "public opinion carried on the oppression."[97] Indeed, according to Beaumont, there was no tyranny worse than one that moderated itself and no bad laws so pernicious as those that now lay dormant but could be reactivated at any moment. "What," he wrote, "is a liberty which I enjoy, only because it does not please a tyrant to take it away?" To this he then added an all-important corollary: "The man who goes to sleep trusting his freedom to the faith of another man deserves to awake a slave." This was precisely the condition to which Ireland and its people had been reduced.[98]

What came next—and again there were clear parallels with the explanatory framework adopted by Tocqueville in *De la démocratie en Amérique*—was a description of the external appearance (or external configuration) of Ireland, but this was a description that focused less on its landscape and geography than the mores of its downtrodden people. Once more, it was an account that relied heavily on firsthand experience of what was being described—Beaumont repeatedly referred to those he had met and what he had seen on his travels—and which did not hesitate to draw comparisons between the fate of the Irish and that of Native and Black Americans. "I have seen," Beaumont wrote, "the Indian in his forests and the Negro in his chains and thought, as I contemplated their pitiable condition, that I saw the very extreme of human wretchedness; but I did not know then the condition of unfortunate Ireland."[99] Like the American Indian, the Irishman was poor and naked but he in contrast lived in a society of luxury and wealth, where he saw people enjoying comforts to which he could not aspire. Nor in his shared destitution did the Irishman enjoy the independence and dignity that alleviated many of the Indian's sufferings. The Irishman, in brief, had "neither the liberty of the savage nor the bread of servitude."[100] "There are misfortunes so far beyond the pale of humanity," Beaumont concluded, "that human language has no words to represent them."[101]

Beaumont detailed at considerable length how this system of oppression worked, showing how an institution such as the parish—which, in England, gave "life and vigour to the principles of popular liberty"—only served further to impoverish the Irish and to promote the Protestant ascendency.[102]

How might this appalling situation be reformed? This was the subject of the second half of the tract. First, Beaumont placed much store in even the limited liberties enjoyed by the Irish population. Liberty, he wrote, might not prevent tyranny and oppression but "it fixes its limits; it is a weapon in the hands of the weak."[103] Each day freedom of the press allowed the evils endured by Ireland to be subjected to merciless publicity. Next, he argued that there was plenty of evidence to suggest that Ireland was becoming a democratic country. Here he cited numerous factors, including the work of the Catholic Association. "It is one of the peculiar characters of the Association," Beaumont wrote, again echoing themes from *De la démocratie en Amérique,* "that it not only keeps a watch on government, but exercises the functions of government itself."[104] This included the setting up of schools and of charitable foundations.

What Beaumont quite definitely did not endorse was the widely advocated policy that the Irish should embark upon mass emigration to remove the "surplus population." "If," he wrote, "by some magical spell, millions of paupers could be at once transported from Ireland, their place would soon be filled by the overflowing of that well-spring of misery which is never dried up."[105]

What, then, was to be done? Somewhat optimistically, Beaumont thought that "violent and sanguinary destruction" could be avoided, although he did believe that there would be a need for the centralisation of power, as this would be the only way that the privileges of the aristocracy could be abolished. In a Tocquevillian vein, Beaumont added that he saw this only as a means to an end and not "as a final form of government."[106] Next, he advocated land reform designed to produce a population of landed proprietors. This, he thought, could be attained through "equitable and legitimate measures," foremost amongst which would be the abolition of primogeniture. Then came the absolute necessity of abolishing the supremacy of the Anglican Church and with that the establishment of an equality of creeds and religious liberty. The selling of the Anglican Church's huge estates in small lots would itself create a large number of new landowners. Thus, Beaumont concluded, "the most indispensable of all religious reforms would lead to the most salutary of all social reforms." Yet Beaumont saw little political will in England to bring about significant reform.[107]

Was Ireland then condemned to eternal suffering? Here, with great prescience, Beaumont saw how the tragedy of Ireland would not let England be, that it would continue to poison British public life for decades to come. "It is this people of paupers, this people of rags, this people of slaves," Beaumont wrote, "that now becomes to its tyrants a source of embarrassment and peril."[108] Obstinacy, he rightly predicted, would only increase the likelihood of civil war and general insurrection. We were, in brief, faced by what Beaumont described as "a situation vast and covered by darkness." This, he believed, would remain the case until "the democratic principle" had worked its way through the world. Only then would the aristocracy have been overthrown, and only this would render "possible an accordance between two peoples condemned to a common life."[109]

In other words, like Tocqueville in *De la démocratie en Amérique,* Beaumont could ultimately do no more than locate Ireland and its destiny within what he saw as the general movement of humanity. This alone assured him that a democratic future was possible for Ireland. But he ended his text with a broader reflection on the immorality and iniquitous consequences of bad government. "There are occurring at the moment," Beaumont wrote, "amongst the two greatest nations that ocean separates, two phenomena of the same nature, which deserve to engage the attention of the world." In the United States, a country where "the progress of humanity [is] so constant and so extraordinary," a "deep and hideous wound" existed: slavery. Despite the efforts of religion and humanity, he wrote, "the leprosy is extending, it is blighting pure institutions, it is poisoning the felicity of the present generation, and already depositing the seeds of death in a body full of life." At the same time, Beaumont continued, "England exhausts herself in useless efforts to shake off a nation which she took six centuries to conquer and struggles vainly under the miseries of her slave." Why had both these nations reached such a sad and similar situation? Both, Beaumont answered, had committed "a primary act of violence, followed by a long course of injustice," and both, he added, would voluntarily give up these pernicious paths if they could, but to do so was not easy. "When the solemn violations of morality and justice have been continued for centuries," Beaumont wrote, "the deep perturbation which they have produced in the moral order must endure long after they have ceased." The tyrant who recognised his errors, in other words, could not escape the consequences of his iniquity. There was, Beaumont added, "happiness in recognising that selfishness, injustice, and violence bring with them retributions as infallible as their excesses." This, therefore, is how Beaumont ended his analysis of the evils inflicted upon the unfortunate nation of Ireland: "There are those who believe that individuals and peoples are led by fatality to crime. This opinion is false; it is injurious to humanity which, by such a theory, cannot be acquitted of crime without being deprived of virtue. The crimes of peoples, like those of individuals, are voluntary, not necessary acts. There is nothing necessary but the consequence of crimes; nothing predestined but their expiation."[110]

If Tocqueville did not join Beaumont on his second trip to Ireland, it was not to be long before he resumed his travels. In 1836, and on what appears to have been a belated honeymoon, Tocqueville set off for Switzerland with his wife. The first glimpse we have in Tocqueville's correspondence of this new journey comes in a letter to Louis de Kergorlay, sent from Strasbourg and dated 16 July. In some respects it must be regarded as one of the most compelling and intimate of Tocqueville's many letters. It began by recounting that Tocqueville had stayed in Metz with his friend, Eugène Stoffels, and his wife. Madame Stoffels, he reported, was a lot more impressive than he had been led to believe from "the incoherent accounts of her husband." Yet, he continued, only the kindness of the Stoffelses had made his stay tolerable. For it had been in Metz, where Tocqueville's father had been appointed as government prefect in 1817, that Tocqueville had first fallen in love. Early one morning, he wrote to Kergorlay, he had made his way to the Préfecture and asked permission to enter the garden. It was hard, he continued, to express the emotion he felt after an absence of thirteen years. To Kergorlay, Tocqueville wrote, all would have looked the same, but to Tocqueville himself each minor change had "plunged him into the most profound sadness." Then he had found one of his father's old servants, someone who had known the family of his first love, Rosalie Malye. Her sister, Amélie, he learned, had died in childbirth. As for Rosalie, she had two children and was happy, and was still living in the nearby town of Bitche. I could not resist, he told Kergorlay, "writing her a note that she could show to her husband in the same way that I might show it to Marie in which I told her of my sorrow at the death of her sister and the pleasure I felt on learning that she was happy and well." He did not feel, he wrote, a regret for past times but "an overwhelming sentiment of the weakness of the human heart which lets go so quickly of what it believed so firmly grasped, of the fleeting passage of time, of the mutability of man, his lack of constancy, of the emptiness and nothingness of life." He was, Tocqueville told Kergorlay, only too pleased to leave the city.[111]

Yet, as Tocqueville was to report to Pierre Paul Royer-Collard from Baden in late August, what had been intended to be a pleasure trip quickly turned into an attempted health cure. Not for the last time, Madame de Tocqueville had fallen ill, and they had been obliged to leave Berne to take the waters at the famous spa town. "Imagine," Tocqueville wrote, "a fairly deep ravine above which hang three or four houses inhabited by bathers; below, a torrent which runs noisily over rocks and towards which flow small streams of warm water forced to pass through channels to emerge finally through faucets; surround all of this with a lukewarm and lightly sulphuric atmosphere and you will have a fairly accurate picture of the place." Fortunately, he told Royer-Collard, he had thrown a few books rather haphazardly into his trunk before leaving Paris and thus, as Madame de Tocqueville bathed (to seeming little effect in the sulphuric waters), Tocqueville had set about reading Machiavelli, Bossuet's *Histoire des variations des églises protestantes,* and Plato's *Laws.*[112] Indeed, Tocqueville somehow found time to write a substantial commentary on Machiavelli's *History of Florence.*[113] In Berne, as he was to do on all of his travels, Tocqueville also wrote a set of notes, mainly on the Swiss constitution.[114] What fun the newlyweds must have been having.[115]

Despite Switzerland's long-established reputation as a country of peace and bourgeois normality, the country was in a state of near civil war. As the British historian Christopher Hughes wrote, this was a "time of freebooters, of assassins and usurpations, of adventurers and fiery speeches."[116] Tocqueville was none too impressed by what he saw. From Berne he told Francisque de Corcelle that he had come to Switzerland more as an admirer of nature than as a philosopher, but every time he read a newspaper or entered a conversation he felt compelled to try to understand what he had learned. Thus, he wrote, "in my capacity as an *American,* I have already conceived a very lofty disdain for the federal constitution of Switzerland, which I unceremoniously call a league and not a federation." A government of this kind, he continued, "is the most lax, powerless, blundering and incapable that one could imagine" and was fit only to lead a people to anarchy. The monarchical state of England was a hundred times more republican. How, Tocqueville pondered, could this be explained? The answer, he conjectured, had nothing to do with differences of race—an explanation, Tocqueville added, that he would only ever accept when all else failed—but lay in the little-known fact that "communal liberty" was at best a recent development in most of the Swiss cantons. The urban bourgeoisie governed the countryside in the same centralised way as royal power had done in France.[117]

Tocqueville's notes on the Swiss constitution confirm the poor impression he had quickly formed. There were cantons, he remarked, but no Switzerland. In most of these, he continued, the majority of people lacked any sense of "self-government"; the Swiss habitually abused freedom of the press; they saw associations much as the French did, as a revolutionary means rather than as "a slow and quiet way to arrive at the rectification of wrongs"; they had no sense of the benefits derived from "the peaceful and legal introduction of the judge into the domain of politics"; and, finally, "at the bottom of their souls the Swiss show no deep respect for law, no love of legality, no abhorrence of the use of force, without which there cannot be a free country." In summary, Tocqueville concluded, "someone who travels across the United States feels involuntarily and instinctively the powerful sense that the institutions, taste and spirit of liberty blend with all the habits of the American people." Similarly, one could not imagine that an Englishman could live under anything other than a free government. But, he continued, "if, in the majority of the Swiss cantons, violence destroyed the republican constitution one senses that, after a short period of transition, the people would soon accustom themselves to their loss of liberty." Liberty, in short, had no deep roots in the mores of the Swiss.[118]

In fact, Tocqueville had already alluded to the weaknesses of the Swiss constitution in the first volume of *De la démocratie en Amérique.* There, when distinguishing the Constitution of the United States from the constitutions of Switzerland, the German Empire, and the Dutch Republics, he had remarked that "among these different peoples, the federal government has always remained deficient and weak, while that of the Union conducts public affairs with vigour and ease." This was true of America, Tocqueville concluded, because the Americans had deployed what amounted to "a great discovery in the political science of today"—namely, that the federal government should not only have the right to pass laws but also to execute them. By contrast, Tocqueville wrote, "In all the confederations that have preceded the American Union of today, the federal government, in order to provide for its needs, applied to individual governments. In the case where the prescribed measure displeased one of them, the latter could always elude the need to obey." The result was "civil war or slavery or inertia."[119]

This judgement was very much confirmed by Tocqueville's stay in Switzerland during 1836. His notes frequently make the point that the Swiss had not wished to establish a federal government but a defensive league. Consequently, the federal executive was powerless, the legislative branch was confined and constrained, and there was no federal judicial power. In sum, the Swiss did not have a government to speak of.

This remained Tocqueville's view in the years to come. To a Swiss correspondent, Auguste de la Rive, he voiced concern and regret at the overturning of Geneva's aristocratic constitution in November 1841, only for him to add three years later, as political and religious disputes intensified, that the Swiss confederation looked to him "to be more divided, more troubled and, consequently, weaker than it has ever been." As for a possible remedy, he told De la Rive, he saw none.[120]

This was a view that Tocqueville repeatedly articulated by way of comparison with the happier experience of the Americans. In 1845, he published two short articles on Switzerland in *Le commerce.*[121] If the first expressed his considerable concern that Europe's great powers were seeking to interfere in the internal affairs of Switzerland in ways that were contrary to the diplomatic and strategic interests of France, the second strongly reiterated his view that the "anarchy" of Switzerland derived primarily from its hopeless and ineffective constitution. The solution, he suggested, lay not in destroying the federal constitution altogether and establishing a "unitary republic" but rather in learning lessons from America. "Let us compare," Tocqueville wrote, "the constitution of the United States of America with that of Switzerland: Congress has no more rights than the Diet,[122] so why does Congress do what the Diet does not do? Because it has instruments which belong to it in its own right; because, in order to put its wishes into effect, it has no need, as is the case with the Diet, to borrow its means of action from another power." If and when, he concluded, "the taxpayer refuses to pay, the soldier to march, and the customs officer to obey, it has its courts which represent only itself and which oblige the citizens to obey its laws." Nor was this an idle matter. "Upon the tranquillity of Switzerland," Tocqueville wrote, "may depend the peace of Europe."[123]

Two years later a short-lived civil war broke out in Switzerland with the formation of the Sonderbund (or secret alliance) by seven predominantly Catholic cantons. Again, Tocqueville was to have his say, this time in a lengthy commentary on *De la démocratie en Suisse* by the Genevan writer Antoine-Elysée Cherbuliez. For the past fifteen years, Tocqueville commented, Switzerland had been in a situation of almost permanent revolution. Its government was "irregular in its behaviour, precipitate in its decisions, and tyrannical in its actions."[124] The Federal Constitution of Switzerland was "the most imperfect of all the constitutions of its kind yet to be seen in the world." This time Tocqueville compared it unfavourably to the constitution of the state of New York.[125]

Yet, as always, Tocqueville saw events in Switzerland from a much broader perspective. "What is happening in Switzerland," he wrote, "is no isolated phenomenon. It is a particular instance of a general movement that is hastening the ruin of the entire fabric of European institutions. The stage may be small, but there is greatness in the play." Nowhere else, he continued, "is the democratic revolution which is shaking the world taking place in such strange and complicated circumstances."[126]

Tocqueville delivered this commentary to the Académie des sciences morales et politiques in January 1848, a matter of a few weeks before France itself was engulfed by revolution and the Second Republic came into being.

It is perhaps this circumstance that also explains why Tocqueville insisted on including this seemingly obscure text as an appendix to the twelfth edition of *De la démocratie en Amérique* published later that year as France grappled not only with its own civil war but the arduous task of framing a new constitution. Clearly Tocqueville felt that there were lessons for France to learn from what he had seen in Switzerland.

CHAPTER FIVE

Algeria

It was not only the domestic circumstances of Alexis de Tocqueville and Gustave de Beaumont that changed during the 1830s. Both men resolved to enter politics, and both, after defeats in the parliamentary elections of 1837, were elected to the Chamber of Deputies in 1839—Tocqueville in March of that year and Beaumont in December.[1] As a parliamentarian Tocqueville used the expertise he had gained in America to make a series of interventions on subjects he knew well—most notably, prison reform and the issue of slavery. But, like many Frenchmen of his class and generation, he felt deeply France's post-1815 international humiliation and, for all of his admiration of England, he came strongly to believe that France needed to combat British imperial expansion, especially in North Africa. In line with this, Tocqueville was to establish himself as one of the French Parliament's foremost authorities on Algeria.[2] To that end, he travelled to Algeria twice: in 1841, with his brother Hippolyte and Gustave de Beaumont; and in 1846 with his wife, Mary. These trips, and the extensive writings on Algeria that preceded and postdated them, are without doubt the most controversial aspects of his life and career.[3]

The decision to send an expeditionary force to invade the Regency of Algiers (nominally part of the Ottoman Empire) and its environs was made in January 1830.[4] Tocqueville saw that the purpose of this invasion was in part to bolster political support for a regime that was fast entering its last days.[5] The actual invasion began on 14 June. From the outset it was beset with difficulties, not least the fierce resistance of its inhabitants. Nor was it to be without controversy. Tocqueville was fortunate (if that is the right word) to receive a firsthand account of the initial French attack from Louis de Kergorlay, who served as an officer in the French artillery. It makes for unedifying reading. "The Arabs or Bedouins," Kergorlay told Tocqueville, "are a squalid and despicable race" and so much so that they could not understand why the French did not cut the throats of their prisoners. The best way to deal with them, Kergorlay wrote, was with either bayonets or shells. Moreover, Kergorlay was strongly of the view that, once the war was over, the French should set about colonising the area. This, he told Tocqueville, would be a good way to destroy the ascendancy enjoyed by the English in the Mediterranean. He also saw that the establishment of a colony would require the settlement of a European population.[6] Ever the adventurer, in 1833 Kergorlay appears to have suggested that he and Tocqueville should buy land in Algeria. Nothing came of this.[7] However, it was at this time that Tocqueville made his first inquiry about learning Arabic.[8]

We also know that Tocqueville was not overly optimistic about the capacity of the French to establish overseas colonies. When he and Beaumont were in the process of completing their study of the penitentiary system in the United States, they penned a short text entitled "Quelques idées sur les raisons qui s'opposent à ce que les français aient de bonnes colonies." The extent to which these comments were inspired by their visit in 1831 to French Canada is difficult to gauge, but at the time Tocqueville expressed his disappointment that his fellow French citizens showed such little interest in the fate of their compatriots on the other side of the Atlantic. The foremost difficulty, Tocqueville and Beaumont now argued, was to be found in the "French genius." The French had a natural taste for quiet pleasures and the domestic hearth, and so it was almost impossible to convince "the poor and honest population of our countryside to leave their homeland to seek their fortune." If ever they did find themselves on another shore, they showed no great inclination to cultivate the land and to make anything of it, trapped as they were by "the charms of an idle and drifting life."[9]

To the difficulties arising out of the French national character were to be added those emanating from France's political traditions. In brief, the habits of administrative centralisation were ill suited to the running of colonies. "If," Tocqueville and Beaumont wrote, "the central government finds it impossible to assess wisely and to resolve in good time the difficulties that arise in a nearby province of the country, this will be even more the case when it has to concern itself with problems arising three thousand leagues away." In addition, the political education received by French subjects left them ill equipped and unwilling to direct their own affairs. "If individual energy and the art of governing oneself are useful in all societies," they wrote, "this is even more so in those that begin and develop as colonies in forced isolation." The English, if not the French, had understood this, as the experience of the New World amply demonstrated. Thus, Tocqueville and Beaumont concluded, "we must recognise, because experience proves this to be the case, that to found a colony is for France to give the country up to an enterprise full of risks and with no guarantee of success."[10]

For all of these doubts, Tocqueville was undeniably attentive to the possibilities of a French presence in North Africa. Evidence of this is found in two "Lettres sur l'Algérie" published in the Versailles-based newspaper *La presse de Seine-et-Oise* during the summer of 1837.[11] The first began with a confession by Tocqueville to his readers: he had never been to Algeria. This, he wrote, was not something of which he was proud, as "I take the everyday view that in order to inform others about something, it is useful to know it oneself, and that to know something well, it is not without use to have seen it."[12] The best he could do therefore was to rely upon the testimony of his friends and "make it as little apparent as possible that I have never seen the things I am trying to portray."[13]

What followed was an account of "what Algeria was before our conquest." This amounted to a detailed portrayal of the character and practices of the distinct populations (or "principal races") that inhabited the area—the nomadic Arabs on the coastal plains, the sedentary Berbers (or Kabyles) in the mountains—as well as a description of earlier Turkish domination in the region. Of the Kabyles, Tocqueville wrote that had Jean-Jacques Rousseau known them, "he would have found men subject to a form of social police and who nonetheless are almost as free as the isolated individual who enjoys his uninhibited independence in the heart of the woods."[14] As for the Arabs, "like all half-savage peoples, they esteem power and force above all else."[15] The "supposed Turkish government" was dismissed as "not truly speaking a government but a continuation of conquest, a violent exploitation of the vanquished by the victor."[16]

Tocqueville's second letter on Algeria could not have been more different in tone and substance. Here we see a young man eager to convince his potential electors not only of his expertise but also of his political acumen. What he sought to offer was a way forward from the military impasse in which France now found itself. Tocqueville began by asking his readers to imagine that France had been invaded by the emperor of China and that the emperor had set about governing his new territory without any regard to the laws, religion, customs, administrative practices and languages of his conquered people. Such, he suggested, was the way France had sought to impose its rule upon Algeria. The administration of the past had been destroyed completely and, in its place, had been substituted a French administration that had no knowledge of the customs and practices of the people it now ruled over. "I ask you," Tocqueville wrote, "to try to picture these agile and indomitable children of the desert entwined into the thousand formalities of our bureaucracy and forced to submit to the slowness, to the procedures, to the paper documents and minutiae of our centralised administration."[17] The result was anarchy. The wiser course—here Tocqueville spoke with some prescience—would have been to "have put ourselves in the place of the defeated" and to "for a time have bent to their ways," to have accepted their traditions and respected their practices.[18]

Mistakes having been made, what was the way forward? Of one thing Tocqueville was certain: it was not in the French interest that the indigenous Arabs should be united under one ruler. "Our present safety, and concern for the future," he wrote, "demand that there be at least three or four."[19] Beyond this, Tocqueville affirmed, in Algeria the French "must take care to give up this taste for uniformity" and understand that "it would be as dangerous as it is absurd to apply the same rules" to different peoples.[20] In short, where the French and Arabs lived together, different legislations should apply. Likewise, the legislation that governed the French in Africa should not be exactly the same as that in France. "We need in Africa, as in France, and indeed even more so than in France," he continued, "essential guarantees for the individual living in society; there is nowhere where it is more necessary to establish individual liberty, respect for property, and guarantees of all rights than in a colony."[21]

Given this, what were Tocqueville's hopes for the new colony? "The future," he wrote, "seems to be in our hands . . . with time, perseverance, ability and justice, I have no doubt that we will be able to raise a great monument to our country's glory on the African coast."[22] How did Tocqueville justify such optimism? In part, by conjecturing that the Arabs would "sell land readily and cheaply" and thus that a foreign population "could easily establish itself . . . without causing them to suffer." As a result, the French, "richer and more industrious" than the Arabs, would come to "occupy a large part of the land without violence" and "peacefully." It was therefore "easy to foresee a time in the near future when the two races will be intermingled." "Everything I have learned about Algeria," Tocqueville added, "leads me to believe that this possibility is not as fanciful as many people imagine."[23] Moreover, he was persuaded that, although the Arab population preserved "a lively faith" in Islam, the power of these religious beliefs was steadily waning, such that, if the French could convince the Arabs that Islam was "in no danger under our domination," enmities arising from religious passions could be "extinguished." Nor did Tocqueville believe that the "civil customs" of the Arabs would prevent "a communal life" with the French. "I have no doubt," he wrote, "that they would adopt our style of life should we give them a lasting interest to do so."[24] There was then no reason to believe that time would not see the amalgamation of "the two races." God, Tocqueville concluded, was not stopping it; only human shortcomings were.[25]

All of this, as Tocqueville again acknowledged, was seen "from a distance" and "in ignorance of the details."[26] Perhaps this explains why Tocqueville drew no parallels between what he had seen firsthand of the dire fate of Native Americans and the likely outcome of French colonisation for the indigenous population in Algeria. At this point, Algeria appeared to offer little else but prosperity, racial harmony, and national prestige. What mattered now was that Tocqueville should see the country for himself. It was this, as he was to tell his electoral agent in Normandy, which was to become his next "great journey."[27]

It was to be a journey prepared with typical thoroughness. We know that Tocqueville read and annotated a considerable portion of the Koran during 1838.[28] Whilst he saw that the "Koran contains more or less all the general moral principles contained in all religions," there was much of which he clearly disapproved, not least the call to jihad and the sanction of violence against idolaters and Jews. To Francisque de Corcelle in the same year, he admitted that the Koran made for a tiring but instructive read, adding that he was "not yet tempted to become a Muslim."[29] Two days later, he told Louis de Kergorlay that, if the Koran was undoubtedly an advance on polytheism, he could not see that it was in any way superior to the Gospels.[30] In both letters he described Islam as at best an able compromise between "spiritualism and materialism, the angel and the beast." Its overall impact upon humanity had been "more harmful than salutary."[31]

Tocqueville next worked his way through a considerable amount of official documentation, most notably the French Ministry of War's *Le tableau de la situation des établissements français dans l'Algérie*.[32] By his own admission, what Tocqueville did not read was what he described to Gustave de Beaumont as "the books of [Amédée] Desjobert and company." His excuse was one we have heard before: as he told Beaumont, he wanted to avoid polemical material that might confuse his thoughts.[33] This was a significant omission, as Desjobert was not only a fellow parliamentary deputy but also, as Jennifer Pitts has shown, an articulate critic of French attempts to colonise Algeria by force. In Desjobert's view, trade was preferable to attempted military conquest—the costs of which, he believed, would far outweigh any possible benefits. He also questioned whether a new colonial empire in North Africa was necessary for the restoration of French national prestige.[34]

Nonetheless, Tocqueville sought to familiarise himself with the situation of Algeria before the French conquest and with how it was operating under French colonial rule. What he read about property rights, the justice system, taxation, commerce and industry, shipping, fishing, and much more was by no means reassuring. He saw that Islamic conceptions of property rights stipulating that most property was inalienable were not conducive to the project of colonisation. He thought it absurd that the French law of patents had been introduced into Algeria and that a forestry service had been introduced when there were no forests. But what concerned him above all was that since 1830 the French had set about introducing a system of arbitrary rule and governance. "It is inconceivable," Tocqueville wrote, "that in our day a nation that calls itself liberal should have established, close to France and in the name of France, a government so disordered, so tyrannical, so irksome, so profoundly illiberal . . . and so very alien to the elementary notions of a good colonial regime." One saw, he continued, "men, generals and administrators who . . . seize with delight the occasion at last to act free from all hindrances and to satisfy passions and tastes inflamed by constraint in a country whose exceptional situation serves them as a pretext."[35]

There was more to such a "monstrous state" than this. France, Tocqueville wrote, was "a country where life was sweet and secure." Why would anyone leave it in order to live in another country where property could be sequestered, where the system of justice was barbarous, where there was no freedom of the press, no freedom of education, no system of representation, and where the state operated without even the limited constraints observed in France? Worse still, having accepted all this and finally arrived in Algeria, the new immigrant would find that "the caprice of a governor could, with a *lettre de cachet,* exile him from the country, ruin his new life, and in a moment destroy his future."[36]

The conclusions reached by Tocqueville after this extensive reading of official documentation were succinctly summarised in a letter written to Francisque de Corcelle in September 1840. Studying this material, he confided, had confirmed his previous opinions but had also added an element of sadness. "I think," he wrote, "that we will never achieve in Algeria all the great things that have deluded us and that, when all is said and done, we have a pretty paltry possession." Nevertheless, Tocqueville continued, he remained more convinced than ever that "there was no middle course between complete surrender and, if I do not say conquest, complete domination." To wish to live in a small part of the country whilst being surrounded by an Arab power which could only survive by waging war against France was not a practical option.[37]

The context here was something that Tocqueville did not comment on directly—namely, the fact that the French Army in Algeria had suffered serious military reverses (most notably at the Battle of Macta in June 1835) with heavy casualties. An attempt to bring peace to the region had been made through the signing of the Treaty of Tafna in 1837. If this entailed a recognition of elements of French imperial sovereignty on the part of Abd-el-Kadar, the leader of the Algerian tribes, it also involved the secession of approximately two-thirds of the country to him. In effect, French occupation was restricted to the Mediterranean ports and coastal region. This uneasy peace came to an end in 1839 when the French Army had sought to break out of this narrow enclave, only to meet stiff and successful military resistance again at the hands of Abd-el-Kadar and his well-disciplined fighters. What followed was sporadic violence between the French occupying forces and the indigenous population, leading in February 1841 to the appointment of General (later Marshal) Thomas-Robert Bugeaud as French governor-general.

Bugeaud was intent on securing military victory by any means. This he was to do to great effect and with considerable controversy, most notably through the deployment of a scorched-earth strategy—the so-called razzia—designed to starve the population into submission. Later were to come the infamous *enfumades,* where those—including women and children—who had taken refuge in caves were asphyxiated and sometimes the caves walled up. Abd-el-Kadar was eventually to surrender in December 1847. For our purposes, what matters is that we recognise that at the time when Tocqueville was undertaking his preliminary studies of Algeria, political opinion in France was at best ambivalent about the wisdom and merits of French intervention in North Africa. This ambivalence was only to deepen in the 1840s.[38] A century-long tragedy was beginning to unfold.

Tocqueville and Beaumont had originally planned to depart on what Tocqueville described as their "political pilgrimage" in September 1840, but the so-called Oriental Crisis of that year and the subsequent signing of the Convention of London by Great Britain, Austria, Prussia, and Russia (to the exclusion of France) guaranteeing the integrity of the Ottoman Empire convinced them that it was best to stay in Paris. It was not beyond the bounds of possibility that France and Great Britain would again be at war with each other—something, to the dismay of John Stuart Mill, that Tocqueville appeared almost to welcome.[39] National pride was again at stake, and, as he wrote to Pierre-Paul Royer-Collard, he had "always believed that what remains of the best of our country is national pride, a pride often puerile and boastful, but which, for all its ridiculousness and weaknesses, is still the most powerful feeling we possess and the most powerful tie that binds this nation together."[40] Such a view, and one he repeated elsewhere, was not unimportant in shaping Tocqueville's response to French involvement in Algeria after 1840.

So it was that after much delay, and with his brother Hippolyte as his and Beaumont's travelling companion, Tocqueville eventually set sail from Toulon on 4 May 1841, arriving in Algiers three days later. What followed was far from what had been planned. Once again, Tocqueville's correspondence and his notebooks provide us with a detailed description of his travels. Moreover, they bear many of the hallmarks of his travels across America. First, Tocqueville had to reach the Mediterranean coast of France, a not insignificant journey before the advent of rail travel. From Valence on the River Rhône he told his wife that this part of France was far more beautiful than he had imagined. He also told her that, much to his annoyance, he had come down with rheumatism. The same letter introduces us to a theme that was to figure prominently in many of those subsequently written from Algeria: he was missing his wife, both emotionally and, by his own frequent admission, sexually. One should not leave home, he told her, when one is happy.[41] It is difficult to know exactly what to make of this. In July 1840 Tocqueville had told Beaumont that he was the only person with whom he would like to visit Algeria, but the Tocqueville marriage was evidently in trouble, and it is hard not to conclude that these repeated expressions of affection were an attempt at reassurance. If we are to believe what Tocqueville wrote, he committed no sexual infidelities whilst in Algeria.

From Valence Tocqueville and his companions took the boat to Avignon and Marseilles, and then on to Toulon, arriving on 2 May. It was only because he and Beaumont were parliamentary deputies, he told his wife, that they were able to get tickets for the ship to Algiers. Having a day to spare before their departure, the two men visited Toulon's arsenal and prison. Tocqueville's rheumatism was much improved, but he was coughing constantly. It was, he wrote, "only a throat cough which does not tire me." All looked set fair for their three-day crossing of the Mediterranean. The sea was as still as a millpond. Nonetheless, Tocqueville was suffering from seasickness by the following day. This was as nothing to the agonies endured by his brother who, Tocqueville recounted, had seemed on the verge of falling away entirely in a fit of apoplexy. By the second evening they had reached Minorca, and two days later they were approaching the coastline of Africa.

Tocqueville was in raptures. First in view was the Cap Caxine, with Algiers behind it. It was, he told his wife, very misty, and before them stretched a

Algiers (Antiqua Print Gallery / Alamy Stock Photo)

long line of furrowed and very green hills that reminded him of the coast of Normandy. Soon the sun had dispersed the mist and "the true Africa appeared": the Atlas Mountains, the Bay of Algiers, the hills that surrounded the town, the whole spectacle sparkling in the sun. Then, to add to Tocqueville's joy, a small boat appeared with his good friend Francisque de Corcelle on board.

What came next very much recalls the manner in which Tocqueville had responded to his first sightings and impressions of America in 1831. His head was in a spin. "Despite the fact that I had read a lot of material," he told his father, "the actual appearance of the places surprised me and as for the inhabitants, for the moment, I see such a prodigious diversity in their opinions that I feel a kind of intellectual dizziness."[42] A similar message was conveyed to his wife, Mary. "I would like to speak to you of Algiers," Tocqueville wrote three days after his arrival, "but it is a place so strange, so different from everything I have seen, so disorderly and so full of contrasts, that my mind is still so confused that I know not what to think or say."[43] There followed a passage that vividly recalls the letter he had sent to Ernest de Chabrol in June 1831 from New York when he had asked his friend to visualize a country peopled by all the nations of the world, all eagerly going about their business. "Imagine," Tocqueville said to his wife, "a collection of all the races, all the costumes, all the languages, European, Asiatic, Arab, Moorish, Kabyle, Negro, each with its own attitudes, all enclosed within a space too small to hold them, bustling away in the labyrinth of the streets of Algiers; imagine too the *swarming* of all this motley multitude and you will have only an imperfect idea of the first sight of this strange town which, for all the disorder that reigns, seems nevertheless blessed with an exceptional energy and from the chaos of which a world will emerge." To his father, he compared Algiers to something from one of the tales of *One Thousand and One Nights.*[44]

Nor was Tocqueville slow to make comparisons with what he had seen in America. On 7 May he wrote in his notebook, "The entire lower town [of Algiers] seems in a state of destruction and reconstruction. On all sides, one sees nothing but recent ruins, and buildings going up; one hears nothing but the noise of the hammer. It is Cincinnati transported onto the soil of Africa."[45] Tocqueville made a similar remark three weeks later when he arrived in what was then the new port of Philippeville. "We disembarked at six o'clock," he recorded. "The town looks American. Two years ago, a single shack. Now 5,000 souls. Houses thrown pell-mell on the hills amid Roman ruins. Disorder, confusion, life."[46]

Like many a traveller to Algeria both before and since, Tocqueville was immediately struck by its natural beauty. To Mary he wrote, "Yesterday we travelled through the neighbourhood. The area roundabout is magnificent. A very picturesque country. A prodigious vegetation this time of year. All of this dotted with charming Moorish houses, orange trees, lemon trees, and a multitude of trees from the south in flower."[47] He said much the same to his father. The temperature was perfect, the sun a pure blue, and the air constantly fresh. The surroundings were magnificent. "At this time of year," Tocqueville concluded, "this country is one of the most beautiful and one of the healthiest that one could live in."[48]

Nonetheless, he sensed immediately that beneath this natural beauty less agreeable things were afoot. If Algeria resembled America, it was also because the colonists were busily destroying what the indigenous population had built. As he confided in his notebook almost immediately upon arrival, "The French are substituting broad arcaded streets for the Moors' tortuous allies. This is a necessity of our civilisation. But they are also substituting their architecture for that of the Moors, and this is wrong." More than this, Tocqueville saw that, for all the surrounding beauty, the French were prisoners in their encampments. As he observed in both his notebooks and in a letter to his wife, one could not travel more than three leagues outside Algiers without fear of being beheaded. Beyond that point began war and what he described, using the English word, as the *wilderness.* One saw not a house or even a tent, only the occasional Arab riding in the distance. "We saw the promised land," he told his wife, "but who knows if the French will ever enter therein?"[49] A comment in his notebooks was even more to the point: "A promised land if one did not have to farm it with a rifle in one's hand."[50]

Tocqueville was undaunted by the challenges that such a dangerous situation might throw up. No sooner had he arrived in Algiers than General Bugeaud returned there with an army flush with military success. As Bugeaud planned his next expedition he offered to take Tocqueville and his travelling companions with him. So, on the evening of 14 May, Tocqueville set out by boat for Mostaganem, arriving there two days later after what was a delightful voyage across a calm sea. "We found ourselves," he told his wife, "in a small town of which the French have burnt down half. The rest is very picturesque." The plan now was to accompany Bugeaud and his army as they advanced on Abd-el-Kadar's desert capital of Tagdempt. A letter to his father and one to Louis de Kergorlay indicate that Tocqueville had already worked out that, in Abd-el-Kadar, the French faced a formidable opponent and one aided by the fanaticism of his followers, but Tocqueville did everything he could to reassure his wife that the forthcoming "military promenade" was no more dangerous than a walk round the park. There was, he told her, nothing to fear from the Arabs, and in any case he and his friends would be surrounded by an army.[51] He similarly tried to reassure his father that he should not be concerned about the safety of Hippolyte de Tocqueville.

Yet Tocqueville did not leave from Mostaganem with Bugeaud's army. At the last moment, and with good cause, he was prevailed upon to stay behind on grounds of his ill health. Beaumont remained with him, but his brother and Corcelle duly marched off into the desert, the former, Tocqueville told his father, "on a very beautiful horse, with a tent." Tocqueville himself was distraught and heartbroken. Nothing, he declared, had ever upset him so much in his entire life. "The moral in all this," he told his wife, "is that one should not embark on such travels when one is in a poor state of health and *married*."[52]

As unreconciled as he was to this turn of events, Tocqueville now resolved to see as much of Algeria as he could, travelling first by boat with Beaumont to the west of the country to visit Oran and Mers-el-Kébir, returning to Algiers on 22 May. They next planned a journey eastward down the coast by boat to Philippeville and then on to Constantine by land. Tocqueville was clearly charmed by the journey to Philippeville and by what he had seen. It was, he told his brother Édouard, the most beautiful journey that he and Beaumont had ever made. The sea was as calm as a river and the weather had been magnificent, without being too hot. Not only this, but they had travelled along a coast the like of which Tocqueville had rarely seen in his life. High mountains covered by trees and pastures up to the summit plunged down into the sea. Through these mountains could be seen charming valleys covered with sheep. It was, he announced, undoubtedly the most beautiful part of the country, even, as he also acknowledged, if you set foot there you were likely to be shot at by the local Kabyle population.[53] Having reached Philippeville with his expectations high, Tocqueville was not to make it to Constantine.

Nonetheless, it was after the decision not to leave with Bugeaud that, for the first time, a clear sense of the purpose of Tocqueville's visit to Algeria emerged. As André Jardin has observed, it was at this point that we see again "the indefatigable investigator whom we saw plaguing the Americans with questions."[54] Upon arrival in Algiers, Tocqueville had told his father that he hoped "this journey will be useful both for us and for the country."[55] His spirits somewhat revived, he informed his wife that he could now see that his earlier annoyance had been "puerile" and that his "real aim in coming to Africa was not to follow soldiers but to study the country as a politician." So, he reported, he and Beaumont had put themselves to work. For the previous week, they had "seen many people, taken lots of notes, and assembled a great number of excellent documents." Their approach was now that of "serious men." Idly strolling about was over. Their trip would indeed serve some useful purpose.[56]

The substance of Tocqueville and Beaumont's conversations and investigations was, as always, recorded in Tocqueville's notebooks. Although these were nowhere near as extensive as the notes taken in America, they provide a vivid picture of what Tocqueville saw and heard. Everything Tocqueville had previously feared might be the case in Algeria proved to be true. His dismay was palpable. As one of his interlocutors, one M. Lepécheux, told them, "here we have the most extreme abuses of French centralisation, applied to a colony—that is, the kind of country that can least bear such a system." Ill-advised and arbitrary decrees rained down from Paris. Endless formalities enforced inaction. Money was wasted. Civil officials thought only of returning to France. Another interviewee, the attorney general—"a very mediocre man, very discouraged, and homesick"—told them that "nothing will come of Algiers; it is a country we should leave as quickly as possible." Worse still was the fact that the military acted much as it wanted and with obvious contempt not only for the Arab population but also towards the civil authorities and the French colonists themselves. "Nothing but force and terror," Tocqueville heard the commander of the Philippeville garrison say of the Arabs, "succeeds with these people." As for the colonists, the same man, the magnificently named Jean-Baptiste-Simon-Arsène d'Alphonse, regarded them as nothing but "a bunch of scoundrels . . . thieves who would be nothing without us." "Listening sadly to these things," Tocqueville commented, "I wondered what could be the future of a country subjected to such men, and where this flood of violence and injustices would end, if not in the revolt of the natives and the ruin of the Europeans?" "What is apparent," he went on, "is not only the coarseness and the violence natural to military power, but the ardent and unintelligent hatred of the soldier for the civilian. . . . We have encountered this imbecilic sentiment at all levels, and General Bugeaud personifies it."[57]

These last remarks were written on 30 May 1841. The following day Tocqueville and Beaumont set out for Constantine, an anticipated journey of three days, and one, he told Édouard de Tocqueville, that was easily made with little risk either to one's life or health. Not for the last time, things did not go according to plan. On either the next day or the day after, Tocqueville came down with dysentery, losing consciousness twice. He had been so weak, he told Mary once he was back in Toulon, that he had been unable to walk and had had to be brought back to Philippeville on a horse-drawn cart, after which, with little sign of physical improvement, he took the first opportunity he could to return to French soil. "My poor love," he wrote, "despite the happiness I feel at having escaped that murderous climate, I feel mortally sad." What had occurred in Philippeville had been "only the culmination of a constantly sickly state in which I had been since my departure from Paris." He had only felt well, he now confessed, for the first two or three days after his arrival in Algiers. To this he then added the following remark: "There is not a brother, or a nurse or a guard, who could have cared for me as well as Beaumont did. . . . Throughout this whole business he showed towards me a devotion that I will never be able to repay."[58]

The next day Tocqueville and Beaumont began their long journey back to Paris, where they arrived over a week later on 21 June. Getting from Lyons to Paris alone had taken them three days, and, prior to that, the Rhône had not been easily navigable. In terms of his own morale, Tocqueville told his wife, the return to Paris had not been as awful as he had feared. His health was also improving, and he could now eat. But there was no hiding the sense of disappointment he felt. He was fed up with everything and with himself. "I cannot reconcile myself," he wrote from Marseilles, "to the way this journey ended when I and others expected so much from it and, instead of thanking God that nothing worse occurred, my unhappy spirit is tormented constantly by thoughts of what I could have done and did not do." Worse still, Tocqueville felt a sense of guilt. "Poor Beaumont," he wrote, could not entirely hide "the cruel disappointment he feels." "I," he continued, "only went to Africa to collect ideas to present in parliament and in certain respects I have attained that goal, although incompletely; but he wanted to write a book and needed to do so to pay for his trip." He spent his time consumed by these "distressing thoughts."[59]

In fact, Tocqueville managed to get over this anguish pretty quickly. Similarly, the sexual ardour he had frequently referred to in his letters from Algeria seems to have assuaged (much to the annoyance of his wife, who had to wait a further ten days before he showed up in Normandy).[60] The truth was that, upon his arrival in the French capital, Tocqueville heard the news that Jean-Gérard Lacuée de Cessac, one of the forty members of the Académie française, had died. Tocqueville started his campaign to replace him immediately with what turned out to be success in December of that year.[61]

A question remained as to what use, if any, Tocqueville and Beaumont were to make of their travels to Algeria. Tocqueville still had some recovering to do. He had arrived in Tocqueville, he told Pierre-Paul Royer-Collard, in "a state of convalescence." As late as October 1841, he reported to his brother Édouard that his health was not that bad, but he could work little and had to live a quiet life. The same letter complained that, for the past three weeks, the weather in Normandy had been so awful that he had scarcely dared to take a step outdoors. The following month he was still complaining, this time telling Beaumont that he was suffering from a violent fever that might be a return of his Algerian illness.

Yet Tocqueville was undoubtedly working, if not at full pace.[62] "During this unhappy summer," he told Édouard de Tocqueville, "I have tried to put the finishing touches to a few pieces of work, including my notes on Algeria."[63] The same month Beaumont told Tocqueville that he had been mulling over his own notes on Algeria and wondering what to do with them. Despite the fact that he felt he needed a second trip to Algeria to complete his inquiries, he wrote, "I am inclined to put pen to paper and, if possible, quickly write a volume in six weeks to two months in which I would develop the following three themes: 1. the defects and unproductiveness of a purely warlike system; 2. the necessity of combining colonisation with war; 3. the necessity of putting in place in Africa the foundations of a civil society and what ought to be its bases."[64]

Tocqueville replied almost immediately to say that he could not think of a better way for Beaumont to spend the next two months than in writing about Algeria. "It is a very important question," he commented, "about which we are sufficiently well informed to be able to put many new and true ideas into circulation. To do so would be of use to the country, of use to us, and, I would add, to me, as we cannot be separated on this subject." Tocqueville then added that, for the past three months, he had been working "in fits and starts" on writing something on the same subject. "I will send you this *factum,*" he continued, "whenever you wish. It is badly and loosely written like all work done over several occasions and without a view to publication. Accuracy and detail are missing everywhere, as I had no documents to hand. They are still in Paris."[65]

A month later, on 15 November, he wrote to Beaumont to say that his brother Hippolyte was bringing the text to Paris. He had just reread it for the first time, he told Beaumont: "In it there are a few ideas which appear to me to be good but almost all of them are yours or are known to you. They are connected together by lots of useless padding."[66]

The above remarks are important to bear in mind when we examine the content of Tocqueville's text.[67] In short, it was not intended for publication (and indeed was not published until 1962), was written in haste, and was, at best, an undeveloped sketch of his thoughts. It also very clearly reflected the precise moment in which it was written. Tensions and rivalries between France and Great Britain, especially over the Orient, remained as strong as ever, and it was in the context of the major diplomatic crisis of 1840 that French policy began its decisive shift towards establishing territorial sovereignty in North Africa.[68]

"I do not believe," Tocqueville began, that "France can think seriously of leaving Algeria. In the eyes of the world such a withdrawal would be a clear indication of our decline."[69] By staying, on the other hand, France's "influence in the general affairs of the world would be strongly increased." Moreover, were France to quit, another European power would undoubtedly replace it. "In brief," he wrote, "it is clear to me that, whatever happens, Africa has henceforth entered into the movement of the civilised world and will not leave it."[70] France then needed to press ahead and, in Tocqueville's view, this meant that it had to complete the processes of both domination and colonisation as quickly as possible. "Domination," Tocqueville stated, "is the necessary means we must use to achieve the untroubled possession of the coastal region and the colonisation of a part of the territory." This needed to be "the real and serious goal" of France's efforts."[71]

What followed from this conclusion was stark in the extreme. "I have often heard people in France," Tocqueville wrote, "find it wrong that we burn harvests, that we empty silos, and finally that we seize unarmed men, women and children." These, he countered, were "unfortunate necessities" and ones to which any people who chose to wage war on Arabs "is obliged to submit."[72] "I believe," he continued, "that the right of war authorizes us to lay waste to the country and that we must do it, either by destroying harvests during the harvest season, or by continually making those rapid incursions known as razzias, the purpose of which is to seize men or herds of animals."[73] Nor did Tocqueville think that this war would be speedily brought to a close. Thus, the French had to learn how to wage war "more economically and with less loss of life." His big idea was the creation of special regiments that "have Africa as their exclusive and particular destination, composed of soldiers selected for this task and led by officers who have themselves chosen this path"[74]

The key argument that Tocqueville sought to advance was that domination was only a means to secure colonisation. There was, he argued, no way of knowing when the war would end, so colonisation—in essence, the importation of a European population into Algeria—had to begin immediately. In addition, a European population settled in Algeria would make the continuation of the war "easier, less costly, and more decisive" by providing a secure base for France's armies.[75]

But what area of Algerian territory should France seek to colonise? Here it is tempting to suggest that Tocqueville drew lessons from what he had observed in America. "In order to colonise to any great extent," Tocqueville wrote, "it would necessarily involve not only violent measures but also evidently iniquitous ones. We would have to dispossess several tribes and transport them elsewhere, where they most likely would be less well off."[76] For pragmatic reasons alone, Tocqueville argued, this was a course of action that ought to be avoided. "Is it not, he commented, "finally time to show, even if only in a tiny corner of the desert, that people can ally themselves with France without losing their fortunes or their lives?"[77] Tocqueville's recommendation, therefore, was that France should focus on colonising the area around Algiers. "In Algiers, at least," he wrote, "we shall only be dispossessing tribes that have always been at war with us." The "best way" to achieve this, Tocqueville continued, was to erect a "continuous barrier" around the territory. Nor should that land be returned once war was over.[78]

Yet, in Tocqueville's opinion, the dispossession of the indigenous population was not the most difficult part of the task facing France. That part was the creation of a populous and flourishing colony and, as Tocqueville and Beaumont had observed, the French were going about this in entirely the wrong way. "It must never be forgotten," Tocqueville wrote, "that the colonists are not serfs but independent and active agents who can decide not to come and not to stay as they wish."[79] The settler needed to be able "to settle where he likes and farm as he chooses." He needed financial incentives and to be able to trade unhindered with metropolitan France. The "constraints and obligations" imposed upon him by the French government should be minimised. The settler's village in Algeria "should call to mind the community where he lived at home." None of this was the case. "Our current situation," Tocqueville concluded, is "ruinous for the treasury, destructive for our influence in the world, and above all precarious."[80] Worse still, France would fail "unless we profoundly modify the institutions that now govern the country." Those institutions, Tocqueville recorded, were "violent, arbitrary, tyrannical, and, at the same time, weak and incompetent."[81] There was both too little and too much centralisation. The colonial governor lacked power but officials in Paris interfered where they were not required. Institutional failings were matched by human vices; to be found there, Tocqueville wrote, were "an enormous number of individuals whom one would not dare to employ in the bright light of publicity in France."[82]

Moreover, this bad situation was compounded by the fact that institutional arrangements changed every day. Nothing was solid or stable. "Not only," Tocqueville continued, "do the colonists not find the protective institutions that exist in their homeland but they have absolutely no idea what institutions they will have tomorrow."[83] In sum, it could not be said that a society or a social body existed. "For myself," Tocqueville concluded, "I declare in all honesty and after thorough examination that, if I were condemned to live on the coast of Africa, I would much rather live in the Regency of Tunis than in Algiers."[84] The astonishing thing was that anyone went to live there at all. Fundamental reforms were therefore required. Arbitrary government and the excessive power of the military had to be ended.

We do not know what Beaumont made of Tocqueville's text. Nor do we know why Beaumont did not write his proposed volume on Algeria.[85] However, late in 1842 he published an initial set of five articles entitled "État de la question d'Afrique" in the daily paper *Le siècle*.[86] As Beaumont explained to Tocqueville, the paper's editor, François-Adolphe Chambolle, had pressed him to respond to the publication of General Bugeaud's *L'Algérie, des moyens de conserver et d'utiliser notre conquête.* "When I see," he told Tocqueville, "the deplorable course we are following in Africa and the surrender of this great question to someone like General Bugeaud, I feel a certain satisfaction in expressing my views; on some points they might be ill founded but in essence I think that they are right."[87] Not unimportantly, these articles were published anonymously.

As might be imagined, Bugeaud's pamphlet was an attempt to justify the (often controversial) policies he had pursued in Algeria.[88] Central to this was Bugeaud's argument that, even when hostilities had ceased, France should maintain an army of eighty thousand men in Algeria and that the army itself should act as the principal vehicle of colonisation through the building of roads, bridges, villages, and so on. He also suggested that the military could settle on the land with their families. In Bugeaud's view, a civilian government was inconceivable. With none of this did Beaumont agree, and to make his case he deployed a set of arguments that he and Tocqueville had developed during and since their visit to Algeria. In brief, Beaumont contended that there could be no worse system of government for a new colony than military despotism. No one would choose to settle in a country "under the violent caprice of a soldier." What was needed was a guarantee of the right to property and the creation of civil institutions. Only then would the people and the necessary capital for investment be forthcoming.[89]

What makes this brief interlude especially interesting is that Bugeaud mistakenly concluded that Tocqueville was the author of the articles. Writing from his military encampment in Algeria, he informed the readers of *Le siècle* that there could be no doubt as to the author's identity, as he was clearly recognisable by his "style" and his "unambiguous opinions." He was, Bugeaud continued, "a well-known writer" and a parliamentary deputy and someone towards whom he had extended his hospitality when the author had visited Algeria (a hospitality cut short, he pointed out, by the author's ill health). The implication was that Tocqueville was both uninformed about his subject and ungrateful towards his hosts.[90] Two days later, Beaumont was obliged to disclose that he had been the author, adding, for good measure, that, if he respected Bugeaud as a soldier, he doubted his aptitude to run a government.

A week or so later Beaumont published two further articles designed to clarify his position. "I have always believed," he wrote, "that the question of our settlement in Africa would be resolved on the day when we have grouped ourselves around Algiers and established on the soil an agricultural population sufficient for the town and the army to live off the produce of its work and thus to make both soldiers and settlers independent of trade with the Arabs and the support of France."[91]

In the months that followed, correspondence between Tocqueville and Beaumont declined dramatically. But travel continued to preoccupy both men. At the end of August 1843 Beaumont wrote to Tocqueville from Nice, then part of the kingdom of Piedmont-Sardinia. Beaumont's wife had not been well, and they had decided to spend time in the warmth of the Mediterranean littoral. Having been unimpressed by what they had seen in Cannes and Antibes, they suddenly decided to cross the frontier. "Everything here," Beaumont wrote, "is ravishing": the climate, the sea, the Alps, "a town French in language, English in its cleanliness, and Italian with its sun." To add to his joy, the journey from Paris had only taken six days and had not been at all tiring.[92]

Tocqueville was delighted to receive the news and congratulated Beaumont on escaping from what he referred to as the bug-infected shacks of the French south for the comfort and cleanliness to be found beyond the border. "There are times," he confided, "when I am so tortured and so little in control of myself here that I dream of getting away for a month or two in a foreign country."[93] It was over a month before Beaumont replied, and when he did, it was only to assure Tocqueville that his time had been spent swimming and walking by the sea. On many occasions, he wrote, he and his wife had asked themselves whether Tocqueville would enjoy such a simple life—for a day, perhaps, they concluded, and then Tocqueville would wish to flee as quickly as possible.

Tocqueville meanwhile had been busy writing articles on the slavery issue and studying the British Empire in India.[94] He was also following developments in Algeria, where it had been reported that one of Louis-Philippe's sons, the duc d'Aumale, was to be appointed as commander of the province of Constantine. Tocqueville correctly suspected that Aumale would become the next governor-general. No reply was forthcoming from Beaumont until the beginning of December, by which time Tocqueville was getting annoyed with his friend. When, at long last, he did hear from Beaumont—still relaxing in Nice—it was to receive the unexpected news that Beaumont was planning another visit to Algeria. The health of Madame de Beaumont, it appeared, was much improved and, as he was so close to the port of Toulon, it seemed an opportune moment to make a short visit to the French colony. It would, he told Tocqueville, add to their knowledge of the subject and, upon his return, they could discuss writing an article together for *Le siècle.*[95]

We know little of Beaumont's short visit. He left Toulon on 10 December and arrived back in Marseilles in early January 1844. Much had changed, he reported to Tocqueville in a letter written from Algiers on 18 December. If the war was not yet won, Abd-el-Kadar had been reduced to insignificance and the threat of insurrection marginalised. People travelled in relative safety and in great numbers. Business was thriving. Property prices had tripled. The work of colonisation also continued apace. New villages, some built by the military, others built by the civil authorities, were springing up everywhere, each connected by newly built roads. Everywhere, Beaumont wrote, he found infantry battalions clearing or sowing land in readiness for the arrival of settlers. And this vital work was due to be extended in the future. Beaumont then added the following remark. The army, he wrote, "is the only thing here that carries out its task nobly and gloriously." The civil administration, by contrast, was "lamentable," the sum of its efforts being either to sleep, regulate, or expropriate. Beaumont also recounted that he had been invited to dinner by Marshal Bugeaud, recently returned from Oran. They were now, he told Tocqueville, the "best friends in the world" and he had done well not to let himself be seduced by Bugeaud's "graciousness." Furthermore, as part of his charm offensive, Bugeaud had arranged for Beaumont to make a visit to the Algerian interior with his general staff. Such a journey, he told Tocqueville, would enable him better to understand the Arabs.[96]

This friendly reception did not prevent Beaumont from being critical of Bugeaud. He tackled questions, he told Tocqueville, that he did not understand. The army, for all its utility, was at times an obstacle to progress. The civilian population was looking forward to the arrival of the new governor-general. To them any change seemed better than what presently existed. Nevertheless, Beaumont now seemed optimistic about the future of Algeria. "This Africa business," he told Tocqueville, "is truly of immense interest, and the more I see it, the more I believe that we can make something big out of it for France."[97]

What Beaumont was also eager to let Tocqueville know was that he had been working hard. Even though he was short of time and many of the visits he made were unprofitable, he told Tocqueville, "I am taking as many notes as I can." But, he confided, there was no Tocqueville there "to generate ideas through the thrust of discussion."[98] The last remark gains significance when we consider the reply received by Beaumont upon his return to France. "I strongly approve of your trip to Africa," Tocqueville wrote. What Beaumont had recounted pleased him greatly. More than this, Tocqueville hoped that "this journey will put an end to the divergence that existed between our thoughts on the question of domination and the war." "I have," he continued, "such a long and dear habit of being of the same opinion as you that I have been pained and worried to find myself in disagreement with you on an important matter." Here we can only partly guess at the cause of disagreement. "As you know," Tocqueville wrote, "I have for long thought and said that in Africa administrative tyranny is much more to be feared than military tyranny." Beaumont, it seems, had thought the reverse.[99]

Any hopes that Tocqueville might have had that disagreements with Beaumont were a thing of the past were to be dashed. Just over a year later they were to be embroiled in a very public quarrel and one that almost brought their friendship to a bitter end. The subject matter that caused their fall out was, in its day, considered to be a very important one: Should the state have a monopoly over secondary education? Tocqueville thought not, and for his pains was characterised as a closet legitimist by the editor of *Le siècle,* François-Adolphe Chambolle. Beaumont responded immediately, publishing an open letter announcing that he would no longer write for *Le siècle* and citing his loyalty to his "oldest friend" as the reason. This proved not to be enough for Tocqueville (who clearly expected Beaumont also to endorse the position he had taken), with the result that Beaumont received what at best might be described as a rude and somewhat self-pitying letter of protest.

Beaumont was understandably hurt, and Tocqueville soon realised that he had behaved badly, but it took a few years before their friendship regained its intimacy and vigour.[100] The significance of this is that Tocqueville undertook his next trip to Algeria not with Beaumont as his companion but his wife, Mary. Indeed, Beaumont was not told of it until the very last minute.

In contrast to Tocqueville's first visit to Algeria, little information about his second visit is available. Those of his notes that remain are fragmentary. But we do have a clear picture of the issues that were preoccupying Tocqueville prior to his departure. We know that Tocqueville became increasingly interested in the British Empire in India,[101] and so much so that in 1843 he wrote a lengthy sketch for a book on the subject. What intrigued him (and here the contrast with the French experience in Algeria is self-evident) was the manner with which the British had been able to acquire such an immense empire with ease and almost by accident. In part, Tocqueville's conclusion was that India had been ready for "conquest and servitude." It was a country of disunited small tribes rather than a "great people." The caste system alienated the vast majority from those who held power. Centuries of invasion by Persians, Afghans, and Mughals had made the Hindu population indifferent to the race and religious faith of their rulers. Nor had the British faced stiff military resistance. Great armies disintegrated before "one or two European battalions." India, in short, had been "at the mercy of Europe."[102]

Yet Tocqueville also saw that British success in India owed much to the peculiar arrangements that had been put in place to administer and govern this vast territory. If the East India Company had been left to pursue its commercial interests, political power resided with the British state. It alone governed. Crucially, Tocqueville argued, the British had then established a clear separation between the military and civil authorities, with supremacy accorded to the latter. A Bureau of Control, based in London and with representation at the highest level of British government, had also been established. "What appears marvellous in all this," Tocqueville concluded, "is the facility with which such a vast and complicated machine works."[103]

Thus, when in the spring of 1846 a parliamentary commission composed largely of his political friends was set up to examine the question of Algeria,

Tocqueville sought to draw upon the British experience for guidance. This was evident in his correspondence with Henry Reeve, the English translator of *De la démocratie en Amérique.* In March of that year, Tocqueville asked Reeve to explain how the army in India was organised. In particular, he wanted to understand the command structure that allowed for the coordination of the regular British Army and the indigenous Indian Army. What, he asked, was the relationship between the war ministry and the ministry responsible for the colonies?[104] The following month Tocqueville turned his attention to the process of colonisation itself, extending his interest to the British colonies in Australia, New Zealand, and South Africa. "Is it possible," he asked Reeve, "to provide an accurate idea of the actual way in which colonisation operates in these different colonies? For example, how, by whom, and under what conditions is land distributed? To what type of people is land handed over? Are they isolated individuals? Are they financial companies? In the latter case, how do they operate? If they are isolated individuals, to what class do they generally belong? Are they poor or rich?" Tocqueville also wanted information on how the British government "indirectly encouraged the work of colonisation." Beyond the maintenance of law and order, did the government engage in public works? Did it build roads, for example? All these details, Tocqueville told Reeve, were important to him. But Tocqueville had one last question to ask. "In Africa and New Zealand, like us in Algeria," Tocqueville wrote, "you have to fight against the indigenous population. What influence does this fact have upon the nature and progress of colonisation?"[105]

One day later, on 5 April 1846, Tocqueville took up these themes again in a long letter to his friend, General Louis de Lamoricière. Lamoricière was a key player in France's Algeria policy, and Tocqueville was eager to find out exactly where he stood on the central issues then under discussion. He began therefore by sketching out what he took to be the various ways in which French "domination over the Arab people" could be established. These, Tocqueville argued, were three in number and each one had been used by conquerors in the past: the French could turn the people against their aristocratic leaders, buy off certain families by giving them individual property rights, or give lands confiscated from unfriendly tribes to those likely to support the French. The latter strategy, Tocqueville conceded, amounted to turning them into fellow usurpers. Tocqueville's point was that for the conquerors to succeed, the "*assiette,*" or site of power, had to be relocated. "One makes use of the ambition of some," he wrote, "to counter the hostility of others." Moreover, "this was the essential method used by the English in India." "Can nothing similar," he asked, "be done in Africa?" Certainly, "judging by the number of caliphs and aghas who have turned their back on us at the first whiff of gunfire," all that the French had tried so far had met with limited success.[106]

What conclusions was Tocqueville prepared to draw from this? Above all, he told Lamoricière, "in Africa, as everywhere else, war alone is not sufficient as a means of consolidating conquest." It was undoubtedly the first step to success. Resistance had to be overcome and the moral strength of the vanquished had to be worn away. But, he argued, if it was war that began all conquests, "it is politics alone that made them long-lasting." This, he added, was as true in the time of Alexander the Great as it was in that of Marshal Bugeaud. To this Tocqueville appended the observation that the problems faced by France in Algeria were not due to a lack of goodwill or courage but rather to ignorance.[107]

Here matters might have stood, but upon learning that the sending of his letter would be delayed, Tocqueville added a long postscript. He had heard, he wrote, that it was Lamoricière's view that European colonisation in Algeria should be restricted to the triangle defined by the towns of Oran, Mascara, and Mostaganem. Was this territory free? If not, and if it were occupied by Arabs, how did Lamoricière intend to turn the land over to Europeans? It was important, Tocqueville wrote, that, as far as possible, France had right on its side and that this was acknowledged by the indigenous population.[108]

Next, he asked Lamoricière if he believed that the European and Arab populations could live side by side. "For my part," Tocqueville commented, "I think this mixture of the two populations very desirable in certain respects, but I doubt that it is a possibility." Occasionally, he continued, a civilised people combined with a barbarous people, but this was only when the former was weak and the latter was strong. When one of the two was the more civilised and the stronger, no such coming together took place. Rather, the dominant group destroyed or drove away the other. "I would wish passionately," Tocqueville wrote "that this was not the case in Africa, but I have little hope of it."[109]

Finally, Tocqueville enquired, were the land to be free "in one way or another," how did Lamoricière think that it ought to be colonised? "The fate of our entire future in Africa," Tocqueville wrote, "lies in the solution to this question." Tocqueville made his own position clear. It was entirely proper, he wrote, that the government should play an "indirect" role in the process—protecting the safety of individuals, building roads, avoiding the imposition of heavy taxation, and so on—but "to take a poor man from France, bring him to Algeria, decide where he will live, build him a house, clear land for him and then go and find another poor devil to live by the side of him . . . seems both absurd and ridiculous." It was akin, Tocqueville observed, to the building of Potemkin villages. We must, he concluded, "abandon a system which consists in planting men in the way one plants asparagus, one by one."[110]

Here Tocqueville could draw upon what he had seen with his own eyes in America. "What a great example!" he wrote. There was to to be found "a people who each year advances four or five leagues across a front of more than four hundred leagues." Yet, the people doing this were not the European emigrants who arrived in vast numbers in America. They stayed in the inhabited areas. On the contrary, it was "American landowners, small capitalists, who, with greater or lesser resources, set out to make their fortune on the frontier." These, Tocqueville concluded, were precisely the type of people who should be drawn to Algeria. Everything had been done to discourage them.[111]

This was not to be Tocqueville's only reference to the American experience. In July 1846 he wrote to one of his closest acquaintances in the United States, Francis Lieber, and in doing so again raised the question of the colonisation of Algeria. "It is impossible," he told Lieber, "to deal with the colonisation of Africa without thinking of the great examples given by the United States on this issue." How, he asked, could he find out more about this process and what could Lieber tell him about it? When Lieber replied in September, Tocqueville must have been disappointed, although not surprised, by what he read. "The cases of America and Algeria," Lieber wrote, "are essentially different." "The Teutonic race and the Irish," he explained, "have a readiness of emigration which the French have not." The American preferred to live in "perfect independence" and was not "half as social as the Frenchman who loves his coffee house with all the buzz of talk and clicking of the domino." Under American law, the land belonged to the first person who settled it. That land was "fine and fertile" and fit for the same purposes as that from which the settler had emigrated. The settler had "no enemies, except Indians, who recede with the buffalo." And "what are they," Lieber added, "compared to your Arabs?" In America, there also existed "an instinctive impulse of establishing governments with the principle of vitality and self-action *within*." Finally, the emigrant felt not a "feeling of debasement" but one of pride, "for the Western settler considers himself more a man than the Philadelphian." He had no Paris or "belle France" to long for as "he is in America and means to stay forever in the West."[112] What Tocqueville made of this discouraging reply can only be guessed at.

In the meantime, Jules Dufaure had presented his report on the administration of Algeria before the French Parliament, and Tocqueville spoke to it on 9 June. What Tocqueville sought to do in his speech was to set out what he took to be an accurate picture of the problems France faced and where the remedies might lie. He began by stating what he now clearly regarded as a stark, if regrettable, truth—namely, the idea of maintaining a French presence in Africa, with the help and support of the indigenous population, was, for the present at least, a "chimera." He had no more desire to "expel" the indigenous population than he had to "exterminate" them, but "to trust the goodwill of the natives to keep us in Africa," Tocqueville continued, was "a pure illusion." Thus, the future of "French domination," in Tocqueville's opinion, now rested upon "the arrival on African territory of a European population," and, specifically, an agricultural population.[113]

The truth, as Tocqueville struggled to tell his fellow parliamentary deputies, was that this population did not as yet exist. "You have created villages," he told them, but "half of their inhabitants are dead and the other half live in misery." Here Tocqueville was careful to acknowledge Marshal Bugeaud's military prowess. He was, Tocqueville declared, "the first to have applied, everywhere at the same time, the type of war that in my eyes, as in his, is the only type of war practicable in Africa" and he had done so "with unequalled energy and vigour." But, he continued, Bugeaud had done nothing to establish "a European society in Africa." Indeed, he had actively sought to prevent it for the simple reason that he did not believe that to do so was either useful or possible. Thus, Tocqueville told Parliament, the whole enterprise had been "surrendered to the miserable rivalries of subaltern officials," to contradictory measures, disobedience, and dissension. This was "the deplorable, humiliating spectacle" that France had presented to the world.[114]

What was to be done? First, Tocqueville agreed with those of his fellow deputies who believed that a "special ministry" needed to be established to coordinate all of France's activities. More than this, he believed that Algeria had to cease to be a matter of secondary concern. It was, he stated, "the country's greatest task" and stood "at the forefront of all the interests France has in the world." His worry was that "this immense African question" would sink "as usual back into oblivion."[115]

There could then be no doubt as to the significance Tocqueville attached to the Algerian question or to the importance he gave to his forthcoming visit there. First there was the matter of securing reelection to Parliament, something Tocqueville did with ease in August 1846. His address of thanks to his electors in Normandy spoke of the need to combine peace, the protection of France's legitimate interests, and national grandeur. People, he recognised, wanted honest and strong government, and of their newly elected representative they expected independence of both heart and mind. No return to the ancien régime and no new revolution, Tocqueville declared to his provincial audience, were his maxims.[116]

A letter to Louis de Kergorlay, written only a few weeks later and dated 11 September 1846, disclosed all of Tocqueville's incorrigible enthusiasm at the thought of what was now hopefully to come. "I am undertaking this trip," he wrote, "with the liveliest curiosity and the conviction that I am doing something that is useful."[117] By doing nothing imprudent he hoped to avoid the unhealthy consequences of the Algerian climate. The same message was conveyed to Francisque de Corcelle. "I have no desire to go to Africa to be sick," Tocqueville wrote, "and am very resolved to do nothing that could produce this outcome." His plan therefore was to stay in and around Algiers for the best part of two months and soak up the atmosphere. Having his wife with him, Tocqueville believed, would make it all the easier to turn down offers of travel across the country.[118]

Tocqueville set off for the Mediterranean coast in early October. Writing from Arles in the south of France, he told Kergorlay that, so far, the journey was going well and that his wife was seemingly enjoying herself. Travelling as a family, he remarked, "is a thoroughly charming way of living on condition however that your wife knows how to do without her comforts and can amuse herself with what amuses you or at least interest herself in the things you find interesting."[119] A week later, having spent several sleepless nights in an insalubrious hotel in Marseilles, things were not quite so rosy. A combination of fatigue and her period, Tocqueville told his father with what even today strikes us as surprising candour, had laid his wife low and this had now turned to diarrhoea. "I have no desire," he continued, "to take her with an upset stomach to a country where stomach upsets are so common." They had therefore decided to postpone their departure by steamship from Toulon by ten days. "Life in general and the life of travellers in particular," Tocqueville concluded philosophically, "are full of these accidents."[120]

Fortunately, as Tocqueville told Beaumont a mere two hours before they weighed anchor on 28 October, he had brought plenty of books and documents with him and all had served admirably as reading fodder during his ten days of enforced respite. His hope was that, as his stay was only to last for two months, this would better enable him to get to work as soon as he reached Algiers.

It is also evident that, to his own satisfaction, Tocqueville had now decided what the big issue to be addressed was. "It is obvious," he wrote to Beaumont in the same letter, "that, however important questions relating to the government of the Arabs and the war are . . . the principal question for me . . . is the administration and the establishment of European society."[121] This view was stated even more clearly in a letter written to Francisque de Corcelle from Marseilles that same month. Here he insisted that "the question of Africa, in all its variety and all its grandeur, can be summarised as follows: how to establish in Africa a French population with our laws, our mores, our civilisation, whilst, with regard to the indigenous population, giving due consideration to the claims of justice, humanity, our self-interest well understood and our honour." Moreover, he told Corcelle, he intended to approach these questions with a completely open mind. Experience had taught him, Tocqueville wrote, that one only had imperfect knowledge of things one had studied in isolation. "I therefore leave behind in France," he concluded, "all the ideas that I have come across by hearsay, firmly resolved to consider every issue as if I had heard about it for the first time."[122]

Tocqueville's hope that he could get to work immediately upon his arrival in Algeria proved to be the case. A letter written to Jules Dufaure from Algiers on 6 November confirmed that, although he had not left the city, he had met "a multitude of persons of all types." He was working from morning to dusk trying to acquire an accurate understanding of things and people. Everywhere and without exception, he reported, he was told that Bugeaud opposed the development of civil society. As for the civil administration, it either worked badly or not at all. Everything was arranged such that it took longer than in metropolitan France. The worst of it, Tocqueville continued, was the "profound anarchy that reigned and that presented the most deplorable spectacle one could imagine." These, at least, were his "first impressions."[123]

As Tocqueville had hoped, upon this occasion he did not fall ill. Indeed, a letter from his wife to his brother Édouard confirmed that she had scarcely ever seen him in better mental or physical form.[124] This Tocqueville himself attributed not only to his intention to be prudent but also to what, in a letter to Beaumont, he referred to as a form of "training" akin to that of "the amateurs of the jockey club." "I know," he wrote, "that if a life of travelling, even of the most tiring kind, is salutary for my health, nothing is more perilous for me than the transition from a sedentary existence to the former." So, for over a month Tocqueville had gone riding every day in and around Algiers, gradually building up his strength. It was only when he felt sufficiently hardened, he reported, that he had accepted the invitation of General Bugeaud to travel with him across the country.[125] Using his wife as an excuse to stay in Algiers appears to have been forgotten.

The same letter to Beaumont, written from the port of Bône (now Annaba) on the northeastern extremity of French Algeria, detailed the journey Tocqueville made. With Bugeaud and his military entourage he had set out over land for the port of Oran, some 250 miles west of Algiers. This was done on horseback, covering around 30 miles a day, and sleeping in a tent. "The whole trip," he told Corcelle upon his return to Algiers at the beginning of December, "was of great interest."[126] What Tocqueville told neither

Beaumont nor Corcelle was that he was also accompanied by three parliamentary deputies. Also present was a journalist, Auguste Bussière, and it is thanks to him that we have a more detailed picture of what Tocqueville saw and did.[127]

Bussière, and presumably Tocqueville, was under no doubts about Bugeaud's intentions. "On this trip," Bussière wrote, "the aim of the Marshal was to show the advantages that his system of administration and colonisation had over all forms of civil administration." That this was indeed the intention is confirmed by a letter sent by one M. Dussert, deputy director of civil affairs for the province of Constantine and Philippeville, to Marèchal de Castellane on 1 January 1847. Having assured Castellane that the New Year had begun much as it had done previously in a state of administrative anarchy and that Bugeaud continued with his project of "military colonisation," he added that he and his colleagues had also recently received a party of parliamentary deputies. Everything, he reported, had been done to subject them to the "phantasmagoria of Arab fantasy," throwing "powder in their eyes" such that they left believing that "they had seen and perhaps even understood a country about which they knew not even the first thing."[128]

For not even the best propagandist do things always go to plan. Bussière's account began with a description of the villages outside Algiers placed under military control. Death and hardship had ravaged the colonial population. Soon afterwards Bugeaud found himself face-to-face with disgruntled settlers, all complaining about the enforced regulations under which they were obliged to work. Then, in Bussière's words, they left "the civil territory to enter what was called the mixed territory," a land without roads, villages and bridges, climbing through the Mouzaïa Pass, site of a famous and bloody battle in 1840 between French troops and those led by Abd-el-Kader. There they met two lone Frenchmen, on foot and unarmed, travelling from Médéa to Blida. Interrogated by Bugeaud, and to his delight, they reported that they felt perfectly safe. As Bussière put it, "Four deputies could therefore testify to France of the respect the government already inspired in the indigenous population and of the confidence that the Europeans had in its strength." This incident, Bussière wrote, was much discussed in subsequent days.

Next was the town of Médéa. Here, Bussière commented, he and his fellow travellers were in the presence of "full military government," with Bugeaud again boasting of the "excellence of a system of free administration and free justice." This was contradicted by the settlers who saw only evidence of arbitrary power. That evening, again showing his irritation at the criticisms he had heard, Bugeaud proposed a toast to the army, praising its discipline, resignation, and courage. With great tact, Tocqueville responded by proposing a toast to the union of the army and the civil authorities.[129]

After Médéa, they journeyed into barren and largely uninhabited territory, stopping a day later at the encampment of the *bachagda* Bou-Alem.[130] "Judging by European standards," Bussière observed, his house "gave no indication of the power or rank of the chief who lived there, but in such a situation and compared to a camel skin tent it was the equivalent of a Louvre or a Versailles." The house was opened to them, and later came a meal of couscous, Arab sweets, and lamb. From here, Bussière recalled, Tocqueville and his companions descended "from hill to hill, through rolling country," when suddenly two or three groups of bedouin horse riders approached them at great speed and with guns blazing, something they continued to do throughout the day.[131] This, presumably, was part of the display of Arab fantasy referred to by Dussert.

They then climbed to the ancient mountain town of Miliana, now "entirely French in construction." A visit to a "magnificent" hospital constructed by the army was followed by dinner with the camp commander, General Levasseur. But here again things did not go according to plan for the hosts. The civilian population spoiled the show, forming a delegation to voice their complaints about poor municipal administration and the need for a new justice of the peace. Bugeaud castigated them for their ingratitude towards the army and sent them on their way. Two days later, having arrived at Orleansville (now Chlef), Bugeaud continued to vent his annoyance. What do these people want? he raged. Are they mad? They need us at every moment and can do nothing without us, he continued, but they want to be rid of us. When Colonel (later Marshal) Saint-Arnaud joined in, he scarcely helped matters. Having boasted of the things the army did for the settlers, he added that, if they gave him the least trouble, he'd put them "headfirst into a silo." One of his officers did the best he could to salvage the situation.[132]

It was at this point that Tocqueville announced that he intended to leave Bugeaud and return to Algiers. Bussière left with him, as did two of the other parliamentary deputies. What had Tocqueville made of this experience, and how had he responded to the "Arab fantasy" placed before him? Two letters written by those who had observed him provide an answer. The first is the letter already cited by Dussert. Tocqueville, he there wrote, was the only one of the four deputies who, "as far as he could, evaded the official stratagems." The second is a letter written by Colonel Saint-Arnaud to his brother shortly after Tocqueville's departure. Annoyed by the constant questioning he had received from the four deputies, he wrote that "M. de Tocqueville affected to some degree a profound, rational, methodical sort of observation."[133]

To return to Algiers, Tocqueville and his companions set off for the port of Ténès. Now they were to be accompanied by a Lieutenant-Colonel Conrobert and a dozen cavalry men. Their journey took them across the Dahra mountain range, an area where heavy fighting had taken place the previous year. Looking at the formidable terrain, Bussière commented, one could understand how hard this war had been for the French soldiers. There they came across a lone Frenchman who had set up a farm and somehow survived the hostilities. Conrobert then decided that they would have lunch at the camp of one of their most famous Kabyle opponents, a man of notorious cruelty, now humbled and reduced to feeding uninvited guests. "We looked at him," Bussière recorded, "with the kind of curiosity that might inspire a ferocious beast powerless to devour his onlookers."[134]

Having arrived at Ténès via the magnificent valley of Oued-Allalah, Tocqueville and his fellow deputies set off by steamboat not for Algiers but for Oran. Tocqueville, according to Bussière, had his doubts about this, in part for what were described as "family reasons," but was prevailed upon to agree. They were met by General Lamoricière and made a tour on horseback of the surrounding area. According to Bussière, Tocqueville spent the entire time talking to members of the Arab Bureau. Dinner in the evening was enlivened by the arrival of a young army officer with news that a group of French soldiers had been released from captivity. The following day they set off by boat in stormy weather for Algiers, stopping off at various points along the way, eventually arriving on 30 November.

No sooner had Tocqueville returned to Algiers than he wrote a long letter to Corcelle, recounting his travels and impressions and commenting on how much he had missed having a "*compagnon de voyage*" with whom he could converse and share ideas. However, the issue Tocqueville chose to highlight was the fate of the indigenous population. They existed, Tocqueville told Corcelle, in a condition of complete submission and prostration. To this was to be added their acute poverty. Everywhere people begged for food. Famine reigned. People lived only to survive. So, Tocqueville reported, there was little chance of further insurrection before the next harvest. But calm did not mean peace. "The hatred that exists between the two races," he wrote, "is truly awful to behold; the hearts of our officers are full of scorn and anger and one sees all too clearly that, in their eyes, the Arabs are nothing but maleficent animals." Yet one thing gave him cause for hope. "I was surprised and charmed," Tocqueville confided to Corcelle, "to see the immense progress we have made in our understanding not only of the practices, laws, and mores of the Arabs but also of their persons." "I spent many days," he wrote, "compiling biographies of the people I saw."[135]

While all this was going on, Tocqueville's wife, Mary, appears to have spent the greater part of her husband's absence contentedly cocooned in her room and evidently enamoured by what little of the country she had seen. The balmy climate, pure air, and stunning vistas over mountain and sea, she recounted, had great appeal. Nonetheless, with each day that her husband failed to return her anxieties increased. She feared that Bugeaud was up to no good.

Yet, no sooner had Tocqueville and Bussière returned than they left Algiers to make a weeklong journey "*au hazard*" across the Sahel massif and the Matidja plain. They were accompanied by two cavalry men and a brigadier. The intention was to visit the numerous settler villages to be found there and thus to see how the process of colonisation was working. In village after village, they saw the same thing: hardworking people ground down by illness, a harsh climate, poor soil, and a lack of resources. In many cases, the settlers had simply returned home to France. Few were they who possessed enough money to invest in their farms. It must have made for a depressing few days.[136]

Of the remainder of Tocqueville's stay we have only the scantiest detail. Letters to both Beaumont and Corcelle tell us that Tocqueville and his wife had been invited by General Marie-Alphonse Bedeau to visit Constantine. Accordingly, on 10 December they set off by boat for the small port of Stora, near Philippeville, where Bedeau was to provide a coach to complete the rest of their journey. Unfortunately, bad weather forced them to take refuge at

Bône, where they remained until at least 18 December.[137] We can only assume that all went to plan after this, as Tocqueville and his wife set sail for France on 29 December, returning to Paris, and what Tocqueville described to Corcelle as the "*collier de misères,*" on 10 January 1847.[138]

What happened next? A month later the government presented two bills before the French Parliament, one concerning special funding required for Algeria, the other relating to the establishment of "agricultural camps" (i.e., military colonisation). Without going into the detail of the negotiations which followed, Gustave de Beaumont suggested that both bills be examined by a parliamentary committee of eighteen members. Tocqueville was chosen as chairmen and parliamentary rapporteur. Accordingly, Tocqueville presented two reports to Parliament in May and June 1847.[139] Here it is important to acknowledge that, when he did so, Tocqueville spoke in the name of the committee and not in a personal capacity. He explicitly acknowledged that at times he was voicing the views only of the majority of the committee. He also reported minority opinion, and this itself is worth dwelling upon as it shows that Tocqueville was fully aware of the arguments against the colonialist strategies he was to advocate. Specifically, Tocqueville told Parliament that two members of the committee (we can presume that these were Amédée Desjobert and Victor Destutt de Tracy) "have contested the humanity and wisdom of attempting such an enterprise."[140]

This is how Tocqueville summarised their views. The minority, he reported, believed that "The country to be colonised is not empty or populated only by hunters, like certain parts of the New World; it is already occupied, possessed, and cultivated by a population that is agricultural and often sedentary. To introduce a new population into such a country is to lengthen the war and to pave the way for the inevitable destruction of the indigenous races." They also believed that Europeans, and especially their children, could not acclimatise to the Algerian climate. Neither view, Tocqueville continued, was endorsed by the majority nor, clearly, by Tocqueville himself.[141]

What, then, was the view presented before Parliament by Tocqueville? Most obviously it bore the heavy imprint of all that he had seen and learned from his two visits to Algeria. To take but one example, in opposing the plan to establish "agricultural colonies," Tocqueville drew upon what he had observed when he and Bussière had crossed the Sahel and the Matidja plain. Much of the land, he told his fellow parliamentarians, was still uninhabited and uncultivated. Those that lived there endured a poor and precarious existence, decimated by illness and misery.[142] Similarly, the recommendations made by Tocqueville were based on his detailed knowledge of the failings of both the military and civil administrations in Algeria. "We believe," he declared, "that the vices of the administration in Algeria are among the principal shortcomings that have afflicted us in this country, and that administrative reform is the most pressing of all our needs evident today."[143] Most everything had been centralised in Paris and what remained had been centralised in Algiers. Administrative authority had been separated from political authority. There was no coordination of policy. No business was finished on time, and everything was undertaken with incredible slowness. There was a lack of good officials. Costs were exorbitant. So Tocqueville continued, sparing no one, least of all Bugeaud, from his criticisms.[144]

Did this mean that France would be best advised to quit Algeria? Far from it. The commission majority unambiguously embraced and defended the project of colonisation. "The European population has arrived. Civilised and Christian society has been founded," Tocqueville told Parliament. "Now it is only a matter of deciding under what laws it must exist and what must be done to hasten its development."[145]

Tocqueville's message was therefore perfectly clear. The ambition, he stated, should be to establish "the extension of France itself across the Mediterranean." This, he specified, was "not a matter of creating a new people, with its own laws, its customs, its interests, and, sooner or later, its separate nationality, but of establishing in Africa a population that resembles us in everything."[146]

Accordingly, Tocqueville addressed two interrelated questions: How were indigenous peoples, and the European settlers, to be governed? The latter can de dealt with quickly. Tocqueville built upon his earlier theme that Algeria had to be governed in such a way that potential colonisers would want to live there. Moreover, his proposals were completely in line with the liberal agenda he had developed and defended elsewhere. "It must not be imagined," Tocqueville argued,

> that the method to follow to create and develop new societies differs much from that which must be followed to keep old societies prospering. Do you want to attract Europeans to a new country and make them stay there? Then make it such that there are institutions there that they recognise from home or that they hope to find there; that civil and religious liberty exist; that individual freedom is assured; that property is easily acquired and well protected; that work is unrestricted; administration simple and prompt; justice impartial and swift; that taxes are light and commerce unrestrained; that economic conditions are such that one can easily achieve a comfortable existence and often wealth: in a word, ensure that people are as well off and, if possible, better off than in Europe.[147]

For good measure, Tocqueville added calls for greater freedom of the press and the participation of citizens in municipal government.

More interesting were the comments made by Tocqueville about Algeria's indigenous population. He began his first report to Parliament with a set of striking comments. France submitted "as a demonstrated truth," he stated, that "our domination in Africa should be firmly maintained." He next asserted that the geographical limits of that domination were now known. Third, he claimed that France at last knew how to fight the war it had been waging for the best part of seventeen years. "We came to understand," he told his fellow deputies, "that we faced not a real enemy but the population itself." The army had learned that troops had to be as mobile as possible and that "if we could not occupy the houses of the inhabitants, we could nevertheless seize harvests, capture herds, and arrest people."[148]

How, Tocqueville next asked, might the number of French soldiers in Algeria begin to be reduced? His answer was blunt in the extreme. "The real and permanent obstacle," Tocqueville insisted, was "the attitude of the indigenous people towards us." The task therefore was to modify this attitude. To that end, Tocqueville's committee recommended a series of measures, beginning with the structure of government. The basic principle was that political power could not be relinquished to the leaders of the indigenous population and had to be in the hands of the French. However, most of the secondary powers, he declared, should be exercised by the inhabitants of the country. The third maxim was that French power should seek to enlist the support of what Tocqueville defined as "already existing authorities." "A new government, and especially a conquering government," he explained, "can easily give physical power to its friends, but it cannot transfer moral power and force of opinion that it does not itself possess."[149]

Next Tocqueville addressed the question of how the French should treat the indigenous population. Here he set out the (what might sound implausible) argument that the French had treated the Arab population with a combination of undue gentleness and unwarranted harshness. Free transport had been provided for those who wished to visit the tomb of the Prophet, but towns had been "invaded, turned upside down, and sacked." The result had been to make "Muslim society much more wretched, more disordered, more ignorant, and more barbarous." Both excesses therefore must be avoided. There was, Tocqueville continued, "neither utility in allowing, nor a duty to allow, our Muslim subjects exaggerated ideas of their own importance, nor to persuade them that we are obliged to treat them under all circumstances precisely as though they were our fellow citizens and equals." What they were owed was "exact, but rigorous, justice" and "good government" at all times.[150]

What this meant, Tocqueville explained at length, was "a power that guides them, not only towards our interest, but in theirs; that shows itself to be truly attentive to their needs; that sincerely seeks to provide for them; that is concerned for their well-being; that looks to their rights; that works ardently for the continual development of their imperfect societies; that does not believe itself to have completed this job when it has obtained submission and taxes; that, in a word, governs them and does not restrict itself to exploiting them." What this did not mean was that the indigenous population should be encouraged to embrace "our mores, our ideas, our practices." It was not "along the road of European civilisation," Tocqueville suggested, that they should be pushed.[151]

Tocqueville's report then addressed two specific issues. The first was schooling for the indigenous population, and in particular the teaching of religion. It would be a "great imprudence," Tocqueville argued, to let the Islamic religion "die out in superstition and ignorance." Above all, its teaching should not be ceded "to fanatics and imposters." Second, he spoke to the all-important question of land distribution. "In conquering Algeria," Tocqueville asserted, "we did not intend, like the barbarians who invaded the Roman Empire, to take possession of the territory of the conquered." This did not mean that the French could not take possession of the lands required for European colonisation, but only that "it strictly obliges us, for the sake of justice and good policy, to indemnify those who own them and enjoy their use." Experience had shown, Tocqueville suggested, that this could be done easily. Crucially, he then argued that the ties of the indigenous population to their lands should be strengthened "rather than transporting them elsewhere." The latter was not only "impolitic" but also made enemies of the two populations. This in turn was followed by an insight. "Civilised peoples," Tocqueville stated, "often oppress and dispirit barbarous peoples by their mere contact, without intending to, and, so to speak, without knowing it." This, he continued, "was how, without recourse to the sword, the Europeans in North America ended by pushing the Indians off their territory. We must take care that it is not the same for us."[152]

What, finally, did Tocqueville's report suggest might be gained by such a strategy? No government, however wise and benevolent, could unite populations whose history, laws, and religion were so opposed, but what could be hoped for was "not to eradicate the hostile sentiments that our government inspires, but to weaken them; not to make our yoke liked, but to make it seem more and more tolerable; not to overcome the repugnance that Muslims have always displayed for a foreign and Christian power but to make them discover that this power, despite an origin they disapprove of, can be useful to them." In short, the aspiration was to build not a "community of ideas" but "a community of interests" resting upon mutual benefit. The alternative, of seeing the indigenous population as "merely an obstacle to be pushed aside or trampled underfoot," could only mean that "sooner or later Algeria would become a battlefield, a walled area, where the two peoples would have to fight without mercy, and where one of the two would have to die." "Let us not in the middle of the nineteenth century," Tocqueville concluded, "begin the history of the conquest of America again."[153]

This was not to be Tocqueville's final word on Algeria before Parliament. A month or so later, in July 1847, he again intervened, this time in a debate concerning the budget for Algeria for the following year. He made two powerful points. The first concerned the fate of a Muslim holy man called El-Arbi.

El-Arbi had sought to welcome the French into Constantine; for this he had been beheaded and his possessions confiscated. Later, Tocqueville reported, when the French had occupied the town, no effort had been made by the French authorities to restore his property to his family. Did this, Tocqueville asked, not sully the honour of France and reduce its moral authority among the Arab population? The second point related to what Tocqueville saw as the unjustified and unwise closure of Muslim charitable institutions. Here, he declared before the parliamentary chamber, "I will not speak to you about what happens in the parts of Algeria that I have not passed through but I will tell of what occurs in Algiers, of what I can verify and have seen myself." As a result of this policy, Tocqueville affirmed, the population of Algiers had been deprived of charitable assistance, casting them down into "hunger, illness, death and destitution." Much the same could be said of those who administered the Muslim faith. Most Muslim clerics, Tocqueville reported, were now less well paid than street porters and lived in a condition of "shameful penury." Muslim schools had similarly fallen into decay for lack of funding. "When," he declared, "Muslims see that we, who claim to be above all others a civilised nation, who claim to bring civilisation to them, are bringing about the disappearance of all the edifices able to maintain the knowledge they possessed, when they see us destroy their places of religious observance and allow their schools to decay, what deep contempt do you not expect them to have towards our government?" "The result," Tocqueville concluded, "arouses their indignation; the means of attaining it appears shameful to them."[154]

Tocqueville spoke once more in Parliament about Algeria, this time under the changed political environment of the Second Republic. He repeated his long-standing argument that Algeria should be subject to the rule of law rather than rule by military and administrative decree.[155] After this, he made no further visits there and he wrote nothing of substance on the subject. A topic that had fascinated him for the best part of eighteen years or more was quietly dropped.

What sense can be made of Tocqueville's travels to Algeria and of the views he expressed based on what he had seen? First, we should note that Algeria was the only non-Christian country that he visited and the only country he visited where France was actively engaged in fighting a war (and a brutal one at that). As was the case with the other countries he visited, he travelled extensively (again with at times damaging consequences for his health) and assiduously (preparing thoroughly, constantly taking notes, speaking with as many people as possible), always trying to see the complex phenomena before him with an objective eye.

Yet, the argument goes, in Algeria his judgement failed him. He failed to condemn the violence inflicted upon the indigenous population. He underestimated the cultural and economic damage that would be caused by the process of French colonisation. He wildly overestimated the ease with which France could establish its imperial domination. This was especially so with regard to the acquisition of property by the settler community.

All this rings true, and we now inhabit an age where, with ease and with the supposed benefits or arrogance of hindsight (if not moral superiority) we presume to judge those who went before us and to find them wanting, both politically and ethically. Indeed, there are those who believe that what Tocqueville wrote about Algeria invalidates *everything* else that he wrote or said. Yet, we should note that, unlike many of his contemporaries, Tocqueville did not resort to theories of racial superiority to justify his defence of French policy. Indeed, he was later to be categorical in his condemnation of the racialist theories expounded by his friend Arthur de Gobineau in his *Essay on the Inequality of the Human Races.* "Christianity," he told Gobineau in 1857, "seeks to make all men brothers and equals. Your doctrine makes them cousins at best. . . . Here there are only victors and vanquished, masters and slaves by right of birth."[156] Nor can this be dismissed as a passing remark on Tocqueville's part. As early as 1838—precisely the time when Tocqueville began to interest himself seriously in Algerian affairs—he wrote a letter to Ferdinand d'Eckstein, rebutting the latter's claim that, in Tocqueville's words, there existed "radical differences between the different human races and that these differences produce permanent and insurmountable inequalities." This assertion, Tocqueville replied, went against "the most sacred" of his beliefs and nothing he knew about the "general history of peoples" or that he had seen of the "different races" that inhabited the "new world" led him to such a conclusion. "I find it therefore highly improbable," he wrote, "that there exists a natural and permanent inequality among the great human family and this would have to be proved to me down to the very last detail before I would accept such claim." This, he continued, was because he knew "nothing more dangerous for the future of humanity than such a doctrine." It was in its name that the slavery that so "dishonours the Christians of the new world" had been established and that its original occupants of that land had been deprived of their property "with a completely philosophical calm." Were such a doctrine to be accepted across the world, Tocqueville concluded, it would not only paralyse the efforts of men and numb their courage but also provide succour to "all the tyrants of the present and those of the future."[157] In this context, it is important to recognise that Tocqueville also advocated the abolition of the last remnants of slavery in Algeria, a practice then limited to Black Africans.[158] Nor, it should be remembered, was Tocqueville uncritical of French policy or unforthcoming in expressing the view that both prudence and justice dictated that the indigenous population of Algeria needed to be treated with both respect and dignity.

The fact remains that Tocqueville did endorse France's colonial project and that he did so despite seeing firsthand the scale, difficulties, and violence it entailed. Why? Three principal reasons stand out. First, Tocqueville felt strongly the sense of national humiliation visited upon France in the post-Napoleonic age. To be a great power again France needed an empire. It was a matter of national status and pride.[159] A quotation from a letter written on the eve of the thirtieth anniversary of the Battle of Waterloo nicely highlights the ambivalences of Tocqueville's general position. "I would have preferred," he told his electoral agent in Normandy, "that Napoleon had been defeated from inside the country by liberal ideas, but only after having given the English a good beating."[160] Second, he believed that, if properly managed, the project of colonisation in Algeria offered the opportunity to improve the well-being of France's own population. The unemployed and the idle could become patriotic and productive settlers. Lastly, while Tocqueville did not endorse a theory of racial superiority, like many others in his day he certainly believed that European civilisation was culturally superior to the imperfect Muslim civilisation he had studied when reading the Koran and had witnessed on his voyages. European rule, if practised properly, would be enlightened rule, and all, including the indigenous population, would ultimately benefit from it.[161]

Should we then agree with Melvin Richter's statement that, when the issue of Algeria forced Tocqueville to choose, "he placed nationalism above liberalism, the interests of 'progressive' Christian countries above the rights of those who were not"?[162] Perhaps, but to do so would be to forget that, for the greater part of the nineteenth century, the claims of liberalism and nationalism were often not seen as contradicting each other. It is also to forget that Tocqueville was a forceful and unrelenting critic of the arbitrary nature of French colonial rule and that the plight of the indigenous Algerian population was never far from the forefront of his preoccupations. As Ewa Atanassow has argued, "Tocqueville sought to make the best of a situation, which from the outset he considered tragic."[163] Above all, what Tocqueville's speeches, notebooks, and letters reveal is someone intent on seeing things firsthand (despite the physical hardships and dangers this might entail) and a traveller never less than inquisitive and observant, uncowed by the power and authority of those around him, determined to get to the truth of the matter, and always ready to learn from those he met. Those travels also left Tocqueville with powerful impressions of the country that were never to leave him. To Nassau Senior in 1855 he wrote, "The natural harbour of Algiers and its surroundings have always remained in my memory as being among the most beautiful things I have seen in the world." Even in winter, the sky had a brightness that outshone anything he had seen. In the same letter, Tocqueville also indicated that he was delighted to learn that the fortification of Algiers was making good progress, turning it into the equivalent of Gibraltar. "Sooner or later," he told Senior with an accurate eye to the future, "the Mediterranean will be the theatre of a great conflict, and then the position of Algiers could be of great importance."[164]

It is strange how the memory works and how a place of violence can be remembered for its beauty, but in Algeria, as in America, Tocqueville's travels were not without purpose nor without lasting effect upon him.

CHAPTER SIX

Italy

Alexis de Tocqueville spent the 1840s as something of an underperforming politician in the July Monarchy of King Louis-Philippe. Always a poor speaker, he never quite made the grade. "In the end," he wrote, "I came to live almost always in a state of morose isolation." What most troubled him about these years in public life was "the constant doubt in which [he] was forced to live." Surrounded by the numerous dynastic parties of the day, all of whom were much like each other, he could not see where truth or falsehood lay. Nor could he decide on the best way forward.[1]

Yet he came to realise before many others were to do so that the Orleanist regime was in deep trouble. Writing to Francisque de Corcelle in the autumn of 1847 from Normandy, Tocqueville commented, "Here people seem calm, even apathetic, little preoccupied by politics, without any pronounced preference for any idea or a particular person, but in a surprising way full of a profound and quiet contempt for those who govern and administer the country, and infested with the unshakeable belief that everything is either sold or given as a favour and that political immorality is the general and habitual atmosphere in which the political world moves." He shook with terror when he viewed this spectacle, but not since the July Revolution of 1830 had he been so convinced that France faced the trials of revolution. Sooner or later the storm would come.[2] As he told his parliamentary colleagues in January 1848, they were lulling themselves to sleep on an active volcano.[3]

When a month later the February Revolution burst forth and Louis-Philippe (as plain Mr. Smith) fled to England with his family for a life in exile, Tocqueville knew exactly where he stood. There was, he saw immediately, no chance of preserving or restoring the monarchy. Only a republic was now possible, Tocqueville told Eugène Stoffels, and everything boiled down to whether France would have a good or a bad republic.[4] His firm hope, he told Paul Clamorgan in early March, was that good sense would prevail and that France would find itself with a properly constituted republic "like that of the United States."[5]

Tocqueville repeated this argument that same month in both his election campaign circular and in his responses to the president of the Valognes electoral committee, telling the latter that upon the ruins of the French monarchy he wished to see built something akin to the "great and very happy" republic he had seen with his own eyes in "another hemisphere."[6] From the outset Tocqueville's greatest fear was that this possibility might be derailed by what he did not hesitate to describe to Nassau Senior as the "prodigious ignorance" of the masses who naively believed not only that the state "could save them from poverty but also provide them with comfort and happiness."[7] If it was to survive, the republic needed to be protected from the wilder excesses of socialism.

To that end, as a member of the newly elected Constituent Assembly, Tocqueville (with Gustave de Beaumont's assistance) did his best to ensure that France would adopt a constitution that copied as far as possible that of the American republic, the example of the United States providing him with ample evidence upon which he drew confidently as a member of the drafting committee for the new constitution.[8] In parliamentary debates he denounced calls for a recognition of the right to work (then the great rallying cry of socialists such as Louis Blanc), here pointing out that America was not only "the country in the world where democracy is practised to the greatest extent" but also that it was the one where socialist doctrines "have the least currency."[9] Moreover, with a rifle on his back, he enthusiastically supported the brutal repression of the popular uprising in June 1848 prompted by the closure of Blanc's (largely ineffective) National Workshops. "This is not a riot," Tocqueville wrote of these events at the time; "it is the most terrible of all civil wars, a war of class against class, of those who have nothing against those who have something." At stake were not just the shape of France's political institutions but "property, the family, civilisation, everything that makes life worth living." Defeat would bring with it "the reddest of Republics."[10]

Having witnessed the street violence firsthand—"all known means of warfare," he told one of his friends from the Cotentin Peninsula, "are being used" and few prisoners were being taken by either side—Tocqueville's relative optimism quickly faded away. So, too, did his faith in the good sense of the French population. To Eugène Stoffels the following month he confided that, although the republic appeared safe for the moment and order had been restored, he no longer believed in "the future" and no longer expected to see "a government established in our country that is at once well-ordered, strong and liberal." "This ideal," Tocqueville wrote, "was the dream of my youth," but he could now see that it would not come to pass. The France he saw before him was a country cast out "on a stormy sea with no shore in sight." This did not mean that France would necessarily suffer "an endless succession of revolutions," but "the disease is chronic" and "will persist longer than anyone imagined." "It is not only a specific form of government that seems impossible," Tocqueville continued, "but any durable form of government whatsoever." France, in short, was destined to oscillate between liberty and despotism, "without being able to endure one or the other for long."

Tocqueville was astute enough to realise that it would not do to attribute the uprising of June 1848 to the actions of "the dregs of humanity" (as some were wont to do). Among those who marched and fought, he countered, were many who believed sincerely that society was founded upon deep injustice and that it needed radical reform. "It is this kind of revolutionary religion," Tocqueville concluded, "that our bayonets and canons will not destroy."[11]

Tocqueville's concerns about the future of France were only magnified in the following months and then confirmed when Louis-Napoleon Bonaparte, nephew of Napoleon I, was elected president of the republic in December 1848. By October 1848 Tocqueville was already anticipating the possibility of a coup d'état and an ensuing descent into "violence, illegality and tyranny."[12] Writing to Paul Clamorgan shortly before election day, he commented, "I am convinced that to vote for Prince Louis is to vote for a crisis that with limited delay will cause us to leave the Republic, although I do not know how or where it will lead us."[13] This proved to be all too true and Tocqueville's fears only grew over time and so much so that, by November 1849, he felt able to conclude that Louis-Napoleon was "a monomaniac who will only give up the imperial idea with his last breath."[14]

Nevertheless, and despite his desperate need for rest and against his better judgement, for five months in the latter half of 1849 Tocqueville served as French foreign minister.[15] "I knew well," he was later to explain, "that I would only pass through the government and not stay in it; but I hoped to remain for long enough to perform some signal service to my country and to enhance my reputation while doing so."[16]

It was only after this last sorry episode was brought unceremoniously to a close at the end of October 1849 that Tocqueville, already in ill health, retired to his country estate in Normandy and began to reflect on these bitter experiences. One thing is immediately apparent. Tocqueville quickly resolved that the best course of action for Beaumont and himself was to distance themselves from unfolding political developments. "Every day," he told Beaumont, "we are walking not quickly but inevitably towards a crisis."[17] What we also know is that, no sooner had Tocqueville arrived at his home in Normandy with his wife, Mary, in June 1850, than he began to write his recollections of events surrounding the February Revolution of 1848 and his own involvement in them. At the end of that month he told Jean-Jacques Ampère that he was surprised at the ease with which he had adapted to a life of isolation and idleness but, he added, "I scribble a bit every morning."[18] Two weeks later he asked Paul Clamorgan if there were collections of Paris newspapers for 1848 in nearby Valognes, adding "in my solitude and not wishing to either speak and even less to commit myself to serious work, I thought that this retrospective reading might interest and amuse me."[19]

Here were the beginnings of a text that Tocqueville never quite finished and that he wrote not for public viewing but as a "form of mental relaxation": his *Souvenirs*.[20] "The best use that I can make of my leisure," Tocqueville wrote in the opening paragraph, "seems to be to retrace these events, to portray the men I saw take part in them, and thereby, if I can, catch and engrave on my memory the chaotic features that make up the uncertain physiognomy of my time."[21] A first (imperfect) edition of *Souvenirs* was not published until 1893. With some justification, it might be regarded as Tocqueville's third masterpiece.

But Tocqueville and his wife were also ill. In March 1850 he developed the first overt symptoms of the tuberculosis that was to kill him nine years later. Writing to Richard Monckton Milnes from Paris in April he informed him that "for the last six months our house has been a veritable place of misery. When the wife recovers, the husband falls ill, and thus it continues."[22] And so it was that Tocqueville applied for leave of absence for six months from his parliamentary duties and that he returned to convalesce in Tocqueville. If, despite his initial concerns, the long journey from Paris to Normandy had no adverse consequences (the sea between Le Havre and Cherbourg, Tocqueville recorded, was "a little choppy" but, for once, with no ill effect on his stomach), by early July he could report to Francisque de Corcelle that, although not fully recovered, his health was improving. A month later he told Corcelle that he was "visibly returning to the condition he was in before the spitting of blood."[23] This was certainly the impression of Nassau Senior, who stayed at the Tocqueville château from 16–27 August, the two men going for long walks and conversing interminably.[24]

Yet, as was repeatedly to prove to be the case, Tocqueville's optimism and his trust in his doctors was misplaced. A particularly exhausting early September—when Tocqueville had travelled to Cherbourg to attend a state visit by Louis-Napoleon, and where he was obliged to make a speech[25]—left him feeling weaker than he had been since his return to Normandy and, as winter approached, he became increasingly nervous about the consequences for his health of the inclement climate of the Cotentin Peninsula. Already, by early August, Beaumont (who had just lost his five-year-old daughter Alix) was recommending that Tocqueville should follow the sun, wintering in Nice or possibly Algiers, Seville, Malaga, or Madeira, but a visit to see his doctor in Paris in October convinced Tocqueville that he should head for Naples or Sicily, returning to France in the spring.[26] In other circumstances, Tocqueville told Madame de Kergorlay, he would have been pleased but it was sad to be doing something, however agreeable, because of poor health.[27]

Tocqueville and his wife (and their cook) left Paris at the end of October. The following day he wrote to Francisque de Corcelle from Dijon.[28] "Although," he commented, "I have a very pronounced, if not a passionate, taste for travel, I begin this trip only with a certain nervousness and a heavy heart." Nevertheless, his prediction was that, if relations between the president and parliament might well worsen, an open rupture would not occur and, if so, he would not "regret his absence but delight in it, since I know nothing more tiring, more irritating, or sadder than what we have done during the last year, floating on a stormy sea without a wind or current and far from the coast." His plan, he told Corcelle, was to stay in the place with the best climate, probably Palermo. Eight days later Tocqueville wrote to Beaumont from Marseilles in a similarly gloomy mood. "I leave France," he wrote, "with a profoundly sad heart and a mind full of the most dreadful thoughts." Not even the expectation of travelling and the sight of new things, he added, could free him "as it had done before" from these painful preoccupations. The chances were, Tocqueville concluded, that little good or enjoyment would come from this trip.[29]

What followed had all the hallmarks of one of Tocqueville's nightmare journeys. To Beaumont, Tocqueville announced that he and Mary intended to take the packet boat from Marseilles to Civitavecchia via Genoa and Livorno and then travel overland to Rome and on to Naples (the latter, Tocqueville added, suited him better than travel by sea). However, on the expected day of their departure, the mistral began to blow, and the sea turned rough. So, fearing a bad crossing, departure was postponed to the following day. Buoyed by the knowledge that the boat Tocqueville and his wife were now to take was better and faster than the one they had originally intended to board and that fine weather looked to be in store for the next three days, they duly set off on 11 November.

All went well until they were delayed in Genoa. News that quarantine restrictions had been lifted in Naples meant that their very small ship was inundated by a "multitude of English families." One could not imagine such a crowd of people, he told Beaumont. The bridge and saloon were so full that he and his wife could hardly move. Worse was to follow. Between Livorno and Civitavecchia, and at night, they were hit by violent winds. The deck was awash. "Men, women and children," Tocqueville continued, "took refuge in any way they could in the saloon, pressed together like slaves on a slave ship." So many people were piled on the stairs that it was impossible to get out. "Add to this," Tocqueville wrote, "that everyone was seasick, and you can guess at the awfulness and devastation." The worst of it was that, in these crowded conditions, Tocqueville feared that he might suffocate. Fortunately, he was able to open a nearby skylight which, although it meant that he got drenched, allowed him, as Tocqueville put it, to survive. This "at the time was the only thing that mattered." When they docked the following day, the storm had calmed, the disembarking passengers looking as if they came from "another world."

Poor Madame de Tocqueville had such horrible memories of their journey, Tocqueville told Beaumont, that he could not see her wishing to go to sea again for many months, if at all. So, after a day's respite, they set out from Civitavecchia to Rome, where they stayed for only one night. Had he stayed longer, Tocqueville explained, he would have been obliged to see the pope and others with whom he had been in contact whilst foreign minister but equally he would have found himself again in the world of politics and of the kind that "pleased [him] the least."[30]

Tocqueville and his wife thus arrived in Naples on 21 November. Things hardly got better. He reported to Beaumont on 24 November that since their arrival they had had "strong winds, rain, hailstorms and thunder." Four days later he told Corcelle that he and his wife were not entirely over the tribulations of their sea crossing, adding that, with the exception of two beautiful days, the weather had been awful, the sirocco wind blowing with an "extreme violence." In such circumstances, Tocqueville reported, the Mediterranean was not a pretty sight.[31]

Yet the poor weather was as nothing compared with the displeasure Tocqueville felt at what he saw all around him. Italy, he told Beaumont, was "incomparably beautiful," but what a people, "what unimaginable filth, what rags and tatters, what vermin." One would have to go, Tocqueville continued, to the "most ghastly streets of Algiers to find something as foul as what one sees at every moment in the streets of Naples." "I believe," he wrote, "that the great party of order here in Naples contains a greater disinterestedness than ours, but, on the other hand, it has to be agreed that ours has a lot fewer lice."[32] The only well-dressed people were priests and soldiers—indeed, Tocqueville told Charles de Rémusat, he had never seen such well-turned out priests and soldiers[33]—but people in general were poverty stricken.

Tocqueville's description of political realities in Italy was equally scathing. To Corcelle (whom Tocqueville had appointed to a position at the Vatican when Tocqueville had been foreign minister) he wrote as follows: "A few revolutionary elements half destroyed, no liberal opinion, the restriction of all conceivable liberties combined with the mockery of a free constitution in which no one believes, a king who continues to die of fear although there is no cause to be frightened and whose cowardice turns a natural softness into tyranny, five or six thousand people detained without trial, and a completely happy people in the midst of all this squalor: there, it seems to me, is a reasonably accurate picture of this country."[34] Only five days later Tocqueville added to this litany of national misfortune in a letter to Beaumont. "In the whole dictionary of the French language," he wrote, "I cannot find words which adequately express the pity and contempt that this miserable people and, even more so, these miserable Italian governments inspire in me." Here were governments which did not even know how to make use of the despotism they adored, which used the resources of the country only to procure soldiers, and whose soldiers stupidly suppressed good as well as bad passions.[35] To Madame de Circourt, Tocqueville confided that he did not reproach "these miserable little Italian princes" for not wanting constitutional government as their peoples were hardly in a condition to accommodate such a regime but he did reproach them for "understanding so badly the profession of despot" and for misusing it as foolishly and stupidly as their subjects did their liberty.[36] Italy, Tocqueville told Victor Lanjuinais, was "easily the most unpleasant country that I have ever visited on my travels."[37]

Nor did Tocqueville spare France from blame for this deplorable situation. Writing to Jules Dufaure from Sorrento on 22 December, he commented that the pleasure and satisfaction derived from feeling well were spoilt by the sight of "all the moral illnesses" he saw around him. He had, Tocqueville continued, developed not only a taste for liberty but also the habit of enjoying it, and he found therefore that he could "not live in a country, even a foreign one, where all conceivable liberties are repressed or destroyed." For someone who had always lived in a society characterised by dynamism and independence, it was hard to understand the "moral malaise" and "intellectual anguish" felt in one where the actions of people were constrained, where everyone was silent, and where it was as if thought was paralysed. "I feel," he told Dufaure, "a mental suffering analogous to that which I experienced ten months ago when I was gasping for air and could not take a deep breadth."[38]

But, as he then remarked, Italy was not China. It was one of France's neighbours, and such had been France's "prodigious influence" that he could not contemplate its sad state "without thinking regrettably about the unfortunate consequences of our actions." This was true in general—when the French made a revolution at home, Tocqueville wrote, they spread anarchy across Europe—but the February revolution in particular had done "irreparable harm" to Italy. It had precipitated a political movement that could only have ended well if it moved slowly but which had handed the fate of the country into the hands of revolutionaries. "It is terrifying and saddening," Tocqueville reflected, "to see how many seeds of liberty have been miserably wasted, trampled underfoot, and destroyed during this last three years by those who only paid lip service to liberty." Never, he concluded, had man's "perversity" and "thoughtlessness" been more fully displayed.[39]

If Tocqueville's stay in Italy subsequently improved, his grim view of Italian political and social realities did not. To Beaumont in early January 1851 he confided that the worst side of his stay was that he could study all kinds of things, except Italy. "Fear, ignorance, and a deep indifference towards everything amongst which people live here," he continued, "closes all mouths." Nor was it easy to meet people. "Middle-class Italians," Tocqueville wrote, "are not bothered about visiting you because they do not want you to visit them and they do not want you to visit them because they live in hovels of which they are ashamed and which nevertheless they have no wish to transform into clean and comfortable apartments." How could one learn from people, he asked, who themselves had no desire to learn anything? He would, he continued, willingly forgive them their "slaps on the back and their superlatives" if they showed the curiosity of those "rustic Americans" who "spat in our faces" but from whom every day they had learnt "something new or useful."

For want of anything better, Tocqueville could only learn from what he saw with his own eyes. And what he saw every day was a population that was "very courteous, very soft, very docile, not at all thievish, very ignorant, strongly superstitious and, in a way, arrested in a condition of childhood: children happily born but badly brought up." It was, he reflected, subjects like this who enabled Italian governments to survive but how sad, he continued, that "governments were precisely always as rascally as the mores of their subjects allowed them to be."[40] Why had he bothered travelling four hundred leagues, Tocqueville mused, only to learn bad lessons?

Tocqueville's letters to Corcelle and Beaumont also show that, as had been the case many times in the past, he was missing his friends and family in France. "It is," he wrote to Beaumont, "a great and precious thing to have a true friendship like ours." To Corcelle (whose wife was now pregnant) he confided that the distance from friends was made worse by the time it took for letters to arrive and for replies to be received.[41] He was also finding their accommodation in Naples ruinously expensive. One thing was instantly apparent. Any plans to travel south to Sicily had to be abandoned due to Madame de Tocqueville's unwillingness to endure another sea crossing.

Sorrento, the plain and bay (Stephen Dorey—Bygone Images / Alamy Stock Photo)

Thus, waiting upon the advice of Jean-Jacques Ampère, Tocqueville and his wife resolved to rent a house in Sorrento, just south of Naples, where, he had learned, furnished properties could be found fairly cheaply. The ever-cautious Beaumont was not convinced of the merits of the Sorrento climate in winter, warning Tocqueville on hearsay that it would likely be colder than Palermo or even Pisa and Nice and advising him that someone with respiratory problems ought not to go too often to the sea; but, as is evident from the accounts received by all his friends in France, Tocqueville was more than pleased with what they had found in their new accommodation at the Belvedere Guerracino. "I am writing to you," he told Eugène Stoffels at the end of December, "from a little town situated on one of the edges of the bay of Naples, opposite the city and Vesuvius." One could not imagine, Tocqueville continued. "a more delicious region" or, up to now, "a milder climate." The palazzo they had rented was surrounded by olive and orange trees on a hill looking out over the sea.[42] To Louis de Kergorlay he wrote that "the location is charming, the house in which we live very well positioned, very well furnished, and, in sum, infinitely agreeable." There were also walks beyond number.[43]

There was, of course, something very different about this journey abroad from all the others that Tocqueville had made thus far. When Tocqueville travelled to America, to Algeria, to England and Ireland, he did so primarily to study aspects of that country, be it prisons, the poor law, the system of colonial administration, and so on. Upon this occasion, as Tocqueville told Paul Clamorgan, he was in southern Italy with one purpose in mind: to recover his health.[44] Moreover, from what Tocqueville was quick to tell his friends, this seemed to be working. On 30 December, he told Eugène Stoffels that he was in "excellent" health and so much so that he hoped that when he returned to Paris he would do so with the strength to resume an active public life.[45] On the same day Tocqueville penned a similar message to Madame de Circourt, commenting that the wonderful climate was having a better impact than he had dared hope for.[46] Beaumont received similar news: already, Tocqueville wrote, he could feel the beneficial effects of the "admirable" climate and again he expressed the hope that when he returned to Paris in the spring it would be with "a restored health" and feeling stronger than he did before falling ill.[47] Tocqueville wrote again to Beaumont in early January 1851, reporting this time that he and his wife "continue to be enchanted by [their] stay." Madame de Tocqueville, it was true, had been ill with "her usual problems," and Tocqueville's stomach had not always been behaving itself, but these "crises" were rare and short-lived; what mattered was that his lungs were fine and he did not hesitate, therefore, to tell Beaumont that he was "in good health." Nor, it might be added, did Tocqueville hesitate from telling Beaumont that what he had heard about the "freshness" of the Sorrento climate was mistaken. "Never," he wrote, "have I seen in France a month of May as continually warm and beautiful as the month of December that has just come to a close." All that was missing was what Tocqueville described as "the poetry of May, the energetic return of all beings to life and the universal awakening of nature." Not once, he announced proudly, had the night temperature dropped below six degrees centigrade.[48]

If the climate greatly pleased Tocqueville, so did the peace and quiet that he and his wife were enjoying in Sorrento. He told Madame de Circourt that he was living like a hermit. To this he added that he now realised that he preferred living with books rather than with their authors. The former, as opposed to the latter, had "no need to speak about themselves and not the least regret in hearing good said about others." What was more, they could be put down and taken up as one wished.[49] In a letter to one of his many English correspondents, Mrs. Rosalind Phillimore, Tocqueville remarked that he was spending his time with people from past centuries rather than from the nineteenth century.[50] To Beaumont, he explained that, since their arrival, he and his wife had been living in "complete solitude." "We feel the desire for company," he wrote, "but not the need of it, since our isolation does not weigh heavily upon us."[51] Likewise, Tocqueville told his brother Édouard that he was far from certain that he missed the company of others and even less certain that they were "suffering from not having it."[52]

Nonetheless, at the end of December Tocqueville reported to Eugène Stoffels that, if he had "less need of it than at one time," he was short of companionship. The same letter also reported that Tocqueville was expecting the imminent arrival of Jean-Jacques Ampère and that the probability was that he would be staying with the Tocquevilles for the duration of their stay.[53] A letter to Beaumont, dated 5 January 1851, indicated that Ampère was due to arrive in the next five or six days and that his room, of which Tocqueville was clearly very proud, was now ready.[54] Significantly, in the letter to Madame de Circourt cited above, Tocqueville was at pains to exclude Ampère from those authors he had no wish to see. "The least of the merits of this author," Tocqueville wrote, "is that he writes, and I already know from experience that there is no more agreeable and pleasant company than his when one is living away from others."[55]

Ampère duly arrived and stayed with the Tocquevilles until early March. Not only this but, shortly after Tocqueville's death, he provided a brief sketch of how their time had been spent together. He was not to be the only visitor. On 8 December Nassau Senior, with both his wife and his daughter Minnie, arrived in Naples, to be greeted by Tocqueville at the dockside on what, according to Minnie Senior, was "a blazing hot day." In the following weeks, again according to Minnie Senior, Tocqueville "came over to Naples" to join the Seniors in their "sightseeing." Six weeks later, on 25 January 1851, the Seniors moved into the ground floor of the house occupied by the Tocquevilles at Sorrento.

Tocqueville had met Senior on his first visit to London in 1833. Although they subsequently saw each other infrequently, they maintained a lengthy correspondence and over time became firm friends. "Among our friends abroad," Senior's daughter later wrote, "there was no one whom my father loved and valued more than Alexis de Tocqueville."[56] Moreover, from May 1848 onwards, and with Tocqueville's knowledge and approval, Senior began taking extensive notes of their conversations. This he also did during his stay with the Tocquevilles in Sorrento, with the result that his notes, combined with Ampère's short sketch, provide an abundance of detail about Tocqueville's winter sojourn. It makes for fascinating reading and tells us much about Tocqueville.

No sooner had the Seniors arrived in Naples than they dined with the Tocquevilles in Sorrento.[57] From Castellmare to Sorrento, Senior recorded, the coastline was "indescribably beautiful," sinking abruptly into the water. Having had lunch at a local tavern, Tocqueville and Senior set out for a long walk in the orange groves up the hill. Their conversation turned to what else but the recent upsurge of anti-Catholic sentiment in England following the reestablishment of the Roman Catholic diocesan hierarchy by Pope Pius IX in September 1850. "I look to England," Tocqueville reportedly told Senior, "as the great source and the great example of political wisdom and moderation." England's recent "burst of intolerance," he continued, had "set a miserable example of bigotry and violence."[58] Two days later Tocqueville and the Seniors set out to climb Mount Vesuvius. Here we can do no better than cite the account provided by Senior's daughter, Minnie. "[Tocqueville] and I went up Vesuvius together. My father and mother remained at the Hermitage,[59] for they would not walk or submit to be carried up the mountain; but M. de Tocqueville and I started, each led by a guide with a leathern strap over his shoulder, to which we clung, our feet sinking at every step into burning cinders. Every now and then we halted, exhausted, but our guides cried 'Coraggio,' and on we went. My companion confessed afterwards that he was always in hopes of my giving up, but I did not flinch, and we were amply repaid by a glimpse of the infernal regions which we fancied we obtained when we looked down into the crater."[60] If Nassau Senior's notes are to be believed, after what must have been an exhausting day he and Tocqueville then spent the evening in the company of the Neapolitan historian and politician Carlo Troja,[61] and, later still, with Lady Mary Holland, resident at the Palazzo Roccella in Naples. The following morning Tocqueville was back again for breakfast and a visit to the gardens of the Palace of Capodimonte.[62] Three days later Tocqueville declined to participate in a visit to Pompei due to the bad weather, but on 27 December he and Senior were out walking again in the mountains above Sorrento. The year 1851 began with breakfast with one of the rising stars of British politics, the future prime minister William Ewart Gladstone and his wife, wintering *en famille* in Naples due to the poor health of their daughter Mary.[63] Regrettably, neither Senior nor Gladstone left a record of the conversation, but the evidence suggests that Gladstone had an equally dim view of the Neapolitan government, shortly afterwards describing it as "struggling to protect its utter illegality by a tyranny unparalleled at this moment."[64]

By the time that Ampère arrived in early January a pattern had been set of visits, walks, and conversation, and this was much as it continued over the next few weeks until the departure of the Seniors for Rome on 21 February. Sometimes Tocqueville, Senior, and Ampère went out alone; at other times they were accompanied by their female companions on donkeys. Strenuous walks over the mountains and along the coast were interspersed with discussions about Talleyrand, what Prince Louis-Napoleon might have learnt and not learnt when he lived in England, the future of the French Constitution, the reform of the poor laws, the worldliness of the Anglican clergy (of which Tocqueville was not impressed), the excellence of the Russian Army, the memoirs of Louis XVIII, and much more. If Ampère compared the magnificence of imperial Rome unfavourably to that of Thebes, Tocqueville praised "the clearness, the finesse, the gaiety and yet the simplicity" of Voltaire's writing style, placing him ahead of Montesquieu, Buffon, and Rousseau as a writer. A visit to the Convento Camaldoli saw Tocqueville pointing out the resemblance between the current situation in France and the moment before the Coup of 18 Fructidor. Four days later, as Tocqueville, Senior, and Ampère walked to the Deserto di Sant'Agata, the conversation turned to what France had hoped to gain from the Roman expedition of 1849, with Tocqueville providing a surprisingly spirited defence of his own involvement as foreign minister in this controversial military escapade. "The whole purpose of my correspondence," Senior reported Tocqueville as saying, "was to induce the pope to grant liberal institutions to his people."[65]

Each day seemed to bring a new expedition and a new conversation. On 1 February Tocqueville, Ampère, and Senior set out for the ruins of Paestum by coach to see the three ancient Greek temples. The following Friday the three men walked over the mountains to Scaricatori on the Bay of Salerno with their baggage, there to take a rowboat along the coast to Amalfi. "Our boatmen," Senior recorded, with perhaps a little too much enthusiasm, "rowed standing like the Venetians, an exercise which brings all the limbs into play, and gives them fine erect figures." What followed were two very serious days of sightseeing. Time and time again Senior's notes refer to the spectacular beauty of the scenery they travelled through. He also commented on the terrible roads and the shameless beggars they met on their way. Of course, conversation was not always serious, littered as it was by numerous anecdotes. Much amusement was had at the discomfort of the English arising from their knowledge that the "throngs of Americans" now descending upon France and Italy were taken to be their compatriots. Winter came for only a few days around the middle of February.[66]

Ampère's later recollections only serve to confirm the picture painted by Senior's notes. Even by the standards of the climate of Naples, he recalled, the weather was remarkably beautiful and pleasant. Almost every day they were able to go for long walks, collecting violets from the side of the road on their return to present to Madame de Tocqueville, who was waiting for them on the terrace. For, as physically "frail" as he was, Ampère confirmed, Tocqueville was a "great walker," his instinct being always to go in a straight line, climbing over a hedge, a ditch and even a wall when required. "Sometimes," Ampère remembered, "we stopped in some lovely spot, with the sea and the sky of Naples before us. Out of breath, we rested for a moment, and then the conversation resumed." And what fine and erudite conversations they had, Ampère recalled. Tocqueville's "inexhaustible mind," Ampère wrote, "never displayed more activity and more freedom than in moments like these, moving without haste or break and with gentle and variable flow from one subject to another. Subjects succeeded each other without effort, from matters of the highest importance to ingenious remarks and the most pointed anecdote, delivered with an aimiable playfulness and kindly mischief." All of this was done with an elegance and perfection of expression from which Tocqueville was never able to depart.[67]

There were two other things about Tocqueville that Ampère remarked upon. The first was something that he had first noticed when he had visited the château de Tocqueville and something rare, he felt, amongst those who spent their time in the world of ideas and public affairs: "a lively and poetic sense of nature," demonstrated in Tocqueville's passion for light, the mountains and the sea. "When, during our excursions," Ampère recollected, "we found ourselves before a magnificent vista I saw him stop and fall into ecstasy." In those moments, Ampère commented, Tocqueville was as much a poet as Chateaubriand.[68] The second thing Ampère noticed was that Tocqueville was at times discouraged and disheartened. Ampère recognised that in part this was because of the worries he had about his health. It arose too out of a spirit of perfectionism and the sense that he might not attain it in the writing he was now beginning to contemplate. But Tocqueville's discouragement was also a "political discouragement," something which weighed upon and often overwhelmed him. "At Sorrento," Ampère wrote, "I recall that, when the newspapers contained something that might distress him, Madame de Tocqueville took care that they should not fall into his hands during the evening. for fear that he would have a very bad night."[69]

For all of Tocqueville's claim in a letter to Paul Clamorgan that he had sought to avoid anything that would deflect from the goal of restoring his health, we know from Tocqueville's letters to his friends that whilst in Sorrento he continued to follow political developments in France closely, and that, as Madame de Tocqueville saw, they continued to distress him.[70] Writing to one of his parliamentary colleagues at the end of January, he confessed that he was very pessimistic about the future, adding "I believe that we are struggling in vain and that the nation is leading us away from liberty."[71]

We also know from these same letters that it was not to be long after his arrival in Sorrento that Tocqueville turned his thoughts to writing again. For all that he hugely enjoyed the beautiful landscape and incomparable climate, Tocqueville realised that if he did not find something to occupy his mind he would quickly become bored.

Already by mid-December 1850 Tocqueville was writing to Louis de Kergorlay as follows: "I brought some books here and intend to continue what I had already begun at Tocqueville this summer, with much spirit and pleasure, which was an account of what I saw during the Revolution of 1848 and after, events and men."[72] Two weeks later Beaumont received the same news, Tocqueville informing him that he had taken up the writing of *Souvenirs* once more and that it was now his habit to spend his mornings "giving some nourishment to my mind." Again, Tocqueville emphasised that what interested him were the events and people he had seen at close quarters. The latter, Tocqueville wrote, "are pretty nasty models, of whom I paint fairly mediocre pictures, but a gallery of contemporaries is often more pleasing to see than the most beautiful portraits of the most illustrious dead."[73] Tocqueville admitted to both Corcelle and Adolphe de Circourt that, in part, he was seeking a form of distraction from his worries about France but, as he made clear in a letter to Eugène Stoffels in late December, after years in politics, when the opportunity had not existed, he was eager to start writing again. Moreover, Tocqueville felt that these (mostly wasted) years had made him a better judge of men and of how politics worked, and thus better placed to fulfil the task he was now setting himself.[74]

How did Tocqueville see his recent past from the vantage point of the Belvedere Guerracino in sunny Sorrento? Tocqueville's letter to Kergorlay announcing that the writing of *Souvenirs* was again underway emphasised (as he was to do in the opening paragraph of the text) that the success of the enterprise depended upon his recollections of 1848 never coming before the public. Only if this were the case could he voice "free judgements" upon his contemporaries and himself. The first part of the text was written in the summer of 1850 when Tocqueville had returned to his family home in Normandy.

It provided a sorry description of a France reduced to a corrupt appendage of the interests of the bourgeoisie, with King Louis-Philippe, a man whose defects mirrored those of his age, as its figurehead. "The spirit peculiar to the middle class," Tocqueville wrote, "became the general spirit of government; it dominated foreign affairs as well as domestic policy. This spirit was active, industrious, often dishonest, generally steady, sometimes reckless through vanity and egoism, timid by temperament, moderate in all things except the taste for well-being, and mediocre, a spirit that, if mixed with that of the people or the aristocracy, can work wonders but that alone never produces anything except a government without virtue and without greatness."[75] Government therefore took on the features of a trading company operating solely for the private benefit of the new ruling class.[76] Tocqueville's "sombre predictions" of the fate awaiting such a regime, he recalled, were met by "insulting laughter." Gradually the idea took root in his mind that France was marching towards a revolution. Nonetheless, as Tocqueville readily admitted, on the eve of the revolution he went to bed unaware that he had seen the last day of the July Monarchy.[77]

The second (and by far the largest) part of *Souvenirs* was written in Sorrento. It covered the period from the outbreak of the revolution in February 1848 until the time immediately after the June days when Tocqueville was involved in the framing of the new constitution. It began with a series of important reflections on the causes of the revolution. "For my part," Tocqueville began, "I hate those absolute systems that make all the events of history depend on great first causes linked together by a chain of fate and thus banish, so to speak, men from the history of the human race." Rather, he believed that "many important historical facts can only be explained by accidental circumstances and that many others are inexplicable." Chance was an important factor in all that we saw occurring in what he described as "the theatre of the world." But, for all that, Tocqueville was equally convinced that "chance can do nothing that has not been prepared in advance." Thus, in his view, the February Revolution was born of general causes "fertilised" by accidents.[78]

These causes, in Tocqueville's opinion, were many and included, inter alia, what he described as the dramatic increase in the labouring population of Paris (many of whom were unemployed); the passion for material pleasures; the democratic disease of envy; the rise of economic and social theories encouraging the view that poverty could be abolished; the contempt with which the ruling class was held; the centralisation of power, meaning that control of Paris was all that was required to bring about a successful revolution; and, last but not least, "the mobility of everything, institutions, ideas, mores and people, in a moving society which had been shaken by seven great revolutions in less than sixty years."[79] The main accidents were likewise many in number: the clumsiness of the opposition, which, in wanting reform, had prepared the way for riots; the inconsistent manner in which those riots were repressed, "at first harshly, then abandoned"; the sudden disappearance of government ministers which left new ministers without the means to reestablish the threads of power; the mistakes of those very ministers who proved themselves incapable of rebuilding what they had so skilfully destroyed; the indecision of the military; the absence from France of the only two members of the royal family—Louis-Philippe's sons, the prince de Joinville and the duc d'Aumale—who enjoyed any popularity; and, if this were not enough, the "senile imbecility" of Louis-Philippe himself, something that "nobody could have foreseen and which, after the event, remains almost unbelievable even today."[80]

These, Tocqueville admitted, were causes of the revolution that he could now think about calmly and comfortably but, as he recalled, on the afternoon of 24 February his mind had been preoccupied by what would come of these events. "I had," he wrote, "spent the best years of my youth in a society that seemed to be regaining prosperity and grandeur as it regained its liberty; I had conceived the idea of a regulated and orderly liberty, controlled by religious beliefs, mores, and laws; I had been touched by the joys of such a liberty, and it had become my life's passion; I had felt that I could never be consoled for its loss, and now I clearly saw that I must give it up forever."[81]

What he knew was that several revolutions, one after the other, would make the enjoyment of such an orderly liberty impossible for a long time to come. It was, as Tocqueville put it, to be the fate of his generation to live their lives between "the alternative reactions of license and oppression." The July Monarchy, in short, had not brought the French Revolution to a close, as he had hoped.[82]

Tocqueville continued his narrative, recalling that the night of 24 February passed "without incident, although the streets did not cease to resound to shouts and rifle fire until the morning." The following day he had set out across Paris to see what had happened to his two nephews, both of whom were attending a Catholic boarding school in the Rue Madame, close to the Luxembourg Palace. If the streets were quiet and half deserted, two things had struck him: first, the "uniquely and exclusively popular character" of the revolution and the absolute power it had given to the people; and second, the fact that so little hatred was displayed by the lower classes at their moment of victory. Nevertheless, what Tocqueville saw on that day was that "the February Revolution seemed to have been made entirely outside and against the bourgeoisie."[83] The people stood alone and were in sole possession of power. In his perambulations, Tocqueville saw not one former agent of public authority—not a single soldier, gendarme or policeman—and even the National Guard had vanished. The people alone carried arms and protected public buildings. Many people had therefore anticipated violence and looting, but oddly, Tocqueville remembered, the atmosphere was one of languor. With the monarchy vanished, the battlefield was empty and "the people no longer saw clearly what enemies remained to be pursued and brought down."[84] Nonetheless, the shock of the revolution had reduced society itself "to dust" and a competition quickly ensued to determine what "new edifice" should be put in its place. Most of these theories, Tocqueville wrote, came under the common name of socialism; and it was socialism, he believed, that would "remain the defining feature and the most redoubtable memory of the February Revolution."[85]

Tocqueville quickly pointed out that it was no part of his enterprise to inquire why the February Revolution had had this socialist character but, from the vantage point of distance, he drew two conclusions. The first was that given that the "ridiculous" theories of socialism had been proposed by so many people, nothing, he wrote, "is more worthy of the serious attention of philosophers and statesmen than the backcloth on which they worked." The second conclusion followed from the challenge posed by socialism to what Tocqueville regarded as "the constituent laws of modern society." Would those laws, he now asked, ever be modified and abolished, and replaced by others? This, Tocqueville wrote, seemed impracticable. However, he continued,

> the more I study what the world was like and the more I see in detail of the world of today, when I consider the prodigious diversity to be found there, not only with regard to laws but in the principles of laws and the different forms that the right to property has taken and continues to take today in the world, whatever people might say, I am tempted to believe that what are called necessary institutions are often only institutions to which we are accustomed and that, when it comes to the constitution of society, the realm of the possible is far wider than the people who live in any particular society imagine.[86]

If Tocqueville did not want to analyse why the February Revolution had been defined by socialism, nor was it his intention to provide a history of the revolution. Rather, he wrote, what he wanted to do was "retrace [his] own actions, thoughts and impressions" during this time and discover the reasons that had determined his conduct through "this labyrinth." The big question he had faced was whether he wished to be a simple spectator of the revolution or to involve himself in events. Here Tocqueville rehearsed all the reasons why he had been so unhappy as a politician during the July Monarchy, not least his early discovery that he "did not possess what was necessary to play the brilliant role [he] had dreamed of."[87] So, Tocqueville recorded, somewhat to his surprise he had felt a sense of liberation when it all came to an end. No longer would he be subject to distasteful monotony and mediocrity and no more would he need to witness the petty passions and vulgar perversity of his parliamentary colleagues. But, as he also acknowledged, the revolution had destroyed this world and, as he saw it at the time, what lay ahead might require different skills and ones that he possessed. Moreover, he was still young and had few wants, no children, and had a devoted wife whose support he could rely on. "I therefore decided," Tocqueville wrote, "to throw myself headlong into the arena and sacrifice my wealth, peace of mind and life to defend not a particular government but the laws that constitute society itself."[88]

What followed in the remainder of the text written in Sorrento was a vivid account of how Tocqueville duly threw himself into the fray. However, it included an important admission. "It is a mistake to suppose," Tocqueville wrote, "that events stay in the memory simply because of their importance or greatness: it is more often the little things that make a deep impression on the mind and stay in the memory."[89] Tocqueville therefore admitted that, apart from the repeated calls of "Vive la république," he had only the dimmest recollection of the opening of the Constituent Assembly on 4 May. Of his election to the assembly, he remembered that everyone was for the republic, but what sort of republic people wanted was far from clear. Quoting his own election address, Tocqueville specified that his republic was not one of a "dictatorship exercised in the name of liberty."[90] He also remembered that the prevailing sentiment among his Norman constituents was a "universal hatred and terror" of Paris. Above all, this experience was tinged with the profound sadness of seeing his family home empty and deserted, the fires out and the clocks run down, with only his dog to greet him. "Believe me," Tocqueville wrote, "that it was then and there that I fully understood the bitterness of revolutions."[91]

Returning to Paris, Tocqueville was shocked to see that it contained thousands of armed workmen, many without work and dying of hunger. He saw immediately that if there had been more mischievous revolutionaries than those of 1848, there had been none more stupid. "By establishing universal suffrage," Tocqueville wrote, "they believed that they were calling the people to support the revolution, whereas in truth they were only arming them against it."[92] It came therefore as a painful surprise to those who had made the revolution that they did not receive the people's votes, something they attributed to the nation's ignorance and lack of gratitude.

Nor did Tocqueville spare his fellow parliamentarians from his criticism. Taken as a whole, Tocqueville believed that the membership of the assembly was an improvement upon any he had previously seen. Many of its members were sincere, disinterested, honest, and even courageous. Oddly, it contained more landowners and more clergy than had been the case during the Restoration. "I counted," Tocqueville recalled, "three bishops, several vicars general and a Dominican." But one thing he noticed immediately was the eagerness of many members of the assembly to be seen to be imitating the days of the National Convention between 1792 and 1795. If this involved exhortations to wear the dress of the convention—in particular, a white waistcoat in the style of Robespierre—it also meant that those possessing the most revolutionary opinions sat themselves, as revolutionary tradition dictated, on the highest benches in the chamber. Looking out at these people, Tocqueville wrote, was "like the discovery of a new world." They spoke, he recalled, "a jargon that was neither the French of the ignorant nor that of the literate but that had the defects of both." A constant stream of personal insults and humorous remarks poured down from them.[93]

Another form of imitation was what Tocqueville regarded as the vaguely ridiculous reenactment of the allegorical festivals of the 1789 revolution. One was the Festival of Concord on 21 May, organised by the provisional government at great expense even though it had no money. Tocqueville admitted that on the day he took his place by the École militaire with pistols in his pockets. Once there, he was promised "fraternal confusion" in the form of peasants and maidens dressed in white and singing patriotic songs as well as oxen with gilded horns. The reality was that the brawny white-clad maidens, some three hundred in number and more used to wielding a washerwoman's beetle than strewing flowers, threw their bouquets into the crowd with such force that they fell like hailstones. A tall young girl then recited an ode in honour of the poet Alphonse de Lamartine, one of the great heroes of the revolution, with a face, Tocqueville recounted, so fearsomely contorted that she looked as if she was suffering from epilepsy. As for "fraternal confusion," much of this was in evidence but "without disorder," for, as Tocqueville commented, "we are a strange people: we cannot survive without the maintenance of law and order when we are well behaved, but when we are in the middle of a revolution it seems to become unnecessary."[94]

Lamartine, then, in Tocqueville's words, at "the height of his fame," was subject to particular scorn. "I do not think," Tocqueville recollected, "that, in the world of ambitious egoists in the midst of which I lived, I have ever met a mind so empty of any thought of the public good than his." Lamartine alone seemed always ready to turn the world upside down to amuse himself. Never, Tocqueville wrote, had he known anyone less sincere or more contemptuous of the truth.[95] Usually, he continued, he found Lamartine surrounded by "petitioners" and "political beggars," because "every revolution ruins a certain number of men and, amongst us, a ruined man always relies on the state to retrieve his losses."[96]

If anything, the aged revolutionary Auguste Blanqui fared even worse in Tocqueville's account. The memory of his appearance at the rostrum, Tocqueville wrote, had ever since filled him with disgust and horror. "He had," he remembered, "emaciated and sullen cheeks, pale lips, the look of someone ill, nasty and filthy, with the sallow pallor of a musty corpse; no linen was visible beneath his old black frockcoat that clung to his thin and fleshless limbs: he looked as if he had lived in a sewer and had just remerged from it."[97] "I have always thought," Tocqueville added a few pages later, "that in revolutions, and above all in democratic revolutions, madmen (real madmen, and not those referred to metaphorically as being mad) have played a very considerable political role."[98] As for socialist Louis Blanc, Tocqueville damned him with faint praise. On the day that the parliamentary chamber was invaded by an armed and unruly mob, Tocqueville wrote, for once Blanc made a good speech. "I never thought that he possessed talent except on that day, as I do not regard talent as the art of fashioning brilliant but empty phrases, which are like beautifully engraved plates with nothing on them." Tocqueville could not resist pointing out that, upon this occasion, Blanc did not have a stool brought forward him for him to stand on in order that his head might be seen above the speaker's rostrum. He was, Tocqueville commented, "almost a dwarf."[99]

Despite this unpleasant company, Tocqueville recorded that initially he had been happy in this environment. For the first time since entering public life, he felt that he was moving in the direction of the majority and in a way that was in accord with his "tastes, reason and conscience." "I agreed with them," Tocqueville wrote, "on two important points: I had absolutely no faith in the monarchy . . . [and] no cause to defend other than that of liberty and human dignity."[100] Nonetheless, the days that followed the Festival of Concord were ones of anxious anticipation. Everyone knew that a crisis was looming and that the issue that would bring it to a head was the fate of Blanc's National Workshops. Outside Paris, Tocqueville remembered, the fear of socialism made the republic more and more hated. It was then, Tocqueville recalled, that the name of Louis-Napoleon first came to the fore, the nation increasingly behaving like "a flock of frightened sheep running hither and thither." Tocqueville had no doubt that France was on the eve of a terrible struggle. It was then, for the first and last time, that he met the writer George Sand at the Paris house of his English friend, Richard Monckton Milnes. Placed next to Madame Sand at the table, Tocqueville admitted that, despite his prejudices against her, he was charmed by her wonderful expression, her intelligence, and her simplicity of manners and language. Above all, Tocqueville remembered her remark, "Try to encourage your friends, Monsieur, not to drive the people out into the streets by rousing or offending them, just as I hope to persuade my friends to have patience; because, if the fighting breaks out, believe me, you will all perish."[101] The long-awaited crisis duly arrived in the form of the June Days uprising. Tocqueville devoted two full chapters to these events and their aftermath, but the conclusions he reached were not much different from the immediate impressions he recorded in his letters to his friends. This was class struggle, and of an especially brutal kind. Women played as important a part as men, carrying their passions as housewives into battle. "They counted on victory," Tocqueville wrote, "to ease the circumstances of their husbands and to help them bring up their children."[102] As gunfire spread across Paris and barricades closed the streets, an old woman with a vegetable barrow rushed at him in a sort of frenzy. "Her hideous and terrible expression," Tocqueville wrote, "horrified me, as it so clearly displayed the fury of demagogic passions and rage let loose by civil wars."[103] As the outcome of the insurrection lay in the balance, he recalled, Paris "resembled a city of antiquity whose citizens defended the walls like heroes because they knew that, were the city taken, they would themselves be led into slavery."[104]

In the days that followed, Tocqueville trudged the streets, satisfying his curiosity to know how the battle against the insurrection was playing out. Such, Tocqueville concluded, were the "necessary and fateful" June days. They did not extinguish the "revolutionary fire" in France but they did deliver "the nation from the oppression of the workers of Paris." But Tocqueville quickly realised something else. If the struggle of the June days had been necessary, he saw that, after them, "the nation's character would be somehow changed; a love of independence would be succeeded by a fear of and perhaps a distaste for free institutions; after such an abuse of liberty, a backlash was inevitable." At first, he argued, this was hardly visible to the naked eye, but this movement had now become "impetuous and irresistible."[105]

At this point, the narrative written at Sorrento changes focus. Now, as Tocqueville's stay in Italy drew to a close, he turned his attention to the framing of the new constitution in the latter half of 1848, something in which both he and Beaumont had played a key role as members of the Committee for the Constitution, and not always with complete success. Tocqueville's account of the committee's proceeding reads as a recitation of dashed hopes, muddled thinking, and incompetence. "Looking at the committee as a whole," he wrote, "it is very easy to see that nothing very remarkable should have been expected of it." Its members, most of whom understood no system of government other than monarchy or had gleaned their ideas from what they had read in the newspapers, "bore little resemblance to those men, so sure of their aim and so well acquainted with the means of attaining it, who drafted the American constitution sixty years ago with Washington in the chair." Moreover, the committee constantly had an eye on what was happening outside Parliament. In brief, and after much bluster and posturing, the constitution that was ratified on 4 November 1848 had two key components: in deference to revolutionary tradition, it adopted the idea of a sovereign unicameral parliamentary chamber, and from the American experience it borrowed the practice of a powerful executive or president legitimised by election based on universal male suffrage. As his statements at the time and his comments in *Souvenirs* testify, Tocqueville had grave doubts about both. "I declare," he wrote from Sorrento, "that I have never been more unhappy on any other committee I have served on." By his own admission, Tocqueville (along with Beaumont) also made "a serious error" and one he feared (rightly) that would have "unfortunate consequences."[106]

From the outset Tocqueville was concerned that a strong executive could pose a threat to the existence of the republic, and this concern was only heightened by the decision to elect the president by means of direct, male universal suffrage. As Tocqueville recorded, his view was that either the prerogatives of the president had to be subject to strict limits or election had to be indirect (as was the case in the United States). Anything else risked disaster. Tocqueville's big mistake, based on what he and Beaumont had seen in America of the way in which the reelection of the president encouraged corruption and excessive patronage, was then to propose that the president could not be reelected for a second term. "Our minds," he confessed in Sorrento, "were not supple or quick enough to turn around and see that as soon as it was decided that the citizens themselves would directly elect the President, the damage was irreparable, and that any rash attempt to hinder the people in their choice would only increase it." "This vote and the great influence I had on the result," Tocqueville wrote, "is the most painful memory that remains with me of this time."[107] That Louis-Napoleon was elected as president by a landslide—only just over a month after the constitution was ratified—must have only added salt to Tocqueville's wounds.

This much is already well known, but what makes this final section of Tocqueville's Sorrento text so worth reading are his more general reflections on the attitudes and opinions of those he was surrounded by and of the French people. "There is no nation," he wrote, "that feels less attachment to its government than the French nation, and none knows less how to do without it. As soon as the nation sees that it must walk unaided, it suffers from a sort of giddiness, which makes it think that at any moment it is going to fall into the abyss."[108] Similarly, Tocqueville became convinced that one thing, at least, was safe from the ravages of revolution: the French system of administrative centralisation[109]. "In France," Tocqueville saw, "there is almost only one thing we cannot make: a free government; and only one thing that we cannot destroy: centralisation." Above all, he came to the conclusion that the French, if they had lost the taste for monarchy, sought to preserve its spirit. "Under such conditions," Tocqueville wrote, "what could a president elected by the people be, if not a pretender to the throne. The institution could only suit someone who wanted to use it to help turn presidential power into royal power."[110] Here it should be noted that these remarks were made in the spring, before Louis-Napoleon carried out his coup d'état in December 1851. They also provide us with important clues as to the intellectual project that was to dominate the remaining years of Tocqueville's life.

For all of its incisive commentary and biting portraits of his contemporaries, much of *Souvenirs* reads as an exercise in self-justification. If only Tocqueville's advice had been followed, the republic would have been saved.

Yet, when in solitude he looked at himself in the mirror, he could not hide his own failings. He knew that he had misjudged the political forces of the day. He accepted that his own recommendations for a new constitution made the ignominious fall into Bonapartist dictatorship almost inevitable. He knew that his achievements were mediocre at best. To his friend Louis de Kergorlay he wrote from Sorrento, "I am better in thought than in action."[111]

Worse still, as he wrote in the same letter, for a man who had no traditions, who belonged to no party, and had "no cause other than that of liberty and human dignity" it was now all but impossible not to feel a stranger in his own land.[112] As Tocqueville wrote to Francisque de Corcelle shortly before he left Sorrento, "I entered public life under liberal and constitutional institutions, and I am adamant about not remaining in public life without them."[113] If Tocqueville's health had been (temporarily) restored by his winter in the sun, it was far from certain what his return to France would bring. It was certainly his hope that he would be able to rejoin his friends in the struggle that he knew lay ahead. "The responsibility for being absent during critical times," he told his former ministerial colleague, Jules Dufaure, on 12 March, "seems to me to be more difficult to bear than the acts I might commit were I present. Thank God! I am reaching the end of my time away and I will soon retake my place among you."[114] To another of his Sorrento correspondents, Arthur de Gobineau, Tocqueville expressed the same sentiments but in more colourful prose. "Politics," he wrote, "is like an old hussy from whom you cannot disentangle yourself long after you have ceased to love her."[115]

CHAPTER SEVEN

Sorrento and Saint-Cyr-sur-Loire

Alexis de Tocqueville was already turning his thoughts to leaving Sorrento by the end of February 1851 but, as he explained to his friend Gustave de Beaumont, he continued to be concerned about the health of his wife, Mary, and he worried that their return journey might be as unpleasant as their outward voyage had been. According to Tocqueville, his wife had only left the grounds of their house on five or six occasions during their stay. As for his own health, if his stomach continued to give him problems, he was feeling better and his peace of mind was restored, and so much so that he was even beginning to see others in a more positive light and, no less importantly, to believe that the political status quo might survive until his return to Paris.[1] Nonetheless, such was Tocqueville's concern about the planned return journey and his fear of the consequences for his wife's health of a carriage journey across what passed for French roads that he asked Jean-Charles Rivet if new railway lines had been opened north of Dijon. Once more, however, the travel plans of the Tocquevilles were disrupted, their departure in early April being postponed—much to Tocqueville's relief, as the most "dreadful storm" swept across the Bay of Naples on their planned day of departure—and they eventually set off for Marseilles on 14 April, returning safely (and seemingly without incident) to Paris at the end of the month.

What is clear is that Tocqueville's dislike and disapproval of Italy had not diminished during his stay. To an unknown correspondent on the day before his departure he wrote, "I find myself in a country where one sees and one feels all the conceivable excesses that arise from a government that is absolute and beyond control, in much the same way that, in our own country, we so often encounter those produced by anarchy. I confess that the one is no better than the other, both being different forms of baseness but forms of baseness in both cases. It is sufficient to see both countries to become a passionate supporter of moderate liberty, if one was not one already."[2]

For all that Tocqueville was determined to return to Paris, Beaumont and others continued to advise him that he should remain in Sorrento, in part for health reasons but also because his return to active politics, they believed, would serve little or only "occasional" purpose. With each day, Beaumont wrote, he became less convinced that there was "anything to be done and anything to be undertaken that might be both honourable and worthwhile to attempt." The chances of returning to a politics that was "wise, peaceable, and responsible," he told Tocqueville in what was to be his last letter to Sorrento, seemed "more or less utopian." Political adventurism, according to Beaumont, was now the order of the day.[3]

In the third part of his *Souvenirs,* written in Versailles to the west of Paris during the autumn of 1851, Tocqueville provided a vivid portrait of the Louis-Napoleon with whom he had worked when a government minister. If this portrait pinpointed the president's faults—he was much given to vulgar enjoyments and had a confused and incoherent mind—it was also generous enough to acknowledge that, as a private individual, he had some attractive qualities. Louis-Napoleon, Tocqueville recalled, had an easygoing temperament and displayed a perfect simplicity, as well as an element of personal modesty. He could also feel and evoke affection. But Tocqueville quickly perceived two other things about the president: Louis-Napoleon firmly believed that he was the instrument of destiny; and, after ruling France for four years, this was not a man who would be prepared to return quietly to private life. "Even to prevent him," Tocqueville wrote, "from throwing himself into some dangerous enterprise during his term of office seemed very difficult unless one could find a way to divert or restrain his ambition." This, Tocqueville confessed, was precisely what he had sought to do when he had served as a minister and to the point that he had proposed to the president that the constitution could be amended with the goal of allowing his reelection. As far as possible, Tocqueville wrote, "I made great efforts to please him."[4]

Tocqueville referred to this strategy in a letter written to Francisque de Corcelle from Sorrento in February 1851. "Once Louis-N was elected," he told Corcelle, "I immediately thought that the best thing was to try to reach an understanding with him, not to overthrow the republic but to modify it in such a way as to create a greater place for him within it." Unfortunately, Tocqueville recalled, the political leaders of the day had not seen it that way, naively believing that they could control and dispatch a man they regarded as an imbecile, with the result that France was now facing "a great national movement which is leading us not only out of the republic, but, momentarily at least, out of our liberty." In this situation, Tocqueville now admitted, "if the nation no longer wants the republic, I would be just as happy to slide into a constitutional monarchy with L.-N, who is there, rather than with great effort go looking for another ruler whom we do not have at the ready and who would leave us as divided as we are." The problem, as Tocqueville readily conceded, was that Louis-Napoleon would "never reduce himself to submitting to even the indirect influence of a parliament" and therefore to ruling as something like a constitutional monarch. "He would rather remain the temporary president of a republic," Tocqueville concluded, "than become a constitutional prince and one subject to the control of an assembly."[5]

Given this analysis of what was possible, it is difficult to know what to make of the course of action pursued by Tocqueville immediately upon his return as a member of the Constituent Assembly in Paris. In brief, Tocqueville set about trying to secure a revision of the constitution such as to allow Louis-Napoleon to stand again for election as president (in the knowledge that, if he were allowed to stand again, his victory would be assured). If the pursuit of this goal saw Tocqueville appointed rapporteur to the parliamentary committee charged with making proposals for constitutional revision, it also involved a face-to-face meeting with the prince-president in mid-May where Tocqueville set out what he took to be the various options open to him. As Tocqueville knew, Louis-Napoleon was no fool, and both men must have known that the possibility of constitutional revision to allow a second consecutive presidential term was slim indeed. This proved to be the case. For his part, upon hearing that Tocqueville's proposal for constitutional revision had not been carried,[6] Louis-Napoleon set about planning a coup d'état, something he and the French Army effected with great efficiency on 2 December 1851.

In the interim, and with the French Parliament prorogued for three months, Tocqueville first returned to Normandy (without his wife, who was again ill), where his duties as a member of the *conseil-général* kept him busy until early September. He returned to Versailles exhausted and not in the best of health but also with a firm view of the state of opinion in his *département*. "I think," he wrote to Beaumont, "that I have discerned this: no passion and virtually no support for the President of the Republic; a general tolerance for those who do not like him but an almost universal endorsement for reelecting him *because he is there*."[7] The reappointment of the president, most probably by unconstitutional means, seemed the most likely outcome.

What Tocqueville was less certain about was what he and Beaumont should now do. "Like you," he wrote to Beaumont, "I think that we should remain not neutral but in reserve, and, as you say, we should above all avoid committing ourselves to civil war in the hope of being able to intervene at the last moment, and, if the President wins, we should stand firm on issues of constitutional liberty." "There is," he continued, "only one line that I can be sure always to follow: to fight for the triumph of our liberties for as long as this crisis continues or go down with them." All else, Tocqueville believed, was of secondary importance.[8]

In the meantime, as again he told Beaumont, Tocqueville's intention was to resume the writing of his *Souvenirs,* something he duly did on 16 September. To Henry Reeve, two months later, Tocqueville commented that he was attempting to isolate himself from both his time and his country, the political spectacle before him being so distressing that he was hiding himself away in "literature."[9] Nevertheless, Tocqueville clearly sensed what was on the horizon. His stay in Sorrento, he informed Nassau Senior only four days before Louis-Napoleon's coup d'état, now appeared to him like a "tranquil and charming refuge" placed between the two "shipwrecks" of the February Revolution of 1848 and "what will follow."[10]

For all its meticulous planning, the coup d'état did not go entirely to plan. Some two hundred parliamentary representatives (including Tocqueville and Beaumont) rushed to the National Assembly, only to find their entry blocked by troops. They next convened in the *mairie* of what was then Paris's tenth arrondissement, whereupon they passed a unanimous motion deposing the president and indulged themselves in other futile heroics. Eventually they were all marched off by the army through the streets of Paris and placed under arrest in the riverside barracks of the Quai d'Orsay. The next day Tocqueville, along with fifty or so other deputies, was transferred in a prison van used to transport common criminals to the military prison in Vincennes on the eastern edge of Paris. He had no idea how long he would be detained or where Beaumont had been imprisoned. That evening, after a visit from his valet, Tocqueville was told that he could be released, but he refused to go while his fellow deputies remained.[11] He did, however, leave on 4 December. Throughout, as his notes to her testify, Tocqueville's primary concern was that his wife should not be worried about his well-being. He was also pleased that he had remained calm and strong and had acted "like a man who had done his duty."[12]

Tocqueville left behind two detailed accounts of these few days. The first appeared anonymously in *The Times* in London on 11 December 1851. It was designed to convince an English audience of the illegality of what had taken place and to encourage the English not to lend their support to what he described as "military saturnalia."[13] The second is found in a record of a conversation Tocqueville had with Nassau Senior and others in Paris on New Year's Eve 1851. Remarkably, Tocqueville was able to see a lighter side to his imprisonment. "The gayest time that I ever passed," Tocqueville recounted, "was in the Quai d'Orsay. The elite of France in education, in birth, and in talents, particularly in the talents of society, was collected within the walls of those barracks." After being penned in for a couple of hours in the courtyard, he told the assembled guests, he and the duc de Broglie tore a chicken apart with their hands and teeth for something to eat. That night, instead of sleeping, he and his fellow inmates exchanged "anecdotes, repartees, jokes and pleasantries." Many hired straw mattresses from the soldiers but, being too idle to bother, Tocqueville chose to lie on the floor in his cloak. "Things amused us in that state of excitement," he told his friends, "which sound flat when repeated."[14]

Yet Tocqueville patently felt deeply humiliated by the indignities inflicted upon him. He was also incandescent with rage at the crime that had been committed and at what he saw as the way the French people had so easily adapted themselves to its outcome. "I know," he wrote to his brother Édouard on 7 December, "that the coup is over, the crime committed, and that the only thing to do for the moment is to submit"; but, he continued, he had no need to be told (as his brother was seeking to tell him) that "the people are quite amenable to the new regime and were prepared in advance to forgive any violation of liberty and legality." This he understood only too well, for he knew this "tired, nervous, half-rotten France, which asks only to obey whoever will ensure its material well-being." "Our souls," Tocqueville went on, "are so degraded that it is not only peasants, bourgeois and shopkeepers who will readily sacrifice liberty, dignity and the country's honour" for peace and quiet and the assurance that they can sell their wares. The salons of Paris were full of the nation's elite—"would-be gentlemen" and "weak, silly women"—who were so scared and so fearful for their wealth that "what has happened and is still happening—the ignominy of the new regime—fills them with joy." It was, Tocqueville wrote, "an awful spectacle" and so much so that it was "almost unbearable." He felt, he told his brother in what was to become an oft-repeated refrain, a stranger in his own country.[15]

A week or so later Tocqueville told Jean-Bernardin Rouxel, the mayor of Tocqueville, that what had happened in Paris was "abominable" and that the French nation so passionately desired to enjoy its material comforts that it was "unworthy of being free."[16] Talking to Nassau Senior over afternoon tea on 21 December, Tocqueville apparently commented, "This is a new phase in our history. Every previous revolution has been made by a political party. This is the first time that the army has seized France, bound and gagged her, and laid her at the feet of its new ruler."[17]

The question now was what, if anything, Tocqueville was going to do. Writing to Beaumont in mid-January 1852 he reported that he was so upset by what he was seeing and hearing in Paris that he was unable to work. The publication of the new constitution, which Tocqueville regarded as "the most despotic" France had ever seen, did nothing to raise his spirits. Nor did his realisation that this was a regime that was going to last for some time to come. All that remained, he told Beaumont, was the role of spectator. In February he remarked similarly to his brother Édouard that he had "no desire to serve [his] country in its present condition." It was therefore with great regret but some relief that Tocqueville resigned from his position on the departmental *conseil-général* to begin a new life he described to Beaumont as internal exile.

Tocqueville's only consolations were that there was no alternative course of action and that, as he would be out of public life, he could develop new habits and new interests. By mid-April he was telling Beaumont that he was now working, but "lazily."[18] We also know that he had started to visit the Bibliothèque royale in the afternoons. "The life that I am leading," he told Beaumont, "does not displease me but the view of this country that I glimpse from over the top of my books grieves me greatly."[19]

In the early summer of 1852, Tocqueville left Paris for his home in Normandy, from where he told his father that for the moment there was nothing better to be done "than distance oneself and write." With Jean-Jacques Ampère as a house guest, Tocqueville told Beaumont that he, his wife, and Ampère were living like Benedictine monks.[20] "Each one of us," he told his father, "works in our cell and we come together briefly over meals. Nothing could be more agreeable for people of our temperament than such a life."[21] As for what Tocqueville was now writing about, he told Beaumont that he had still not found a subject but he was searching for one with "despairing energy." Two weeks later, on 16 July, Tocqueville reported to Beaumont that he had now sketched out a chapter.[22]

What *was* Tocqueville writing about? A clue to the answer can be found in the aforementioned letter to Jean-Bernardin Rouxel dated 14 December 1851. Having told Rouxel that he would distance himself from public life until such time as genuine representative institutions had been restored, Tocqueville continued by stating that "for a long time I have had in my head the subject of a new book which, in anticipation of the events that have just occurred, I started last winter in Sorrento and which I now ardently desire to have the leisure to continue." As soon as the good weather returned, he added, he planned to travel to Tocqueville and stay there until the book was finished.[23] Duly arrived that summer in Normandy, he wrote from Tocqueville in July to another of his Cotentin acquaintances, Zacharie Gallemand, telling him, "I believe that I have acquired the right to live a little for myself" and as such, he continued, he had taken up his studies again and had begun work on a project he had "thought about for a long time." A month later, in a second letter to Gallemand, Tocqueville was more specific about the nature of his studies. "Being no more than a mere nothing in the present," he wrote, "I am seeking to live usefully in the past; and the hard work I have undertaken leads me to make a very detailed and, if possible, more accurate examination than has been done so far of what was the condition of French society at the moment when the Revolution transformed it so harshly and doubtless too quickly, but nonetheless to the great advantage of the generations that followed." He had already read a work by Étienne Le Royer de la Tournerie on feudal rights in Normandy, Tocqueville told Gallemand, but he was now seeking advice on possible other source material that Gallemand, himself a sizeable landowner, might be familiar with.[24]

In brief, Tocqueville had begun working on what was to become *L'ancien régime et la révolution*. As these comments show, this was something he had been thinking about since his stay in Sorrento.

It was as early as 1836 that Tocqueville had first published an essay on French society and politics prior to the Revolution of 1789. This he did in a text written at the request of John Stuart Mill, who published it in the *London and Westminster Review*.[25] In it are to be found several of the themes that were to figure prominently in the book Tocqueville was eventually to publish (to great acclaim) in 1856. The first was that the French nobility constituted a distinct caste possessing enormous privileges, attached only to the semblance of power rather than its exercise, and distanced from the daily interests of ordinary citizens. "Men were born noble," Tocqueville wrote; "they did not become so." The second was the coming into existence during the eighteenth century of a literary class. Denied access to public affairs, these "ambitious men" took refuge in the study of letters and the pursuit of literary glory. Yet if they occupied a brilliant position, it was ill defined. They shared the pleasures of the great and saw all the privileges reserved for superiority but were denied tasting those advantages. "Equality," Tocqueville wrote, "was thus placed before their eyes as a phantom which fled before them in proportion as they approached to seize it." Accordingly, they "might be heard railing at privileges even in the palaces of the privileged."[26]

Next, Tocqueville insisted that the widely held view that it was only with the Revolution of 1789 that the division of landed property took place was mistaken. All the revolution did, he claimed, was extend this process across the whole country. According to Tocqueville, landed property had been "silently" passing out of the hands of the nobles and becoming divided among the people for some time, and it was these changes in land distribution that "facilitated, in a singular manner, the great political revolution that was about to take place." "The France of that day, with her *noblesse,* her state religion, her aristocratic laws and customs, was already," Tocqueville affirmed, "the most democratic nation of Europe." Moreover—and this Tocqueville believed was in stark contrast to the experience of England—"in France, the extension of royal power to embrace every part of the public administration regularly kept pace with the rise and progressive development of the democratic classes." Royal power penetrated ever deeper into the management of local affairs, always, he argued, to the exclusion of the nobility and enthusiastically supported by lawyers who "obeyed the instincts of their position" and "lent themselves to the despotic purposes of kings." Increasingly subject to a uniform system of administration, the French came to comprise "the most firmly bound together" nation in Europe. In sum, prior to the Revolution of 1789, "royal power had assumed, directly or indirectly, the management of everything and had no longer . . . any limits but that of its own will."[27]

Tocqueville also saw the great paradox that haunted any account of France prior to 1789. As the constitution became more despotic and liberty disappeared from institutions, the attachment to a sense of a right to individual liberty, the right to direct one's own affairs, became all the stronger and penetrated ever more deeply not only among the enlightened classes but also among the minds of the people. Once this had occurred, absolute and arbitrary power could only be perceived as a usurpation. It was, Tocqueville concluded, "a great, though a common, error to believe that the spirit of liberty in France had its birth with the revolution of 1789. It had always been one of the distinctive characters of the nation; but this spirit had only shown itself in intervals and, as it were, by fits."[28]

It was Tocqueville's conclusion to his essay that best gave evidence of the theme that, when developed at length in *L'ancien régime et la révolution,* was, in the words of his biographer Hugh Brogan, "to transform the historiography of the Revolution for good": the continuity of French history through and beyond the immediate revolutionary period.[29] As Tocqueville succinctly expressed it, "the effects . . . said to be produced by the French Revolution are usually exaggerated." "Without doubt," he continued, "there never was a revolution more powerful, more rapid, more destructive and more creative than the French Revolution. It would, however, be deceiving ourselves strangely to believe that there arose out of it a French people entirely new, and that an edifice had been erected whose foundations had not existed before. The French Revolution has created a multitude of accessory and secondary things; but of all the things of principal importance, it has only developed the germs previously existing. It has regulated, arranged and legalised the effects of a great cause, but has not been itself that cause."[30]

So, the revolution had only carried further and introduced into law an already existing equality of conditions. It had completed, but had not begun, the union of the country into one administrative body. It had not created a centralised power but had made it "more skilful, stronger and more enterprising." Finally, the revolution had not given birth to the democratic idea of liberty but had given the French nation the appearance, if not the reality, of sovereign power. "All that the revolution has done," Tocqueville therefore concluded, "would have been done, sooner or later, without it. It was but a violent and rapid process, by the aid of which the changes already effected in society were extended to the government; laws were made to conform themselves to manners; and the direction already taken by opinions was communicated to the outside world."[31]

How the French Revolution of 1789 was to be understood was a contentious issue from the outset but, as Tocqueville's 1836 text suggested, the widely held assumption was that it had denoted a radical break in French history.[32] Here Edmund Burke had led the way, and we should not therefore be surprised to learn that, as he worked on the writing of *L'ancien régime et la révolution* in the early 1850s, Tocqueville was to read the entire corpus of Burke's work on the French Revolution, only for him to conclude, inter alia, that Burke had been too close to the events of the revolution to be able properly to comprehend them. Burke had consequently been wrong to see the revolution, in Tocqueville's phrase, as a "French accident" and "the momentary product of a perfidious art."[33] "The real weakness of the nobility, envy, vanity in the middle classes, poverty, the agonies of the feudal system among the lower classes, ignorance: all these," Tocqueville wrote in his notes, "were powerful and ancient causes which only asked to be made fertile."[34] In the

1856 text, and as an explicit rebuttal of the Burkean view, he affirmed that, if the revolution had taken "the world by surprise . . . it was the result of a very long process, the sudden and violent climax of a task to which ten generations had contributed." Moreover, Tocqueville claimed, when the revolution was viewed from an appropriate distance we could see that, as radical as it had appeared, its "only effect was to abolish the political institutions which for several centuries had reigned unopposed among the majority of European peoples, and which we usually call feudal institutions." This, he conceded, was enough to bring about an "immense revolution" for the reason that these institutions were deeply interwoven with the religious and political fabric of Europe but, Tocqueville insisted, the revolution did not "destroy everything."[35]

One thing is certain: Tocqueville's reading and detailed research convinced him that in the course of the eighteenth century two dominant, and not necessarily compatible, ruling passions had developed among the French. The first, as he explained in *L'ancien régime et la révolution,* had the deeper roots and was "a violent and inextinguishable hatred of inequality," a passion that led the French to want "to build a society where men were as alike and conditions were as equal as humanity could allow." The second, of more recent origin and more intermittent in existence, was a desire "to live not only equal but free."[36] By the end of the ancien régime, Tocqueville believed, these two passions existed with comparable sincerity and strength, coming together at the start of the revolution "to inflame the whole heart of France at one and the same time." "This," Tocqueville enthused, was "'89, a time of inexperience, doubtless, but of generosity, of enthusiasm, of virility, and of greatness, a time of immortal memory" during which the French were proud enough to believe that "they could be equal in freedom." Amid democratic institutions were placed free institutions and, "with a single blow," all those laws that "had taken from the nation its free enjoyment of itself, and had put the government alongside each Frenchman, to be his tutor, his guardian, and, if need be, his oppressor" were removed.[37]

Nonetheless, with the passing of the "vigorous generation" that had begun the revolution, Tocqueville continued, the love of liberty was discouraged and weakened amongst "anarchy and popular dictatorship" and the country "searched gropingly" for a master and for absolute government. This,

Tocqueville added, was something easily understood "by the genius of he who was going to be at one and the same time the continuer of the Revolution and its destroyer."[38] Consequently, Tocqueville argued, France "recovered possession of centralisation in its ruins and restored it" and thus "from the very bowels of a nation that had just overthrown the monarchy suddenly came forth a power more extensive, more detailed, more absolute than that which any of our kings had exercised." Napoleon (described in the text simply as "*le dominateur*") and his government subsequently fell, but what was most substantial in his work remained, with the result, in Tocqueville's memorable phrase, that, ever since, the French had "limited [themselves] to placing liberty's head on a servile body" and had been pleased to provide their government "with the habits, ideas and laws that despotism needs in order to rule."[39]

L'ancien régime et la révolution was therefore a deeply political work of history and one that explained to its French readers why France had not been able to establish an enduring political regime characterised by the liberty of the individual and the rule of law. In a way, it served to demonstrate at length a truth that Tocqueville had already expressed privately—namely, that the French were not fit for liberty. Still, the political context in which it was written clearly had an enormous bearing upon its content. Most obviously, the text itself was for the most part written under the early years of the Second Empire established by the new emperor of the French, Napoleon III, on 2 December 1852. But the original idea for the book predated the establishment of the Second Empire and the coup d'état of December 1851.

An important part of the setting here was the self-conscious creation of a myth of Napoleon Bonaparte as the symbol of French greatness and military glory following his death in 1821, a process which arguably reached its high point with the return of Napoleon's mortal remains from the island of Saint Helena in the South Atlantic to Paris in 1840 in what was an elaborate and expertly choreographed ceremony of some considerable proportions and expense. The intention of the mythmakers (among whom was the politician and historian Adolphe Thiers, then writing a twenty-volume history of the Consulate and the First Empire) was to use this celebration of Napoleon's achievements and of France's imperial past to strengthen the sense of national unity and increase the popularity of the July Monarchy. As a tactic it failed miserably and did much to foster the later popularity of Louis-

Napoleon and thereby to secure his extraordinary election to the presidency of the Second Republic.[40]

That Tocqueville did not buy into this dangerous strategy was amply illustrated by the speech he made in April 1842 following his election to the Académie française. Custom dictated that Tocqueville's oration be a eulogy of his predecessor at the academy, who, in this case, had been Jean-Gerard Lacuée de Cessac, a former minister under Napoleon during the First Empire. Tocqueville thought long and hard about what to say and how to say it, but in the end succeeded only in damning Lacuée de Cessac with faint praise and telling his distinguished audience in no uncertain terms that the First Empire had been a despotism the like of which no other country had ever seen. As for Napoleon, he was, Tocqueville announced, "as great as a man can be without virtue."[41] The speech was not a great success but, as Hugh Brogan has correctly observed, it gave a clear sense of the direction in which Tocqueville's mind was moving.[42] What Tocqueville could not have known (or possibly even expected) was that the shadow of the emperor would so quickly reappear on the political stage in the form of his nephew.

We know that Tocqueville's thoughts had returned to this subject by the summer of 1850 when he received a visit to the family château from Nassau Senior and his family. As always, their conversations and walks were far ranging but, on 19 August, Senior raised the subject of Thiers's *Histoire du Consulat et de l'Empire,* the publication of which had been an enormous success. Tocqueville was unimpressed. It was too long and too detailed, he told Senior, and had no appreciation of the intrinsic and external causes that had created Napoleon. Thiers did not adequately explain how it was that Napoleon did what he did or why he chose to do it. Nor did he paint a full picture of Napoleon's private character. "The History of the Empire and the History of the Emperor," Tocqueville concluded, "are still to be written." To this, according to Senior's notes, he added, "I hope one day to write them."[43]

A matter of months later, Tocqueville set off on his journey to Italy, with the stated purpose of his trip being to restore his health. But it was not long before Tocqueville started writing, telling Louis de Kergorlay on 15 December 1850 from Sorrento that he had recommenced work on *Souvenirs.*

Remarkably, that same letter also informed Kergorlay that, while waiting for inspiration on *Souvenirs* to return, Tocqueville had contented himself "with musing about what could be a new book," to which he added that "for a long time" he had been troubled by "the idea of attempting a great work once again." But, he asked, "what subject am I to take up?" Two considerations, Tocqueville told Kergorlay, immediately guided his choice. The first was that the possibility of success rested upon finding a subject that would interest the public. The second was that it had to be a subject capable of animating the writer himself. "I am," he told Kergorlay, "the man least fit in the world for going up with any advantage against the current of my mind and my taste." To date, Tocqueville continued, no subject had completely pleased him, but now that he had begun running down "the slope of mature years" he had been looking more seriously for "the mother-idea of a book."[44]

It had then to be "a contemporary subject," as only things of the present interested both the public and himself. One possibility was "an ensemble of reflections and insights on the current time, a free verdict on our modern societies, and a forecast of their probable future," but, Tocqueville conceded, "I do not see the whole" and "lack the weft to make the cloth." He thus needed to find "a solid and continuous basis of facts" for his ideas. This, Tocqueville now saw, he could only do when "writing history," as only this allowed him "to paint the men and affairs of our century" and permitted him to "make one picture out of all of these paintings." And no period could be better "chosen for painting" than "the long drama of the French Revolution." Here, Tocqueville believed, was a period that ran from 1789 to the present day and that was "not only grand, but remarkable and even unique." It also threw "a vivid light on the period which preceded it."[45]

Even so, Tocqueville admitted to Kergorlay, doubts remained about how to deal with such a subject. "My first thought," Tocqueville confided, "had been to redo M. Thiers' book in my own manner; to write the narrative of the Empire, avoiding only expatiating on the military part." The problem was that it would turn the book into "a very long-term enterprise." It would also demand the skill to "handle the fabric of the facts," and this was not an "art" Tocqueville thought he possessed. "What I have best succeeded in until now," he wrote, "is in judging facts rather than in recounting them." Finally,

Tocqueville believed, "there is a certain affectation in taking up again the road that M. Thiers has just followed."[46]

Thus, Tocqueville explained, another way of envisioning this project had come to mind. It would, he wrote, "no longer be a matter of a lengthy work, but of a rather short book, one volume perhaps." Nor would it "properly speaking" be a history of the empire, but "a collection of reflections and judgements on that history." The principal concern would not be to "recount the facts" but rather to illuminate the diverse causes which gave rise to these facts and their consequences: "how the empire came about, how it was able to establish itself in the midst of the society created by the Revolution; what were the means used; what was the *true* nature of the man who founded it; what caused his success; what caused his reverses; the passing influence and the durable influence which he exercised on the destinies of the world and in particular on those of France." Here, Tocqueville hoped, was "material for a very great book."[47]

For all that this had become clear in Tocqueville's mind, one major worry, he told Kergorlay, remained: how he could successfully combine what he termed "the mixture of history properly so-called and historical philosophy." "I lack," Tocqueville wrote, "the infinite art that would be necessary to choose well the facts that must, as it were, support the ideas; to recount them enough for the reader to be led naturally from one reflection to another through an interest in the narrative, and not to tell too much of them in order that the character of the work remains visible." The "inimitable model" here, he believed, was Montesquieu's *Considérations sur les causes de la grandeur des Romains et de leur décadence.* Nonetheless, Tocqueville concluded, "I am proud enough to believe that I am better suited than anyone else to bring to such a subject a great freedom of mind and to speak without passion and unreservedly of men and events." Towards men, he wrote, he had "neither love nor hate" and, as for "those things called constitutions, laws, dynasties and classes," they had no value for him apart from "the effects they produce." In brief, he told Kergorlay, he had "no *cause* other than that of liberty and human dignity."[48]

Eleven days later Tocqueville wrote a letter similar in content (if not length) to Gustave de Beaumont. Again he repeated his intention not to write a history in the style of the "celebrated books" already published but rather to write something designed "to understand the cause, the character and the significance of the great events that form the principal links in the chain" of the times. Several things are worthy of note here. Having had the idea of writing another book for some time, he told Beaumont, he had put himself to finding a new subject "while hiking through the mountains of Sorrento." Next, for all of the detail of the project he had provided to Kergorlay, Tocqueville remarked that all this was still "a cloud which floats before my imagination." He also assured Beaumont that these thoughts were "absolutely" for his eyes only.[49]

There is something remarkable about this. Tocqueville had travelled to Italy in what turned out to be an ultimately vain attempt to recover from the first ravages of tuberculosis. The priority was a relaxing winter stay in a warm climate for the benefit of his health. Whilst in Sorrento Tocqueville not only turned again to his *Souvenirs* (and wrote the greater part of it there) but also used his contemplative walks across the mountain scenery to clarify his thoughts about what would ultimately be *L'ancien régime et la révolution.* It is easy to understand why Madame de Tocqueville and many of his friends constantly worried about Tocqueville's tendency to push himself up to and beyond his physical capacities.

It was in his piazza in Sorrento that Tocqueville produced his first detailed sketches of what he then intended to be the content of his second great book. Here there is an element of scholarly controversy. It is beyond doubt that in Sorrento Tocqueville produced a general plan and chapter outline for the book in December 1850.[50] Robert Gannett Jr. believes (with good cause) that Tocqueville also there penned a shorter note entitled "Idée originaire, sentiment générale et primitif du sujet," although it has been conventionally dated as written in 1856.[51] Both texts point in the same direction, but if commentary is restricted to only the first text, indisputably written in Italy, it is clear that at this time the focus of Tocqueville's thoughts was the figure of Napoleon Bonaparte. Remarking again that he wanted to look beyond the facts, he wrote, "I would like to show what [Napoleon] in his prodigious enterprise really took from his own genius and how the situation of the country and the spirit of the times helped him; to make it known how and why at that moment this disobedient nation ran to servitude of its own accord; with what incomparable art he discovered in the Revolution's most demagogic works everything which was fitting to despotism and made it come forth naturally." Tocqueville also wanted "to contemplate the effort of this almost divine genius" to restrain human liberty and how, under the weight of the administrative machine Napoleon had created, society was "repressed and suffocated, becoming sterile." As for Napoleon's foreign policy and conquests, Tocqueville's ambition was "to paint the furious ride of his fortunes across peoples and kingdoms." "What more extraordinary picture," Tocqueville's note read, "of human power and weakness is there than that of this impatient and changeable genius constantly making and unmaking his work himself, ceaselessly tearing out and replacing the limits of empires and making nations and sovereigns despair." Finally, he wrote, "I would like to make understood the series of excesses and mistakes by which [Napoleon] precipitated his own downfall; and, despite these errors and excesses, follow closely the immense trace he has left behind in the world, not only as memory, but as influence and lasting action."[52]

What followed were brief outlines of eleven chapters, plus a list of people to be consulted (including Adolphe Thiers) and suggestions for documents to be checked (unpublished memoirs, letters, diplomatic documents, police archives, manuscripts, official publications, and so on). Tocqueville also listed engravings and caricatures published at the time. One chapter outline contains the injunction "Do not dwell at length on his battles." Another has the line, "Torpor and sleep of the human spirit in the midst of all this great noise of victory." Still another reads, "The actor, charlatan, petty, even vulgar, side of the great man." "Here," Tocqueville wrote, "are great objects which I glimpse." His guiding methodological maxim was nonetheless clear enough: "to tell and to judge at the same time."[53]

When Tocqueville returned from Sorrento in the spring of 1851, he immediately took up his parliamentary duties and sought unsuccessfully to bring about a revision of the constitution to allow Louis-Napoleon to stand again for president. With the failure of this initiative, he next returned to his family home in Normandy and then spent the autumn in Versailles, where he worked on the part of his *Souvenirs* covering his time in office as minister of foreign affairs. Immediately following the coup d'état in December 1851, Tocqueville's thoughts turned to the project he had sketched out the previous winter in Sorrento and, although only intermittently and half-heartedly, he worked on this through the early part of the following year in Paris. During this time he made extensive notes on the periods of the Directory and the Consulate, with special attention being devoted to texts by Benjamin Constant from the 1790s, the memoirs of the Marquis de Lafayette, and also those of the counterrevolutionary Jacques Mallet du Pan and the politician Antoine Thibaudeau. Tocqueville also spent time at the National Archives.

As a letter to Beaumont indicates, writing on his new project seems to have begun in earnest once Tocqueville returned to Normandy in July 1852.[54] The same message was conveyed to Louis de Kergorlay six days later, except on this occasion Tocqueville indicated that "one or two chapters are already sketched out."[55] To this Tocqueville added that he had not "begun the book with what ought to be its beginning." Rather, he continued, he had started with the material he had collected in Paris and where he "felt the most desire to write." "What I have written," Tocqueville told Kergorlay, "forms the picture of the period which preceded 18 Brumaire and the state of mind which brought about that coup d'état."[56] The attraction of this approach, he made clear, was that "despite great differences there are many similarities between the time of which I am speaking and that which we have just been through."[57] In short, Tocqueville rightly saw parallels between the coup d'état masterminded by Napoleon Bonaparte in 1799 and that of his nephew in 1851.

Yet, as François Furet and Françoise Mélonio have written, "at that time Tocqueville had already changed the object of his research."[58] Having started his inquiries with the rise of Napoleon Bonaparte in the 1790s, Tocqueville now realised that he had to go further back in French history, and specifically to the period prior to 1789. We have already seen this in the letter Tocqueville wrote to Zacharie Gallemand, in which he indicated that he had been turning his attention to the issue of feudal rights in prerevolutionary Normandy. A letter written to Gallemand one week later, and dated 28 August 1852, provides further evidence of this shift of perspective. Building upon his earlier indication that his purpose was "the general study [of] the true condition of France at the moment when the great Revolution burst forth," Tocqueville now continued by saying that his objective "was not to understand what the feudal regime was at the time of its greatest strength but to gain an idea of the abuses, the constraints, the burdens, the humiliations and small tyrannies which still remained when it was finally destroyed." What he wanted to know, he now told Gallemand, was "how landed property was divided in 1788" and "what were the number of property owners, great or small." "How," Tocqueville wrote, "was land divided up at the moment of the great earthquake of 1789: that is the question."[59]

Further evidence of this change in Tocqueville's focus is not difficult to find. To his friend Pierre Freslon on 7 September 1852 he wrote that "with regard to the burdens that the feudal system visited upon the French and in particular upon the agricultural class in 1789, after the loss of much time and an intellectual indigestion arising from a diet of very weighty but insubstantial documents, I am arriving, I think, at a clear and accurate idea of these burdens and their weight." "You would laugh," he added, "if you could see a man who has written so much on democracy surrounded by specialists in feudal law and bent over old land registers and dusty records."[60]

Why Tocqueville abruptly changed his field of inquiry need not detain us, but it is clear that he became increasingly convinced that an understanding of the French Revolution could not be reached without an appreciation of the deep sense of grievance felt by the French peasantry towards the remnants of the feudal system. Indeed, Tocqueville came to see that those grievances only increased as the obligations imposed by feudalism lessened—and so much so that Tocqueville's investigation of the prerevolutionary feudal system was to preoccupy him for the best part of the next four years.

This had numerous dimensions, of which one of the most significant was to be another journey, this time to the village of Saint-Cyr-sur-Loire, not far from the town of Tours, where Tocqueville resided from June 1853 until May 1854. As with the recent visit to Italy, this decision was partly determined by Tocqueville's (and Madame de Tocqueville's) continuing ill health and thus the need once more to find somewhere protected from the winter chill of the Normandy coast.[61] Tocqueville also needed to find somewhere that was inexpensive, as his finances were in poor shape.[62] At first he thought of living just outside Paris, but in a state of discouragement about both his health and the lack of progress he was making on the study of the

Indre-Loire, Tours, 1881 (Antiqua Print Gallery / Alamy Stock Photo)

ancien régime, by the early summer he was thinking of a "quiet provincial spot" and one ideally in the Loire Valley.[63] What followed were a series of letters from Beaumont (whose own property was in the Sarthe, just north of the Loire Valley) detailing houses for rent in the region. "It is absolutely necessary," Tocqueville wrote at the beginning of May, "that the residence should be well positioned, in a dry spot and not subject to being covered by fog."[64] A contract was signed by early May and the Tocquevilles moved into a villa on the banks of the River Loire called Les Trésorières on 1 June.

"The countryside, the house, the garden, the distance to Tours," Tocqueville told Beaumont, "all these things please us and we are already relishing the thought of the rest we are going to enjoy."[65] Indeed, Tours was so close, he told Francisque de Corcelle, that he set his watch by the sound of its church bells.[66] Tocqueville wrote to Adolphe de Circourt that it was like living on a "desert island."[67] Nearby, he told another acquaintance, was what would be regarded as a "charming valley if one had never left Touraine."[68] Tocqueville also reported to Corcelle that, quite fortuitously, there lived nearby a certain Dr. Bretonneau, a "famous" physician, who seemed "a very likeable old chap."[69] As ever, a Tocqueville trip was not without its setbacks and inconveniences. Much to Madame de Tocqueville's distress, it turned out that the house was full of bedbugs. Not only this but, upon arrival, Tocqueville's dog was very ill. Tocqueville himself fell ill two weeks later with rheumatism in his neck, preventing him from both going for walks and from sleeping.

Nevertheless, he was delighted to be living within easy travelling distance of the Beaumont family (whom the Tocquevilles were to visit in both the autumn and spring).[70] After one very cold winter's night, he told Corcelle that not even in Sicily or Africa had he seen a sky "more full of stars or more sparkling."[71] As had been the case in Sorrento, friends also came to visit. In addition to Beaumont, these included Ampère, the Corcelles, Kergorlay, Jean-Charles Rivet, Victor Lanjuinais and, from England, Harriet Grote and the inevitable Nassau Senior (with whom Tocqueville made several day trips to see some of the famously beautiful Loire châteaux). True to form, Tocqueville quickly established a daily routine. "I rise at half-past five," he told Mrs. Grote, "and work seriously till half-past nine; then dress for *déjeuner* at ten. I commonly walk half an hour afterwards, and then set to on some other study—usually, of late, in the German language—till 2.00 p.m., when I go out again and walk for two hours, if weather allows." In the evenings Tocqueville and his wife read together and went "to bed at 10.00 p.m. regularly every night." He also told Mrs. Grote that, after eight months of seclusion, he had come to regard society as something he "could do without."[72] He did not regret, he told another of his correspondents, "not being what people call a great figure."[73] It was certainly better for his spirits, he told Circourt, than a life amongst "the sterile agitation of the salons of Paris," even if, as he frequently acknowledged, it meant that he had nothing to recount in his letters except details of his health.[74] Most of the news that he heard about politics, Tocqueville explained to Corcelle, came from his local peasant barber, who passed on what he had heard from his other clients.[75] He told Léon Faucher in February 1854 that he knew as much about what was going on in France as he would have done were he living in Honolulu.[76] The Tocquevilles made no effort to make any friends in the vicinity although, on Corcelle's recommendation, they did invite the archbishop of Tours, Cardinal Morlot, to dinner.[77]

For all of Tocqueville's contentment with his quiet and uneventful life, his mood did from time to time slip over into one of melancholy. As he told Madame de Circourt, he sensed that he no longer knew either his compatriots or his contemporaries. He lived "like an old man among a new people."[78] To his former ministerial colleague, Odilon Barrot, Tocqueville wrote that the two of them belonged to another age. They were, he told Barrot, "species of antediluvian animals that it will soon be necessary to place together in the cabinets of natural history museums to show how, in the distant past, there were beings so singularly constituted as to love liberty, legality and sincerity." These tastes would be seen as so strange that they would be attributed to bodily organs no longer possessed by the inhabitants of the modern world.[79]

Most importantly, Les Trésorières was situated close to the departmental archives of the Indre-et-Loire in nearby Tours and it was here, under the capable guidance of its young archivist, Charles de Grandmaison, that Tocqueville was to spend much of his time during his stay. Fortunately, Grandmaison left a delightful and touching memoir of Tocqueville's visits and one that suggests that working with Tocqueville on the preparation of his work on the ancien régime was the highlight of his professional career. Tocqueville, Grandmaison recalled over twenty years later, simply appeared one misty morning at the archives unannounced. Having previously seen Tocqueville at the manuscript department of the national library in Paris, Grandmaison immediately recognised his slender and tired-looking visitor and instantly provided Tocqueville with several bundles of documents to look through. Satisfied with what he had seen, Tocqueville announced that he would return on the following day, which he duly did around midday, carrying a black leather ministerial portfolio. "He immediately set to work," Grandmaison recollected, "and began by examining the correspondence of the *intendants* to the different ministers." Tocqueville came back in the following days, only for Grandmaison to realise that a reader of such renown was attracting the curiosity of others in the building. He thus suggested that Tocqueville move into his own office and it was here, overlooking the *préfet*'s kitchen garden, that he worked on a "modest and old desk" for much of the next twelve months.[80]

Gradually, according to Grandmaison, Tocqueville's natural reticence in the company of others was overcome, and "little by little" there was established "the kind of intimacy that can exist between two people of different ages and of unequal worth."[81] At one point in his memoir, Grandmaison observed simply that Tocqueville was the very embodiment of what, in the seventeenth century, people would have seen as an *honnête homme,* someone who combined a fine intelligence and the pleasures of the mind with exquisite politeness and charming manners.[82] Towards the end of summer Grandmaison was invited to dinner at the Tocqueville "*hermitage.*" The owner of the house, Grandmaison recounted, had had the singular idea of filling the house with busts of famous men placed between the windows. At the front there was a lawn, beyond which was an extensive vegetable patch and fruit garden and rows of linden trees. In addition to the Tocquevilles, Ampère was also present. The meal was simple, "without luxury and refinement." But what Grandmaison remembered above all was the conversation. First it turned to the trip that Ampère had recently made to America, where he had seen towns with universities which at the time of Tocqueville's visit only twenty years earlier had been nothing but villages. "The question of slavery," Grandmaison continued, "was not forgotten, the two interlocutors seeing it as the cause of a fearsome conflict between the North and the South, although neither saw that it would break out so soon." They talked about Tocqueville's book, with Grandmaison writing that Tocqueville was kind enough to tell Ampère that, if he now had a clearer idea of its content, this was due not only to the archives he had consulted but also to his conversations with the archivist. After dinner they walked in the garden, the setting sun turning the hillsides of the nearby valley the colour of crimson, and where they spoke of the Bay of Naples and about Sorrento. Like many other acquaintances of Tocqueville, Grandmaison saw that, for all that he had immersed himself in the study of "the moral world," this had in no way stifled Tocqueville's appreciation of "the beauties of nature."[83]

Conversations also took place between Tocqueville and Grandmaison at the archives, usually just after Tocqueville's arrival and never for more than a half hour (a routine, Grandmaison noted with some amusement, that Tocqueville observed scrupulously). These conversations, Grandmaison informed his readers, were by no means always about the ancien régime. Politics scarcely figured at all, although Grandmaison recalled that Tocqueville could not prevent himself from making some comment about the woeful situation of the country from time to time. Tocqueville spoke to Grandmaison about Napoleon III and, from Grandmaison's account, he did so in similar tones to those he was to employ in his description of the prince-president in his *Souvenirs.* Louis-Napoleon, Tocqueville apparently told Grandmaison, was the only intelligent person he had ever met with whom conversation served no purpose. Yet, Grandmaison commented, Tocqueville never spoke about the emperor with bitterness. The outbreak of the Crimean War revealed another aspect of Tocqueville's character to Grandmaison: "the strength and depth of his patriotism." "Never," Grandmaison wrote, "did I discern a word or a thought that he did not wish for the success of our army."[84]

Upon occasion their conversations touched upon subjects beyond the borders of France. Tocqueville had famously ended the first volume of *De la démocratie en Amérique* with the prediction that, in the near future, the United States and Russia would emerge as the world's two superpowers, the one achieving its victories by the ploughshare, the other by the soldier's sword. Grandmaison's account indicates that this remained Tocqueville's view and, furthermore, that he now regretted that he would not have the opportunity to write a book on Russia to match that of his study of the United States. Grandmaison also correctly alluded to the fact that Tocqueville had been reading about Russia since his arrival in Tours. Specifically, during June 1853 Tocqueville had made extensive notes on a volume entitled *Études sur la situation intérieure de la vie nationale et les institutions rurales de la Russie* by the German writer and lawyer August von Haxthausen. Again, Grandmaison's memory served him well when he remembered that Tocqueville had found Haxthausen's book both very boring and very instructive.[85]

None of this material on Russia made its way into the published version of *L'ancien régime et la révolution,* but it was central to Tocqueville's ambition to develop a comparative perspective on the history of French absolutism. Moreover, Tocqueville's notes show that Haxthausen's description of the lives of the Russian peasantry very much accorded with the conclusions that Tocqueville himself had been reaching about the ancien régime. Under the heading "The Coming Destruction of Serfdom," Tocqueville wrote out the following quotation from the first volume of Haxthausen's text: "In our day, anyone with any sense admits that it is impossible to maintain serfdom in its present form for very long. Everyone in Russia knows it. But how to get there without producing a revolution? That is the question of the day." This observation, Tocqueville wrote, was all the more impressive for the fact that Haxthausen had some sympathy for the system, but what he saw, according to Tocqueville, was "the weakening of the old nobility which still lived on the land and shared the ideas and mores of the peasant; its substitution or its transformation into agents of the government without any point of contact with the agricultural class; the absenteeism of all the large landowners and, as a consequence of all these things the *obrog,* an arbitrary tax on the peasant's individual worth." In addition, and despite the oppression and isolation of the agricultural class, there existed, in Tocqueville's words, "an ordered and civilised government which spreads, without knowing it and often without wanting it, the ideas of modern civilisation" and thereby "finally gives people those things which make them miss all the more those things they still lack."[86]

Here was a description of nineteenth-century Russia that had distinct parallels with the picture of eighteenth-century France that Tocqueville was steadily building up from his reading in the Tours archives, not least in its account of the way in which an absent and functionless nobility facilitated the creation of what Tocqueville here described as a "vast, detailed and paperwork-loving centralisation." It also helped to inform one of the most original and important insights contained within *L'ancien régime et la révolution*—namely, that governments are most vulnerable not when things get worse but at the point where they start to get better. As Tocqueville wrote, "patiently endured for so long as it seemed inevitable, a grievance appears unbearable once people conceive the possibility of removing it."[87]

"One sees in Haxthausen," Tocqueville wrote to Beaumont, "a truly extraordinary picture that alone justifies putting up with the boredom of reading his work; namely his presentation of a people still held in the clutches of serfdom and of communal property and nevertheless benefitting to an extent from the institutions and even, in certain respects, participating in the spirit of the democratic and civilised times in which we live." "On the one side," Tocqueville continued, "we have the attachment of the serf to the land typical of the tenth century: on the other, we have the perpetual movement of place and status which characterises the Americans." This in turn conjured up another comparison with America. It was not just Haxthausen's writing style that made for a boring read, he told Beaumont, but also the picture of Russian society he was presenting where ideas, laws, and customs and even the smallest details of objects were "so perfectly uniform." This, Tocqueville wrote, "makes me think of an America without enlightenment and liberty, a democratic society to be frightened of."[88]

Tocqueville said much the same to Circourt. He had never felt less like visiting the "Empire of the Tsars," he wrote, than after reading Haxthausen's book. "What above all would make this society uninhabitable for me," Tocqueville commented, "would be the boredom. . . . Uniformity in liberty has also seemed to me to be boring, but what can one say about complete uniformity in servitude, about these perfectly similar villages, populated by people perfectly alike, doing the same things, in the midst of the most profound intellectual sleep?" "I'd much prefer disordered barbarism," he told Circourt.[89]

According to Grandmaison, the other country that figured prominently in his morning conversations with Tocqueville was Germany. Grandmaison knew that Tocqueville had "courageously" embarked on the study of the language and that Tocqueville was already thinking of visiting the country once his time in the Loire came to an end. He also understood that Tocqueville was interested in Germany because he believed it to be the place in Europe where the ideas and institutions of the ancien régime had best survived.[90]

But Tocqueville's primary purpose in visiting the archives in Tours was not to converse but to work. A letter written by Tocqueville to Pierre Freslon one week after his first arrival at the archives gives a clear sense of what had been his starting point. In Tours, Tocqueville told Freslon, he had found "not exactly a rare treasure, but a precious deposit," although one containing an "enormous amount of useless dust." Moreover, Tocqueville continued, much of what could be "swallowed" was unlikely to take up much space in the book he was contemplating writing. It would, he wrote, "be a big mistake to restrict myself only to painting the Ancien Régime. But I am obliged to understand it thoroughly . . . so as to present its principal features, and above all to be in a position to judge and to indicate how it had an effect on the revolution that destroyed it." Tocqueville's hope was that this would not be time wasted—something, he added, that he was "often tempted to think when seeing the days which follow one after another and the time which passes without producing anything else than a mountain of notes from which will finally emerge a small chapter of thirty pages."[91]

Grandmaison's memoir confirms Tocqueville's account of how he was spending his time. Tocqueville's difficulty was to decide just how far back into French history he should go. Initially, Grandmaison recalled, Tocqueville's plan was to focus his research on materials from the reign of Louis XI in the latter half of the fifteenth century onwards. However, given that Tocqueville's knowledge of the earlier period was, in Grandmaison's words, at best "vague and superficial" and that he only worked from documents and not secondary sources, this seemed to Grandmaison a somewhat unwise approach, and he managed therefore to convince Tocqueville to concentrate his efforts on the period immediately prior to the revolution. Thus, Grandmaison recalled, Tocqueville "threw himself with great energy into the reading and study of the documents that I spared no effort in finding for him in the chaos of our still poorly arranged collection." He devoured everything placed before him with the "patience and scrupulousness of a Benedictine monk," accumulating piles of notes and extracts. Never, it seems, did Tocqueville ask directly for help. "My role," Grandmaison wrote, "was limited to the finding and providing of the things that I thought likely to interest him and to lead him to the goal he wanted to reach."[92] And so it continued day after day until the arrival of winter, when the bad weather inclined Tocqueville to make the four-kilometre walk there and back to the archives less often. By then, as Grandmaison again accurately recorded, the preliminary stages of Tocqueville's research were over, and it was time to write.

What documents Tocqueville consulted during this period has been excellently pieced together by Gannett. He estimates that between July and November 1853 Tocqueville produced over 330 pages of reading notes, divided into twenty-two subsections, each of which represented between four days to four weeks of work. Moreover, as eighteen out of the twenty-two subsections are dated, it is possible to trace the evolution of Tocqueville's inquiries. Throughout, according to Gannett, Tocqueville sought to "discern the way the royal administration intersected each day with the lives of the French population." He also devoted much attention to the erosion of popular participation in public affairs. The important point is the conclusion reached by Gannett. It was these studies, Gannett writes, "that by the end of the summer would contribute to a complete reformulation of the concept and scope of the book on the French Revolution."[93]

How different, then, might have been the content of *L'ancien régime et la révolution* had Tocqueville not fortuitously decided to journey to the Loire Valley and had he not found such a talented and enthusiastic archivist to help him in his research. If there are errors in his description and analysis of the ancien régime, these can on occasion be also attributed to this experience. Had Tocqueville not been in the archives in Tours, where village records had all but disappeared, the conclusions he reached about the absence of local democracy under the ancien régime might have been very different.

Shortly after the publication of *L'ancien régime et la révolution* in 1856 Tocqueville sent a letter to Charles de Grandmaison. "Without you and your archives," he wrote, "I would not have been able to write the book that I have just published."[94] No doubt Grandmaison felt a good deal of legitimate pride in reading these kind and generous words from a man he so greatly admired. Still, Grandmaison, as much as anyone else, knew that if the book proved to be a success, it owed much not only to Tocqueville's intelligence and clarity of thought but also to his determination, despite illness and often plagued by self-doubt, to work meticulously through the archives and to grind out his text page by page, often painfully slowly. The latter was what Tocqueville did in his house just down the river from Tours and the archives.

In early September 1853 Tocqueville told Kergorlay that he had not worked much, in part because of the many visitors he had received, but also because his stomach was once again causing him problems. Only a week or so later, when excusing himself for not writing to Corcelle, he explained his silence by referring to the life he was leading as a kind of "voluntary tread mill" where he could only "think of raising one foot after another until the wheel stops."[95] Yet on 23 September he told Pierre Freslon that he was putting his books and his old papers aside and starting finally to write his own volume. "Up to the present," he wrote, "I have only been preparing myself and I am beginning to get both annoyed and to be bored by this lengthy noviciate." His plan was to throw out the words of the first chapter "somehow or other" and then see if he had the makings of a "great book." "I need," Tocqueville continued, "to make a success of this first effort in order to have the courage to continue to move forward." To this he added that his work in the archives at Tours had shown him that "one finds a thousand new incentives to hate the Ancien Régime but few new reasons to like the revolution." One can see, he told Freslon, that "the Ancien Régime was weakening rapidly and of its own accord under the weight of the passing of time and as a consequence of the imperceptible change in ideas and in mores." With a little more patience, it would have been possible to transform rather than destroy it.[96]

In early October Tocqueville told Ampère that he was now "firmly resolved" to put pen to paper, although ominously he added that what he had previously seen clearly about his book was now "surrounded by a cloud that gets ever thicker."[97] A couple of weeks later a similar message was received by Kergorlay. He had nothing of interest to report, Tocqueville told Kergorlay, but preparatory work on his book would finish at the end of the month and then the real work would begin.[98] Tocqueville was honest enough to admit to Léonce de Lavergne that he had as yet produced "absolutely nothing" and feared that he would never make sense of all the archival papers he had devoured.[99] Worse still, Tocqueville told Adolphe de Circourt on 16 October that the only thing that displeased him about his present "retreat" was that it led "his friends to believe that I have worked a lot and that I am going to leave here with a weighty volume under my arms." Unhappily, he recounted, nothing could be further from the truth. Indeed, he was alarmed by the lack of progress he had made over the last four months. "It is so long since I have had the opportunity to *write*," Tocqueville then confessed, "that I do not know if I have completely forgotten the craft."[100] To Harriet Grote he reported that, after four unproductive months, he felt that what had happened to him was akin to what happened to "prisoners who, seeing before them an immense amount of free time, always put off the work they want to undertake until the following day and often arrive at the end of their imprisonment or of their life without even beginning a project that they could easily have finished among the distractions of the world."[101]

On 3 November Tocqueville wrote to Pierre Freslon again to say that writing would now start the following week. "I promise you," he told Freslon, "that I approach the arrival of this moment in a state of great anxiety and with a kind of terror."[102] Beaumont was sent a letter on the same day containing the identical piece of information, except that in this case Tocqueville indicated that he was suffering from "mortal anxiety."[103] Remarkably, after all the reading he had done and all the dusty papers he had worked his way through in the Tours archives, Tocqueville was still voicing doubts about the whole project to Freslon. "What will I do," he asked, "if I realise that what I have taken for precise ideas are only vague suggestions, if what I have taken to be original and new thoughts are true but well-known notions?." If this did not come off, Tocqueville wrote, "I will not know what to do." Such were the depths of his misgivings that he again voiced his concern that there was no longer anything resembling a reading public in France. "Of all the aristocracies," Tocqueville wrote, "the one that up to now the Revolution has most destroyed is the literary aristocracy."[104]

For all of these doubts and misapprehensions, Tocqueville wrote to Ampère on 18 November to say that there was only good news to report. While his health was not all that might be desired, Tocqueville related, it was much improved, and he felt strong enough to walk to the archives three times a week. He had finished his preparatory reading three days previously and was intent on ordering no more books from the libraries in Paris. "So here I am," he wrote, "on the edge of the great divide."[105] Happily, over the next couple of months Tocqueville did make some progress. "I am completely absorbed by my work," he informed Beaumont in mid-December, "and, although it is going slowly, I do at least have the pleasure of seeing it move forward a little every day."[106] On New Year's Day 1854, he wrote to Ampère to say that the first chapter—"the aim of which is to show what was the true goal of the Revolution"—was "more or less" sketched out and that the writing of the second chapter had been begun. "It is in this chapter," he wrote, "that I will place the product of the huge note taking that I have done over the last year."[107] At the end of January Tocqueville told Beaumont that he hoped to have some chapters for him to read in the spring. Pierre Freslon received a similarly positive message that same month.

The evidence suggests that these had not been easy days. To Beaumont, towards the end of December, Tocqueville indicated that the winter cold was already having a damaging effect on his health and that this was preventing him from working as quickly as he had been doing. He was like the gold digger whose mine had fallen in on his head, he told Beaumont, feeling crushed by the weight of his notes and "and no longer knowing how to get out with my treasure."[108] Tocqueville's New Year's Day letter to Ampère struck a similar tone. "There are times," he told Ampère, "when I feel very pleased with myself and as delighted with my work as a fool could be, [but] at other times I am at the bottom of an abyss of despair" and so much so, he wrote, that he had never missed Ampère more and never more needed his advice on how to structure and develop his argument and how not to tire the reader with too much detail.[109]

This continued to be the pattern during Tocqueville's remaining months in the Loire Valley. In early March he wrote a long letter to his nephew, Hubert de Tocqueville, then a young man in his early twenties. Tocqueville's two previous letters to his nephew in January and February had very much been those typical of a kindly uncle offering career advice (in this case, beware of working for the administrative machinery of the state), but upon this occasion Tocqueville took the trouble to explain how he was and, most importantly, what he had been doing with his time. As he was often wont to do in his letters, Tocqueville began by reporting on his and his wife's health. Here there was good news and this despite the recent changeable weather and cold north wind which had done little to help his rheumatism. Next Tocqueville turned to his work and here, for once, his mood was one of relative optimism. His book, he told his nephew, was advancing slowly and he could not see its end but its form and content were becoming ever sharper in his mind and his hope was that the "first part" would be finished by the time he left his "retreat" at the end of May. If Tocqueville persisted in saying the subject of his book was the French Revolution and that he was thinking of writing two volumes, he made it clear that he "had devoted the last year doing something that had not ever been done before"—namely, studying the ancien régime with a view "to explaining why this great Revolution took place in France; why it had the character it did; but also to explain why many events occurred subsequently and to locate the origin of a whole plethora of habits, attitudes and propensities that we believe to be new but which have their roots in the government of the Ancien Régime." If, Tocqueville commented, he could get this done he would not consider his time at Saint-Cyr to have been wasted.[110]

By the end of March Tocqueville's mood had changed again. He wrote to Kergorlay to say that he feared that he would be leaving Saint-Cyr with only a half volume sketched out and nothing finished.[111] He lacked, he wrote, both the time and the inspiration to do any better and was already feeling in "absolute need" of some sort of distraction before taking up his scrawling (*barbouillages*) again. Towards the end of April, Tocqueville reported to Beaumont that he had been confined to his bedroom for the last week with neuralgia and unable to work.[112]

The usually reliable Grandmaison made one mistake in his account of Tocqueville's stay in the Loire Valley. "In April 1854," he wrote, "Tocqueville left Touraine, taking with him an immense quantity of notes and a book that was well advanced." Perhaps the book was not as well advanced as Grandmaison might have imagined, but what is certain is that Tocqueville did not leave his retreat by the river until the end of the following month. Grandmaison was, of course, correct when he observed that it would take a further two years before *L'ancien régime et la révolution* was to be published. Remarkably, Tocqueville remained plagued by doubts about both its value and reception right down to the moment of publication[113]—an event overshadowed by the death of his father only a matter of days before—and even into the spring of 1856 there was uncertainty about what the title would be. In February of that year Tocqueville reported to Beaumont that his publishers in Paris, Michel Lévy, were strongly in favour of *La révolution française* and it was only after much discussion that this was resolved in favour of the title for which it has subsequently become well known.[114] Later that month the printers returned the manuscript to Tocqueville because it was illegible, thereby further delaying the process of publication.[115]

There can be no doubt about the importance of Tocqueville's stay in Saint-Cyr-sur-Loire nor about what he had achieved during the time he had spent in the archives in Tours. It was here that the empirical groundwork that informed what was to become his second masterpiece was undertaken and here that the ideas which were to inform its content came to be fully formed. It was here, too, that—in relative isolation—the writing of that masterpiece began and here also that a chance encounter with a young and enthusiastic archivist was to have such a decisive importance in shaping the subsequent historiography of the French Revolution.

But Tocqueville's journey to the Loire had successfully served another purpose. On 17 July 1854 he wrote to one of his American friends, "I left Saint-Cyr at the end of last month, having almost fully achieved the goal I had in mind when I initially went there (a thing so rare in this world as to be worth noting). There the health of my wife has been completely restored and I have restored mine to the state in which I was two years ago. I am still not a vigorous man but, God be praised, nor am I any longer a sick man."[116] By this time Tocqueville and his wife were already in Germany, and another episode in Tocqueville's travels had begun.

CHAPTER EIGHT

Germany

Alexis de Tocqueville's interest in Germany was long standing.[1] In this he was little different from the majority of educated French citizens for whom Germany was the home of philosophy and of music. Possibly the earliest expression of Tocqueville's interest is to be found in a letter to Henry Reeve, dated 21 September 1836. "I expect," he told Reeve, "to make an extended visit to Germany in a year's time." "The problem is," he added, "that I do not know the language."[2] This was a subject that Tocqueville would return to time and time again in future years. Only a few weeks later, he confirmed this interest when he told his close friend Louis de Kergorlay that "after England the country that I have always most wanted to travel through is Prussia. Everything that I have heard said about it leads me to believe that there is no country that more merits being examined carefully."[3]

Kergorlay was himself planning an extended visit to Germany, and in the weeks that followed this was to be a recurring topic in their letters. Was it the case, Tocqueville wanted to know, that the government of Prussia, whether through principle or instinct, deprived its subjects of political liberty whilst at the same time granting them a set of "secondary liberties" compatible with absolute monarchy? More specifically, he asked Kergorlay to make inquiries about provincial government and the limits of centralisation. It was not, Tocqueville commented, by drawing examples from republican or semirepublican peoples that French centralisation and, what he termed, "the antiliberal multitude" could be challenged but by citing the experience of peoples subject to absolute government. No sooner was Kergorlay on his way to Germany than Tocqueville was asking for information about what

Kergorlay had seen and expressing his excitement about what he would learn upon Kergorlay's return. How, he asked, were the French seen and judged by the Germans? What did they make of France's recent revolution and its consequences? For the most part, Tocqueville imagined, they probably felt neither favour nor hatred but indifference.[4] By the end of December, Tocqueville was asking Kergorlay how the Prussian education system operated and in particular how the law compelling children to attend school worked and to what effect. He also wanted to know what role local authorities had in the provision of education.[5] For his part, if Kergorlay laboured to improve his own command of the German language, he quickly saw that the stereotypical romantic images the French had of Germans bore little relation to reality. Almost nothing of the "interior life" of this vast country was known to us, he told Tocqueville. "When one thinks," he added, "that between the Kalmyks and us, there is only Germany, one cannot be indifferent to its future." That future, Kergorlay saw clearly, would be played out against a backdrop of the conflicting claims of nationalism and liberalism, Protestantism and Catholicism, Prussia and Austria.[6]

The subject of Germany would continue to feature prominently in Tocqueville's correspondence with Kergorlay in the years to come. Tocqueville also built up an extensive list of German correspondents with whom during the 1840s he largely exchanged views about prison reform. The most important of these was Leo von Thun-Hohenstein, future Austrian minister of education and religion.[7] Tocqueville first met Thun in Paris in 1835 and they were to remain in contact over the next twenty years. However, in the late 1830s and early 1840s, Tocqueville's time was mostly taken up with the completion of the second volume of *De la démocratie en Amérique* and with his attempts to forge a new political career in Paris. If there was a second foreign country that most exercised his interest in these years it was Algeria and not Germany.

It was not until 1844 that Tocqueville again turned his thoughts to Germany in a serious way. That year he resumed contact with Thun, announcing that he had not given up the idea of visiting Germany but did not know when and how this might be possible. Specifically, he asked Thun if he could recommend one or two contributors who might write articles on Germany for the newspaper he now co-owned, *Le commerce.* "I believe," Tocqueville wrote, "that it is in the interest of France as much as possible to establish bonds of friendship in central Europe; and the best means of doing this is to show her what is going on there."[8] When Thun himself declined the invitation and suggested no one else, Tocqueville next turned to Francis Lieber in the United States. Would he, Tocqueville asked, possibly care to write about America for *Le commerce* and might he also be able to recommend possible contributors from Germany? "We are extremely interested," Tocqueville informed Lieber, "in every detail concerning what is going on in Prussia, the German Customs Union, commerce in the Baltic Sea, the general movement of public opinion in northern Germany." "If," he continued, "you could find us good contributors either in Prussia with regard to general politics or in Hamburg to cover the industrial and commercial affairs of northern Germany, you would render us an extremely great service."[9] Again Tocqueville was to be disappointed. "I deeply regret," he wrote to Lieber in December 1844, "that you have not been able to find a correspondent for us in Germany. Nonetheless, I was expecting this. Germany is still the country of silence, and I fear that it will never be different, at least in our lifetimes."[10]

That Tocqueville's interest in Germany was not diminished by this disappointing experience was confirmed two years later when he wrote to Kergorlay about the latter's own plans to publish something on contemporary German affairs. "Like you," Tocqueville wrote, "I believe that, taking everything into account, Germany now presents the biggest, the most interesting, and the most productive study of politics that one could devote oneself to." The same letter affirmed Tocqueville's intention to visit Germany in 1847. "Between now and then," he wrote, "I have therefore a considerable interest in concerning myself with this country in as much as political life allows me, not admittedly by working on it, but by making contact with as many Germans as possible."[11]

Tocqueville did not get to Germany in 1847, but the dramatic and revolutionary events of 1848 in Berlin and the Rhineland, and the impetus they gave to the cause of German unification, were to lead to his first visit in 1849. Tocqueville came quickly to an assessment of the significance of what was unfolding on the other side of the Rhine. Writing to Gustave de Beaumont, now French ambassador in London, in August 1848 he commented, "I believe that what is happening in Germany is of a nature to produce new common interests between us and England that did not exist six months ago. If the letters that I am receiving from Germany paint things in their true colours, the movement in support of the union of the German race is something much stronger and more serious than I had previously believed. The passion of populations for this idea appears to be sincere and deep, and the princes will be compelled to give way to it." This was not all. "Nothing," Tocqueville continued, "would be more to be feared for us than such an outcome: it is only the imbeciles of our diplomatic service who do not see it this way." England too had much to fear, for, Tocqueville wrote, "who says German unification, also says a significant extension of the Zollverein,[12] large industrial and maritime enterprises in the Mediterranean and the Baltic Sea, the dissolution of Hanover."[13]

This concern about the implications for France of moves towards German unification was only accentuated by the further threat of war arising from nationalist opposition to Austrian rule in northern Italy. "The most terrible threat to France at this time," Tocqueville told Beaumont some six weeks later, "is war." Its likely outcome, he believed, would be "the preponderance of the great military powers of Germany." From this Tocqueville drew the conclusion that the most important priority was to preserve peace, even if this meant what in another letter to Beaumont he termed "the preservation of the old territories of Italy." War, he told Beaumont, would mean "the end of the world." News of what Tocqueville described as a "bloody insurrection" in Berlin in October only increased his fears. Germany, he wrote, "is in a mess from one end to the other."[14]

In the months that followed, not only was Tocqueville appointed French representative to an international conference in Brussels designed to facilitate mediation between Austria and Piedmont,[15] but he also did his best to extend his list of German acquaintances in Paris. In January 1849, for example, he met Karl Wilhelm von Willisen, the Prussian envoy. Yet Tocqueville was again ill. As early as September 1848 he had told Beaumont that he was exhausted and had had to take a break for a few days. He returned to this subject in a letter to Paul Clamorgan in mid-January, indicating that he had been obliged to request leave from his work in the French Parliament.[16]

In March he told Clamorgan that he had been suffering from a "sickly lethargy" for the past two months which had thrown him into a state of "inertia and inaction." Then, on 6 May, he wrote to Clamorgan, "I will definitely leave tomorrow. I have had enough. A few days of rest are absolutely necessary. During this time, I want to live without letters, without newspapers, to replace the violent commotion amidst which I have been living for the last year with an absolute calm."[17] On 9 May, Nassau Senior received a similar message. Apologising to Senior for not being able to see him when he was in Paris, Tocqueville wrote that "my health has been so shaken by the ferment and demands of this last year that my doctors have ordered me to avoid Paris for some time so as to get the rest and relaxation that have become essential for me."[18] The truth was that, by the time that he wrote this letter, Tocqueville was already in Brussels with his wife, Mary.

The above account accords broadly with the notes made by Tocqueville in April 1851 for that part of his *Souvenirs* that was meant to cover the period from June to October 1849. Although never written up in final form, we there read, "I fall ill; I remain very much out of touch with what is going on in the Assembly in the first months of 1849. At the end of April I go for a trip along the Rhine in the hope of recovering my health."[19] However, if Tocqueville was clearly mistaken about the date of his departure, so too do the letters he wrote to Beaumont at the time tell a somewhat different story about Tocqueville's intentions. As ill as he might have been, finding out what was going on in Germany and not his health was uppermost in his thoughts.

First, there is something that these letters pass over without comment—namely, that Tocqueville and his wife travelled from Paris to Brussels by train. As he was such an observant traveller, one might have expected some reflection upon what presumably must have been a new and possibly exciting experience. After all, the Paris-to-Brussels railway had only been opened in June 1846, thereby reducing what had been a journey of three to four days by stagecoach to one of just twelve hours in relative comfort. Next, when Tocqueville wrote to Beaumont from Brussels, he made no mention of a trip down the Rhine for health reasons but rather announced his intention to travel as soon as possible directly to Berlin. "I need," he wrote, "to see people from all the political parties." The "men of the resistance," he commented, were easily accessed but not those of "movement." Perhaps Beaumont, or possibly Emmanuel Arago (who had represented France in Berlin in the latter half of 1848) might possibly suggest some names?[20]

Three days later, having abandoned the idea of travelling as far as Berlin—his wife's health, Tocqueville reported to Beaumont, was probably not up to such a long journey "even by train"—Tocqueville was in Bonn. The plan now was to reach Frankfurt, where the new national parliament had been sitting since April 1848. It was, Tocqueville told Beaumont, very important that he should get there as soon as possible as, up until now, the journey he had made had been that of "a pure *tourist*" and this, he added, was not an "occupation" for which he had ever been remotely suited. Moreover, Tocqueville wrote, "even the most determined tourist would have been disappointed by the awful weather" they had experienced since leaving Paris. So, the fact was that he had "seen nothing" and had "nothing to tell" Beaumont. Indeed, Tocqueville reported, if he had seen anything at all it was only the "tranquillity" that reigned throughout the country. Far from being "excitable" and "agitated," people were just going about their ordinary business. "I can hardly believe," he told Beaumont, "that great revolutionary convulsions might come out of a place that is so united and immobile in appearance." That at least, Tocqueville added, was his "*impression.*"[21]

On 18 May, Tocqueville was writing to Beaumont from Frankfurt. Somewhat amusingly, given what he had told Clamorgan on the eve of his departure, he was now complaining that no one was writing to him from France. More importantly, his impression that all was calm in Germany was being very considerably revised. The newspapers, he wrote, would be telling Beaumont that Germany was in crisis and "nothing could be truer." Indeed, Tocqueville had arrived in Frankfurt at a moment of high drama. Having spent much of the latter half of 1848 discussing whether the way forward for national unification lay in either a greater or smaller Germany (the latter would have excluded Austria), on 27 March 1849 the Frankfurt Parliament voted to approve a new monarchical constitution and on the following day elected King Frederick William IV as the hereditary emperor. On 21 April, the Prussian king made known his refusal of this offer and by the time that Tocqueville arrived in Frankfurt not only had the prime minister, Heinrich von Gagern, resigned from what amounted to a provisional government on 10 May, but all of the Prussian deputies and most of the conservative deputies had withdrawn from the Parliament, thereby crushing the hopes of German liberals for a constitutional settlement to the crisis. During May there were popular uprisings in Dresden, parts of Bavaria, Baden, and elsewhere in support of the Frankfurt Parliament, but its days were numbered. On 31 May the Parliament, now no more than a rump, relocated to Stuttgart, only for it to be closed on 18 June when Württemberg dragoons entered the building where it was sitting.

Even though he had just arrived, Tocqueville quickly assessed this situation with remarkable accuracy. The moderates, who had wanted unification without destroying the old order, he told Beaumont, had failed to secure the support of the German princes and, in particular, the King of Prussia, and now found themselves paralysed and dominated by a revolutionary majority. Many of the small German states were in a similar position. On the other side stood the larger states, with Prussia at their head, now ready to take the route of resistance, supported above all by their armies. There were then two governments and two Germanies facing each other with no possibility of compromise. "You should be able to see this from afar as well as I can," he told Beaumont, "but what you can have no idea of is the unutterable confusion that exists in this country at the moment, the widespread unrest, the revolutionary hotbeds that are multiplying everywhere amidst this excessive decentralisation, and, more than anything else, the profound ignorance professed by everyone about the immediate future." In Frankfurt itself, Tocqueville observed, a struggle between the Parliament and the regent, Archduke Johann of Austria,[22] had now officially begun (on 16 May the regent had appointed Maximilien Grävell as prime minister, to the dismay of the Parliament) and this struggle, he continued, could easily descend into the streets. "My bags are packed," he told Beaumont, "and I am ready at any moment to take the train and reach the Rhine."[23]

Where, however, would all of this lead? Tocqueville had little doubt that ultimately the German princes would be victorious, and this was so because behind them stood the "only organised force" that existed in Germany: the army. If, he conceded, certain parts of the army had shown weaknesses—most notably in Baden, where, Tocqueville reported, officers had been either killed or chased away and replaced by non-commissioned officers and men from the ranks[24]—this was quite definitely not the case with the Prussian army which, Tocqueville wrote, he expected to "hold firm."[25] And this was despite the fact that the Prussian army faced a "revolutionary party" that was, in Tocqueville's opinion, much like the one that existed in France—namely, one that was "violent, rash, only ever obeying its passions and not its reason." But, Tocqueville believed, a Prussian victory would not solve anything. "This country," he told Beaumont, "appears to me to be deeply agitated and discouraged by a revolutionary spirit, a distaste for existing institutions, and vague passion for change."[26]

Moreover, as Germany was a country without "a head or a centre," it would be impossible to defeat the revolution "in one shot." Likewise, Tocqueville saw no reason to believe that, "even during this formidable crisis," Prussia would abandon the policy it had pursued for the last century. Correctly guessing that Frederick William IV had turned down the imperial crown offered to him by Parliament on the assumption that he could secure it by other means more to his liking, Tocqueville saw this as a very risky strategy. "He is," he told Beaumont, "playing a game where both his throne and his life are at risk and it is pretty stupid of him to imagine that he can augment his power at a time when he will struggle to retain the power he already has."[27] Tocqueville also thought that the German territories along France's borders would become a hive of revolutionary activity and that the deployment of French troops to counter it would risk "unleashing the revolutionary passions of Germany" against France. This, Tocqueville concluded, was something that Beaumont should pass on and repeat to any policy makers considering such a response.[28]

Despite concerns about both his own and his wife's health, Tocqueville told Beaumont, the decision to travel to Frankfurt had been an excellent one. "The spectacle that I have before my eyes," he wrote, "excites my interest to the highest degree and every day gives me countless new ideas about things that I believed I already knew." Yet, for all that Frankfurt had given him a sense of the forces of revolution, Tocqueville now saw that his trip would be incomplete without a week in Berlin, "the head and the home of the forces of resistance." It would be a great shame, he wrote, if, for the sake of a week, such a useful trip was to be wasted. His plan was now to return to Paris at the beginning of June rather than the end of May. Of course, Tocqueville added, all of this "will depend on any news that I receive from France."[29]

As with so many of the trips undertaken by Tocqueville, things were not to turn out as planned. Tocqueville ended his letter of 18 May to Beaumont by complaining, once more, that he was not receiving any mail from France. This was to change the following day when Tocqueville received a letter from Beaumont, dated 15 May, urging him to return to Paris as soon as possible. The country, Beaumont wrote, was facing a moment of the gravest crisis. The French Parliament was dissolving into chaos and it was likely that a new government would be formed. No sooner was Beaumont's letter received than Tocqueville cancelled his intended trip to Berlin, announcing that he would leave Frankfurt the following day and be in Paris as quickly as possible. As his parting shot to Beaumont on political events in Frankfurt, Tocqueville again asserted that it was more and more likely that victory would lie with the princes. The moderates, he wrote, were in a "state of demoralisation and confusion" whilst, for its part, the "revolutionary element" was in no position to continue the struggle alone. Tocqueville correctly predicted that those parliamentary deputies who remained would soon leave the city. Once more, he stated his view that the victory of the princes would solve nothing.[30]

What followed has an all too familiar ring about it. Four days after writing to Beaumont from Frankfurt, Tocqueville next wrote from Bonn. "My dear friend," he began, "at the time of writing, I should have been with you, but a kind of unbelievable fate attaches itself to this journey." His wife's health, Tocqueville reported, had forced him to delay his departure for forty-eight hours. When he and his wife finally embarked on the Rhine for Cologne, his wife had become so unwell that they had been forced to disembark at Bonn, where Tocqueville very much feared they would be forced to remain for the next few days. It was nothing very serious, Tocqueville confided, but complete rest was required. Tocqueville made no effort to disguise his frustration at this turn of events. "I do not need to tell you," he wrote, "of the annoyance and fevered impatience I am feeling," a situation made worse by his knowledge that everyone in Paris believed him already to be on his way. "To be away from my country and from my friends at a moment like this," Tocqueville continued, "is a bitter experience and I have regretted many times having left." Tocqueville went so far as to suggest that his preoccupation with French affairs had prevented him from taking any deep interest in what he had been seeing in Germany.[31]

Tocqueville's intention was now to leave immediately for Cologne, one hour's journey away, where he believed he had a "the slim hope" of finding a letter from France or at least some French newspapers, and then return immediately to his "poor wife." For her part, Tocqueville told Beaumont, his wife had several times suggested that he should set out for Paris alone but "how," he asked, could she be "left ill in a foreign country where we do not know a soul"? However, he continued, if something were to occur in Paris which "absolutely demanded" his return, Beaumont should let him know immediately. "If," Tocqueville wrote, "I need to come back, I will do so, and then I will return here to find my wife and bring her back, as it is absolutely impossible that she can come back on her own."[32]

When Tocqueville got to Cologne he there found a letter, dated 21 May, from his friend Jean-Charles Rivet.[33] Tocqueville did not disclose the precise content of Rivet's letter to Beaumont—in essence, Rivet gave details of a dinner where eight of Tocqueville's political allies had sat down to discuss their possible role in the unfolding political crisis—but its content was such, Tocqueville told Beaumont, as only to increase his desire to return. And, for all of his concern for his wife, this was precisely what Tocqueville did, leaving the following day. "I hope," he told Beaumont, "to arrive on Friday and thus to attend the dinner that has always taken place, I hope, on this day. The only thing is that I do not know in which restaurant it takes place. I would be very pleased if you could drop off a note with the details at my home."[34] Just over a week later, on 2 June, Tocqueville was appointed minister of foreign affairs in the new government headed by Odilon Barrot. Politics, the "old hussy" referred to by Tocqueville in his 1851 letter to Gobineau from Sorrento, appears to have been irresistible.

This proved to be both a short and unhappy experience. "It was a sad fate," Tocqueville wrote in his *Souvenirs,* "to be Minister of Foreign Affairs of such a country at such a time." Nonetheless, it is from Tocqueville's account of these five months in *Souvenirs* that we get the clearest sense of the conclusions that Tocqueville was to draw from his first visit to Germany. Written in Versailles in the autumn of 1851, Tocqueville began his narrative with his return to France in May 1849. "It was," Tocqueville wrote, "while I was busy watching one of the acts of the great drama of the European revolution unfold in Germany that unexpected and alarming news drew my attention back to France and her affairs." He started off, he recalled, as soon as he received this news, and when his wife fell suddenly ill, she "pressed" him to continue his journey without her, something he "did, but reluctantly." As Tocqueville acknowledged, he "was leaving her alone in a country still ravaged by civil war." Correctly remembering that he had arrived in Paris on 25 May, he then went on to say, less accurately, that "the very evening of my arrival I learned that some of my friends were dining together at a little restaurant on the Champs-Elysées." He rushed there, according to his account, listened to what the likes of Jules Dufaure, Beaumont, Francisque de Corcelle, and others had to say, and then drew several conclusions, one of which was that he would not refuse a ministerial position if a good opportunity arose.[35]

The ministerial brief that Tocqueville inherited was something of a poisoned chalice. At the time, he recalled, the position of France in Europe was both "difficult and weak." In particular, he had to deal with a president whose lack of preparedness to deal with foreign affairs was unmistakable. "One of his fantasies," Tocqueville wrote, "was to forge an alliance with one of the two great powers of Germany, with whose support he planned to redraw the map of Europe and thereby erase the territorial boundaries drawn around France by the treaties of 1815."[36]

Nevertheless, Tocqueville returned from Germany having drawn two conclusions. First, as he wrote in his notes, "Germany is suffering from a revolutionary disease that may be arrested but which cannot be cured, and this disease is inexorably destroying the old society"; and, second, "that the next phase will be the complete triumph of the princes and of military power."[37] Tocqueville also came to see that the 1848 revolution in Germany was not the product of a single cause. "It had been product," he wrote, "of both the general spirit of the times and the ideas of unity particular to the Germans."[38]

When he took up office, this story, as Tocqueville knew, was far from being played out. Germany had never seemed more divided or disturbed. The fall of the Parliament in Frankfurt had not restored order but had left a freer field for anarchy. Revolutionary demagogy had been defeated, but the desire for German unity had not been eradicated. Rather, as Tocqueville saw clearly, "the king of Prussia undertook to appropriate it and use it for his own purposes."[39] The whole of Germany was now filled with Prussian soldiers. Indeed, no sooner had Tocqueville taken up his post than, on 26 May, Prussia, Saxony, and Hanover signed the so-called Alliance of the Three Kings. "Thus," Tocqueville wrote, "Prussia suddenly became dominant across a vast territory stretching from Memel to Basle, with some twenty-six or twenty-seven million Germans marching under its orders."[40]

As minister of foreign affairs, Tocqueville understood all too well that France was distrusted by its European neighbours and he consequently resolved that France should not intervene in what he termed the "German crisis." He thus limited his efforts to seeking to ascertain the intentions of the Russian tsar and to trying to find a solution to the huge numbers of failed revolutionaries (or, in Tocqueville's word, "adventurers") who had taken refuge in Switzerland. As he recalled, he had tried to get the Swiss to see reason, but to little effect. "Nothing," Tocqueville wrote, "is equal to the pride or presumption of the Swiss."[41]

For all that Tocqueville acknowledged the limited possibilities before him, he was under no illusions as to the long-term significance of what he had witnessed in Germany. "There was," he wrote, "a more serious question that I asked myself: is it in France's interest that the bonds of the German Confederation be tighter or looser?" In other words, should France seek to facilitate the emergence of Germany as a "single nation" or should it rather seek to ensure that it remained "an ill-assorted aggregation of disunited peoples and princes"? Arguably, this has been the most important question facing French foreign policy makers for the past two hundred years or more. For his part, Tocqueville rightly saw that French policy had traditionally sought to maintain a divided Germany but was this, he asked, still the right policy? When, he argued, only Poland and a "semibarbarous Russia" lay beyond Germany, it might have made sense, but the question now to be asked was whether Russia presented a real threat to Europe. "As someone who thinks that our West is threatened with sooner or later falling under the yoke or at least the direct and irresistible influence of the Tsars," Tocqueville wrote, "I think that it is in our primary interest to encourage the union of all the Germanic races to oppose this." The state of the world, Tocqueville concluded, was new and France therefore should "not be afraid to strengthen our neighbours so that they might one day be in a position to help us in repelling the common enemy." The tsar himself, Tocqueville added, saw what an obstacle a united Germany would be to his ambitions.[42]

Tocqueville saw that this was not the right time to try to resolve this issue. He was also convinced that from late 1849 onwards the tide had very much turned against Prussia's hegemonic ambitions. Free of the fear of revolution, the German princes were less eager to lend their support. Moreover, having defeated the forces of Hungarian independence, Austria now sought to reassert its position in Germany. "When," Tocqueville wrote, "the king of Prussia found himself again face to face with his powerful rival, behind which he perceived Russia, his courage suddenly failed him," with the result that (for the time being at least) the German Confederation of 1815 was reinstated.[43] Thus, Tocqueville concluded, of the great upheaval of 1848 in Germany, there soon remained only two visible traces. The first was that the small German states were even more dependent upon the large German monarchies than they had been before. The second was that what had remained of Germany's feudal institutions had suffered irreparable damage. "From one end of Germany to the other," Tocqueville observed, "ground rents in perpetuity, seigneurial tithes, compulsory labour, rights of transfer, hunting, justice, which constituted a great part of the wealth of the nobility, remained abolished. The kings were restored, but the aristocracies did not recover."[44] The fate of Germany's ancien régime was a subject to which Tocqueville would soon return.

Following the coup d'état of December 1851 Tocqueville retired from public life and, although dogged by ill health, began in the following months to turn his mind slowly to writing his projected study of France at the time of the Revolution of 1789. Nonetheless, with the completion of his account of his ministerial involvement in German affairs in *Souvenirs,* Tocqueville's interest in Germany was not to be brought to an end. Indeed, it was to remain with him until his death. Not only this, but what Tocqueville had learned of Germany in 1849 and what he would learn of it over the next few years was to be integral to shaping the structure and argument of *L'ancien régime et la révolu-*

tion. Why, Tocqueville wanted to know, had the German experience been so different from that of France, and how could this be explained?

We catch a glimpse of Tocqueville's interest in this question in his correspondence with Arthur de Gobineau. Writing to Tocqueville in April 1852, and presumably in response to an earlier inquiry from him, Gobineau set out his thoughts on what Tocqueville might usefully read on German life and society. His starting point was that the source of new ideas in Germany was to be found in philosophy, theology and historical scholarship. One could say this about any country in the world, Gobineau wrote, "but in Germany, the impact has been more direct and has led more quickly to application because the universities have played a much bigger role in society than among us." He then recommended a reading of the "polemical writings" of Martin Luther and Erasmus and of contemporaries such as Ulrich von Hutton. For the seventeenth century he suggested Gottfried Wilhelm Leibniz and, for the eighteenth century, both Moses Mendelssohn and Gotthold Ephraim Lessing. Gobineau concluded by suggesting biographies of Johann Wolfgang von Goethe and Friedrich von Schiller (especially the latter). This, Gobineau insisted, was just for starters.[45]

In reply, Tocqueville expressed his thanks but had to admit that, unless he could find translations, this information was of no use to him. "Note," he wrote, "that I am much less interested in the causes that produced a revolutionary state of mind in Germany towards the end of the last century than I am in the extent and the character of this state of mind, the places where it was dominant, and the symptoms through which it manifested itself." To that extent, Tocqueville continued, he felt that he might learn more about Germany from less distinguished and less well-known texts. "Works on Germany written by foreigners around this time, accounts of travels," he concluded, "might throw light on the subject that interests me." To this list Tocqueville also added private memoirs.[46]

Shortly afterwards, on 21 May, Tocqueville received a similar letter from Adolphe de Circourt. Circourt's list of suggested authors and texts was more extensive than that provided by Gobineau and included French authors such as the counterrevolutionary Augustin Barruel as well as more famous writers such as Voltaire, Jean le Rond D'Alembert and the Marquis de Condorcet, but again the list was intended to help Tocqueville come to an understanding of the intellectual developments across Europe that had preceded the revolution.[47] Interestingly, in his response Tocqueville indicated that, if he was aware of Barruel's work, he had not read it. This, he told Circourt, was because he disagreed with what he knew to be Barruel's basic premise—namely, that the French Revolution was the product of a conspiracy. Yet, in line with Tocqueville's view that it was permissible to speak of a European, and not just a French, revolution, the greater part of his reply focused on Germany.

Tocqueville's starting point was an acknowledgment of his "profound ignorance of things German" but, he went on, there was one aspect of the philosophical and political history of Germany in particular that he did not understand. In France, Tocqueville wrote, philosophy had moved in the same direction as practical ideas and mores. Theory taught that tradition had no value whatsoever and that old things were useless. In Germany, by contrast, this appeared not to have been the case. There, philosophical and social ideas had gone in the opposite direction to practice and mores, stressing the importance of tradition and seeking in the past both a rationale for the present and a guide for the future. This, Tocqueville believed, appeared still to be the case, and he found it hard to comprehend. "I cannot conceive," he wrote, "that the scholarly theories of a people should be so different from the thinking that every day guides its conduct, especially in a country like Germany where theory usually plays such a large role in the production of facts." Did this mean, Tocqueville asked, that the German revolutionary mind had followed a different path from that of France? If so, what path had this been? Of one thing Tocqueville seemed sure: both French and German thought had condemned the present, "but one side wanted to abolish it in order to adopt a new plan whilst the other wanted to rebuild it on old foundations."[48]

By the time that Tocqueville was writing this letter to Circourt he had already returned to his home in Normandy and was soon to begin writing the first draft chapters of what he hoped would be his history of the French Revolution. Despite this, his enquiries about Germany continued. For example, he asked his nephew Hubert to visit a reading room in the Passage de l'opéra in Paris with a view to taking out a subscription to a German newspaper and then, in November, he asked his nephew to borrow several books from the library for him: these included Friedrich Nicolai's account (in French translation) of his travels in Germany and Switzerland in 1781, a work generally regarded as one of the most important books on the intellectual and political situation of Germany at the end of the eighteenth century.

The extent of Tocqueville's ongoing interest in Germany was most clearly evidenced when he wrote to Christian von Bunsen in January 1853. Bunsen was then serving as Prussian ambassador in London and had been recommended to Tocqueville by his English friend, Harriet Grote. Bunsen was also known to both Nassau Senior and Henry Reeve. Having presented his apologies and signalled that he had left public life, Tocqueville went on to explain that he had now set about studying "the circumstances that had accompanied the beginning of our revolutions, or rather our revolution as there is only one, and one that still lives on and is not near to being finished." He therefore wanted to place himself at the moment of the revolution's birth and to gain a clear idea of the first impressions of those who had seen, however indistinctly, these events from abroad. "Unfortunately, and much to my regret," Tocqueville then wrote, "I do not know Germany. Up until now I have lived almost exclusively in the English world. I imagine that during the last sixty years the Germans have published memoirs, collections of letters or diplomatic papers which shed light on what I seek to find out. I do not know of them and consequently cannot acquire them. From the beginning, the French Revolution must have given rise, either directly or indirectly, to writings which reflect what were widespread opinions. My semi-ignorance of German and my almost complete ignorance of Germany (which happily is not incurable) deprive me of this necessary information."[49]

Bunsen did not reply until the end of April but, when he did, he recommended a reading of texts by Barthold Niebuhr, Ernst Arndt, August Rehberg, and Johann Droysen, all of which were imbued with antirevolutionary and anti-French sentiment. Bunsen also told Tocqueville that writers such as Kant, Herder, and Goethe had at first looked sympathetically upon the revolution, only for Napoleon's invasion to cause an upsurge in German patriotism. Tocqueville's own reply, written shortly before his departure for Saint-Cyr, contained the not unimportant announcement that, once settled in the Loire Valley, he intended to begin learning German. His hope, he further confirmed, was to have a good understanding of the language within a year. "My very definite plan," Tocqueville wrote, "is next year to visit this Germany which has always interested me but which to date I have never wished to visit, convinced as I am that one can only see with pleasure and benefit those peoples whose language one knows." Tocqueville's wish was to meet and speak with Bunsen before he undertook his trip.[50]

Tocqueville's plan to learn German was undoubtedly aided by Gustave de Beaumont's own decision to do the same thing. He wrote to Tocqueville to this effect in January 1853, in his case indicating that he thought that six months would be sufficient to finish the job. Like Tocqueville, he was at something of a loose end (having lost his parliamentary salary, he was also in financial difficulties) and had now resolved to write a history of Austria. Tocqueville immediately voiced his approval and later in the year he and Beaumont were jointly to take out a subscription to the liberal *Kölnische Zeitung*. Its content, as well as their mutual difficulties in learning German, was now to become a frequent topic in their correspondence. Tocqueville, it seems, tried to read it every day and he certainly felt that its pages were teaching him much about the situation of contemporary Germany—he was shocked, in particular, to learn of the extent of the animosity in Germany, especially among liberals, towards Russia[51]—but any significant progress in learning German continued to elude him. Few of his friends and correspondents were now to be spared being told that he was too old to learn this "abominable" and "diabolical" language. He was not bored by the hours he was spending learning German, he told Adolphe de Circourt in October 1853, but he was depressed by his failure to improve. French, he wrote, was a language that led the confused mind towards light but "German adds the obscurities of language to the obscurities of intelligence. Are you even sure that the native population of Germany always understands what it reads and what it writes? I am beginning to doubt it."[52] A few months later, Tocqueville told Madame de Circourt that, for all that he was enjoying his studies, he could not get used to the "guttural" sound of German. Was it, he wondered, possible to say "sweet nothings" in such a language?[53] Perhaps Tocqueville's considered view was best revealed in his remark that the great French diplomat Talleyrand must have been thinking of German when he had commented that speech had been given to man in order to hide his thoughts.[54]

Yet, for all these frustrations and difficulties, Tocqueville never wavered from his view that learning German was indispensable not only for any future trip to Germany that he might make but also for the research he now had in mind on the ancien régime. In a letter written in May 1853 Tocqueville indicated to Christian von Bunsen that he was planning a trip to Germany. He mentioned this idea again to Kergorlay in September of that year and then to Harriet Grote two months later. By the spring of the following year Tocqueville's plans were taking definite shape. "Around the beginning of June," he told Jean-Jacques Ampère, "we will make our way directly to Bonn and remain there for at least a month or six weeks. If I do not find enough to occupy me, I will travel up and down the Rhine valley, our base remaining in Bonn. Around August or the end of July we will move elsewhere, staying for about the same length of time. I am thinking of Berlin or Dresden, as it seems to me that it is there that I will find the greatest number of intelligent people capable of providing me with lots of ideas about Germany." However, as Tocqueville explained, this still remained only a "project," as the cloud on the horizon was a cholera epidemic in England and Paris that, Madame de Tocqueville feared, might soon spread to Germany. "She wonders," he wrote, "if it is wise for people who have just been very ill and who are still in delicate health to go rushing across a country during an epidemic when they can be pretty sure to remain sheltered from the plague by spending the summer at home."[55]

But the thought of having to spend a summer by the sea in Normandy was not Tocqueville's only worry. He was clearly concerned that some of his friends—most notably Nassau Senior and the always demanding Harriet Grote—would seek to join him in Germany. Tocqueville's letter to Senior in May was therefore a masterpiece in evasion. He still hoped to go to Germany, he told Senior, but this very much depended on his health. He and his wife would only make their decision after they had left their house in the Loire and once they had visited Tocqueville's father at Compiègne, north of Paris. They had thought, Tocqueville continued, to establish a base where Madame de Tocqueville would remain, but given the fragility of his own health it now seemed likely that he would take his wife with him on his travels. Moreover, Tocqueville wrote, "I am not going to Germany to see certain places in particular but to go here and there where documents and people might lead me."

It was therefore impossible for him to sketch out an itinerary in advance as "it is in the nature of such a trip that it is made haphazardly." Tocqueville ended by saying that he felt that Senior and their "excellent friend Mme Grote" would have a clearer idea of their plans than he did of his own.[56] That Tocqueville remained anxious that his English friends would track him down was apparent from a letter he sent to Circourt in early June. Again, his theme was that what made such a trip enjoyable was being able to go about as one pleased and according to one's fancy. He would, he told Circourt, much prefer to know where his friends intended to be so that he might go to see them than tell them in advance where he planned to be. Above all, Tocqueville wanted to retain his freedom of movement and he therefore asked Circourt to share nothing of his plans.[57]

However, it is clear from a letter sent to Circourt on 1 June that Tocqueville now had a very precise idea of where he intended to go in Germany and what exactly he wanted to find out. His intention, Tocqueville told Circourt, was to leave around the middle of the month, probably for Bonn, where he would stay for approximately six weeks. He then planned to go to Dresden, which he would use as a base from which to make various excursions. "As for my principal aim," he continued, "I want above all to know in what state Germany found itself at the moment when the French revolution burst forth; what our contact with Germany produced there, either at the level of ideas or the military; and finally . . . what principally occurred in that great country up to the time when it rose up en masse against us." What had occurred prior to this *levée en masse,* Tocqueville wrote, "greatly excited [his] curiosity." To that end, therefore, he asked Circourt what places he would be best advised to visit, what books he should read and, above all, who were "the most important individuals to consult." In line with a past practice with which we are already familiar, Tocqueville also asked if Circourt would kindly provide him with letters of introduction.[58]

Circourt's reply must have been everything that Tocqueville wished for. He sent three letters of introduction. The first was to the Countess von Oriola, "a charming person, well-read, gifted and very well connected across Germany." Her husband was a brigadier in the cavalry and one of the best soldiers in the Prussian Army. The second was for Friedrich Dahlmann, "the flower and light" of the University of Bonn, a historian and someone who had played a "brilliant and, above all, very honourable" role in the political debates of 1848–1849. He could tell Tocqueville about everything that Bonn had to offer in terms of books and people. He also had links with the "elite of the intellectual world" in Dresden, Leipzig, Jena, and Halle. The third person was Charles Monnard, a Swiss, who had recently moved from the University of Lausanne to Bonn, "an honest man, enlightened, industrious" and someone "very familiar with Germany, without having lost sight of France." He was also already familiar with Tocqueville's writings. As to where Tocqueville might go, in literary terms Dresden was only a shadow of its former self. The same, "unhappily," could be said of Weimar. By contrast, Berlin brought together all the brilliant ideas previously spread across northern Germany. Going first to Bonn struck Circourt as a good idea, in part because on the way Tocqueville could pass through Charlemagne's Aix-la-Chapelle and see the Gothic art of Cologne. If, when he had "set up his tent," Tocqueville wanted more introductions, guidance on where to go or what to read, Circourt concluded, he should not hesitate to ask. A reply would be there within a week.[59]

Tocqueville had then prepared his visit to Germany with typical thoroughness. He had made great efforts to learn German; taken steps to familiarise himself with German ideas and contemporary events; and had planned his itinerary. He knew the questions he wanted answered, and why; and he had his valuable letters of introduction. Tocqueville was also in good health. What could possibly go wrong?

Tocqueville and his wife arrived in Bonn on 19 June, having stopped off in Brussels on the way to see their friends, the Lamoricières, now living in enforced exile.[60] Despite the continuous rain, the journey had gone well, although somewhat ominously Tocqueville reported to Kergorlay and others that his wife, Mary, had been extremely fatigued by the experience. All his wife's old problems caused by travelling, he told Ampère, had reappeared: kidney pains; the impossibility of remaining in a carriage for more than five or six hours; difficulties with walking. Tocqueville hoped that the cause was a period of continuous movement after what had amounted to virtual inactivity for the past year.[61] Nonetheless, the Tocquevilles quickly established themselves in a small furnished apartment at 18 Koblenzer Strasse, close to the Rhine and facing the gardens of the university. There were charming walks nearby and plenty of fresh air.

The Tocquevilles also found themselves welcomed into Bonn society. On the day after their arrival, Tocqueville renewed his acquaintance with Christian-August Brandis, professor of philosophy at the University of Bonn. Brandis did no more than invite Tocqueville and his wife to what Tocqueville assumed would be a small gathering that evening. To his surprise, as he told Ampère, it turned out to be a meeting of the "university en masse," a huge get-together of professors and their wives, complete with an "immense supper" where "the locals had eaten like the Germans of the sixteenth century." Everyone, Tocqueville reported, had welcomed them with great kindness and both he and his wife had been "delighted" by their evening, even though they had met so many people that they could not remember their names. Tocqueville's intention was to meet them all again as soon as possible and "draw from them whatever I can."[62] As later correspondence shows, Tocqueville was greatly to enjoy the company of these distinguished scholars and was delighted to be welcomed into their homes. Almost always, he told Theodore Sedgwick, he had found "a genuine simplicity of habits and good-heartedness of character" and it had not taken him long to "feel like one of them."[63]

This was much to be expected. As with his previous travels, Tocqueville's aim was to "immerse [himself] as much as possible in the atmosphere of German mores and ideas," something from which, he told Sedgwick, he was "fortunate to derive great pleasure."[64] This was all the more intriguing as these mores were so different from those of France. Tocqueville therefore lived only among Germans and spoke with them only about their own country. He read only German books and newspapers. He was living, he told Léonce de Lavergne, "a completely Germanic life."[65] Were it not for the fact that he did not have a late evening meal, he reported to Gobineau, he'd be taken for a genuine inhabitant of the country.[66] It was this very satisfying experience—his time, Tocqueville told Beaumont, was being spent "excellently, usefully and agreeably"—that encouraged Tocqueville from the outset to stay as long as possible in Bonn. As he told both Francisque de Corcelle and Adolphe de Circourt, he felt that he would learn more about Germany by getting to know one place well and at his leisure than by travelling hither and thither across this "vast space."[67] With the onset of the summer holidays, he told Lavergne, he would no doubt be obliged to move on, "wandering across the country like an ordinary traveller, seeing lots of hostels, lots of new faces, and plenty of land and water, without learning anything."[68] Immersing himself in the life of another country, Tocqueville commented, also enabled him to forget his own country. The only problem, as he repeatedly reported to his friends, was his continuing lack of proficiency in speaking German. "I am beginning," Tocqueville told Gobineau, "to understand books moderately well but conversation still remains only a sound."[69] While his wife spoke German to the best of her ability, he could only aspire to "speak gibberish."[70]

Tocqueville was, as usual, quick to make use of his letters of introduction. He wrote on 30 June to Adolphe de Circourt to say that he had already met (the heavily pregnant) Countess von Oriola—"a very witty, likeable and completely charming woman," Tocqueville wrote[71]—and it was to be through her that he met her husband, a man Tocqueville found to be hugely impressive and interesting, and that he was also to meet her sister, Armgart von Armin. All three spoke a perfect French, and Tocqueville's primary concern was that he should not take too much advantage of such delightful and amiable company. Tocqueville also introduced himself to Friedrich Dahlmann. Unfortunately, he reported to Circourt, Dahlmann only spoke French with difficulty, but every time they met, Tocqueville came away having learned something useful.[72] As for Charles Monnard, he and Tocqueville were to meet soon after the latter's arrival. Not only did Monnard put Tocqueville in touch with other German academics, most notably Hugo Hälschner, but the two men were to continue a correspondence after Tocqueville's return to France.

Tocqueville's requests for assistance from Circourt were not yet at an end. No sooner had Tocqueville arrived in Bonn than he set himself to work with what he described to Lavergne as a "*furia francese*."[73] Circourt received a similar message in Tocqueville's letter of 30 June. He had, Tocqueville reported, immediately thrown himself headfirst into a study of "the chaos of the Germanic ancien régime," his plan being to learn something of "the old social and administrative constitution of Germany." From the outset he had hit upon a seemingly insoluble problem arising from what he could now see as the great dissimilarities evident across different parts of this large country. "To reduce all these differences and, sometimes these contrasts," Tocqueville wrote, "to a common general idea is impossible." The best way forward was therefore to focus upon the individual parts of the country, providing a set of less general but more detailed and precise accounts that might over time reveal a "moderately fair" picture of the whole.[74]

Even here Tocqueville faced a problem. "In the part of Germany where I am," he told Circourt, "the ancien régime has been so completely destroyed for such a long time that one meets very few people who can say with any accuracy what it was like." More than this, the corner of Germany where he found himself was probably of the least interest to him because, with the exception of political institutions, the ancien régime on the banks of the Rhine closely resembled the ancien régime of France. In brief, Tocqueville saw that of greater interest were those parts of Germany which had most preserved "the social and administrative structure of the Middle Ages" and these, he had been led to believe, were best found in Westphalia, Hanover, Brandenburg, and Mecklenburg. Consequently, what Tocqueville wanted was to be put in touch with "the old aristocracy of the old Germany, people among whom the manners and traditions of the old institutions might be met and who still live among the remains of this antediluvian world." "For someone," Tocqueville continued, "who has seen American society which, so to speak, is leading modern Europe in the direction of the future, there is nothing more novel or more intriguing than seeing societies which are heading in the direction of the past." Would it be possible, he therefore asked, for Circourt to render him the great service of indicating which people might best suit his purposes and of providing him with letters of introduction? If so, Tocqueville concluded, he intended to leave his wife behind in Bonn and make a trip towards either the north or the east of Germany.[75]

Circourt, as always, was true to his word, sending Tocqueville a detailed reply only four days later. For someone who willingly admitted that the world Tocqueville wanted to secure entry into was not one he knew well, he still managed to produce an impressive list of names and contacts. He also suggested that the Countess von Oriola might be of assistance, as her family had owned a large estate in Mecklenburg. Circourt likewise offered to provide letters of introduction should Tocqueville decide to relocate to Berlin.

None of this was to be required. For the time being, Tocqueville was perfectly happy beavering away in the library of the University of Bonn, taking advantage of the many contacts he had made among the university's academics, and enjoying the delights of what he described to Pierre Freslon as "a little provincial town."[76] Tocqueville also read the recently published *Germany from 1670 to 1814, or Sketches of German Life from the Decay of the Empire to the Expulsion of the French* by Mrs Sarah Austin.[77] "I am working a lot," Tocqueville told Beaumont in early August, "and I hope that, even if I do not come to understand Germany, I will at least have an idea of what it is most important for me to know about her."[78] As for the subject of his endeavours, this Tocqueville frequently described to his correspondents as a "dead Germany." If Beaumont wanted to know what things were like in 1754, Tocqueville added, this was something he could talk about for hours.[79]

Once more Tocqueville was to find himself struggling due to his lack of command of the German language. Since his arrival in Bonn, Tocqueville explained to Circourt, his "greatest difficulty had been to make understood what I wanted to know and to frame questions sufficiently clearly and precisely to produce helpful responses." He was steadily getting there, but when the complexity of an idea and the obscurity of technical terms was joined to the inherent difficulty the language presented to him, "even in its simple and ordinary form," he "lost [his] way" and advanced only with a "heart-breaking slowness." Tocqueville also admitted to Circourt that another of his principal concerns was an inability to identify and obtain the books that would be useful to him. "The Germans," he wrote, "publish so many books that among them there must be some that respond precisely to what I want to know." Fortunately, Tocqueville conceded, when he was in difficulty, he could always rely on the "gentlemen of the university" to enlighten him, something they always did "obligingly."[80] Tocqueville was also not above asking Circourt and Ampère, both of whom spoke fluent German, for assistance.

For all these difficulties, Tocqueville felt that he was making progress and that, if he tried hard, he would get something out of his trip. He did this, in part, by employing precisely the same methods he had previously used on his travels to America and elsewhere. For example, early on he drew up a lengthy questionnaire which clearly identified the information he sought to obtain and which helped him structure his conversations with his distinguished German acquaintances. First and foremost were a series of questions about the position of the nobility in Germany under the ancien régime:

Was it a closed aristocracy, only to be entered by birth? Did it enjoy considerable privileges, such as the exclusive right to certain positions and tax exemptions? Did the aristocracy take part in rural government and administer justice? Crucially, and in light of what Tocqueville had discovered about the ancien régime in France, did the German aristocracy elicit "violent jealousies and great hatreds"? Next came a set of questions relating to the division of land and the relations between classes: Was landownership divided? Did peasants own land? Were there representative assemblies? Was the bourgeoisie confined to the towns, or did it extend to the countryside? Did the bourgeoisie have tax exemptions? Was it separated from the nobility by the rights it possessed or by habits and pretensions? Was the bourgeoisie hostile to the nobility? How did the nobility recruit its members? Was its membership, as in France, largely composed of public officials? Regarding the rural lower classes, Tocqueville wanted to know whether they were still "attached to the soil." What feudal dues still weighed heavily upon them? And where and in what proportion were they landowners? At the bottom of the list was a simple entry for the Catholic Church. Another asked whom to contact in Westphalia.[81]

Whilst in Bonn, Tocqueville repeatedly put these questions to his willing German colleagues. At the end of June, for example, Tocqueville had a series of conversations with Ferdinand Walter, professor of law at the University of Bonn and a member of the Prussian National Assembly in 1848. From Walter, Tocqueville learned, inter alia, that, with a few exceptions, the principle of German nobility was birth; that feelings of contempt and envy scarcely existed between nobles of different origin; and that, "to a certain extent," German nobles had enjoyed the same privileges and tax exemptions as their French counterparts. The nobility, Tocqueville heard, had had exclusive rights to certain occupations (as military officers and court officials, for example), as well as rights to exclusive ownership of such properties as mills and ovens. They extracted feudal dues and through their law courts exercised "real police power" over the countryside. All these things, Walter told Tocqueville, were moderated and regulated by law and did not give rise to complaints. Moreover, many peasants had already become landowners and, according to Walter, the differences between the noble and the commoner were less noticeable and less humiliating than those that had existed in France. It was also Walter's view that, if little in the actual structure of German institutions had changed by the eighteenth century, the spirit in which they functioned had changed dramatically. Much of this, Tocqueville admitted, he did not understand and required confirmation. He also recorded his view that Walter seemed to have "a soft spot for the Ancien Régime."[82]

Over the next few weeks Tocqueville had similar discussions with Charles Monnard, and two other Bonn professors, Christian-August Brandis and Hugo Hälschner (all three of whom held liberal views like Tocqueville's own). Again, Tocqueville focused much of his questioning on the subjects of peasant landownership, the division of land, rules of inheritance, and the extent to which serfdom had existed into the eighteenth century and beyond. On the latter, Hälschner confirmed that serfdom had existed throughout Germany in the eighteenth century, even if in certain regions its characteristics had been significantly weakened. Tocqueville also quizzed his three Protestant interlocutors on the position of the Catholic Church in Germany, and specifically in Prussia. Four themes emerged that are particularly worthy of note. Each was to continue to preoccupy Tocqueville, and all four were to find their way into *L'ancien régime et la révolution*.

The first concerned the influence of French ideas in Germany. According to Hälschner, Tocqueville recorded, "the whole German intellectual movement of the eighteenth century had in large part a French origin."[83] Second, the German experience confirmed that it was not only in France but across Europe that the old society of the Middle Ages was no longer viable. "Everything," Tocqueville noted, "which had formed the real life of medieval society, not only its life, but its strength and energy, was precisely what was languishing and dying." Everything that lived and moved was contrary to the general inequality and diversity of that society and sprang from a moral and intellectual order concerned with rights, equality for all, mildness, and toleration. Third, the decline of the medieval order had been accompanied by a rise of absolute government. "It was only around the middle of the eighteenth century," Tocqueville wrote, "that people thought of submitting themselves to the control of the state." Formerly independent towns now required the authorisation of the state to carry out their activities, with an agent of the state charged with overseeing what went on. Everything that related to general government by the nobility was swept away by Frederick the Great, leaving them individually with only the government of the countryside. Fourth, and finally, this process was greatly aided by resort to the principles of Roman law, principles used to subvert the ancient liberties derived from Germanic law. Roman law, Tocqueville deduced, "has done more . . . to disorganise, disjoint, and finally destroy the old society of Europe, to create centralisation and equal dependence, to replace turbulent freedom with orderly and tranquil servitude, than the princes themselves."[84]

Not unimportantly, Tocqueville ended his notes on these conversations by posing two questions, both of which were to frame his thinking and writing in the years that were to remain to him. Was, he asked, a revolution necessary to destroy the old society and introduce a new one? To this he replied that it was in Prussia that one could best see how an old society could be both destroyed and transformed peacefully, "the old edifice subsiding without breaking." This, Tocqueville wrote, was a perspective that he should not lose from sight. Second, if the Prussian *Landrecht* (general state laws) had done much to modify and regulate the old order, would these changes have taken place without the French Revolution? "Was it not thanks to the violent revolution in France," Tocqueville asked, "that the old society was able to transform itself little by little in countries other than France"? This, Tocqueville recorded, was "a question to examine."[85]

As letters to both Beaumont and Pierre Freslon confirm, there was one definite conclusion that Tocqueville had arrived at by the end of July. "As I have told you," Tocqueville wrote to Beaumont, "since my arrival I have lived in the Germany of the last century and, when considering why the Revolution took place among us rather than there, I see with a certain satisfaction that the ideas I had of her without knowing the country and based purely upon abstract reasoning appear to be fully confirmed by the facts. The political condition, and above all the social condition, of this country seems to me to be exactly what I had imagined."[86] It was this knowledge, Tocqueville told Freslon, that gave him the courage to continue on his chosen path.[87]

It was only after Tocqueville had been in Bonn for three weeks that he wrote his first letter from Germany to Gustave de Beaumont. Prior to his departure from France, Beaumont had written to Tocqueville to inquire about the plans for his journey and there took the opportunity to set out some of the issues that were preoccupying him in his own enquiries. Was it the case, he wondered, that the future of Germany would be "liberal, constitutional, and parliamentary"—as the period prior to 1848 had indicated—or would socialism and communism lead Germany unerringly towards "absolute power"? In brief, Beaumont asked, "have we more reason to hope for the triumph of liberal ideas than to fear the final victory of despotism?"[88] Tocqueville's response was one with which his other correspondents would soon become familiar. He had been so engrossed in his historical enquiries that he lived in "total ignorance" of matters relating to contemporary Germany. Of the general political situation of the country and what it thought of what was happening in Europe, he had no idea.[89]

Francisque de Corcelle was one of the friends who received a similar response. Writing on 22 July, Tocqueville told Corcelle that his impressions of Germany were at best vague and incomplete. This was not by chance. He was, Tocqueville wrote, no longer a politician and he had sought to replace the passions of politics by those of erudition. Nevertheless, he was from time to time obliged to speak of those things about which other people spoke and thus, in "fits and starts," he had acquired some "general ideas" about what he saw around him. Put bluntly, for all of Tocqueville's insistence that since his arrival he had only been interested in a "dead Germany," he was very much interested in what he saw around him of the "living Germany."[90]

Germany, Tocqueville told Corcelle, appeared, like France, to be affected by a "great political languor." There were many signs of this, but the "illness" seemed much less severe than that afflicting France and would probably not last for as long. Moreover, a turning away from politics did not denote a general turning away from ideas. Scientific and literary life flourished, and poetry remained popular. Lots of books were published, finding a considerable number of readers. Thinking concerned itself with things other than physical well-being. Even in politics, the "despondency" one saw derived more from a sense of confusion than from a "cooling" towards political liberty. People continued to have faith in "free institutions" and continued to believe that they were most worthy of respect and love (something, Tocqueville added, that was not true of France). Germany, Tocqueville wrote, "is confused, perplexed and unaware of the paths it must take but it is not broken and, so to speak, reduced to nothing as we are." With regard to international affairs, "everyone" was "visibly impassioned" against Russia and this made them more favourable to France than they might otherwise have been.[91]

Tocqueville next turned his reflections to philosophy, and in particular to that of Hegel. This was a topic he had discussed in his conversations with Brandis and Monnard. As Tocqueville correctly observed, the philosophy of Hegel had occupied an important place in German life for fifty years. It had been promoted and endorsed by governments precisely because it asserted their legitimacy and taught that they merited obedience. Nevertheless, as Tocqueville again correctly observed, this doctrine had given rise to the "anti-Christian" and "antispiritualist" schools of thought that had sought to pervert Germany over the last forty years and, in the form of socialism, to the ideas that had caused so much confusion in 1848. Once opened, Tocqueville wrote, this Pandora's box had produced all kinds of "moral infirmities" from which the German people still suffered. Yet, he continued, the evidence indicated that a "general reaction" had set in against this "sensualist and socialist philosophy" and that it was no longer "preached" in the universities.[92]

Here Tocqueville was on less sure ground. Socialist ideas were to play an increasingly important (and damaging) role in German politics and society. However, Tocqueville believed this to be the case in part because, in parallel to this "philosophical revolution," "everyone" had told him that a revival of religious sentiment (of all faiths) was taking place right across Germany. This, Tocqueville told Corcelle, had been a point made especially by the Catholic professors from the University of Bonn whom he had spoken with. Catholicism, they had affirmed, was in a stronger position than it had been for more than a century and this they attributed above all to the liberty enjoyed by the Catholic Church and especially its complete separation from the state. This, of course, was a view Tocqueville had heard expressed earlier by members of the Catholic clergy both in the United States and Ireland, and it provided Tocqueville with further proof that the Catholic Church in France should pursue the same course.[93]

The final thing Tocqueville reported to Corcelle he considered to be of no less importance. Nowhere in Germany, he commented, had he seen any sign of the "stupefaction" caused among most people in France by "the terror of socialism." People obsessed by this "nightmare" in France breathed easily, and nowhere had he heard it said that gendarmes had to be placed at everyone's doors to protect them from being "robbed or having their throat cut by a neighbour." "This," Tocqueville concluded, "seems sufficient to establish a profound difference between Germany and France, because among us when one gets back to the root of everything that happens, that is said and that is done, one always finds the same guiding and central emotion: fear."[94]

Elsewhere in Tocqueville's correspondence a less positive view of Germany emerged. For all his protestations to the contrary, Tocqueville did, for example, venture a few opinions to Beaumont about contemporary Germany. One thing Tocqueville had noticed was the relative lack of interest among the public in parliamentary debates. This, he told Beaumont, was generally attributed to the unimportant position occupied by the Prussian representative chamber, but in his view it had more to do with widespread "lukewarm" attitude towards politics. Whilst in Germany, Tocqueville argued, one did not witness the "moral tiredness" sadly evident in France and people retained "a confidence in the future." It was evident that "the institutions of absolute government did not engender a great sense of unease and impatience and that mores and customs tended strongly in this direction."[95]

This in turn encouraged Tocqueville to make a further observation (and one he repeated in almost exactly the same words to one of his American correspondents, Theodore Sedgwick). Since their arrival in Bonn, Tocqueville told Beaumont, he and his wife had been fortunate to be received into several families, and from this he had concluded that there was much to be admired in the private lives of Germans. But, he added, what poor citizens they make! "When I see," Tocqueville wrote, "the long usage they have made of absolute power, the mildness of this power, the traditions of liberty effaced by mores, centralisation, the pursuit of positions, and an all-embracing dependence everywhere, I ask myself if they could ever be very different from what they are."[96] Summarising this sorry state of affairs, Tocqueville told Sedgwick that Germans were fit only for servitude or revolution.[97]

That Germans made such poor citizens gave Tocqueville another cause for grave concern. Recently, Tocqueville recounted, he had met a Prussian who had served for ten years in the United States and who had told him that, in the previous year, 140,000 people had emigrated from Germany to America. Previously such emigrants had been poor, but now they included the well-off and even the rich. Relatively few came from Prussia, most hailing from the small states of central Germany or from Baden, Bavaria, and Württemberg. "All of these Germans," Tocqueville had been told, "take their ideas with them to the United States and, to a certain extent, hold on to them. They preserve their language; do not mix much with the natives of the country; on the whole remain together; and, although, through a process of imitation, they finish up adopting some American political practices, often by the second generation, they remain a distinct and foreign element." This, Tocqueville told Beaumont, convinced him that the biggest threat facing America came from the rapid introduction of people not belonging to the "English race" and, furthermore, that "the final success of democratic institutions" was not beyond question.[98] Again, Tocqueville made a similar point to Sedgwick. "What can you do with these people," he asked bluntly, "when they arrive among you in America?"[99]

Thus, Tocqueville wrote to Freslon at the end of July, for all that people in Germany continued to believe in the utility of political liberty and preserved their faith in representative institutions, it was by no means certain that the liberal cause would prevail. In Germany, as in France, mores and customs cleaved to despotism; society had lost all habit of governing itself; the state intervened everywhere in the details of individual life; and public life lacked strength and means of expression. "I am beginning to believe," Tocqueville told Freslon, "that nowhere on this vast continent will I find a place where it would please me to live."[100]

Then disaster struck. On 5 August, Tocqueville wrote to Ampère to say that his wife had fallen ill three days previously. The problem was rheumatism in her right hand. The least movement caused severe pain, and she was now swathed in bandages. Tocqueville's intention was still to leave Bonn around the middle of the month, first to spend a couple of weeks in Heidelberg, and then to travel to Dresden via Frankfurt and Leipzig. However, he told Ampère, should his wife remain ill and should cholera continue to spread across Germany, it was possible that they would be forced to return to France.[101]

Two weeks later, on 20 August, Tocqueville wrote to Beaumont from Mainz. Although there had been a small improvement in his wife's condition it was still not possible for her to move either her arm and hand and thus, on the advice of a "celebrated doctor" in Bonn, they had been advised that Madame de Tocqueville should take the waters in Wildbad, to where Tocqueville and his wife were now travelling. He had not hesitated to encourage his wife to make this journey, Tocqueville told Beaumont, but he still felt "cruelly frustrated." "I will not hide the fact," he wrote, "that very probably this will reduce the rest of our trip to Germany to nothing and will deprive me not only of some of the pleasure but also of some of the utility that I was expecting from it." A stay of even only three weeks in Wildbad would see the approach of winter and make the trip to Dresden less likely. To make matters worse, the Tocquevilles' finances were not in good shape, and a stay in a spa town was likely to prove expensive. Moreover, for all that the time in Bonn had gone "excellently," Tocqueville knew that he needed more time to come to an understanding of the mores and institutions of a country such as Germany. Indeed, Tocqueville told Beaumont, he had only seen the stay in Bonn as a preparation for more serious studies. He was trying to hide all of this from his wife, Tocqueville told Beaumont, and hoped that he was succeeding.[102]

Somehow this seems unlikely. The Tocquevilles arrived in Wildbad on 22 August. Two days later Tocqueville wrote again to Ampère, his frustration very evident. His trip, he told Ampère, was "completely spoilt" and his efforts in Bonn had been rendered "almost useless." Yet Tocqueville was clearly not reconciled to his fate. Madame de Tocqueville, he reported, was of the view that he and Ampère should still meet in Dresden. This, Tocqueville thought, would be too far away from his wife but, if Ampère were to be passing through Frankfurt, could they possibly join him there? He knew several people in the city whom it would be useful to see, and they could then go to Heidelberg to see Christian von Bunsen. "A trip of eight to ten days like this with you," Tocqueville wrote, "would be as agreeable as it would be useful."[103] Not even this proved to be possible, and what followed sounds to have been utterly dismal.

On 29 August Tocqueville wrote to Francisque de Corcelle to recount the "misfortunes" that had befallen him and his wife. Corcelle would, he began,

The Spa Bad Wildbad, Black Forest (iStock.com)

probably have some difficulty finding Wildbad on the map. "Look at the mountains of the Black Forest, near the border of Württemberg and Baden, about an equal distance between Karlsruhe and Stuttgart," he wrote, "and, if you have a good map, you will possibly see a village named Wildbad in German or the *bain sauvage.*" Nowhere, Tocqueville told Corcelle was better named, as Wildbad was lost amongst an endless labyrinth of mountains covered with fir trees from top to bottom. It was "a kind of desert in the middle of which had been built two or three hotels and a bath house." This, Tocqueville declared, was now their home. They knew not a soul and lived, Tocqueville wrote, "among such a great number of the hunchbacked, the twisted, the one-armed, the lame and the crippled that I am beginning to believe that a healthy person with the use of his two arms is an exception among the human race."[104] The description provided by Tocqueville to Circourt was scarcely more encouraging. He was living, he told Circourt, "between two fir tree woods at the bottom of a gorge so deep that the sun rises two hours later and goes down two hours earlier than it does for the rest of humanity."[105] Whether Tocqueville was consoled by Gustave de Beaumont's suggestion that Wildbad sounded very much like the Saginaw, Michigan, that he and Tocqueville had visited in America when they had wished to travel to where no one else lived, and that "a society of bathers" attested to a "level of civilisation unknown among the red skins," can only be guessed at.[106]

Things only got worse. To Ampère on 6 September Tocqueville recorded that, for all Madame de Tocqueville had been undertaking her bathing sessions, there had been no improvement. In fact, things had deteriorated. Not only did he have to dress and feed his wife "like a child" but she was now experiencing pain in her left leg, with the result that she could only go out in a wheelchair. Tocqueville was clearly worried by this lack of improvement. However, a letter to Circourt confirmed that Tocqueville had managed to find a Protestant pastor who came to him each day for an hour to give him lessons in German.[107] Tocqueville also acquired some books on the laws of the Duchy of Württemberg and of Swabia which, "for want of anything better," he began to study and became interested in.[108] But this was small recompense for what had been lost. In Bonn, he told Ampère, he had studied books and met "men of science," and it had been in Dresden and Bonn that he had intended "to apply these general theories to the Germany which lives, to confront ideas acquired in this way with the world of practice, to put professors face to face with those who governed and ran things." None of this would now be possible. His trip to Germany had therefore been "completely spoilt" and was "a unique opportunity wasted." Not just this, but the intended fruits of this journey were things necessary to him and things that he would not be able to take up again for a long time.[109]

So, after twenty-four thermal treatments and little sign of improvement in his wife's health, on 20 September the Tocquevilles set off for home (with the loyal Ampère in tow). They stopped off in Heidelberg to spend forty-eight hours with their good friends, the Lamoricières, before travelling on to Brussels, and then crossed the border into France at Valenciennes where, Tocqueville told Corcelle, their bags were searched and all printed material, of whatever kind, was confiscated. "As I approached the frontier," he wrote to Beaumont just over a week later, "I felt a profound sadness and wanted to turn back. I had just spent three months in a country which, when compared to ours, can be called a country of liberty, and the idea of again breathing the air of a France so enslaved and so happy in her servitude oppressed me." Never had he returned to his own country with such little sense of joy, and this had not changed in the few days that had since elapsed. "I find," he told Beaumont, "that it was much easier to learn to live among foreigners than it is to live at home."[110] A day later he wrote much the same thing to Circourt. "I breathed," he wrote, "much more easily amongst foreigners," adding that "a certain amount of time will be necessary before I get used to the air of my homeland."[111]

When Tocqueville returned to France, he could not face the prospect of staying in Paris—cholera was still rife in the city—and thus he and his wife (and Ampère) took up residence with Tocqueville's father in Clairoix, near Compiègne. Their little house was pretty and surrounded by trees, but "horribly humid," and so, with his wife still ill, the Tocquevilles next rented a house a few kilometres away, with the intention of remaining there for two months. Situated on the edge of the forest and in a sunny location, its only drawback, Tocqueville told Beaumont, was that it was in audible distance of the royal kennels. Listening to "the dogs of His Majesty," he wrote, made him think that "they formed the only assembly in present-day France which could make itself heard outside its walls."[112] Nonetheless, the Tocquevilles were happy there, eating, sleeping and reading in the same room, enjoying their walks together, and they did not move back to Paris until April of the following year, Tocqueville making the occasional visit to pick up the books and papers he needed and to attend the reception of Monsignor Dupanloup into the Académie française. He was living, he told Circourt, like a snail in its shell.[113]

But Germany was far from being forgotten. Tocqueville commented to Odilon Barrot that he could write a book about everything he had seen there.[114] No sooner had Tocqueville returned to France than he was writing to Charles Monnard, asking to be remembered to the many friends he had made in Bonn. A later letter pointedly asked Monnard to tell the doctor who had recommended the thermal baths in Wildbad as a cure for his wife's rheumatism that she was still unwell. Tocqueville's correspondence with Beaumont again took up the thorny and long-standing question of with which German newspaper, if any, the two of them were to take out a subscription. As before, there were to be problems with delivery, but Tocqueville was still pleased that every week he had before him a few pages of German that he felt "obliged" to read. We also know that Tocqueville and his wife continued to spend their evenings reading aloud in German.[115] To Monnard he wrote to say that he had neither abandoned German nor had lost Germany from view and that what happened on the other side of the Rhine remained of great interest to him.[116]

Tocqueville also tried to make sense of what he had seen in Germany and what, despite his disappointments, he might have achieved. He could not say, Tocqueville told Corcelle, that he had come to know Germany, but he had acquired "a certain facility in understanding what was happening there and what people said about it." This, he acknowledged, was "already something," as the French and German peoples were so different from one another. The "great work of assimilation" that was taking place across the civilised world was such that many of the external aspects of the two countries—institutions, social habits, and customs—were now much alike, but what remained different was what "one did not see," the way that people saw the world and were affected by what they saw, "the inner person" who had preserved the "original imprint" lost by the "outer person." "It is this invisible Germany," Tocqueville wrote, "about which I came to acquire some ideas" and, to that extent, he concluded, the journey he had made could not be considered as having been "completely without utility."[117] Kergorlay received an equally upbeat message. "Although my trip to Germany was so cruelly disrupted by [my wife's] illness," Tocqueville commented, "I was able to draw real profit from it. As I knew precisely the things above all that I wanted to clarify I was able to focus there and then on these things and, in a very little time, to gather lots of useful ideas."[118]

What were these ideas? In terms of politics, Tocqueville was not sure if the "paralysis" evident in France was not even greater in Germany. If the institutions of public life had been withdrawn from France, such institutions—representative assemblies, a limited freedom of the press, and so on—continued to exist in the greater part of Germany but "the old tradition of order and moderation in government seems numbed and overthrown." Germany, Tocqueville pointed out to Corcelle, had not even received the "imperfect political education" provided to France by thirty-six years of representative government. To that extent, the Germans not only did not understand the means through which political liberty was established and maintained but they also hardly understood the very idea of liberty. They preserved "the mores that the absolute government of the last two centuries had given them." The "great pipe dream of German unity" filled their imaginations far more than "the image of regular liberty" and, to that end, they were prepared to pardon all the abuses of absolute government.[119]

This did not mean that, if Germany was at rest, it was also stable. Germany, Tocqueville wrote, "sleeps but she sleeps standing up, and the least shock could throw it to the right or the left." There reigned a general discontentment; the idea of stability was absent; the old traditions had been destroyed; and a respect for old ways, for established rules, and for those who exercised royal power had been extinguished. As evidence of this, Tocqueville here appealed to something he had learned from one of his conversations in Bonn: the numbers of Germans who were emigrating to America in search of new laws and a new country. Nevertheless, he was convinced that it would be a long while before any political movement gained the initiative in Germany. The Germans, he wrote, "are easy to stir up but they do not stir themselves up." At least, Tocqueville added, "I do not think so."[120]

Nor did Tocqueville believe that the Revolution of 1848 had not left its mark on Germany and that society was again resting on the foundations that had existed before the "great perturbation." It was almost possible to say, he told Corcelle, that "our Revolution of 48 has had a more considerable impact upon Germany than our Revolution of 89." Certainly, those parts of the "old constitution of Europe" that the first had left intact had been "reduced to dust" by the second, and it was from this moment that "the abolition of an infinite number of privileges" limiting civil liberty could be dated. Moreover, this part of the 1848 revolution, Tocqueville argued, had been warmly embraced by those rulers who had felt most threatened. Nothing, he added, "has ever done more to bring to light a truth that I have long recognised—namely, that the great movement of humanity that began among us sixty five years ago advances towards liberty only by fits and starts, but is driven towards equality by an irresistible and continuous force."[121]

Tocqueville was also led to reflect upon German attitudes towards France. "When I was in Prussia," he told Corcelle, "I was struck by the fact that public opinion in the country displayed a hostility towards Russia, but in the army this was not the case." There, it was Austria and France which were the principal objects of hatred. And this, Tocqueville recognised, made any French intervention, whether peaceful or warlike, on the other side of the Rhine infinitely more difficult than it had been at the time of the Revolution of 1789. Anti-French sentiment was so widespread that it risked uniting everyone against them.[122] And how, Tocqueville asked his nephew Hubert de Tocqueville, could this be otherwise? "We overturned the world," he wrote, "disrupted every nation, spilt torrents of blood, overturned or undermined thrones, shook societies to their foundations, and all in the name of ideas, emotions and beliefs that we ourselves seem squalidly to have abandoned."[123]

Equally, Tocqueville remained fascinated by how moves towards German unification would play out and how, in the context of the Crimean War, Prussia and Austria would play their respective hands. Austria, Tocqueville correctly observed, was receiving less and less support from the smaller German states but Prussia, he suggested to Circourt, was widely and increasingly discredited within Germany.[124] Tocqueville also believed that Austria and Germany displayed many of the same characteristics. This was revealed in another letter Tocqueville sent to his nephew, Hubert de Tocqueville, now serving as an attaché at the French embassy in Vienna. From what he had seen "last year in Germany," what his nephew now told him of Austria seemed correct. "The salient feature of what is happening in Austria," Tocqueville wrote, "is, on the one hand, the disappearance of the old feudal organisation bequeathed by the Middle Ages and, on the other hand, the organisation of a new world for the sole benefit of the State and of centralisation." The old local powers were disappearing and, in their place, central government was taking control. The whole of Germany, Tocqueville contended, presented the same picture to a greater or lesser extent. In fact, this was true of the entire continent. "Everywhere," he wrote, "the liberty of the Middle Ages is being abandoned, not in favour of modern liberty, but to return to ancient despotism, because centralisation is nothing other than a modernised form of the administration of the Roman Empire."[125]

Most importantly, having returned to France, Tocqueville was in good health and eager to get to back to his writing, with the result that he had completed what was to be part two of *L'ancien régime et la révolution* before he left Compiègne for Paris in April 1855. Here, too, the fruits of Tocqueville's trip to Germany were to be clearly visible.[126] Crucially, Tocqueville's knowledge of property rights and the feudal system in Germany enabled him to support his seemingly paradoxical conclusion that, although the feudal burdens placed upon the French peasantry were light and rare in comparison to those endured in Germany, it was in France that those burdens were felt most acutely and with the greatest resentment.

On 18 February 1855, Tocqueville wrote again to Charles Monnard. He did so first to inquire about Monnard's forthcoming book on Switzerland and, second, to ask of him "a small service." Looking over the notes he had made the previous summer in Bonn on "the old Germany" and also those he had made in Wildbad on the laws in Württemberg and Swabia, he saw that the latter were in "almost complete agreement" with "the general principles of German law" he had learned about in Bonn. For this, Tocqueville acknowledged, he had largely to thank Monnard's "excellent neighbour," Hugo Hälschner. Nevertheless, many of the things they had discussed remained shrouded in "semidarkness." "I am very interested," Tocqueville wrote, "in settling some of these questions, because they are directly related to the subject which interests me at the moment and I cannot risk putting before the public arguments that are not solidly grounded." Would it therefore be possible, Tocqueville inquired, for Monnard to ask Hälschner if he might write to him directly to seek clarification on these matters? Ideally, Tocqueville added, it would be preferable if Hälschner replied in French. There was no rush, as Tocqueville did not expect to get on to this before the spring or early summer.[127]

Subsequent letters written by Tocqueville to Monnard up to August 1855 indicate that Tocqueville had not as yet taken up the offer of assistance from both Monnard and Hälschner—his work had taken him in another direction, he told Monnard—but references to what Tocqueville had learned from them are evident in Tocqueville's published text. This is especially the case in Tocqueville's extensive notes, where he refers to the manner in which Roman law replaced Germanic law, the passage from feudal to democratic monarchy, the decline of Germany's free cities, the abolition of serfdom in Germany, Frederick the Great's law code, peasant property holdings in Germany, and the division of land along the Rhine.

Central to Tocqueville's argument in *L'ancien régime et la révolution* was his claim, bolstered by a study of the political institutions of France, England, and Germany, that out of the "incoherent mass" that Europe had become after the overthrow of the Roman Empire, there had suddenly emerged a set of uniform laws. "As I progressed in this work," Tocqueville wrote, "I was astonished at the sight of the incredible similarity to be found among their laws and I admired the way such different and separate peoples had given themselves such similar laws." If these laws varied infinitely in detail and according to place, he observed, they always had the same foundation and so much so that he came to know in advance that, if he looked at old German legislation, he would find something substantially similar in England and France. Governments conducted their business according to the same principles; political assemblies had the equivalent powers and were composed of the same elements; society was divided along equivalent lines; the nobility occupied an identical position and enjoyed the same privileges; the constitutions of the towns resembled each other; and the countryside was governed in a similar manner. Just as importantly, the condition of the peasantry varied little and land was owned, inhabited, and farmed in the same way. And this was true, Tocqueville wrote, from Poland to the Irish Sea. "These were not different people," he argued, but were "very much the same everywhere."[128]

Having established this point, Tocqueville next stated that it was "no part of [his] subject" to explain how the "ancient constitution of Europe" had been "weakened and become dilapidated"; it was, he argued, sufficient to recognise that, by the eighteenth century, it was "half ruined" everywhere. Yet, Tocqueville's notes to this part of the text do precisely that and do so by reference to what he had learned in Germany. By the end of the Middle Ages, Tocqueville argued, Roman law had become "the principal and almost only study of German jurists." Accordingly, they applied Roman law to everything that resembled it in German institutions and to anything that had even the most distant analogy with the law code of Justinian. They thus introduced a "new spirit and new practices" into Germanic law, gradually transforming the latter to such an extent that by the seventeenth century it was no longer recognisable. In so doing, the conditions of many in German society, most notably that of the peasantry, were worsened, with many of those who had until then been able to preserve "all or some of their liberties and property" losing them through "scholarly" comparisons with the conditions of slaves and long-term leases.[129]

The "useless" attempts to oppose this gradual transformation could, Tocqueville argued, be clearly seen by reference to the history of Württemberg. From the birth of Württemberg in 1250 until its creation as a duchy in 1495, Tocqueville wrote, its legislation was "entirely indigenous; it was composed of customs, of local laws made by towns or by manorial courts, and statutes promulgated by the Estates; only ecclesiastical matters were regulated by a foreign law, that of canon law." After 1495, the character of legislation started to change with the intrusion of Roman law: those who had studied law in foreign universities entering government and taking over control of the higher courts. Those who represented the feudal system and the towns made all kinds of protests about what was going on and at first appeared to have been successful, but to no avail. Roman law, Tocqueville contended, "soon ended up by entirely driving out national law from a large part of legislation and by planting its roots even on the ground where it allowed this legislation to survive."[130]

German historians, Tocqueville wrote, had offered two explanations of this triumph of foreign over indigenous law: the first was that it arose from a movement which prized the literature and languages of antiquity and which felt "contempt" for the "intellectual products of the national spirit"; and the second argued that the legislation of the Roman Empire was part of the heritage of the Holy Roman Empire. Neither, Tocqueville argued, was sufficient to explain why Roman law was introduced across the entire continent of Europe at the same time. Rather, Tocqueville wrote, "I think that this arose from the fact that, at that time, the absolute power of rulers was establishing itself everywhere on the ruins of the old liberties of Europe," and thus from the fact that Roman law, "a law of servitude," served their purposes. To summarise this point, Tocqueville then quoted, almost word for word, a note he had made in conversation with Hugo Hälschner in Bonn: "Roman law, which everywhere had improved civil society, had tended everywhere to degrade political society, because it had chiefly been the work of a very civilised and a very subjugated people." In essence, Tocqueville concluded, what was being witnessed was the passage from feudal inequality to democratic equality, from feudal monarchy to democratic monarchy. There followed what was "a golden age of princes, during which they enjoyed both stability and omnipotence, things which usually exclude each other: they were as sacred as the hereditary chiefs of a feudal monarchy and as absolute as the masters of a democratic society."[131]

If this process was less marked in eastern than in western Europe, Tocqueville argued, it was nonetheless visible everywhere, and this included Germany, a country "where the old constitution of Europe had kept more of its original characteristics than in France." Even there, Tocqueville pointed out, many of the old institutions had been destroyed. Yet, he noted, the "decrepitude" of the old order could best be observed by considering those institutions that remained despite "the ravages of time" rather than those that had gone forever. To illustrate this, the example that Tocqueville chose was that of the free cities of Germany. In the thirteenth and fourteenth centuries, he wrote, these cities had been "rich and enlightened republics." They were "the sanctuaries of wealth, art and knowledge, the mistresses of Europe's commerce, the most powerful centres of civilisation." The free cities retained this position into the sixteenth century but by that date, Tocqueville argued, their "decadence had come," a process hastened by the later Thirty Years' War. Their populations and their wealth declined; the arts deserted them "to shine in the new cities created by sovereigns, and which represent the new world"; and their governments, whether aristocratic or democratic, were charged with dishonesty. By the eighteenth century what remained was only a "hollow façade." "Their ancient customs," Tocqueville wrote, "seemed to be operating; the magistrates that they had established bore the same names and seemed to perform the same functions; but the activity, the energy, the communal patriotism, the manly and fertile virtues that they had inspired, had disappeared." Only Hamburg remained; elsewhere the old institutions had collapsed without changing their appearance.[132]

The German experience, therefore, showed that all the powers of the Middle Ages that still survived had been struck down by the same decay and decline. Anything that was even associated with the ancient constitution lost its vitality. The aristocracy lapsed into a "senile debility," as too did any form of political liberty that had preserved its medieval character. Similarly, provincial assemblies retaining their old constitution came to hinder the progress of civilisation rather than aid it. They were seen as being foreign to the new spirit of the age. Their very antiquity brought discredit upon them and they inspired more hatred the less power they had. Again, by way of supporting evidence, Tocqueville referenced a German source, upon this occasion a "contemporary" German author said to be "a friend of the old regime." "The existing state of things," the author is quoted as saying, "seems to have become generally offensive to everyone and sometimes contemptible. . . . Even our housekeepers can no longer put up with old furniture."[133]

As Tocqueville observed, there was something paradoxical about this. "In Germany, as in France," he wrote, "society was extremely active and always growing more prosperous." Looked at carefully, this served only "to complete the picture," because what could be seen was that "everything that lived, acted and produced was of recent origin, and not merely new, but in contradiction with the old." The monarchy now possessed different attributes. The administration of the state everywhere extended itself over the wreckage of local institutions. A hierarchy of government officials increasingly replaced the government of the nobility. "All of these new powers," Tocqueville wrote, "acted according to procedures and followed principles either unknown to or rejected by the men of the Middle Ages."[134]

Why did Tocqueville feel it necessary to include this examination of the decline of the ancient constitution in Germany in his account? His answer was simple in the extreme, and it tells us much about why he set such great store by the time, however much it had been unavoidably curtailed, he had been able to spend there. "Whoever has studied and seen only France," Tocqueville wrote, "will never understand anything about the French Revolution."[135]

Tocqueville continued this line of argument in the key opening chapter of the second part of *L'ancien régime et la révolution*. At first glance, Tocqueville wrote in its opening sentence, one thing was surprising: "the Revolution, whose real purpose was to abolish what remained of the institutions of the Middle Ages, did not break out in those countries where these institutions were best preserved and where their constraints and their severity were most felt by the people." Rather, it broke out where the people were the least oppressed.[136]

To prove this point, Tocqueville then showed that, by the end of the eighteenth century, there was almost no part of Germany where serfdom had been abolished.[137] Most of the soldiers who had fought in the armies of Frederick the Great and of Maria-Theresa of Austria, Tocqueville argued, were "true serfs."[138] Peasants could not leave their estates and were subject to manorial justice. They could not change their profession nor marry without their master's consent. Compulsory labour still existed. If the serf could own land, its ownership was still uncertain, the serf being required to cultivate land and sell produce in an approved way.

To support his argument, Tocqueville drew principally upon the law code of Frederick the Great. Here, Tocqueville contended, was a document that, at its heart, rested upon the "democratic, but not liberal" principle that the ruler was the sole representative of the state as well as the agent and servant of society. To that end, the ruler was authorised to direct and regulate all individual actions. Among the chief duties of this "all-powerful agent of society" was that of the preservation of public safety and that of making peace and war. The ruler "alone must make laws and general regulations." All associations and public establishments that existed within the state were subject to the ruler's inspection and direction.[139]

Yet, Tocqueville wrote, "beneath this completely modern head" was to be seen "a completely gothic body." The inhabitants of the countryside largely remained in "hereditary servitude." The privileges of the nobility were untouched. The bourgeoisie existed as a separate group from the peasantry, but the code also recognised the existence of an "intermediate class" composed of high officials, the clergy, and university professors. This group in turn occupied an inferior position to the nobility. They could not buy noble lands and, in general, could not be presented at court. In brief, Tocqueville argued, despite Frederick the Great's "contempt" for the old constitution of Europe, he did not believe that it was time to dispense with the "wreckage."

So, Tocqueville wrote, "this new law code . . . is the most authentic and the most recent legislative document that gives a legal basis to the very feudal inequalities that the [French] Revolution was going to abolish throughout Europe."[140]

Nothing similar, Tocqueville contended, had existed in France for many years. With the exception of one or two recently conquered eastern provinces, the last vestiges of serfdom had disappeared. Peasants came and went, bought and sold their goods, and worked much as they liked. Indeed, they had ceased to be serfs and had become landowners, the beneficiaries of the division of land that had preceded the revolution. Yet, they felt the weight of the feudal system more than their German counterparts, who, for the most part, did not own their land and where the nobility still largely remained in charge of the administration of the countryside. This was so, Tocqueville insisted, primarily for two reasons. First, the administration of the countryside was now largely undertaken by the officials of the state, thus relieving the nobility of any useful function. Second, as landowners the peasants felt the full weight of the feudal dues and privileges that still remained. "Imagine," Tocqueville wrote,

> the French peasant of the eighteenth century . . . so passionately in love with the land that he devotes all his savings to buying it at any price. . . . However, there remain the same neighbours who tear him from his fields and force him to work elsewhere without pay. If he wants to defend his crops against their game, these people forbid it; the same people wait for him at the crossing of a river to demand a toll. . . . Imagine the situation, the needs, the character, the passions of this man and calculate, if you can, the amount of hatred and envy stored within his heart.[141]

Here was Tocqueville's answer to the question of why the revolution had broken out in France and not elsewhere, and it was an argument that he could not have made without the knowledge he had acquired in Bonn of the "dead Germany." However, Tocqueville had one more piece of conclusive evidence to support this all-important conclusion. Although in general the numbers of small landowners in eighteenth-century Germany were very low, it was in the regions mostly situated on the banks of the Rhine that peasants were property owners and where they enjoyed a level of freedom comparable to that of the French peasant. "It was also there," Tocqueville pointed out, "that the revolutionary passions of France spread most quickly and where they have always been the most ardent." Those parts of Germany that had remained impermeable to these passions were those where nothing similar had yet to occur.[142]

On 28 May 1856 Tocqueville wrote to his father to tell him that "the last word of the last page" of *L'ancien régime et la révolution* had been written and all that now remained to be done was the correction of the proofs. After this "the book will be launched upon the world," something he viewed with an element of trepidation. Their age, he believed, was little inclined to welcome the success of ideas such as his own. Indeed, it was not inclined to welcome ideas of any kind.[143] Tocqueville's fears proved groundless, the first edition being received with almost universal and widespread praise and selling out by August of that year. Tocqueville's publisher, Michel Lévy, hastily published a second edition in October and then a third in July 1857.[144]

Tocqueville was understandably delighted by the reception of *L'ancien régime et la révolution* in France,[145] but he was also eager to ensure that it was being read outside France, including Germany. At the beginning of July Tocqueville had copies sent to both Monnard and Hälschner by way of thanks for the help they had offered in Bonn. A copy was also sent to Bunsen at the same time, Tocqueville hoping that "it contains several new things that will not be without interest." In October Tocqueville wrote again to Monnard, indicating that he was aware that the book was being commented upon in "some important newspapers and reviews" in Germany and that he had been told that a translation into German was already underway. The translation, by Arno de Boscowitz, duly appeared in 1857. More intriguing was Tocqueville's remark to Monnard that "the approbation" that the "first part" of his work had received encouraged him "to get back to work so as to complete the second" and that, on this subject, he was in need of advice.[146]

In brief, having spent the years between 1852 and 1856 trying to come to an appreciation of the inner workings of the ancien régime and thereby understand why the revolution had broken out in France rather than elsewhere, Tocqueville now reverted back to what he had originally intended to be the subject of his inquiry: the revolution itself. This was exactly what Tocqueville had announced he would do in his foreword to the 1856 text. Having stated in the opening sentence that his "book is not a history of the Revolution," he then went on to say that his "intention" was "to follow the same Frenchmen with whom I have lived so intimately under the old regime through the vicissitudes of this long Revolution; to see how, having been formed by the old regime, they were changed and transformed by events, whilst nonetheless never changing their nature and continually reappearing before us with a slightly different physiognomy but always as being recognisable." He would, Tocqueville wrote, start with the first moment of 1789—"a time of youth, of enthusiasm, of pride, of generous and sincere passions"—when a love of equality and a love of liberty shared a place in their hearts, before showing how those same French people, "forgetting liberty," came to desire nothing more than to be "the equal servants of the master of the world" and how "a stronger and much more absolute government than that which the revolution had overthrown, recovered possession of and concentrated all power, did away with all the freedoms so dearly bought, and put vain idols in their place." His account would stop, Tocqueville wrote, at the point where the revolution seemed to him to have "just about finished its work and given birth to a new society." By way of conclusion, he would therefore "consider this society" and try "to look into our future." To this Tocqueville added the following: "A part of this second work is sketched out but still unworthy of being offered to the public. Will I be able to finish it? Who can say? The fate of individuals is still more hidden than that of peoples."[147]

As his biographer, André Jardin, commented, Tocqueville's statement that a part of the second volume was already sketched out was "a pure product of his imagination."[148] We also know that Tocqueville was not able to finish this project before he died in 1859. However, it was on this project that Tocqueville worked intermittently (and, for the most part, at his home in Normandy) between June 1856 and September 1858 (when he set out first for Paris and then for Cannes, where he would die the following April). As with the writing of the first volume, Tocqueville's correspondence allows us to follow the often convoluted composition of his never-to-be completed manuscript. He found the sheer volume of documentation available to him overwhelming. "To read everything is impossible," he told Prosper Duvergier de

Hauranne; "to choose is dangerous."[149] As Tocqueville recounted to Pierre Freslon, he also found it difficult to view the revolution with sufficient distance, thus finding himself distracted by unimportant and passing facts whilst not seeing "the principal and fundamental parts of the picture."[150] Nonetheless, for all his habitual doubts and uncertainties,[151] Tocqueville seems from the outset to have had a strong sense of what his subject matter was. As early as September 1856 he told Pierre Freslon that, "properly speaking," his objective was "to paint the ideas and feelings of the nation during the revolutionary epoch."[152] A month later he wrote much the same thing to George Cornewall Lewis, telling him that his goal was "rather to paint the movement of the feelings and ideas which successively produced the events of the Revolution than to recount the events themselves."[153] Tocqueville also had a clear understanding of how this was to be achieved.

To paint that picture, he told Louis de Kergorlay, he had to date found only one means, and that was "to live through each moment of the Revolution with its contemporaries by reading not what had been said about them or what they subsequently said about each other but what they themselves said at the time."[154] In short, Tocqueville's focus was on the ideology of those who participated in the revolution—an ideology, he told Kergorlay, that was a "kind of new and unknown virus"—and to understand this he began with an examination of what he described as "the state of mind" in Europe, and in particular in Germany, prior to 1789. To that end, the librarians of the Bibliothèque impériale in Paris were kind enough to send Tocqueville countless official documents and pamphlets to read—sometimes, he told Beaumont, up to 150 at a time.[155] This is why Tocqueville had written to Monnard and why he had asked for his help.[156]

"You know," Tocqueville told Monnard, "that for me it has never been a question of knowing only the ideas and emotions in France that had prepared the revolution and had accompanied its development." Accordingly, he continued, he attached an "infinite price" to knowing what the "true state of thinking" was in Germany at the time. "The different emotions of hope, of love, of hatred that [the revolution] inspired on the other side of the Rhine," he wrote, "are for me a part of its history," and he therefore wanted to penetrate into "the soul" of Germany, to shed light on the different responses the revolution had evoked. He had learned German, he declared, with this sole end in mind. Consequently, what Tocqueville wanted from Monnard was guidance on where to look. Above all, Tocqueville wrote, he wanted books "heavily impregnated" with the spirit of the times. Letters written by contemporaries, he believed, were the most "precious" documents of all. After these came monographs that drew upon these letters and upon other texts which came from the period. So too, Tocqueville thought, brochures inspired by the passions of the day could be very useful. As an example of what Tocqueville had in mind, he cited a work already drawn to his attention by Monnard: a life of the German patriot Friedrich Perthes written by Perthes's son.[157] In essence, Tocqueville wrote, everything relating to the French Revolution in Germany was of the highest interest to him, but especially material relating to the period from 1785 to 1800. All of this, Tocqueville reminded Monnard, had been the subject of an earlier conversation between the two men. The only thing was that he had not known then what he now knew he was looking for. How, Tocqueville therefore asked, could he obtain the work by Charles Engelbert Oelsner written under the pseudonym of Luzifer? Were the letters of Georg Forster worth reading? What was the title of the book published by Johann Gottlieb Fichte in 1794 about the French Revolution? Did the journals of Friedrich von Gentz cover the period he was interested in? Was Christian von Dohm's *Denkwürtigkeiten meiner Zeit 1778–1806* worth consulting for his purposes? None of this, Tocqueville concluded, came from "a vain curiosity" but from "a serious desire" to instruct himself.[158]

After duly consulting his colleagues Hugo Hälschner and Johann Löbell, Monnard replied on 29 November. Not only did he indicate that he and Hälschner were prepared to lend Tocqueville some of the books he needed, but he also provided a long list of other authors and titles that Tocqueville might usefully read. Tocqueville's own reply, dated 1 February 1857, confirmed that he was making his way, albeit slowly, through many of these texts.[159] He had acquired a copy of the first volume of Ernst Brandes's *Betrachtungen,* as well as copies of Forster's correspondence and Joachim-Heinrich Campe's volume of letters written from Paris during the revolution. He was presently reading the first volume of Georg Heinrich Pertz's life of the Baron vom Stein but not, he told Monnard, learning too much as Stein entered "too late upon the scene." Tocqueville also expressed his thanks for the kind offer that he could borrow Oelsner's text, which, he confirmed, was definitely not available in the Bibliothèque impériale.

Tocqueville took detailed notes on many of these texts, often transcribing long quotations to which he no doubt intended to return if and when he had the opportunity to put his second volume into something like its final form. This was not to be, but from the manuscripts that survive it is clear that references to Germany were largely to be confined to the very opening chapter devoted to an examination of the "violent and shifting restlessness of the human mind immediately prior to the Revolution" and to a later section detailing "what made the Revolution victorious abroad."[160]

Tocqueville's opening remarks were such as to argue that, in the ten or fifteen years preceding the revolution in France, the human mind throughout Europe "surrendered itself to irregular, incoherent and bizarre movements such as had not been seen for centuries." The idea of human greatness and of the omnipotence of reason was combined with a contempt for the corruption and rottenness of the age and society in which people lived. This "intellectual disturbance" and "secret revolt" against the institutions of the past, Tocqueville noted, was characteristic of Germany and was to be found in all German philosophy, history, poetry, and novels. Friedrich-Heinrich Jacobi's "insipid philosophical novel" *Woldemar* was, for example, "full of diatribes against the present and predictions of an imminent catastrophe." Nothing, Tocqueville wrote, better showed the extent to which all "the eccentricities of a leisured, restless and literary society" had spread throughout Europe. It was a book that exaggerated "with the heaviness and clumsiness of a German setting all the defects of the French mind of the time."[161] Even the traders and merchants of Germany's great commercial cities, Tocqueville observed, embraced these intellectual habits, breaking off from their labours to discuss "the great questions relating to human existence, the human condition, happiness."[162]

As for the question of what made the revolution victorious outside France, Tocqueville was again to make use of a series of German texts—Campe's letters and the biography of Perthes, for example—to show the "enthusiasm" and the "enchantment" for the revolution that spread across Europe after the storming of the Bastille. Having noted Campe's "naive and boundless enthusiasm caused by the sight of Paris," Tocqueville then went on to write that "what strikes him most is the sweet, happy, well-ordered appearance of the population. No disorder: a volunteer police force to which everyone hastens to submit voluntarily. No bad language. No quarrels. The picture of a city perfectly governed without a government." The French, Tocqueville commented wryly, freely provided this "*trompe-l'oeil* to the spectator." Campe, Tocqueville noted, was similarly impressed by the "*gamins de Paris*" who, in a fit of patriotism and enthusiasm for freedom, armed themselves, provided themselves with flags and drums, going through the streets in large groups and appearing to take part in the maintenance of order.[163] The overall conclusion reached by Tocqueville after his extensive reading of German texts was best captured in his remark that "in times when passion begins to gain control over the conduct of human affairs, it is less what people of experience and knowledge think that deserves attention than what fills the imagination of dreamers."[164]

There is much that might be said about this and the other conclusions reached by Tocqueville from his study of these German texts. As perceptive as ever, they provide an insight into the delusions of the revolutionary mind. However, here it is sufficient to have established that, after his return to France in 1854, Germany continued to remain central to Tocqueville's intellectual preoccupations and to function as a principal point of comparison with the history of France. As Tocqueville told Pierre Freslon on 8 October 1856, it was only by reading German source material that the "universal character" of the French Revolution could be understood.[165] For all of that, during these years Tocqueville did not restrict his interests to a Germany of the past.

This was most evident in a series of letters Tocqueville wrote to his nephew, Hubert de Tocqueville, newly appointed as a diplomatic attaché to the French embassy in Berlin. Berlin and Prussia, Tocqueville wrote in a tone of great authority, "are the homes of enlightenment in Germany." Although, he commented, the political influence of Prussia had recently declined, its influence over the thinking and mores of Germany was still predominant. As for the Prussians, they were "quite superior, often full of a rather noisy national vanity disproportionate to the role that Prussia now plays in the world."[166] There was nevertheless a lively and "in some respects, fertile" intellectual life there, and the University of Berlin was "indisputably" the first in the country. Moreover, it was university professors and administrators—especially those of the highest rank—who in Prussia held a position of influence that they held nowhere else, and it was these people, Tocqueville told his nephew, that he should endeavour to get to know. As for Prussia itself, everywhere it bore the imprint of Frederick the Great, and to understand the country all of his works needed to be studied.[167]

Tocqueville's next letter, written in February 1857, waxed lyrical about the genius of Schiller. "If I knew German well enough to judge on such a matter," he wrote, "I would say that Schiller appears to me to be at least Goethe's equal as a poet: as a human being, he is infinitely superior."[168] Tocqueville also suggested that his nephew should read a general history of the eighteenth century by the Heidelberg historian Friedrich Schlosser, a book which had itself been recommended to Tocqueville by the great German historian Leopold von Ranke.[169] Letters written later in the year to his nephew included introductions to Ranke, the celebrated jurist Friedrich von Savigny, Armgart von Armin, the historian Friedrich von Raumer, and, last but not least, the geographer and naturalist Alexander von Humboldt.

Yet for all Tocqueville's admiration for the vigour of German intellectual life, his antipathy towards aspects of the country was never far from the surface. He was pleased, Tocqueville wrote, that his nephew had met Alexander von Humboldt, but, he continued, he wondered if "the worth of Monsieur Humboldt had not been a little inflated by German vanity." He was undoubtedly a "person of distinction" in the history of the human mind but it was "above all in Prussia that one finds the loud and confident admiration that the Germans have for themselves as a nation and a race." It was, Tocqueville told his nephew, this character trait that had always most struck him about them, sometimes irritating him, but, for the most part, simply making him laugh. As individuals, they were in general "simple and good-natured," but, when it came to their country, they were "insufferably conceited." To hear them speak, one would think them "the first of the human races," whereas in reality "they form, and always have formed, the most *lifeless* of all the great civilised nations of modern Europe." Their "national spirit" was one of "clumsy awkwardness."[170]

A letter written in February 1858 dwelt further upon the hostility between Germany and France. "I came back from Germany three and a half years ago," Tocqueville wrote, "convinced that, in our neighbours on the other side of the Rhine, we had the most irreconcilable of enemies." Whatever might be the desire of governments to form an alliance, the people themselves dragged their leaders in other directions. This, Tocqueville argued, was among the most "disastrous" consequences for France of its First Empire. "If," he told his nephew, "you were to read the German literature that immediately precedes the French Revolution, you would be struck by the attraction that the Germans showed at the time for everything that was French." Already there existed a reaction against France, but it was "literary reaction." Hearts still turned "naturally" towards France and the first revolutionary wars had done little to change this. "War," Tocqueville wrote, "ravaged Germany; but the French mind delivered it from the vices of the old regime; and despite the violence of our proconsuls and our wars, the provinces of the Rhine much preferred to belong to us than to remain under the domination of their former masters." It was "the long, exhausting and, above all, contemptuous oppression" exercised by the empire in Germany that had united the entire German nation against France, setting alight hostile passions that had survived long after the causes that had given them birth had disappeared. Henceforth, whatever France did, it would never find a true ally in Germany, having turned its "natural allies" into its "worst enemies." Crueller still, the "animosity" of the Germans prevented them from understanding the French; and their "excessive vanity" made their "bad feelings" all the more visible and still more unpleasant. This, Tocqueville concluded, was in marked contrast to the English who, for all their justified pride, did not feel the need to make the French feel worthless. Contact with the English, he wrote, had never caused him to feel the "impatience always aroused in him by the national self-satisfaction of the Germans."[171]

Oddly, given this philippic, Tocqueville ended the letter by remarking that he hoped his nephew would profit from his time in Berlin to learn to speak and to read German. If he did so, Tocqueville wrote, it would be something he would congratulate himself on for the rest of his life. Nor, it seems, had Tocqueville abandoned hope of liberal reform in Germany. In January 1858 Crown Prince William of Prussia was appointed prince regent, immediately nominating a liberal, Karl-Anton von Hohenzollern-Sigmaringen, to head the Prussian government and thereby initiating what was seen as a "new era" of constitutional government. Thanking his nephew for providing him with details of the new "liberal government," Tocqueville indicated that this news had caused him "great pleasure." It was to be hoped, he replied, that the Prussians would "begin this path with prudence and modesty," as the whole question boiled down to knowing "whether this limited liberty is large enough and effective enough to give the nation the sense that it participates in the nation's affairs and is happy with it." That said, things were going in the right direction and in the best way to "establish the new institutions and to allow them to bear fruit at the earliest opportunity."[172]

This optimism seems only to have strengthened during the year. Now very ill and convalescing in Cannes, Tocqueville wrote to Christian von Bunsen in December 1858 to say that, when he was in need of consolation, he turned his eyes to Bunsen's country as "the only one on the continent of Europe that at the moment gives cause for satisfaction among those who love the sight of regular liberty." Please God, he wrote, that the Prussians should be inspired by moderation and be prevented from "losing their newly acquired liberty by wanting prematurely to make use of a full liberty" of the kind enjoyed by a long-established constitutional monarchy such as England. One got there "only gradually and to the extent that mores and customs conformed to the laws." Moreover, constitutional monarchy was "a complicated machine" that needed to be handled by skilled workmen. His only regret, Tocqueville concluded, was that Bunsen had not been called to join the new government, as who more than he had studied "the workings of those noble institutions that Prussia has just given itself."[173]

What Tocqueville would have made of subsequent developments can be easily surmised. In early 1860 the Prussian government presented two bills before Parliament intended to increase expenditure on the military and to enable military reform. This brought the new constitutional system to a standstill and heightened tension between the liberal deputies in Parliament and the political and military establishment. In 1861, and again in 1862, Parliament was dissolved, but to no effect, merely confirming the intractability of the disagreement. Newly crowned as king, William I considered abdication, but then, in September 1862, he appointed Otto von Bismarck to head the government. "It is not by speeches and majority resolutions that the great questions of the time are decided," Bismarck famously declared before Parliament that same month, "but by iron and blood." What followed were three victorious wars in quick succession—against Denmark in 1863, Austria in 1866, and France in 1870—and the unification of Germany, the new German Empire being proclaimed in the Hall of Mirrors in the Palace of Versailles on 18 January 1871.[174]

In brief, in the short space of a decade, all of Tocqueville's forebodings about Germany's enmity towards France and about its national conceit had been realised. Rather than as a beacon of constitutionalism and liberty, as Tocqueville had hoped, a united Germany had become a bastion of militarism, casting what was to be a fateful shadow over Europe for many years to come. There can, however, be no doubt as to the enduring nature of Tocqueville's fascination with and interest in Germany and of the key place it occupied in his analysis of the nature of the ancien régime and its progressive disintegration. Indeed, it could be argued that Germany came to occupy a position of centrality in his thinking similar to that occupied earlier by America. If what Tocqueville had learned of German history enabled him to understand why revolution had first broken out in France, so too the German experience, like that of America, revealed facets of how a democratic society had emerged out of the ruins of an aristocratic world. The German experience also taught Tocqueville—if further evidence were needed—the difficulty of establishing liberty upon a secure foundation in such a society. Would the America of the 1850s teach Tocqueville the same lesson?

CHAPTER NINE

America and England Revisited

The fact of the matter is that references to America are almost completely absent from Alexis de Tocqueville's *L'ancien régime et la révolution* and from the projected second volume. The most detailed reference appears in a comparison of the effect of administrative centralisation in Canada and the United States. "It is," Tocqueville began, "in the colonies that can best be judged the form of the metropolitan government because it is there that all its characteristic traits are usually enlarged and become more visible." In French Canada, he argued, there had been no obstacles to the extension of central power—the nobility was almost nonexistent, for example—and therefore it had come to pass that municipal and provincial institutions as well as individual initiative were not permitted. The government in Paris sought to meddle in all things and all manner of artificial procedures, and regulations designed to impede the activities and prosperity of the population had been introduced. In Algeria one would have thought oneself, Tocqueville wrote, "under the full grip of modern centralisation." Indeed, in both countries, one was in the presence of "a government that was almost as numerous as the population" and that wanted to "foresee everything," "take everything over," and that believed it understood the interests of the governed better than they did themselves.[1]

In contrast, in the United States there existed an "exaggerated" form of the English system of decentralisation. Towns acted as "independent municipalities" and as kinds of "democratic republics." Government was no longer involved in anything whilst individuals, "uniting together, do everything." Curiously, the very absence of the "upper classes," which had made the inhabitants of French Canada even more submissive to government than those in France, had had the opposite effect in the English colonies of making the inhabitants "more and more independent of authority." The "material consequences" of these two contrasting methods of colonisation, Tocqueville concluded, could be seen in the respective size of their populations. At the time of the English conquest, that of Canada stood at sixty-three thousand, whilst that of the English colonies stood at three million. More importantly, if, in Tocqueville's opinion, both colonies had ended up by establishing "the foundations of an entirely democratic society," for as long as Canada remained French, "equality was joined with absolute government," whilst in America equality was "combined with liberty."[2]

Here were familiar Tocquevillian themes deployed in the unfamiliar context of an account of the rise of absolutist and centralised government in eighteenth-century France. The same was true of other references made to America in Tocqueville's examination of the ancien régime and the approach of the French Revolution. Studying the constitution of rural parishes in the Middle Ages, for example, Tocqueville was surprised to discover that, "transported suddenly far from feudalism," these medieval parishes had become the townships of New England. In France, by contrast, they had been "clasped in the powerful hand of the state."[3] Likewise, the manner in which religious unbelief established itself as the general and dominant passion of the French in the eighteenth century was contrasted with what Tocqueville took to be the commonplace American view that a civilised society—and, "above all, a free society"—could not survive without religion. Even with the help of complete freedom of the press, Tocqueville wrote, "the antireligious doctrines" of the French never gained much acceptance in America.[4]

Tocqueville extended this comparison to include conflicting visions of the role of reason in society. It was said of eighteenth-century philosophy, Tocqueville argued, that it was characterised by a "kind of adoration for human reason." In truth, he countered, this amounted to little more than the adoration with which certain *philosophes* adored their own reason. "Never," Tocqueville wrote, "has less confidence in common sense been shown. . . . Genuine and respectful submission to the will of the majority was as foreign to them as submission to divine will." In this they were very far from the respect shown by the English and Americans for the feelings of the majority of their fellow citizens. Among the latter, reason was "proud and self-confident but never overbearing; thus, it has led to liberty, whereas for us it has hardly done anything else but invent new kinds of servitude."[5]

Tocqueville likewise commented upon the way in which the rule of law and local liberties were respected in America and not in France and that, while Paris by 1789 had succeeded in "devouring" the French provinces, no American citizen believed that the people of New York could decide the fate of the United States and this, despite the fact that "today New York has as many inhabitants as Paris had at the moment when the Revolution burst forth."[6] Finally, Tocqueville also suggested that the way in which the French word *gentilhomme* had travelled to America with the English, and there extended in meaning to designate all citizens "without distinction," summarised "the history of democracy itself."[7]

Where Tocqueville added something distinctively new to what he had previously written about America was in his brief reflections upon America's place in the thinking of those who had made the Revolution of 1789. The American Revolution, Tocqueville acknowledged, aroused much sympathy in Europe, and not only in France. For all of their lack of understanding of the event's importance, people were moved by it and all heard its faraway sound as a sign and prophecy that "new times were coming." From this, Tocqueville argued, came "the universal idea of change" and the "strange malaise" that led people to believe that their present condition was unbearable. However, Tocqueville's point was that, if it was true that the American Revolution had had a great influence upon the French Revolution, this was less to do with what had actually been done in America than that it seemed to make "more evident and more striking" what the French already thought they knew. "The Americans," Tocqueville wrote, "gave substantial reality to what we were already dreaming about."[8] To that extent, Tocqueville argued, it was only after the Anglomania of the French Revolution's first leaders had been abandoned that "those who marched after them" sought to imitate what they thought had been achieved in the United States. And the very worst of those imitators, Tocqueville concluded, were those who had never been there, for it was these very people "who had taken from the United

States the abstract principles of their constitution without having understood the necessity of certain conservative applications of these principles that had been made in America."[9]

Did this relative absence of America in Tocqueville's second masterpiece mean that it had now become a subject of little interest to him? Had Tocqueville been so shaken by the dramatic and painful events of the Revolution of 1848 and the creation of Napoleon III's Second Empire that he no longer believed that American democracy provided lessons from which he and his contemporaries might profit? One thing is certain: despite encouragement from his American friends, who were eager for Tocqueville to see firsthand the material prosperity and cultural sophistication of the country, he was not to travel to the United States again.

A brief glance at *De la démocratie en Amérique* is sufficient to remind us that, as Tocqueville completed his text in 1840, he was far from believing that we could be sure of the shape of the newly emerging democratic society he had glimpsed on his journey. The society he had sought to portray, Tocqueville wrote in his concluding chapter, had only just been born, and time had "yet to set its form." What would disappear and what would survive was almost impossible to make out; as the past no longer illuminated the future, we moved forward in a shadowy darkness. Much of what Tocqueville saw of the "spectacle of this universal uniformity," he wrote, saddened him and filled him with a sense of regret at the passing of a society which no longer existed; yet he also saw that in the future that awaited us it would not be a matter of trying to retain any of the advantages provided by the inequality of conditions but of seeking to secure the benefits offered by equality. "We must not aim to make ourselves similar to our fathers," Tocqueville concluded, "but to work hard to attain the type of grandeur and happiness that is appropriate to us."[10]

Thus, as he reached what he described as "the final end of my journey," Tocqueville saw both "great dangers" and "great evils" ahead. Nonetheless, he was strengthened in his conviction that the latter could be "avoided or limited" and that "to be honest and prosperous, it is still enough for democratic nations to want to be so." Hence, it was a mistake to believe that peoples were "never masters of themselves" and that, out of necessity, they were forced to obey an "insurmountable and unintelligent force that arises from previous events, from race, from the soil, or from climate." Yes, Tocqueville wrote, providence had traced around every one of us "a fatal circle" but, "within its vast limits," individuals and peoples were "powerful and free." The nations of today therefore could not but create social conditions that were equal but, Tocqueville wrote in the very last sentence of the book, it "depends on them whether equality leads them to servitude or liberty, to enlightenment or barbarism, to prosperity or misery."[11]

These remarks were plainly directed towards Tocqueville's French readers. What the French made of developments towards an equality of conditions, Tocqueville's message ran, was in their own hands. Approached intelligently and wisely, there was no need to fear the future. Hope could replace foreboding. Yet, in Tocqueville's opinion, this was not to be the case. France, as subsequent events were to show, had not chosen the path of democracy and liberty but rather that of the democratic despotism of the Second Empire.

However, Tocqueville's remarks were applicable elsewhere, and especially to the United States. In *De la démocratie en Amérique* Tocqueville had presented a largely favourable picture of a relatively stable democracy built around a decentralised political system, a vigorous associational culture, a recognition of the virtues of self-interest well understood, and a flourishing religious life. The potentially damaging impacts of individualism, materialism, and the tyranny of the majority were kept in check. Yet, the final chapter of the first volume had accurately pinpointed some of the challenges the union was likely to face in the future. The first, and gravest, of these was the existence of slavery in the South. It existed like a cancer within the American body politic, eating away at the foundational principles of American democracy. To this were to be added a set of destabilising factors arising from the restlessness and constant agitation of life in America associated with what Tocqueville saw as the all-conquering spirit of American capitalism and the displacement of an ever-growing population westwards. Soon America was destined to become a major military and maritime power; hence Tocqueville's famous comparison of the destinies of Russia and America, each moving on a seemingly endless course of expansion.

At the time of his writing, Tocqueville was of the view that the strengths of American democracy, manifested not least in a shared faith in a better future and immense national pride, far outweighed its weaknesses. But could this be guaranteed to remain the case? Would the practices of American democracy become corrupted and tarnished? Would the forces that held America together decline in potency? Would those who defended slavery and servitude gain victory over the supporters of liberty and justice? In brief, would America betray the hopes that Tocqueville had placed in it?

These questions were not always at the forefront of Tocqueville's preoccupations—especially in the 1840s when, with literary success achieved, he turned his energies towards launching his career as a parliamentary deputy. Nonetheless, and although intermittently, Tocqueville kept up a correspondence with many of those he had met in America, seeing them when they visited Europe and continuing to solicit information about their homeland. Tocqueville was also to follow developments as the United States expanded west to the Pacific and south towards Texas and Mexico. Tocqueville saw that the movement of people and trade into the Mississippi River valley would inevitably encourage American expansion into the Caribbean, making it "the Mediterranean of the New World." The evidence suggests that, as time went on, Tocqueville became increasingly uneasy about the scale and rapidity of American territorial aggrandisement.

The Revolution of 1848 found Tocqueville not only determined to fight off the threat of popular radicalism but also eager to stress what he continued to see as the merits of the American constitution for his fellow citizens. In that context, he quickly made his way to the home of Richard Rush, an American minister to France, in search of information about the current workings of the American constitution. These exchanges were vividly recorded by Rush. "We had much conversation on the new form of government for France, especially as regards the federative principle and centralization," he wrote after his dinner with Tocqueville and the distinguished American historian George Bancroft on 30 April 1848.[12] For Tocqueville, these conversations must have seemed like something of a refresher course, reminding him of the days in the 1830s when he had been writing about the nature of the federal constitution and grappling to understand the potential dangers of a tyranny of the majority. In a series of speeches, most notably one he made before the citizens of Cherbourg on 19 March 1848, Tocqueville called for greater union between France and America, arguing that the two republics should "stretch their arms across the seas that separate them." Where Europe had seen discord, wars and revolutions, he told his audience, democratic and republican America "has not had even a riot."[13] That year Tocqueville also added a new preface to the twelfth edition of *De la démocratie en Amérique.* Whether this had been planned before the revolutionary upheaval of February is uncertain, but there could be no doubting the timeliness of its appearance.[14] Whether France was to have a disorderly republic or a peaceful republic, Tocqueville wrote, was a question that America had solved over sixty years earlier. There the "principle of the sovereignty of the people" had reigned unchallenged and, there too, the country had constantly increased in population, in territory and in wealth. Where else, Tocqueville asked, could France find "greater hopes and greater lessons"?[15]

There was one blot on this seemingly rosy landscape. When Tocqueville was appointed minister of foreign affairs at the beginning of June 1849, a minor diplomatic incident blew up between France and the United States. The cause of this incident was the behaviour of Guillaume Tell Poussin, the American representative in Washington, DC.[16] Diplomacy before the age of rapid communications was never an easy affair, and this was certainly the case when messages had to be transported back and forth across the Atlantic by ship. Tocqueville, with typical aristocratic courtesy, tried to be as evenhanded as he could be, but little seemed capable of assuaging the anger of the American administration at what its secretary of state, James Middleton Clayton, saw as Poussin's dishonourable behaviour.[17] Tocqueville did not mention this episode when he provided an account of his time as minister of foreign affairs in his *Souvenirs,* but the bitterness it caused him can best be gauged by referring to two letters he wrote to Gustave de Beaumont at the time of the dispute. In the first, written on 5 October 1849, Tocqueville not only indicated how "horribly frustrated" he was by the news he was receiving from America but also that he had suffered "some very disagreeable damage to [his] reputation" as a consequence. In the second, written exactly one week later and as a resolution to the dispute was in sight, he simply commented, "what animals these Americans are."[18] To Sir Henry Lytton Bulwer, the British ambassador in Washington, Tocqueville spoke of "American vanity."[19]

In the wake of the Revolution of 1848 Tocqueville was by no means alone in believing that the US Constitution and American democracy more generally might offer guidance to the French as they set about writing their own new republican constitution. The text of America's constitution was retranslated and republished, and the press in France published numerous articles examining its supposed strengths and weaknesses.[20] However, once France had been subdued by a new Bonapartist despotism and with hopes of a moderate and viable republican constitution now dashed, it is noticeable that Tocqueville (like his French compatriots) turned less and less to America as the model republic. Slavery, the possibility of secession by the US South, America's ever-growing industrial power, and its imperial ambitions: these now became the principal sources of Tocqueville's interest and preoccupation.

That Tocqueville remained eager to relive his earlier visit to America was amply shown by the enthusiasm with which he greeted the departure of one of his closest friends, Jean-Jacques Ampère, for the United States in September 1851.[21] No sooner had Tocqueville received Ampère's first letter from New York than he wrote back enthusiastically to say that he was longing to know in which direction Ampère intended to travel. "The United States," he wrote, "are so well-known to me and still so present after twenty years that you will not be able to go anywhere where I cannot follow you in my thoughts." He also admitted that he would be very eager to talk with Ampère on his return, to find out what he had "seen in the same way, what he had seen differently, what has changed over the last twenty years, not only with regard to the superficial and material aspects of society but fundamentally." "It is impossible," Tocqueville added tellingly, "that the very temperament of the people has not deteriorated amid such rapid growth."[22]

There were indeed few places where Tocqueville would not have been able to follow Ampère in his thoughts, as in many respects their journeys were very similar. Ampère met many of the distinguished Americans that Tocqueville had spoken with during his stay. These included Theodore Sedgwick, with whom Ampère crossed the Atlantic,[23] and John C. Spencer, author of the preface to the first American edition of *Democracy in America,* who again affirmed that Tocqueville had been mistaken in his fears about a possible tyranny of the majority in the United States.[24] Ampère spent time in

New York City and Boston, as well as Washington, DC, a city, he remarked, where there are "houses without streets and streets without houses."[25] He journeyed to Quebec and there, like Tocqueville, saw and heard remnants of the old France. A few days later, he arrived in the early morning at Niagara Falls, finding himself, like Tocqueville and Chateaubriand before him, in the presence of a spectacle that was at once extraordinary, miraculous, and sublime.[26] He travelled up the Hudson River (comparing it unfavourably with the Rhine) on a steamboat as far as Albany and marvelled as he stood before the extraordinary richness and splendour of the unspoilt, silent, and primitive forest. He, too, learnt of the sorrowful plight of Native Americans.[27]

How, if at all, did Ampère answer Tocqueville's question about what had changed in America since his own visit twenty years earlier? Had there been the deterioration in American society that Tocqueville anticipated? Ampère answered this questioning directly in a letter he wrote to Tocqueville from New York in November 1851. With regard to fundamentals, he told Tocqueville, nothing much had changed. The ascendancy of the majority, the energy of individuals, the ability of associations to perform functions elsewhere carried out by government: all these continued to exist "in their essentials." Ampère did, however, identify two major changes. The first arose from the rapid extension of the railways, which he argued, was having a major impact on the development of all parts of the Union, including the West. The second came in the form of a more profound change that, he believed, could well transform the "fundamental policy" of the United States: "a disposition to interfere in the affairs of Europe." Here Ampère specifically had in mind the invitation to the United States of the controversial failed Hungarian revolutionary Lajos Kossuth—with much exaggeration, he reported, the newspapers were dreaming of an "antiabsolutist crusade" against tsarist Russia and the bombardment of Saint Petersburg—but, he believed, this new disposition had its origins in the 1846–1848 war against Mexico and was getting stronger by the day.[28]

In his published account of his visit, *Promenade en Amérique,* Ampère's response to Tocqueville was less direct. Most concerning of all, Ampère wrote, was the constant and unceasing flow of immigrants, not all of whom were healthy and eager to earn an honest living.[29] Ampère also observed that in the new states to the West—Ohio, Indiana, and Illinois—the "democratic principle" prevailed far more than it did in the older states of the East. Their constitutions were "very democratic" and open to frequent revision. Electoral mandates were of short duration (in Indiana, for example, for one year only). Above all, "democratic fanaticism" forbade the formation of associations out of "the immoderate fear" that they would encourage "aristocratic" tendencies and the oppression of the individual—thereby, in Ampère's opinion, destroying the principle and practice that had been the source of the "strength and greatness" of the country: "the voluntary concordance of individual actions towards a common goal."[30] Most seriously, Ampère worried that new developments in America ran the risk of favouring instincts that were harmful to the preservation of liberty. Did these, he wondered, encourage the transfer of "the insatiable love of gain from private morals, where it already holds too much sway, to public morality, to the general life of the country?" The United States, Ampère concluded, was formed "under the discipline of severe virtues." Americans should be fearful that it might perish through the weakening of the principles that had inspired its independence, its strength, and its constitution.[31]

Having returned to France via Jamaica and the Azores, it was not long before Ampère made his way to Normandy and the Tocqueville family home, where he was to spend over two months from July through to September. In a letter to Henry Reeve, Tocqueville provided an endearing portrait of how this time was spent. "M. Ampère," he wrote, "is working to write up the journey that he has just made to the United States. He occupies the top of the tower and, for my part, I scribble away beneath him on the first floor. From time to time, we meet in the library and, in the presence of Mme de Tocq[ueville] who completes the assembly, we read together what we have written, we comment, we make critical remarks, we praise each other, and the time passes agreeably enough."[32] To Francisque de Corcelle, Tocqueville simply reported that he and Ampère "spoke almost always only about America and about literature."[33] As for Gustave de Beaumont, he neatly summarised the benefits of this arrangement when, upon hearing from Madame de Tocqueville that Ampère was treating them to "delightful readings," he commented that it must be a great pleasure for Tocqueville to recommence the "great journey" they had undertaken together "without leaving the drawing room" of the Tocqueville château.[34]

We have no details of the content of these reading sessions and conversations, but Tocqueville's subsequent pronouncements on America—mostly to be found in his many letters to his American correspondents—reveal clear parallels with some of the apprehensions about the future of the United States voiced in Ampère's text. Specifically, when pieced together to provide a coherent whole, Tocqueville's letters reveal an increasingly pessimistic assessment of America during the 1850s and one haunted ever more by the prospect of civil war.

This was with good cause. In 1854 the Kansas-Nebraska Act overturned the Missouri Compromise of 1820, thereby reopening the question of the extension of slavery westwards by allowing settlers in each new territory to determine whether or not slavery would be allowed on the basis of "popular sovereignty." Violent confrontations followed between pro- and anti-slavery elements, leading to what was dubbed Bleeding Kansas. Two years later, Charles Sumner, one of Tocqueville's closest American associates, was severely beaten over the head on the floor of the US Senate for denouncing what he termed "the Crime against Kansas" and the barbarity of slavery.[35] In 1857, immediately following the inauguration of James Buchanan as president, Chief Justice Roger B. Taney delivered the *Dred Scott* decision asserting that Congress had no power to deprive persons of their property in slaves. Those who had written the US Constitution, Taney intoned, had considered people of African descent to be "beings of an inferior order, and altogether unfit to associate with the white race, either in social and political relations, and so far inferior that they had no rights which the white man was bound to respect."[36] By the time of Abraham Lincoln's inauguration as president in 1861, seven southern slave states had seceded from the Union. A month later, on 12 April 1861, the Civil War began.[37]

As we know, Tocqueville was deeply troubled by the existence of slavery in America, arguing in the first volume of *De la démocratie en Amérique* that it was "the most formidable of all the evils that threaten the future of the United States." This was not a view from which he was to waver. Tocqueville had been pleased when his own parliamentary report on the abolition of slavery in the French colonies was translated and published in America in

1840 by the wife of Harvard University professor Jared Sparks.[38] However, when writing to Sparks to express his thanks, Tocqueville voiced the view that he had "little hope" that his text would make "a useful impression." Slavery, he told Sparks, "has deeper and stronger roots in your soil than anywhere else" and he therefore doubted that either man would see its end. "It is sad for me to realise," Tocqueville wrote, "that, as your nation grows, slavery expands with it to such an extent that it makes humanity wail."[39] Nevertheless, this deep concern remained largely hidden in Tocqueville's public pronouncements up until 1852. It is after this date that his worries about the future of the United States grew considerably.

This took various forms, but one thing did not change: Tocqueville's sense of self-identification with America. In a letter to Theodore Sedgwick written on 4 December 1852, for example, he described himself as "half an American citizen" and as Sedgwick's "compatriot."[40] Likewise, in a later letter to Edward Vernon Childe, Tocqueville used the label "half Yankee" to describe himself, adding that what was then happening in America "must be of interest to all civilised people."[41] To Charles Sumner, as late as 1858, he referred to himself as "a friend of America and of humanity."[42]

Yet, in the earlier of these three letters, Tocqueville also remarked that he viewed with "apprehension" what he depicted as the "spirit of conquest, and even plunder" that was becoming ever more manifest in American politics. This, he told Sedgwick, was not a "sign of good health" from a country which already had more land than it could fill, and he was saddened by the prospect of American aggression towards Cuba. In Europe, he continued, the United States was seen "as the pit of the abyss from where nothing but a putrid stench comes out." A week later he wrote to Jared Sparks in a similar vein. Casting himself as someone who desired "the prosperity and greatness" of America, Tocqueville wrote that the country had "nothing to fear but from itself, from the excesses of democracy, the spirit of adventure and of conquest, the sentiment of and excessive pride in its strength, and the passions of youth." Not only did Tocqueville recommend a policy of moderation "among such great good fortune," but he also strongly counselled that America should avoid military entanglements with the European powers—an eventuality, he believed, that could have serious and grave repercussions on the nation's internal affairs.[43] Four years later Tocqueville became alarmed at the prospect of war between the United States and Great Britain after President Franklin Pierce recognised the military adventurer William Walker as head of the legitimate government of Nicaragua after the so-called Filibuster War. To Sedgwick, Tocqueville recommended extreme caution on the part of the United States and the hope that a peaceful compromise could be found.[44]

More than this, something of the fundamental character of American life and society appeared to be under challenge. If Tocqueville continued to reference the practical good sense of the Americans and their bounteous good fortune, he seemed less and less confident that these would be enough to see the country through the challenges ahead. Asking Theodore Sedgwick if the Know-Nothing party was "as dangerous to the internal peace of the Union as it seems to us from afar," he commented that the cause of liberty appeared threatened not only by recent examples of "popular disorder" in the West but also by "the violent, intolerant, and lawless spirit that seems to be spreading throughout a good part of the Union."[45]

This was a theme that Tocqueville took up again in 1856 in a letter to Francis Lieber. Was there any truth, he asked, in what was now the widely held opinion that "the very foundations" of American mores and political practices were under threat? "People affirm," Tocqueville wrote, "that the part of the population in the States that still has violent mores and uncouth habits increasingly sets the tone for the rest; that acts of personal violence, the cases of people taking justice into their own hands, are becoming more and more common and to such an extent that many peaceful people carry arms with them in case they have to resort to legitimate self-defence." To this was to be added what Tocqueville referred to as "the imperfect state of the justice system" wherein the election of judges at the whim of "the multitude" and the political parties was such as to offer no legal guarantees to the individual.[46]

There were other aspects to the American malaise. One, identified by Tocqueville in a letter to Edward Vernon Childe in 1857, was "the government of the country by the least honest, if not the least capable, part of the nation." This, Tocqueville wrote, could be explained by the fact that "domestic prosperity and external peace" had encouraged the people to indulge their natural love for "courtiers and flatterers." It was to be hoped that, in a time of crisis, they would "place their confidence in better hands."[47] A letter written that same month announced Tocqueville's agreement with Theodore Sedgwick that "the greatest danger threatening the northern states" was "the corruption of democratic institutions." This, Tocqueville told Sedgwick, was something the seeds of which he had seen when he was in the United States, but he was surprised that it had spread more quickly than he had then feared.[48] In March 1858 Tocqueville reported to Charles Sumner that public opinion in Europe was increasingly convinced that "in America the majority of public officials lack moderation, sometimes probity, above all education, and that they belong to a race of political adventurers, an energetic and intelligent race, but one that is violent, vulgar and without principles." He did not necessarily subscribe to this view, and he suffered when he heard it expressed, Tocqueville wrote, but "I am led to believe that in your country the movement of an unlimited democracy often elevates to the government of society men who are more aptly made for obedience than leadership and that, *in general,* those who govern are inferior to the governed."[49]

What also worried Tocqueville, as it had Ampère, was the arrival of a "prodigious number of foreigners" on American soil. As we know, this was something that Tocqueville had commented upon when he was in Germany, but he was to return to this theme on several occasions later in the decade. "Unfortunately," Tocqueville told Sedgwick in August 1856, "each new day brings so many foreign elements that soon you will no longer be yourselves." Tocqueville's fear was that "having so many races" in America would undermine what he termed its "natural condition," encouraging Americans only further to separate themselves from one another.[50] Three months later, Tocqueville repeated the point, suggesting that America was being turned into "a new people," but to this he added that he was also fearful of the appearance of "a new race of desperate gamblers" brought forth in a still half-empty land by America's prosperity. This race, he observed, combined "the passions and the instincts of the savage with the tastes, needs, vigour and vices of civilised men." The world, Tocqueville remarked, had never seen anything like it before, and it was hard to know where it would lead should such people gain "the upper hand" in the country's affairs.[51] That Tocqueville was worried about the fate of his financial investments in several American railway companies cannot have eased his growing disquiet.

The fact was, as Tocqueville told Sedgwick, that from a European perspective America looked more and more as if it was approaching a time of revolution and that it had "strangely abused the advantages given to [it] by God," advantages that had allowed it "to commit great errors with impunity." "From this side of the ocean," Tocqueville then observed, "you have become the *puer robustus* of Hobbes," a country that inspired little faith in its wisdom and a fear of its power, that was seen as "an unpredictable and dangerous force" and, being so, "upset all of the friends of democratic liberty and delight[ed] all of its opponents." The numbers of those who would be pleased to see America "fall into great shame and great disgrace" grew every day.[52]

Tocqueville used Thomas Hobbes's image of the *puer robustus* or "stout boy" as a description of America on two subsequent occasions in letters to Nassau Senior and Francis Lieber, both dated September 1856.[53] For Hobbes, the idea denoted a figure who rebelled against order and authority and who was therefore a threat. For Tocqueville, it was clearly intended to convey a sense of bad behaviour and immaturity on the part of the American republic and its citizens. Here was a country and a people increasingly infused with an excessive hunger for adventure and conquest, a prey to imperial ambitions, its institutions and its democracy victims of instability and corruption, and one ever more losing the national character and mores that had marked it since its point of departure.

Yet, as threats to the future of the Union, these were as nothing compared with that posed by the continued existence of slavery and its likely extension into the new territories of the American West. Where Tocqueville stood on this issue was given its clearest expression in a "Testimony against Slavery," published in the 1856 edition of the *Liberty Bell,* an antislavery publication edited by Maria Weston Chapman since 1839. Solicited by Chapman herself, Tocqueville's statement appeared in a section headed "The Historic Point of View," alongside contributions from Jules Michelet, Charles de Montalembert, and other eminent French writers.[54] "As a persevering enemy of despotism everywhere," Tocqueville declared, "I am pained and astonished by the fact that the freest people in the world is, at the present time, almost the only one among civilised and Christian nations which yet maintains personal servitude." To this, he added that, "as an old and sincere friend of America," he was uneasy at seeing the way in which slavery was damaging both its progress and reputation as well as compromising the future of the Union. "As a man too," he concluded, "I am moved at the spectacle of man's degradation by man, and I hope to see the day when the law will grant equal civil liberty to all the inhabitants of the same empire, as God accords the freedom of will, without distinction, to the dwellers upon earth."[55]

Tocqueville prefaced this statement by indicating that he did not feel that, as "a foreigner," it was for him to tell people in the United States how and when slavery should be abolished.[56] In subsequent correspondence with both Theodore Sedgwick and Edward Vernon Childe, he stressed that he did not support the position of the "abolitionist party"—of those, Tocqueville wrote, who "believed in the possibility of destroying slavery in the old states"; but those same letters, written following the election of James Buchanan as president and the apparent "triumph of the cause of slavery" it represented, made absolutely clear that he regarded the "extension of this horrible evil" as an abomination. This, he told Sedgwick, "would seem to me to be one of the greatest crimes that human beings could commit against the general cause of humanity."[57] To Childe, Tocqueville wrote that the introduction of slavery into new states amounted to the spreading of "this horrible plague" to parts of the earth previously free of it and to imposing "all the crimes and miseries accompanying slavery on millions of future people." All of this, he concluded, was "a crime against humanity" and seemed "both dreadful and unpardonable."[58] To Sedgwick in April 1857 Tocqueville wrote that the sight of what was occurring "makes me despair and horrifies me." "I thank God," he continued, "that I am not placed in the painful situation of being obliged either as a citizen to jeopardise such a great present good as the Union, or as a human being to allow a dreadful plague over a large part of the inhabitable earth, and perhaps for as long as the world will last."[59] A letter written to Jared Sparks in July of that year linked the issue of slavery not only to that of "the future of the Union" but also to "that of liberty in the world." Certainly, following the election of Buchanan as president, and as he told Henry Reeve in England, Tocqueville saw the descent into civil war as being increasingly likely.[60] From an American visitor by the name of Beckwith, Tocqueville came to understand that the supporters of slavery in the South were far more inclined to violence than he had previously realised and that civil war was far from improbable.[61]

The scale of Tocqueville's disappointment and bitterness can only be guessed at. Having witnessed firsthand France's slide into popular despotism under the Second Empire, he now found himself watching from a distance a country in which he had placed such high hopes seemingly and steadily losing the habits, ideas and mores that had allowed a democratic republic to flourish long after the providential moment and chance of its birth. Those institutions and practices—the federal constitution, self-interest well understood, and religion primary among them—that had bound the country together over a vast and empty continent had less and less purchase in a society increasingly characterised by greed, materialism, and corruption. Worst of all, slavery was not receding before the enlightenment of experience, as Tocqueville had predicted in 1835, but was now the subject of renewed and determined efforts to preserve and extend its existence, thereby threatening the very existence of the United States by perpetuating not the equality but the inequality of conditions.

Writing to Francis Lieber in September 1856 Tocqueville reflected that, having now reached the age of fifty-one, he was "over the top of the mountain" and could only descend from there. "I often gain comfort from this," he wrote, "when seeing how little worldly affairs turn out as I would have liked them to." He had wished to see a "free Europe" but now realised that the "cause of liberty" was more compromised than at any time since his birth. "Your America itself," Tocqueville told Lieber, "to which once turned the dreams of all those who lacked the reality of liberty has, in my view, given little satisfaction to the friends of liberty for some time." Indeed, he went on, it was as if the "despots of the old world" were happy to see the Americans show their subjects "the follies and vulgarities that liberty gives rise to" in order that they might be cured "of the desire ever to be free."[62] As Tocqueville had to admit to Nassau Senior, the changes that had occurred since his visit to America were such as to make the country "more and more difficult to understand."[63]

In contrast to the relative absence of references to the United States in *L'ancien régime et la révolution,* references to England abound, and so much so that the English experience served as a constant point of comparison with that of France. This comparison came in many forms, but the example of English society worked not only to illuminate the character of the ancien régime but also as an illustration of how an aristocratic society could both survive and adapt to new realities. For example, Tocqueville reported that one of the things that most struck French émigrés when they arrived in England was the absence of police. This filled them with surprise and even contempt for the English, the idea that this might have something to do with a conception of liberty completely eluding them. By contrast, in France almost everyone had become convinced that only the government could preserve public order. Everybody, Tocqueville wrote, wanted a squad of mounted constabulary by their front door. No one suspected that "behind the protector might well hide the master." Similarly, in France no one thought that a business could succeed without the involvement of the state. Even farmers believed that if agriculture was not progressing, it was because the government was not giving them enough advice or support. Hence, they called for government inspectors and public honours for those who grew the best crops. "Inspectors and medals!" Tocqueville commented wryly, "this is a suggestion that would never have dawned on a farmer from the county of Suffolk."[64]

The most sustained point of comparison in Tocqueville's narrative related to the characters and circumstances of the English and French aristocracies. During the eighteenth century, Tocqueville wrote, the gradual impoverishment of the nobility was to be seen not only in France, where the feudal system was reaching its end, but across the European continent. No new form of aristocracy was replacing it. The exception to this rule was England. There the opposite was to be noticed. "The old noble families which still existed," Tocqueville wrote, "had not only preserved but greatly increased their wealth," remaining "first in riches as well as in power." Moreover, those "new families" that had risen up beside them had only succeeded "in imitating their opulence without surpassing it."[65]

There was a more important difference between the two aristocracies. "Everywhere that the feudal system was established on the European continent," Tocqueville continued, "it ended up by becoming a caste system: in England alone it again became an aristocracy." In other words, birth was not its distinguishing feature and this, Tocqueville argued, was not only unique among modern nations but "alone" allowed us to understand "the peculiarities of [England's] institutions, mind and history." It was this, rather than England's Parliament, its liberty, its openness and its jury system, that had made the country so different from the rest of Europe. In short, "England was the only country where the caste system had not merely been changed but actually destroyed." Nobles and commoners engaged in the same business activities, joined the same professions, and "even more significantly" married each other. In France, "after sixty years of democracy," old and new families still avoided joining through marriage as much as possible.[66]

In Tocqueville's view, there had for long been no nobility in England in the "limited sense" in which it was understood elsewhere. This, he believed, was a "unique revolution" lost in the depths of time, but its effects were still very visible. It could, for example, be seen in the English language. Here Tocqueville again drew upon an observation he had made first in the 1830s and on subsequent occasions—namely, that, as social ranks became more mixed in England, the definition of a "gentleman" was steadily extended to cover more people lower down the social scale.[67] Likewise, if inequalities in taxation hardly existed in England, where they did it was in cases introduced in favour of the poor. Interestingly, Tocqueville also argued that, if the English aristocracy and the middle classes had remained so closely united, this was not, as was usually believed, because of the openness of the aristocracy but rather due to the fact that its shape was "indistinct" and its boundary "unknown." It was less a case of being easy to join the aristocracy than it was of not knowing whether one had joined. Anyone who got close to the aristocracy could think they were part of it and share in its glory and power.[68] No less importantly, a mutual attachment to English liberties forced the aristocracy and middle classes to remain on good terms "in order to be able to reach an understanding when necessary."[69] "The English aristocracy," Tocqueville wrote, "was by nature more haughty than that of France, and less disposed to be familiar with those who lived beneath it; but the demands of its situation forced it to do so." It was prepared to do anything to lead, even pretend to consider its inferiors as its equals. Crucially, the English aristocracy had taken upon itself "the heaviest public burdens, so that it would be allowed to govern."[70]

Nothing, Tocqueville argued, could have been less true of the French aristocracy. "Among us," he wrote, "it has taken the opposite course from that which we have seen among the English," becoming ever more exclusive. The word *gentilhomme* had preserved its original meaning because France had "preserved the caste itself, as separate as it has ever been from all others." The nobility and the third estate became more and more isolated and estranged from one another and no longer came together in public life, seeing themselves not merely as rivals but as enemies. The tax exemptions of the nobility grew from the fifteenth century onwards and were nowhere more visible and resented than in France. Tocqueville also argued that Edmund Burke had been mistaken in thinking that the right of the bourgeoisie to buy offices had produced an open aristocracy analogous to that of England. "Although very easy to cross," Tocqueville wrote, "the barrier that separated the French nobility from the other classes was always fixed and visible, always recognisable to those who remained outside." The system of ennoblements therefore only increased the hatred felt by the commoner for the nobility and was only further strengthened by "the envy which the new noble inspired among his former equals."[71] Finally, the French nobility was content to give up its role in government as long as its privileges were maintained.[72] All of this, Tocqueville stated, was such that, when the different classes of the ancien régime came back into contact with each other, they did so only to tear each other apart. "Even today," he wrote, "their jealousies and their hatreds survive them."[73]

There were other comparisons made by Tocqueville between England and France. He was struck by the fact that the English—not even those most connected to contemporary French society—had never been attracted by the irreligious philosophy of the French eighteenth century. "All those," Tocqueville wrote, "who had something to fear from revolutions hastened to come to the aid of established beliefs." Political parties found it in their interest to defend the Church of England.[74] Likewise, the English did not share the "contempt" for the dead shown by the administrations of the ancien régime. The reference here was to the enforced sale of charitable bequests, thereby putting them to uses not intended by the donor. The "meticulous scruples" of the English would have ensured that they would never have done such a thing. Rather, the whole force of the social body would have been deployed to ensure a respect for the last wishes of each citizen. For Tocqueville this was no minor point. As he wisely observed, the French had "forgotten that the best means to teach people to violate the individual rights of the living is to take no account of the will of the dead."[75]

England also gave evidence of another important principle and one that Tocqueville gleaned from his reading of Sir William Blackstone's *Commentaries on the Laws of England*—namely, that "nations have the ability to prosper despite the imperfections which are found in the secondary parts of their institutions, when the general principles, the very principles which animate it, are fertile." Here the mistake of the French had been to believe that the greatness and power of a people was determined by the simplicity and coherence of its legal system. For all of its many flaws, its inordinate complexity and outdated machinery, Tocqueville observed, "there was no country in the world where . . . the great end of justice was as completely attained as in England; where every person, whatever their rank, and whether they pleaded against an individual or against the ruler, was more sure of being heard, and found in all the courts of the country better guarantees for the defence of their fortune, their liberty and their life."[76] No country in Europe was more prosperous, nowhere was individual property more secure and extensive, and no society was more solid. None of this, Tocqueville argued, came from the excellence of a particular law but from "the spirit which animates English legislation as a whole."[77]

There was a further, and important, aspect to this comparative history that intrigued Tocqueville. "If one reads carefully what Blackstone says of the feudal system in England," he wrote, "one remains convinced, despite some efforts by the author as was his custom to combine some Saxon institutions with it, that we have under our eyes the same identical institution as that which was known in France; perhaps more complete and more systematic, because it had been introduced all at once and by the most advanced feudal people of the period, the Normans."[78] At the outset, in other words, the French and English systems were remarkably similar. As Tocqueville put it, there was "perfect parity at the point of origin." The differences appeared subsequently, and here Tocqueville again deployed the argument that if in France there had emerged a caste, in England "there came out of it, from very early on, an aristocracy." Why this had occurred in England as opposed to another of the countries of Germanic origin Tocqueville admitted he did not precisely know. "Among the English," he wrote, "I think that caste, if it ever existed in such an exclusive manner as among us, was gradually disorganised by the purchase of noble lands by wealthy commoners, who took rank among the nobility, in such a way that little by little the influence and the importance given to rights by birth was transferred to landownership, even without birth."[79] Moreover, the absence of monetary privileges attached to noble estates owned by nobles and of monetary penalties on noble estates owned by commoners was such as to bring the distinction between the nobility and commoners to an end whilst at the same time allowing the preservation of the political power and social influence—in brief, the privileges—of the wealthy and "in particular of the possessors of landed wealth."[80]

For Tocqueville, why this occurred was arguably less interesting than the consequences of its occurrence. "For me," he wrote, "everything which today is characteristic of England, political freedom, decentralisation, in a word *self-government,* proceeds from it."[81] By the same token, its nonoccurrence in France served to explain why the monarchy had been able to establish "absolute power on the ruins of feudal liberties." It was for this reason that it had been necessary to have "royal officials, royal interference and, finally, centralisation." As Tocqueville remarked, "local administration is only practicable, can only produce the expected effects and attach hearts and minds to its continuance, when it is exercised by a population represented by all the educated, rich, honoured, respected individuals who are to be found there."[82]

Most importantly of all, these different national trajectories helped explain why the English Revolution of 1640 and the French Revolution of 1789 had been so very dissimilar. Both, Tocqueville conceded, shared an instinctive desire to secure "civil and intellectual emancipation as an absolute right." To that extent the two revolutions were "both part of the great movement of the modern human mind." However, if "both revolutions had liberty and equality as goals, the immense difference between them was that the English Revolution was made almost solely for liberty, while the French Revolution was made chiefly for equality." The second major difference was that the "multitude" had played a leading role in the Revolution of 1789 whilst in England it had only ever played a secondary role, the dominant players being large sections of the upper and middle classes, supported by the organised power of the army. As Tocqueville explained, "The English Revolution used old powers by extending them, rather than creating new powers."

Finally, if the French Revolution was antireligious, the English Revolution was "more religious than political." When, Tocqueville argued, one observed the ease with which Charles I faced down his opponents when they raised only political arguments, one was led to wonder whether, "without the religious complications, England would have let itself be carried along by the current which at that time was leading all of Europe towards absolute power."[83]

There was a further point of comparison to be made. If the English Revolution had overturned the entire political constitution of the country to the point that even the monarchy was overthrown, it had scarcely touched the nation's secondary laws and had left most customs and practices intact. Not everything was changed at the same time, and English society, although shaken at the summit, remained stable at its base. The revolution had been limited in its effects. France, by contrast, had seen many revolutions since 1789 that had changed the structure of government from top to bottom. Yet, Tocqueville maintained, the disorder they had produced had been short-lived and had been barely noticed by the majority of the people. This was because, according to Tocqueville, the administrative structure of the state had remained in place, changes being limited to those who ruled and the forms of central power. The secondary powers of the state—those things which touched ordinary citizens on a daily basis—remained largely the same and were administered by the same people in much the same way. Crucially, according to Tocqueville, this had not been the case prior to 1789, when an administrative revolution had swept away agents, principles, and practices, turning public administration completely upside down: "A certain regular order continued to reign in the most important and most general affairs, but already no one knew any longer whom to obey, nor whom to speak to, nor how to conduct themselves in the small and individual matters that form the daily routines of social life." In such circumstances, Tocqueville wrote, it took only "one last blow . . . to produce the greatest upheaval and the most frightening confusion there ever was."[84] England had been spared this terrible fate.

Writing to Mrs. Sarah Austin in the late summer of 1856, Tocqueville told her that, as she was already aware, he saw "England as [his] second intellectual home." He did so in the context of the extremely favourable reception bestowed upon the English edition of *L'ancien régime et la révolution*. Nothing, he told Mrs. Austin, could be more agreeable. "The approval of distinguished people who live in your country," he wrote, "will always be considered by me to be one of the best rewards for my efforts."[85] Accordingly, Tocqueville was delighted to receive the praise of friends such as Nassau Senior and George Cornewall Lewis (as well as John Stuart Mill) and to read the flattering reviews in *The Times, The Spectator,* and other important publications of the day. "It is," Cornewall Lewis wrote, "the only book I ever read, which satisfied my mind as taking a thoroughly sound and rational view of the causes and character of the French Revolution." "The only fault I have to find in your volume," he continued, "is that there is not enough of it."[86]

Given what we now know of the positive light in which England was portrayed in Tocqueville's text we should not be unduly surprised by this widespread praise from his English readers. But was Tocqueville's relationship with England and the English always so unambiguously positive and empathetic as this would suggest? And would it remain so into the 1850s, when Tocqueville was again to travel to England?

As we know, Tocqueville twice visited England in the 1830s. If he was charmed by many aspects of English society, he was also slightly bemused by what he saw. England looked to be keeping the providential forces of democracy at bay. Tocqueville also caught a glimpse of an emerging industrial society in cities such as Birmingham and Manchester. In Ireland he witnessed the impact of English colonialism in all its harsh and unforgiving reality. Yet for all that Tocqueville returned to France after his visits with a generally positive impression of what he had seen and learned, he remained acutely aware of the mutual incomprehension that characterised the relationship between the two countries. To this was also to be added an understanding that the interests of England and France were not always in harmony. There was something about the overbearing demeanour of the English and their almost contemptuous disregard for France that irked the patriotic Frenchman.

This was repeatedly evident from Tocqueville's reaction to the Second Egyptian-Ottoman War of 1839–1841.[87] Like many a politician and commentator of his day, Tocqueville saw that the key to the future of the eastern Mediterranean and the Middle East more generally lay in the fate of the rapidly crumbling Ottoman Empire. He correctly understood that, if only to thwart Russian ambitions in the region, the policy of the British government would be to support the Ottomans against the Pasha of Egypt, Mehmet Ali. France, Tocqueville believed, should side with neither Russia nor England, but he was adamant that France's voice should be heard and that the future of the Ottoman Empire should not be decided by Russia and England alone. When, therefore, in 1840 Britain, Russia, Prussia, and Austria resolved to force Egypt to withdraw its forces from Syria without consulting the French, Tocqueville was all too ready to contemplate war against Britain (as indeed were many of his fellow citizens). To John Stuart Mill, he wrote, "Like me, and like all sensible people, you must have groaned at seeing the close alliance of our two countries broken," but, he went on, "after the manner in which the English government has acted towards us, not to have shown a sense of injury on the part of our politicians would perhaps have been to wound and to extinguish a national passion which we will need one day." That passion, Tocqueville made clear, was national pride. "The conduct of your government towards us," Tocqueville concluded, "has, in my opinion, been inexcusable, and I have been greatly saddened in seeing the English people allow the party in power to pursue such a policy."[88] Mill agreed with Tocqueville that the British government was "very culpable" but with the main thrust of Tocqueville's argument he had no sympathy. "The whole of the feeling which has arisen in this country," he wrote, "has arisen . . . from the demonstrations since made in France—from the signs of rabid eagerness for war, the reckless hurling down of the gauntlet to all Europe, the explosion of Napoleonism and of hatred to England, together with the confession of Thiers & his party that they were playing a double game, a thing which no English statesman could have avowed without an entire loss of caste as a politician."[89]

The relationship between Tocqueville and Mill never recovered after this exchange. Nor did Mill's attempted correction succeed in changing Tocqueville's hostile stance towards England. The alliance with England, Tocqueville wrote, is "based on the understanding that we can do nothing on the seas and that we do not need external trade (which is not the case) and moreover it does not allow us any significant expansion on the continent. It is founded on this and this alone: we are allowed to exist but are forbidden from expanding, whereas it allows the English to expand continually."[90] Consequently, France could not stand aside and let England and Russia decide the destiny of the Orient. It could not display resignation and must be among "the first rank." It was therefore in the "immediate interest" of France that "the commercial, industrial and political power of England should not be augmented in the Mediterranean."[91] The policy of a return to peace with an alliance with England as the means—the policy pursued by the French government under François Guizot—had to be abandoned.

Tocqueville struck a similarly hostile pose towards England in a series of four articles devoted to issues relating to the Franco-Tahitian War that had begun in 1844.[92] Again England and France did not come to blows, but there was significant diplomatic tension between the two countries, the British government preventing France from annexing Tahiti and the nearby Leeward Islands. At one point the Tahitian queen, Pomare IV, took refuge in the British consulate (later going into exile on a British warship). Although aware that France had again suffered humiliation at the hands of the British government, Tocqueville was careful to stress that he would regard war with England as "a great misfortune" but he denied with equal force that an alliance with England was a necessary element of French policy. First and foremost, the interests of France and England were far from being identical. England, Tocqueville wrote, was an industrial and trading power and it was this that drove England forward. To survive, all markets had to be open to it. England needed, he continued, "to be mistress of the seas; she needs not only to be powerful; she needs to be all powerful." With such a nation, a close friendship was only possible on one condition, and that was for it "to give up those things where it wants to be all powerful."[93] France could not abandon the seas to English control.

It was from this perspective that Tocqueville sided with the United States in its dispute with England over the control of the Territory of Oregon. Already Tocqueville appreciated that America was fast becoming a major commercial and maritime power and that it would soon begin to challenge England's global supremacy. "It is not through any alliance," Tocqueville wrote in 1846, "that America serves our interest, but through her greatness; it is by dividing up the seas, by reestablishing a maritime equilibrium."[94] Was the time when on the other side of the ocean an ally was emerging, he asked, the moment to abandon the struggle against Great Britain? If so, never would France establish an equal relationship with its rival.

The so-called Affair of the Spanish Marriages, where the British government sought unsuccessfully to block French plans for the marriages of Queen Isabella of Spain and her younger sister, the Infanta Louisa Fernanda, did nothing to assuage Tocqueville's antipathy towards British ambitions and behaviour.[95] Tocqueville, like some of his parliamentary colleagues, was clear that no more concessions should be made to the British foreign secretary, Lord Palmerston.[96] Nonetheless, and as Tocqueville argued in a letter to Francisque de Corcelle, given the situation in which France found itself, friendly relations with the English government were "indispensable" and to the point that France had to be prepared to "sacrifice everything that did not affront her honour."[97]

For Tocqueville, the situation can barely be said to have improved with the advent of the Second Republic and his time as minister of foreign affairs between June and October 1849. Writing in his *Souvenirs* Tocqueville recorded that, in a situation where France (with reason) was distrusted by its neighbours, it was left with nothing else to rely upon but the "the sterile goodwill" and "lukewarm" support of the English.[98] Tocqueville was also very much aware that, in the revolutionary year of 1848, England had been the "only country in Europe where the ground [did] not shudder." Not even Beaumont's appointment as French ambassador to London (and his residence in the magnificent surroundings of Hertford House in Manchester Square) could do much to forge a common policy to thwart Austrian interventions in northern Italy. At best, Beaumont told Tocqueville, England might adopt a position of "kindly neutrality." Then came France's misjudged military expedition to Rome and further British criticism of French policy—criticism that Tocqueville, now a government minister, did his best to refute.

A series of letters written by Tocqueville to Henry Reeve over the summer of 1849 was withering in its contempt for what he clearly regarded as the naive posturing of the British political class. Could they not see, Tocqueville asked, with what "extreme moderation" France was conducting this "unhappy war"? Did they not recognise that, for all they had been obliged to take Rome by force, the French were "the only friends and guarantors of liberty in Italy"? Did they not see that, if the Austrians, Neapolitans, and

Spaniards had found themselves before the walls of Rome there would have taken place "a very real bombardment" of the city and not the "imaginary bombardment" of which France had been accused by the English consul? Did they not appreciate that a victory for Austria and their allies would lead not only "to the overthrow of the [Roman] Republic but to the extinction of all liberty and the return, pure and simple, to the government of priests?" The truth of the matter, Tocqueville suggested, was that English politicians were blinded by their "old animosity toward the French" and he found it strange that it "should be the English, and among the English, principally the old Tories who attack us."[99]

Correspondence with Lord Normanby, the British ambassador in Paris, gave further evidence of Tocqueville's irritation. One issue concerned the imprisonment of a certain Dr. Giacinto Achilli by the Roman authorities. A former Dominican priest, Achilli had converted to the Protestant faith and taken on the role of missionary. He also possessed a British passport issued in Malta. It was not clear what crime, if any, Achilli was guilty of, but Lord Palmerston, the British foreign secretary, let it be known to Tocqueville that he expected the French to exert pressure to secure his release. From what Tocqueville knew of Achilli, he was "a scoundrel," but, as he told Adolphe de Circourt, "he had the sympathy of the *saints* of England, all of whom will move heaven and earth against us and against the Pope while he remains in prison." The pleasure of punishing this "poor devil," Tocqueville wrote, was not worth such a price. Rather than be subject to "Anglican fanaticism," the best thing for France was to have Achilli released or to let him escape.[100] Tocqueville therefore was only too willing to comply with the wishes of the British government but, with only thinly disguised sarcasm, he told Normanby on 23 August 1849 that "Lord Palmerston speaks easily of Roman liberties but his language is strongly redolent of the Protestant and the Islander; we, who are governmentally Catholic and Continental and who are constrained not to speak but to act on questions relating to Italy, are by contrast obliged to restrict ourselves to what is possible and practicable."[101]

Tocqueville was similarly brusque in response to Normanby's inquiries about French intentions relating to the blockade of the Rio de la Plata. England and France had been engaged in a drawn-out dispute with Argentina since 1832 but, in early 1849, Lord Palmerston concluded a separate treaty with the Argentinian dictator, Juan Manuel de Rosas, leaving the French to defend Montevideo, capital of the Oriental Republic of Uruguay, against Argentinian aggression. It was rumoured that the French were thinking of sending out a military force and of setting up a new colony in Uruguay. Despite enthusiasm in some quarters for such a policy, this was quite definitely not Tocqueville's view, and he made it known to Normanby that his intention was to bring this business to an end as soon as possible.[102] Tocqueville made this as clear as he could in a letter to Henry Reeve. There was not a single French soldier, he told Reeve, ready to board ship. His hope was that a proposed treaty with the Argentinians would be ratified by the French Parliament. Moreover, the French would do nothing without communicating with the English. Nonetheless, Tocqueville continued, "you are so constituted, you others on the other side of the Channel, that at the least movement we make you are always ready to cry that we are about to undertake some great adventure from which you may suffer." The French, he wrote, had lots of more important things to deal with but if they were to go to war against such an "impertinent rascal" as Rosas—a man who did not cease to insult France and all other civilised nations, Tocqueville remarked—where would be the great crime in it?[103]

Beneath this lay Tocqueville's acute awareness that British and French interests did not always coincide and that a slavish acceptance by the French of British foreign policy interests could lead to potentially catastrophic outcomes. So, too, as in Tocqueville's writings on Algeria, the positions taken by him were driven by the powerful patriotic sentiment that France needed to escape from the humiliating position it had been placed in by the other European powers after the defeat of Napoleon and the signing of the Treaty of Vienna.

Given this long-standing irritation with the haughty disdain displayed by the British government towards France, it is no surprise that Tocqueville took some quiet pleasure in the military and administrative embarrassments occasioned for Britain by its woeful and incompetent performance in the Crimean War after it began in October 1853.[104] At the outset, Tocqueville appeared pleased that Britain and France would be fighting alongside each other, especially as their Russian adversary was the bastion of despotism in Europe,[105] but whatever enthusiasm he might have had was quickly dissipated by the litany of failings displayed by the British Army and its aristocratic officers (Lord Raglan, the commander in chief, figuring among the most incompetent). Writing to both Francisque de Corcelle and Adolphe de Circourt in January 1855, Tocqueville was led to reflect upon the immense reputational damage that would be suffered by Britain as a consequence of its military shortcomings and the extent to which Britain's enemies would see it as an adversary less to be feared.[106]

As Tocqueville remarked to both men, it amused him somewhat to point this out to his English friends. There are many examples of this, but the set of letters written to Nassau Senior at the time provides ample illustration. Expressing his pleasure at the good relations that apparently existed between the French and British Armies,[107] Tocqueville went on to say that he was less pleased by British management of the war. "The English would be mistaken," he wrote, "if they did not see that what is happening at the moment has sensibly diminished their moral force in Europe." This was an unpleasant truth, but Tocqueville saw proof of it everywhere. "The heroic courage of your soldiers is universally and unreservedly praised," he continued, "but I have found it widely believed that the importance of England as a military power in the world has been greatly exaggerated; that it is utterly lacking in military talent when it comes to both administering and fighting a war; and that, even in the most pressing of cases, it cannot raise a large army." Tocqueville had never heard such hostile language about England since he was a boy, he wrote, and he saw that this mounting contempt would, on the French side, make war between the two nations easier than at any time since the fall of Napoleon. "From a continental perspective," he added, "a nation which cannot raise enough troops to meet its needs is a nation much diminished in our respect." Such a nation lacked grandeur and patriotism.[108]

In Tocqueville's opinion, British military failings reflected a deeper malaise and were pregnant with possible long-term consequences. First, these events posed a great threat to the position of the aristocracy in English society. As he told Senior, "it will suffer severely from the rebound if it does not make great efforts to show itself capable of lifting itself up again, and it would make a mistake if it believed that, by fighting bravely on the field of battle, it will retain the direction of government." The truth of the matter, Tocqueville told Beaumont, was that as a result of these disasters the English political world was in complete disarray and its institutions were gravely undermined. At its service England now had neither "the wisdom and vigour of its old masters, nor the coarse but powerful passion that democracy gives to its children in America." It possessed only a mediocre and weak government that had shown itself incapable of meeting the needs of war and was just as likely to prove incapable of meeting those of peace. As Tocqueville reminded Harriet Grote, the English will have seen the great advantages that centralised government possessed in times of war and would not readily forget this experience. Given that the British Army remained the only one in the world where only gentlemen were officers, it was also likely that it would be subject to revolution. Revolutions in the army, Tocqueville added, were rarely restricted to the army alone.[109] Fortunately, he wrote, the English people remained calm, but their first protests would be dangerous.

So, too, had the cause of liberty been weakened by British military and administrative incompetence. From their position of weakness, Tocqueville told Senior, the British now dared not say anything that might offend the "master of France."[110] As Tocqueville suggested to Circourt, the British had been contaminated by their "intimate and extended" contact with the French Army and the French government.[111] To Beaumont, he wrote that for Britain's opponents it was evident that "the liberty of the English does not give birth to the miracles that people say but, on the contrary, disturbs and troubles the undertakings in which it is involved." For France, therefore, the evident superiority of the French Army provided proof of the merits of absolute government whilst also indicating to the French emperor that he might be better advised in forging alliances with the other despotic powers of Europe.[112] "As imprudent as it is to speak of a foreign country," Tocqueville told Nassau Senior, "I venture to say that the English would be mistaken to believe themselves so separated from the rest of the world that what occurs across the whole of the Continent will not have an influence upon its own institutions." No European nation, he wrote, would remain forever different from the others, not even Britain, "despite the sea" and its "mores and institutions." "We will not perhaps see the truth of what I say in our own lifetimes," Tocqueville concluded, "but those who come after us are sure to see it; and I would have no fears depositing my letter with a notary for it to be reread fifty years from now."[113]

One person who followed news of the war in the Crimea closely was Marie de Tocqueville (neé Mary Mottley), Tocqueville's English wife. "As much as her eyes allow," Tocqueville wrote to Harriet Grote, "she devours the reports from the Crimea in *The Times,* and what she reads there both saddens her greatly and moves her." One could only hope, Tocqueville told Grote, that accounts of the parlous conditions and sufferings of the British Army were exaggerated. It was hard to believe that a country as rich and as well informed as Britain could so badly foresee what the needs of its army might be.[114] Tocqueville and his wife might also have had cause to wonder whether the British were happy with the outcome of a war which had cost so much blood and money and where France and Napoleon III alone appeared to have profited from the struggle. The French and the British, Tocqueville wrote in a later letter to Harriet Grote, were two such very different peoples of such incompatible characters that they could not "marry each other with impunity." One might also speculate as to what Madame de Tocqueville would have made of her husband's remark to Gustave de Beaumont that the English showed astonishing naïveté in their "national egoism." "In their eyes," Tocqueville wrote, "the enemies of England are complete rogues and their friends are great men." This, according to Tocqueville, encapsulated the English understanding of human morality.[115]

Yet for all of this disenchantment with the English and their government, Tocqueville continued to value his English friendships greatly, and few things gave him greater satisfaction than the praise he received from England. As Tocqueville wrote to George Cornewall Lewis, then chancellor of the exchequer in the British government, "Today England is the sole country in the world where, in the same person, one can meet one of the best *scholars* of the day and the administrator of the finances of a great empire." He would not, Tocqueville assured Cornewall Lewis, pose questions similar to those he had posed to Cornewall Lewis to any of France's finance ministers.[116]

It was to be Cornewall Lewis who would suggest to Tocqueville that he should again travel to England, this time with a view to visiting the British Museum in London in order to consult its extensive contemporary publications on the French Revolution. The head of the library, Cornewall Lewis told Tocqueville, reported that the collection is "in excellent order, well catalogued, and is a collection containing many small works and most easily consulted." Cornewall Lewis further reassured Tocqueville that, although books could not be taken out of the library, everything would be done to "facilitate" his research. Cornewall Lewis also felt sure that Lord Clarendon, the foreign secretary, would grant Tocqueville "all reasonable facilities" to consult the diplomatic papers of the period.[117] Seven months later, in June 1857, Tocqueville arrived in London.

As with all of Tocqueville's journeys, much forward planning was involved.[118] Reeve was immediately written to and asked to find an apartment that Tocqueville might rent. When this proved impossible, Reeve provided names and addresses of hotels. He also invited Tocqueville to stay at his home at 62 Rutland Gate in Knightsbridge. Best of all, Reeve secured honorary membership of the Athenaeum for Tocqueville. Tocqueville was clearly looking forward to seeing old friends again and to enjoying some stimulating conversation. Along with the complete destruction of public life, he told Harriet Grote, the despotism of the Second Empire had also made the French "exceedingly stupid."[119]

Once more, things did not go quite to plan. No sooner had Tocqueville arrived in London than he made his way to the library of the British Museum. After his first day there, he told his wife, Mary, he returned "dazed and overwhelmed." Just imagine, he wrote, enough documents on the French Revolution to fill the Tocqueville château from top to bottom. He would need at least six months to get even a general idea of the enormous number of things to be found there. Worse still, and contrary to what Cornewall Lewis had reported, the collection had not been catalogued.[120] Tocqueville did not hide either his frustration or his disappointment. "In truth," he wrote to Sir Anthony Panizzi, head of the library, "my studies have not had the result that I was hoping for." The British Museum, Tocqueville conceded, undoubtedly possessed "the most magnificent" collection of texts on the French Revolution that existed. It contained the complete works of many of the writers of the revolutionary period and runs of newspapers that were more complete than could be found elsewhere. But, Tocqueville continued, "for all the anonymous pamphlets (these are numberless) which, without being of great intrinsic interest, have the advantage of enabling us to know the impression produced by particular events or changes in public opinion . . . there is no means of profiting from them until such time as a chronological catalogue has been prepared." So, Tocqueville reported, having failed to work out how to access the material, he had given up and had resolved to take up his work again once the library had found both the time and financial resources to produce an inventory.[121]

To his wife, Tocqueville was less circumspect in his comments. The British Museum, he wrote, "will have been for me a complete *humbug*. There are immense riches to be found there, it is true, but no means of accessing them. It is as if one plunges one's hand without looking into a pond full of fish. Sometimes by chance you might catch one but how many more escape one's grasp."[122] Tocqueville made similar comments to both Gustave de Beaumont and Jean-Jacques Ampère after he had returned to France. Estimating the number of pamphlets to be in the region of twelve thousand, he told Beaumont that he had wasted many hours in the library and, for the most part, had succeeded "only in collecting dust."[123]

Tocqueville fared better on his visits to the State Papers Office. Here, Tocqueville told Beaumont, were to be found all the government's diplomatic papers, bound together carefully in large volumes. The rule was that no papers dated after 1789 were to be made available, but an exception had been made in Tocqueville's case and he had therefore been able to consult all of the diplomatic correspondence from 1789 to 1793 (the date at which relations had been broken off between France and Great Britain). He had discovered little of great interest, Tocqueville wrote, but he had found what he believed to be fairly conclusive proof that the English had not played the "Machiavellian role" frequently attributed to them. Certainly, they had not been saddened by French difficulties but "nothing indicated that they had tried to make them worse." It was also amusing to see, he commented, that, for all of their own experience of revolution, the English had little suspected what would come out of the French Revolution.[124]

Thus, as Tocqueville told Beaumont, the "utilitarian side of the trip" was far from being a success.[125] However, there were to be many compensations. As Nassau Senior's daughter, Minnie Simpson, was later to write, upon Tocqueville's arrival in London he was "received with a perfect ovation."[126]

Here, too, there was to be the occasional mishap. Tocqueville set off for England on 18 June, leaving his wife, Mary, behind him and travelling only with his incompetent servant Auguste. Given the latter's lack of a knowledge of English and of England, he was, Tocqueville told his wife, more of a hindrance than of use. Crossing the English Channel there was a "magnificent sky" and, despite a "slightly swelling sea," Tocqueville was able to report that he had not been sick. Their boat arrived in Folkestone at nine o'clock in the morning. Having had breakfast, the two men set off for London, completing the journey by train in only three hours. Awaiting them was something of a calamity. Their hotel was fully booked and would remain so for the next ten days. All the nearby hotels were similarly fully booked due to a "grand musical festival" taking place at the Crystal Palace.[127] Tocqueville was therefore compelled to go from door to door in search of accommodation, before finally finding "a very beautiful but horribly expensive apartment" on Albemarle Street (just off Piccadilly). Writing to his wife that evening, he indicated that the following day he planned to see Henry Reeve and together find more suitable accommodation. Having seen no one, he also admitted to being lonely and, worst of all, that he worried that his change of address might mean that he would not receive his wife's letters. "I love you," he signed off, "and embrace you from the bottom of my heart."[128]

Tocqueville's day was not yet over. At one o'clock in the morning, he reported to his wife, he was awoken by "an awful commotion." The sky was full of thunder and lightning. A great storm was sweeping across the city. It was, Tocqueville wrote, "very beautiful, but the person staying above me, either due to the heat or due to *fashion,* had left his window completely open, with the result that his apartment was quickly turned into a lake, the water penetrating between the floorboards and soon falling like a cascade into my own room." Tocqueville was obliged to jump on his bed and protect his belongings, using the pots at his disposal to collect the falling water. After about an hour he went back to bed and "slept like a log."[129]

What followed was a rather typical bout of Tocquevillian self-pity. Up until now, he told Mary on the second day of his stay, all he had experienced had been "the inconveniences of a foreign country." "I had forgotten," he wrote, "the many little habits that characterise English life and I have still to pick up my easy use of the language, with the result that everything is difficult." He had spent the day traipsing across the vast city and had still to find accommodation he liked or could afford. To make matters worse, it was exceptionally hot and, as a result, he found that he could not sleep at night.[130] He had turned down offers of lodging from both Reeve and Senior for fear that he would have to invite them to his home in Normandy in return.[131]

Tocqueville's "great preoccupation" was to work out how to protect himself "from the world." Hardly had he arrived, Tocqueville wrote, than he had been inundated with invitations from all manner of people. His solution, he told his wife, was to decide that he would not dine out in the evenings. Nonetheless, amidst all this commotion, he could not rid himself of a sense of isolation and loneliness. "Perhaps," Tocqueville wrote mournfully, "when I am better set up, I will look with more interest at the things I find around me."[132]

By the following day, Tocqueville reported rather sheepishly, things had somewhat improved. He had slept well. The weather was cooler. And, best of all, he had received two letters from his wife, letters, Tocqueville told her, that reminded him what an important place she had in his life and his affections. Now he was resolved to enjoy his time in England. Furthermore, Tocqueville was now installed in the Athenaeum, the "magnificent palace" from which he had no intention of moving. He did, however, admit to an element of melancholy and regret. "Instead of stirring up feelings of joy as it had done twenty years ago," Tocqueville wrote, "the vision of this society which is so free, so well organised, so bound together and so prosperous, filled my heart with an envious sadness (the worst of sadnesses)." When, he went on, the principal goal of one's life has been to make one's own country into something similar, it was hard to find any consolation in seeing such an ambition "so completely and so miserably" come to grief. "Here," he concluded, "I have all manner of personal satisfactions, but as a Frenchman I feel constantly in a state of inferiority and humiliation."[133]

The New Athenaeum, 1851 (Stephen Dorey—Bygone Images / Alamy Stock Photo)

Still, the pleasurable side of Tocqueville's travels was now underway. First came a visit to Kent House in Knightsbridge, home of the Cornewall Lewises and of Lady Thereza Cornewall Lewis's brother, Lord Clarendon. Sunday afternoon was spent *en famille,* the Cornewall Lewises, according to Tocqueville, showing all their usual simplicity and cordiality. Many questions were asked about Madame de Tocqueville's health. The following evening Tocqueville travelled out to Richmond on the western edge of the city to visit George and Harriet Grote, unexpectedly staying the night and engaging in "uninterrupted *chit-chat*" until ten o'clock. The Grotes, Tocqueville confided to his wife, were clearly a little bored with each other! The next morning Tocqueville rose before his hosts and returned to London. "The countryside," Tocqueville wrote, "is the charm and the glory of England." He could see how "*rural*" he had become by the enjoyment he felt at seeing all the details of English country life.[134]

There followed in quick succession a visit from Jacob Pleydell-Bouverie, son of the Third Earl of Radnor, lunch with Lord Stanhope (attended by the

Duke and Duchess of Argyle and the eminent historian Thomas Babington Macaulay),[135] breakfast with the Seniors, and a meeting with Lord Clarendon (who, like his sister, was "very amiable"). Tocqueville turned down an invitation to dinner with Lord Palmerston (preferring, he told Mary, to dine quietly on his own at the Athenaeum, "where everything that might agreeably occupy a reasonable man" was to be found). He also turned down invitations from Lord and Lady Charlemont, Lord and Lady Stanhope (thus, regretfully, missing the opportunity to stay at Chevening House in Kent) and the Duchess of Argyle, as well as dinner at the home of Lord and Lady Granville. In the latter case, however, Tocqueville agreed to attend after dinner, there finding most of the principal ministers of the British government and many of "the finest ladies of England." To Tocqueville's pleasure it turned out that his recent book had been the topic of conversation over dinner. As soon as he entered the room, he found himself "surrounded, flattered and praised" and so much so that he felt hugely embarrassed and did not know what to do with himself.[136]

It was that evening that Tocqueville learned from Lord Clarendon that Prince Albert, husband of Queen Victoria, wished to meet him. The audience took place a couple of days later, Tocqueville and the Prince Consort speaking together for over an hour. Tocqueville found the prince to be a "singularly sensible" person and someone not only of wide knowledge but also free of prejudice; and, so much so, he told his wife, that upon leaving "I was able to say to him without flattery that of all the remarkable things I had seen in England up until now the thing most worthy of being remembered was his conversation." There was much more, Tocqueville wrote, that he could say about the meeting but, swiftly and incongruously moving on, he turned in the next sentence to Marie's most recent letter. "I see," he commented, "that your bowels have been somewhat affected by your stay in Paris and by the heat: this worries me a lot and makes me forget about all the princes of the world."[137]

Despite his protests (he had too much to do, he was eager to leave London as soon as possible, and so on), Tocqueville's socialising continued apace. He saw his fellow French liberal, Victor Lanjuinais, and also found himself seated regularly at table with the writer Prosper Mérimée, now a supporter of the Second Empire and close associate of the imperial family. One highlight remained: a visit to see Cornewall Lewis at 11 Downing Street. Like many people since, Tocqueville was struck by the modesty of the surroundings. "In a big ugly brick building blackened by smoke," Tocqueville wrote, "one comes across a small door with a copper door knocker and a plaque of the same metal on which is written 'The Chancellor of the Exchequer.'" Next door, he reported, was another small door of the same size where Lord Palmerston, the prime minister, resided. Twenty steps further on was a room about as big as the billiard room at Tocqueville, lined with simple furniture and not well lit. This, he continued, was the room where the government ministers deliberated and "it was here that the first Pitt decided on the measures which have assured the greatness of England and its maritime supremacy around the globe; and here too that his son directed the gigantic struggle against the French Revolution." For most of his compatriots, Tocqueville conceded, these achievements would be diminished by the "extreme meanness of the location," but for him it was precisely "the extreme simplicity" of the place that gave it its grandeur and that gave grandeur to those "actors who knew how simply to play the first roles in the drama of the world." He was distressed at seeing how little he had in common with his own country.[138]

Next came a visit to the Houses of Parliament with Cornewall Lewis. "A hidden aversion," Tocqueville told his wife, "had always prevented me from going there." Recently rebuilt after the fire that had burnt down much of the building, "everything is new, magnificent, with a great affectation for Gothic architecture and great care to appear old." To look at it, Tocqueville wrote, one would think that it was soon destined to perish, but the way business was done in both chambers was "simple and practical" with little attention to eloquence and the vain pomposities of language. This, he mused, must have had more to do with the nature of the institution than race as "in Congress the Americans are often as theatrical and as noisy as we are."[139] It also seems that Tocqueville paid a visit to the three sons of former king Louis-Philippe, living in exile in Twickenham to the west of London. To Francisque de Corcelle he indicated that he had done this without any political motive and only as "a mark of respect and sympathy."[140]

Throughout his stay in London, Tocqueville continued to be showered with compliments. On one occasion, he recalled, he entered a room and saw a very old man reclining in a huge chair. Without standing up, the gentleman shook his hand and told him in English that Tocqueville had written the greatest book of the century. This, it turned out, was John Singleton Copley, Lord Lyndhurst. He was, Tocqueville told his wife, "the oldest representative of what remains of old England." On the whole, Tocqueville's health held up, although in the early part of July the demands of the London season—"la vie *déréglée,*" as he described it to Richard Monckton Milnes—had clearly got the better of him. Happily, having received a visit from a Dr. Ferguson, who recommended that Tocqueville should live like a hermit for a few days, he was able to report to his wife on 10 July that "the stiffness, headaches and lack of appetite" had passed and that he was again looking forward to what he would be doing.[141]

Tocqueville also took to walking back from the British Museum at the end of the day to his hotel on Albemarle Street through "the disreputable little streets" inhabited by the working class of London. Here was the ugly reverse side of the beautiful coin that he usually had before his eyes. If, he wrote, the poor, working-class districts of Paris were unsettling to see, "the poor of the cities of England have a more miserable appearance than do ours." The filthy conditions in which they lived under a "rain of coal dust" were horrendous. There was, Tocqueville observed, "no country where there are more people who want to be *somebody* and who, to attain that end, are prepared to do all manner of things unknown elsewhere. But I believe that all those who are reduced to be a *nobody* fall lower down the social scale than anywhere else." This in turn induced Tocqueville to indulge in "a bit of philosophy." "As you know," he told his wife, "there still exists a kind of freemasonry in Europe between members of the former upper classes who understand each other with the merest of whispers and speak openly to each other." Sometimes, Tocqueville wrote, he amused himself in London by talking with the distinguished ladies he met, all of whom treated him as one of their own, only to discover that they were possessed of the "same vanities and the same prejudices" that had destroyed the French aristocracy." So why did they receive "so affably" all those—Tocqueville cited as examples the Reeves and the Seniors—whom they found so boring and to be their inferiors? The answer, according to Tocqueville, was fear, and "because they are living in a country where you have to reckon with everybody, and above all those who speak, write and act." From this he concluded that it was more necessary than ever to shout "*Vive la liberté!*"[142]

It was not long before Tocqueville felt the need to get out of London. This he did on two occasions: first, by visiting the estate of Lord Hatherton in Staffordshire and, second, by staying with his old friend, Lord Radnor, in Berkshire. Both men, in their different ways, were for Tocqueville the very models of English aristocracy. When Tocqueville arrived in England in mid-June, the first thing he noticed as he journeyed from Folkestone to the capital was that England and France were far less dissimilar than they had been when he had first visited the country. Nothing, he told his wife, so clearly demonstrated the "material progress" made by France over the last twenty-five years. But one thing still surprised him: the attention given to all the details of the countryside, to "everything resembling the cultivation of a garden." There were no great châteaux or grand houses along the way, but everything was neat and clean, and nothing offended the eye.[143] This was a frequent theme in his letters from England. Occasionally, as when he travelled on the train from London to Wiltshire, Tocqueville was inclined to reflect upon the monotony of the English countryside—"who has seen one corner of England," he wrote, "has seen the entire island"—but all too frequently he found it impossible to resist the picture postcard idyll of English country life. On one occasion he described a house he visited just south of London. Such a house in France, Tocqueville wrote, would be "a miserable shack." In England, by contrast, it is "a little cottage where everything is pleasant to see. At the front is a little garden, full of magnificent flowers, which one crosses by a little path artistically laid out in small pebbles as large as walnuts; a brilliantly polished little front door; a small sitting room where everything is neat and tidy; and finally, on the other side of the road, a Gothic church in the middle of beautiful meadows surrounded by magnificent trees, and, in the background, green hills."[144] Tocqueville was not the first or last visitor to England to find this utterly irresistible.

He was similarly charmed by what he saw when he visited Hatherton's property at Teddesley. Edward Littleton, First Baron Hatherton, had a distinguished political career lasting over forty years but, for Tocqueville, he was first and foremost a "*gentleman farmer*" and someone who devoted considerable money and effort to the modernisation of his very extensive (and very lucrative) land holdings. Hatherton's house, Tocqueville reported, was very ugly and not very large. Everything was being renovated, the "venerable *housekeeper*" being unsure if there was anywhere for them to sleep when they arrived. As for Hatherton, he was, according to Tocqueville, "simplicity itself." No sooner had the two men arrived than Hatherton took Tocqueville to see the various properties on his estate. Everything was on a grand scale and, most importantly, Tocqueville saw immediately that there was much that could be imitated on the less advanced and smaller scale farms of France. Tocqueville was immensely impressed by the accommodation provided for the pigs—"it is," he wrote, "cleaned from top to bottom everyday and the manure removed and there is not a single sty that is not much cleaner than the house of Madame Bono"[145]—but he was also surprised that on such a large estate and in such a wet climate there was not a single granary. The wheat and hay were kept in stacks in the open air, thereby preserving it for longer. Tocqueville also learnt much about the food provided for animals during the winter and the various fodder crops that were easy to grow. Above all, he saw that the land had been improved by drainage.[146]

Also of great interest to Tocqueville were the conditions in which the workers both lived and laboured. Hatherton, Tocqueville recorded, had built a number of brick houses which were "very pleasant to live in" and that were rented out. Each had the same aspect: "a little garden with flowers next to the house, and the rest with potatoes; a clean interior." The rent was three pounds a year, with labourers receiving fifteen shillings a week in wages. All of this was enough to ensure "a reasonably comfortable existence." As an encouragement to neatness, Lady Hatherton had established prizes for the best-kept gardens. She also devoted considerable time to the local schools. "What greater opportunity to do good," Tocqueville commented, "than to possess such a great fortune and to live throughout the year amid a population that depends directly upon you." It would, he reflected, require a hundred times more effort and know-how to achieve the same amount of good in France.[147]

Having seen the workers' cottages, Tocqueville was next taken to see one of the tenant farms. It was a farm of three hundred acres and was rented for £350 per year. It resembled, Tocqueville observed, a large farm on the outskirts of Paris. The farmhouse was "a very agreeable residence," surrounded by pretty flower beds and was better maintained than the prettiest houses in the suburbs of large French towns. Upon their arrival, the family was playing music together. The master of the house, Tocqueville wrote, was a young man who looked as much of a gentleman as his landowner. The kitchen, he noted, was cleaner than any of the staircases and floors of the Tocqueville château. Most striking of all was Tocqueville's overall conclusion. "It has to be said," he told his wife, "that here the cultivation of soil rests upon an entirely different system from our own." This, Tocqueville continued, was " a system with both its weaknesses and its strengths, but it has had the result of creating a breed of farmer who is a veritable entrepreneur of the agricultural industry and who, as a consequence, bears no resemblance to our peasant farmer."[148] In a subsequent letter to Hatherton, dated 1 September 1858, Tocqueville made the point that the English had "an agriculture of capitalists" whilst in France they still had "an agriculture of peasants."[149]

Their tour complete, Tocqueville and Hatherton returned to the house for dinner, prepared by the housemaid. At Tocqueville's request, they then visited the servants' quarters where, from Tocqueville's description, he witnessed the hierarchical arrangements typical of many an English country house at the time: a large dining room where all the servants ate and a smaller one where the "aristocracy" of the staff ate their pudding and drank their tea separately and enjoyed their own select company. Last of all, they arrived at the "very comfortable" apartment of the housekeeper, from where she directed the activities of the entire household. Tocqueville subsequently wrote to Hatherton to thank him for his visit. "I have never seen so many things," he wrote, "that so greatly interested me in such a short space of time."[150]

To gauge fully the significance of Tocqueville's description of Lord Hatherton and his estate in Staffordshire it needs to be placed alongside the description provided of Lord Radnor and his home at Coleshill House in Berkshire five days later. There was "no one in the country," Tocqueville wrote to his wife, "who is more respected and who leads a life more replete with benevolent and useful deeds" than Lord Radnor. He was "in good health despite his seventy-eight years, which he refers to with serenity; he takes a lively interest in the affairs of his country although he no longer wishes to take part in them; he concerns himself with everything that can be of use to the people living around him; in everything he does he sets an example worthy of imitation; and is surrounded by his children, various friends and universal admiration." Radnor's household, Tocqueville continued, was like the man himself. He lived in a fine country house, surrounded by a beautiful park, where everything conveyed a sense of "peaceful grandeur." There was no "vain luxury," only "an attention to the least details that contribute to the tranquillity and comfort of life." The servants were well turned out but were without the overdone, gilded appearance that Tocqueville had upon occasion found shocking in some of the great houses of England. The food was good, without any unnecessary luxury, and one served oneself as if it were a simple family dinner. Unfortunately, Tocqueville spoilt this delightful portrait by adding as his final remark the comment that Radnor's daughter, Lady Mary, was "very ugly and, were it not for the fact that her face had a kindly expression, she would be physically very disagreeable."[151]

Here, then, was evidence of what Tocqueville had long searched for and hoped to find: an aristocracy that had maintained its role in the affairs of local life and that continued to use its wealth and influence for the general benefit of all concerned. To that extent, it was the very antithesis of the functionless and privileged nobility of the France of the ancien régime, and thus it played a crucial role in preserving the stability, prosperity, and liberty that characterised English society. And it was as such that it was described by Tocqueville to his friends after his return home at the end of July.

"You can well imagine," Tocqueville told Louis de Kergorlay, "that I did not spend my time in England without casting a curious eye about me." And what he had seen was that England seemed yet more aristocratic than it had done when he had last visited the country over twenty years earlier. The "democratic agitation" of those years had passed, and "not only did the aristocracy appear more securely established than ever but the nation is clearly happy to leave government in the hands of a very small number of families." The aristocracy therefore governed less as a result of its "preponderant strength" than as a consequence of the "tacit and voluntary consent of the other classes."[152] To his distant relative, Laurette de Pisieux, comtesse de Montboissier, Tocqueville commented that the "aristocratic institutions" of England seemed stronger and less contested than when he had first visited England in the 1830s.[153]

It was this, Tocqueville later explained to Kergorlay, that explained why the practices of "self-government" persisted in England. There were,

Tocqueville conceded, many defects in the administration of English local government and the superiority of central government in certain areas was acknowledged. However, "there existed not only powerful individual opinions but also an unconquerable public prejudice opposed to the extension of its sphere." This, Tocqueville believed, had several causes but foremost was "the place of the aristocracy in English society." "The aristocracy," Tocqueville wrote, "is sufficiently enlightened to understand that, the day when central government becomes master of the administration of the country, it will have lost its raison d'être." Behind this lay the "confused but strong feeling" that, for all of its faults, this system and the idea of doing things for oneself was integral to the "public prosperity" of England and had made it "the richest and the most free" of countries. "It is this passion for being one's own master," Tocqueville wrote, "that today essentially characterises the English race." The French had it in respect of their private lives, but "the English race has it to its highest degree in their local public life."[154]

Reflecting upon what he had seen, Tocqueville told Francisque de Corcelle that he did not envy England either its wealth or its power but he had breathed freely when, "for the first time in many years," he had been in a place where there were no "class hatreds and jealousies." But there was a second dimension to this picture of English life that Tocqueville felt worthy of note, and again it was something that he had not witnessed for some considerable time. In England, he explained to Corcelle, he had seen "the perfect agreement between religious morality and political morality, private virtues and public virtues, Christianity and liberty." In a similar vein, Tocqueville told Corcelle that in England he had "heard Christians of all denominations recommend free institutions not only as necessary for the public good but for the morality of all societies." Not once had he observed "the kind of moral monstrosity that can be seen across virtually the entire continent, where it is the religious who recommend despotism and where it is left to rascals to recommend liberty."[155] As Tocqueville told Kergorlay, religious sentiment in England remained strong without being fervent and destructive of other human passions.[156]

Tocqueville had previously commented upon one example of such moral monstrosity in a letter he had sent to Corcelle prior to his trip to England. In brief, Tocqueville had been outraged that the French Roman Catholic newspaper *L'univers* had voiced its support for James Buchanan rather than for the abolitionist John C. Frémont in the American presidential election of 1856. "I weep," Tocqueville had written, "at thus seeing the Church seemingly becoming the upholder of brutal force and tyranny across the face of the earth."[157] Given this earlier remark, Corcelle now concluded that Tocqueville was attacking the entire Catholic Church. This, Tocqueville replied firmly, was not the case, and, in rebutting this charge, he was again to have the opportunity of stressing the particularity and importance of what he had seen whilst in England. He had not been making a comparison between Catholicism and Protestantism, he pointed out, but between England and the Continent: hence his reference to "all denominations." Furthermore, Tocqueville wrote, "the truth is that I never met an English Catholic who was not as strong a supporter of the free institutions of his country as any Protestant, nor one who made a distinction between two parts of morality: one which relates to public morality and with which it is not necessary to concern oneself; a second which relates to private virtues and which alone requires observance." Not once, he emphasised, had he met an English Catholic, layperson or cleric, who made such a distinction.[158] Again, Tocqueville asserted that his comparison had not been one between religions but between countries. But Tocqueville was in no doubt as to the importance of this comparison and its significance. In England he had found a country where "religion and liberalism are in agreement" and he had delighted in it. Moreover, he wrote, "the sight of the opposite had weighed upon and oppressed my soul since my youth." "I expressed this view," Tocqueville concluded, "over twenty years ago in the introduction to the *Démocratie.* I feel this today as strongly as I did when I was still young; and I doubt that there has been a single idea that has been as present in my mind since I have been in the land of the living."[159]

Tocqueville voiced a related conclusion to Kergorlay, and again it was one that emphasised the extent to which what Tocqueville had seen in England confirmed in him the truth of what had been long-held convictions. There was, he told Kergorlay, "not a single one of my theoretical ideas about the practice of political liberty" that had not been corroborated anew by "everything I saw with my own eyes." The more he had penetrated the details of the way things were carried out in England, "the more these truths seemed proven." Nonetheless, despite this appearance of aristocratic ascendancy and stability, Tocqueville saw no reason to believe that "the movement which imperiously pushes all other nations in an antiaristocratic direction" would not, over time, lead England along the same path. Centralisation would little by little win the day, but so slowly, Tocqueville suggested, that it would hardly be noticed. The present state of affairs therefore seemed destined to continue for some time to come and for as long as the aristocracy ran things well. A great setback or a series of errors, Tocqueville conceded, could easily bring other classes into government, but, he wrote, it seemed that this was well understood "even among the class which governs and this understanding will doubtless preserve them for many years from their downfall."[160]

No sooner had Tocqueville returned home than he set about sending effusive letters of thanks to many of those who had so warmly welcomed him into their houses. He was undeniably touched by the affection shown towards him and pleasantly surprised by the esteem in which he was held by what amounted to the British political elite of the day. Yet for the "avalanche of compliments" he received from their "lordships and ladyships," Tocqueville was never able to shake off a sense of sadness during his stay in London. From where, he mused to his wife, did this come? Was it from a feeling of isolation to which he was not accustomed? Was it, on the other hand, a consequence of the hubbub and excitement of the "magnificent society" in which he now found himself? Was it the emptiness that came after a time "so full of vanity and pride"? He did not know the answer, but, Tocqueville wrote, "the bottom of my soul is full of a melancholy and at times a despondency that will disappear, I hope, only when I breathe another air than that of London." Tocqueville saw then that there were two sides to his temperament, for as much as he enjoyed and was excited by life in high society, he quickly tired of it and became troubled by it, sensing that he was losing his bearings. Yet, once he had returned home, he admitted, he missed such a life and it was only slowly that calmness and tranquillity returned to him. "Then," he explained to his wife, Mary, "what pleased me, pleases me even more, what hurt me loses its harshness, a state of moral well-being comes over me, and, to the extent that this condition continues, its charms increase and a thousand new pleasures, a thousand sweetnesses, not previously seen, reveal themselves every day in a way of life that nevertheless always feels the same."[161]

In short, if Tocqueville's visit to England had confirmed political intuitions held since he had visited America, it also revealed something of which he had long been aware in his own character: the inquisitive and enthusiastic traveller always missed the comforts of home and the intimacy of those he loved.

For all of the grand figures that Tocqueville saw in London and the grand houses he visited, there was one person of a more modest position that he was determined to see: his wife's brother, Joe. Joseph Mottley had joined the Royal Navy in 1812 and, it seems, had had a far from brilliant career. In 1845 Tocqueville had written to the then British prime minister, Sir Robert Peel, asking that he might secure his brother-in-law's promotion.[162] Twelve years later, Tocqueville appears to have been given a similar mission by his wife. On this occasion, he went in person to see Sir Charles Wood, the first lord of the Admiralty. As Tocqueville told his wife, he could well understand why her brother had not advanced in his career. As a servant of the state, he clearly had many strengths, but, when it came to his own affairs, he was certainly maladroit. He was at one and the same time both likeable and frustrating. Yet Tocqueville manifestly enjoyed his time with the various members of the Mottley family he met, and it seems that Tocqueville's approach to Sir Charles Wood was successful, with Joseph Mottley reporting in August that he had been promoted to captain.

Tocqueville's visit to Sir Charles Wood had another unanticipated, but very welcome, outcome. On 10 July, Tocqueville wrote to his wife not only to report on his first conversation with Wood about her brother but also to report that Wood, upon learning that Tocqueville lived near Cherbourg, had suggested providing a vessel of the Royal Navy to transport him there from Portsmouth. Were he still minister of foreign affairs, Tocqueville told Mary, he could not have asked for more than this. Indeed, for someone who suffered terribly while travelling at sea, the prospect of arriving five leagues from home without difficulty was irresistible. Thus, having visited the naval dockyards in Portsmouth and dined with the admiral in charge, Tocqueville duly set off (in what he described to Ampère as a "princely" fashion) on 20 July, waking up the next morning, he told Henry Reeve, almost able to see the smoke from the chimneys of his house.[163] His arrival, Tocqueville reported to Beaumont, was greeted with great bewilderment by the local population:

"expecting to see some prince descend from the boat, they saw only your obedient servant."[164] To Jean-Charles Rivet, Tocqueville recounted that he had been mistaken for a high-ranking government official returning after a visit to Queen Victoria's residence at Osborne on the Isle of Wight.[165] According to Hugh Brogan, the imperial government prohibited all mention in the press of Tocqueville's unusual return.[166]

No sooner had Tocqueville returned to his family home than for the next two months he and his wife were besieged by family and friends. Not the least of these visitors was the American senator Charles Sumner. Although pleased to be back in Normandy, Tocqueville did have to admit that what he had seen in England had rather spoilt his first impressions of his native country. His village seemed less clean than before his departure, his fields less well farmed, and his house uglier. What he missed most, he told Lady Thereza Cornewall Lewis, were the massive trees scattered everywhere about the English landscape. These, he wrote, were an "aristocratic institution" about which he felt very envious.[167]

That same letter, written on 5 August, also indicated that Tocqueville and his wife were both "very worried" and "constantly preoccupied" by what was then occurring in India.[168] Indeed, as a subsequent letter to Lady Thereza Cornewall Lewis revealed, his wife spoke and thought about was happening in India ceaselessly, to the point that she was having sleepless nights. Despite marrying a Frenchman, he confided, she had remained profoundly English in her "heart, habits and ideas."[169] What was the source of anxiety in India?

From early May 1857 a large-scale rebellion against the British East India Company had been underway.[170] The scale of the rebellion was a threat to British imperial rule and, when Delhi fell to the insurgent army in the middle of the month, British officials and their families were massacred. Worse was to follow for the British (as well as for the Indian population, which suffered thousands of deaths through British military retribution), and it was not to be until the summer of 1858 that British forces started to gain the upper hand. Hostilities finally ended in early 1859.[171]

Given that Tocqueville had only returned from London a matter of weeks before news of the Indian Rebellion filled the pages of the press—indeed, the evidence suggests that Tocqueville had been at the home of the eminent Liberal Party politician, Lord Granville, when news of the rebellion first arrived by telegraph[172]—how did he respond to these momentous events? Did he recalibrate his views on the success and stability of the English political system and the place of the aristocracy within it? Did Tocqueville seek to draw parallels between what was now occurring in India and what he had seen on his own earlier visits to the French colony in Algeria? Here we should remember that Tocqueville had spent some considerable time during the 1840s studying the British experience in India and that he had compared it favourably to that of the French experience in North Africa. He had been impressed by the seeming ease with which the British had been able to establish an immense empire on the Indian subcontinent and by the administrative and military arrangements put in place to secure their rule.

"There has never been anything so extraordinary under the sun," Tocqueville told Lady Thereza Cornewall Lewis in October 1857, "than the conquest and, in particular, the government of India by the English." Nothing had so drawn the attention of the world to this small island. To that extent, he told Lady Thereza, the loss of India would undoubtedly cause great damage to the position of England and could not be done with impunity.[173] Similarly, Tocqueville told Prosper Duvergier de Hauranne that events in India represented the most dangerous crisis facing England since the war with America.[174] If the rebellion spread, he explained to Victor Lanjuinais, England would disappear from the political map of continental Europe (and to France's potential advantage).[175]

Yet, from the outset, Tocqueville remained confident that, for all of the immense challenges ahead, the English would emerge victorious from the struggle, in part because he was convinced that the "insurgents" had no overall plan. If Delhi was retaken, he predicted to Adolphe de Circourt, they could well "scatter like dust."[176] He also believed that the English would be driven by a "heroic and just" instinct to keep India "at any price."[177] Tocqueville wrote to Reeve that he believed that, if it employed all its resources and determination, there was nothing that was impossible for the English nation.[178]

Tocqueville could also understand—or, at least, thought he could understand—why the rebellion had occurred. He offered several explanations to his English friends. Writing to Lady Cornewall Lewis, Tocqueville suggested that the present "insurrection" owed more to "general" than to "accidental" causes. Principally, he argued, "the English, who are the only civilised people which continues to govern itself as an aristocracy, are led by a singular twist of fate to destroy or weaken aristocracy everywhere it governs." This, with prudence, they had done for over one hundred years in India, reaching compromises with the indigenous princes and ruling elites compatible with English rule. But these indigenous groups, Tocqueville maintained, had come to realise that it was only a matter of time before they lost all power and they had resolved to rebel against the destiny that was being prepared for them. England's good fortune was that many of these "little princes" had chosen to remain spectators in the struggle.[179]

Tocqueville set out a related argument to Henry Reeve. There were many people in France, Tocqueville wrote, who said that the English had repressed the Hindu population. "I believe," he responded, "the opposite; and I think that your danger arises rather from the fact that, in drawing them closer to civilisation and in giving them fairer ideas on government and administration, you have made them more dangerous for their masters and have diminished the prestige of the latter."[180] Tocqueville also expressed to Reeve the view that one of the principal causes of the rebellion lay in the distance that separated the European army officer from the Asian soldier. For all that the British had done to ensure the fair and generous treatment of the indigenous troops, Tocqueville wrote, never had there existed less camaraderie among companions in arms, and so much so that differences of "civilisation and race" placed such great distance between them that "at every instance, the one saw himself not as being the equal of the other, but as not resembling the other." To that extent, he concluded, the rebellion was not an uprising against oppression but against pride.[181] The English, Tocqueville told Eugénie de Grancey, had the misfortune of irritating the very people they helped through their laws, whereas the French often found themselves liked despite their humiliation of their subjects.[182]

To Lord Hatherton, Tocqueville presented another argument, and one, he told Gustave de Beaumont, he had heard from the mouth of Lord Palmerston. "In the past," Tocqueville wrote to Hatherton, "I wanted to write a book about the settlement of the English in India and, to this effect, I collected and read many documents about the country." Although he had long since given up this idea, one thought had remained with him from these studies—namely, "that for over one hundred years the English had not done for the Hindu population what might have been expected of them from their enlightenment and their institutions." They had done no more than try to soften and improve the institutions of the preexisting indigenous governments. This was so, Tocqueville argued, because India had been the most hidden part of the British governmental system and, moreover, it had been consciously hidden from view by the East India Company. This had deprived the English of a knowledge of Indian affairs that would have allowed them to use all their undoubted abilities to improve and repair the failing institutions that existed there.[183]

It was Tocqueville's view, therefore, that the English would be best advised to dissolve the East India Company and to place Indian affairs before parliamentary and public scrutiny (which was exactly what was to be done). He also told Hatherton that he feared that Britain would be obliged to establish a permanent standing army, as only this would enable it to secure its position in India.[184] What Tocqueville did not agree with was Henry Reeve's suggestion that the English should now seek to establish a large colonial population in India. Whilst omitting any reference to the French experience in Algeria, Tocqueville replied that he had always noticed that wherever a European population had been introduced among "imperfectly civilised populations," its "real or imagined superiority" was so wounding to the pride of the indigenous population that it caused "more anger than any political oppression." This, he feared, would be especially so in the case of the English, who were the "most haughty" of all the European nations.[185]

This point was repeated by Tocqueville when he commented on Reeve's proposal to Lord Hatherton, except that on this occasion he explicitly referenced the failures of French policy in North Africa. "In Algeria," he told Hatherton," the Arabs and the Kabyles are more irritated by the presence of our settlers than they are by that of our soldiers." A better strategy for India therefore would be for the English to introduce "the general principles which make Europe rich and enlightened" and thereby show the Hindus the advantages of European civilisation. Contact with a European population would only increase "their prejudices and their repugnance."[186] Of one other thing Tocqueville was absolutely sure: in securing its victory over the rebellion, the English must not allow "the barbarism of savages" to be followed by "the barbarity of the civilised."[187] "You only have the right to be the masters of these pitiless savages," he told Lady Cornewall Lewis, "because you are worth more than they are." The legitimate right to punish did not entail the right to commit massacres in turn (as Tocqueville feared rightly might be the case).[188]

Above all, Tocqueville saw that British rule could only rest upon consent and not upon force, and that if this consent was lost the position of Britain in India would be well nigh untenable. He also understood that had the rebellion in India occurred three years earlier—at the time of British military failures in the Crimea—the difficulties faced would have been even greater, and perhaps fatal to British interests. England therefore found itself in a precarious and fragile position. As Tocqueville told Ampère, England was now like a large lobster in the process of shedding its shell. In normal circumstances it had nothing to fear, but at that moment the smallest fish could cause it a dangerous injury. In such circumstances, England needed peace in Europe and (regrettably, as far as Tocqueville was concerned) an alliance with the France of Napoleon III more than ever. Events in India had therefore the potential to be the great setback that Tocqueville feared might sweep away the system of aristocratic government in England. But he also viewed these events from a broader perspective and one now likely to cause offence. There could not be a person under the sun, Tocqueville wrote to Ampère, who could be indifferent to what was occurring in India, as these were events of relevance to "the general destiny of the human race."[189]

As Tocqueville made clear in letters to both Henry Reeve and Nassau Senior, what was at stake was the future of civilisation and the progress of humanity. "There cannot be a civilised nation in the world," he told Senior, "which should rejoice at seeing India escape from the hands of Europeans and thereby fall into a state of anarchy and barbarism worse than before the conquest."[190] This view was expressed in even starker and more uncompromising terms in a letter to Adolphe de Circourt, dated 25 October 1857. Tocqueville did not regret the defeat of the Hindus, he wrote, as "the general interests of humanity would have been compromised by their victory and it would have led only to the restoration of barbarism amidst one of the most numerous of human families. Moreover, England, despite its faults (which are many), is when all is said and done the only country of political liberty that still exists in Europe and I have no desire whatsoever that the friends of servitude who swamp us should have the joy of seeing this last refuge trodden under foot by savages."[191]

Conclusion

Cannes

There remained one last long journey for Alexis de Tocqueville to make, but this was not to be until the late autumn of 1858. For the time being, life resumed something akin to its normal pattern. Back at the Tocqueville château after his visit to England, guests came and went. Tocqueville continued to busy himself with improvements to his estate. He also did his best to press ahead with his book on the French Revolution but (not for the first time) progress was slow. Having told Jean-Jacques Ampère in early August that he was impatient to make a start, he wrote a month later to say that, although he was working, it was to no effect. By November he was able to report progress but, he told Ampère, he still had no idea where he was heading. The only recompense had been an autumn of extraordinary beauty. In February 1858 Tocqueville was in better spirits. Despite ("like almost everyone in France") having had influenza, he had done as much on his book as he could at Tocqueville. "I have quit the land of the shadows where I have groped in the dark for too long," he told Ampère, and now saw the way forward. Tocqueville's plan was therefore to return to Paris, where he would work in the archives and libraries for several months collecting material.[1]

This he did at the very end of March (leaving his wife, Mary, behind in Normandy), with the intention of staying in the capital until the end of June, if not longer. Tocqueville's hope was that this would give him enough time to complete the research he needed to do. All he had to show for his recent endeavours, he told Ampère, were incomplete sketches of a few chapters that were not fit to show anyone.[2] As had been the case so often in the past, Tocqueville was to be disappointed. To his wife he wrote that he felt lost among "an ocean of papers," adding that the whole project saddened him so much that he felt like giving up entirely. When he was writing *De la démocratie en Amérique,* he told her, he had had none of the advantages he now enjoyed, but then he had had "youth, passion, faith in a cause, and hope," all of which seemed to have now deserted him. In a letter written in early May, Tocqueville observed that there existed a "distressing inconsistency" between his mind and his body. If the former was like that of a thirty-year-old who wanted to act and achieve great things, the latter was that of someone who felt like a frail ninety-year-old.[3] To Charles de Montalembert, Tocqueville wrote that he felt "overwhelmed" by the task he had set himself and that, since his return to Paris, the only consequence of his work had been to prevent him from seeing his friends.[4] Moreover, Tocqueville disliked staying in a hotel and he missed both his wife and his home very badly. "I fear," he told Mary, "that our meadows, our sheep, our kid goats and our pigeons interest me more than the French Revolution."[5] If he saw friends—for example, Nassau Senior and Gustave de Beaumont—he had no taste for the social obligations of life in Paris, finding these occasions arid and insipid. Nevertheless, Tocqueville had to acknowledge that a solitary existence free from domestic distractions had enabled him to find and identify the manuscripts and books he would need to work on if he were to complete his task.

For all his talk of three months in the libraries and archives of Paris, Tocqueville was back in Normandy by early May. It turned out that Madame de Tocqueville was unable to join him in Paris—for once it was through no fault of her own that her plans were unavoidably changed—and thus, with great enthusiasm and self-confessed joy, Tocqueville set off immediately for the quiet and rest of home and the delights of planting trees, sowing grass, and looking out at the sea.[6] Now the plan was to return to Paris with his wife during the winter and then resume his scholarly endeavours. Briefly there was an idea to take the waters somewhere, as Tocqueville's wife was still suffering from rheumatism, but this came to nought. As he explained to Francisque de Corcelle, Mary now positively feared travel, being of the opinion that one lost more in travelling long distances to find a remedy for an illness than one was likely to gain from the remedy itself. She was probably right, Tocqueville mused.[7]

Thus, apart from seeking to ensure that Tocqueville's agricultural improvements yielded a good harvest (which, with the help of fine weather, they did),[8] the big event of the summer was the official inauguration by Emperor Napoleon III of the Paris-to-Cherbourg railway at the beginning of August, an occasion designed to coincide with celebrations marking the completion of the second basin of the Cherbourg naval dockyard and a state visit by Queen Victoria and her husband. One can easily imagine Tocqueville's discomfort. Having long advocated the extension of the railway to Cherbourg, he now found it turned into an imperial propaganda exercise. The only monarch he would pay his respects to, he told Richard Monkton Milnes some two weeks before the celebrations, was the English queen.[9] To Harriet Grote he wrote to say that he could take no pleasure in seeing the emperor take credit for something for which he was not responsible. Tocqueville was also aggrieved that he could not replicate the kindness shown to him by Prince Albert when he had been in England. To avoid any awkwardness, he thought that it might be best to be elsewhere on "urgent business."[10]

Whether it was because, as he told Harriet Grote, people might interpret such a response as evidence of a big sulk or simply as a futile gesture on Tocqueville's part is not clear, but the fact is that not only did he not go away but he also showed himself perfectly happy to welcome any number of British and French guests to his home during the festivities and afterwards. Although Tocqueville could not bring himself to attend any of the official celebrations, he could not resist looking down on the "magnificent spectacle" of the French and British fleets from the nearby coastal cliffs at Fermanville. The sound of the firing of thousands of salutes and the smell of gun powder, he told many a friend, reached as far as the Tocqueville château. On the surface, then, all seemed well. However, in the second week of August, Madame de Tocqueville fell ill, losing her voice, and taking to her bed. Worse still, and as a flurry of letters to friends and family in early September revealed, Tocqueville was increasingly concerned about his own health.[11]

All these letters disclose that Tocqueville had been unwell for the previous six months and that he now understood that action of some kind was required. That this was the case is revealed in letters to Gustave de Beaumont, in particular, but also to other friends. In April Tocqueville wrote to Beaumont to say that if the problems with his throat had cleared up, his stomach was worse than it had been for some time. The following month, having returned home, he reported that, if he was not ill or in pain, he was suffering from a form of "physical exhaustion" that, he believed, was a product of the spring weather and of "mental exhaustion." On 17 June Tocqueville wrote to Beaumont with the extremely distressing and alarming news that he had been coughing up blood. He had written to Dr. Bretonneau but had received no reply.[12] A week or so later he made the same report to Jean-Charles Rivet and Nassau Senior, indicating that he was incapable of work, suffering from bronchitis, and had been unable to speak. The letter to Senior also reported that Tocqueville had tried to convince his wife that they should spend the summer in the south of France, but that she had cited the difficulties and length of the journey, the summer heat, and Tocqueville's own poor health as reasons for staying put.[13] To Beaumont in early July, Tocqueville suggested that he was feeling a little improved but, he admitted, the "verve" he had acquired in Tours had all but disappeared. Harriet Grote received a similar message. He was suffering, Tocqueville told her, from "*un certain malaise de corps,*" and, although there had been no repetition of the blood spitting, he had since "not been the same man."[14]

Tocqueville's intention was to visit his doctors in Paris in mid-September, a trip he hoped that would now be made all the easier with the opening of the Paris-to-Cherbourg railway. This was indeed to be the case. The journey, he told his wife, had been made as if by "magic." He had had his morning chocolate drink at his hotel in Valognes and set off a half hour later, arriving at Caen at 11:15 a.m., where he enjoyed an excellent lunch of filet of beef and potato purée. By 5:30 p.m. he was in Paris, where he walked to his hotel and found himself wondering if he had really covered such a long distance in so short a time. Moreover, he had not been fatigued by the journey and had one of the best night's sleep he had had in a long time.[15]

The next day Tocqueville saw Dr. Andral and Dr. Charruau separately, both of whom concluded that Tocqueville was suffering from a problem with his bronchial tubes and (seemingly) that it was not much for him to be worried about. In their medical wisdom, a treatment of vesication was prescribed. This amounted to applying an irritating substance to the skin in order to cause blisters for a period of three weeks. Tocqueville set off for home the following morning, eager as always to see his wife as quickly as he could. He arrived, he told Adolphe de Circourt, "extremely tired, very put out, and very unwell."[16]

Remarkably, Tocqueville's health seemed to improve over the next couple of weeks—to the point, he told his brother Édouard, that he was beginning to wonder whether his illness deserved the attention he had bestowed upon it. The remedies looked to be working, and the noises coming from his chest had ceased. Over the next couple of weeks (as was to be the case over the next few months), Tocqueville had both his good and his bad days, and he returned to see his doctors before the end of the month to hear their assessment of how he was progressing. Again, the train journey went well, Tocqueville arriving not feeling unduly tired and with an appetite, only for his own optimism to be confirmed the next day by Dr. Charruau's assessment that he was improved, if not completely cured. Later that afternoon, Tocqueville set out for a walk but made a quick return to his hotel due to the strong wind. As ever, he was concerned about his wife's well-being in his absence, fearing that running the Tocqueville estate would prove too much for her. A letter from her, received on 1 October, brought tears to his eyes. "Who would ever have imagined," Tocqueville replied, "that a man who had such a passionate desire to spread out into the world would have come to attach his being so strongly to a small corner of the earth and to his inner life."[17]

That afternoon, having walked down the Rue de Rivoli, Tocqueville saw both of his doctors together. They agreed that Tocqueville's general state of health was good and (deploying their medical expertise to the full) decided to replace the treatment of vesicatories with that of "*un caustique,*" which (as far as one can make out) amounted to putting something like nitric acid into the oesophagus through the back. It was, by Tocqueville's account, a very painful operation and one that left him considerably discomforted for the next couple of days. One can perhaps understand Tocqueville's irritation when his wife appeared to suggest that he was exaggerating his fears about his health. If he was melancholic, he replied, it was because he saw that in future his life might well be dogged by illness and medical treatments.[18]

For some time there had been talk between Tocqueville and his wife of heading south for the winter, despite the disruption and inconvenience it would inevitably cause. But where would they go? Tocqueville's clear preference was for Rome, in part because his good friend Jean-Jacques Ampère was now resident there. Given, Tocqueville asked Ampère, that the railway on the French side of the Alps stopped at the foot of Mont Cenis, was the massif over to Italy difficult to cross? Was there likely to be snow from late October onwards? Would it be possible to hire a coach to make the journey, or would it be necessary to take a public carriage? Once across the Alps, what was the best way to get overland to central Italy? Would he and his wife be able to find a comfortable furnished apartment in Rome that would not be too expensive? Most importantly, Tocqueville asked, would the Rome climate be suitable for someone who had bronchitis or who had just had it?[19]

For all this typical attention to detail and preparation, two weeks later Tocqueville was obliged to tell Ampère that he would not be seeing him in Rome as it had now been resolved that he and his wife would spend the winter in Cannes (then little more than a small village on the Mediterranean coast). Dr. Andral, Tocqueville reported, would have allowed him to travel as far south as Pisa but what, Tocqueville commented, was the point of travelling all that way to live in such an "insignificant city"? The climate in Cannes, Tocqueville added, was reportedly very mild; he and his wife had found a nice house where they could live; and, as it was in France, Tocqueville could make use of the public libraries. As he told Beaumont, it also suited Madame de Tocqueville's inclination to travel no further than she was forced to. Despite his obvious disappointment, Tocqueville's hope was that his wife would now quickly join him in Paris and that the two of them (and their servants) would set off as soon as possible and no later than the end of October. On one point Tocqueville was mightily relieved: any idea of sending him to convalesce in Madeira or Africa had been dropped. The south of France would be quite adequate to protect him from the worst of the winter weather.[20]

Unavoidably, Tocqueville's wife's arrival in Paris was delayed by the numerous tasks involved in closing the family château for the winter. In the interim, Tocqueville tried to get out for walks whenever he could, but while he waited, as he told Corcelle, he felt tired, ill and alone. He was also largely unable to talk. His short note to Corcelle was written with what he described as "*une plume de malade.*"[21] When his wife did eventually arrive on 16 October, she was, as Tocqueville told Beaumont, both "stressed and tired." It was not clear, Tocqueville added, which one of them, if either, would complete the long journey ahead without becoming ill.[22]

What followed was worse than anything Tocqueville might have imagined.[23] The Tocquevilles left Paris by train on 28 October. Four days later, having stayed overnight in Dijon, Lyons, and Valence, they arrived in Aix-en-Provence. A strong and glacial north wind had followed them down the Rhône Valley, the river flooding its bridges. He had never seen, Tocqueville told Léonce de Lavergne, a storm "so violent and so cold." It was, as Tocqueville expressed it, "*le sublime de l'horreur*."[24] "Each day," Tocqueville told his brother Édouard, had "tired and disheartened [him] terribly."[25] The next day they set out by coach for a further three days of travel, snow falling all the way from Fréjus to Cannes.

Both Tocqueville and his wife were completely exhausted upon arrival. They were, as Tocqueville told both Francisque de Corcelle and Jean-Charles Rivet, "*à bout des forces.*" He was so tired, he told Édouard de Tocqueville, that he could not possibly have gone any further. The whole journey, Tocqueville reported to Beaumont, had been "abominable," and the only thing he now dreamt about was taking to his bed. Moreover, the bad weather had continued. The mountains around them were covered in snow, he told Beaumont, and there was frost every night.[26]

At first Tocqueville was so exhausted and the weather so bad that he could not leave the house. The icy cold was followed by torrential rain. So far, he told Édouard de Tocqueville, "the beautiful climate of the south of France has been nothing more than a myth."[27] Nonetheless, Tocqueville was pleased with the doctor he had taken on, later supplementing the efforts of Dr. Sève with those of a Dr. Maure from nearby Grasse. The programme he had been advised to follow, he told Beaumont on 11 November, was not to go out, because it was cold; not to speak, because this would help his bronchial tubes; not to receive visitors; and, above all, not to get bored or melancholic.[28] Such was the need to recover from the journey, he wrote in the same letter, that even serious reading was for the moment unthinkable. Yet, Tocqueville added, he had never felt so strongly the need for books to occupy and interest him.

Cannes (Chronicle / Alamy Stock Photo)

In search of undemanding reading, Tocqueville's thoughts turned to memoirs covering the beginnings of the Revolution of 1789. Beaumont was asked to let him know of "interesting books *of any kind*" that might have recently appeared.[29] Adolphe de Circourt received a similar request in a letter sent the following day. With serious work being impossible, Tocqueville wrote, he was in need of books that would amuse without tiring him. He particularly liked good travel books, he told Circourt, books that told him about "the different countries of the world." New discoveries in Africa excited his curiosity in particular, as, he continued, did anything to do with the Far East, Siberia, and recent Russian conquests in the Pacific Ocean.[30] Tocqueville's publisher, Michel Lévy, received a request for books from his catalogue.

When Tocqueville next wrote to Beaumont two weeks later it was to report that he was feeling much better and that the weather was now wonderful. He was able to go out for walks, which helped his appetite, and eating was giving him back some of his strength. He also reported that he was very happy with the house he had rented, very much feeling at home among the orange and olive trees with the sea nearby. "It is," he wrote, "a very lovely location."[31] However, to this he added that "no location is lovely to live in for an ill body and a sad soul." If his friend had seen him in some very painful circumstances, Tocqueville told Beaumont, none was as "cruel" as the situation he now found himself in. Upon his arrival in Cannes, he explained, he had been so exhausted that he had believed he would die.[32] To make matters worse, the two servants he and his wife had taken on were pretty much useless.[33] Worse still, his wife, Mary, was also very ill, both physically and emotionally. According to Tocqueville, she had lost half her weight since they had left Paris. Here he was, he told Beaumont, at the end of the world, in a place that no one passed through, without friends, with no living parents, and with brothers who had let him leave Paris on a terrible journey without any thought of accompanying him. It was hard, he commented, not to feel downcast and bitter.[34]

Over the next few weeks, and into December, Tocqueville continued to report that his own heath was improving, even if only slowly.[35] Briefly, at least, the Mediterranean sunshine had reappeared, and Tocqueville had been able to get out and to walk as much as his diminished strength allowed. If this continued, he told François Mignet, he thought that he might be fit enough to leave Cannes in the spring.[36] His spirits had also been raised by the appearance of his brother Hippolyte, who was now to stay with him on and off for the next few months. No letter Tocqueville wrote was complete without a medical bulletin, all of which indicated that exercise and fresh air were getting his body back in working order, that his stomach (always a key indicator to his general health, he reminded Beaumont) was functioning well, and that the problem with his bronchial tubes was certainly no worse, if not slightly improved. He was now able to read during the day, and in the evening a young seminarist came to read to him for a couple of hours (albeit with a strong Provençal accent and accompanied by his mother). The downsides were insomnia and a need constantly to rest his voice. Tocqueville also remained deeply worried about his wife, who had now developed a problem with her larynx necessitating painful treatment and long periods of silence.[37] So, too, he admitted to being bored, but, he told Ampère, it was the thought of walking through the mountains and being cured that sustained him through his convalescence.[38]

For all of Tocqueville's understandable concern and self-pity, his letters still displayed a strong interest in the well-being of his friends. In Beaumont's case, Tocqueville sought to convince him (correctly) that he should agree to write an introduction to what would be a new edition of Beaumont's book on Ireland. As for Corcelle, Tocqueville busied himself (successfully) from the autumn of 1858 through to the spring of the following year with ironing out obstacles to the marriage of his daughter Marthe to Adolphe Pineton de Chambrun, a man initially thought not to be suitable by the Corcelles. Tocqueville also continued to show a fatherly interest in the affairs of Edward Lee Childe, a worthless individual who clearly had no more ambition than to live off the considerable wealth of his American father. He wrote sympathetically to Ampère, gracefully accepting that the latter's emotional (if entirely platonic) attachment to the invalid Louise Guillemin kept him in Rome. Despite the distance that now existed between them, Tocqueville continued to correspond intermittently with Louis de Kergorlay, telling him at the end of November that for all of the differences in the lives they led Kergorlay remained "the only person" who fully understood the way he thought. Tocqueville also continued to concern himself with the well-being of the son of his cousin, Eugénie de Grancey, then serving with the French Army in Indochina. Beaumont and Corcelle offered to join Tocqueville in Cannes but, in both cases, they were told that their presence was not required.

Tocqueville's situation seemingly continued to improve into late December. If he complained to Edward Lee Childe that he found his "intellectual solitude" a cause of increasing "listlessness," he reported to Beaumont on 24 December that, if not cured, he was certainly much improved. He was sleeping well and had regained his appetite. His stomach was in better shape than it had been for the past year. The weather, too, was "almost always magnificent," with the result that he was able to walk for two hours on most days. That said, the bronchial problems persisted and, if he coughed less frequently, on occasions there were still small amounts of blood in his spit. This, Tocqueville admitted, frightened him terribly. Still, Tocqueville told Beaumont, his doctor assured him that he would leave Cannes completely recovered.

It was also the case that Madame de Tocqueville was much improved, although from what Tocqueville said it seems that even now she could barely speak and had great difficulty walking. Tocqueville's brother Hippolyte was also still there, even if Tocqueville wondered how he managed to put up with what he was having to endure. For the most part he found himself sitting between two mutes and the long evenings, from which he rarely exempted himself, were crushingly boring. Fortunately, Tocqueville reported, Hippolyte had found some people from Parisian society ("a senator, a deputy, [and even] an imperial chamberlain") in Cannes with whom he could go on long walks.[39] If there was one thing that annoyed Tocqueville it was reports in the press that he was gravely ill. This, he wrote to one of his correspondents in Normandy, a M. Lemoigne Dutaillis, was quite definitely not the case, and his doctor assured him that "next summer [he] would return completely cured to Tocqueville." "Let us hope," he concluded, "that heaven hears our prayers."[40]

This appears to have remained Tocqueville's view until early March, when, in some desperation and distress, he wrote to Beaumont urging him to make his way to Cannes as quickly as possible. Prior to this, Tocqueville had had a considerable setback during January, and so much so that he was not even fit enough to write to his friends. Such had been the pain, Tocqueville told Beaumont in mid-February, that he had not been able either to eat or sleep for three weeks and he had spat blood for ten days. To make matters worse, Tocqueville had also had a bladder infection.[41] Yet all the notes sent to his friends and family from early February onwards reported that he was again on the mend, that his appetite and physical strength were returning, and, most welcome of all, that his doctors assured him that there had been "extraordinary progress" with his bronchial problems. Indeed, Tocqueville was being told that a full recovery could be expected within three months. Moreover, the delightful spring weather was just what was needed for convalescence, and he was starting to go outdoors. He was, Tocqueville told Corcelle, like "a lizard in the sun."[42] He was reading again—he told Pierre Freslon that he been reading the memoirs of Miot de Mèlitot as well as Gibbon's *Autobiography*[43]—and once more he asked Circourt for suggested reading on politics and literature. Tocqueville also received a copy of *On Liberty* from John Stuart Mill, to whom he not only expressed his sincere thanks but also his condolences at the news of the death of Mill's wife.[44]

Not everything gave such cause for optimism and hope, however. Tocqueville continued to worry that his doctors were not telling him the truth. As he told his brother Édouard, he was still suffering from insomnia and constipation. Most of all, Tocqueville remained very concerned about his wife's well-being. If her throat problem was getting better, she remained ill and (from the sound of it) very depressed.[45] Tocqueville was also irritated that someone had declared that he had been too ill to receive letters. "The letters of my friends," he told Corcelle, "are my sole consolation and the only intellectual pleasure allowed me."[46] On 3 March Tocqueville wrote to Ampère in Rome to say that there was absolutely no need for him to make the journey to Cannes. The January crisis has passed, and there was nothing for Ampère to be worried about.[47] Two days later, a letter to Circourt indicated that he was receiving a certain number of foreign visitors. This, he commented, did much to extend his horizons.[48] On 8 March he also wrote a long letter to Horace Hammond, British Consul in Cherbourg, about the likelihood of war between France and Austria.[49] On 10 March Tocqueville told Victor Lanjuinais that he was on his way to a full recovery.[50]

For all that, on 4 March Tocqueville had already written to Beaumont, pleading with him to come to Cannes. His brother Hippolyte had now left, and his other brother, Édouard, staying with his wife in nearby Nice, was about to do the same. Tocqueville and his wife were thus alone, and he was frightened by the condition his wife was now in. "She is ill," Tocqueville wrote, "more ill than she has been for a month; it is clear that she is reaching the limit of her physical and *moral* strength." He had no idea where this might lead. You alone, Tocqueville told his friend, "can put us back on track," with "your gaiety, your courage, your high spirits, the complete knowledge you have of us and of our affairs." Tocqueville knew that he was asking a lot of Beaumont but, he thought, a couple of weeks in Cannes would be all that was needed. He begged Beaumont not to be too angry with someone who was imposing such a heavy burden upon him, but think rather "of the unhappy man, the friend of more than thirty years, who fears all kinds of misfortune if you do not come to his aid." Lest Beaumont be unsure about what to do next, Tocqueville then informed him that it was best to take the train from Paris to Marseilles (a journey of nineteen hours) and then the coach for Nice, which would get him to Cannes in twenty-three hours. A cab would take Beaumont from the town to their house for forty sous.[51] Beaumont arrived on 11 March.

From this point onwards, the number of letters sent and received by Tocqueville was considerably diminished and the primary source of information on his last weeks is to be found in the letters sent by Beaumont to his wife, Clémentine.[52] Beaumont had clearly been very worried about Tocqueville's health and what was happening in Cannes from early January onwards. What concerned him most was the silence and absence of information. Towards the end of the month he was able to speak to Émilie de Tocqueville in Paris and her comments, based on daily letters from her husband Hippolyte, only served to confirm his worries. "He no longer goes out at all, two nuns sit up at his bedside, and he no longer utters a single word," Beaumont wrote.[53] Tocqueville had subsequently shown some improvement during February, but Beaumont must have arrived in Cannes in early March with a sense of deep foreboding, and, as it turned out, with just cause.

"I do not know if my first impressions deceive me," Beaumont wrote to his wife on the day after his arrival, "but I have, alas, been deeply saddened by them." Any thought that Tocqueville's wish to see him had been either overzealous or the mere flattery of a friend was to be discounted immediately. His journey was not only justified but necessary. "My arrival alone," Beaumont continued, "caused him such emotion that he was unable to speak to me for some moments, finding only tears and sobs to show his joy at seeing me. Just now he was telling me that he felt himself to be dying of sadness and isolation, and that in coming I had saved his life." Already Beaumont had his doubts about whether this would be possible. He had spoken to Tocqueville's doctors immediately and, although they had not given up hope of a recovery, they did not hide the gravity of the situation. From what they told him, Tocqueville had one damaged lung, and problems with his stomach and digestive tract, as well as with his chest and nerves. He also had a constant fever. "At night," Beaumont wrote, "the invalid always has a nun close to him, he does not cough up blood, but he coughs frequently, and his spittle is not free of pus." No doctor in the world,

Beaumont added, would not struggle with such a situation. Fortunately, Beaumont reported, the nuns were looking after Tocqueville well—they were, he wrote, polite and intelligent, and their care was enlightened—but he had quickly understood that Madame de Tocqueville required as much care as her husband.[54] She had therefore agreed to let Beaumont take over some of the housekeeping duties. Beaumont also convinced her that there was no possibility that she and her husband could return to Normandy. He read to them during the day, and when guests came—for example, Lord Brougham and Christian von Bunsen[55]—Beaumont struck up a conversation to interest and distract his friends.[56]

The bleakness and desperation of the situation was not slow in dawning on Beaumont. "I find it hard to hope," Beaumont told Clémentine, "when I see an ill so deep." "The misfortune," he wrote a day later on 14 March, "goes beyond all that one can imagine; the future is dark; and the present is of a devastating sadness." Mornings were spent dealing with the primary care of the "invalid." The doctors visited. Lunch took place. If fine weather allowed, a short walk followed. The post and newspapers arrived in the late afternoon, followed by callers who were received if Tocqueville was up to it. Dinner was at 6:00 p.m., but, Beaumont wrote, "come the evening, it is like the grave." Tocqueville, he wrote, "tries not to fall asleep, dozes off constantly, and makes an effort to wake up, fearing that early slumbers will harm the night's sleep." "I believe," Beaumont told Clémentine, "that I am doing some good, but one has the feeling of battling against the impossible."[57]

Beaumont worked hard at trying to improve Madame de Tocqueville's mental state—it would be a great help, he told his wife, if she could recover her voice—and also set about trying to find a young doctor who might be willing to join the Tocquevilles in Cannes and act as both Tocqueville's doctor and a secretary who could read to him, take down dictation, and so on. Such a person would bring some life and company to the house.[58] Beaumont also saw that it was an "immense misfortune" that the Tocquevilles did not have children. For the rest, it was a question of watching over both Tocqueville and his wife and doing his best to comfort both as best he could.[59]

At times this proved well nigh impossible. Writing on 16 March, Beaumont commented that possibly Tocqueville's biggest weakness as an invalid was a lack of patience.[60] It was alien to his temperament and, due to his incapacity to display it, he only harmed himself. "He is restless and torments himself," Beaumont told his wife. "He wants to go outside," he continued, "as soon as he is indoors, and wants to return inside as soon as he had gone out; he wants to read but is not strong enough to do so, and wants to be read to but cannot listen; he becomes impatient when we talk and disturb him, then loses patience even more when we are silent near him; as he is in an almost continual state of somnolence, he would like to be kept awake, yet he is irritated when we wake him." Everyone—including the nuns and the servants—found Tocqueville difficult to deal with, but especially Marie de Tocqueville. "Madame de Tocqueville opened her heart to me at one point," Beaumont wrote on 21 March. She was, he reported, "absolutely discouraged, worn out, exhausted, overwhelmed and unfortunately a little detached from her poor husband, whose condition has taken more strength from her than she can give. She spoke to me with despair of her desire to be dead; it is her desire to escape everything; she sees her husband ardently wishing to live; all her own desire is to see him end before he crushes her." Beaumont's fear was that Madame de Tocqueville would not be able to bear it for much longer and, as he put it, "her head will crack."[61]

Some days started better and looked more promising than others. At times, there were signs of recovery and Tocqueville appeared healthier. He was able to walk for up to thirty minutes, even though he was reduced to "walking as slowly as a ninety-year-old." On occasions Tocqueville was able to speak and he coughed less. If he had an appetite, he complained that the food always tasted bitter. He was alternatively despondent and hopeful (even talking about working on the second volume of his book on the French Revolution). Yet, the pain suffered by Tocqueville was continually evident and, for all that Beaumont acted as though he had complete confidence in the future, he saw no detectable signs of progress in Tocqueville's condition. "It is with good reason," Beaumont wrote to Clémentine, "that it is called consumption; for there is a daily dwindling of strength, without any corresponding restoration." When Beaumont asked Dr. Maure what hope of a recovery there might be, he gloomily compared Tocqueville to a ruined man with only twenty francs to his name and who plays it on the lottery. "He could win a castle," Maure stated, "but the chances are one in a thousand."[62] When Beaumont hinted that he might return to Paris, the idea produced what he described as a "nervous convulsion" in Tocqueville and the idea was quietly and quickly dropped.[63]

On 23 and 24 March, Beaumont's letters to his wife reported some minor improvement. Tocqueville had had several good nights. He had a stronger appetite and felt less weak when walking. He was coughing less. Just as welcome was an improvement in the condition of Madame de Tocqueville. She had started to speak again, was almost fully rested, and her spirits were lifted. The weather too was kind. For light relief, they read Edmond About's *Le roi des montagnes,* a tale of a young German botanist and two English women kidnapped by brigands in Greece. Tocqueville still seemed unaware of the gravity or nature of his illness. For all the "unimaginable" unhappiness of the Tocquevilles, Beaumont wrote, "I sometimes find my hopes returning." In eight to ten days, he told his wife, he thought the Tocquevilles would be "back on course."[64]

All changed the following day. Tocqueville had slept well, but that morning he started coughing up blood again. Suddenly the end seemed nearer, although the doctor managed to convince Tocqueville that the blood had come not from his lungs but from a nasal cavity. When Beaumont asked him how long Tocqueville might have left, he replied "a few months." Tocqueville himself was terrified and spent the entire day in a state of depression. He told one of the nuns caring for him that, if he vomited blood again, he feared it would be the end of him. Beaumont had never seen Tocqueville so low, reporting to his wife that at most he was eating soup with a fresh egg and that, if he got out of bed, he did not leave his room. In these unfortunate circumstances, Beaumont told Clémentine, he could not contemplate leaving.[65]

The next day was no worse, but no better, although Tocqueville was calmer. As Beaumont contemplated this "abyss of sadness and distress," he again was led to wonder whether his presence had been of benefit. On Sunday, 27 March, he hurried off to mass so as to be back with the Tocquevilles by lunchtime.[66] The next day, Tocqueville seemed worse and the doctor ordered stronger doses of laudanum, reducing Tocqueville to a soporific and lethargic state and even greater depression. By 30 March there had been further decline, Beaumont reporting that Tocqueville had spent his time trying to find a physical position which would make his sufferings less intolerable. Tocqueville's doctor now confirmed that his life was "hanging on a thread." Tocqueville appeared, Beaumont told his wife, "more dead than alive," "the fatal claws of death" being visible on his face. Most people, he thought, would have given up on life by this point. Even the weather now became unfavourable, with violent storms during the night. "Maybe some divine grace," Beaumont wrote, "might be able to give us another one to two months."[67]

From then on, the day's ambition was to make it to the evening, Tocqueville weakening a little more every day, moving at most from one armchair to another. Tocqueville's brother Édouard briefly came over from Nice, but he proved to be more of a hindrance than a help. It would "be breaking the habit of a lifetime," Beaumont wrote, for Édouard to be of "any great assistance" to his brother and sister-in-law. Remarkably, Beaumont still hoped that they might win some time, and he remained resolved not to fail in his duty to his friend. "I go straight in front of me," he told Clémentine, "with no other plan but to do each day what shows itself to be necessary."[68] Nonetheless, on 1 April he reported that disease now devoured Tocqueville, and that he seemed to be "becoming extinguished little by little." He ate almost nothing. Beaumont now considered Tocqueville to be "lost" and it was therefore for Madame de Tocqueville, he told his wife, that he stayed on, so "alone and abandoned" was she.[69] Tocqueville's doctors still continued to deceive him about the seriousness of his condition.[70] In Beaumont's opinion, Madame de Tocqueville also did not see that disaster was imminent. The search for a secretary-cum-doctor went on.[71]

On 4 April Édouard de Tocqueville arrived with his wife with the intention of staying with his brother and sister-in-law. Édouard's son, Hubert, planned to arrive in the next few days. As Beaumont reported to his wife, they "gently" pressed him to return home, knowing full well that he had problems to deal with under his own "roof."[72] Having promised to recall him if there was the slightest need and with the blessing of Tocqueville and his wife, Beaumont agreed to leave Cannes immediately and return to Paris, which, as he told Tocqueville in what was to be his last letter to him, he passed through "like a bullet." Despite this haste, Beaumont appears to have had enough time to find a young "*sécretaire-médecin*" by the name of Thadée Dujardin-Beaumetz, who arrived in Cannes on 10 April. Beaumont's letter assured Tocqueville that he would be pleased by the qualities of this new recruit (to which Beaumont added that he was jealous of the person who had replaced him and that he thought constantly of their time together in Cannes).

As ever, Beaumont sought to strike an optimistic note, assuring Tocqueville that with the arrival of the fine spring weather his strength would quickly return.[73] One cannot begin to imagine the torments suffered by Beaumont.

On 10 April, Lord Brougham wrote to Henry Reeve to say that he had spoken with Dr. Sève, who had indicated that it was now only "a matter of days." So, he told Reeve, "all is nearly over."[74] This proved to be true. Tocqueville died on 16 April 1859. He had written his very last letter to Ampère on 9 April, asking him to come to Cannes and indicating that he could no longer put one foot in front of another.[75] Ampère arrived in Marseilles the day after Tocqueville had died. Kergorlay arrived on the day that this letter was sent and was with Tocqueville at the end, along with Hippolyte and Édouard de Tocqueville. Madame de Tocqueville, according to a note written by Dujardin-Beaumetz to Francisque de Corcelle, did not leave her husband's bedside. "He remained calm," Dujardin-Beaumetz wrote, "was able to talk a little, listen to a short reading."[76] Towards late afternoon, Tocqueville passed away.

There has since been some uncertainty about the extent to which, on his deathbed, Tocqueville became reconciled to the Catholic faith of his youth. This confusion in part arises from Beaumont's later comment that "Tocqueville's end was as Christian as his life." People, Beaumont commented, "have spoken of conversion, and this is wrong; he did not have to convert, because there had never been the slightest trace of irreligion in him."[77] What seems certain is that Tocqueville did make confession and, that on 6 April, he received Communion, lying on his chaise longue. He made it known that he did so willingly, although undoubtedly after considerable encouragement from his wife. The account provided by Beaumont makes clear that Tocqueville did so on condition that it was understood that this did not mean that he was now prepared to accept all the dogmas of the Catholic Church.[78]

Tocqueville's coffin was taken to Paris and then to Tocqueville, in Normandy, where he was buried on 10 May. His grave was marked by a simple wooden cross.

In 1861, only two years after Tocqueville's death, Gustave de Beaumont published a two-volume collection entitled *Œuvres et correspondance inédites d'Alexis de Tocqueville.* A year later, the Boston publisher Ticknor and Fields published a slightly revised English-language version as *Memoir, Letters and Remains of Alexis de Tocqueville.*[79] As Andreas Hess has rightly argued, "this first edition of Tocqueville's unpublished writings and letters is both a declaration of admiration and deep friendship with the deceased and the portrait of a moral man." This was achieved not only through Beaumont's selection of Tocqueville's writings but also in the long introductory memoir provided by Beaumont where, to quote Hess again, "Man and work are not seen as separate but as one entity."[80] "We have tried," Beaumont wrote, "to paint the author, the philosopher, and the statesman, but who can paint the man himself, his heart, his grace, his poetical imagination, and at the same time his good sense?"[81] Nonetheless, this is precisely what Beaumont set out to do.

Tocqueville, Beaumont wrote, possessed not only great talents but a variety of them. He was as brilliant in conversation as he was as a writer. He also possessed, according to Beaumont, the even rarer talent of being a good listener. He chose his friends well and never lost a friendship. Moreover, Tocqueville found time for everything and, in Beaumont's words, "never omitted a duty or a social obligation." He had little regard for rank and a high regard for personal merit. Above all, "his only aim was the pursuit of truths useful to his fellow-creatures and no other ambition than to augment their welfare and their dignity." His, Beaumont wrote, was "a great intelligence united with a noble heart."[82]

To that end, Beaumont provided what was to be the first biographical sketch of Tocqueville's short life, beginning with a brief description of his upbringing and how he and Beaumont met, and ending with an account of the heartrending last days in Cannes. It is a portrait that confirms much of what we have seen in this volume. From his early days as a *juge auditeur* in Versailles, Tocqueville displayed not only the superiority of his mind but also "the rare faculty of generalisation." His political opinions were formed early, and seeing the democratic nature of the revolution that was sweeping through society, Tocqueville quickly realized that the fundamental question to be addressed was how to reconcile the equality that separated and isolated men with liberty and how to prevent the power generated by democracy from becoming tyrannical and despotic. Tocqueville was not an abstract or metaphysical thinker but someone whose speculations always had "a practical and definite objective." Indeed, Beaumont went so far as say that Tocqueville was "little versed" in philosophy and had little taste for its controversies. It was this practical bent to his intellect, Beaumont contended, that led Tocqueville to "consider the past as in so far as it related to the present and foreign peoples only with a view to his own country."[83]

Likewise, Tocqueville had little time for books reliant upon secondary sources and the opinions of others. He alone, he believed, possessed the key to the question he was seeking to answer, and this key was always to be found in the original sources. Beaumont also confirmed that if in America the two men conversed incessantly and thought "so much the same on all things," a division of labour quickly emerged, with Tocqueville giving himself up to the study of American institutions and Beaumont focusing upon the material that would inform his novel *Marie.*[84]

It was in this biographical memoir that Beaumont drew attention not only to Tocqueville's enthusiasm for travel but also to the manner in which he travelled. As he pointed out, Tocqueville was no ordinary traveller, but someone driven in his travels by the spirit of inquiry and investigation. Beaumont remarked that, for Tocqueville, there could be "no obstacle to a journey deemed necessary for his work, not even the preservation of his life."[85] This was undoubtedly true.

In making these remarks and by providing a wide selection of previously unpublished material, Beaumont's overt ambition was to present Tocqueville to the public in "a new light" and to introduce this public to a Tocqueville known previously only to his intimate friends. Thus, Beaumont began his first volume with extracts from Tocqueville's unpublished travel notes from Sicily. This was then followed by two other previously unpublished texts based loosely on Tocqueville and Beaumont's journey into the American wilderness, *Course au Lac Onéida* and *Quinze jours au désert.* Beaumont made the point that, once returned from America, Tocqueville did not limit his researches to French sources, journeying several times to Germany and England in search of primary research material. He also told his readers that, as Tocqueville was a man who "could not live without thinking, nor think without writing," he had left behind many unfinished manuscripts and that these included not only his notes on England but, most substantially of all, extensive commentary on British rule in India. Finally, Beaumont drew attention to Tocqueville's extensive private correspondence, a correspondence stretching in some cases over several decades and including correspondents not only from France but from across Europe and North America. Beaumont was in no doubt that Tocqueville excelled as a letter writer, his letters being on a par with anything that he had published during his lifetime. Published for the very first time, it was these letters, Beaumont wrote, that would make Tocqueville "known and loved as a man."[86]

Beaumont's achievement was immense. It was largely due to his editorial work, to cite Andreas Hess, that the foundations of much of Tocqueville's later "reception, celebration and reputation" would rest and, no less importantly, that "Tocqueville became the Tocqueville we know today."[87] The present volume has sought to build upon the picture presented by Beaumont by focusing upon the place of travel in both Tocqueville's life and in shaping his thinking. Accordingly, if it has examined Tocqueville's best-known and justly famous writings, *De la démocratie en Amérique* and *L'ancien régime et la révolution,* it has also concentrated on Tocqueville's notebooks; his correspondence with family, friends and public figures; his parliamentary speeches and reports; and what in his day remained unpublished manuscripts.

This book began by looking at why people travel and how they have travelled, seeking to explore the very different motivations and goals involved. As we saw, Tocqueville was typical of many travellers, past and present, whose motives were often various and not easily reconciled with each other. One thing that is striking about Tocqueville's travelling is the extent to which his sense of the need to travel conflicted with his feeling of loneliness when travelling and his desire to be home among familiar surroundings and those he loved. Another is the contrast between the physical determination he always displayed when travelling and his own physical frailties (which became ever more evident over time). Nor, for all that he tried, could Tocqueville always free himself from the cultural preconceptions and national prejudices that have bedevilled so many a traveller as they have tried to make sense of their new and alien surroundings.

So, too, do we need to take note of the fact that the nature of travel was transformed dramatically over the course of Tocqueville's lifetime. One example of this is found in the duration and character of the journey from Tocqueville's home in Normandy to the French capital. What began for him as a very uncomfortable and arduous two-day journey by stagecoach or boat had, by the end of his life, been transformed into a quite pleasant seven- or eight-hour journey by train (with, as we have seen, an enjoyable lunch on the way). If Tocqueville's most authentic experiences of the American wilderness were enjoyed on horseback or in a canoe, it remains the case that he travelled across much of America in the relative comfort of a paddle steamer. For all of that, as Tocqueville's many awful journeys at sea testify, in his day travel could still be something of a daunting and, at times terrifying and existential, challenge—none more so than his trip from France across the Atlantic. And, of course, Tocqueville was never to recover from the physical demands made upon him by his final misjudged journey from Paris to Cannes.

It is also the case that Tocqueville's travels coincided with the appearance of a nascent tourist industry and all the paraphernalia that went with it. As Beaumont commented in his memoir, "When Alexis de Tocqueville was travelling over North America to study its institutions, and to penetrate to the very heart of the people, an Englishman, the very pleasantest companion possible, was visiting the same country, with no other aim than to discover the varieties of game peculiar to the climate, and especially the different races of wild duck. There were also two very distinguished Frenchmen, whose society was very agreeable, looking for picturesque landscapes for portraits."[88] Tocqueville, in short, was far from being the only European to visit America, and the paths he trod up the Hudson River valley and to Niagara Falls were already well trodden by people from across the globe. Even the Sicily that Tocqueville visited in the 1820s was fast ceasing to be the legendary island of brigands. As for Cannes, for all that it remained a small fishing port, it had already been "discovered" by the English and by a few Russian aristocrats.

Yet, as Beaumont remarked, Tocqueville travelled "differently" from those for whom travel was merely an agreeable pastime and source of amusement, from those who saw nothing and were looking for nothing. For Tocqueville, travel was only ever a serious undertaking and something to be planned and prepared for with meticulous care and attention (even if those plans and preparations often went awry). He did not feel that he could write about another country without having been there and seen it, as best and as thoroughly as he could, with his own eyes. If this was true of America in particular, it was also most evidently the case with Algeria. Once arrived in a foreign country (and this, as we have seen, was true even on his honeymoon in Switzerland), Tocqueville applied himself with diligence and determination to meet as many people as he could and to see as many things as he could, taking meticulous notes and then working up these first impressions into more considered general observations and reflections. It was first impressions such as these that most famously provided the starting point for what became arguably the greatest and most influential book ever written about America.

Even in its published form, there remained ample evidence of the first person in Tocqueville's *De la démocratie en Amérique.* The same is true of Tocqueville's visits to both Algeria and England, where what he had seen was deployed to formulate and inform not books but policy recommendations and parliamentary reports about topics as varied as local government, Poor Law reform, and colonial expansion.

Travel therefore, as Beaumont again observed, was for Tocqueville never a matter of "mere vague curiosity." It always served a purpose. Yet, Tocqueville's journeys, when not imposed upon him by sheer necessity, were undoubtedly inspired by what at times appears as an almost insatiable inquisitiveness and sense of adventure. The most obvious example of this was Tocqueville's decision to head west as far as he could in search of the American wilderness. Much criticised by later commentators as a frivolous distraction, Beaumont argued that this journey (one that took up far more time that had been originally envisaged) had a "serious motive" arising from Tocqueville's awareness that "one of the first conditions of American prosperity" lay in the vast amounts of yet unoccupied space that lay before it and therefore that some "exploratory survey" of this land had to be made. This does not ring as being entirely true but, with his "mind full of memories" of Chateaubriand, there was no way that Tocqueville could ever have returned to France without seeing virgin forests, lone pioneers and, above all, American

Indians (for all that they had now been reduced to miserable wretches). In so doing, to cite Beaumont again, Tocqueville advanced "in the forest to the outer limit of civilisation."[89]

Clearly Tocqueville's journeys to Algeria fit into this picture of intrepid adventure. At the time of his visits, it was a country at war and Tocqueville did not hesitate to set out with the French Army into enemy territory. A less obvious case is found in Nassau Senior's description of Tocqueville striding out across the mountains behind Sorrento regardless of the physical obstacles in his way. We might also remember that, when still a young man, Tocqueville's family was very worried that his and Kergorlay's hike across the Swiss Alps would turn into a reckless disaster. As for examples of inquisitiveness, these are too numerous to mention, but wherever Tocqueville went it was never without his notebook and never without a set of questions that he was determined to answer and lists of people he sought to meet and speak with. One of the more charming (and least-known) examples must be the manner in which Tocqueville toured the farms owned by Lord Hatherton in England. Who, from a man who grappled with the most important and pressing political matters of the day, would have expected such genuine interest in pigs and pigsties and the use of guano? But such was the range of interests that this remarkable person encompassed. Travel also opened Tocqueville's eyes to the iniquities of the world. Foremost among these were the poverty and oppression he saw visited upon the Catholic inhabitants of Ireland, the brutal and relentless destruction of the Native American peoples, and, of course, the enslavement of America's Black population. Those eyes, it can be argued, were opened less than they should have been when confronted with French colonisation of Algeria and the violence this inevitably involved. So, too, did Tocqueville's perambulations around the streets of Paris evoke little sympathy for the plight of the Parisian poor.

However, as Seymour Drescher has commented, Tocqueville's "appetite for personal observation far exceeded his life's itinerary."[90] This serves to explain why Tocqueville never published serious studies of either India or Russia, two countries that fascinated him over a period of decades but which he was never able to visit. What he could not see with his own eyes, Tocqueville tried to make up for by reading travel literature (something he often did with his wife by the fireside on a winter's evening, up until the end of his life). If friends, for example, Beaumont and Kergorlay, were visiting foreign countries, he solicited them for information, advising them how best they might make use of their visit and the questions they ought to be asking. In both cases, he actively encouraged their respective interests in Ireland and Germany. Tocqueville's letters to friends and acquaintances in the United States constantly asked for information about the most recent political and economic developments there. He took great pleasure from hearing Ampère recount his own voyage around America. Many of the friendships made by Tocqueville—for example, with Nassau Senior and George Cornewall Lewis—came as a result of his travels, as did his close association with those Americans with whom he continued a correspondence for well over twenty years. Moreover, Tocqueville was not slow in developing a sense of self-identification with the places he visited. This was especially true of America and England, both of which he regarded as second homelands. And, of course, Tocqueville was strongly of the view that to understand a country properly and from the inside one had to learn the language (a commitment that caused him hours of toil and anguish). Most importantly of all, travel underpinned the most serious and sustained of Tocqueville's intellectual endeavours.

There is much that can be said and has been said about what Tocqueville himself came to describe as his "new science of politics." One of its oddities is that Tocqueville largely chose to ignore texts written by other authors on the subjects he was writing about. This included books about the United States such as that written by Michel Chevalier. More seriously, critics have argued that Tocqueville's analysis of America was at best superficial and impressionistic, and from this it has been concluded that an absence of methodological rigour on Tocqueville's part is sufficient to cast doubt on the objectivity and validity of any conclusions or recommendation he might have reached not only about the United States but about other countries.

This book has contested this claim, arguing that Tocqueville approached his inquiries with a level of methodological self-awareness and sophistication that was unusual for the age and certainly unusual for the subject matter under discussion. But even if this were not the case, it would not undermine the argument that travel for Tocqueville was a lifelong undertaking and one not limited, as might easily and incorrectly be believed, to a single visit to the United States as a young man. Moreover, a focus on Tocqueville's travels enables us to see that a large proportion of his writings are structured around an extensive set of comparisons between the countries he knew and visited and those whose pasts he studied. Of these the most striking are the core comparisons between France and the United States and between France and the Anglo-American world more generally. There are many others; the comparisons between England and Ireland, and Canada and America, being just two. The comparison of American and Swiss democracy is another. So, too, it could be argued that the conclusions Tocqueville reached about the French experience in Algeria were informed, often explicitly, by a comparison with the British imperial experience in India and elsewhere. As we have seen, a similar emphasis and reliance upon comparison was evident in Tocqueville's historical writings and was given its clearest statement in his remark, quoted above, that "whoever has studied and seen only France will never understand anything about the French Revolution." It was for this reason that Tocqueville went to Germany to study its feudal constitution and to England to find what amounted to an alternative history—one of the preservation and the flourishing of liberty—to that of France.

None of these comparisons were peripheral to Tocqueville's intellectual preoccupations. All served to help him grapple with what he considered to be the central questions he sought to answer, and those questions themselves were about a journey. Time and time again in his writings Tocqueville resorted to the metaphor of travel, frequently casting himself as a traveller crossing from one shore of a river to another and, perhaps most famously of all, as one who leaves the walls of a great city to climb a nearby hill in order to gain a clearer view of the whole. That whole, as he described it in *De la démocratie en Amérique,* was of "the whole future of the English race in the New World," but, in truth, Tocqueville's view took in more than this. What as a traveller he observed was itself a journey: the journey not just of American society but of European societies more generally from inequality to equality and from aristocracy to democracy. Once begun, as Tocqueville saw, it was a journey that could not be stopped or reversed and that could at best only be modified and moderated.

In short, travelling with Alexis de Tocqueville helps us to understand not only the man and his ideas but also much about our past and, as the America he so admired seemingly disintegrates before our eyes, quite probably our future.

APPENDIX: Reading Tocqueville

NOTES

ACKNOWLEDGEMENTS

INDEX

Appendix: Reading Tocqueville

TOCQUEVILLE IN ENGLISH TRANSLATION

Throughout this volume, I have almost exclusively quoted French texts of Tocqueville's writings, but ample English resources exist. Most English-language publications concern Tocqueville's visit to America and his later reflections on the French Revolution. Thus, relatively little of Tocqueville's extensive correspondence is available.

In recent years several new editions of *Democracy in America* have been published by the University of Chicago Press, Penguin, and the Library of America (the latter translated by Arthur Goldhammer). The most complete text, containing Tocqueville's extensive notes now held at Yale University's Beinecke Rare Books and Manuscript Library, is that edited by Eduardo Nolla and translated by James T. Schleifer and published by the Liberty Fund in 2009 in four majestic volumes with continuous pagination. This edition was originally published by Vrin in Paris in 1990. The Liberty Fund edition is a bilingual edition and the product of many years of dedicated scholarship.

Similarly, there have been several editions of Tocqueville's text on the ancien régime and the French Revolution, published under a variety of titles. The first edition I owned was published by Doubleday in 1955, and Oxford University Press published another in 1988. The most recent edition was translated by Alan S. Kahan and edited by François Furet and Françoise Mélonio. It appears in two volumes as *The Old Regime and the Revolution* (Chicago, 1998–2001).

Among recent editions of Tocqueville in English, several merit special mention for both their quality and their relevance to the subject matter of this book. These include two volumes edited by Olivier Zunz and translated by Arthur Goldhammer: *Alexis de Tocqueville and Gustave de Beaumont in America: Their Friendship and Their Travels* (Charlottesville, VA, 2011), and *Recollections: The French Revolution of 1848 and Its Aftermath* (Charlottesville, VA, 2016). *Writings on Empire and Slavery,* edited and translated by Jennifer Pitts (Baltimore, 2001), remains an invaluable source for those interested in Tocqueville's views on Algeria, and *Journeys to England and Ireland,* edited by J.-P. Mayer, translated by George Lawrence and K. P. Mayer (New Haven, CT, 1958), endures as the classic edition of Tocqueville's travels in those lands. English translations of other works by Tocqueville and by Tocqueville and Beaumont follow.

Beaumont and Tocqueville

On the Penitentiary System in the United States and Its Application in France, edited by Thorsten Sellin, translated by Francis Lieber (Carbondale, IL, 1964).

Tocqueville and Beaumont on Social Reform, edited and translated by Seymour Drescher (New York, 1968).

Tocqueville

The "European Revolution" and Correspondence with Gobineau, edited and translated by John Lukacs (Garden City, NY, 1959).

Recollections, edited by J.-P. Mayer and A. P. Kerr, translated by George Lawrence (New York, 1971).

Alexis de Tocqueville: Selected Letters on Politics and Society, edited by Roger Boesche and translated by James Toupin and Roger Boesche (Berkeley, CA, 1985).

Memoir on Pauperism, edited by Gertrude Himmelfarb and translated by Seymour Drescher (Chicago, 1997).

The Tocqueville Reader: A Life in Letters and Politics, edited by Olivier Zunz and Alan S. Kahan (Oxford, 2002).

Tocqueville on America after 1840: Letters and Other Writings, edited and translated by Aurelian Craiutu and Jeremy Jennings (New York, 2009).

Letters from America, edited and translated by Frederick Brown (New Haven, CT, 2012).

TOCQUEVILLE IN FRENCH

The first edition of Tocqueville's writings was edited by Gustave de Beaumont as *Œuvres et correspondance inédites d'Alexis de Tocqueville* (Paris, 1861), 2 vols. A revised version was almost immediately published in the United States and Great Britain as *Memoir, Letters and Remains of Alexis de Tocqueville.* Subsequent to this, Beaumont and Mme. de Tocqueville edited the *Œuvres complètes d'Alexis de Tocqueville* (Paris, 1864–1866), 9 vols.

Gallimard's publication of the *Œuvres, papiers et correspondances* is all-encompassing, spanning seventy years, from 1951 to 2021. It includes:

Œuvres Complètes I: *De la démocratie en Amérique* (Paris, 1951), 2 vols.

Œuvres Complètes II: *L'ancien régime et la révolution* (Paris, 1952), 2 vols.

Œuvres Complètes III: *Écrits et discours politiques* (Paris, 1962, 1985, 1990), 3 vols.

Œuvres Complètes IV: *Écrits sur le système pénitentiaire en France et à l'étranger* (Paris, 1984), 2 vols.

Œuvres Complètes V (1): *Voyages en Sicilie et aux États-Unis* (Paris, 1957).

Œuvres Complètes V (2): *Voyages en Angleterre, Irlande, Suisse et Algérie* (Paris, 1958).

Œuvres Complètes VI (1): *Correspondance anglaise: Correspondance avec Henry Reeve et John Stuart Mill* (Paris, 1954).

Œuvres Complètes VI (2): *Correspondance anglaise: Correspondance et conversations d'Alexis de Tocqueville et Nassau William Senior* (Paris, 1991).

Œuvres Complètes VI (3): *Correspondance anglaise* (Paris, 2003).

Œuvres Complètes VII: *Correspondance étrangere: Amérique, Europe continentale* (Paris, 1986).

Œuvres Complètes VIII: *Correspondance d'Alexis de Tocqueville et de Gustave de Beaumont* (Paris, 1967), 3 vols.

Œuvres Complètes IX: *Correspondance d'Alexis de Tocqueville et d'Arthur de Gobineau* (Paris, 1959).

Œuvres Complètes X: *Correspondance et écrits locaux* (Paris, 1995).

Œuvres Complètes XI: *Correspondance d'Alexis de Tocqueville avec P.-P. Royer-Collard et avec J.-J. Ampère* (Paris, 1970).

Œuvres Complètes XII: *Souvenirs* (Paris, 1964).

Œuvres Complètes XIII: *Correspondance d'Alexis de Tocqueville et de Louis de Kergorlay* (Paris, 1977), 2 vols.

Œuvres Complètes XIV: *Correspondance familiale* (Paris, 1998).

Œuvres Complètes XV: *Correspondance d'Alexis de Tocqueville et de Francisque de Corcelle; Correspondance d'Alexis de Tocqueville et de Madame de Swetchine* (Paris, 1983), 2 vols.

Œuvres Complètes XVI: *Mélanges* (Paris, 1989).

Œuvres Complètes XVII: *Correspondance à divers* (Paris, 2021), 3 vols.

Œuvres Complètes XVIII: *Correspondance d'Alexis de Tocqueville avec Adolphe de Circourt et avec Madame de Circourt* (Paris, 1983).

Three volumes of Tocqueville's works have been published by the prestigious Bibliothèque de la Pléiade: *Œuvres,* vol. 1 (Paris, 1991) contains Tocqueville's travel notes (from Sicily, America, Switzerland, and Algeria); his notes on India; and a representative selection of political writings and speeches. *Œuvres,* vol. 2 (Paris, 1992) contains the text of *De la démocratie en Amérique* plus extensive notes. *Œuvres,* vol. 3 (Paris, 2004) contains the two volumes of *L'ancien régime et la révolution* and *Souvenirs.*

Also useful is *Lettres choisies; Souvenirs,* edited by Françoise Mélonio and Laurence Guellec (Paris, 2004). As the title suggests, this volume contains not only the text of the *Souvenirs* but also a very extensive selection of Tocqueville's private correspondence with a wide range of correspondents.

Notes

1. EMBARKING

1. Sara Wheeler, *O My America! Second Acts in the New World* (London, 2013), 7.

2. Cheryl B. Welch, "Tocqueville in the Twenty-First Century," in *The Cambridge Companion to Tocqueville,* ed. Cheryl B. Welch (New York, 2006), 1–20.

3. Robert D. Putnam, *Bowling Alone: The Collapse and Revival of American Community* (New York, 2000), 24; Dana Vila, "Tocqueville and Civil Society," in Welch, ed., *The Cambridge Companion,* 216–44.

4. See Jon Elster, *Alexis de Tocqueville, the First Social Scientist* (Cambridge, 2009).

5. *De la démocratie en Amérique* is tome I of Tocqueville's *Œuvres complètes* (Paris, 1961). Other French editions are available, including volume 2 of Tocqueville's *Œuvres,* published by the Bibliothèque de la Pléiade (Paris, 1992). There are several English language editions, but I use the Liberty Fund edition, *Democracy in America,* ed. Eduardo Nolla and trans. James T. Schleifer (Indianapolis, 2010), which is a bilingual edition, with both the French and English texts having the same pagination; the reference here is to page 3. Hereafter, aside from the Liberty Fund edition of *Democracy in America,* all translations are my own. Henceforth, volumes of the *Œuvres Complètes* will be cited as *OC.* For bibliographical details, see the Appendix.

6. There are two standard biographies of Tocqueville: André Jardin, *Tocqueville: A Biography* (Baltimore, 1998); and Hugh Brogan, *Alexis de Tocqueville: Prophet of Democracy in the Age of Revolution* (London, 2006). A third must now be added to this list: Olivier Zunz, *The Man Who Understood Democracy: The Life of Alexis de Tocqueville* (Princeton, NJ, 2022).

7. Tocqueville used the charming word *gentilhommière;* Tocqueville to Lord Hatherton, 15 July 1857, in *OC,* VI (3), 246. Two English guests left vivid descriptions of the château and its environs. Henry Reeve wrote, "This château is only about two and a half miles from the sea, but the wisdom of three hundred years ago placed it in a valley instead of on the height, and one has five miles to walk for the views. . . . [T]he charm of the view, wood and water is indescribable. . . . [T]he population here have been little affected by chances and changes, and retain their picturesque dresses and primitive habits." Henry Reeve, quoted in John Knox Laughton, *Memoirs of the Life and Correspondence of Henry Reeve,* 2 vols. (London, 1898), 1:371–72. Writing shortly after Tocqueville's death in 1859, Minnie Senior (M. C. M. Simpson) was similarly taken by what she saw. The château, she wrote, "was built of granite, the modern part in the time of Louis XIII. The rest is very ancient, especially three round towers. . . . The park consists of about thirty acres, and is traversed by a fine avenue leading to the front of the house. To the west the ground rises to a wild common overlooking the sea and a green plain covered with trees and hedgerows, and studded with picturesque towers and spires of the eleventh, twelfth and thirteen centuries." M. C. M. Simpson, *Many Memories of Many People* (London, 1898), 62–63.

8. Tocqueville to Madame Swetchine, 26 February 1857, in *OC,* XV (2), 313–16. The relatively brief correspondence between Tocqueville and Madame de Swetchine, beginning in 1855, amounts to an extended discussion of Tocqueville's sense of doubt and uncertainty in the world and his sense of alienation from the society in which he lived; see *OC,* XV (2), 245–324.

9. Brogan, *Alexis de Tocqueville,* 278.

10. Tocqueville to Mrs. Sarah Austin, 26 November 1835, in *OC,* VI (3), 49–50. Tocqueville made a similar remark in a letter to Francisque de Corcelle, 12 April 1835, in *OC,* XV (1), 52–54.

11. Tocqueville to John Stuart Mill, 18 December 1840, in *OC,* VI (1), 330. In a letter written to the aged politician and philosopher Pierre-Paul Royer-Collard, Tocqueville wrote that the second volume of *De la démocratie en Amérique* would be "much more about the general effects of equality on mores than about the particular effects that equality has produced in America." He wondered whether this would be "a flaw" and whether his readers would follow him onto this new terrain, acknowledging that, if this was a flaw, it was now irreparable; Tocqueville to P.-P. Royer-Collard, 30 August 1838, in *OC,* XI, 71. Subsequent to the publication of the second volume, Tocqueville told Royer-Collard that it was "little read and badly understood"; Tocqueville to P.-P. Royer-Collard, 15 August 1840, in *OC,* XI, 92.

12. See Ross Carroll, "The Hidden Labors of Mary Mottley, Madame de Tocqueville," *Hypatia,* no. 33 (2018): 643–62. Carroll argues that Mary Mottley did not confine herself to "domestic-management and emotional-support" roles, acting rather as "Tocqueville's political and intellectual interlocutor" (643). According to Carroll, Tocqueville saw his marriage to his wife as a fusion of both hearts and minds. To Tocqueville's great regret, he and his wife had no children. It should be noted that Mary Mottley converted to Catholicism shortly before her marriage.

13. That Tocqueville felt deeply ill at ease in the world of politics receives ample confirmation in a long letter he wrote to Royer-Collard in 1841. "I feel," Tocqueville wrote, "an almost insuperable repugnance towards associating myself in a permanent way with any of the politicians of our day and, as for the parties which divide our country, there is not one with which I would care to establish a link"; Tocqueville to P.-P. Royer-Collard, 27 September 1841, in *OC,* XI, 108.

14. Tocqueville to Édouard de Tocqueville, 7 December 1851, in *OC,* XIV, 272.

15. Tocqueville, *Souvenirs, OC,* XII.

16. Tocqueville himself saw that his book would please no one apart from the "friends of liberty," and these could be "counted on the fingers of two hands"; Tocqueville to Marie Mottley, February 1856, in *OC,* XIV, 594.

17. See Annelien de Dijn, *French Political Thought from Montesquieu to Tocqueville: Liberty in a Levelled Society?* (Cambridge, 2008).

18. Tocqueville, *L'ancien régime et la révolution,* in *OC,* II (1), 248.

19. Tocqueville to Louis de Kergorlay, 15 December 1850, in *OC,* XIII (2), 230.

20. Tocqueville, "Mon instinct, mes opinions," in *OC,* III (2), 87.

21. Tocqueville, *L'ancien régime et la révolution,* 217.

22. See Tim Hannigan, *The Travel Writing Tribe: Journeys in Search of a Genre* (London, 2021); and William Atkins, "On Staying at Home," *Granta,* no. 157 (2021): 6–9. Atkins's short introduction to what is a volume of new travel writing provides a lucid statement of the dilemmas that face the contemporary traveller. "When any long-haul flight can plausibly be described as an act of violence," he writes, "we'd all do well to learn to dwell better, to know and love our patch more deeply" (9).

23. Seneca, *Letters from a Stoic* (London, 1969), 188–89.

24. Jean-Jacques Rousseau, *Émile* (London, 1974), 414, 416.

25. Xavier de Maistre, *Voyage autour de ma chambre* (Hamburg, 1794), 3–4. It could be argued that painters, rather than writers, have best appreciated what can be gained from focusing upon a small space over a long period of time. Take, for example, John Constable; he never travelled abroad but drew constant inspiration from a very small part of the East Anglian landscape along the River Stour to Flatford Mill.

26. John Stuart Mill, *On Liberty and the Subjection of Women* (London, 2006), 156.

27. Johann Winckelmann, *Reflections on the Imitation of Greek Art,* in *Winckelmann: Writings on Art,* ed. David Irwin (London, 1972), 6–85.

28. Dale Townshend, "Terror and Wonder: The Gothic Imagination," in *Terror and Wonder: The Gothic Imagination,* ed. Dale Townshend (London, 2014), 10–37.

29. The continental alternative to the English Lakes and Scotland were the Swiss Alps. As Tim Blanning, *The Romantic Revolution* (London, 2010), 143, writes, "The Alps were everything the romantics liked—irregular, particular, sublime, organic, terrifying, original."

30. See Édouard de Tocqueville, *Voyage en Angleterre, en Écosse et en Irlande* (Paris, 2022). This fascinating document was found by the late Barbara Wright of Trinity College Dublin.

31. It is interesting to note that, in today's world of mass tourism, those with any pretensions to superiority prefer to refer to themselves as *travellers* rather than *tourists.* London's Travellers Club, founded in 1819, remains a very sophisticated and exclusive place; see John Martin Robinson, *The Travellers Club: A Bicentennial History 1819–2019* (London, 2019).

32. On the growth of foreign travel in Europe, see Orlando Figes, *The Europeans: Three Lives and the Making of a Cosmopolitan Culture* (London, 2019), 210–56.

33. Tocqueville to Francisque de Corcelle, 29 August 1854, in *OC,* XV (2), 111.

34. Brian Dolan, *Ladies of the Grand Tour* (London, 2001), 5–6, writes, "Travel helped women to develop views on the opportunities and rights to education, it guided those seeking separation from unhappy domestic circumstances, it worked to improve mental and physical health abroad, and it turned many into writers, arbiters of fashion, and *salonnières.*" See also Emily Thomas, *The Meaning of Travel: Philosophers Abroad* (Oxford; 2020), 163–76. "The history of travel," Thomas writes, with considerable justification, "is largely a history of men" (169). Thomas also points out that many early women travellers found it easier to dress as men. For an example of recent attempts to recover the experiences of women travellers, see Mary Morris, ed., *The Virago Book of Women Travellers* (London, 2013).

35. Bruce Chatwin, *Anatomy of Restlessness* (New York, 1997), 75.

36. Moses leading the Israelites out of Egypt is one of the earliest examples of this. So, too, in the Muslim faith, where the concept of *hegira,* or flight, marking the departure of the prophet Mohammed from Mecca to Medina, has a central place.

37. A modern equivalent is "mindfulness tourism"; see Nat Segnit, *Retreat* (London, 2021), 14–16.

38. See Gustave Flaubert, *Flaubert in Egypt: A Sensibility on Tour,* ed. Francis Steegmuller (London, 1972).

39. It should be remembered that one of the earliest forms of travel was that of the religious pilgrimage; see Peter Stanford, *Pilgrimage* (London, 2021). This ancient tradition has been much revived in the twenty-first century, as the thousands of New Age backpackers trudging their way up to Machu Picchu testify.

40. See David Pryce-Jones, *Treason of the Heart: From Thomas Paine to Kim Philby* (New York, 2011).

41. Étienne Cabet, *Réalisation d'Icarie* (Paris, 1847), 33.

42. See Gregory Claeys, *Searching for Utopia: The History of an Idea* (London, 2011), 129–39.

43. For an account of the community of Auroville in India, see Akash Kapur, *Better to Have Gone: Love, Death, and the Quest for Utopia in Auroville* (London, 2021).

44. Paul Preston, *A People Betrayed: A History of Corruption, Political Incompetence and Social Division in Modern Spain 1874–2018* (London, 2020), 1–25.

45. Frances Trollope, *Domestic Manners of the Americans* (New York, 2003), 1.

46. Charles Dickens, *American Notes* (London, 2004), 125–41.

47. Victor Jacquemont, *Correspondance inédite de Victor Jacquemont avec sa famille et ses amis, 1824–1832,* 2 vols. (Paris, 1867), 1:152–94. See also Aurelian Craiutu, "A Precursor of Tocqueville: Victor Jacquemont's Reflections on America," in *America through European Eyes: British and French Reflections on the New World from the Eighteenth Century to the Present,* ed. Aurelian Craiutu and Jeffrey C. Isaac (University Park, PA, 2009), 117–42.

48. For a full account of this dystopian vision of the United States, see Georges Duhamel, *America the Menace: Scenes from the Life of the Future* (New York, 1974). See also Richard Kuisel, *Seducing the French: The Dilemma of Americanization*

(Berkeley, CA, 1993); and Jean-Philippe Mathy, *Extrême-Occident: French Intellectuals and America* (Chicago, 1993).

49. Trollope, *Domestic Manners,* 9.

50. Contemporary academic literature refers here to the "travellee."

51. For a sustained reflection on the value of travel, see Thomas, *The Meaning of Travel.*

52. J. P. Brissot de Warville, *New Travels in the United States of America, Performed in 1788* (London, 1792), xxxviii.

53. Lady Emmeline Stuart-Wortley, *Travels in the United States during 1849 and 1850,* 3 vols. (London, 1851), 1:vi.

54. John Graham Brooks, *As Others See Us: A Study of Progress in the United States* (New York, 1908), 176, 179.

55. Laboulaye is credited with being the person who first had the idea for the Statue of Liberty; see Francesca Lidia Viano, *Sentinel: The Unlikely Origins of the Statue of Liberty* (Cambridge, MA, 2018).

56. See Richard Switzer, ed., *Chateaubriand's Travels in America* (Lexington, KY, 1969). As Switzer writes in the introduction, "It remained for Chateaubriand, one of the great writers of fiction, to present primitive America in so vivid a way that his ideas were to influence generations to come" (xi).

57. Claude Lévi-Strauss, *Tristes tropiques* (London, 1973), 17.

58. Achille Murat, *Esquisse morale et politique des États-Unis de l'Amérique du Nord* (Paris, 1832), 3.

59. See Tocqueville to Basil Hall, 19 June 1836, in *OC,* VI (3), 51–52.

60. C. F. Volney, *Œuvres de C. F. Volney,* 8 vols. (Paris, 1825–1826), 4:v.

61. Frederick Marryat, *A Diary of America, with Remarks on Its Institutions,* 6 vol. (London, 1839), 3:53–71.

62. Tocqueville to Ernest de Chabrol, 24 January 1832, in *OC,* XVII (1), 157.

63. Montesquieu, *The Spirit of the Laws,* ed. Anne M. Cohler, Basia C. Miller, and Harold S. Stone (Cambridge, 1989), 310.

64. Jean-Jacques Rousseau, *Confessions* (Harmondsworth, UK, 1973), 377.

65. See Alan Levine, "The Idea of America in European Political Thought: 1492 to 9 / 11," in Craiutu and Isaac, eds., *America through European Eyes,* 17–42; and Tzvetan Todorov, *The Conquest of America* (New York, 1985).

66. See Stephen Brooks, *America through Foreign Eyes: Classic Interpretations of American Political Life* (Oxford, 2002). Recent scholarship has cast a darker picture: see David Stannard, *American Holocaust: Columbus and the Conquest of the New World* (Oxford, 1992) and Kirkpatrick Sale, *The Conquest of Paradise: Christopher Columbus and the Conquest of the New World* (New York, 1991).

67. Tocqueville, *Democracy in America,* 44.

68. Tocqueville's most recent biographer, Hugh Brogan, speaks of him as a "bold, energetic, enthusiastic" traveller; see Brogan, *Alexis de Tocqueville,* 64. Eduardo Nolla, "Editor's Introduction," in Tocqueville, *Democracy in America,* clii, is more eloquent: "Travelling, roads and trips: these are all very Tocquevillian things."

69. Tocqueville to his father, 1 July 1841, in *OC,* XIV, 223.

70. See Tocqueville's reports on this subject in *OC,* X, 622–47, 665–73, 694–702, and 721–24. The project was completed in 1858.

71. For a discussion of the theme of how people moved around France, see Graham Robb, *The Discovery of France: A Historical Geography* (London, 2007), 231–49.

72. Eugen Weber, *Peasants into Frenchmen: The Modernization of Rural France, 1870–1914* (London, 1979), 3.

73. Tocqueville to Marie Mottley, 14 March 1848[?], in *OC,* XIV, 507.

74. Tocqueville to Eugène Stoffels, 18 October 1831, in *OC,* XVII (1), 124.

75. Tocqueville to Marie Mottley, 1837, in *OC,* XIV, 412.

76. Tocqueville to Marie Mottley, 21 August 1851[?], in *OC,* XIV, 53.

77. See Tocqueville to Victor Lanjuinais, 16 November 1857, in *OC,* XVII (3), 443; Tocqueville to Louis Bouchitté, 14 February 1858, in *OC,* XVII (3), 469.

78. Tocqueville to Jean-Jacques Ampère, 26 June 1850, in *OC,* XI, 187.

79. Tocqueville to Madame de Circourt, 5 December 1857, in *OC,* XVIII, 428.

80. Tocqueville to Gustave de Beaumont, 1 July 1855, in *OC,* VIII (3), 324; Tocqueville to Gustave de Beaumont, 8 August 1855, in *OC,* VIII (3), 331.

81. Tocqueville to Mrs. Harriet Grote, 1 October 1856, in *OC,* VI (3), 216. Somewhat incongruously, the same letter includes Tocqueville's complaint that John Stuart Mill had not responded to the receipt of a copy of *L'ancien régime et la révolution* that had been sent to him.

82. Tocqueville to N. W. Senior, 15 November 1857, in *OC,* VI (2), 206, emphasis in the original.

83. Tocqueville to Lord Radnor, 19 August 1857, in *OC,* VI (3), 265–66.

84. Tocqueville to Louis de Loménie, November 1857[?], in *OC,* XVII (3), 445. A slightly earlier letter reflected that, at a time when no great services could be rendered to one's country, being an importer of pigs did at least bring some benefit to the community; Tocqueville to Laurette de Pisieux, 21 September 1857, in *OC,* XVII (3), 428.

85. Tocqueville to Lord Hatherton, 7 August 1857 and 6 March 1858, in *OC,* VI (3), 260–62, 291, emphasis in the original.

86. Tocqueville to his father, 25 November 1855, in *OC,* XIV, 318.

87. Tocqueville to Francisque de Corcelle, 6 July 1855, in *OC,* XV (2), 138.

88. Tocqueville to Camille d'Orglandes, 14 October 1835, in *OC,* XVII (1), 261.

89. Tocqueville to Eugénie de Grancey, 15 February 1858, in *OC,* XVII (3), 471.

90. Tocqueville to Adolphe de Circourt, 23 December 1856, in *OC,* XVIII, 357.

91. Tocqueville to Marie Mottley, 23 August 1834, in *OC,* XIV, 395–96.

92. Tocqueville to Francisque de Corcelle, 4 August 1855, in *OC,* XV (2), 143.

93. Tocqueville to Gustave de Beaumont, 2 November 1845, in *OC,* VIII (1), 568.

94. Tocqueville to Lord Hatherton, 6 March 1858, in *OC,* VI (3), 291.

95. Tocqueville to Louis de Kergorlay, 3 February 1857, in *OC,* XIII (2), 325.

96. Tocqueville, *Voyage en Sicile,* in *OC,* V (1), 49.

97. Tocqueville to his mother, 15 May 1831, in *OC,* XIV, 85.

98. Tocqueville to his father, 4 July 1831, in *OC,* XIV, 114.

99. Tocqueville to Madame Swetchine, 7 January 1856, in *OC,* XV (2), 268.

100. Tocqueville to Madame de Circourt, 2 September 1853, in *OC,* XVIII, 103.

101. Tocqueville to Marie Mottley, 19 June 1857, in *OC,* XIV, 597. Tocqueville had used the same image, this time explicitly referring to the "forests of America," when, in a letter to Madame Swetchine, he had spoken of "the sense of intellectual and moral isolation" he felt living among his contemporaries; Tocqueville to Madame Swetchine, 20 October 1856, in *OC,* XV (2), 298.

102. Tocqueville to his mother, 8 October 1829, in *OC,* XIV, 52.

103. Tocqueville to Charles Stoffels, 31 June 1834, in *OC,* XVII (1), 204.

104. Tocqueville to his father, 24 August 1833, in *OC,* XIV, 172–74, 29 April 1835, in *OC,* XIV, 175–77.

105. Tocqueville to his father, 24 August 1833, in *OC,* XIV, 173. In later years Tocqueville acquired a servant by the name of Eugène. The experience proved not to be entirely satisfactory, with Tocqueville complaining on one occasion that both his cap and briefcase had been left on the mail coach. "Never," he wrote to his wife, "have I lost so many things whilst travelling than I have since travelling with a servant"; Tocqueville to Marie Mottley, 30 August 1849[?], in *OC,* XIV, 547. Later still, Tocqueville had another servant, one by the name of Auguste. As their journey to London in 1857 illustrated, this, too, proved to be an unhappy experience; it was not clear, Tocqueville wrote, which one of them was the servant; see Tocqueville to Marie Mottley, 30 June 1857, in *OC,* XIV, 598; and Tocqueville to Marie Mottley, 11 July 1857, in *OC,* XIV, 622. Auguste also proved to be useless when Tocqueville was ill in Cannes.

106. See Tocqueville to Gustave de Beaumont, 30 January 1849, in *OC,* VIII (1), 336, where Tocqueville, in a "state of crisis," contrasts his passion for action with his "nervous weakness" and what he referred to as his "feminine sensibility."

107. Tocqueville to Gustave de Beaumont, 25 October 1829, in *OC,* VIII (1), 91–96.

108. Gustave de Beaumont, "Notice sur Alexis de Tocqueville," in *Œuvres et correspondance inédites d'Alexis de Tocqueville,* 2 vols. (Paris, 1861), 1:31–33. See also Gustave de Beaumont, "Extrait du journal de Beaumont," in *Lettres d'Amérique 1831–32* (Paris, 1973), 200–202.

109. Tocqueville to Ernest de Chabrol, 16 January 1832, in *OC,* XVII (1), 157.

110. Tocqueville to Alexandrine de Tocqueville, 22 May 1835, in *OC,* XIV, 180.

111. Tocqueville to Gustave de Beaumont, 26 August 1835, in *OC,* VIII (1), 154.

112. Tocqueville to Marie Mottley, 12 June 1841, in *OC,* XIV, 435.

113. Tocqueville to Édouard de Tocqueville, 22 December 1850, in *OC,* XIV, 260.

114. Tocqueville to Richard Monckton Milnes, 9 July 1857[?], in *OC,* VI (3), 245.

115. In a letter to Francisque de Corcelle, Tocqueville remarked that it was his and his wife's habit to be ill one after the other; Tocqueville to Francisque de Corcelle, 1 January 1853, in *OC,* XV (2), 68.

116. Tocqueville to Jean-Jacques Ampère, 4 July 1855, in *OC,* XI, 286.

117. In a letter to Francisque de Corcelle, where Tocqueville referred to the illnesses he had suffered from for almost thirty years, he commented that his body rebelled against changes of environment; Tocqueville to Francisque de Corcelle, 20 November 1855, in *OC,* XV (2), 153.

118. See Tocqueville to Jean-Jacques Ampère, 27 September 1840, in *OC,* XI, 145; and Tocqueville to Jean-Jacques Ampère, 2 October 1853, in *OC,* XI, 223. See also Tocqueville to Adolphe de Circourt, 16 October 1853, 109–10; Tocqueville to Adolphe de Circourt, 7 December 1853, in *OC,* XVIII, 121; and Tocqueville to Francisque de Corcelle, 26 September 1840, in *OC,* XV (1), 151–52.

119. Tocqueville to N. W. Senior, 31 March 1851, in *OC,* VI (2), 128.

120. Reeve, quoted in Laughton, *Memoirs of the Life and Correspondence of Henry Reeve,* 1:272.

121. Beaumont, "Notice sur Alexis de Tocqueville," 21–23.

122. Tocqueville to Gustave de Beaumont, 15 June 1852, in *OC,* VIII (3), 51.

123. This was the view of another of Tocqueville's closest friends; see Jean-Jacques Ampère, "Appendice," in *OC,* XI, 442.

124. In a letter, Beaumont counseled Tocqueville against endangering his health during his impending visit to Algeria by asking too much physically of himself. Having pointed out that the presence of Madame de Tocqueville might temper his activities—no sleeping in a tent or eating the local dish of couscous—Beaumont pointed out that Tocqueville would constantly be tempted to push himself to the limit. He also reminded Tocqueville that he and horses had never been a great combination. See Gustave de Beaumont to Tocqueville, 10 October 1846, in *OC,* VIII (1), 590–91.

125. Beaumont, "Notice sur Alexis de Tocqueville," 24–26.

126. See Tocqueville, "Le Jardin," in *OC,* V (2), 234–38.

127. Beaumont, "Notice sur Alexis de Tocqueville," 21.

128. Tocqueville to his father, 7 May 1835, in *OC,* XIV, 178.

129. Tocqueville to Alexandrine de Tocqueville, 22 May 1835, in *OC,* XIV, 180.

130. Tocqueville to his father, 16 July 1835, in *OC,* XIV,184.

131. Tocqueville to Marie Mottley, 9 May 1841, in *OC,* XIV, 418.

132. Tocqueville to Gustave de Beaumont, 29 September 1846, in *OC,* VIII (1), 587.

133. Tocqueville to Gustave de Beaumont, 28 October 1846, in *OC,* VIII (1), 592.

134. Tocqueville to Lord Radnor, 19 July 1857, in *OC,* VI (3), 248.

135. Tocqueville to Louis de Kergorlay, 10 October 1836, in *OC,* XIII (1), 408–9. Whether Kergorlay fully embraced this advice is not exactly clear, but in a subsequent letter Tocqueville congratulated him on showing "the true spirit of travel"; Tocqueville to Louis de Kergorlay, 10 November 1836, in *OC,* XIII (1), 417.

136. Tocqueville to Charles Stoffels, 11 February 1836, in *OC,* XVII (1), 273–74.

137. Tocqueville to Louis de Kergorlay, 4 July 1837, in *OC,* XIII (1), 460.

138. Tocqueville to Jean-Jacques Ampère, 9 June 1854, in *OC,* XI, 243.

139. See Matthew Mancini, *Alexis de Tocqueville and American Intellectuals* (Lanham, MD, 2006).

140. See Hélène Tuzet, *Voyageurs français en Sicile au temps du romantisme (1802–1848)* (Paris, 1945); and, in particular, 7–51, "Comment on voyageait en Sicile avant 1848." Tuzet begins her account by saying that "for anyone tackling a trip to Sicily at the beginning of the nineteenth century both real courage and banal curiosity were required" (7). All travellers, she continued, confirmed that the picture painted to them was of a country "immersed in barbarism and infested by brigands" (7). There were no roads and, outside the main cities, accommodation was primitive in the extreme. Like Tocqueville, most people had no alternative but to travel by mule. That said, according to Tuzet, by the 1820s something like "modern tourism" was beginning to emerge and journeys came increasingly to follow a set "model." Francesco Ferrara published the first guide to Sicily, *Guida dei viaggiatori agli oggetti più interessanti a vedersi in Sicilia* (Palermo, 1822). Tocqueville is not mentioned in Tuzet's fascinating volume.

141. In later letters to Italian correspondents, Tocqueville suggests that, at the time, he spoke Italian "almost fluently." Those same letters indicate that by the early 1840s this was a facility that Tocqueville had lost; see Tocqueville to C. di Tottigiani, 9 April 1842, in *OC,* VII, 291; and Tocqueville to P. S. Mancini, 3 February 1845, in *OC,* VII, 306–7.

142. Tocqueville to Édouard and Alexandrine de Tocqueville, 15 March 1830, in *OC,* XIV, 55. Tocqueville also commented on the favourable climate of the Bay of Naples.

143. Tocqueville to G. Campo, 17 March 1827, in *OC,* VII, 281.

144. According to Tuzet, *Voyageurs français en Sicile,* 223–44, few visitors to Sicily failed to make this ascent, and all left detailed accounts of what they had seen.

145. In a letter to his childhood friend Eugène Stoffels, Tocqueville indicated that, in his view, this text contained only "a few pages" of which he had "a high opinion"; Tocqueville to Eugène Stoffels, 21 February 1831, in *OC,* XVII (1), 74.

146. Tocqueville, *Voyage en Sicile,* in *OC,* V (1), 33–54.

147. See Tocqueville to Joseph-Alexandre von Hübner, 29 August 1849, in *OC,* VII, 316–18; and Tocqueville to Henry Reeve, 5 July 1849, in *OC,* VI (1), 103–5.

148. Tocqueville to G. Massari, 8 June 1851, in *OC,* VII, 323–24.

149. Tocqueville to Auguste de la Rive, 6 April 1857, in *OC,* VII, 360.

150. Tocqueville to his mother, 8 October 1829, in *OC,* XIV, 52.

151. Tocqueville to Gustave de Beaumont, 25 October 1829, in *OC,* VIII (1), 91–92.

2. AN AMERICAN JOURNEY

1. On Tocqueville and America, see George Wilson Pierson, *Tocqueville in America* (Baltimore: 1996); James T. Schleifer, *The Making of Tocqueville's "Democracy in America"* (Chapel Hill, NC, 1980); Leo Damrosch, *Tocqueville's Discovery of America* (New York, 2010); and Arthur Kaledin, *Tocqueville and His America: A Darker Horizon* (New Haven, CT, 2011).

2. See Tocqueville to Charles Stoffels, 26 August 1830, in *OC,* XVII (1), 63–65; Tocqueville to Charles Stoffels, 4 November 1830, in *OC,* XVII (1), 68–70; Tocqueville to Auguste Henrion, 17 October 1830, in *OC,* XVII (1), 65–68; and Tocqueville to Auguste Henrion, 19 November 1830, in *OC,* XVII (1), 70–73. Tocqueville justified his decision to rally to the new regime by saying that the alternative was a republic and anarchy, and, to that extent, he had done his duty as a Frenchman.

3. Tocqueville to Marie Mottley, 17 August 1830, in *OC,* XIV, 376–77. A letter to Mary Mottley gave a vivid sense of the horror and despair he had felt as the violent events of the so-called Trois Glorieuses unfolded; see Tocqueville to Marie Mottley, 30 July 1830, in *OC,* XIV 375–6. A similar description is found in Tocqueville to Eugène Stoffels, 18 October 1831, in *OC,* XVII (1), 124.

4. Tocqueville to Hippolyte de Tocqueville, 18 August 1830, in *OC,* XIV, 71–72.

5. Tocqueville to Charles Stoffels, 26 August 1830, in *OC,* XVII (1), 64.

6. Gustave de Beaumont, "Notice sur Alexis de Tocqueville," in *Œuvres et correspondance inédites d'Alexis de Tocqueville,* 2 vols. (Paris, 1861), 1:15.

7. Tocqueville to Charles Stoffels, 4 November 1830, in *OC,* XVII (1), 70.

8. Tocqueville to Gustave de Beaumont, 4 March 1831, in *OC,* VIII (1), 105–106.

9. Beaumont, "Notice sur Alexis de Tocqueville," 1:16.

10. Tocqueville to Eugène Stoffels, 21 February 1831, in *OC,* XVII (1), 73–74.

11. Tocqueville to Camille d'Orglandes, 29 November 1834, in *OC,* XVII (1), 213.

12. Gideon Minor Davison, *Tournée à la mode aux États-Unis* (Paris, 1829).

13. Tocqueville to the Abbé Lesueur, 30 June 1831, in *OC,* XIV, 110. Tocqueville made a similar reference in a letter to his mother, pointing out that this was "*le voyage à la mode*"; see Tocqueville to his mother, 19 June 1831, in *OC,* XIV, 105. See also Richard H. Gassan, *The Birth of American Tourism: New York, the Hudson Valley, and American Culture, 1790–1830* (Amherst, MA, 2008).

14. For a vivid account of the demands of an Atlantic crossing, see Victor Jacquemont, *Correspondance 1824–1832,* 2 vols. (Paris, 1993), 1:69–91.

15. Jacques Portes, *Fascination and Misgivings: The United States and French Opinion, 1870–1914* (Cambridge, 2000), 21–25.

16. Tocqueville to his mother, 26 April 1831, in *OC,* XIV, 6–80; Tocqueville to Eugène Stoffels, 28 July 1831, in *OC,* XVII (1), 94–95. See also Tocqueville to Ernest de Chabrol, 18 May 1831, in *OC,* XVII (1), 75, where Tocqueville recalled the effects arising from "the solitude and monotony of the Ocean."

17. Tocqueville to his mother, 14 May 1831, in *OC,* XIV, 80.

18. Tocqueville to Émilie de Tocqueville, 9 June 1831, in *OC,* XIV, 102.

19. Tocqueville to Louis de Kergorlay, 18 May 1831, in *OC,* XIII (1), 224.

20. Tocqueville to his mother, 18 May 1831, in *OC,* XIV, 81–82.

21. Tocqueville to Eugène Stoffels, 28 July 1831, in *OC,* XVII (1), 95.

22. Tocqueville to his mother, 14 May 1831, in *OC,* XIV, 82.

23. Tocqueville to Eugène Stoffels, 28 July 1831, in *OC,* XVII (1), 95–96.

24. Tocqueville to his mother, 15 May 1831, in *OC,* XIV, 84.

25. Tocqueville to Eugène Stoffels, 28 July 1831, in *OC,* XVII (1), 96.

26. Tocqueville to his mother, 15 May 1831, in *OC,* XIV, 117.

27. Tocqueville to the Abbé Lesueur, 28 May 1831, in *OC,* XIV, 95.

28. Tocqueville to his mother, 24 October 1831, in *OC,* XIV, 144.

29. Tocqueville to Émilie de Tocqueville, 9 June 1831, in *OC,* XIV, 102–3.

30. Tocqueville to the Abbé Lesueur, 28 May 1831, in *OC,* XIV, 97.

31. Tocqueville to his mother, 24 October 1831, in *OC,* XIV, 143.

32. Tocqueville to his mother, 17 July 1831, in *OC,* XIV, 117.

33. For details of the Fourth of July ceremony, see Tocqueville to Ernest de Chabrol, 16 July 1831, in *OC,* XVII (1), 97–99.

34. Tocqueville to his mother, 25 December 1831, in *OC,* XIV, 161.

35. Damrosch, *Tocqueville's Discovery,* xix.

36. "I have never heard a more horrible sound," Tocqueville wrote, "than that of water rushing into the ship"; see Tocqueville to Ernest de Chabrol, 28 November 1831, in *OC,* XVII (1), 149.

37. Tocqueville to Ernest de Chabrol, 26 November 1831, in *OC,* XVII (1), 147.

38. Tocqueville to Ernest de Chabrol, 27 December 1831, in *OC,* XVII (1), 153.

39. Tocqueville to Ernest de Chabrol, 14 January 1832, in *OC,* XV, 157.

40. Tocqueville to Émilie de Tocqueville, 9 June 1831, in *OC,* XIV, 102.

41. Tocqueville to Eugénie de Grancey, 10 October 1831, in *OC,* XVII (1), 111.

42. Tocqueville to Édouard de Tocqueville, 28 May 1831, in *OC,* XIV, 91–92.

43. Tocqueville to Ernest de Chabrol, 9 June 1831, in *OC,* XVII (1), 87–88.

44. Tocqueville to Ernest de Chabrol, 9 June 1831, in *OC,* XVII (1), 88–89.

45. Tocqueville to Ernest de Chabrol, 9 June 1831, in *OC,* XVII (1), 89.

46. Tocqueville to Louis de Kergorlay, 29 June 1831, in *OC,* XIII (1), 225–27.

47. Americans visiting France were similarly shocked by the fact that cafés, restaurants, and shops opened on Sundays for business as usual.

48. Tocqueville to Louis de Kergorlay, 29 June 1831, in *OC,* XIII (1), 227–31. The place of religion in American society made a frequent appearance in Tocqueville's letters from America. With time, he came to see that his initial impressions were mistaken and that religious faith in America was less inert than he had first thought.

49. Tocqueville to Louis de Kergorlay, 29 June 1831, in *OC,* XIII (1), 231–34.

50. Tocqueville, "Première Impressions," 15 May 1831, in *OC,* V (1), 293–94.

51. Tocqueville to his mother, 6 December 1831, in *OC,* XIV, 152–54. Emphasis in the original.

52. Tocqueville to his father, 3 June 1831, in *OC,* XIV, 100–102.

53. Tocqueville to Louis de Kergorlay, 29 June 1831, in *OC,* XIII (1), 234–35.

54. Tocqueville to Louis de Kergorlay, 18 May 1831, in *OC,* XIII (1), 224.

55. Tocqueville to Ernest de Chabrol, 7 October 1831, in *OC,* XVII (1), 108.

56. See Antoine Redier, *Comme disait Monsieur de Tocqueville* (Paris, 1925), 93–103. Redier's view is that "the first stone of the edifice" is to be found in the letter to Chabrol.

57. Tocqueville to his father, 3 June 1831, in *OC,* XIV, 100.

58. Tocqueville to his mother, 27 September 1831, in *OC,* XIV, 137. See also Tocqueville to Ernest de Blosseville, 10 October 1831, in *OC,* XVII (1), 117, where Tocqueville wrote, "Since arriving in this country, we have seen so many people and so many things that when we want to speak about America our mind is immediately presented with such a confused mass of ideas that we do not know where to begin."

59. Tocqueville to his father, 7 October 1831, in *OC,* XIV, 139.

60. Tocqueville to his mother, 24 October 1831, in *OC,* XIV, 144.

61. Tocqueville, *Democracy in America,* ed. Eduardo Nolla and trans. James T. Schleifer (Indianapolis, 2010), 4.

62. Tocqueville, *Democracy in America,* 503, emphasis added.

63. Pierson, *Tocqueville in America,* 77–78.

64. In addition to Schleifer, *The Making of Tocqueville's Democracy,* see James T. Schleifer, "Tocqueville's Journey Revisited: What Was Striking and New in America," *Tocqueville Review* 27, no. 2 (2006): 403–23.

65. Tocqueville, *Democracy in America,* 1043.

66. Tocqueville, *Democracy in America,* 27.

67. Tocqueville, *Democracy in America,* 944.

68. Tocqueville, *Democracy in America,* 610.

69. Tocqueville, *Democracy in America,* 118, 896, 919, 922.

70. Tocqueville, *Democracy in America,* 475.

71. Tocqueville, *Democracy in America,* 698.

72. Tocqueville, *Democracy in America,* 91, 97.

73. Tocqueville, *Democracy in America,* 463.

74. Tocqueville, *Democracy in America,* 719.

75. Tocqueville, *Democracy in America,* 402–26.

76. Schleifer, "Tocqueville's Journey Revisited," 414.

77. Tocqueville, "A MM. Les électeurs de l'arrondissement de Valognes," in *OC,* III (2), 42.

78. In addition to the texts of Chateaubriand cited herein, see Marc Fumaroli, *Chateaubriand: Poésie et terreur* (Paris, 2003), 323–76. In English, see Richard Switzer, ed., *Chateaubriand's Travels in America* (Lexington, KY, 1969).

79. François René de Chateaubriand, *Chateaubriand's Travels in America,* trans. Richard Switzer (Lexington, KY, 1969), 91.

80. Chateaubriand, *Travels in America,* 44.

81. Chateaubriand, *Travels in America,* 42.

82. Chateaubriand, *The Memoirs of François-René, Vicomte de Chateaubriand,* trans. Alexander Teixeira de Mattos, 6 vols. (New York, 1902), 1, 228.

83. Tocqueville, "Première rencontre avec les Indiens," in *OC,* V (1), 223–24.

84. Tocqueville to Émilie de Tocqueville, 7 September 1831, in *OC,* XIV, 131–32. See also a set of similar observations in Tocqueville to Eugénie de Grancey, 10 October 1831, in *OC,* XVII (1), 113–14. Chactas was Atala's lover in Chateaubriand's novella. Beaumont's description of the first Indians that he and Tocqueville met was even more dismissive. "Generally speaking," he wrote "the Indians are quite ugly. The women are hideous. Their complexion is dark copper, their mouths wide, their hair long and dirty. There is something savage in their features, and nothing noble and dignified in their bearing. Their taste for strong liquor has reduced them to brutes"; see Gustave de Beaumont to Ernest de Chabrol, 24 July 1831, in *Lettres d'Amérique 1831–32* (Paris, 1973), 103.

85. Tocqueville, "Quinze jours dans le désert," in *OC,* V (1), 379.

86. Tocqueville, "Cahier portatif no 1," in *OC,* V (1), 155.

87. Tocqueville, "Première rencontre avec les Indiens," in *OC,* V (1), 225.

88. Tocqueville to his mother, 25 December 1831, in *OC,* XIV, 159.

89. Tocqueville, "Cahier portatif no 1," in *OC,* V (1), 155.

90. Tocqueville to Eugénie de Grancey, 10 October 1831, in *OC,* XVII (1), 112–13.

91. Tocqueville, "Quinze jours dans le désert," 350–55, 376.

92. Beaumont provided a fictional account of this journey; see Gustave de Beaumont, *Marie ou l'esclavage aux États-Unis* (Paris, 1843), 162–77.

93. Tocqueville, "Quinze jours dans le désert," 370–71.

94. Tocqueville, "Quinze jours dans le désert," 376–81.

95. Tocqueville, "Quinze jours dans le désert," 382–84.

96. Tocqueville, "Cahiers portatif No 2", in *OC,* V (1), 176–77.

97. Tocqueville to Eugénie de Grancey, 10 October 1831, in *OC,* XVII (1), 112–13. In addition to Tocqueville's travel notes, see Tocqueville to his father, 14 August 1831, in *OC,* XIV, 123–26. For his part, Beaumont provided a detailed

account of this journey in a letter to his brother; see Gustave de Beaumont to Achille de Beaumont, 11 August 1831, in *Lettres d'Amérique,* 117–27. One thing that Beaumont recorded was that among the other passengers was an Englishman by the name of Vigne, whom he described as "a good fellow and intrepid traveller." Although his account makes no mention of Tocqueville and Beaumont as fellow travellers, see Geoffrey T. Vigne, *Six Months in America* (Philadelphia, 1833), 137–50.

98. Tocqueville to his mother, 21 August 1831, in *OC,* XIV, 127. Both Beaumont, *Lettres d'Amérique,* 128–30, and Vigne, *Six Months,* 150–53, provide further details of this two-day visit. Beaumont's view was that Chateaubriand's description of the falls was "very imperfect." Beaumont also reported that their days were spoilt by the attentions of an English lady, Miss Clemens. He had earlier described her to his brother Achille as someone with an "ardent and very romantic imagination"; see Gustave de Beaumont to Achille de Beaumont, 11 August 1831, in *Lettres d'Amérique,* 120.

99. Tocqueville to Charles Jules Xavier de Dalmassy, August 1831, in *OC,* XVII (1), 104.

100. Tocqueville to his mother, 25 December 1831, in *OC,* XIV, 160.

101. Tocqueville, *Democracy in America,* 515, note a.

102. Tocqueville, *Democracy in America,* 515–16.

103. Tocqueville, *Democracy in America,* 494–500.

104. Tocqueville, *Democracy in America,* 465–66, 175.

105. Joel Poinsett, "Cahiers Non-Alphabétiques 2 et 3," in *OC,* V (1), 151.

106. Jared Sparks, "Cahiers Non-Alphabétiques 2 et 3," in *OC,* V (1), 96, emphasis in the original.

107. Tocqueville, "Cahiers Non-Alphabétiques 2 et 3," in *OC,* V (1), 91.

108. Tocqueville, *Democracy in America,* 466–67.

109. Tocqueville, *Democracy in America,* 475, 479, 472.

110. Tocqueville, *Democracy in America,* 479.

111. Tocqueville, *Democracy in America,* 452.

112. Tocqueville, *Democracy in America,* 453.

113. Tocqueville, *Democracy in America,* 454–55.

114. Tocqueville, *Democracy in America,* 455.

115. Tocqueville, *Democracy in America,* 455.

116. Tocqueville, *Democracy in America,* 455–60.

117. Tocqueville, *Democracy in America,* 516–17, emphasis in the original.

118. Tocqueville, *Democracy in America,* 526, 529, 547.

119. Tocqueville, *Democracy in America,* 549.

120. Tocqueville, *Democracy in America,* 517.

121. Tocqueville, *Democracy in America,* 557.

122. Tocqueville, "Cahier Alphabétique B," in *OC,* V (1), 246–47.

123. Tocqueville, "Cahier E," *OC,* V (1), 289.

124. Tocqueville, *Democracy in America,* 553–55.

125. Tocqueville, *Democracy in America,* 561.

126. Tocqueville, *Democracy in America,* 581.

127. Tocqueville, *Democracy in America,* 625.

128. Tocqueville, *Democracy in America,* 600–601.

129. Tocqueville, *Democracy in America,* 604–6.

130. Tocqueville, *Democracy in America,* 634, 630, 612.

131. Tocqueville, *Democracy in America,* 641–45.

132. Tocqueville, *Democracy in America,* 653, 655.

133. Tocqueville, *Democracy in America,* 649–56.

134. Léon Faucher, "De la démocratie aux États-Unis," *Le courrier français,* 24 December 1834. Note that this review was published prior to the publication of *La démocratie en Amérique.*

135. *Le journal des débats,* 25 March 1835.

136. *Journal général de l'instruction publique et des cours scientifiques et littéraires,* 21 May 1835.

137. *Le semeur, journal religieux, politique, philosophique et littéraire,* 4 March 1835.

138. *Le bon sens, journal de la démocratie,* 5 February 1835.

139. *Le semeur, journal religieux, politique, philosophique et littéraire,* 4 March 1835,

140. *L'écho français,* 11 February 1835.

141. *Le national de 1834,* 7 June 1835.

142. Sir William Blackstone was the author of the *Commentaries on the Laws of England* (Oxford, 1765–1769).

143. *Le moniteur du commerce,* 27 December 1835.

144. All of the review articles herein are conveniently located in Yale Tocqueville Manuscripts, Beinecke Rare Book and Manuscript Library, Yale University, MS Vault Tocqueville, CXI.

145. On Reeve, see John Knox Laughton, *Memoirs of the Life and Correspondence of Henry Reeve,* 2 vols. (London, 1898). On 25 February 1835, Reeve recorded that *De la démocratie en Amérique* was "a work of first-rate order," but he declined to translate it because he saw Tocqueville as "a philosophical opponent." When Reeve met Tocqueville for the first time in Paris in early March he realised his mistake, telling his mother that Tocqueville was "a very agreeable man" and that, having nearly finished the book, he saw that "my first impression as to its democratic tendency was entirely erroneous." "He regards Democracy," Reeve wrote, "as the inevitable lot of Europe, and as an evil which we had best prepare to meet, as we cannot escape it." From that time onwards, Reeve recalled in 1872, "I lived in the intimacy of unbroken friendship with Alexis de Tocqueville"; Henry Reeve, quoted in Laughton, *Memoirs of the Life and Correspondence of Henry Reeve,* 1:42, 47, 50.

146. Olivier Zunz, "Tocqueville and the Americans: *Democracy in America* as Read in Nineteenth-Century America," in *The Cambridge Companion to Tocqueville,* ed. Cheryl B. Welch (New York, 2006), 359–61.

147. Edward Everett, "De Tocqueville's *Democracy in America,*" *North American Review,* no. 43 (1836): 178–206.

148. Tocqueville to Henry Reeve, 21 November 1836, in *OC,* VI (1), 36.

149. Tocqueville to Gustave de Beaumont, 22 November 1836, in *OC,* VIII (1), 175, emphasis in the original.

150. In a letter to John Stuart Mill, Tocqueville indicated that he agreed with Everett's criticism: "I was often obliged [to generalize] so that people in Europe could see clearly the general character of the country I wanted to bring out"; Tocqueville to John Stuart Mill, 19 September 1836, in *OC,* VI (1), 315.

151. Everett, "De Tocqueville's *Democracy in America,*" 179, 184, 197, 198, 203.

152. Everett, "De Tocqueville's *Democracy in America,*" 180–84.

153. Everett, "De Tocqueville's *Democracy in America,*" 188–92.

154. For an account of Tocqueville's stay at the house of Spencer in Canandaigua, see Tocqueville to Émilie de Tocqueville, 25 July 1831, in *OC,* XIV, 121–22. Tocqueville was particularly taken by the blue eyes of Spencer's two daughters.

155. John C. Spencer, "Preface to the American Edition," in *Democracy in America,* by Alexis de Tocqueville (New York, 1838), iii, vi, vii.

156. Spencer, "Preface," iii–v.

157. Spencer, "Notes by the American Editor," 451–53.

158. Spencer, "Preface," v.

159. Tocqueville to J. C. Spencer, 20 September 1838, in *OC,* VII, 71. Tocqueville did indeed make alterations to the seventh French edition of *De la démocratie en Amérique.*

160. See Zunz, "Tocqueville and the Americans."

161. Garry Wills, "Did Tocqueville 'Get' America?," *New York Review of Books,* no. 51 (2004): 52–56. In his article Wills somewhat misleadingly makes use of the following quotation: "To acquire information about institutions and public establishments, etc., etc., we really have to see people, and the most enlightened people are in the best society." Contrary to the impression given, this is in fact a quotation from a letter written not by Tocqueville but by Beaumont to his brother; see Gustave Beaumont to Jules de Beaumont, 26 May 1831, in *Lettres d'Amérique,* 51.

162. Wills, "Did Tocqueville 'Get' America?"

163. Wills, "Did Tocqueville 'Get' America?," 52.

164. Wills makes a subtle distinction here between "visited" and "passed through." By Wills's definition, Tocqueville passed through, rather than visited, Hartford, Connecticut.

165. Wills, "Did Tocqueville 'Get' America?," 53.

166. Pierson, *Tocqueville in America,* 724.

167. Pierson, *Tocqueville in America,* 758–59.

168. Pierson, *Tocqueville in America,* 764–67.

169. Tocqueville to his mother, 14 May 1831, in *OC,* XIV, 82.

170. Tocqueville, "Cahiers Non-Alphabétiques," in *OC,* V (1), 95–99.

171. Tocqueville, *Democracy in America,* 49.

172. Michael Drolet, *Tocqueville, Democracy and Social Reform* (Houndmills, UK, 2003); Richard Swedberg, *Tocqueville's Political Economy* (Princeton, NJ, 2009). See also Michael Drolet, "Democracy and Political Economy: Tocqueville's Thoughts on J.-B. Say and T. R. Malthus," *History of European Ideas* 29, no. 2 (2003): 159–81.

173. Seymour Drescher, *Dilemmas of Democracy: Tocqueville and Moderation* (Pittsburgh, 1968), 52–53.

174. See Jeremy Jennings, "Democracy before Tocqueville: Michel Chevalier's America," *Review of Politics,* no. 68 (2006): 398–427.

175. Tocqueville to Émilie de Tocqueville, 28 November 1831, in *OC,* XIV, 147.

176. Tocqueville, "Cahier E," 2 December 1831, in *OC,* V (1), 281.

177. Tocqueville, "Cahier E," in *OC,* V (1), 285. See also Tocqueville to his mother, 6 December 1831, in *OC,* XIV, 152–54.

178. Tocqueville, *Democracy in America,* 560.

179. Tocqueville to his father, 20 December 1831, in *OC,* XIV, 154–57.

180. Tocqueville, *Democracy in America,* 558n36.

181. Tocqueville, "Cahier E," in *OC,* V (1), 289–92.

182. Tocqueville, *Democracy in America,* 972–79.

183. Tocqueville, "Cahiers E," in *OC,* V (1), 292.

184. Tocqueville, *Democracy in America,* 4, note c, brackets in the original.

185. Tocqueville, *Democracy in America,* lxxxi–lxxxiii.

186. Tocqueville to Gustave de Beaumont, 3 December 1836, in *OC,* VIII (1), 176.

187. Pierson, *Tocqueville in America,* 766. Olivier Zunz has restated this point; see Zunz, "Tocqueville and the Americans," 367–69.

188. Jared Sparks, quoted in Richmond Laurin Hawkins, "Unpublished Letters of Alexis de Tocqueville," *Romanic Review* 19, no. 3 (1928): 195.

189. Jared Sparks, quoted in Herbert B. Adams, *Jared Sparks and Alexis de Tocqueville* (Baltimore, 1898), 39.

190. Jared Sparks, quoted in Adams, *Jared Sparks,* 44.

191. Tocqueville, "Cahier E," in *OC,* V (1), 96.

192. Tocqueville, "Cahiers Non-Alphabétiques 2 et 3," in *OC,* V (1), 115. Tocqueville used this comparison in the text of *Democracy in America;* see Tocqueville, *Democracy in America,* 419.

193. Tocqueville, *Democracy in America,* 414n4.

194. Tocqueville, "Cahier Portatif no 3," in *OC,* V (1), 187–88; Tocqueville, "Cahier Alphabétique B," in *OC,* V (1), 246–47.

195. Tocqueville, *Democracy in America,* 413–14.

196. Tocqueville, *Democracy in America,* 416–18.

197. Tocqueville, *Democracy in America,* 419. Given that Tocqueville was familiar with the writings of James Fenimore Cooper prior to his departure (and that Cooper's writings were already well known in France) it is difficult to know what to make of this comment.

198. Tocqueville, *Democracy in America,* 421.

199. James T. Schleifer, *The Chicago Companion to Tocqueville's "Democracy in America"* (Chicago, 2012), 92.

200. Tocqueville, *Democracy in America,* 28.

201. Tocqueville to Louis de Kergorlay, 18 October 1847, in *OC,* XIII (2), 209.

202. Tocqueville to his father, 3 June 1831, in *OC,* XIV, 101.

203. Tocqueville to Édouard de Tocqueville, 28 May 1831, in *OC,* XIV, 92.

204. Tocqueville to his father, 3 June 1831, in *OC,* XIV, 99–100.

205. See Tocqueville, "Appendix 2: A Fortnight in the Wilderness," in *Democracy in America,* 1309. This text was first published by Beaumont in 1861.

206. Tocqueville to the Abbé Lesueur, 30 June 1831, in *OC,* XIV, 112.

207. Tocqueville to his mother, 24 October 1831, in *OC,* XIV, 143.

208. Tocqueville to Ernest de Chabrol, 18 May 1831, in *OC,* XVII (1), 76.

209. Tocqueville to Felix le Peletier d'Aunay, 7 June 1831, in *OC,* XVII (1), 86.

210. Tocqueville to Édouard de Tocqueville, 28 May 1831, in *OC,* XIV, 92.

211. Tocqueville to his father, 3 June 1831, in *OC,* XIV, 100, emphasis in the original.

212. Tocqueville to Ernest de Chabrol, 18 May 1831, in *OC,* XVII (1), 78.

213. Tocqueville to Édouard de Tocqueville, 20 January 1832, in *OC,* XIV, 165–66. Tocqueville later expressed a similar view about his attempts to write about Algeria, saying that he would need to stay there for at least two years to understand the country; see Tocqueville to Gustave de Beaumont, 28 October 1846, in *OC,* VIII (1), 592. That this was a deeply held view on Tocqueville's part is confirmed by a letter to Hubert de Tocqueville, where Tocqueville congratulated his nephew (then residing in Germany) on "not having the pretension to have grasped the whole truth about a country so different from ours in a matter of a few months"; Tocqueville to Hubert de Tocqueville, 27 May 1858, in *OC,* XIV, 347.

214. Tocqueville to an unknown correspondent, 8 November 1831, in *OC,* XVII (1), 138, 140.

215. Tocqueville to Louis Bouchitté, 11 October 1831, in *OC,* XVII (1), 118; Tocqueville to Ernest de Chabrol, 27 December 1831, in *OC,* XVII (1), 153.

216. Tocqueville to Ernest de Chabrol, 17 September 1831, in *OC,* XVII (1), 106–7.

217. Tocqueville to Édouard de Tocqueville, 20 January 1852, in *OC,* XIV, 165.

218. See, for example, Tocqueville to Louis de Kergorlay, date unknown, in *OC,* XIII (1), 364–68.

219. Tocqueville to Gustave de Beaumont, 8 October 1839, in *OC,* VIII (1), 380. Tocqueville expressed similar sentiments in his letters to Francisque de Corcelle; see, in particular, Tocqueville to Francisque de Corcelle, 25 June 1838, in *OC,* XV (1), 99–101.

220. Tocqueville, *Democracy in America,* 16. In 1852 Tocqueville was to sketch out in greater detail what he took the "science of politics" to be, distinguishing it in the process from the "art of government"; Tocqueville, "Discours prononcé à la séance publique annuelle de l'Académie des sciences morales et politiques du 3 Avril 1852," in *OC,* XVI, 229–42.

221. Tocqueville, *Democracy in America,* 4.

222. James T. Schleifer, "Tocqueville's *Democracy in America* Reconsidered," in Welch, ed., *The Cambridge Companion,* 124.

223. See Harvey C. Mansfield Jr. and Delba Winthrop, "Tocqueville's New Political Science," in Welch, ed., *The Cambridge Companion,* 81–107; and Aurelian Craiutu, "What Kind of Social Scientist was Tocqueville?," in *Conversations with Tocqueville,* ed. Aurelian Craiutu and Sheldon Gellar (Lanham, MD, 2009), 55–81.

224. Sheldon S. Wolin, *Tocqueville between Two Worlds: The Making of a Political and Theoretical Life* (Princeton, NJ, 2001), 140–41.

225. Tocqueville, *Democracy in America,* 27–28.

226. Tocqueville to Francisque de Corcelle, 12 July 1836, in *OC,* XV (1), 67.

227. Tocqueville, *Democracy in America,* 30–31.

228. Tocqueville, *Democracy in America,* 3, note a.

229. It might be added that Tocqueville was also very conscious that, as a twenty-nine-year-old, he lacked personal experience. To that extent, he told his cousin that if he had not produced "a good book," it was the best that he could do "for the moment"; Tocqueville to Félix Le Peletier d'Aunay, January 1835, in *OC,* XVII (1), 219.

230. Tocqueville and Beaumont arrived in Memphis on 17 December 1831, bound for New Orleans. As the river was frozen, they could not depart, and spent their time walking and shooting in the woods; see Pierson, *Tocqueville in America,* 93–99.

231. Tocqueville to Gustave de Beaumont, 21 February 1855, in *OC,* VIII, 3, 271–72. The same episode is recounted in a letter from Beaumont to his brother; see Gustave de Beaumont to Achille de Beaumont, 5 December 1831, in *Lettres d'Amérique,* 203. That Tocqueville's enthusiasm for shooting game remained undiminished is revealed in Tocqueville to Gustave de Beaumont, 24 August 1852, in *OC,* VIII (3), 70.

3. PRISONS, SLAVERY, AND A TRIP TO CANADA

1. Tocqueville to Gustave de Beaumont, 1828 or 1829, in *OC,* VIII (1), 75.

2. Tocqueville to Gustave de Beaumont, 5 October 1828, in *OC,* VIII (1), 71.

3. Tocqueville to Gustave de Beaumont, 8 May 1830, in *OC,* VIII (1), 98.

4. Tocqueville to Gustave de Beaumont, 4 October 1829, in *OC,* VIII (1), 89.

5. See Seymour Drescher, "Tocqueville and Beaumont: A Rationale for Collective Study," in *Tocqueville and Beaumont on Social Reform* (New York, 1968), 201–17. The most extensive account of the relationship between the two men is to be found in Andreas Hess, *Tocqueville and Beaumont: Aristocratic Liberalism in Democratic Times* (London, 2018).

6. Gustave de Beaumont to his father, 25 April 1831, in *Lettres d'Amérique 1831–32* (Paris, 1973), 27–28.

7. Gustave de Beaumont to Tocqueville, 15 August 1848, in *OC,* VIII (2), 19.

8. Gustave de Beaumont to Tocqueville, 6 June 1831, in *OC,* VIII (1), 107–8.

9. Gustave de Beaumont to Tocqueville, 26 June 1850, in *OC,* VIII (2), 277.

10. Gustave de Beaumont to Tocqueville, 25 December 1854, in *OC,* VIII (3), 256.

11. Richard Monckton Milnes, Lord Houghton, *Commonplace Book 1842–1843,* quoted in *OC,* VI (3), 317.

12. Tocqueville to his father, 17 August 1835, in *OC,* XIV, 192.

13. Drescher, "Tocqueville and Beaumont," 214.

14. M. C. M. Simpson, *Many Memories of Many People* (London, 1898), 55. To this day, relatively little has been written on Beaumont, but for an insightful sketch of his career and personality, see G. W. Pierson, "Gustave de Beaumont, Liberal,"

Franco-American Review, no. 1 (1937): 307–16. For a recent study that seeks to establish the importance of Beaumont's texts, see Sara A. Benson, "Democracy and Unfreedom: Revisiting Tocqueville and Beaumont in America," *Political Theory* 45, no. 4 (2017): 466–94. See also Margaret Kohn, "The Other America: Tocqueville and Beaumont on Race and Slavery," *Polity* 35, no. 2 (2002): 169–93; Kohn refers to Beaumont as Tocqueville's "often overlooked collaborator."

15. Tocqueville, *Democracy in America,* 1041–51, 1037.

16. Gustave de Beaumont to his brother Jules, 4 July 1831, *Lettres d'Amérique,* 81.

17. Gustave de Beaumont, *Lettres d'Amérique,* 41, 48, 66, 80–81, 98, 147, 170, 173, 186.

18. Gustave de Beaumont to his mother, 17 July 1831[?], in *Lettres d'Amérique,* 98

19. Gustave de Beaumont to his sister-in-law Félicie, 26 October 1831, in *Lettres d'Amérique,* 170.

20. Gustave de Beaumiont to his brother Achille, 8 November 1831, in *Lettres d'Amérique,* 173.

21. Gustave de Beaumont to his sister-in-law Félicie, 26 October 1831, in *Lettres d'Amérique,* 170.

22. Gustave de Beaumont to his father, 25 April 1831, in *Lettres d'Amérique,* 24, 28.

23. Gustave de Beaumont to his brother Jules, 26 May 1831, in *Lettres d'Amérique,* 52.

24. Gustave de Beaumont to his father, 29 June 1831, in *Lettres d'Amérique,* 70.

25. Gustave de Beaumont to his brother Jules, 16 September 1831, in *Lettres d'Amérique,* 147; Gustave de Beaumont to his brother Achille, 25 September 1831[?], in *Lettres d'Amérique,* 156; Gustave de Beaumont to his mother, 7 October 1831, *Letttres d'Amérique,* 159.

26. Gustave de Beaumont to his mother, 7 October 1831, in *Lettres d'Amérique,* 160.

27. Gustave de Beaumont to his sister-in-law Félicie, 26 October 1831, in *Lettres d'Amérique,* 169–70.

28. Gustave de Beaumont to his brother Achille, 8 November 1831, in *Lettres d'Amérique,* 173–75.

29. Gustave de Beaumont to his father, 16 May 1831 in *Lettres d'Amérique,* 43–44.

30. Beaumont's wife, Clémentine, was La Fayette's granddaughter.

31. Gustave de Beaumont to his brother Achille, 18 June 1831, in *Lettres d'Amérique,* 67.

32. Gustave de Beaumont to his sister Eugénie, 1 December 1831, in *Lettres d'Amérique,* 185.

33. Gustave de Beaumont to his brother Jules, 26 May 1831, in *Lettres d'Amérique,* 53; Gustave de Beaumont to his father, 25 April 1831, in *Lettres* d'Amérique, 28.

34. Gustave de Beaumont to his father, 16 May 1831, in *Lettres d'Amérique,* 41.

35. Gustave de Beaumont to his brother Jules, 4 July 1831, in *Lettres d'Amérique,* 80; Gustave de Beaumont to Ernest de Chabrol, 2 August 1831, in *Letttres d'Amérique,* 112.

36. Gustave de Beaumont to his father, 16 May 1831, in *Lettres d'Amérique,* 41–42.

37. Gustave de Beaumont to his mother, 7 June 1831, in *Lettres d'Amérique,* 58–59.

38. Gustave de Beaumont to his brother Achille, 25 September 1831[?], in *Lettres d'Amérique,* 158.

39. Gustave de Beaumont to his sister Eugénie, 14 July 1831, in *Lettres d'Amérique,* 90–92.

40. Gustave de Beaumont to his sister Eugénie, 14 July 1831, in *Lettres d'Amérique,* 92.

41. Gustave de Beaumont to his brother Jules, 4 December 1831, in *Lettres d'Amérique,* 193–94.

42. Gustave de Beaumont to his brother Jules, 4 December 1831, in *Lettres d'Amérique,* 193–94.

43. Tocqueville to his mother, 19 June 1831, in *OC,* XIV, 105.

44. See the notes made by Beaumont of their conversations with John Nielson in Gustave de Beaumont, *Lettres d'Amérique,* 131–37, 141; and Tocqueville's notes in *OC,* V (1), 74–85.

45. Tocqueville, "Cahier Alphabétique A," in *OC,* V (1), 210–11.

46. Tocqueville to the Abbé Lesueur, 7 September 1831, in *OC,* XIV, 129.

47. Gustave de Beaumont to his father, 5 September 1831, in *Lettres d'Amérique,* 139.

48. Gustave de Beaumont to his brother Achille, 11 August 1831, in *Lettres d'Amérique,* 123.

49. Tocqueville to the Abbé Lesueur, 7 September 1831, in *OC,* XIV, 129.

50. Tocqueville, "Cahier Alphabétique A," in *OC,* V (1), 213–17.

51. Tocqueville, "Cahier Alphabétique A," in *OC,* V (1), 211–19.

52. Gustave de Beaumont to his father, 5 September 1831, in *Lettres d'Amérique,* 140–42.

53. Tocqueville to the Abbé Lesueur, 7 September 1831, in *OC,* XIV, 129.

54. Tocqueville, "Cahier Alphabétique A," in *OC,* V (1), 211.

55. Gustave de Beaumont to his father, 5 September 1831, in *Lettres d'Amérique,* 139.

56. Tocqueville to the Abbé Lesueur, 7 September 1831, in *OC,* XIV, 130.

57. Tocqueville, "Cahier Alphabétique A," in *OC,* V (1), 218.

58. Tocqueville to the Abbé Lesueur, 7 September 1831, in *OC,* XIV, 130.

59. Tocqueville, "Cahier Alphabétique A," in *OC,* V (1), 210, 211, 216.

60. Tocqueville, "Cahier Alphabétique A," in *OC,* V (1), 215–17.

61. Gustave de Beaumont to his father, 5 September 1831, in *Lettres d'Amérique,* 140.

62. Tocqueville, "Cahier Alphabétique A," in *OC,* V (1), 210–11.

63. Tocqueville, "Cahier Alphabétique A," in *OC,* V (1), 218. Tocqueville's interest and concern about the fate of French Canadians and their colonised status is shown in a letter to Henry Reeve, 3 January 1838, in *OC,* VI (3), 55–7. French Canadians, he wrote, formed "a separate people in America, a people which has a distinct and robust sense of its nationality . . . with its own language, religion, laws and mores." Tocqueville also referred to French Canada in his *L'ancien régime et la révolution.*

64. Tocqueville, "Enquête sur le pénitencier de Philadelphie," in *OC,* IV (1), 329–41.

65. Tocqueville and Gustave de Beaumont, "Lettre au ministère de l'intérieur écrite à Auburn, le 14 juillet 1831," in *OC,* IV (2), 21–40.

66. Gustave de Beaumont to his brother Jules, 16 September 1831, in *Lettres d'Amérique,* 150.

67. Gustave de Beaumont to his father, 16 May 1831; Gustave de Beaumont to his sister Eugénie, 14 July 1831, in *Lettres d'Amérique,* 45, 92.

68. Gustave de Beaumont to his sister-in-law Félicie, 26 October 1831; Gustave de Beaumont to his brother Achille, 8 November 1831, in *Lettres d'Amérique,* 167, 176.

69. Tocqueville to Edward Everett, 6 February 1833, in *OC,* VII, 54.

70. Tocqueville to Gustave de Beaumont, 4 April 1832, in *OC*, VIII (1), 111–12.

71. Tocqueville to Gustave de Beaumont, 10 April 1832, in *OC*, VIII (1), 115.

72. Tocqueville to Gustave de Beaumont, 17 May 1832, in *OC*, VIII (1), 118.

73. Tocqueville, "Description du Bagne de Toulon (Mai 1832)," in *OC*, IV (2), 43–61; Tocqueville, "Notes prises par Tocqueville sur les prisons de Genève et de Lausanne," in *OC*, IV (2), 64–75.

74. Michelle Perrot, "Tocqueville méconnu," in *OC*, IV (1), 23–25.

75. Tocqueville to Gustave de Beaumont, 1 November 1833, in *OC*, VIII (1), 137.

76. James T. Schleifer, *The Chicago Companion to Tocqueville's "Democracy in America"* (Chicago, 2012), 18.

77. Tocqueville and Gustave de Beaumont, "Note sur le système pénitentiare et sur la mission confiée par M. le ministre de l'intérieur à MM Gustave de Beaumont et Alexis de Tocqueville," in *OC*, IV (1), 49.

78. Beaumont to his mother, 7 June 1831, in *Lettres d'Amérique*, 57.

79. Tocqueville to Félix Le Peletier d'Aunay, 7 June 1831, in *OC*, IV (2), 14.

80. Tocqueville to Ernest de Chabrol, 20 June 1831, in *OC*, XVII (1), 92.

81. Tocqueville to Félix Le Peletier d'Aunay, 7 June 1831, in *OC*, IV (2), 19.

82. Tocqueville to Félix Le Peletier d'Aunay, 7 June 1831, in *OC*, IV (2), 14–20.

83. Tocqueville and Beaumont, "Lettre au ministre de l'intérieur écrite à Auburn," 21–28.

84. Tocqueville and Gustave de Beaumont, "Lettre écrite à Philadelphie le 10 novembre 1831 sur le système pénitentiare adopté en Pennsylvanie," in *OC*, IV (2), 29–40.

85. Tocqueville to Honoré-Ambroise Langlois, 17 August 1838, in *OC*, X, 98–104.

86. Tocqueville and Gustave de Beaumont, "Système pénitentiare aux États-Unis," in *OC*, IV (1), 96. See also Roger Boesche, *Tocqueville's Road Map: Methodology, Liberalism, Revolution and Despotism* (Lanham, MD, 2006), 149–68.

87. Tocqueville and Beaumont, "Système pénitentiare," 231.

88. Tocqueville and Beaumont, "Système pénitentiare," 53. That Tocqueville continued his support for the Philadelphia system and that he was aware of its controversial nature is evident from later correspondence with Italian and German experts. To Carlo di Torrigiani he wrote, "It is obvious that, if a man can be led to repent of his misconduct, it is above all when, placed before God and a

priest, he is entirely separated from the world and his accomplices"; Tocqueville to Carlo di Torrigiani, 9 April 1842, in *OC,* VII, 292.

89. Tocqueville and Beaumont, "Système pénitentiare," 215.

90. Tocqueville and Beaumont, "Système pénitentiare," 235–41.

91. Tocqueville and Beaumont, "Système pénitentiare," 245–47. See also Tocqueville to a member of the Sociéte des sciences morales de Seine-et-Oise, 29 March 1836, in *OC,* XVII (1), 277–82. Here Tocqueville not only reaffirmed his faith in the system of solitary confinement but also made clear that France had much to learn from America in terms of how prisons were built and how cheaply this could be done.

92. Tocqueville, *Democracy in America,* 407–9.

93. Evidence of the continued importance Tocqueville attached to this issue can be seen in Tocqueville to Nathaniel Niles, 15 June, 1843, in *OC,* VII, 88–9; Tocqueville to Nikolaus-Heinrich Julius, 2 May 1843, in *OC,* VII, 294–95; and Tocqueville to Pasquale Stanislao Mancini, 3 February 1845, in *OC,* VII, 306–7.

94. Tocqueville, "Chambre des Députés, session de 1843, rapport fait au nom de la commission chargée d'examiner le projet de loi sur les prisons par M. de Tocqueville, député de la Manche," in *OC,* IV (2), 117–82.

95. Gustave de Beaumont, "La polémique avec Le siècle," in *OC,* IV (1), 471–89.

96. Charles Lucas, "Lettre de Charles Lucas, inspecteur des prisons du royaume, à G de Beaumont et A de Tocqueville, avant leur départ en Amérique," in *OC,* IV (1), 462–63.

97. Tocqueville, "Observations sur le mémoire de M. Ch. Lucas rélatif au régime pénitentiare par MM de Tocqueville, Ch. Lucas et Bérenger," in *OC,* IV (2), 183–213.

98. Christine Dunn Henderson, "Tyranny and Tragedy in Beaumont's Marie," in *America through European Eyes: British and French Reflections on the New World from the Eighteenth Century to the Present,* ed. Aurelian Craiutu and Jeffrey C. Isaac (University Park, PA, 2009), 145.

99. Tocqueville, *Democracy in America,* 29n1, 548n30.

100. Gustave de Beaumont, *Marie, or Slavery in the United States; A Novel of Jacksonian America,* ed. Alvis L. Tinnin, trans. Barbara Chapman (Stanford, CA, 1958).

101. Gustave de Beaumont, *Marie: Ou, l'esclavage aux États-Unis; Tableau des mœurs américaines* (Paris, 1842), 1; hereafter, all quotations from *Marie* are from this edition.

102. Beaumont, *Marie,* 218.

103. Beaumont, *Marie,* 1.

104. Tocqueville, "Cahier Portatif No 3," in *OC,* V (1), 191–92.

105. Beaumont, *Marie,* 3–4.

106. Beaumont misquotes the title of the play in both his letters from America and in his novel.

107. Beaumont, *Marie,* 8, 28–30.

108. Beaumont, *Marie,* 221–65.

109. Beaumont, *Marie,* 256.

110. Beaumont, *Marie,* 63–64.

111. Beaumont, *Marie,* 87.

112. Beaumont, *Marie,* 83.

113. Beaumont, *Marie,* 258.

114. Tocqueville, "Rapport fait au nom de la commission chargée d'examiner la proposition de M. de Tracy, relative aux esclaves des colonies," in *OC,* III (1), 41–78. In a letter to John Stuart Mill, Tocqueville wrote that, in producing this report, he had gone out of his way not to stir up "colonial passions," adding, "but you know the settlers, they are all the same, whatever country they come from; they go completely mad as soon as you talk of being fair to their Blacks"; Tocqueville to John Stuart Mill, n.d., in *OC,* VI (1), 326.

115. For a pathbreaking study, see Benedict Gaston Songy, "Alexis de Tocqueville and Slavery: Judgments and Predictions (PhD diss., St. Louis University, 1969).

116. Tocqueville, "Rapport fait au nom de la commission," 42–5.

117. Tocqueville, "Rapport fait au nom de la commission," 49–59.

118. Tocqueville, "L'Emancipation des esclaves," in *OC,* III (1), 79–111.

119. Tocqueville to Gustave de Beaumont, 9 October 1843, in *OC,* VIII (1), 506. Tocqueville offered similar praise in the fifth of his articles in *Le siècle,* describing it as "a fine book and one that will last"; Tocqueville, "L'Emancipation des esclaves," in *OC,* III (1), 101.

120. Tocqueville, "L'Emancipation des esclaves," in *OC,* III (1), 80.

121. Tocqueville, "L'Emancipation des esclaves," in *OC,* III (1), 105.

122. Tocqueville, "Intervention dans la discussion de la loi sur le régime des esclaves dans les colonies," in *OC*, III (1), 112–26.

123. Tocqueville, "Intervention dans la discussion de la loi," in *OC,* III (1), 124–25.

124. Tocqueville, "Intervention dans la discussion de la loi" in *OC,* III (1), 117–18. For a critical appraisal of these interventions on slavery by Tocqueville, see Nick Nesbitt, "On the Political Efficacy of Idealism: Tocqueville, Schoelcher, and the Abolition of Slavery," in Craiutu and Isaac, eds., *America through European Eyes,* 91–114.

4. ENGLAND, IRELAND, AND SWITZERLAND

1. Tocqueville, "Voyage en Angleterre de 1833. Notes, idées et observations que j'ai receuillies en Angleterre pendant le séjour de cinq semaines que j'y ai fait en 1833," in *OC,* V (2), 9–43. See also Seymour Drescher, *Tocqueville and England* (Cambridge, MA, 1964).

2. Tocqueville to Laurette de Pisieux, 5 July 1833, in *OC,* XVII (1), 191.

3. Tocqueville to his mother, 7 August 1833, in *OC,* XIV, 171–72.

4. Tocqueville to Marie Mottley, 14 August 1833, in *OC,* XIV, 388–89.

5. Tocqueville to Gustave de Beaumont, 13 August 1833, in *OC,* VIII (1), 124.

6. Tocqueville to his father, 24 August 1833, in *OC,* XIV, 173.

7. Tocqueville to Gustave de Beaumont, 13 August 1833, in *OC,* VIII (1), 125.

8. Tocqueville appears to have been slightly mistaken, as the bishop referred to here was Archbishop Richard Whately.

9. Tocqueville to Marie Mottley, 27 August 1833, in *OC,* XIV, 389–91.

10. Édouard de Tocqueville, *Voyage en Angleterre, en Écosse et en Irlande* (Paris: 2022), 96–98.

11. Tocqueville to Marie Mottley, 30 August 1833, in *OC,* XIV, 391–4.

12. Tocqueville to his father, 24 August 1833, in *OC,* XIV, 174.

13. Tocqueville to Marie Mottley, 30 August 1833, in *OC,* XIV, 391–4.

14. Gustave de Beaumont to Tocqueville, 24 August 1833, in *OC,* VIII (1), 129.

15. Tocqueville, "Voyage en Angleterre de 1833," in *OC,* V (2), 14.

16. Tocqueville to Gustave de Beaumont, 13 August 1833, in *OC,* VIII (1), 124.

17. Gustave de Beaumont to Tocqueville, 6 October 1833, in *OC,* VIII (1), 132.

18. Tocqueville, *Democracy in America,* 49–51.

19. Tocqueville, "Mémoire sur le paupérisme," in *OC,* XVI, 117–39. Tocqueville appears to have had a dim view toward this essay; see Tocqueville to Prosper

Duvergier de Hauranne, 4 May 1837, in *OC*, XVII (1), 320, where he wrote, "I confess to you in all frankness that I would have preferred not to have produced this small piece of writing." For a commentary on both of Tocqueville's *mémoires* dealing with the subject of pauperism, see Richard Swedberg, *Tocqueville's Political Economy* (Princeton, NJ, 2009), 136–44.

20. Tocqueville, "Mémoire sur le paupérisme," in *OC*, XVI (2), 117–18.

21. Tocqueville, "Mémoire sur le paupérisme," in *OC*, XVI, 127. This was a theme that Tocqueville returned to in his later (and originally unpublished) "Second mémoire sur le paupérisme," in *OC*, XVI, 140–57. Here his point was that, as the French economy was less exposed to the external market, "commercial crises" would not be as "frequent, as widespread and as severe as in England"; "Second mémoire sur le paupérisme," in *OC*, XVI, 145.

22. Tocqueville, "Mémoire sur le paupérisme," in *OC*, XVI (2), 133.

23. Tocqueville, "Voyage en Angleterre en 1833," in *OC*, V (2), 36.

24. Tocqueville, "Voyage en Angleterre en 1833," in *OC*, V (2), 37.

25. Tocqueville, "Voyage en Angleterre en 1833," in *OC*, V (2), 37–39.

26. Tocqueville, "Voyage en Angleterre en 1833," in *OC*, V (2), 39.

27. Tocqueville to Mrs. Elizabeth Belam, 4–5 September 1833, in *OC*, VI (3), 38.

28. Tocqueville to Léon von Thun-Hohenstein, 2 February[?] 1835, in *OC*, VII, 283. The content of Tocqueville's letter suggests that he was sending Thun a copy of Nassau Senior's famous report on the English Poor Laws. Tocqueville also recommended that Thun read Thomas Malthus's *Essay on the Principle of Population*.

29. Tocqueville to his father, 29 April 1835, in *OC*, XIV, 175.

30. Tocqueville to Virginie Ancelot, 28 April 1835, in *OC*, XVII (1), 233–34.

31. Tocqueville to Marie Mottley, 5 May 1835, in *OC*, XIV, 397.

32. For an account of one of these dinners see Tocqueville to Virginie Ancelot, 19 June 1835, in *OC*, XVII (1), 249.

33. Tocqueville to his father, 29 April 1835, in *OC*, XIV, 175; Tocqueville to Virginie Ancelot, 28 April 1835, in *OC*, XVII (1), 233.

34. Tocqueville to John Stuart Mill, June 1835, in *OC*, VI (1), 291. Tocqueville recorded a similar experience on top of a stagecoach in 1834 when he was obliged to travel back from the Beaumont family château to Paris overnight in cold conditions. On this occasion, although he was awoken when a basket of chickens

fell on his head, he acknowledged that being of a small build had its advantages; Tocqueville to Jules de Beaumont, 18 September 1834, in *OC,* XVII (1), 208.

35. Tocqueville to Alexandrine de Tocqueville, 22 May 1835, in *OC,* XIV, 179–80.

36. Tocqueville to his father, 29 April 1835, in *OC,* XIV, 175. See also Michael Wheeler, *The Athenaeum: More Than Just Another London Club* (New Haven, CT, 2020), 71–108.

37. See Tocqueville's description of a day he spent in Manchester, which began with a copious breakfast with a local doctor and included visits to a charitable organisation, the town hall, a poor Irish quarter, a large factory, and a barracks. This was followed by dinner and an evening spent with a local scientific society. It would be difficult, he told Mary Mottley, "to lead a more hectic existence"; Tocqueville to Marie Mottley, 1 July 1835, in *OC,* XIV, 398.

38. Tocqueville, "Voyage en Angleterre et en Irlande de 1835," 11 May 1835, in *OC,* V (2), 51. See also Tocqueville to Matthieu Molé, 19 May 1835, in *OC,* XVII (1), 237–38, which develops this point at length.

39. Tocqueville to John Stuart Mill, June 1835, in *OC,* VI (1), 294. Tocqueville made it clear that he sided with the English democrats, arguing that this strategy was the only way of saving society from "barbarism and slavery."

40. According to the diaries of Mrs. Senior, Tocqueville visited the Seniors eight times between his arrival in London on 24 April and his departure on 24 June. To this day, although now largely forgotten, Nassau Senior remains a controversial figure. This is largely due to the fact that he is often seen as one of the authors of the Poor Law Amendment Act of 1834 (which brought work-houses into existence) and because of his apparent indifference to the fate of the Irish population during the Irish Potato Famine of 1845. There can be no doubt about the strength of the friendship between Tocqueville and Senior.

41. Tocqueville, "Voyage en Angleterre et en Irlande de 1835," in *OC,* V (2), 54.

42. Tocqueville, "Enquête sur la corruption électorale," in *OC,* XVI, 88–111. The greater part of Tocqueville's evidence related to the working of the secret ballot in France. Interestingly, at the end of the discussion the topic turned to the use of secret ballots in the United States, with Tocqueville venturing the opinion that "the greatest advantage" of their use lay in protection against the tyranny of the majority (108).

43. Tocqueville to his father, 7 May 1835, in *OC,* XIV, 178. Tocqueville was to make the same point and the same contrast between America and England after

his return to France in a letter to Mathieu Molé, September 1835, in *OC,* XVII (1), 253–54: "One can," he wrote, "compare America to a large forest crossed by a multitude of straight roads leading to the same place. It is only a matter of going to the roundabout to see everything at one glance. But in England, the roads cross each other, and it is only by following each one of them that one arrives at a clear idea of the whole."

44. Tocqueville, "Voyage en Angleterre et en Irlande de 1835," in *OC,* V (2), 60.

45. Tocqueville to Mathieu Molé, 19 May 1835, in *OC,* XVII (1), 235–40.

46. Tocqueville, "Voyage en Angleterre et en Irlande de 1835," 1 June 1835, in *OC,* V (2), 64.

47. Tocqueville, "Voyage en Angleterre et en Irlande de 1835," 7 July 1835, in *OC,* V (2), 90.

48. Tocqueville, "Voyage en Angleterre et en Irlande de 1835," in *OC,* V (2), 67–68.

49. In a letter to Mary Mottley, Tocqueville wrote that even Dante would have struggled to invent a more awful punishment than living in these hideous dwellings; Tocqueville to Marie Mottley, 1 July 1835, in *OC,* XIV, 398.

50. Tocqueville, "Voyage en Angleterre et Irlande de 1835," in *OC,* V (2), 80–81.

51. Tocqueville, "Voyage en Angleterre et Irlande de 1835," 2 July 1835, in *OC,* V (2), 78.

52. Tocqueville, "Voyage en Angleterre et Irlande de 1835," in *OC,* V (2), 78–82.

53. Tocqueville, "Voyage en Angleterre et Irlande de 1835," in *OC,* V (2), 90–91; emphases in the original.

54. Drescher, *Tocqueville and England,* 66.

55. Tocqueville to Lord Lansdowne, 21 August 1835, in *OC,* VI (3), 44.

56. Tocqueville, "On the Social and Political Condition of France," *London and Westminster Review,* no. 25 (1836): 138. This text was written for and translated by John Stuart Mill. It contained many of the ideas that were to inform the writing of Tocqueville's *L'ancien régime et la révolution.* In French it is published as "État social et politique de la France avant et depuis 1789," in *OC,* II (1), 31–66.

57. Tocqueville, *Democracy in America,* 982–83.

58. Tocqueville, *Democracy in America,* 984–85.

59. Tocqueville, *Democracy in America,* 1249.

60. Tocqueville, "Voyage en Angleterre et Irlande de 1835," 11 May 1835, in *OC,* V (2), 49.

61. Tocqueville, *Democracy in America,* 1223–31.

62. Tocqueville, *Democracy in America,* 1232–34.

63. Tocqueville, *Democracy in America,* 1249–53.

64. Tocqueville, *Democracy in America,* 1280–81, 1244.

65. See Andreas Hess, *Tocqueville and Beaumont: Aristocratic Liberalism in Democratic Times* (London, 2018), 66–75.

66. It also seems likely that Mill later sent Beaumont a "very important pamphlet" written by Revans about Ireland; John Stuart Mill to Tocqueville, 7 January 1837, in *OC,* VI (1), 318. Nassau Senior wrote extensively on Ireland over a period of many years; see, in particular, Nassau William Senior, *Journals, Conversations and Essays Relating to Ireland* (London, 1868). His general view was that Ireland's "material evils" had their roots in her "moral evils" and that these were "insecurity, ignorance and indolence" (33).

67. Tocqueville, "Voyage en Angleterre et Irlande de 1835," in *OC,* V (2), 93–95.

68. Tocqueville, "Voyage en Angleterre et Irlande de 1835," in *OC,* V (2), 97–98.

69. Tocqueville to Eugénie de Grancey, 26 July 1835, in *OC,* XVII (1), 251.

70. Tocqueville, "Voyage en Angleterre et Irlande de 1835," 20 July 1835, in *OC,* V (2), 111.

71. Tocqueville, "Voyage en Angleterre et Irlande de 1835," 26 July 1835, in *OC,* V (2), 131–33.

72. Tocqueville, "Voyage en Angleterre et Irlande de 1835," in *OC,* V (2), 133–34. See also Tocqueville to his father, 16 July 1835, in *OC,* XIV, 184.

73. Tocqueville to Gustave de Beaumont, 26 August 1835, in *OC,* VIII (1), 154.

74. Tocqueville to Eugénie de Grancey, 26 July 1835, in *OC,* XVII (1), 251. Letters to both John Stuart Mill and Henry Reeve apologised for Tocqueville's hasty departure from England: Tocqueville to John Stuart Mill, 12 July 1835, *OC,* VI (1), 295; Tocqueville to Henry Reeve, 11 July 1835, *OC,* VI (1), 26.

75. Tocqueville to Eugénie de Grancey, 7 August [September?] 1835, in *OC,* XVII (1), 255–56.

76. Tocqueville to Gustave de Beaumont, 26 August 1835, in *OC,* VIII (1), 154.

77. Tocqueville to Marie Mottley, 1835, in *OC,* XIV, 399, emphasis in the original.

78. Tocqueville to Mathieu Molé, September 1835, in *OC,* XVII (1), 253.

79. Tocqueville to John Stuart Mill, 10 April 1836, in *OC,* VI (1), 309.

80. Tocqueville to Lord Radnor, 28 August 1835, in *OC,* VI (3), 45–47.

81. Tocqueville to Lord Radnor, 28 August 1835, in *OC,* VI (3), 47–48.

82. Tocqueville to Lord Radnor, 28 August 1835, in *OC,* VI (3), 48.

83. Tocqueville, "De la situation intérieure en Irlande," in *OC,* III (2), 472–77; Tocqueville, "L'Irlande et l'Angleterre," in *OC,* III (2), 478–82. Both articles cite Beaumont and draw heavily upon his investigations in Ireland.

84. See Tocqueville, "On the Social and Political Condition of France," 137–69.

85. Gustave de Beaumont, *L'Irlande, sociale, politique et religieuse,* 2 vols. (Paris, 1839–1842); Beaumont's text was translated immediately upon publication by W. C. Taylor, and that edition was recently republished as *Ireland: Social, Political, and Religious* by Harvard University Press (Cambridge, MA, 2006); to help the non–French speaking reader I have referred to the English text where possible but, on occasions, have amended Taylor's version. With just cause, Beaumont was not happy with Taylor's translation; see Gustave de Beaumont, "Observation relative à la traduction anglaise de M. L Dr W.C.Taylor," in *L'Irlande, sociale, politique et religieuse,* 2 vols. (Paris, 1863), 2:319–23. Beaumont pointed out that not only was material removed for the translation, but material was also added by the translator. In general, the translation is reasonably accurate, except where Taylor makes significant additions.

86. Gustave de Beaumont to Tocqueville, 27 July 1837, in *OC,* VIII (1), 212–13. Only the thought of his and his wife's visit to the "paradise" of the Tocqueville family château on their return to France, Beaumont wrote, sustained them in their "purgatory."

87. Gustave de Beaumont to Tocqueville, 27 July 1837, in *OC,* VIII (1), 212–16.

88. Gustave de Beaumont to Tocqueville, 26 October 1839, in *OC,* VIII (1), 391–92. Beaumont wrote that "I would have preferred to have written half of your *Democracy* than my two volumes on Ireland" (391).

89. Beaumont, *L'Irlande* (Paris: 1839–1842), 1:1–2.

90. Beaumont, *L'Irlande,* 1: 3.

91. Beaumont, *L'Irlande,* 1: 3–4.

92. Beaumont, *L'Irlande,* 1: 4.

93. Beaumont, *Ireland,* 5.

94. Beaumont, *Ireland,* 43.

95. Beaumont, *Ireland,* 14.

96. Beaumont, *Ireland,* 55.

97. Beaumont, *Ireland,* 67.

98. Beaumont, *Ireland,* 72.

99. Beaumont, *Ireland,* 130.

100. Beaumont, *Ireland,* 130.

101. Beaumont, *Ireland,* 132.

102. Beaumont, *Ireland,* 170.

103. Beaumont, *Ireland,* 213.

104. Beaumont, *Ireland,* 221.

105. Beaumont, *Ireland,* 281.

106. Beaumont, *Ireland,* 302.

107. Beaumont, *Ireland,* 332.

108. Beaumont, *Ireland,* 375.

109. Beaumont, *Ireland,* 375.

110. Beaumont, *Ireland,* 376–77.

111. Tocqueville to Louis de Kergorlay, 16 July 1836, in *OC,* XIII (1), 380–82.

112. Tocqueville to P.- P. Royer-Collard, 25 August 1836, in *OC,* XI, 18–21.

113. Tocqueville, "Notes sur Machiavel," in *OC,* XVI, 541–50. Tocqueville was generally unimpressed by Machiavelli. Writing from Baden he told Kergorlay that for Machiavelli "the world is a grand arena from which God is absent"; Tocqueville to Louis de Kergorlay, 5 August 1836, in *OC,* XIII (1), 390.

114. Tocqueville, "Remarques sur l'histoire suisse," in *OC,* V (2), 171–88.

115. Tocqueville confided to John Stuart Mill that the trip to Switzerland had been a big mistake, referring to a "miserably wasted" three months; Tocqueville to John Stuart Mill, 19 September 1836, in *OC,* VI (1), 314. To Henry Reeve, Tocqueville complained that he had lost only two months; Tocqueville to Henry Reeve, 21 September 1836, in *OC,* VI (1), 35.

116. Christopher Hughes, *Switzerland* (New York, 1975), 110.

117. Tocqueville to Francisque de Corcelle, 27 July 1836, in *OC,* XV (1), 70–71.

118. Tocqueville, "Remarques sur l'histoire Suisse," 176–77.

119. Tocqueville, *Democracy in America,* 251–55.

120. Tocqueville to Auguste de la Rive, 15 February 1842, in *OC,* VII, 289–90; Tocqueville to Auguste de la Rive, 22 December 1844, in *OC,* VII, 304–5. Tocqueville was similarly pessimistic about Switzerland when he wrote to De la Rive in 1853; Tocqueville to Auguste de la Rive, 29 March 1853, in *OC,* VII, 330–31.

121. Tocqueville, "La Suisse en 1845," in *OC,* III (2), 463–71.

122. "The Diet" is a reference to the Tagsatzung, or Swiss federal parliament.

123. Tocqueville, "La Suisse en 1845," 468–70.

124. Tocqueville, "Sur *La démocratie en Suisse,*" in *OC,* XVI, 212. The text is translated as "Report on Democracy in Switzerland," in *Tocqueville on America after 1840: Letters and Other Writings,* ed. and trans. Aurelian Craiutu and Jeremy Jennings (New York, 2009), 354–69.

125. Tocqueville, "Sur *La démocratie en Suisse,*" in *OC,* XVI, 214–15.

126. Tocqueville, "Sur *La démocratie en Suisse,*" 203–204.

5. ALGERIA

1. Tocqueville described his three-week campaign as a "*grande entreprise gastronomio-électorale,*" commenting that he had dined out every night and that each dinner had lasted for at least three hours; Tocqueville to Francisque de Corcelle, 9 October 1838, in *OC,* XV (1), 102. He returned to this theme the following year in a letter to Pierre-Paul Royer-Collard when he recounted that the only time his electors came together was over "immense dinners." Most, he added, did not know that Adolphe Thiers was the prime minister: Tocqueville to P.-P. Royer-Collard, 15 August 1840, *OC,* XI, 89–90. In another letter to Royer-Collard he proffered the view that his fellow residents of the Cotentin Peninsula were "honest, intelligent, religious enough, passably moral" but "poor citizens": Tocqueville to P.-P. Royer-Collard, 23 June 1838, *OC,* XI, 64.

2. Tocqueville's writings on Algeria are largely contained in *OC,* III (1). The exception are his "Notes du voyage en Algérie de 1841," in *OC,* V (2), 189–218. Jennifer Pitts has translated a sizeable portion of these texts; see Jennifer Pitts, ed., *Alexis de Tocqueville: Writings on Empire and Slavery* (Baltimore, 2001).

3. In addition to the introduction by J.-J. Chevallier and André Jardin to *OC,* III (1), 7–32, see Melvin Richter, "Tocqueville on Algeria," *Review of Politics* 25, no. 3 (1963): 362–99; Cheryl B. Welch, "Colonial Violence and the Rhetoric of Evasion: Tocqueville on Algeria," *Political Theory* 31, no. 2 (2003): 235–64; Cheryl B. Welch, "Out of Africa: Tocqueville's Imperial Voyages," in *Tocqueville's Voyages: The Evolution of His Ideas and Their Journey beyond His Time,* ed. Christine

Dunn Henderson (Indianapolis, 2014), 304–34; Jennifer Pitts, *A Turn to Empire: The Rise of Imperial Liberalism in Britain and France* (Princeton, NJ, 2005), 204–39; and Roger Boesche, "The Dark Side of Tocqueville: On War and Empire," in *Tocqueville's Road Map: Methodology, Liberalism, Revolution, and Despotism* (Lanham, MD, 2006), 109–25. See also Domenico Losurdo, *Liberalism: A Counter-history,* trans. Gregory Elliott (London, 2011), 233–40. Losurdo's conclusion is that Tocqueville's "identification with the regime of white or Western supremacy . . . seems to have been total" (240). A word of caution comes from Lucien Jaume. On the colonisation of Algeria, he writes, Tocqueville's "thought evolved continually and should not be interpreted in the light of a few 'sensational' quotes from various letters and texts or of his support at one point for Bugeaud's *enfumades*"; Lucien Jaume, *Tocqueville: The Aristocratic Sources of Liberty* (Princeton, NJ, 2008), 305. See also André Jardin, *Tocqueville: A Biography* (Baltimore, 1998), 318–42. For recent assessments, see Alan Kahan, "Tocqueville: Liberalism and Imperialism," in *French Liberalism from Montesquieu to the Present Day,* ed. Raf Geenens and Helena Rosenblatt (Cambridge, 2012), 152–68; and Ewa Atanassow, "Colonization and Democracy: Tocqueville Reconsidered," *American Political Science Review* 111 (2017), 83–96. See also Lina Benabdellah, "On Tocqueville in Algeria and Epistemic Violence," Al Jazeera, 7 June 2020, which argues that Tocqueville's writings on Algeria are a form of "epistemic violence against people of colour."

4. For a judicious and insightful account of French policy in Algeria, see David Todd, *A Velvet Empire: French Informal Imperialism in the Nineteenth Century* (Princeton, NJ, 2021), 2–122. Todd's overall thesis is that after 1815 the French preference was to build an "informal" empire based upon trade and commerce rather than the possession of colonial territories. "The one significant exception to this pattern," Todd argues, "was the extremely brutal and formal colonization of Algeria in the mid-century. However . . . Algeria can also be construed as the unintended product of a failed project of informal colonialism" (71). In other words, it was only when the French policy of informal domination and collaboration with Abd-el-Kadar failed that the French government embarked "on a deliberate policy of territorial conquest" and that members of the French elite (including Tocqueville) came to endorse "the most savage phase of the conquest between 1840 and 1847" (77).

5. See the series of letters written by Tocqueville during the late spring of 1830 to his brother Édouard and his sister-in-law Alexandrine: 15 March 1830, in *OC,* XIV, 55–58; 24 March 1830, in *OC,* XIV, 59–61; 6 April 1830, in *OC,* XIV, 61–64; 29 April 1830, in *OC,* XIV, 64–66; 6 May 1830, in *OC,* XIV, 66–69. Historians have traditionally emphasised the domestic origins of the Algiers expedition, but

as Todd, *A Velvet Empire,* 93, notes, the Bourbon monarchy's "imperial ambitions" consisted in "a limited coastal settlement and informal rule, rather than full territorial conquest."

6. Louis de Kergorlay to Tocqueville, 22 June 1830, in *OC,* XIII (1), 189–96; 27 June 1830, in *OC,* XIII (1), 196–98; 8 July 1830, in *OC,* XIII (1), 198–201; 29 July 1830, in *OC,* XIII (1), 202–6; 7 August 1830, in *OC,* XIII (1), 206–9.

7. With the establishment of the July Monarchy, Kergorlay left the army. He subsequently became embroiled in the plot led by the duchesse de Berry to restore the Bourbons to the throne, for which he was arrested and later found innocent. Kergorlay's letters to Tocqueville largely amount to a tiresome litany of unfulfilled projects (of which one of the most enduring was his attempt to find a wife).

8. Tocqueville to [Antoine-Isaac?] Silvestre de Sacy, n.d. [1833–1834?], in *OC,* XVII (1), 194–95.

9. Tocqueville and Gustave de Beaumont, "Quelques idées sur les raisons qui s'opposent à ce que les français aient de bonnes colonies," in *OC,* III (1), 35–40 (37). Another argument, and one not advanced by Tocqueville, was that demographic stagnation after 1815 meant that France had no surplus population to export.

10. Tocqueville and Beaumont, "Quelques idées," 39–40.

11. Tocqueville, "Deux lettres sur l'Algérie (1837)," in *OC,* III (1), 129–53.

12. This was a pointed jibe at commentators who believed that they could speak with authority about Algeria without visiting it.

13. Tocqueville, "Deux lettres" 130.

14. Tocqueville, "Deux lettres," 131.

15. Tocqueville, "Deux lettres," 135.

16. Tocqueville, "Deux lettres," 138.

17. Tocqueville, "Deux lettres," 142.

18. Tocqueville, "Deux lettres," 144.

19. Tocqueville, "Deux lettres," 149.

20. Tocqueville, "Deux lettres," 150.

21. Tocqueville, "Deux lettres," 150.

22. Tocqueville, "Deux lettres," 151.

23. Tocqueville, "Deux lettres," 151.

24. Tocqueville, "Deux lettres," 152.

25. Tocqueville, "Deux lettres," 153.

26. Tocqueville, "Deux lettres," 149.

27. Tocqueville to P. Clamorgan, 25 April 1841, in *OC,* X, 175.

28. Tocqueville, "Notes sur le Coran," in *OC,* III (1), 154–62. For an assessment of Tocqueville's views on Islam, see Alan S. Kahan, *Tocqueville, Democracy, and Religion* (Oxford, 2015), 182–89.

29. Tocqueville to Francisque de Corcelle, 19 March 1838, in *OC,* XV (1), 98.

30. Tocqueville to Louis de Kergorlay, 21 March 1838, in *OC,* XIII (2), 28–29.

31. In a later letter, Tocqueville wrote that, having completed his studies of the Koran, he had concluded that "there have been few religions as deadly to men as that of Mohammed"; Tocqueville to Arthur de Gobineau, 22 October 1843, in *OC,* IX, 69. The following year Tocqueville wrote that the more he had learned about Islam, the more he was convinced that it was responsible for the "decadence" that afflicted the Muslim world; Tocqueville to Richard Monkton Miles, 29 May 1844, in *OC,* VI (3), 87.

32. Tocqueville, "Notes prises avant le voyage d'Algérie et dans le courant de 1840," in *OC,* III (1), 163–208.

33. Tocqueville to Gustave de Beaumont, 9 August 1840, in *OC,* VIII (1), 421.

34. Pitts, *A Turn to Empire,* 185–89. Following the collapse of cooperation with Abd-el-Kadar, Desjobert advocated the evacuation of French possessions in Algeria.

35. Tocqueville, "Notes prises avant le voyage d'Algérie," 197.

36. Tocqueville, "Notes prises avant le voyage d'Algérie," 206.

37. Tocqueville to Francisque de Corcelle, 26 September 1840, in *OC,* XV (1), 151. See also Tocqueville to Léon Juchault de Lamoricière, 20 December 1840, in *OC,* XVII (2), 112–14, where Tocqueville expressed considerable concerns about the French predicament in Algeria.

38. For a brief account of these developments, see Eugene Rogan, *The Arabs: A History* (London, 2012), 135–47. At the time, French opinion was broadly divided between three possible policies: the extermination or expelling of the Arab population, the abandonment of the colonial project, and the assimilation of the Muslim population. The latter came increasingly to be seen as a delusion, with Muslims thought not to possess the moral and mental capacities appropriate for French citizenship. According to a recent study by Osama Abi Mershed, few liberal thinkers in France considered military conquest and pacification as not

being integral to the task of civilisation and modernisation; see Osama Abi-Mershed, *Apostles of Modernity: Saint-Simonians and the Civilizing Mission in Algeria* (Stanford, CA, 2010).

39. See Tocqueville to John Stuart Mill, 18 December 1840, in *OC,* VI (1), 329–31; John Stuart Mill to Tocqueville, 30 December 1840, 331–33; and Tocqueville to John Stuart Mill, 18 March 1841, 334–36. Tocqueville was enraged by what he saw as the disparaging and disdainful attitude of the British towards France, deeply shocking Mill with his argument that national pride was something that needed fostering and especially so in a "democratic nation" such as France, which could easily be reconciled to its loss of status by the building of railways and personal happiness. Tocqueville even appears to have thought that there was a danger of the English invasion of the Cotentin Peninsula; see Tocqueville to Adolphe Thiers, 31 July 1840, in *OC,* XVII (2), 93–95.

40. Tocqueville to P.- P. Royer-Collard, 15 August 1840, in *OC,* XI, 90.

41. Tocqueville to Marie Mottley, 30 April 1841, in *OC,* XIV, 415.

42. Tocqueville to his father, 12 May 1841, in *OC,* XIV, 216.

43. Tocqueville to Marie Mottley, 9 May 1841, in *OC,* XIV, 418.

44. Tocqueville to his father, 12 May 1841, in *OC,* XIV, 216.

45. Tocqueville, in "Notes du voyage en Algérie de 1841," 191.

46. Tocqueville, "Notes du Voyage en Algérie," 216. See also Tocqueville to Édouard de Tocqueville, 30 May 1841, in *OC,* XIV, 221, where he made an almost identical observation: the town, he commented, displayed "a febrile activity the like of which I had seen nowhere since the United States."

47. Tocqueville to Marie Mottley, 9 May 1841, in *OC,* XIV, 419.

48. Tocqueville to his father, 12 May 1841, in *OC,* XIV, 216.

49. Tocqueville to Marie Mottley, 9 May 1841, in *OC,* XIV, 419.

50. Tocqueville, "Notes du Voyage en Algérie," in *OC,* V (2), 192.

51. Tocqueville to Marie Mottley, 16 May 1841, in *OC,* XIV, 423.

52. Tocqueville to Marie Mottley, 17 May 1841, in *OC,* XIV, 424–25, emphasis in the original.

53. Tocqueville to Édouard de Tocqueville, 30 May 1841, in *OC,* XIV, 221.

54. Jardin, *Tocqueville: A Biography,* 326.

55. Tocqueville to his father, 12 May 1841, in *OC,* XIV, 216. The seriousness of Tocqueville's intentions was disclosed prior to his departure in a letter to his friend, Léon Juchault de Lamoricière, then serving as an officer in Algeria. Asking for advice on who to see, Tocqueville made it clear that he and Beaumont wanted to meet people who could enable them to see "both sides of the subject" and thereby "lead them to the truth"; Tocqueville to Léon Juchault de Lamoricière, 30 March 1841, in *OC,* XVII (2), 125.

56. Tocqueville to Marie Mottley, 28 May 1841, in *OC,* XIV, 430.

57. In addition to Tocqueville, "Notes du voyage en Algérie," see Tocqueville, "Notes journalières s'intercalant dans le livre-journal et y faisant suite (Mai 1841)," in *OC,* III (1), 209–12.

58. Tocqueville to Marie Mottley, 12 June 1841, in *OC,* XIV, 435–36.

59. Tocqueville to Marie Mottley, 13 June 1841, in *OC,* XIV, 437.

60. Upon arrival at his home, it was with some considerable satisfaction that Tocqueville wrote to his father to tell him that his journey from Paris had been completed in just twenty-four hours (half the time, he pointed out, it would have taken his father to do the journey in his youth). Was this not, he wrote, "the most charming way to travel that one could imagine?" Tocqueville to his father, 1 July 1841, in *OC,* XIV, 223.

61. Understandably, securing election became a major preoccupation for Tocqueville over the following months, as many of his letters testify.

62. Clues to the conclusions Tocqueville would reach about French policy in Algeria are found in two letters to Léon Faucher. The situation was so bad, Tocqueville wrote, that it was a wonder that there were any French settlers there at all. He attributed the greatest blame to Bugeaud; Tocqueville to Léon Faucher, 5 July 1841, in *OC,* XVII (2), 134–35; Tocqueville to Léon Faucher, 15 July 1841, in *OC,* XVII (2), 135–37.

63. Tocqueville to Édouard de Tocqueville, 17 October 1841, in *OC,* XIV, 224.

64. Gustave de Beaumont to Tocqueville, 12 October 1841, in *OC,* VIII (1), 448.

65. Tocqueville to Gustave de Beaumont, 12 October 1841, in *OC,* VIII (1), 449–52, emphasis in the original.

66. Tocqueville to Gustave de Beaumont, 15 November 1841, in *OC,* VIII (1), 452–54.

67. Tocqueville, "Travail sur l'Algérie, October 1841," in *OC,* III (1), 213–80.

68. See Todd, *A Velvet Empire,* 97.

69. Tocqueville, "Travail sur l'Algérie," 213.

70. Tocqueville, "Travail sur l'Algérie," 216.

71. Tocqueville, "Travail sur l'Algérie," 221.

72. Tocqueville, "Travail sur l'Algérie," 226–27.

73. Tocqueville, "Travail sur l'Algérie," 228.

74. Tocqueville, "Travail sur l'Algérie," 235.

75. Tocqueville, "Travail sur l'Algérie," 240.

76. Tocqueville, "Travail sur l'Algérie," 242.

77. Tocqueville, "Travail sur l'Algérie," 243.

78. Tocqueville, "Travail sur l'Algérie," 244–45.

79. Tocqueville, "Travail sur l'Algérie," 252.

80. Tocqueville, "Travail sur l'Algérie," 254.

81. Tocqueville, "Travail sur l'Algérie," 255.

82. Tocqueville, "Travail sur l'Algérie," 262.

83. Tocqueville, "Travail sur l'Algérie," 267.

84. Tocqueville, "Travail sur l'Algérie," 268.

85. However, in June 1842 Beaumont submitted a report to the Commission de colonisation d'Algérie on behalf of the parliamentary subcommittee on which he sat. A letter from Beaumont indicates that he had not had enough time to show it to Tocqueville before it was submitted.

86. The articles were published on 26 and 30 November and on 3, 7, and 11 December 1842. They were subsequently republished as Gustave de Beaumont, *État de la question d'Afrique* (Paris, 1843).

87. Gustave de Beaumont to Tocqueville, 16 November 1842, in *OC,* VIII (1), 476.

88. Bugeaud, *L'Algérie, des moyens de conserver et d'utiliser notre conquête* (Paris, 1842).

89. Beaumont, *État de la question,* 18.

90. Bugeaud's letter appeared in *Le siècle* on 28 December 1842. It was dated 14 December 1842.

91. Beaumont, *État de la question,* 49.

92. Gustave de Beaumont to Tocqueville, 30 August 1843, in *OC,* VIII (1), 497–98.

93. Tocqueville to Gustave de Beaumont, 5 September 1843, in *OC,* VIII (1), 499.

94. That Tocqueville had thoughts to write and publish about India as early as 1840 is confirmed in a letter to the editor of the *Revue des deux mondes;* Tocqueville to François Buloz, 2 October 1840, in *OC,* XVII (2), 104–5. The plan was to write a long review of Auguste Théodore Hilaire Barchou de Penhöen's *Histoire de la conquête et de la fondation de l'empire anglais dans l'Inde.* Nothing came of this. However, see Tocqueville to Barchou de Penhöen, 12 October 1841, in *OC,* XVII (2), 149–50.

95. Gustave de Beaumont to Tocqueville, 1 December 1843, in *OC,* VIII (1), 511–14. Tocqueville was less than impressed to receive news of Beaumont's planned visit to Algeria; see Tocqueville to Francisque de Corcelle, 11 December 1843, in *OC,* XV (1), 176.

96. Gustave de Beaumont to Tocqueville, 18 December 1843, in *OC,* VIII (1), 519–21.

97. Beaumont to Tocqueville, 18 December 1843, 522.

98. Beaumont to Tocqueville, 18 December 1843, 522.

99. Tocqueville to Gustave de Beaumont, 27 December 1843, in *OC,* VIII (1), 523–24.

100. See the long letter written to Paul Clamorgan, in which Tocqueville went to some lengths to explain his position on this issue, insisting strongly on his liberal credentials. "I do not want," he wrote, "to be a dupe of the clergy." Tocqueville suggested that Beaumont's failure to support him reflected a lack of courage on the latter's part; Tocqueville to Paul Clamorgan, 14 December 1844, in *OC,* X, 19–23.

101. See Tocqueville to Henry Reeve, 14 September 1843, in *OC,* VI (1), 72–73.

102. Tocqueville, "Ébauches d'un ouvrage sur l'Inde," in *OC,* III (1), 443–55.

103. Tocqueville, "Ébauches," 456–75.

104. Tocqueville to Henry Reeve, 23 March 1846, in *OC,* VI (1), 92–93.

105. Tocqueville to Henry Reeve, 4 April 1846, in *OC,* VI (1), 93–49; and 13/20? April 1846, in *OC,* VI (1), 95–96. The following year Tocqueville wrote to John Stuart Mill asking for information about how the British had established a civil administration in India, with such apparent success; Tocqueville to John Stuart Mill, 23 April 1847, in *OC,* VI (1), 348. Tocqueville was to continue to see parallels between the British colonisation of India and the French experience in Algeria.

106. Tocqueville to Léon Juchault de Lamoricière, 5 April 1846, in *OC,* XVII (2), 353–55.

107. Tocqueville to Lamoricière, 5 April 1846, in *OC,* XVII (2), 355–56.

108. Tocqueville to Lamoricière, 5 April 1846, in *OC,* XVII (2), 357.

109. Tocqueville to Lamoricière, 5 April 1846, in *OC,* XVII (2), 357.

110. Tocqueville to Lamoricière, 5 April 1846, in *OC,* XVII (2), 357–58.

111. Tocqueville to Lamoricière, 5 April 1846, in *OC,* XVII (2), 358.

112. Tocqueville to Francis Lieber, 22 July 1846, in *OC,* VII, 109–12; Francis Lieber to Tocqueville, 25 September 1846, in *Tocqueville on America after 1840: Letters and Other Writings,* ed. and trans. Aurelian Craiutu and Jeremy Jennings (New York, 2009), 87–89, emphasis in the original.

113. Tocqueville, "Intervention dans le débat sur les crédits extraordinaires de 1846," in *OC,* III (1), 293–94.

114. Tocqueville, "Intervention," 295–303.

115. Tocqueville, "Intervention," 303–7.

116. Tocqueville, "Allocution de Tocqueville après l'élection du 1er août," in *OC,* III (2), 81–83.

117. Tocqueville to Louis de Kergorlay, 11 September 1846, in *OC,* XIII (2), 188. Two weeks later Tocqueville informed Corcelle that he had decided to go to Algiers rather than Rome because it was "undoubtedly more useful and required only a marginally longer sea crossing"; Tocqueville to Francisque de Corcelle, 25 September 1846, in *OC,* XV (1), 215.

118. Tocqueville to Francisque de Corcelle, 11 October 1846, in *OC,* XV (1), 218.

119. Tocqueville to Louis de Kergorlay, 8 October 1846, in *OC,* XIII (2), 189.

120. Tocqueville to his father, 16 October 1846, in *OC,* XIV, 245.

121. Tocqueville to Gustave de Beaumont, 28 October 1846, in *OC,* VIII (1), 592.

122. Tocqueville to Francisque de Corcelle, 11 October 1846, in *OC,* XV (1), 219–20.

123. Tocqueville to Jules Dufaure, 6 November 1846, in *OC,* XVII (2), 379–82.

124. Marie de Tocqueville to Édouard de Tocqueville, 26 November 1846, in *OC,* XIV, 247.

125. Tocqueville to Gustave de Beaumont, 14 December 1846, in *OC,* VIII (1), 601.

126. Tocqueville to Francisque de Corcelle, 1 December 1846, in *OC,* XV (1), 223.

127. Auguste Bussière, "Le Maréchal Bugeaud et la colonisation de l'Algérie: Souvenirs et récits de la vie coloniale en Afrique," *Revue des deux mondes* 4, no. 3 (1853): 449–506.

128. M. Dussert to Marèchal de Castellane,1 January 1847, in *Campagnes d'Afrique: 1835–1848; Lettres adressées au Maréchal de Castellane* (Paris, 1898), 503.

129. Bussière, "Le Maréchal Bugeaud," 462–3.

130. In the Ottoman Empire, a *bachagda* was a high administrative official.

131. Bussière, "Le Maréchal Bugeaud," 465–66.

132. Bussière, "Le Maréchal Bugeaud," 471.

133. Maréchal de Saint-Arnaud, *Lettres du Maréchal de Saint-Arnaud, 1832–1854,* 2 vols. (Paris, 1864), 2:83. Saint-Arnaud's letter also gives a sense of the show that was put on for Tocqueville and his colleagues. "We had," he told his brother, "three Homeric meals for eighteen people, a reception and a royal entry at Orleansville, with cannon, troops lining the streets, spectacles, etc." In view of Saint-Arnaud's comment on the way Tocqueville observed the things around him, remarks by Tocqueville in August 1847 to someone about to make his first trip to Algeria merit quotation. "You will hear," Tocqueville wrote, "the most exaggerated and the most contradictory statements: do not come to a conclusion until you have had the time for careful consideration"; Tocqueville to Peter Eugen Obermayer, 27 August 1847, in *OC,* XVII (2), 417.

134. Bussière, "Le Maréchal Bugeaud," 475.

135. Tocqueville to Francisque de Corcelle, 1 December 1846, in *OC,* XV (1), 223–25.

136. Bussière, "Le Maréchal Bugeaud," 477–506.

137. In addition to the bad weather, Tocqueville indicated that he had also been delayed due to the poor health of his wife. Such misfortunes, he added, were fine if they were visited upon "*tourists* and those sight-seeing in Africa" but should be spared those who "travel four hundred leagues from their home to study for themselves questions which interest their country"; see Tocqueville to Marie Alphonse Bedeau, 18 December 1846, in *OC,* XVII (2), 383–84; emphasis in the original.

138. Francisque de Corcelle, 10 January 1847, in *OC,* XV (1), 225.

139. Tocqueville, "Rapport fait par M. de Tocqueville sur le projet de loi relatif aux crédits extraordinaires demandées pour l'Algérie," in *OC,* III (1), 308–79; Tocqueville, "Rapport fait par M. de Tocqueville sur le projet de loi portant

demande d'un crédit de 3 millions pour les camps agricoles de l'Algérie," in *OC,* III (1), 380–408.

140. Tocqueville, "Rapport fait par M. de Tocqueville sur le projet de loi portant demande d'un crédit," 380.

141. Tocqueville, "Rapport fait par M. de Tocqueville sur le projet de loi portant demande d'un crédit," 380.

142. Tocqueville, "Rapport fait par M. de Tocqueville sur le projet de loi portant demande d'un crédit," 384–90.

143. Tocqueville, "Rapport fait par M. de Tocqueville sur le projet de loi relatif aux crédits extraordinaires," 331.

144. Tocqueville, "Rapport fait par M. de Tocqueville sur le projet de loi relatif aux crédits extraordinaires," 330–46.

145. Tocqueville, "Rapport fait par M. de Tocqueville sur le projet de loi relatif aux crédits extraordinaires," 310.

146. Tocqueville, "Rapport fait par M. de Tocqueville sur le projet de loi relatif aux crédits extraordinaires," 347.

147. Tocqueville, "Rapport fait par M. de Tocqueville sur le projet de loi portant demande d'un crédit," 404.

148. Tocqueville, "Rapport fait par M. de Tocqueville sur le projet de loi relatif aux crédits extraordinaires," 316–17.

149. Tocqueville, "Rapport fait par M. de Tocqueville sur le projet de loi relatif aux crédits extraordinaires," 320–21.

150. Tocqueville, "Rapport fait par M. de Tocqueville sur le projet de loi relatif aux crédits extraordinaires," 323–24.

151. Tocqueville, "Rapport fait par M. de Tocqueville sur le projet de loi relatif aux crédits extraordinaires," 324–25.

152. Tocqueville, "Rapport fait par M. de Tocqueville sur le projet de loi relatif aux crédits extraordinaires," 326–28.

153. Tocqueville, "Rapport fait par M. de Tocqueville sur le projet de loi relatif aux crédits extraordinaires," 328–30.

154. Tocqueville, "Intervention à la chambre à l'occasion du vote du budget générale de l'Algérie pour 1848," in *OC,* III (1), 419–25.

155. Tocqueville, "Rapport fait par M. de Tocqueville, au nom de la commission chargée d'examiner la proposition de M. Henri Didier ayant pour objet de faire

nommer une commission spéciale chargée de préparer les lois promises à l'Algérie," in *OC,* III (1), 429–40.

156. Tocqueville to Arthur de Gobineau, 24 January 1857, in *OC,* IX, 277. See also the comments on Gobineau's work in Tocqueville to Adolphe de Circourt, 16 October 1853, in *OC,* XVIII, 110; Tocqueville to Adolphe de Circourt, 7 December 1853, in *OC,* XVIII, 119–20; Tocqueville to Gustave de Beaumont, 13 January 1854, in *OC,* VIII (3), 182; and Tocqueville to Francisque de Corcelle, 10 June 1854, in *OC,* XV (2), 104–5. In the last of these Tocqueville described Gobineau's work as that of "the philosophy of the head of a stud farm" (105).

157. Tocqueville to Ferdinand d'Eckstein, 8 March 1838, in *OC,* XVII (1), 377–78.

158. Tocqueville, "Rapport fait par M. de Tocqueville sur le projet de loi relatif aux crédits extraordinaires," 330.

159. A similar concern for France's national prestige also underpinned Tocqueville's ambiguous response to the French military expedition to Rome in 1849. Naively, as with Algeria, Tocqueville believed that French intervention and the restoration of papal authority would induce the pope to use his temporal power in a more liberal direction.

160. Tocqueville to P. Clamorgan, 17 June 1845, in *OC,* X, 339.

161. This was a view Tocqueville also expressed later when considering the Indian rebellion against British rule in 1857.

162. Richter, "Tocqueville on Algeria," 364.

163. Atanassow, "Colonization and Democracy."

164. Tocqueville to N. W. Senior, 1 April 1855, in *OC,* VI (2), 179. Senior was himself visiting Algeria at the time and Tocqueville's letter provides a commentary on Nassau's rather disappointing experience. In brief, French officials would not speak to him.

6. ITALY

1. Tocqueville, *Souvenirs, OC,* XII, 103–4.

2. Tocqueville to Francisque de Corcelle, 29 September 1847, in *OC,* XV (1), 239.

3. As Tocqueville made clear to his electoral agent in Normandy, he was very proud of this prediction. Never, he wrote, was the prediction of a politician so "promptly realised"; Tocqueville to P. Clamorgan, 25 February 1848, in *OC,* X, 444.

4. Tocqueville to Eugène Stoffels, 7 March 1848, in *OC,* XVII (2), 451–52.

5. Tocqueville to P. Clamorgan, 7 March 1848, in *OC,* X, 450.

6. Tocqueville, "Réponse d'Alexis de Tocqueville au président du Comité Électoral de Valognes le 26 mars 1848," in *OC,* III (3), 48.

7. Tocqueville to N. W. Senior, 10 April 1848, in *OC,* VI (2), 101.

8. In a letter to Paul Clamorgan, Tocqueville had referred to America as his "best subject" on which to speak in parliament; Tocqueville to Paul Clamorgan, 28 January 1846, in *OC,* X, 374.

9. Tocqueville "Discours prononcé à l'Assemblée Constituante dans la discussion du projet de constitution sur la question du droit au travail," in *OC,* III (3), 174.

10. Tocqueville to P. Clamorgan, 24 June 1848, in *OC,* X, 468.

11. Tocqueville to Eugène Stoffels, 21 July 1848, in *OC,* XVII (2), 462–64.

12. Tocqueville to Gustave de Beaumont, 27 October 1848, in *OC,* VIII (2), 81.

13. Tocqueville to P. Clamorgan, 18 November 1848, in *OC,* X, 488. See also Tocqueville to Jean Bernardin Rouxel, December 1848, in *OC,* X, 492–93.

14. Tocqueville to Gustave de Beaumont, 4 November 1849, in *OC,* VIII (2), 233.

15. In the first of three letters written to Paul Clamorgan, Tocqueville spoke of the "sickly torpor" that had afflicted him over the last two months. In the second, he announced his intention to leave Paris and to live without letters or newspapers in a state of "absolute calm." In the third, he explained why he agreed to join the government. Tocqueville to P. Clamorgan, 9 March 1849, in *OC,* X, 514; Tocqueville to P. Clamorgan, 6 May 1849, in *OC,* X, 533; Tocqueville to P. Clamorgan, 15 June 1849, in *OC,* X, 534–35.

16. Tocqueville, *Souvenirs,* in *OC,* XII, 202. In a letter to Arthur de Gobineau, Tocqueville wrote that his ambition had been "to preserve the dignity and influence of [his] country"; Tocqueville to Arthur de Gobineau, 13 September 1850, in *OC,* IX, 153.

17. Tocqueville to Gustave de Beaumont, 28 November 1849, in *OC,* VIII (2), 251.

18. Tocqueville to Jean-Jacques Ampère, 26 June 1850, in *OC,* XI, 187.

19. Tocqueville to P. Clamorgan, 9 July 1850, in *OC,* X, 546. Tocqueville's doctors insisted that he should speak as little as possible.

20. For an excellent English language edition, see Alexis de Tocqueville, *Recollections: The French Revolution of 1848 and Its Aftermath,* ed. Olivier Zunz (Charlottesville, VA, 2017). This text also includes letters and documents relevant to Tocqueville's account.

21. Tocqueville, *Souvenirs,* 29. Writing to Arthur de Gobineau from home in September 1850, Tocqueville indicated that his intention was to provide "a true picture of the state of Europe and of France" during his time in office; Tocqueville to Arthur de Gobineau, 13 September 1850, in *OC,* IX, 153.

22. Tocqueville to Richard Monckton Miles, 13 April 1850, in *OC,* VI (3), 133. Tocqueville told Monckton Miles that "no one had left political life with more satisfaction and less regret than me."

23. Tocqueville to Francisque de Corcelle, 1 August 1850, in *OC,* XV (2), 28.

24. Tocqueville and Senior, *Correspondence and Conversations,* 1:97–143.

25. For Tocqueville's speech to Louis-Napoleon as president of the republic, see Tocqueville, "Discours prononcé le 6 septembre 1850 pour la réception du président de la république à Cherbourg," in *OC,* X, 709–10. Tocqueville used this occasion to make a plea for the extension of the railway to Cherbourg and also to assure the president that the good people of the Cotentin shared a "horror of subversive theories, a taste for order, and a respect for the law." Tocqueville spoke as president of the Conseil générale de la Manche. For Tocqueville's assessment of this occasion, see Tocqueville to Marie Mottley, 6 September 1850, in *OC,* XIV, 547–48; Tocqueville to Arthur de Gobineau, 13 September 1850, in *OC,* IX, 152–53; and Tocqueville to Victor Lanjuinais, 13 September 1850, in *OC,* XVII (2), 690–91. Among other things, Tocqueville recorded that the president arrived four hours late, much to the displeasure of the waiting crowds.

26. Tocqueville to Gustave de Beaumont, 19 July 1850, in *OC,* VIII (2), 285. See also Tocqueville to Victor Lanjuinais, 8 October 1850, in *OC,* XVII (2), 692–93, where Tocqueville voiced his concern that "great political battles" would take place in Paris during his absence in Italy; and a similar letter from Tocqueville to Jules Dufaure, 12 October 1850, in *OC,* XVII (2), 694–95.

27. Tocqueville to Mme L. de Kergorlay, 9 October 1850, in *OC,* XIII (2), 228.

28. See also Tocqueville to Édouard de Tocqueville, 10 November 1850, in *OC,* XIV, 257–58, in which, from Marseilles, Tocqueville indicated that, while in Dijon, he had called to see his niece Denise and her husband Emmanuel. A letter to Beaumont, although it gives no detail, suggests that the journey from Paris to Marseilles was not without "unfortunate incidents"; Tocqueville to Gustave de Beaumont, 24 November 1850, in *OC,* VIII (2), 326. See also Tocqueville to Victor Lanjuinais, 1 December 1850, in *OC,* XVII (2), 697, in which, from Dijon, Tocqueville recorded that the "first part" of their journey had been tiring for his wife and himself but they had not been ill and were in good spirits.

29. Tocqueville to Gustave de Beaumont, 9 November 1850, in *OC,* VIII (2), 310–11.

30. Tocqueville to Gustave de Beaumont, 24 November 1850, in *OC,* VIII (2), 326–27.

31. Tocqueville to Francisque de Corcelle, 28 November 1850, in *OC,* XV (2), 36.

32. Tocqueville to Gustave de Beaumont, 24 November 1850, in *OC,* VIII (2), 328.

33. Tocqueville told Charles de Rémusat, 22 December 1850, in *OC,* XVII (2), 706.

34. Tocqueville to Francisque de Corcelle, 28 November 1850, in *OC,* XV (2), 37.

35. Tocqueville to Gustave de Beaumont, 3 December 1850, in *OC,* VIII (2), 331–32.

36. Tocqueville to Mme de Circourt, 30 December 1850, in *OC,* XVIII, 43.

37. Tocqueville to Victor Lanjuinais, 8 December 1850, in *OC,* XVII (2), 702.

38. Tocqueville to Jules Dufaure, 22 December 1850, in *OC,* XVII (2), 703.

39. Tocqueville to Dufaure, 22 December 1850, 703–4. See also Tocqueville to Francisque de Corcelle, 4 August 1849, in *OC,* XV (1), 349, in which Tocqueville draws attention to the opposition from all parties in Italy towards France: from "the revolutionaries because we have destroyed them; the absolutists, because we are not doing enough for them; and the liberals because we are betraying their hopes."

40. Tocqueville to Gustave de Beaumont, 5 January 1851, in *OC,* VIII (2), 354–55.

41. Tocqueville to Gustave de Beaumont, 24 December 1850, in *OC,* VIII (2), 328; Tocqueville to Francisque de Corcelle, 28 November 1850, in *OC,* XV (2), 37. Tocqueville subsequently observed to Beaumont that the Italian postal system appeared to have been set up in such a way as to discourage people from writing letters; Tocqueville to Gustave de Beaumont, 26 December 1850, in *OC,* VIII (2), 342. He made a similar remark to Charles de Rémusat, commenting that communications between Italy and France were so bad that he might just as well have been in Australia; Tocqueville to Charles de Rémusat, 22 December 1850, in *OC,* XVII (2), 705.

42. Tocqueville to Eugène Stoffels, 30 December 1850, in *OC,* XVII (2), 707–8.

43. Tocqueville to Louis de Kergorlay, 15 December 1850, in *OC,* XIII (2), 229. See also Tocqueville to Édouard de Tocqueville, 22 December 1850, in *OC,* XIV, 260; Tocqueville to Gustave de Beaumont, 26 December 1850, in *OC,* VIII, (2), 343; and Tocqueville to Dufaure, 22 December 1850, in *OC,* XVII (2), 704. Tocqueville's description was later confirmed by two of Tocqueville's visitors.

"We lived," Jean-Jacques Ampère wrote, "in a house situated above the road, a little before Sorrento, on the first slopes of the mountain; from a roof top terrace one saw Naples and Vesuvius to the right; on the left, the eye looked down on small valleys full of orange trees, the fruit gleaming in the sunshine; and from which rose domes, bell towers and white villas; it was an enchanting sight"; Jean-Jacques Ampère, "Appendice," in *OC,* XI, 443. Minnie Senior (M. C. M. Simpson) also wrote that "the Palazzo was beautifully placed half-way up a hill about a mile from Sorrento, and from our loggia and terrace we overlooked the orange-covered plain, the white houses of the town, the sapphire sea, Naples, and the dream-like island of Capri in the distance"; M. C. M. Simpson, *Many Memories of Many People* (London, 1898), 56.

44. Tocqueville to Paul Clamorgan, 10 April 1851, in *OC,* X, 551.

45. Tocqueville to Eugène Stoffels, 30 December 1850, in *OC,* XVII (2), 707. Tocqueville also reported that his wife was in good health.

46. Tocqueville to Mme de Circourt, 30 December 1850, in *OC,* XVIII, 43.

47. Tocqueville to Gustave de Beaumont, 26 December 1850, in *OC,* VIII (2), 344.

48. Tocqueville to Gustave de Beaumont, 5 January 1851, in *OC,* VIII (2), 352. Years later, in his obituary notice for Tocqueville, Ampère wrote that the improvement in Tocqueville's health was such that he and Madame de Tocqueville falsely believed that he had been cured of whatever malady he had been suffering from; Ampère, "Appendice," 442–43.

49. Tocqueville to Mme de Circourt, 30 December 1850, in *OC,* XVIII, 43.

50. Tocqueville to Mrs. Rosalind Margaret Phillimore, 31 December 1850, in *OC,* VI (3), 137.

51. Tocqueville to Gustave de Beaumont, 5 January 1851, in *OC,* VIII (2), 352.

52. Tocqueville to Édouard de Tocqueville, 22 December 1850, in *OC,* XIV, 259.

53. Tocqueville to Eugène Stoffels, 30 December 1850, in *OC,* XVII (2), 707.

54. Tocqueville to Gustave de Beaumont, 5 January 1851, in *OC,* VIII (2), 352.

55. Tocqueville to Mme de Circourt, 30 December 1850, in *OC,* XVIII, 44. Minnie Senior later confirmed this opinion. "There was no one," she wrote, "more amusing than Ampère. . . . He had an astonishing capacity for friendship"; Simpson, *Many Memories of Many People,* 63–64.

56. Simpson, *Many Memories of Many People,* 54.

57. Nassau William Senior, *Journals Kept in France and Italy from 1848 to 1852, with a Sketch of the Revolution of 1848 by the late Nassau William Senior,* ed. M. C. M. Simpson (London, 1871), 3.

58. Simpson, *Many Memories of Many People,* 179–80. Amongst many English Protestants this provoked an angry response and fears of a papal reconquest of England. The following year, the British prime minister Lord John Russell secured the passing of the Ecclesiastical Titles Act, making it an offence for anyone not a member of the Anglican Church to use an episcopal title.

59. The Hermitage was a place where those climbing Mount Vesuvius could rest and refresh themselves.

60. Simpson, *Many Memories of Many People,* 56.

61. Troja was briefly prime minister of the Two Sicilies between 3 April 1848 and 15 May 1848. His political position was broadly liberal and in favour of Italian unification.

62. Senior, *Journals Kept in France and Italy,* 6.

63. Senior, *Journals Kept in France and Italy,* 32; William Ewart Gladstone, *The Gladstone Diaries,* 14 vols., ed. M. R. D. Foot and H. C. G. Matthew (Oxford, 1968–1994), 4:297. Gladstone and Tocqueville had previously met in August 1849 when the former visited Paris.

64. See Richard Shannon, *Gladstone, Peel's Inheritor 1809–1865* (London, 1982), 229–32.

65. That this was the case is amply borne out by the numerous letters written at the time by Tocqueville as foreign minister to French military and diplomatic personnel such as Alphonse de Rayneval, Édouard Drouyn de Lhuys, Alexandre Walewski, and General Louis de Rostolan.

66. See Alexis de Tocqueville and Nassau William Senior, *Correspondence and Conversations of Alexis de Tocqueville and Nassau William Senior from 1834 to 1859,* 2 vols., ed. M. C. M. Simpson (London, 1872), 1:177–243. The greater proportion of these pages were subsequently translated into French; see *OC,* VI (2), 314–60.

67. Jean-Jacques Ampère, "Appendice," in *OC,* XI, 442–44.

68. Ampère, "Appendice," 446.

69. Ampère, "Appendice," 444–46.

70. Tocqueville to Francisque de Corcelle, 21 February 1851, in *OC,* XV (2), 41–43.

71. Tocqueville to Victor Lanjuinais, 31 January 1851, in *OC,* XVII (2), 711.

72. Tocqueville to Louis de Kergorlay, 15 December 1850, in *OC,* XIII (2), 229.

73. Tocqueville to Gustave de Beaumont, 26 December 1850, in *OC,* VIII (2), 343.

74. Tocqueville to Eugène Stoffels, 30 December 1850, in *OC,* XVII (2), 708.

75. Tocqueville, *Souvenirs,* 31.

76. Nassau Senior's notes on his conversations with Tocqueville in Normandy during August 1850 convey the same conclusions about the July Monarchy. For example, Senior records Tocqueville's comment that the regime "rested on the most selfish and grasping of plutocracies"; see Tocqueville and Senior, *Correspondence and Conversations,* 1:134.

77. Tocqueville, *Souvenirs,* 57.

78. Tocqueville, *Souvenirs,* 84.

79. Tocqueville, *Souvenirs,* 84–85. In a letter to George Grote, where Tocqueville argued that France had wanted neither revolution nor a republic, he highlighted just two of these causes: the fact that Paris had become the dominant industrial city in the country and therefore had been able to provide supporters of the republican cause with an "army of workers" when they were needed, and that administrative centralisation allowed Paris to exercise a form of "dictatorship" over the rest of the country; Tocqueville to George Grote, 27 February 1849, in *OC,* VI (3), 118.

80. Tocqueville, *Souvenirs,* 85.

81. Tocqueville, *Souvenirs,* 86.

82. Tocqueville, *Souvenirs,* 87.

83. Tocqueville, *Souvenirs,* 91–92.

84. Tocqueville, *Souvenirs,* 94.

85. Tocqueville, *Souvenirs,* 95.

86. Tocqueville, *Souvenirs,* 96–97.

87. Tocqueville, *Souvenirs,* 102.

88. Tocqueville, *Souvenirs,* 105.

89. Tocqueville, *Souvenirs,* 118.

90. Tocqueville, *Souvenirs,* 102. For the full text, see Tocqueville, "Circulaire électorale," in *OC,* III (3), 39–42.

91. Tocqueville, *Souvenirs,* 114.

92. Tocqueville, *Souvenirs,* 116.

93. Tocqueville, *Souvenirs,* 120–21.

94. Tocqueville, *Souvenirs,* 144.

95. Tocqueville, *Souvenirs,* 126.

96. Tocqueville, *Souvenirs,* 127.

97. Tocqueville, *Souvenirs,* 135.

98. Tocqueville, *Souvenirs,* 139.

99. Tocqueville, *Souvenirs,* 142.

100. Tocqueville, *Souvenirs,* 124.

101. Tocqueville, *Souvenirs,* 150.

102. Tocqueville, *Souvenirs,* 152.

103. Tocqueville, *Souvenirs,* 160.

104. Tocqueville, *Souvenirs,* 166.

105. Tocqueville, *Souvenirs,* 178.

106. Tocqueville, *Souvenirs,* 180, 184.

107. Tocqueville, *Souvenirs,* 190.

108. Tocqueville, *Souvenirs,* 181–82.

109. Tocqueville, *Souvenirs,* 182.

110. Tocqueville, *Souvenirs,* 188.

111. Tocqueville to Louis de Kergorlay, 15 December 1850, in *OC,* XIII (2), 230.

112. Tocqueville to Louis de Kergorlay, 15 December 1850, in *OC,* XIII (2), 233.

113. Tocqueville to Francisque de Corcelle, 21 February 1851, in *OC,* XV (2), 42–43.

114. Tocqueville to Jules Dufaure, 12 March 1851, in *OC,* XVII (2), 713.

115. Tocqueville to Arthur de Gobineau, 28 March 1851, in *OC,* IX, 164.

7. SORRENTO AND SAINT-CYR-SUR-LOIRE

1. Tocqueville to Gustave de Beaumont, 26 February 1851, in *OC,* VIII (2), 377–8. See also Tocqueville to Jean-Charles Rivet, 22 March 1851, in *OC,* XVII (2), 714, where Tocqueville confirmed this account of his own and his wife's health, but Tocqueville admitted that he was still suffering from what he described as "a dark melancholy."

2. Tocqueville to an unknown correspondent, 13 April 1851, in *OC,* XVII (2), 716.

3. Gustave de Beaumont to Tocqueville, 6 April 1851, in *OC,* VIII (2), 387–93.

4. Tocqueville, *Souvenirs, OC,* XII, 211–12, 229, 230.

5. Tocqueville to Francisque de Corcelle, 21 February 1851, in *OC,* XV (2), 41–42.

6. The vote took place on 19 July. For Tocqueville's assessment of its implications, see Tocqueville to Édouard de Tocqueville, 22 July 1851, in *OC,* XIV, 265.

7. Tocqueville to Gustave de Beaumont, 14 September 1851, in *OC,* VIII (2), 407; emphasis in the original. Similar observations can be found in Tocqueville to Marie Mottley, 23 August 1851, in *OC,* XIV, 554–55; and Tocqueville to Marie Mottley, 4 September 1851, in *OC,* XIV, 563.

8. Tocqueville to Gustave de Beaumont, 14 September 1851, in *OC,* VIII (2), 406–11.

9. Tocqueville to Henry Reeve, 27 September 1851, in *OC,* VI (1), 118.

10. Tocqueville to N. W. Senior, 28 November 1851, in *OC,* VI (2), 139.

11. See Tocqueville to the Prefect of Police, Charlemagne de Maupas, 3 December 1851, in *OC,* XVII (2), 734.

12. See Tocqueville's notes sent to his wife during his imprisonment, 2–4 December 1851, in *OC,* XIV, 565–68.

13. Tocqueville's text was sent to Harriet Grote on 8 December 1851, who, at Tocqueville's request, translated it and secured its publication in the *Times* on 11 December 1851. The English text is available as "To the Editor of the Times," *Memoirs, Letters and Remains of Alexis de Tocqueville,* 2 vols. (London, 1861), 1:176–92. The original French text was lost, and the French version now available is a retranslation of the text that is published in the *Times;* see Tocqueville, "Au rédacteur en chef du Times," in *OC,* VI (1), 119–29.

14. Alexis de Tocqueville and Nassau William Senior, *Correspondence and Conversations of Alexis de Tocqueville and Nassau William Senior from 1834 to 1859,* 2 vols., ed. M. C. M. Simpson (London, 1872), 2:9–10.

15. Tocqueville to Édouard de Tocqueville, 7 December 1851, in *OC,* XIV, 271–22. See also Tocqueville to Édouard de Tocqueville, 14 February 1852, in *OC,* XIV, 275–78, where Tocqueville sought to demolish the reasons cited to support the coup—namely, that it would serve to strengthen authority, morality, and religion.

16. Tocqueville to Jean-Bernardin Rouxel, 14 December 1851, in *OC,* X, 561–62.

17. Tocqueville and Senior, *Correspondence and Conversations,* 2:2. See also Tocqueville to Francisque de Corcelle, 13 May 1852, in *OC,* XV (2), 54, where

Tocqueville wrote that "the true aristocracy of the country is now the army. . . . In this regime it is what the old nobility was under the Restoration, the bourgeoisie was under Louis-Philippe, and the workers were under the provisional government."

18. Tocqueville used the same expression in a letter to Victor Lanjuinais; see Tocqueville to Victor Lanjuinais, 18 April 1852, in *OC,* XVII (3), 44.

19. Tocqueville to Gustave de Beaumont, 7 March 1852, in *OC,* VIII (3), 32.

20. This was subsequently to become a frequent refrain in Tocqueville's letters; see, for example, Tocqueville to Louis Bouchitté, 21 October 1855, in *OC,* XVII (3), 220.

21. Tocqueville to his father, 24 July 1852, in *OC,* XIV, 283.

22. Tocqueville to Gustave de Beaumont, 16 July 1852, in *OC,* VIII (3), 62.

23. Tocqueville to Jean-Bernardin Rouxel, 14 December 1851, in *OC,* X, 562.

24. Tocqueville to Zachary Gallemand, 19 July 1852, in *OC,* X, 565–66; Tocqueville to Zachary Gallemand, 20 August 1852, in *OC,* X, 566–68.

25. See Tocqueville, "On the Social and Political Condition of France," *London and Westminster Review,* no. 25 (1836): 137–69. In French it is published as "État social et politique de la France avant et depuis 1789," in *OC,* II (1), 31–66. See also the letters between Mill and Tocqueville, dated June 1835–April 1836, concerning the writing and publication of the text, in *OC,* VI (1), 291–309. Tocqueville worried that his method of writing might be "too French" for a British audience. He also indicated to Mill that working on the text had given rise to a multitude of new ideas and had led him to see numerous connections that he had not previously been aware of. The intention was that Tocqueville should write a series of essays, but unfortunately, and despite promises to the contrary, this was the only one he delivered.

26. Tocqueville, "On the Social and Political Condition of France," 140, 152.

27. Tocqueville, "On the Social and Political Condition of France," 155, 157, 160, 163. Italics in the original.

28. Tocqueville, "On the Social and Political Condition of France," 164.

29. Hugh Brogan, *Alexis de Tocqueville: Prophet of Democracy in the Age of Revolution* (London, 2006), 562. The theme of continuity was subsequently developed by other historians such as Edgar Quinet and Albert Sorel. For a broader discussion of the historiography of the revolution, see Jeremy Jennings, *Revolution and the Republic: A History of Political Thought in France since the Eighteenth Century* (Oxford, 2011), 237–97.

30. Tocqueville, "On the Social and Political Condition of France," 168.

31. Tocqueville, "On the Social and Political Condition of France," 169.

32. For a detailed account of how Tocqueville set about writing *L'ancien régime et la révolution,* see Robert T. Gannett Jr., *Tocqueville Unveiled: The Historian and His Sources for the Old Regime and the Revolution* (Chicago, 2003). For another illuminating study, see Robert T. Gannett Jr., "The Shifting Puzzles of Tocqueville's *The Old Regime and the Revolution,*" in *The Cambridge Companion to Tocqueville,* ed. Cheryl B. Welch (New York, 2006), 188–215.

33. On the reception of Edmund Burke in France, see Jeremy Jennings, "Edmund Burke, the French Revolution and His French Critics," in *The Reception of Edmund Burke in Europe,* ed. Martin Fitzpatrick and Peter Jones (London, 2017), 91–104.

34. Tocqueville, "Quatre jugements sur Burke," in *OC,* II (2), 341–42.

35. Tocqueville, *L'ancien régime et la révolution,* in *OC,* II (1), 95–6.

36. Tocqueville, *L'ancien régime et la révolution,* 247.

37. Tocqueville, *L'ancien régime et la révolution,* 247–48.

38. Tocqueville, *L'ancien régime et la révolution,* 248.

39. Tocqueville, *L'ancien régime et la révolution,* 248–49, in *OC,* II (1), 247–50.

40. See Natalie Petiteau, *Napoléon: De la mythologie à l'histoire* (Paris, 1999), 57–105.

41. Tocqueville, "Discours de M. de Tocqueville, prononcé dans la séance publique du 21 avril 1842, en venant prendre séance à la place de M. le Comte de Cessac," in *OC,* XVI, 251–69.

42. Brogan, *Alexis de Tocqueville,* 405.

43. Tocqueville and Senior, *Correspondence and Conversations,* 1:112–14. Inexplicably, the *Œuvres Complètes* do not include the last sentence. Senior also records Tocqueville as saying that "Napoleon's taste was defective in everything, in small things as well as great ones; in books, in art, and in women, as well as in ambition and in glory; and his idolizers cannot be men of much better taste" (113–14).

44. Tocqueville to Louis de Kergorlay, 15 December 1850, in *OC,* XIII (2), 230.

45. Tocqueville to Louis de Kergorlay, 15 December 1850, in *OC,* XIII (2), 230–31.

46. Tocqueville to Louis de Kergorlay, 15 December 1850, in *OC,* XIII (2), 231–32.

47. Tocqueville to Louis de Kergorlay, 15 December 1850, in *OC,* XIII (2), 232.

48. Tocqueville to Louis de Kergorlay, 15 December 1850, in *OC,* XIII (2), 232–33.

49. Tocqueville to Gustave de Beaumont, 26 December 1850, in *OC,* VIII (2), 342–45.

50. Tocqueville, "Sorrente, décembre 1850—Napoléon", in *OC,* II (2), 301–4.

51. Tocqueville, "Idée originaire, sentiment générale et primitif du sujet," in *OC,* II (2), 29. See also Gannett, *Tocqueville Unveiled,* 176–77n78.

52. Tocqueville, "Sorrente, décembre 1850," 301–2.

53. Tocqueville, "Sorrente, décembre 1850," 302–4.

54. Tocqueville to Gustave de Beaumont, 16 July 1852, in *OC,* VIII (3), 62.

55. The disparity is explained by the fact that Tocqueville was uncertain about whether the material would comprise one or two chapters.

56. The Coup of 18 Brumaire (the date in the French republican calendar) brought Napoleon Bonaparte to power as first consul of France on 9 November 1799.

57. Tocqueville to Louis de Kergorlay, 25 July 1852, in *OC,* XIII (2), 243–44. First published after Tocqueville's death by Beaumont, these two chapters can be found in *OC,* II (2), 269–92.

58. François Furet and Françoise Mélonio, "Tocqueville's Workshop," in *The Old Regime and the Revolution,* vol. 2, *Notes on the French Revolution and Napoleon,* by Alexis de Tocqueville, ed. François Furet and Françoise Mélonio, trans. Alan S. Kahan (Chicago, 2001), 3.

59. Tocqueville to Zacharie Gallemand, 28 August 1852, in *OC,* X, 569.

60. Tocqueville to Pierre Freslon, 7 September 1852, in *OC,* XVII (3), 63–65.

61. See Tocqueville to Gustave de Beaumont, 5 November 1852, in *OC,* VIII (3), 77; Tocqueville to Gustave de Beaumont, 24 January 1853, in *OC,* VIII (3), 83–85; Tocqueville to Gustave de Beaumont, 17 February 1853, in *OC,* VIII (3), 90; Tocqueville to Joseph Boulatignier, 25 April 1853, in *OC,* XVII (3), 85; and Tocqueville to Arthur de Gobineau, 11 October 1853, in *OC,* IX, 200.

62. Like Beaumont, Tocqueville had lost his parliamentary salary. Beaumont lived in a condition of penury ever after.

63. Tocqueville to Gustave de Beaumont, 8 April 1853, in *OC,* VIII (3), 102.

64. Tocqueville to Gustave de Beaumont, 2 May 1853, in *OC,* VIII (3), 117.

65. Tocqueville to Gustave de Beaumont, 4 June 1853, in *OC,* VIII (3), 128. Writing to Ampère, Tocqueville was slightly less complementary about the house, commenting that the furniture was "ugly and old" and that the garden,

although pleasant, was "very small"; Tocqueville to Jean-Jacques Ampère, 2 June 1853, in *OC,* XI, 215. See also Tocqueville to Auguste Vivien, 19 July 1853, in *OC,* XVII (3), 103; Tocqueville to Jules Dufaure, 14 August 1853, in *OC,* XVII (3), 106; and Tocqueville to Léonce de Lavergne, 31 October 1853, in *OC,* XVII (3), 117. Still another description is provided by Charles de Grandmaison, the archivist in Tours. According to Grandmaison, the house was airy, caught the sun, and was protected from the cold northeast wind. However, there was no view, not even of the nearby Loire. It was very much, he concluded, a house for someone who wanted to convalesce; Charles de Grandmaison, "Séjour d'Alexis de Tocqueville en Touraine: Préparation du livre sur l'ancien regime, juin 1853–avril 1854," *Le correspondant,* no. 114 (1873): 934–35. Subsequent to the publication of Tocqueville's *Souvenirs,* Grandmaison published this essay, with a new introduction, as *Alexis de Tocqueville en Touraine* (Paris, 1893).

66. Tocqueville to Francisque de Corcelle, 17 June 1853, in *OC,* XV (2), 75.

67. Tocqueville to Adolphe de Circourt, 13 April 1853, in *OC,* XVIII, 94. To Madame de Circourt in January 1854 Tocqueville commented that, were it not for the fact that one could go out for walks, it would be like living in a "fortified castle"; Tocqueville to Madame de Circourt, 11 January 1854, in *OC,* XVIII, 141.

68. Tocqueville to Léonce de Lavergne, 31 October 1853, in *OC,* XVII (3), 117.

69. Tocqueville to Francisque de Corcelle, 17 June 1853, in *OC,* XV (2), 75. A later letter to Corcelle indicates that Tocqueville was to consult Dr. Bretonneau. The "infallible Bretonneau," Tocqueville wrote in September, "continues to assert that there is nothing serious about my illnesses and that I will make a complete recovery. On this last point, I am absolutely incredulous, and believe my recovery no more certain than that of France. In both cases, the sickness is too longstanding to hope for a complete cure and I limit myself in both cases to wanting a tolerable condition." See Tocqueville to Francisque de Corcelle, 17 September 1853, in *OC,* XV (2), 80. For an account of the relationship between Tocqueville and Bretonneau, see Grandmaison, "Séjour d'Alexis de Tocqueville," 947–48. Grandmaison reports that Tocqueville could never get Bretonneau to talk about what was wrong with him, the good doctor preferring to talk about botanical matters and literature. Grandmaison interprets this to mean that Bretonneau knew that the only thing that was likely to help Tocqueville was rest, advice Tocqueville was not likely to listen to. Bretonneau later caused some considerable scandal when, as a seventy-eight-year-old widower, he married a girl of eighteen; see Tocqueville to Charles de Grandmaison, 17 October 1856, in *OC,* XVII (3), 338–39.

70. See Tocqueville to Gustave de Beaumont, 27 May 1854, in *OC,* VIII (3), 216, where Tocqueville wrote that these were some of the happiest days that he and

his wife had ever spent. See also Tocqueville to Francisque de Corcelle, 11 May 1854, in *OC,* XV (2), 99, where Tocqueville voiced the same sentiments, adding that with the Beaumonts "one could always find something very rare, especially in the countryside: the most intimate and pleasant conversation or the most complete solitude, depending on whether one had a taste for one or the other."

71. Tocqueville to Francisque de Corcelle, 31 December 1853, in *OC,* XV (2), 88. To this observation Tocqueville added that what troubled him on a freezing night like this was "the thought of so many poor people who, at this hour, shivered with cold on the ground with half-empty bellies."

72. Tocqueville and Senior, *Correspondence and Conversations,* 2:58–62. This might simply have been a ploy to encourage Mrs. Grote to bring her stay in Tours to a close. In a letter to Beaumont, Tocqueville indicated that Mrs. Grote had arrived in Touraine expecting to find another Bay of Naples and was therefore complaining bitterly about the climate; Tocqueville to Gustave de Beaumont, 19 February 1854, in *OC,* VIII (3), 193.

73. Tocqueville to Louis Bouchitté, 3 January 1854, in *OC,* XVII (3), 133.

74. Tocqueville to Adolphe de Circourt, 13 August 1853, in *OC,* XVIII, 94.

75. Tocqueville to Francisque de Corcelle, 11 March 1854[?], in *OC,* XV (2), 94. Tocqueville made the same observation to Freslon; Tocqueville to Pierre Freslon, December 1853, in *OC,* XVII (3), 132. It was Tocqueville's barber's view that, if the price of corn continued to rise, there would be need for another revolution and a general pillaging of the rich.

76. Tocqueville to Léon Faucher, 1 February 1854, in *OC,* XVII (3), 141.

77. See Grandmaison, "Séjour d'Alexis de Tocqueville," 929. For Tocqueville's assessment of Cardinal Morlot's qualities after his appointment as archbishop of Paris in 1857, see Tocqueville to Francisque de Corcelle, 28 January 1857, in *OC,* XV (2), 196; and Tocqueville to Madame Swetchine, 11 February 1857, in *OC,* XV (2), 310–11.

78. Tocqueville to Madame de Circourt, 2 September 1853, in *OC,* XVIII, 103.

79. Tocqueville to Odilon Barrot, 26 November 1853, in *OC,* XVII (3), 115.

80. Grandmaison, "Séjour d'Alexis de Tocqueville," 928.

81. Grandmaison, "Séjour d'Alexis de Tocqueville," 928.

82. Grandmaison, "Séjour d'Alexis de Tocqueville," 933.

83. Grandmaison, "Séjour d'Alexis de Tocqueville," 935–36.

84. Grandmaison, "Séjour d'Alexis de Tocqueville," 941–42.

85. Grandmaison, "Séjour d'Alexis de Tocqueville," 943.

86. Tocqueville, "Constitution de la classe agricole en Russie," in *OC,* XVI, 562–68.

87. Tocqueville, *L'ancien régime et la révolution,* in *OC,* II (1), 223.

88. Tocqueville to Gustave de Beaumont, 3 November 1853, in *OC,* VIII (3), 164. One outcome of this exchange of letters was the publication by Beaumont of "La Russie et les États-Unis sous le rapport économique," *Revue des Deux Mondes,* no. 5 (1854): 1163–83. The article amounted to an extended commentary on Haxthausen's text by way of a comparison of the economic performance of the Russian and American economies, Beaumont's view being that the free market American approach was by far the superior of the two. His argument in favour of individual liberty and against the despotism of the state remains relevant and has stood the test of time. Beaumont's article deserves wider appreciation. Tocqueville was delighted that Beaumont took up this subject; see Tocqueville to Gustave de Beaumont, 16 February 1854, in *OC,* VIII (3), 189.

89. Tocqueville to Adolphe de Circourt, 7 December 1853, in *OC,* XVIII, 120–21.

90. Grandmaison, "Séjour d'Alexis de Tocqueville," 943–44.

91. Tocqueville to Pierre Freslon, 9 June 1853, in *OC,* XVII (3), 92.

92. Grandmaison, "Séjour d'Alexis de Tocqueville," 931. For an illuminating account of how Tocqueville worked on *L'ancien régime et la révolution,* see Tocqueville to Prosper Duvergier de Hauranne, 1 September 1856, in *OC,* XVII (3), 315–16.

93. Gannett, *Tocqueville Unveiled,* 81. See also Tocqueville to Mrs. Harriet Grote, 22 November 1853, in *OC,* VI (3), 162, where Tocqueville commented, "When considering all the things that my preliminary study teaches me and all the thoughts it suggests, I have come to realise that what is most missing from those who have wanted to speak about the French Revolution, and even the present time, are true and accurate ideas about what preceded it. I will have, I believe, this advantage over them and I hope to make full use of it."

94. Tocqueville to Charles de Grandmaison, 9 August 1856, in *OC,* XVII (3), 304–5.

95. Tocqueville to Francisque de Corcelle, 17 September 1853, in *OC,* XV (2), 79. Tocqueville wrote "tread mill" in English.

96. Tocqueville to Pierre Freslon, 23 September 1853, in *OC,* XVII (3), 109–10.

97. Tocqueville to Jean-Jacques Ampère, 2 October 1853, in *OC,* XI, 223.

98. Tocqueville to Louis de Kergorlay, 19 October 1853, in *OC,* XIII (2), 268.

99. Tocqueville to Léonce de Lavergne, 31 October 1853, in *OC,* XIII (2), 118.

100. Tocqueville to Adolphe de Circourt, 16 October 1853, in *OC,* XVIII, 109, emphasis in the original.

101. Tocqueville to Mrs. Harriet Grote, 22 November 1853, in *OC,* VI (3), 162.

102. Tocqueville to Pierre Freslon, 3 November 1853, in *OC,* XVII (3), 119.

103. Tocqueville to Gustave de Beaumont, 3 November 1853, in *OC,* VIII (3), 164.

104. Tocqueville to Pierre Freslon, 3 November 1853, in *OC,* XVII (3), 119–20.

105. Tocqueville to Jean-Jacques Ampère, 18 November 1853, in *OC,* XI, 227.

106. Tocqueville to Gustave de Beaumont, 13 January 1854, *OC,* VIII (3) 182.

107. Tocqueville to Jean-Jacques Ampère, 1 January 1854[?], in *OC,* XI, 231–32.

108. Tocqueville to Gustave de Beaumont, 28 December 1853, in *OC,* VIII (3), 177.

109. Tocqueville to Jean-Jacques Ampère, 1 January 1854[?], in *OC,* XI, 232.

110. Tocqueville to Hubert de Tocqueville, 7 March 1854, in *OC,* XIV, 294–95.

111. Tocqueville to Louis de Kergorlay, 23 March 1854, in *OC,* XIII (2), 283.

112. Tocqueville to Gustave de Beaumont, 27–30 April 1854, in *OC,* VIII (3), 209.

113. See, for example, Tocqueville to his father, 28 May 1856, in *OC,* XIV, 324.

114. Tocqueville to Gustave de Beaumont, 17 February 1856, in *OC,* VIII (3), 370. Beaumont himself suggested *Démocratie et liberté en France* as the title.

115. Anyone familiar with Tocqueville's handwriting would not be surprised by this.

116. Tocqueville to Theodore Sedgwick, 17 July 1854, in *OC,* VII, 156.

8. GERMANY

1. For a discussion of this theme, see Françoise Mélonio, "Tocqueville européen: La France et l'Allemagne," *Tocqueville Review* 27, no. 2 (2006): 517–32.

2. Tocqueville to Henry Reeve, 21 September 1836, in *OC,* VI (1), 36.

3. Tocqueville to Louis de Kergorlay, 10 October 1836, in *OC,* XIII (1), 407.

4. Tocqueville to Louis de Kergorlay, 4 December 1836, in *OC,* XIII (1), 423.

5. Tocqueville to Louis de Kergorlay, 26 December 1836, in *OC,* XIII (1), 432.

6. Louis de Kergorlay to Tocqueville, 14 January 1837, *OC,* XIII (1), 439–40.

7. On Thun, see Pieter M. Judson, *The Habsburg Empire: A New History* (Cambridge, MA, 2016), 226–27.

8. Tocqueville to Leo von Thun, 11 November 1844, in *OC,* VII, 302.

9. Tocqueville to Francis Lieber, 18 September 1844, in *OC,* VII, 93–94.

10. Tocqueville to Francis Lieber, 2 December 1844, in *OC,* VII, 100.

11. Tocqueville to Louis de Kergorlay, 11 September 1846, in *OC,* XIII (2), 187.

12. The Zollverein was a customs union established in 1834 that embraced the majority of German states. "No one who looks at a map of the Zollverein states," Christopher Clark writes, "can fail to be impressed by the close resemblance to the Prussian-dominated European state that emerged from the wars of 1864–71"; Christopher Clark, *The Iron Kingdom: The Rise and Downfall of Prussia 1600–1947* (London, 2007), 393.

13. Tocqueville to Gustave de Beaumont, 27 August 1848, in *OC,* VIII (2), 29.

14. Tocqueville to Gustave de Beaumont, 20 October 1848, in *OC,* VIII (2), 71–72.

15. The conference never took place. Tocqueville had hoped to be offered a ministerial position in the government.

16. Tocqueville to P. Clamorgan, 18 January 1849, in *OC,* X, 500. See also Tocqueville to the president of the Assemblée nationale, 8 January 1849, in *OC,* XVII (2), 483–4, where Tocqueville requested leave from his duties.

17. Tocqueville to P. Clamorgan, 6 May 1849, in *OC,* X, 533.

18. Tocqueville to N. W. Senior, 9 May 1849, in *OC,* VI (1), 110.

19. Tocqueville, *Souvenirs, OC,* XII, 279.

20. Tocqueville to Gustave de Beaumont, 8 May 1849, *OC,* VIII (2), 125–36.

21. Tocqueville to Gustave de Beaumont, 11 May 1849, *OC,* VIII (2), 127–28, emphasis in the original.

22. Tocqueville referred to a conflict between the Parliament and the imperial vicar (a post which had ceased to exist with the dissolution of the Holy Roman Empire in 1806). He presumably had the regent in mind.

23. Tocqueville to Gustave de Beaumont, 18 May 1849, in *OC,* VIII (2), 133. See also Tocqueville to Jean-Charles Rivet, 17 May 1849, in *OC,* XVII (2), 498–501, which gives an identical analysis of the situation Tocqueville saw in Germany. In the letter to Rivet, Tocqueville pointed out that any conclusions he had drawn were based upon only eight days in Germany and no knowledge of the German

language. They were therefore at best "very superficial *aperçus.*" Emphasis in the original.

24. Mutiny within the army not only led the Grand Duke of Baden to flee but also to the establishment of a revolutionary provisional government.

25. Tocqueville to Gustave de Beaumont, 18 May 1849, in *OC,* VIII (2), 134. Tocqueville's prediction proved entirely accurate: by the end of July, Prussian forces had crushed the insurrection in Dresden and defeated all insurgent forces. That Tocqueville was deeply concerned—indeed, disapproving—of the brutal manner in which the Prussian forces carried out their task is shown in Tocqueville to Napoléon-Joseph de Bassano, 26 August 1849, in *OC,* XVII (2), 591–93. While the French government had supported action against the insurrection, Tocqueville wrote, it had done so to secure an end to "anarchy" and not to bring about "the destruction of liberty." It had been no part of their intention to effect an "anti-liberal restoration."

26. Tocqueville to Gustave de Beaumont, 18 May 1849, in *OC,* VIII (2), 134.

27. Tocqueville to Gustave de Beaumont, 18 May 1849, in *OC,* VIII (2), 134.

28. Tocqueville to Gustave de Beaumont, 18 May 1849, in *OC,* VIII (2), 134–35.

29. Tocqueville to Gustave de Beaumont, 18 May 1849, in *OC,* VIII (2) 135.

30. Tocqueville to Gustave de Beaumont, 19 May 1849, in *OC,* VIII (2), 137–8.

31. Tocqueville to Gustave de Beaumont, 23 May 1849, in *OC,* VIII (2), 139.

32. Tocqueville to Gustave de Beaumont, 23 May 1849, in *OC,* VIII (2), 139–40.

33. For the text of this letter, see *OC,* XII, 280–81n2.

34. Tocqueville to Gustave de Beaumont, 23 May 1849, in *OC,* VIII (2), 140.

35. Tocqueville, *Souvenirs,* 198–204. Tocqueville was here also gracious enough to pay tribute to what he termed "the courage and good sense" of his wife.

36. Tocqueville, *Souvenirs,* 238.

37. Tocqueville, *Souvenirs,* 280.

38. Tocqueville, *Souvenirs,* 247.

39. Tocqueville's then concerns about the consequences for France of a united Germany were clearly expressed in a letter to General Jacques Aupick, French ambassador in Constantinople, 24 August 1849, in *OC,* XVII (2), 589. Instead of a "divided and weak" Germany, Tocqueville wrote, France would find herself confronted by "a united and powerful" Germany, hostile to France in terms of both its interests and traditions.

40. Tocqueville, *Souvenirs,* 247–48.

41. Tocqueville, *Souvenirs,*246.

42. Tocqueville, *Souvenirs,* 249.

43. Tocqueville, *Souvenirs,* 250. Russia had helped Austria defeat its opponents in Hungary.

44. Tocqueville, *Souvenirs,* 250. This list of lost privileges held by the nobility is taken almost word for word from a letter from Gustave de Beaumont to Tocqueville, 10 October 1849, in *OC,* VIII (2), 194. Beaumont was newly arrived as French ambassador to Austria.

45. Arthur de Gobineau to Tocqueville, 29 April 1852, in *OC,* IX, 194–96.

46. Tocqueville to Arthur de Gobineau, 15 May 1852, in *OC,* IX, 198.

47. Adolphe de Circourt to Tocqueville, 21 May 1852, in *OC,* XVIII, 69–75.

48. Tocqueville to Adolphe de Circourt, 14 June 1852, in *OC,* XVIII, 75–77.

49. Tocqueville to Christian von Bunsen, 2 January 1853, in *OC,* VII, 329.

50. Tocqueville to Christian von Bunsen, 23 May 1853, in *OC,* VII, 332–33.

51. Tocqueville to Adolphe de Circourt, 22 December 1853, in *OC,* XVIII, 128.

52. Tocqueville to Adolphe de Circourt, 16 October 1853, in *OC,* XVIII, 109.

53. Tocqueville to Mme de Circourt, 11 January 1854, in *OC,* XVIII, 142.

54. Tocqueville to Mme de Circourt, 2 October 1856, in *OC,* XVIII, 335. A few months later, Tocqueville told Madame de Circourt's husband that "the most distinguished German authors always took care to cover the clearest of ideas with a little gibberish"; Tocqueville to Adolphe de Circourt, 22 February 1857, in *OC,* XVIII, 380. That this was Tocqueville's firm view is confirmed in Tocqueville to Pierre Freslon, 31 July 1856, in *OC,* XVII (3), 297–98, where Tocqueville commented that, in contrast to the English, with the Germans he was never quite sure what they wanted to say.

55. Tocqueville to Jean-Jacques Ampère, 31 March 1854, in *OC,* XI, 236–37.

56. Tocqueville to N. W. Senior, 21 May 1854, in *OC,* VI (2), 171. Harriet Grote had received a similarly uninformative, if shorter, reply; Tocqueville to Mrs. Harriet Grote, 11 May 1854, in *OC,* VI (3), 168.

57. Tocqueville to Adolphe de Circourt, 5 June 1854, in *OC,* XVIII, 175.

58. Tocqueville to Adolphe de Circourt, 1 June 1854, in *OC,* XVIII, 168–69.

59. Adolphe de Circourt to Tocqueville, 4 June 1854, in *OC,* XVIII, 170–73. Circourt followed this up with another letter in which he suggested other people that Tocqueville might usefully meet in Bonn. He also indicated that he would "religiously" observe Tocqueville's request that he should not disclose his travel plans to anyone; Adolphe de Circourt to Tocqueville, 8 June 1854, in *OC,* XVIII, 176–78.

60. See Tocqueville to Louis de Kergorlay, 2 July 1854, in *OC,* XIII (2), 288; Tocqueville to Francisque de Corcelle, 10 June 1854, in *OC,* XV (2), 102; and Tocqueville to Victor Lanjuinais, 30 June 1854, in *OC,* XVII (3), 161. The Tocquevilles also saw exiled French friends in Spa and Liège.

61. Tocqueville to Jean-Jacques Ampère, 21 June 1854, in *OC,* XI, 246.

62. Tocqueville to Jean-Jacques Ampère, 21 June 1854, in *OC,* XI, 246–47.

63. Tocqueville to Theodore Sedgwick, 14 August 1854, in *OC,* VII, 159.

64. Tocqueville to Theodore Sedgwick, 14 August 1854, in *OC,* VII, 159.

65. Tocqueville to Léonce de Lavergne, 29 July 1854, in *OC,* XVII (3), 162.

66. Tocqueville to Arthur de Gobineau, 22 July 1854, in *OC,* IX, 216.

67. Tocqueville to Francisque de Corcelle, 22 July 1854, in *OC,* XV (2), 105–6; Tocqueville to Adolphe de Circourt, 27 July 1854, in *OC,* XVIII, 191. This remained Tocqueville's view after he returned to France; see Tocqueville to Louis Bouchitté, 15 December 1854, in *OC,* XVII (3), 178.

68. Tocqueville to Léonce de Lavergne, 29 July 1854, in *OC,* XVII (3), 162.

69. Tocqueville to Arthur de Gobineau, 22 July 1854, in *OC,* IX, 216.

70. Tocqueville to Léonce de Lavergne, 29 July 1854, in *OC,* XVII (3), 162. Tocqueville here uses the marvellous French word *baragouiner.*

71. Tocqueville to Adolphe de Circourt, 30 June 1854, in *OC,* XVIII, 180.

72. Tocqueville to Adolphe de Circourt, 27 July 1854, in *OC,* XVIII, 189–90.

73. Tocqueville to Léonce de Lavergne, 29 July 1854, in *OC,* XVII (3), 162.

74. Tocqueville to Adolphe de Circourt, 30 June 1854, in *OC,* XVIII, 180.

75. Tocqueville to Adolphe de Circourt, 30 June 1854, in *OC,* XVIII, 180–81. Two days later, Tocqueville made a virtually identical request to Louis de Kergorlay, indicating that he wanted above all to study the relationship between the old nobility and the peasantry and that he believed that this was best done in East Prussia and Mecklenburg; Tocqueville to Louis de Kergorlay, 2 July 1854, in *OC,* XIII (2), 287.

76. Tocqueville to Pierre Freslon, 30 July 1854, in *OC,* XVII (3), 164.

77. Austin's largely laudatory account of German national liberation from the French was published in 1854. It ends with the first German military crossing of the Rhine in 1814. Throughout, Austin does not disguise her distaste for Napoleon Bonaparte, describing him as someone who flattered the worst and stifled the best of the qualities of the French, thereby turning "their marvellous talents and aptitudes into channels immediately destructive to others, and permanently injurious to themselves"; Sarah Austin, *Germany from 1670 to 1814, or Sketches of German Life from the Decay of the Empire to the Expulsion of the French* (London, 1854), xiii. See also Tocqueville to Madame Austin, 11 September 1855, in *OC,* VI (1), 152. Austin was the aunt of Henry Reeve and was personally known to Tocqueville.

78. Tocqueville to Gustave de Beaumont, 6 August 1854, in *OC,* VIII (3), 228.

79. Tocqueville to Gustave de Beaumont, 16 July 1854, in *OC,* VIII (3), 223.

80. Tocqueville to Adolphe de Circourt, 27 July 1854, in *OC,* XVIII, 189–90. See also Tocqueville to Jean-Charles Rivet, 25 June 1854, in *OC,* XVII (3), 160.

81. Tocqueville, "Voyage en Allemagne," in *Œuvres,* 3 vols. (Paris: 1991–2004), 3:320–21.

82. Tocqueville, "Voyage en Allemagne," 3:321–25.

83. Tocqueville, "Voyage en Allemagne," 3:331.

84. Tocqueville, "Voyage en Allemagne," 3:331–36.

85. Tocqueville, Voyage en Allemagne," 3:338.

86. Tocqueville to Gustave de Beaumont, 16 July 1854, in *OC,* VIII (3), 224.

87. Tocqueville to Pierre Freslon, 30 July 1854, in *OC,* XVII (3), 165.

88. Gustave de Beaumont to Tocqueville, 7 June 1854, in *OC,* VIII (3), 220.

89. Tocqueville to Gustave de Beaumont, 16 July 1854, in *OC,* VIII (3), 223.

90. Tocqueville to Francisque de Corcelle, 22 July 1854, in *OC,* XV (2), 106.

91. Tocqueville to Francisque de Corcelle, 22 July 1854, in *OC,* XV (2), 106–7.

92. Tocqueville to Francisque de Corcelle, 22 July 1854, in *OC,* XV (2), 107–8.

93. Tocqueville to Francisque de Corcelle, 22 July 1854, in *OC,* XV (2), 108–9.

94. Tocqueville to Francisque de Corcelle, 22 July 1854, in *OC,* XV (2), 109.

95. Tocqueville to Gustave de Beaumont, 16 July 1854, in *OC,* VIII (3), 224.

96. Tocqueville to Gustave de Beaumont, 6 August 1854, in *OC,* VIII (3), 228.

97. Tocqueville to Theodore Sedgwick, 14 August 1854, in *OC,* VII, 159.

98. Tocqueville to Gustave de Beaumont, 6 August 1854, in *OC,* VIII (3), 229.

99. Tocqueville to Theodore Sedgwick, 14 August 1854, in *OC,* VII, 159.

100. Tocqueville to Pierre Freslon, 30 July 1854, in *OC,* XVII (3), 165.

101. Tocqueville to Jean-Jacques Ampère, 5 August 1854, in *OC,* XI, 249.

102. Tocqueville to Gustave de Beaumont, 20 August 1854, in *OC,* VIII (3), 232–33.

103. Tocqueville to Jean-Jacques Ampère, 22 August 1854, in *OC,* XI, 251–52.

104. Tocqueville to Francisque de Corcelle, 29 August 1854, in *OC,* XV (2), 110.

105. Tocqueville to Adolphe de Circourt, 1 September 1854, in *OC,* XVIII, 199.

106. Gustave de Beaumont to Tocqueville, 27 August 1854, in *OC,* VIII (3), 234.

107. Tocqueville to George Cornewall Lewis, 19 September 1854, in *OC,* VI (3), 172, indicates that this was a young Lutheran minister by the name of Ehni, whom Tocqueville had previously met in Paris.

108. Tocqueville to George Cornewall Lewis, 9 October 1854, in *OC,* VI (3), 172.

109. Tocqueville to Jean-Jacques Ampère, 6 September 1854, in *OC,* XI, 255.

110. Tocqueville to Gustave de Beaumont, 1 October 1854, in *OC,* VIII (3), 240.

111. Tocqueville to Adolphe de Circourt, 2 October 1854, in *OC,* XVIII, 205.

112. Tocqueville to Gustave de Beaumont, 1 October 1854, in *OC,* VIII (3), 250.

113. Tocqueville to Adolphe de Circourt, 14 November 1854, in *OC,* XVIII, 217.

114. Tocqueville to Odilon Barrot, 11 October 1854, in *OC,* XVII (3), 169.

115. Tocqueville to Mrs. Harriet Grote, 10 August 1856, in *OC,* VI (3), 208; Tocqueville to Adolphe de Circourt, 11 March 1857, in *OC,* XVIII, 386.

116. Tocqueville to Charles Monnard, 14 August 1854, in *OC,* VII, 344.

117. Tocqueville to Francisque de Corcelle, 2 October 1854, in *OC,* XV (2), 118.

118. Tocqueville to Louis de Kergorlay, 19 December 1854, in *OC,* XIII (2), 290.

119. Tocqueville to Francisque de Corcelle, 2 October 1854, in *OC,* XV (2), 118.

120. Tocqueville to Francisque de Corcelle, 2 October 1854, in *OC,* XV (2), 118–19.

121. Tocqueville to Francisque de Corcelle, 2 October 1854, in *OC,* XV (2), 119.

122. Tocqueville to Francisque de Corcelle, 23 October 1854, in *OC,* XV (2), 123.

123. Tocqueville to Hubert de Tocqueville, 25 March 1855, in *OC,* XIV, 308–9.

124. Tocqueville to Adolphe de Circourt, 2 October 1854, in *OC,* XVIII, 206.

125. Tocqueville to Hubert de Tocqueville, 25 March 1855, in *OC,* XIV, 307.

126. See, in particular, Tocqueville, *L'ancien régime et la révolution, OC,* II (1), 93–94, 99–105, 119, 265–72.

127. Tocqueville to Charles Monnard, 26 April 1855, in *OC,* VII, 340–41.

128. Tocqueville, *L'ancien régime et la révolution,* 91–93.

129. Tocqueville, *L'ancien régime et la révolution,* 265.

130. Tocqueville, *L'ancien régime et la révolution,* 265–66.

131. Tocqueville, *L'ancien régime et la révolution,* 266.

132. Tocqueville, *L'ancien régime et la révolution,* 93, 267. These remarks echo precisely the sentiment expressed in Tocqueville's notes of his conversation with Ferdinand Walter on 27 June 1854 to the effect that Germany was "more changed in the spirit than the letter of its institutions." Tocqueville, "Voyage en Allemagne," 3:323.

133. Tocqueville, *L'ancien régime et la révolution,* 93–94.

134. Tocqueville, *L'ancien régime et la révolution,* 94.

135. Tocqueville, *L'ancien régime et la révolution,* 94.

136. Tocqueville, *L'ancien régime et la révolution,* 99.

137. A long note added to the text indicates that, if serfdom was abolished in Baden in 1783, it was not until 1833 that it was abolished in Hohenzollern-Sigmaringen. To this Tocqueville adds that, in those parts of eastern Germany populated by Slavs, serfdom had always been much harsher; Tocqueville, *L'ancien régime et la révolution,* 267–68.

138. Tocqueville, *L'ancien régime et la révolution,* 98.

139. Tocqueville, *L'ancien régime et la révolution,* 269.

140. Tocqueville, *L'ancien régime et la révolution,* 269–70.

141. Tocqueville, *L'ancien régime et la révolution,* 106.

142. Tocqueville, *L'ancien régime et la révolution,* 101, 272.

143. Tocqueville to his father, 28 May 1856, in *OC,* XIV, 324.

144. Tocqueville engaged in a lengthy correspondence with his publisher about the need to bring out new editions as quickly as possible. On the reception of *L'ancien régime et la révolution,* see J.-P. Mayer, "Histoire de l'influence de l'ancien régime," in *L'ancien régime et la révolution, OC,* II (1), 335–55.

145. See, for example, Tocqueville to Gustave de Beaumont, 1 July 1856, in *OC,* VIII (3), 420. Similar letters were received by Charles de Montalembert, Odilon

Barrot, Victor Lanjuinais, François Buloz, Pierre Freslon, Ampère, Corcelle, Circourt, Kergorlay, and others. Tocqueville was not above responding to any criticism the book received. A good example of this is the letter he sent to Léon Plée, author of what he described to Ampère as series of "malicious" articles in *Le siècle* portraying him as "a friend of the Ancien Régime." "No one," Tocqueville told Plée, "has done more than me to bring to light the vices, the errors and the faults of this Ancien Régime, although I do think that among all the bad institutions that it contained there were several things that it would have been desirable to preserve." Tocqueville also insisted that he considered the "principal conquests" of the revolution to have been political liberty, the abolition of privileges, equality before the law, and freedom of religion; Tocqueville to Léon Plée, 31 July 1856, in *OC,* XVII (3), 299–300.

146. Tocqueville to Charles Monnard, 15 October 1856, in *OC,* VII, 354.

147. Tocqueville, *L'ancien régime et la révolution,* 72–73.

148. André Jardin, *Tocqueville: A Biography* (Baltimore, 1998), 513.

149. Tocqueville to Prosper Duvergier de Hauranne, 1 September 1856, in *OC,* XVII (3), 316.

150. Tocqueville to Pierre Freslon, 20 September 1856, in *OC,* XVII (3), 324. See also Tocqueville to Prosper Duvergier de Hauranne, 10 July 1856, in *OC,* XVII (3), 279, where Tocqueville acknowledges the scale and difficulty of the task he had set himself.

151. There are many examples of this that could be cited, but see Tocqueville to his wife, 18 April 1858, in *OC,* XIV, 637: "I am working very hard," Tocqueville wrote, "but am making little progress; I am so lost among an ocean of papers . . . that often I feel a most profound sadness and am ready to give up my project."

152. Tocqueville to Pierre Freslon, 8 October 1856, in *OC,* XVII (3), 331.

153. Tocqueville to George Cornewall Lewis, 6 October 1856, in *OC,* VI (3), 221–22.

154. Tocqueville to Louis de Kergorlay, 16 May 1858, in *OC,* XIII (2), 337.

155. Tocqueville to Gustave de Beaumont, 1 February 1857, in *OC,* VIII (3), 457. See also Tocqueville to Alfred Maury, 13 October 1856, in *OC,* XVII (3), 332–35; and Tocqueville to Jules Ravenel, 25 January 1857, in *OC,* XVII (3), 369–72, where Tocqueville set out what he wanted to achieve and the material he therefore wished to consult. Even so, Tocqueville told Victor Lanjuinais that the books he most wanted were never at hand; Tocqueville to Victor Lanjuinais, 11 February 1857, in *OC,* XVII (3), 377.

156. Tocqueville also asked Circourt for suggested reading on Germany. For his part, Circourt made contact with Leopold von Ranke to seek his advice.

157. For Tocqueville's notes on this biography, see Tocqueville, "Préoccupations universelle que cause la révolution française en Europe," *OC,* II (2), 255–65.

158. Tocqueville to Charles Monnard, 15 October 1856, in *OC,* VII (3), 354–56.

159. See also Tocqueville to Adolphe de Circourt, 22 February 1857, in *OC,* XVIII, 379–80; and Tocqueville to Adolphe de Circourt, 11 March 1857, in *OC,* XVIII, 385–86. Both letters give a sense of the German texts that Tocqueville was reading. Of the text by Georg Forster, for example, Tocqueville wrote (11 March 1857) that "the intoxication that, at its beginning, the principles of our Revolution caused among quite a few German thinkers has never been more visible than in this book." Tocqueville also told Circourt (11 March 1857) that his poor knowledge of the German language meant that he was advancing "as slowly and as laboriously as someone walking across a ploughed field."

160. Tocqueville, "Agitation violente et incertaine de l'esprit humain aux approaches de la révolution," in *OC,* II (2), 33–46; "[La révolution et l'Étranger] Enthousiasme de l'Europe en 1789," in *OC,* II (2), 243–65.

161. Tocqueville, "Agitation violente et incertaine de l'esprit humain aux approaches de la révolution," 34–35.

162. Tocqueville, "Agitation violente et incertaine de l'esprit humain aux approaches de la révolution," 38.

163. Tocqueville, "Ce qui fit vaincre la révolution au-dehors," in *Œuvres,* 3:617–18, emphasis in the original.

164. Tocqueville, "Ce qui fit vaincre la révolution au-dehors,"36.

165. Tocqueville to Pierre Freslon, 8 October 1856, in *OC,* XVII (3), 331–32.

166. Tocqueville had, of course, made a similar observation about the national vanity of the Americans.

167. Tocqueville to Hubert de Tocqueville, 30 October 1856, in *OC,* XIV, 327.

168. Tocqueville to Hubert de Tocqueville, 23 February 1857, in *OC,* XIV, 328–29. Tocqueville was less impressed by Schiller as a historian, describing him as "a great colourist rather than a faithful copier of nature."

169. See Tocqueville to Adolphe de Circourt, 22 February 1857, in *OC,* XVIII, 379, where Tocqueville seemed less than fully impressed by Schlosser's study: "It is a very mediocre work," Tocqueville commented, "but, for a foreigner, it contains lots of very interesting *German* facts." Emphasis in the original.

170. Tocqueville to Hubert de Tocqueville, 8 December 1857, in *OC,* XIV, 337, emphasis in the original. Tocqueville had made similar observations about the German character in a letter written to Henry Reeve five months earlier; see Tocqueville to Henry Reeve, 22 July 1857, in *OC,* VI (1), 236.

171. Tocqueville to Hubert de Tocqueville, 7 February 1858, in *OC,* XIV, 341–42.

172. Tocqueville to Hubert de Tocqueville, 4 April 1858, in *OC,* XIV, 346.

173. Tocqueville to Christian von Bunsen, 27 December 1858, in *OC,* VII, 366–67. See also Tocqueville to Hubert de Tocqueville, 15 November 1858, in *OC,* XIV, 360, where he speaks of the possibility and potential of a "representative monarchy" in Prussia.

174. For a recent history of the rise of Germany in the nineteenth century, see Katja Hoyer, *Blood and Iron: The Rise and Fall of the German Empire 1871–1918* (London, 2021).

9. AMERICA AND ENGLAND REVISITED

1. Tocqueville, *L'ancien régime et la révolution, OC,* II (1), 286–87.

2. Tocqueville, *L'ancien régime et la révolution,* 287.

3. Tocqueville, *L'ancien régime et la révolution,* 119–20.

4. Tocqueville, *L'ancien régime et la révolution,* 205–6.

5. Tocqueville, *L'ancien régime et la révolution,* 306.

6. Tocqueville, *L'ancien régime et la révolution,* 139, 292.

7. Tocqueville, *L'ancien régime et la révolution,* 148–49.

8. Tocqueville, *L'ancien régime et la révolution,* 199.

9. Tocqueville, *L'ancien régime et la révolution,* 157.

10. Tocqueville, *Democracy in America,* 1279–83.

11. Tocqueville, *Democracy in America,* 1283–85.

12. Richard Rush, *Occasional Productions, Political, Diplomatic, and Miscellaneous, Including, among Others, a Glance at the Court and Government of Louis Philippe and the Revolution of 1848* (Philadelphia, 1860), 391. See also Rush's notes for their conversation on 16 April 1848, when Tocqueville quizzed Rush on bicameralism in America (384).

13. Tocqueville, "Banquet populaire de Cherbourg," in *OC,* III (3), 45.

14. The four thousand copies were quickly sold, with two further editions being published later in the year.

15. Tocqueville, "Forward to the Twelfth Edition," in *Democracy in America,* 1373–75. That Tocqueville was aware of the difficulties that this might present in France is revealed in Tocqueville to Ernest de Blosseville, July 1848, in *OC,* XVII (2), 460.

16. There is much that might be said about this curious figure, not least that in 1841 he published *Considérations sur le principe démocratique qui régit l'union américain et d'autres états,* a detailed commentary and refutation of many of the arguments advanced by Tocqueville in *De la démocratie en Amérique.* Prior to 1830 Poussin lived in the United States for seventeen years, where he worked, with considerable distinction, as an engineer in the US Army.

17. For documents relating to this episode, see Tocqueville, "The Poussin Affair," in *Tocqueville on America after 1840: Letters and Other Writings,* edited and translated by Aurelian Craiutu and Jeremy Jennings (New York, 2009), 409–54.

18. Tocqueville to Gustave de Beaumont, 5 October 1849, in *OC,* VIII (2), 181; Tocqueville to Gustave de Beaumont, 12 October 1849, in *OC,* VIII (2), 201–2.

19. Tocqueville to Sir Henry Lytton Bulwer, 16 October 1849, in *OC,* VI (3), 131.

20. For one example among many, see Hyacinthe Colombel, *Quelques réflexions concernant la Constitution qu'on élabore pour la France* (Nantes, France, 1848). Arguably the most significant contributor to these debates was Édouard Laboulaye; see, for example, Édouard Laboulaye, *De la Constitution américaine et de l'utilité de son étude* (Paris, 1850). On Laboulaye, see Walter D. Gray, *Interpreting American Democracy in France: The Career of Édouard Laboulaye* (Newark, DE, 1994). For his part, Tocqueville's rival on American affairs, Michel Chevalier, published a long essay and a series of seven short articles; see Michel Chevalier, "La liberté aux États-Unis," *Revue des Deux Mondes* 3, no. 1 (1849): 91–124; and Michel Chevalier, "Étude sur la Constitution des États-Unis" in *Le journal des débats, politiques et littéraires,* 25 May 1848, 6 June 1848, 15 June 1848, 22 June 1848, 4 July 1848, 11 July 1848, and 21 July 1848.

21. Ampère did not hide the fact that his interest in the United States had been awakened by a reading of *De la démocratie en Amérique* and his friendship with its author. Accordingly, it was to Tocqueville that Ampère's *Promenade en Amérique* was dedicated. See Jean-Jacques Ampère, *Promenade en Amérique: États-Unis—Cuba—Mexique,* 2 vols. (Paris, 1855).

22. Tocqueville to Jean-Jacques Ampère, 6 October 1851, in *OC,* XI, 200–203.

23. Also travelling on the same ship was the famous actress and author Fanny Kemble; Ampère, *Promenade,* 1:4–5.

24. Ampère, *Promenade,* 1:337–42.

25. Ampère, *Promenade,* 2:42–43.

26. Ampère, *Promenade,* 1:62–65.

27. Ampère, *Promenade,* 1:188–91.

28. Jean-Jacques Ampère to Tocqueville, 12 November 1851, in *OC,* XI, 205–6.

29. Ampère, *Promenade,* 1:386–88.

30. Ampère, *Promenade,* 1:213–15.

31. Ampère, *Promenade,* 1:59–72.

32. Tocqueville to Henry Reeve, 8 August 1852, in *OC,* VI (1), 134. Tocqueville also told Reeve that he would be amused by Ampère's "lively, simple and witty accounts."

33. Tocqueville to Franscisque de Corcelle, 7 November 1852, in *OC,* XV (2), 60. Ampère's own recollections of this pleasant and engaging experience can be found in Jean-Jacques Ampère to Mme de Tocqueville, 14 October 1852, in *OC,* XI, 214.

34. Gustave de Beaumont to Tocqueville, 16 August 1852, in *OC,* VIII (3), 69.

35. It took Sumner three years to recover from the severe injuries he sustained.

36. For a discussion of these and other disquieting developments in the 1840s and 1850s, see Jill Lepore, *These Truths: A History of the United States* (New York, 2018), 232–71.

37. For a broader discussion of Tocqueville's views on America during this period, see Aurelian Craiutu and Jeremy Jennings, "Interpretive Essay: The Third Democracy; Tocqueville's Views of America after 1840," in Tocqueville, *Tocqueville on America,* 1–51.

38. Tocqueville, *Report Made to the Chamber of Deputies on the Abolition of Slavery in the French Colonies* (Boston, 1840).

39. Tocqueville to Jared Sparks, 13 October 1840, in *OC,* VII, 82–83.

40. Tocqueville to Theodore Sedgwick, 4 December 1852, in *OC,* VII, 146. See also Tocqueville to Jared Sparks, 11 December 1852, in *OC,* XVII (3), 78–79, where Tocqueville described himself as being "sincerely and deeply" a friend of America.

41. Tocqueville to E. V. Childe, 12 December 1856, in *OC,* VII, 185. See also Tocqueville to Victor Lanjuinais, 8 December 1850, in *OC,* XVII (2), 702, where Tocqueville described himself as being "quasi-Yankee."

42. Tocqueville to Charles Sumner, 28 March 1858, in *OC,* VII, 226.

43. Tocqueville to Jared Sparks, 11 December 1852, in *OC,* VII, 148–49.

44. Tocqueville to Theodore Sedgwick, 6 June 1856, in *OC,* VII, 167–68. Apart from declaring English to be the official language of the country, Walker also reintroduced slavery. After further military adventures in the region, Walker was executed in 1860. His exploits convinced many southerners of the possibility of creating a slave-owning empire in Latin America.

45. Tocqueville to Theodore Sedgwick, 19 September 1855, in *OC,* VII, 163. The Know-Nothings (first known officially as the Native American Party and then simply the American Party) was a short-lived anti-immigrant and anti-Catholic party.

46. Tocqueville to Francis Lieber, 9 October 1857, in *OC,* VII, 215.

47. Tocqueville to E. V. Childe, 2 April 1857, in *OC,* VII, 193.

48. Tocqueville to Theodore Sedgwick, 13 April 1857, in *OC,* VII, 195.

49. Tocqueville to Charles Sumner, 28 March 1858, in *OC,* VII, 227, emphasis in the original.

50. Tocqueville to Theodore Sedgwick, 29 August 1856, in *OC,* VII, 177.

51. Tocqueville to Theodore Sedgwick, 14 October 1856, in *OC,* VII, 182–3.

52. Tocqueville to Theodore Sedgwick, 29 August 1856, in *OC,* VII, 177–8.

53. Tocqueville to Francis Lieber, 1 September 1856, in *OC,* VII, 179; Tocqueville to N. W. Senior, 4 September 1856, in *OC,* VI, (2), 190.

54. Gustave de Beaumont had published his own antislavery testimonial entitled "The United States and Slavery" in the 1852 edition of *The Liberty Bell,* where he wrote, "It is enough to say that I believe in the eventual abolition of slavery in the United States. A people could not be at the head of the Christian world, which is the civilised world, if it preserves within itself an institution which is the very negation of justice, of religion, of liberty, that is to say everything that makes for the power and grandeur of nations" (43–45).

55. Tocqueville to *The Liberty Bell,* in *OC,* VII, 163–64. Tocqueville's text was subsequently republished in *Letters on American Slavery from Victor Hugo, de Tocqueville, Emile de Girardin, Carnot, Passy, Mazzini, Humboldt, O. Lafayette, &c.* (Boston, 1860), 8.

56. Tocqueville to *The Liberty Bell,* in *OC,* VII, 163.

57. Tocqueville to Theodore Sedgwick, 19 February 1857, in *OC,* VII, 189–90.

58. Tocqueville to E. V. Childe, 2 April 1857, in *OC,* VII, 193.

59. Tocqueville to Theodore Sedgwick, 13 April 1857, in *OC,* VII, 195–6.

60. Tocqueville to Henry Reeve, 21 September 1856, in *OC,* VI (1), 207.

61. Tocqueville to Adolphe de Circourt, 4 November 1856, in *OC,* XVIII, 346.

62. Tocqueville to Francis Lieber, 1 September 1856, in *OC,* VII, 179.

63. Tocqueville to N. W. Senior, 21 August 1858, in *OC,* VI (2), 218.

64. Tocqueville, *L'ancien régime et la révolution,* 135–37.

65. Tocqueville, *L'ancien régime et la révolution,* 145.

66. Tocqueville, *L'ancien régime et la révolution,* 145–48.

67. Tocqueville, *L'ancien régime et la révolution,* 148–49.

68. Tocqueville, *L'ancien régime et la révolution,* 152.

69. Tocqueville, *L'ancien régime et la révolution,*159.

70. Tocqueville, *L'ancien régime et la révolution,* 159–60.

71. Tocqueville, *L'ancien régime et la révolution,* 148–53.

72. Tocqueville, *L'ancien régime et la révolution,* 160.

73. Tocqueville, *L'ancien régime et la révolution,* 166–67.

74. Tocqueville, *L'ancien régime et la révolution,* 206.

75. Tocqueville, *L'ancien régime et la révolution,* 234.

76. Tocqueville, *L'ancien régime et la révolution,* 309.

77. Tocqueville, *L'ancien régime et la révolution,* 222.

78. Tocqueville, "Notes sur Blackstone," in *Œuvres,* 3 vols. (Paris: 1991–2004), 3:339.

79. Tocqueville, "Notes sur Blackstone," 3:342.

80. Tocqueville, "Notes sur Blackstone," 3:342.

81. Tocqueville, "Notes sur Blackstone," 3:341, emphasis in the original.

82. Tocqueville, "Notes sur Blackstone," 3:341.

83. Tocqueville, "Ressemblance et dissemblance des révolutions de 1640 et de 1789," 3:343.

84. Tocqueville, *L'ancien régime et la révolution,* 243.

85. Tocqueville to Mrs. Sarah Austin, 29 August 1856, in *OC,* VI (1), 191.

86. Sir George Cornewall Lewis to Tocqueville, 30 July 1856, in *OC,* VI (3), 202–3.

87. See the series of texts devoted to this subject in *OC,* III (2), 255–324.

88. Tocqueville to John Stuart Mill, 18 December 1840, in *OC,* VI (1), 330–21.

89. John Stuart Mill to Tocqueville, 30 December 1840, in *OC,* VI (1), 332–33.

90. Tocqueville, "Note sur les inconvénients de l'alliance anglaise," in *OC,* III (2), 282.

91. Tocqueville, "Intérêts naturels et permanents des grandes puissances dans la question d'Orient," in *OC,* III (2), 315.

92. Tocqueville, "Quatre articles sur Tahiti," in *OC,* III (2), 403–20.

93. Tocqueville, "Discussion de l'Adresse," in *OC,* III (2), 428–29.

94. Tocqueville, "Projet de Discours sur l'affaire de l'Orégon," in *OC,* III (2), 446.

95. See the set of Tocqueville texts devoted to "La question espagnole," in *OC,* III (2), 357–95.

96. Of Palmerston's foreign policy, Orlando Figes, *Crimea: The Last Crusade* (London, 2011), 148–49, notes that "it was Protestant and freedom-loving, energetic and adventurous, confident and bold, belligerent in its defence of the little man, proudly British, and contemptuous of foreigners, particularly those of the Roman Catholic and Orthodox religion, whom Palmerston associated with the worst vices and excesses of the Continent."

97. See Tocqueville to Francisque de Corcelle, 29 September 1847, in *OC,* XV (1), 239–40.

98. Tocqueville, *Souvenirs,* 243.

99. Tocqueville to Henry Reeve, 15 June 1849, in *OC,* VI (1), 99–100; 30 June 1849, in *OC,* VI (1), 101–2; 5 July 1849, in *OC,* VI (1), 103–5; and 19 July 1849, in *OC,* VI (1), 105–7.

100. Tocqueville to Francisque de Corcelle, 14 September 1849, in *OC,* XV (1), 411, emphasis in the original; Tocqueville to Francisque de Corcelle, 24 September 1849, in *OC,* XV (1), 422; Tocqueville to Francisque de Corcelle, 1 October 1849, in *OC,* XV (1), 442. See also Tocqueville to Edmond Drouyn de Lhuys, 29 October 1849, in *OC,* XVII (2), 650–51.

101. Tocqueville to Lord Normanby, 23 August 1849, in *OC,* VI (3), 125–26.

102. Tocqueville to Lord Normanby, 12 September 1849, in *OC,* VI (3), 126–27. See also Tocqueville to Henri Hubert Delisle, 10 September 1849, in *OC,* XVII (2), 606–7, where Tocqueville expresses his doubts about any further French

intervention. For his extensive notes on this subject, see Tocqueville, "L'affaire du Rio de la Plata," in *OC,* III (3), 369–93. See also the report prepared by Beaumont for Tocqueville: Gustave de Beuamont, "Note de Beaumont pour Tocqueville," 1 July 1849, in *OC,* VIII (2), 153–62.

103. Tocqueville to Henry Reeve, 30 July 1849, in *OC,* VI (1), 107–8.

104. See Figes, *Crimea.*

105. See, for example, Tocqueville to William Rathbone Greg, 16 April 1854, in *OC,* VI (3), 165; and Tocqueville to Rosalind Margaret Phillimore, 30 November 1854, in *OC,* VI (3), 175.

106. Tocqueville to Francisque de Corcelle, 23 January 1855, in *OC,* XV (2), 134; Tocqueville to Adolphe de Circourt, 26 January 1855, in *OC,* XVIII, 235.

107. In fact, both armies held each other in mutual contempt.

108. Tocqueville to N. W. Senior, 22 January 1855, in *OC,* VI (2), 173–75; Tocqueville to N. W. Senior, 15 February 1855, *OC,* VI (2), 175–77.

109. Tocqueville to N. W. Senior, 25 February 1855, in *OC,* VI (2), 178; Tocqueville to Gustave de Beaumont, 8 March 1855, in *OC,* VIII (3), 279–80; Tocqueville to Mrs. Harriet Grote, 4 February 1855, *OC,* VI (3), 182.

110. Tocqueville to N. W. Senior, 22 January 1855, in *OC,* VI (2), 176.

111. Tocqueville to Adolphe de Corcourt, 26 January 1855, in *OC,* XVIII, 236.

112. Tocqueville to Gustave de Beaumont, 8 March 1855, in *OC,* VIII (3), 279.

113. Tocqueville to N. W. Senior, 15 February 1855, in *OC,* VI (2), 177.

114. Tocqueville to Mrs. Harriet Grote, 7 January 1855, in *OC,* VI (3), 177.

115. Tocqueville to Gustave de Beaumont, 14 November 1856, in *OC,* VIII (3), 447. Tocqueville made the same point at greater length in a letter to Mrs.Harriet Grote, 31 January 1857, in *OC,* VI (3), 233–34, where he suggested that people incorrectly saw this as an example of Britain's political Machiavellianism. In Tocqueville's opinion, it derived from a simplicity of mind that prevented the English from "perceiving several things at the same time" (234) and from the understandable desire to attribute their actions to more than national self-interest.

116. Tocqueville to Sir George Cornewall Lewis, 6 October 1856, in *OC,* VI (3), 222, emphasis in the original.

117. Tocqueville to Sir George Cornewall Lewis, 3 November 1856, in *OC,* VI (3), 227. See also Tocqueville to Henry Reeve, 21 September 1856, in *OC,* VI (1), 208; and Tocqueville to Theodore Sedgwick, 13 June 1857, in *OC,* VII, 201.

118. See, for example, Tocqueville to Victor Lanjuinais, June 1857[?], in *OC,* XVII (3), 406, where Tocqueville asked about the prices of accommodation and meals in London.

119. Tocqueville to Mrs. Harriet Grote, 31 May 1857, in *OC,* VI (3), 238.

120. Tocqueville to Marie Mottley, 23 June 1857, in *OC,* XIV, 602–3; Tocqueville to Marie Mottley, 25 June 1857, in *OC,* XIV, 605.

121. Tocqueville to Sir Antony Panizzi, 17 July 1857, in *OC,* VI (3), 247–48. An inventory was not made available until 1899.

122. Tocqueville to Marie Mottley, 1 July 1857, in *OC,* XIV, 611–12. Tocqueville used the English word "***humbug.***"

123. Tocqueville to Gustave de Beaumont, 25 July 1857, in *OC,* VIII (3), 490–91.

124. Tocqueville to Gustave de Beaumont, 25 July 1857, in *OC,* VIII (3), 491. Tocqueville repeated these comments about the absence of English intervention in letters to Lord Clarendon, 21 July 1851, in *OC,* VIII (3), 250–51, and to Lady Thereza Cornewall Lewis, 5 August 1857, in *OC,* VI (3), 259. As Tocqueville was not allowed to take any notes, it was arranged that copies would be sent to him in France.

125. See Tocqueville to Léonce de Lavergne, 4 September 1857, in *OC,* XVII (3), 417, where he wrote that, although his stay had been "very agreeable," his time could have been better employed.

126. M. C. M. Simpson, *Many Memories of Many People* (London, 1898), 59. For Tocqueville's own assessment, see Tocqueville to Louis Bouchitté, 25 August 1857, in *OC,* XVII (3), 412, where he wrote that his "flattering" reception owed as much to his principles as it did to his own person.

127. Opened in 1851 for the Universal Exhibition and located in Hyde Park, the Crystal Palace was dismantled and relocated to the south of London in 1854. It became a major tourist attraction; hence the fact that there were no hotel rooms available.

128. Tocqueville to Marie Mottley, 19 June 1857, in *OC,* XIV, 596–7.

129. Tocqueville to Marie Mottley, 20 June 1857, in *OC,* XIV, 597–98, emphasis in the original.

130. Tocqueville to Marie Mottley, 20 June 1857, in *OC,* XIV, 598.

131. Tocqueville to Marie Mottley, 21–22 June 1857, in *OC,* XIV, 599–600.

132. Tocqueville to Marie Mottley, 21–22 June 1857, in *OC,* XIV, 600.

133. Tocqueville to Marie Mottley, 21–22 June 1857, in *OC,* XIV, 600–601.

134. Tocqueville to Marie Mottley, 23 June 1857, in *OC,* XIV, 602, emphasis in the original.

135. Tocqueville was greatly impressed by Macaulay, recording that he had the kindness to speak to him in French. Tocqueville subsequently had breakfast with Macaulay, when, according to the diary of Edward Henry Stanley, the conversation focused on "the state of America." According to Stanley, Tocqueville expressed the view that "disunion" was "not probable"; Edward Henry Stanley, "Un petit déjeuner avec Tocqueville," in *OC,* VI (1), 243–44.

136. Tocqueville to Marie Mottley, 25 June 1857, in *OC,* XIV, 605–6.

137. Tocqueville to Marie Mottley, 29 June 1857, in *OC,* XIV, 610. See Tocqueville's similarly fulsome remarks in Tocqueville to Lady Thereza Cornewall-Lewis, 20 June 1857, in *OC,* VI (1), 353, and in a letter to Mrs. Harriet Grote written at the time of the official visit of Queen Victoria and Prince Albert to Cherbourg: Tocqueville to Mrs. Harriet Grote, 23 July 1858, in *OC,* VI (3), 296. Prince Albert was likewise impressed by Tocqueville.

138. Tocqueville to Marie Mottley, 3 July 1857, in *OC,* XIV, 616.

139. Tocqueville to Marie Mottley, in *OC,* XIV, 3 July 1857, 616–17.

140. Tocqueville to Francisque de Corcelle, 29 July 1857, in *OC,* XV (2), 204.

141. Tocqueville to Marie Mottley, 10 July 1857, in *OC,* XIV, 618. See also Tocqueville to Nassau William Senior, 9 July 1857, in *OC,* XVII (3), 407, where Tocqueville recorded that Ferguson had told him to get as much rest as possible.

142. Tocqueville to Marie Mottley, 2 July 1857, in *OC,* XIV, 614. Tocqueville wrote "*somebody*" and "*nobody*" in English.

143. Tocqueville to Marie Mottley, 20 June 1857, in *OC,* XIV, 598.

144. Tocqueville to Marie Mottley, 30 June 1857, in *OC,* XIV, 611.

145. Madame Bono was one of Tocqueville's neighbours in Normandy.

146. Tocqueville to Marie Mottley, 11 July 1857, in *OC,* XIV, 620–21, emphasis in the original.

147. Tocqueville to Marie Mottley, 11 July 1857, in *OC,* XIV, 621–22.

148. Tocqueville to Marie Mottley, 11 July 1857, in *OC,* XIV, 621–22.

149. Tocqueville to Lord Hatherton, 1 September 1858, in *OC,* VI (3), 301. In this letter Tocqueville not only set out the improvements he was trying to make on his estate—for example, the rotation of crops and the use, for the first time, of liquid guano—but also included a heartfelt invitation to Hatherton to visit him in Normandy.

150. Tocqueville to Lord Hatherton, 1 July 1857, in *OC,* VI (3), 246.

151. Tocqueville to Marie Mottley, 16 July 1857, in *OC,* XIV, 623–24.

152. Tocqueville to Louis de Kergorlay, 4 August 1857, in *OC,* XIII (2), 326–27.

153. Tocqueville to Laurette de Pisieux, 21 September 1857, in *OC,* XVII (3), 427–28.

154. Tocqueville to Louis de Kergorlay, 27 February 1858, in *OC,* XIII (2), 333.

155. Tocqueville to Francisque de Corcelle, 29 July 1857, in *OC,* XV (2), 204.

156. Tocqueville to Louis de Kergorlay, 4 August 1857, in *OC,* XIII (2), 327–28.

157. Tocqueville to Francisque de Corcelle, 28 January 1857, in *OC,* XV (2), 196–97.

158. Tocqueville made a similar point to Kergorlay when he commented upon this aspect of English life. Speaking of Thomas à Kempis's *Imitation of Christ,* he remarked that "it is not *healthy* to detach oneself from life, from its interests, its business, and even its pleasures, when they are honest, and, in teaching this, those who live according to such a book can hardly fail to lose all public virtues at the expense of acquiring certain private virtues." Such a teaching, Tocqueville wrote, ran the risk of producing "the most useless citizens"; Tocqueville to Louis de Kergorlay, 4 August 1857, in *OC,* XIII (2), 328, emphasis in the original.

159. Tocqueville to Francisque de Corcelle, 5 August 1857, in *OC,* XV (2), 206.

160. Tocqueville to Louis de Kergorlay, 4 August 1857, in *OC,* XIII (2), 326–27.

161. Tocqueville to Marie Mottley, 25 June 1857, in *OC,* XIV, 606; Tocqueville to Marie Motley, 27 June 1857, in *OC,* XIV, 607.

162. Tocqueville to Sir Robert Peel, 18 May 1845, in *OC,* VI (3), 96–98. Tocqueville had written to Peel three years earlier about the career prospects of another of his wife's brothers, Henry.

163. Tocqueville to Henry Reeve, 2 August 1857, in *OC,* VI (1), 229.

164. Tocqueville to Gustave de Beaumont, 25 July 1857, in *OC,* VIII (3), 491.

165. Tocqueville to Jean-Charles Rivet, 5 August 1857, in *OC,* XVII (3), 411–12.

166. Hugh Brogan, *Alexis de Tocqueville: Prophet of Democracy in the Age of Revolution* (London, 2006), 606.

167. Tocqueville to Lady Thereza Cornewall-Lewis, 5 August 1857, in *OC,* VI (3), 259.

168. Tocqueville to Lady Thereza Cornewall-Lewis, 5 August 1857, in *OC,* VI (3), 259.

169. Tocqueville to Lady Thereza Cornewall-Lewis, 18 October 1857, in *OC,* VI (3), 273.

170. There is no agreed-upon nomenclature for these events. Until recently they were referred to in Britain as the Indian Mutiny, but other names include the Indian Rebellion, the First War of Independence, the Sepoy Mutiny, the Great Rebellion, and so on.

171. According to David Cannadine, *Victorious Century: The United Kingdom, 1800–1906* (London: 2017), 314, the "Great Rebellion was the greatest nineteenth-century crisis the British Empire faced."

172. See Tocqueville to Léonce de Lavergne, 4 September 1857, in *OC,* XVII (3), 418.

173. Tocqueville to Lady Thereza Cornewall-Lewis, 18 October 1857, in *OC,* VI (3), 275.

174. Tocqueville to Prosper Duvergier de Hauranne, 4 August 1857, in *OC,* XVII (3), 409–10.

175. Tocqueville to Victor Lanjuinais, 2 September 1857, in *OC,* XVII (3), 415–16. See also Tocqueville to Charles de Rémusat, 9 September 1857, in *OC,* XVII (3), 420–1.

176. Tocqueville to Adolphe de Circourt, 17 August 1857, in *OC,* XVIII, 402. After a siege lasting several months, Delhi was retaken in September 1857. This did not, however, bring the rebellion to an end.

177. Tocqueville to Lady Thereza Cornewall-Lewis, 18 October 1857, in *OC,* VI (3), 275.

178. Tocqueville to Henry Reeve, 2 August 1857, in *OC,* VI (1), 230.

179. Tocqueville to Lady Thereza Cornewall-Lewis, 18 October 1857, in *OC,* VI (3), 273–74.

180. Tocqueville to Henry Reeve, 2 August 1857, in *OC,* VI (1), 230.

181. Tocqueville to Henry Reeve, 30 January 1858, in *OC,* VI (1), 254–55.

182. Tocqueville to Eugénie de Grancey, 8 October 1857, in *OC,* XVII (3), 431.

183. Tocqueville to Lord Hatherton, 27 November 1857, in *OC,* VI (3), 281; Tocqueville to Gustave de Beaumont, 17 August 1857, in *OC,* VIII (3), 496.

184. Tocqueville to Lord Hatherton, 27 November 1857, in *OC,* VI (3), 281. Later the British did indeed establish the British Indian Army.

185. Tocqueville to Henry Reeve, 30 January 1858, in *OC,* VI (1), 253–54.

186. Tocqueville to Lord Hatherton, 6 March 1858, in *OC,* VI (3), 289–90.

187. See Tocqueville to Henry Reeve, 18 September 1857, in *OC,* VI (1), 247; Tocqueville to Gustave de Beaumont, 17 August 1857, in *OC,* VIII (3), 496; and Tocqueville to Adolphe de Circourt, 17 August 1857, in *OC,* XVIII, 402.

188. Tocqueville to Lady Thereza Cornewall-Lewis, 18 October 1857, in *OC*, VI (3), 275–76.

189. Tocqueville to Jean-Jacques Ampère, 9 August 1857, in *OC*, XI, 386.

190. Tocqueville to N. W. Senior, 6 August 1857, in *OC*, VI (2), 203. See also Tocqueville to Henry Reeve, 2 August 1857, in *OC*, VI (1), 229–30.

191. Tocqueville to Adolphe de Circourt, 25 October 1857, in *OC*, XVIII, 424. For an assessment of Tocqueville's views on Hinduism, see Alan S. Kahan, *Tocqueville, Democracy and Religion* (London: 2015), 189–93. According to Kahan, "Hinduism, in Tocqueville's view, was an aristocratic or pseudo-aristocratic religion which for centuries had been completely inadequate to the needs of Indian civilization" (189).

CONCLUSION: CANNES

1. Tocqueville to Jean-Jacques Ampère, 9 August 1857, in *OC*, XI, 385–86; Tocqueville to Jean-Jacques Ampère, 15 September 1857, in *OC*, XI, 391; Tocqueville to Jean-Jacques Ampère, 21 November 1857, in *OC*, XI, 396–97; Tocqueville to Jean-Jacques Ampère, 18 February 1858, in *OC*, XI, 400; Tocqueville to Jean-Jacques Ampère, 11 April 1858, in *OC*, XI, 402–4.

2. Tocqueville to Jean-Jacques Ampère, 11 April 1858, in *OC*, XI, 403–4.

3. Tocqueville to Marie Mottley, 18 April 1858[?], in *OC*, XIV, 638.

4. Tocqueville to Charles de Montalembert, 18 April 1858[?], in *OC*, XVII (3), 482–83.

5. Tocqueville to his wife, 4 May 1858, in *OC*, XIV, 644.

6. See Tocqueville to Lord Hatherton, 6 March 1858, in *OC*, VI (3), 290; and Tocqueville to Arthur de Gobineau, 12 May 1858, in *OC*, IX, 293, where Tocqueville indicated that he had developed "a passionate liking" for the life he led in the country, greatly enjoying the combination of intellectual activity and life outdoors. Among the many other letters conveying this same sentiment, see Tocqueville to Jean-Charles Rivet, 8 May 1858, in *OC*, XVII (3), 484; and Tocqueville to Louis Bouchitté, 12 June 1858, in *OC*, XVII (3), 491.

7. Tocqueville to Francisque de Corcelle, 10 June 1858, in *OC*, XV (2), 218.

8. See Tocqueville to Francisque de Corcelle, 27 June 1858, in *OC*, XV (2), 223. Tocqueville told Corcelle that he was becoming "a very distinguished farmer," adding that "a man who has seven thousand bales of hay is not to be treated with disdain."

9. Tocqueville to Richard Monkton Milnes, 22 July 1858, in *OC,* VI (3), 294.

10. Tocqueville to Mrs. Harriet Grote, 23 July 1858, in *OC,* VI (3), 295–96.

11. See Tocqueville to Henry Reeve, 25 July 1858, in *OC,* VI (1), 274–5; Tocqueville to Gustave de Beaumont, 18 September 1858, in *OC,* VIII (3), 597; Tocqueville to Arthur de Gobineau, 16 September 1858, in *OC,* IX, 296; Tocqueville to Édouard de Tocqueville, 16 September 1858, in *OC,* XIV, 351; Tocqueville to Francisque de Corcelle, 10 August 1858, in *OC,* XV (2), 224; and Tocqueville to Adolphe de Circourt, 24 September 1858, in *OC,* XVIII, 497.

12. Tocqueville to Gustave de Beaumont, 8 April 1858, in *OC,* VIII (3), 561; Tocqueville to Gustave de Beaumont, 21 May 1858, in *OC,* VIII (3), 572; Tocqueville to Gustave de Beaumont, 17 June 1858, in *OC,* VIII (3), 576.

13. Tocqueville to Jean-Charles Rivet, 21 June 1858, in *OC,* XVII (3), 494; Tocqueville to N. W. Senior, 30 June 1858, in *OC,* VI (2), 213.

14. Tocqueville to Gustave de Beaumont, 4 July 1858, in *OC,* VIII (3), 583; Tocqueville to Mrs. Harriet Grote, 23 July 1858, in *OC,* VI (3), 294.

15. Tocqueville to Marie Mottley, 13 September 1858, in *OC,* XIV, 651–52.

16. Tocqueville to Adolphe de Circourt, 24 September 1858, in *OC,* XVIII, 497.

17. Tocqueville to Marie Mottley, 1 October 1858[?], in *OC,* XIV, 657.

18. Tocqueville to Marie Mottley, 3 October 1858, in *OC,* XIV, 661–62.

19. Tocqueville to Jean-Jacques Ampère, 20 September 1858, in *OC,* XI, 410–11.

20. Tocqueville to Francisque de Corcelle, 15 October 1858, in *OC,* XV (2), 231.

21. Tocqueville to Francisque de Corcelle, 7 October 1858, in *OC,* XV (2), 229.

22. Tocqueville to Gustave de Beaumont, 23 October 1858, in *OC,* VIII (3), 600. See also Tocqueville to Jules Dufaure, 23 October 1858, in *OC,* XVII (3), 520–21; and Tocqueville to Édouard de Tocqueville, 6 November 1858, in *OC,* XIV, 357 for a description of the parlous condition he was in before leaving Paris.

23. See a letter sent by Tocqueville to one of his contacts in Cannes where he sought to specify what he and his wife would require by way of transport from Aix-en-Provence. Above all else, he wrote, it was necessary that the carriage horses should be "placid" and the coachman "prudent," as Madame de Tocqueville was frightened of travelling by coach, especially across mountains; Tocqueville to Auguste Bonniol, 27 October 1858, in *OC,* XVII (3), 524.

24. Tocqueville to Léonce de Lavergne, 25 November 1858, in *OC,* XVII (3), 533.

25. Tocqueville to Édouard de Tocqueville, 1 November 1858, in *OC,* XIV, 356.

26. Others, including Ampère, Circourt, Kergorlay, Lavergne, Childe, Tocqueville's brother Édouard, and his nephew Hubert, received accounts of this awful journey and the calamitous impact it had had upon its participants.

27. Tocqueville to Édouard de Tocqueville, 13 November 1858, in *OC,* XIV, 358.

28. Tocqueville to Gustave de Beaumont, 11 November 1858, in *OC,* VIII (3), 604.

29. Tocqueville to Gustave de Beaumont, 11 November 1858, in *OC,* VIII (3), 604, emphasis in the original.

30. Tocqueville to Adolphe de Circourt, 12 November 1858, in *OC,* XVIII, 505. The ever-diligent Circourt duly provided a comprehensive list within the week.

31. See also Tocqueville to Hubert de Tocqueville, 15 November 1858, in *OC,* XIV, 360; and Tocqueville to Auguste Borniol, 5 November 1858, in *OC,* XVII (3), 526.

32. Tocqueville to Gustave de Beaumont, 23 November 1851, in *OC,* VIII (3), 606. See also Tocqueville to Louis de Chateaubriand, 29 November 1858, in *OC,* XVII (3), 534.

33. To Édouard de Tocqueville he described one of these servants as a "great twit"; Tocqueville to Édouard de Tocqueville, 13 November 1858, in *OC,* XIV, 359. See also Tocqueville to Jean-Charles Rivet, 5 December 1858, in *OC,* XVII (3), 538–39, where Tocqueville wrote of one of these servants that he had never met someone so incapable of performing the functions for which he had been employed.

34. Tocqueville to Gustave de Beaumont, 23 November 1858, in *OC,* VIII (3), 606–7.

35. See Tocqueville to Jean-Charles Rivet, 5 December 1858, in *OC,* XVII (3), 538, where Tocqueville wrote that, upon arrival in Cannes, he could not take more than one hundred steps without needing a rest, whereas he was now able to walk for over an hour and a half in the mountains.

36. Tocqueville to François Mignet, 9 December 1858, in *OC,* XVII (3), 539.

37. Tocqueville indicated to Beaumont that she could only communicate by writing things down.

38. Tocqueville to Jean-Jacques Ampère, 5 December 1858, in *OC,* XI, 415.

39. Tocqueville to Gustave de Beaumont, 24 December 1858, in *OC,* VIII (3), 611–13. See also Tocqueville to Jean-Jacques Ampère, 30 December 1858, in *OC,* XI, 417–18.

40. Tocqueville to A. Lemoigne Dutaillis, (end 1858), in *OC,* X, 580. Tocqueville wrote to many others, for example Nassau Senior and Frédéric Chassériau, to deny this rumour.

41. See Tocqueville to Prosper Duvergier de Hauranne, 9 February 1858, in *OC,* XVII (3), 552; and Tocqueville to Jean-Charles Rivet, 15 February 1859, in *OC,* XVII (3), 554–55.

42. Tocqueville to Francisque de Corcelle, 5 February 1859, in *OC,* XV (2), 240.

43. Tocqueville to Pierre Freslon, 23 February 1859, in *OC,* XVII (3), 557–58. Tocqueville told Freslon that he thought that "there was nothing more fascinating than memoirs, above all those of celebrated men." See also Tocqueville to Henry Reeve, 25 February 1859, in *OC,* VI (1), 278, where Tocqueville reports that he had been reading about the Roman Catacombs in the *Edinburgh Review.*

44. Tocqueville to John Stuart Mill, 9 February 1859, in *OC,* VI (1), 351–2. It appears that Tocqueville was not to read Mill's famous text.

45. Tocqueville to Gustave de Beaumont, 15 February 1859, in *OC,* VIII (3), 615. Tocqueville reported to Beaumont that she had not written to anyone for two months.

46. Tocqueville to Francisque de Corcelle, 5 February 1859, in *OC,* XV (2), 240.

47. Tocqueville to Jean-Jacques Ampère, 3 March 1859, in *OC,* XI, 419–21.

48. Tocqueville to Adolphe de Circourt, 5 March 1859, in *OC,* XVIII, 535–36.

49. Tocqueville to Horace Hammond, 8 March 1859, in *OC,* VI (3), 308–9.

50. Tocqueville to Victor Lanjuinais, 10 March 1859, in *OC,* XVII (3), 561.

51. Tocqueville to Gustave de Beaumont, 4 March 1859, in *OC,* VIII (3), 615–16, emphasis in the original.

52. These letters and their copyright are held by Yale University's Beinecke Rare Book and Manuscript Library (Yale Tocqueville Manuscripts, MS Vault Tocqueville, Section D. IV, r). Subsequent references to these letters come from this source. These letters have been translated into English by Juliet O'Brien, and the translation was funded by University College Dublin's Seed Funding initiative. I thank Andreas Hess for allowing me to see typescripts of both the French and English versions and for allowing me to cite them. See also Andreas Hess, "How Tocqueville Became 'Tocqueville'—Gustave de Beaumont's Letters from Cannes to the First Edition of *Memoir, Letters, and Remains of Alexis de Tocqueville,*" in *Who Telleth a Tale of Unspeaking Death,* ed. Wolfgang Marx (Dublin, 2017), 75–93. Beaumont subsequently provided a retrospective account of what

transpired in Cannes in his "Notice sur Alexis de Tocqueville," in Tocqueville, *Œuvres et correspondance inédites d'Alexis de Tocqueville,* 2 vols., ed. Gustave de Beaumont (Paris, 1861), 1:113–21.

53. Gustave de Beaumont to his wife, Clémentine, 21 January 1859.

54. Gustave de Beaumont to his wife, Clémentine, 12 March 1859.

55. Tocqueville had first met Brougham in London in 1835, when the latter was the British chancellor of the exchequer. They had subsequently quarrelled in 1843 on the subject of boarding rights off the African coast. See the exchange of letters: Tocqueville to Lord Brougham, 9 February 1843, in *OC,* VI (3), 70–72; Lord Brougham to Tocqueville; 14 February 1843, in *OC,* VI (3), 73–77. Brougham had been one of the first members of the British aristocracy to "discover" Cannes. Knowing that he was resident in Cannes, Nassau Senior suggested that he might call to see Tocqueville.

56. Gustave de Beaumont to his wife, Clémentine, 13 March 1859.

57. Gustave de Beaumont to his wife, Clémentine, 14 March 1859.

58. Gustave de Beaumont to his wife, Clémentine, 14 March 1859.

59. Gustave de Beaumont to his wife, Clémentine, 16 March 1859.

60. The day before, Tocqueville had written to Nassau Senior to indicate that he was living a life of "*solitary confinement*": Tocqueville to N. W. Senior, 15 March 1859, in *OC,* VI (2), 220, emphasis in the original. In a letter to Circourt he spoke of his "profound solitude," adding that "at this moment in time, I would willingly give up all the beauties of nature to be able freely to speak to my friends"; Tocqueville to Adolphe de Circourt, 17 March 1859, in *OC,* XVIII, 539. He made a similar remark in a letter to Kergorlay, commenting that he and his wife were living a life of "the most profound solitude, where one person can only speak very softly and the other one cannot speak at all"; Tocqueville to Louis de Kergorlay, 18 March 1859, in *OC,* XIII (2), 347–48. These were among the very last letters written by Tocqueville.

61. Gustave de Beaumont to his wife, Clémentine, 21 March 1859.

62. Gustave de Beaumont to his wife, Clémentine, 22 March 1859.

63. Gustave de Beaumont to his wife, Clémentine, 21 March 1859.

64. Gustave de Beaumont to his wife, Clémentine, 23 and 24 March 1859.

65. Gustave de Beaumont to his wife, Clémentine, 26 March 1859.

66. Gustave de Beaumont to his wife, Clémentine, 27 March 1859.

67. Gustave de Beaumont to his wife, Clémentine, 30 March 1859.

68. Gustave de Beaumont to his wife, Clémentine, 31 March 1859.

69. Gustave de Beaumont to his wife, Clémentine, 2 April 1859.

70. In a letter to Corcelle, Tocqueville wrote, "I am not ill but only weak." The same letter also expressed Tocqueville's joy that arrangements for the marriage of Corcelle's daughter were now completed; Tocqueville to Francisque de Corcelle, 6 April 1859, in *OC,* XV (2), 243–44.

71. Gustave de Beaumont to his wife, Clémentine, 4 April 1859.

72. Gustave de Beaumont to his wife, Clémentine, 4 April 1859. Beaumont's letters to his wife regularly refer to the serious financial difficulties he and his family were facing and the need to maximise production on their estate. In these difficult circumstances, Beaumont was worried about the health of his wife, in particular.

73. Gustave de Beaumont to Tocqueville, 13 April 1859, in *OC,* VIII (3), 616–19.

74. John Knox Laughton, *Memoirs of the Life and Correspondence of Henry Reeve,* 2 vols. (London, 1898), 2:17.

75. Tocqueville to Jean-Jacques Ampère, 9 April 1859, in *OC,* XI, 423–24.

76. See André Jardin, *Tocqueville: A Biography* (Baltimore, 1998), 531–32.

77. Beaumont, "Notice sur Alexis de Tocqueville," 120. This text merits close reading. Beaumont's point was that, for Tocqueville, Christianity and civilisation were one and the same thing, and that a love of liberty had to be united with a religious faith. In this Beaumont was undoubtedly correct.

78. This account is to be found in *OC,* IX, 13–14n5. It can also be found in translation in Jardin, *Tocqueville: A Biography,* 529. The most complete discussion of this issue is to be found in John Lukacs, "The Last Days of Alexis de Tocqueville," *Catholic Historical Review* 50, no. 1 (1964): 155–70. Lukacs concludes that Tocqueville's beliefs were those of "a tormented Christian and not those of an agnostic aristocrat respectful of the social and political functions of religion" (170).

79. Macmillan also published an edition in London.

80. Hess, "How Tocqueville Became 'Tocqueville,'" 86.

81. Beaumont, "Notice sur Alexis de Tocqueville," 122.

82. Beaumont, "Notice sur Alexis de Tocqueville," 114–15, 122–24.

83. Beaumont, "Notice sur Alexis de Tocqueville," 11–15.

84. Beaumont, "Notice sur Alexis de Tocqueville," 22–23, 26–27.

85. Beaumont, "Notice sur Alexis de Tocqueville," 90.

86. Beaumont, "Notice sur Alexis de Tocqueville," 90–96. Part of Beaumont's first edited volume and the whole of the second volume consists of letters published by Tocqueville. If pride of places goes to letters to friends such as Beaumont himself and other close friends such as Ampère and Kergorlay, also included are letters to such as Albert de Broglie, Pierre Freslon, Harriet Grote, John Stuart Mill, Madame Swetchine, and many others. Only very recently have some of these letters been published in tome XVII of the *OC*.

87. Hess, "How Tocqueville Became 'Tocqueville,'" 78–79.

88. Beaumont, "Notice sur Alexis de Tocqueville," 21–22. Presumably the Englishman referred to here was Godfrey Vigne.

89. Beaumont, "Notice sur Alexis de Tocqueville," 22–24.

90. Seymour Drescher, "Tocqueville's Comparisons: Choices and Lessons," *Tocqueville Review* 27, no. 2 (2006): 480.

Acknowledgements

I first read Alexis de Tocqueville over fifty years ago at my comprehensive school in Nottingham, and in a curious sort of way he has stayed with me ever since. Other writers attracted my enthusiasm and interest, but the more I read of Tocqueville over the years, the more he came to fascinate me and the more impressed I became by him as both a man and a writer. Writing a book about him has not diminished my admiration but only increased it. As I have discovered, time spent with Tocqueville is never wasted.

Anyone writing on Tocqueville owes an enormous debt to the many fine scholars who have worked to complete the publication of the *Œuvres Complètes* over the last seven decades. The writing of my book would have been impossible without their efforts. I am also indebted to the work of numerous individuals who have enriched our understanding of Tocqueville in so many ways. In particular I would like to express my thanks to Richard Boyd, Christine Dunn Henderson, Alan Kahan, Eduardo Nolla, Jennifer Pitts, James T. Schleifer, and Cheryl Welch. I have also enjoyed many lunchtime conversations with Sir Larry Siedentop. Unfortunately, Olivier Zunz's excellent *The Man Who Understood Democracy: The Life of Alexis de Tocqueville* appeared too late for me to incorporate its many insights into this book.

I have had the opportunity to present my preliminary findings at several conferences and seminars. Two stand out for their extraordinary richness and openness of discussion: the first took place at University College Dublin at a seminar organised by Andreas Hess (who also allowed me to make use of translations of invaluable Beaumont manuscript material); the second was a seminar organised by John Adamson at the University of Buckingham. Both provided vivid reminders of what academic life could be at its best.

Over many years I had the good fortune to be invited by Liberty Fund to several conferences devoted to Tocqueville. These were always hugely enjoyable and inspired me to take my reading of Tocqueville further. I learned much from the observations of Henry C. Clark, Simon Green, Daniel J. Mahoney, Filippo Sabetti, David Womersley, and many others. I vividly remember being told by one French participant that Tocqueville was not a liberal (an accolade he reserved only for the later writings of Benjamin Constant and Frédéric Bastiat).

I benefitted greatly from access to many libraries. Two visits to Yale University's Beinecke Rare Book and Manuscript Library were particularly rewarding, as was a visit to Harvard University's Houghton Library. Above all, I am indebted to the London Library and its marvellous staff, who managed somehow to keep the library functioning through months of restrictions in response to the COVID-19 pandemic. I cannot be alone in expressing my sincere appreciation for their efforts. Jennie de Protani, archivist at the Athenaeum in London, was extremely helpful in making available material relating to Tocqueville's election as an honorary member of the club.

Olivia Spraggs at Alamy was wonderfully helpful in facilitating the purchase of images for this volume. Brian B. Bendlin was utterly brilliant as my copy editor, greatly improving my text in the process. Everyone I dealt with at Harvard University Press was fantastically positive in seeing this volume through to publication. Here special thanks go to Emily Silk for her very considerable efforts on my behalf (and for the title of this book). I also thank Mary Ribesky for shepherding the book through production.

The earliest research for this project received generous financial support from the British Academy as well as Indiana University's Institute for Advanced Study (where, under director Ivona Hedin, I was able to spend several very congenial and productive months).

Three essays I have published gave a foretaste of some of the themes discussed in this volume. In 2004, with Aurelian Craiutu, I published "The Third Democracy: Tocqueville's View of America after 1840," *American Political Science Review* 98, no. 3 (2004): 391–404. Thanks to the encouragement of Ed Parsons at Cambridge University Press, this led to the later publication of our edited volume, *Tocqueville on America after 1840: Letters and Other Writings* (Cambridge, 2009). That same year saw the publication of an essay entitled "French Visions of America: From Tocqueville to the Civil War," in *America through European Eyes: British and French Reflections on the New World from the Eighteenth Century to the Present,* edited by Aurelian Craiutu and Jeffrey C. Isaac (University Park, PA, 2009), 161–184. Attendance at a hugely enjoyable conference in Santiago de Compostela, Spain, devoted to Tocqueville produced "Tocqueville's Journey into America," in *Tocqueville's Voyages: The Evolution of His Ideas and Their Journey beyond His Time,* edited by Christine Dunn Henderson (Indianapolis, 2014), 79–110.

A special note of thanks must be expressed to my editor, Ian Malcolm. Ian's support, encouragement, and wise advice over the past years have been invaluable. So, too, has his friendship. I could not have asked for a better editor to work with.

Thanks also go to Daniel Bunyard, Piers Russell-Cobb, and Jeremy Paxman. During the dark days of successive COVID lockdowns, our regular late Friday afternoon conversations over the internet with glass in hand provided endless sources of amusement and lifted my spirits: exactly what was required as I endeavoured to complete my manuscript.

Finally, I offer my heartfelt thanks to Aurelian Craiutu. We met more years ago than I care to remember, and it was Aurelian who first suggested that he and I should work together on Tocqueville. Thus began an immensely productive and enjoyable intellectual collaboration as well as a friendship that I have treasured. It is to him, therefore, that this book is dedicated.

Index